Predicting the Future

An Illustrated History and Guide to the Techniques

ALBERT S. LYONS

*With a literal translation of the original I Ching
by Han-yu Shen and Albert S. Lyons*

HARRY N. ABRAMS, INC., *Publishers*, NEW YORK

For Barbara

Editor: Charles Miers
Designer: Dirk Luykx
Rights, Reproductions, and Photo Research: John K. Crowley
Original Illustrations: Martin Hardy

PAGE 1: Anonymous (German). *The Hand as the Mirror of Salvation.* 1446. Colored woodcut. National Gallery of Art, Rosenwald Collection, Washington, D.C.
PAGE 2: Illuminated page from Tammaso Sardi's *Anima Peregrina: The Mountain of Sciences,* showing Moses, Nebuchadnezzar, and Sardi. Corsini Library, Rome.

Lyons, Albert S., 1912–
Predicting the future: an illustrated history and guide to the techniques / Albert S. Lyons; with a literal translation of the *I Ching* by Han-yu Shen and Albert S. Lyons.
p. cm.
ISBN 0–8109–3708–5
1. Divination. 2. Divination—History. I. Shen, Han-yu.
II. I Ching. English. 1990. III. Title.
BF1751.L96 1990
133.3—dc20 90–32714
CIP

Published in 1990 by Harry N. Abrams, Incorporated, New York
A Times Mirror Company

Printed and bound in Japan

Contents

Preface
7

Introduction
9

Astrology
13

Numerology
157

Tarot
197

Handreading
237

I Ching
281

Tea-Leaf Reading
341

Dreams
353

Selected Bibliography
420

Index
423

Photograph Credits
432

Georges de La Tour. *Fortune Teller.* Oil on canvas, $40\frac{1}{8} \times 48\frac{5}{8}''$.
Metropolitan Museum of Art, New York City. Rogers Fund.

scientific leaders. During recent centuries, the two methods are seen to be different. Those who use spiritual, mystical, magical, and intuitive means are the palmists, numerologists, tarot adepts, tea-leaf readers, and others. The astrologers place themselves in a special category, but their system too is not considered a scientific study of the stars—which today is called astronomy. The secular prognosticators calculate with the techniques of science (statistics; mathematical laws of probability; inductions based on experimentally derived facts). These predictors include insurance actuaries, economic forecasters, stock-market analysts, and even horse-race handicappers. The focus in this book is on the mystical methods that employ an organized system of prediction and that can be taught and learned. Clairvoyance, precognition, and other means of prophecy that presuppose special, spiritual, intuitive talents are not our concern.

Historical works on the mystical systems of prediction have usually been made from the standpoint of either the believer who marshals arguments to prove the truth of the technique or the skeptic who opposes the basis and contentions of the theory. Certainly few descriptions of the methods are without bias, either favorable or antagonistic. I submit that if one wishes to present, as a historian, a summary of the ways in which people have attempted to forecast the future, the beliefs of the writer should be irrelevant. The pertinent considerations are the attitudes, practices, and incentives of the humans about whom he writes, not the preconceived opinions of the author.

Surely there is nothing wrong with praising or with castigating, nor with aiming at a value judgment, if that is indeed the purpose of the historical treatise, but those aims themselves have thereby established the limits of the survey—useful and informative as it may be. An anthropologist who describes the myths and methods of some particular culture under his scrutiny is expected to be careful to offer the material, not from a lofty perch as the foolish fantasies of a benighted people, but rather from the point of view of the practitioners themselves who subscribe to the concepts and activities. So we hope it will be with this book. What role did the various structured systems of prophecy play among humans in the past and what are these techniques as still followed by them at present?

We have chosen seven of the leading methods, without deciding on their validity: astrology, handreading (palmistry), numerology, the tarot, dreams, the *I Ching*, and tea-leaf or coffee-ground divination (tasseology).

Introduction

Say not which cloud has dark'd the light,
Nor whence it came my way,
But tell me how to spend the night,
And shall I see the day.

In a novel of mid-century by Vercors, *You Shall Know Them,* the author addresses the question, what determines that a creature is human and not a beast? The principal characters finally conclude that an organism is human if it has the capacity and propensity to inquire about the meaning of existence and the makeup of the world—indeed even to pose the question itself. Language, tool making, reasoning, and many other attributes are possessed by both animals and humans, but only the quest for explanations, called by some "philosophy," is a characteristic unique to human beings. Whether this analysis is valid is of less concern at the moment than the realization that looking for meanings in the past, present, and future is a very human endeavor.

Especially do we have an interest in the future. When we are young, we daydream of what the coming years have in store for us—love, career, material success. In our later years, we may in addition speculate on the future happenings to those around us, particularly family and friends. When ill, our primary concerns before all others are whether we will get well and how long it will take (the physician calls these estimates "prognosis"). We often try to forestall the inevitability of sickness by diet, immunizations, and various regimens—thus trying to anticipate future events.

Throughout history the means employed by humans of achieving foresight have depended on the state of knowledge and of the prevalent concepts of the time. Primitive peoples, who may be the inheritors of prehistoric practices, seek portents in the casting of sticks and stones. Ancient Mesopotamians looked to the stars and animal entrails for clues. Rulers and subjects for many centuries relied on those specially trained by predecessors or unusually favored by nature or deity to determine what lay ahead. Such were the prophets of the Bible; the *baru* of Babylonia; the sybils and soothsayers of Greece; the augurs of Rome; the astrologers of the Middle Ages; the fortune-tellers and clairvoyants of all times.

In general, the two principal ways of guessing the future may be characterized as the mystical (spiritual) and the materialistic (secular). In ancient civilizations, the two approaches were not separate—astronomy, astrology, and the reading of entrails were all one process, sometimes integrated in the persons of religious and

The chapter on the *I Ching* was a joint effort with my surgical colleague and friend Han-yu Shen, who became deeply involved when I solicited his help. His background, education, knowledge of Chinese, and scholarly attitudes made him particularly suited to probe the implications of each Chinese pictograph. Although I planned and composed the text of the chapter, it was Dr. Shen who studied the individual Chinese characters in the hexagrams and came to grips with the proper literal meanings, as we together sought to select the most precise English word to match each Chinese character. Marion Howe of the Chait Galleries made available for my use the exceptional library on Chinese culture in the galleries.

In the chapter on dreams, Arnold Pfeffer generously corrected and evaluated the parts that dealt with Freudian principles. Roger Pratt gave valuable advice on the tarot chapter. Without the diligence and cooperation of Fred Royce Cohen, I probably would not have been able to complete the manuscript. David Berman made many useful suggestions and obtained special needed items. I am indebted to many others, including Fred Brown, Alix Cohen, Claire Hirschfield, Saul Jarcho, Alexis Karstaedt, Herbert Kessler, Hans Kleinschmidt, Ellen Lerner, Stanley and Ann Lyons, Demetrius Pertsemlidis, Owen Rachleff, Bruce Ramer, Raul Schiavi, Nancy Siraisi, Marvin Stein, and James Yeannakopoulos.

The staff of the Gustave Levy Library at the Mt. Sinai Medical Center, particularly the interlibrary loan and reference departments, were of indispensable assistance. I also much appreciate the help provided by William Schupbach, Dominik Wujastyk, Nigel Allan, and Vivian Nutton at the Wellcome Institute Library in London, where portions of the research were done. The Rare Book Room at the New York Academy of Medicine was also a useful source repository.

At Harry N. Abrams, Inc., my devoted editor, Charles Miers, agonized with me over organization, phraseology, and facts; John Crowley, always the cooperative and knowledgeable gentleman, obtained the needed pictures, sometimes only by dogged persistence; to Dirk Luykx, the designer, belongs the credit for all that is aesthetically appealing in the design; the talented graphic artist Martin Hardy was conscientiously committed to achieving attractive and informative diagrams. Thanks are also due to Cynthia Deubel for her early work on the pictures at the beginning stages of the project and Carey Lovelace, for her early (and later) responsible endeavors in editing.

Finally, Barbara Lyons has been, as always, an essential source of help and encouragement in all my endeavors.

—New York
April 1990

Preface

Colleagues have asked how a surgeon came to write on the subject of prediction. My early interest was aroused during studies and teaching of the history of medicine, since occult methods—especially astrology—were a significant influence for centuries on practitioners of medicine.

Furthermore, I have been impressed by the prime importance, as patients, we place on prediction (the doctor calls this prognosis); whereas, as physicians, our attention to prognosis is last—awaiting diagnosis, the detection of cause, and then the response to treatment. This order of priorities is the reverse of the questions in the patient's mind: how serious is the illness (prognosis); what can be done about it (treatment); what caused it (cause or etiology); only finally, what is the illness called (diagnosis)?

In other fields too, people in all periods have tried to anticipate the future by whatever means were available—and the occult systems were often prominently used. Thus, I was stimulated to look further into the development of those practices. I gave attention to the Far East but my involvement has been principally with Western practices. Although both primary and secondary writings have been pursued, sometimes I had to place reliance on secondary sources—discriminatingly I hope.

The complex discipline of astrology required considerably more than wide reading and attending a few classes. To Faith McInerney, a professional astrologer, I wish especially to express gratitude for her patient, personal instruction, the casting of horoscopes for and with me, and providing a detailed critique of the section on astrological technique. I also thank the astrologer Julian Armistead, who made corrections and suggestions, and Rhoda Urman, astrologer and author, for "vetting" the technical segments.

John Scarborough, a highly respected historian of medicine, pharmacy, and hermeticism, freely and painstakingly examined the portions on the history of ancient astrology. To him I am much indebted for his unstinting help in this and other projects. However, I must emphasize that none of them and none of those who reviewed other chapters are in any way accountable for errors, omissions, or the opinions expressed in the book.

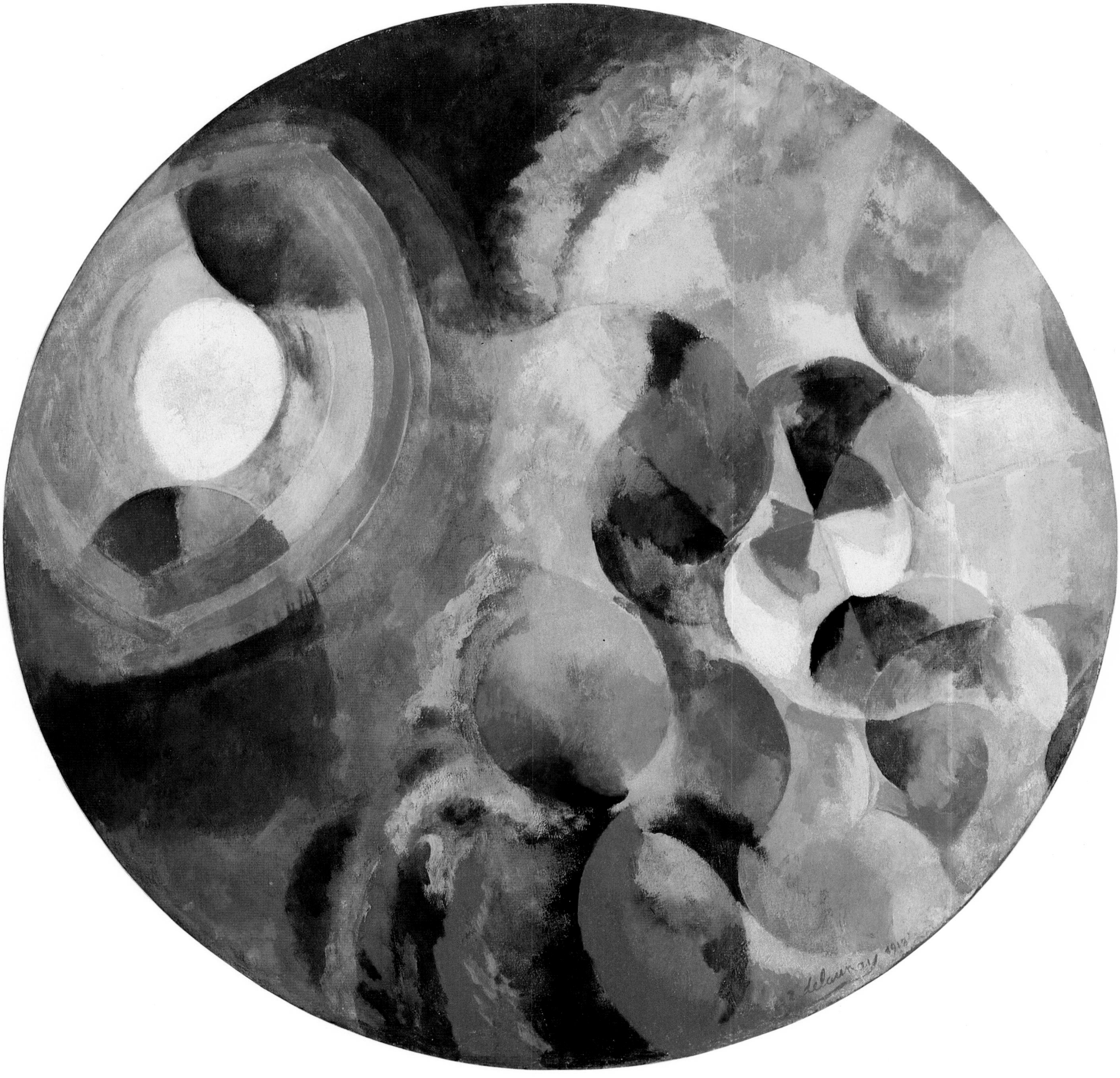

Robert Delaunay. *Sun Disks (Composition Simultanée: Les Disques Soleil)*. 1912–1913. Oil on canvas. Diameter 53″. Collection, The Museum of Modern Art, New York City. Mrs. Simon Guggenheim Fund.

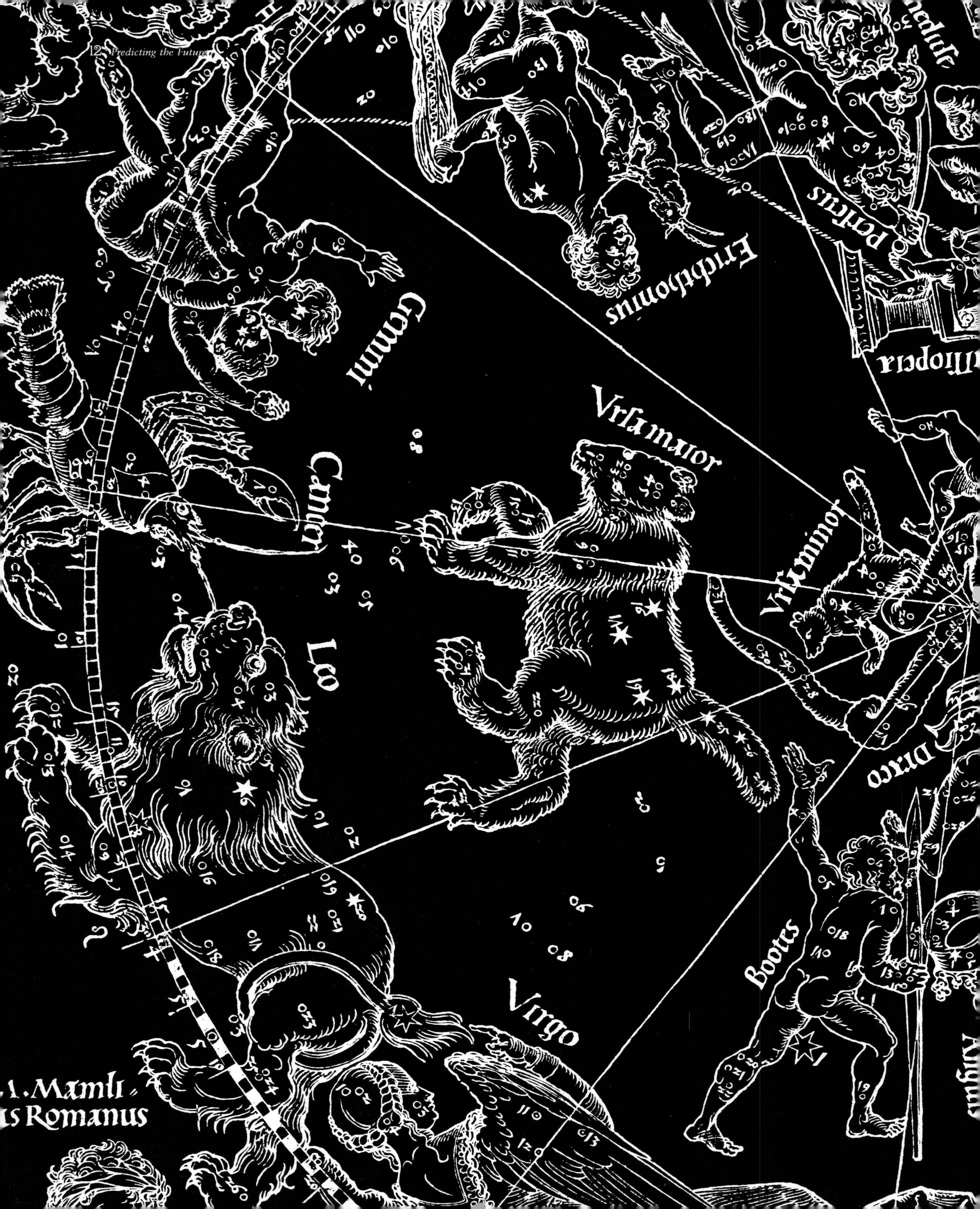
Gemini
Erichthonius
Perseus
Vrsa maior
Vrsa minor
Cancer
Leo
Draco
Bootes
Virgo

Astrology
Andromeda
Pegasus
Cepheus
Equicul
Aquarius
Capricornus
Telum
Avis
Delphinus
Lyra
Aquila
Hercules
Ophiuchus
Sagittarius

les heures du jour
les heures de la nuyt
pompee
Iulius cesar

Astrology

The worlds revolve, some fast, some slow,
Electrons leap, no speck is still,
All move yet know not why they go,
But I can choose; my fate is will.

Astrology is the study of the stars for the purpose of understanding ourselves and anticipating the future. It presupposes that the positions of the planets and other heavenly bodies have an effect on the character of each human and on events on earth.

In astrology, changes in position of the stars are described as if the stars themselves are doing the moving rather than the earth, an assumption that had been perpetuated for thousands of years. Vestiges of this idea remain with us today: we still say that the sun is "rising," "reaching the top of the sky," or "setting" beyond the horizon, because things appear that way and it is more convenient to use those expressions. Modern astrologers, too, know that solar movements are only apparent rather than real. Nevertheless, they refer to the individual positions of the planets as if these bodies are moving around the earth instead of the sun, and they record their locations at various times of the hour, day, and month in relation to us, the observers on earth. One particular band of stars (zodiac constellations) that appears to exist in specific arrangements, moving continuously and regularly but very slowly, also figures prominently in astrology. As the earth revolves around the sun, the sun might seem to move from the area of one constellation to the other during the year—if we were only able to see those clusters during the day when the earth 's surface is receiving the sun's rays.

Human accomplishment is pictured as being in awe of the heavens and its angels. The passage of time determines the victors on earth. The zodiac band marks the path of the sun (but is shown out of correct astrological order). *The Triumph of Time over Fame,* from a French manuscript of Petrarch's *Triumphs.* Bibliothèque Nationale, Paris.

The one apparent constant on earth is the daily alternation between light and darkness, different in various parts of the world and varying in proportions but occurring in regular sequences. The supreme cause of this constant pattern, the sun, on which all life depends, was considered a deity as far back as records go. In any one place on earth the sun rises and reaches a different but consistent height in the sky at different seasons. After a period of time—now called a solar year—the sun starts to rise again at the same spot on the horizon and reaches the same height as it did the year before. As the sun rises daily at the eastern rim of the horizon and sets in the west, it follows a predictable course, reaching higher or lower in the sky at midday, depending on the season and the place on the earth from which it is viewed. This apparent course is called the "ecliptic."

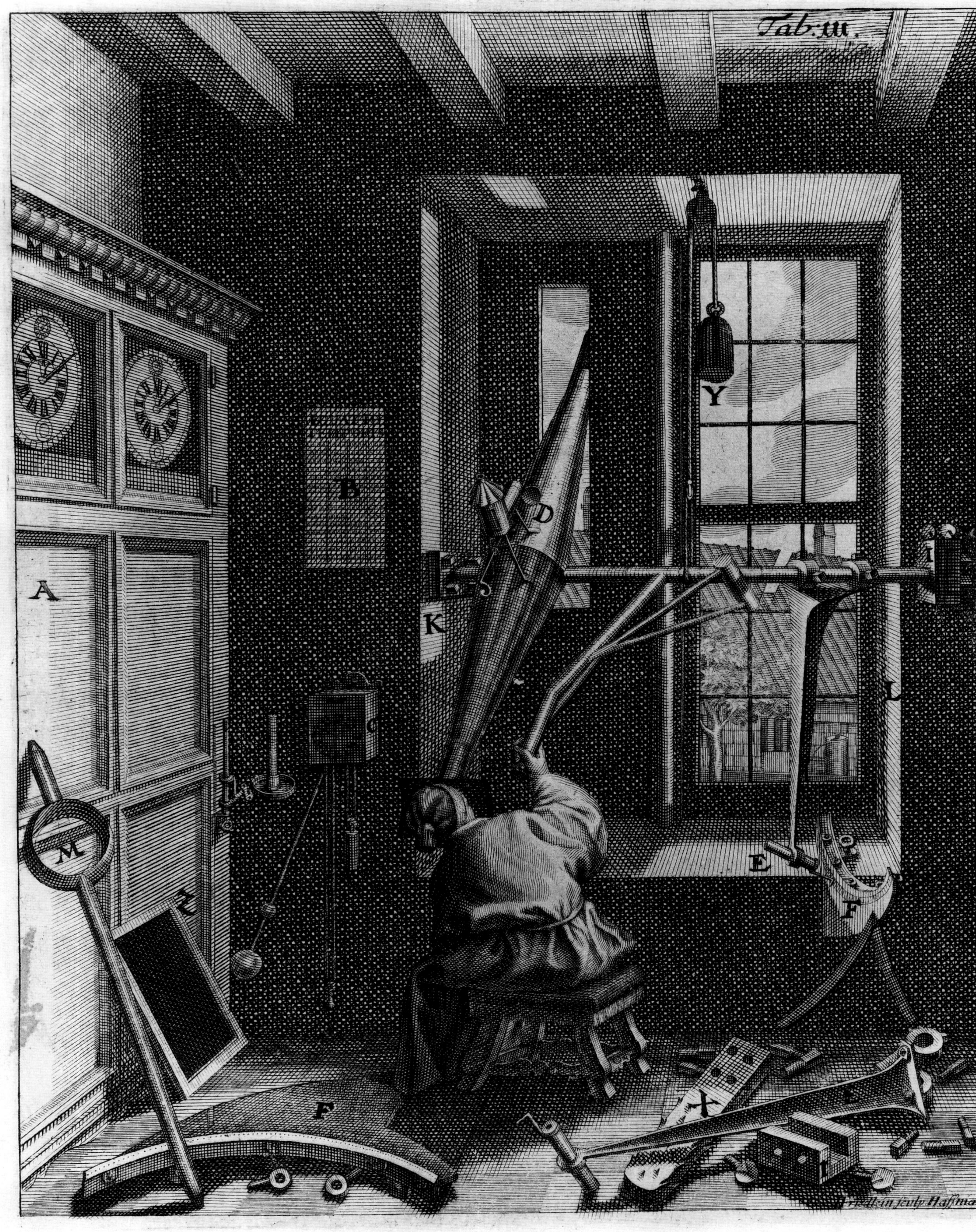
Tab. III.
A
B
D
K
Y
I
L
E
F
M
X
F

The night sky is also filled with bright points of light, in separate clusters, that "move" slowly across the sky during the same period of time (a calendar year) that the sun takes to come back to the points on the horizon where it first rose and set. The clusters have been given names by various cultures—sometimes according to their patterned resemblance to figures, sometimes because of mythological associations. Now they are called constellations, and in astrology they make up the zodiac signs (after the Greek words *zōdion,* meaning "animal figures," and *kiklos zōdiakos,* meaning "circle of animal figures").

Some of these spots of light have been noted to "move" more rapidly and in irregular courses but are not, apparently, synchronized with the steady yearly motion of the constellations or even of the sun and moon. These wandering bodies in Greek times were given the name "planets" (after *planētes*, Greek for "wanderer"). Because the sun and moon also seem to move independently, they too were considered planets, as distinguished from constellations. Although the stars making up the "fixed" constellations that comprise the zodiac are actually not astronomically fixed in relative positions to each other, their distances from earth are so huge that the very tiny movements of each star are hardly noticeable even by telescope.

Indeed, each star in a constellation is itself a sun, probably with its own surrounding planets. All these adjacent solar systems and our own solar system together make up only one galaxy of suns (stars), which astronomers have termed "the spiral galaxy." But in astrology, only twelve clusters (the zodiac) among the many others in our solar system are dealt with.

An engraving showing the eighteenth-century Danish astronomer Roemer with the tools of his science. Bettmann Archive, New York City.

Our own solar system revolves around the center of the spiral galaxy, just as planets revolve around our sun. Whereas our planets take from a few months (Mercury) to hundreds of years (Pluto) to make a complete circle around the sun, our sun itself takes about 225 million years to complete its journey around the center of the galaxy, which itself is moving through space, as are all the galaxies.

Astrology assigns to the arrangements of the heavenly bodies at any one instant a significant influence over events on earth and, in particular, over the makeup and likely future course of a person ("the native") born at that moment. Using astrology to make predictions requires a knowledge of the significance of the established apparatus: zodiac signs, planets, divisions of the sky (houses), the ascendant zodiac sign (at sunrise), the descendant sign (at sunset), the *Medium Coeli* (the zenith of the celestial sphere), the *Imum Coeli* (the nadir), certain other special points, and the positional relationships of all parts to each other (aspects, expressed in degrees).

The positions of the signs and planets at the precise moment of a person's birth (the natal horoscope) are determined by consulting and calculating from astronomical tables (ephemerides) or, today, by receiving the facts through a computerized service. From the information plotted on a diagrammatic wheel, the astrologer interprets favorable and unfavorable features according to laws developed over centuries by his predecessors. By means of the tendencies shown on the wheel, the astrologer may indicate tendencies in a person's makeup, the probable directions of that person's life, the suitability of specific activities and personal relationships, and the inherent dangers that he or she must guard against or compensate for.

The astrologers of centuries past did not hesitate to make firm predictions—they were often dire prophecies—on the basis of what appeared in their diagrams. Modern astrologers rarely do more than suggest probabilities of future

Das sechst Cappittel von ☿ vnd was er bedüttt

Es spricht althabitius das ☿ sig ein ver-
mischter planet vnd ein menlicher vnd ey
tegkliche vnd wirt sin natur geneigt
durch die anderen planeten. Dann ist
er by einem gütten So ist sin natur auch güt
Ist er bey einem bösen So ist sin natur auch
böß. Ist er aber by einem nechtigen so ist sin
natur auch nechtig. Ist er tegig So ist sin
natur auch tegig Vnd hatt zü bedütte
die kleineren brüder. Dorum sich in yemas
geburtt wie sich ☿ hab mit dem herren der
ersten oder mit dem drittter der geburtt. Wan

occurrences, underscoring the free choices that can be exercised to meet the challenges, achievements, and adversities that are revealed by the horoscope reading.

There are several kinds of interpretations of the stars. Natural astrology follows and predicts phenomena in the universe. The separate discipline of astronomy has now taken over this role. Judicial astrology refers to interpreting and predicting happenings on earth according to the movements of heavenly bodies through the sky. One division of this activity is "mundane" astrology, in which the future course of countries, rulers, and world events are predicted. In ancient Babylon this was the primary purpose of sky reading. Genethliacal (or natal) astrology focuses entirely on the personality of individual persons through interpretation of the horoscope at birth. It is the most common astrological activity practiced today. Another type of forecasting by using horoscopes is horary astrology, in which specific questions on the advisability of taking a future course of action are answered. The actual positions of the planets and signs, at the very moment that a question is asked, are scrutinized for the favorable and unfavorable properties on a horoscope wheel drawn up for the precise time when the petitioner poses the question. Electional astrology searches for the most auspicious time for embarking on an enterprise or engaging in an activity by consulting horoscopes plotted for days, months, or years ahead. Medical astrology uses horoscopes for the purpose of predicting and advising on health and illness.

One cannot learn astrology by studying a few treatises or books—and certainly not just by reading this chapter. However, one may be able to obtain enough information here to permit a reasonable understanding of the fundamental tenets, the components of a horoscope and how they can be read (delineated), the historical climate in which astrological ideas evolved, and the current attitudes for and against astrology.

A page from a fifteenth-century German edition of Guido Bonatti's *Liber Astronomicus* showing Mercury and, below him, the two signs that he rules, Gemini and Virgo. Nationalbibliothek, Vienna.

A paleolithic female deity figure from Laussel, France. The figure is holding a bison's horn or moon crescent symbol with twelve line markings (possibly signifying the months). Musée d'Aquitaine, Bordeaux.

History of Astrology

Astrology has its roots in the ancient belief that the stars represent deities who affect the events and affairs of humans on earth. Astrological practices have varied from society to society. Modern astrology is both the accumulation and the distillate of the contributions of philosophers, theologians, scientists, and astrologers of the past. However, any survey of the development of astrology begs some questions on which much disagreement remains: which portion of the ancient knowledge of the heavens is astrology and which is astronomy? Which came first? What was the role of astrology in past cultures?

Astrology can be defined as the reporting of influences on human makeup and behavior by specific planets and particular clusters of stars within the solar system. Astronomy, on the other hand, reports observations on matter and energy within and also beyond the solar system. The purposes of astrology are to understand humans and to predict their probable courses of behavior; the purposes of astronomy are to understand the universe and to predict the likelihood of celestial events and their effects on natural phenomena. Indeed, for centuries astronomers have contributed the calculations and the information that astrologers use.

It is ironic that the word *astrology,* derived from the Greek (*astēr,* for "star"; *logos* for "speech," "discourse," "explanation," or "account") literally implies a study of the stars. This term would fit the practice of observing the stars and correlating the data with explanations or theories, which is actually astronomy. Yet it is the animate human, not the stars, that is the focus of astrologers. Moreover, now it is astronomers, rather than astrologers, who are scanning the stars. On the other hand, the word *astronomy* (*astēr,* Greek for "star"; *nomos* for law) implies pronouncing judgments on the basis of set laws and principles, which is more the practice of astrology. Astronomical theories are propositions to be tested, modified, and disproved as observations and calculations develop. The laws and tenets of astrology remain steadfast.

The stargazers of ancient civilizations were both observers and interpreters. They were properly astronomer-astrologers. To the ancients there were no differences drawn between the disciplines, for it seemed obvious that the sun, moon, and stars were associated not only with time changes and seasonal alterations, but also with natural catastrophes, human biology, and historical upheavals. Add to this the belief in a supreme deity or deities residing in extraterrestrial locations, and the conclusion is obvious: what happens above affects what happens on earth.

When astrology and astronomy were finally divided, astronomers did the observing and recording and astrologers consulted and constructed charts based on the data obtained by the astronomers. This separation of roles began gradually, and its precise timing has been the subject of much argument. We can say that by the Hellenistic period (fourth century B.C. and into the Christian Era) some scientists had already separated their interests, focusing mainly on astronomical concepts and measurements. Also in Hellenistic times, astrological horoscopes came into prominence. But there must have been those who continued to blend physical cosmogeny (astronomy) with personal predictive readings based on the positions of the stars (astrology).

Prehistoric and Pre-Columbian Societies

The amount of astronomical information that prehistoric peoples possessed is a matter of conjecture, but artifacts suggest to recent archaeoastronomers that early humans may have known more than had heretofore been recognized. Evidently some natural phenomena on earth were associated with movements of the bodies in the sky. For instance, large prehistoric megaliths were arranged in various patterns possibly to reflect astronomical occurrences. The great circle at Stonehenge in southern England reveals probable intimate knowledge of the changing seasons, the phases of the moon, and the sun's course. Rings of stones, wooden posts, and mounds of earth in Europe, Africa, and the Americas also had calendric significance and were used for religious, agricultural, and social purposes, in the opinion of modern-day archaeologists. Early humans evidently recognized constellations as well.

However, the extent to which the earliest people linked sky patterns with human behavior is not known. Any culture sophisticated enough to mark the precise times at which the sun would shine through a particular aperture or onto one stone among a circle of rocks—or to know when a particular star would first appear in the sky—must have also wondered about what the stars consisted of and why they were there. The evidence is lacking, however, that prediction by astrological horoscopes—the formalized system that views the stars as determinators of the makeup and activities of individual people—was practiced earlier than the last few centuries before Christ.

Some of today's cultures that we call primitive or undeveloped may give us clues as to what Neolithic people may have thought and believed, although these guesses are only speculation, for contemporary tribal people may well

OPPOSITE: The structure of boulders at Stonehenge on Salisbury Plain in England, created about 1500 B.C., represented a sophisticated calendric system, which appears to have had astronomical associations and possibly was used in religious ceremonies.

BELOW: A statuette of Ishtar, the Babylonian goddess associated with the planet now known as Venus. Third century B.C. Musée du Louvre, Paris.

RIGHT: An illustration from the sixteenth-century *Codex Vaticanus* representing the Aztec concept of Zodiac Man, with star symbols associated with body parts. Vatican Museums, Rome.

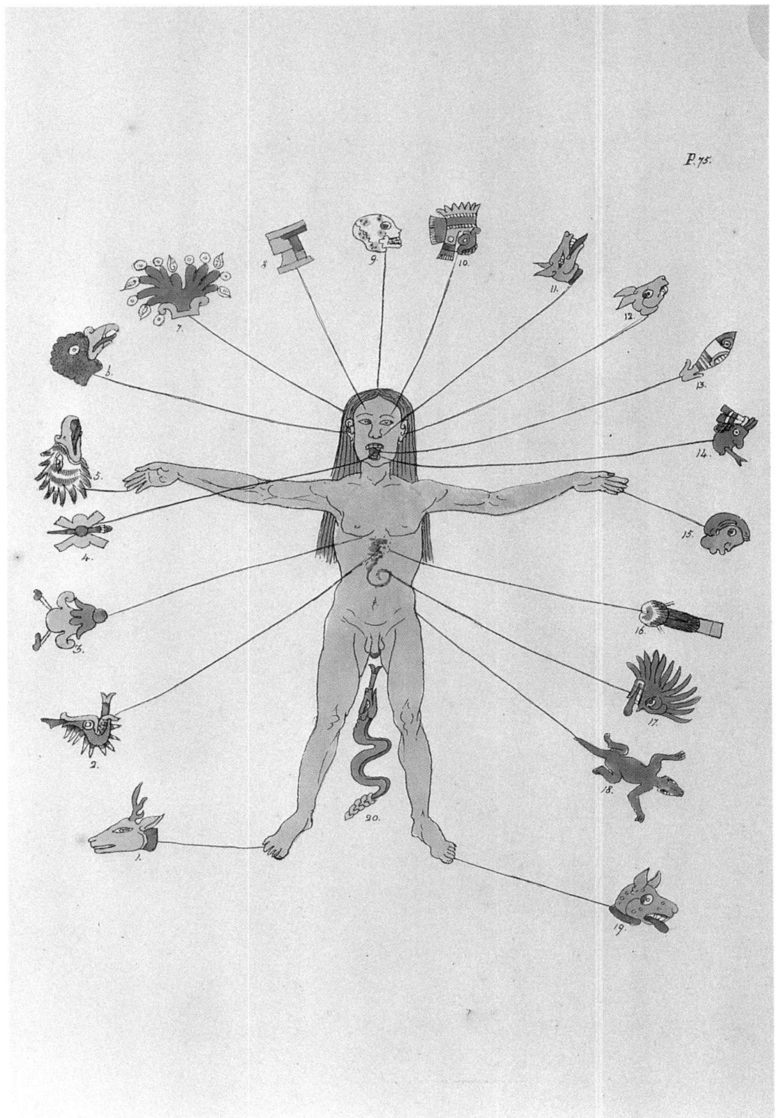

have developed and changed their beliefs over time. In many such societies, the sky bodies are considered to be gods, the abodes of gods, or the location of the souls of the dead. The motions of the sun, moon, and stars, which are used to mark time, and the occurrence of seasons are also seen to exert an influence over human behavior or to signal coming events.

Pre-Columbian Americans' practices are still not completely understood. Their astronomical calculations and religious observances have remained relatively isolated from those of European and Asian peoples, and much of their historical information was destroyed by the conquering Europeans for religious and political reasons. Our sources are chiefly archaeological remains, the glyphs of the Maya civilization, and a scant few writings by missionaries and monks. Nevertheless, it can be deduced that astronomical knowledge in the early American societies was quite profound. Their buildings show astonishing architectural linkages with phenomena in the sky. For example, in Chichén Itzá in Mexico, a great pyramid was constructed that allows the sun's light at the equinox to fall precisely

LEFT: A Mesopotamian limestone boundary stone showing a ruler presenting his daughter to a deity. c.1200 B.C. Height 32¾″. The symbols represent the sun, moon, and Venus (Ishtar). Musée du Louvre, Paris.

BELOW: A seventh-century B.C. Assyrian astrolabe from Nineveh used to make astrological calculations. Diameter 5″. The British Museum, London.

OPPOSITE: A Babylonian clay tablet from about 2000 B.C., recording in cuneiform writing omens based on the positions of the planetary equivalent of Venus (Ishtar). Height 7″. The British Museum, London.

within a secret chamber. The Pre-Columbians evidently recognized the difference between the unchanging clusters (the fixed star groups) and the moving stars (the planets). From tablets and glyphs, scholars have been able to identify constellations known to the Pre-Columbians and to which they assigned favorable or unfavorable meanings.

We can suppose, however, that the principal cultures from which later Western astrology developed were ancient Mesopotamia, Egypt, and Greece.

Mesopotamia

The Mesopotamian civilizations developed in the regions associated with the Tigris and Euphrates rivers (*Mesopotamia* means literally "between two rivers"), located in modern Iraq. The Sumerians, Babylonians, Assyrians, Persians, and other civilizations occupied this part of the world for several millenniums. Virtually all the documentation we have concerning Mesopotamian star practices and principles comes from the ancient tablets on which the Mesopotamians wrote. Much of this information was assembled in a great collection of literature by Ashurbanipal, the Assyrian king of the seventh century B.C.

The peoples of Mesopotamia strongly believed in the power of the heavens to control events on earth. Priests were in charge of discovering, interpreting, and applying the observations of what we now call astrology and astronomy. (The Greeks and Romans used the term "Chaldean" to refer to priest-astrologers of Mesopotamia and even to their own experts who had studied among the Babylonians; but to this day the term is still rather vague in meaning.) Since they were the educated and the supervisors of religious observance, the priestly class was logically expected to be the observers and calculators of heavenly happenings. Theology, astrology, and astronomy were inseparable. The gods acted through the stars or were themselves the stars. Natural phenomena were all under heavenly influence and belonged to the same overall discipline.

Prediction was of the highest importance. Indeed, of the three types of Babylonian priests, the *baru,* whose function was to prognosticate, stood highest. The ziggurats, the

K.160

An ancient mosaic on the floor of the synagogue at Beth Alpha, Israel, showing zodiac symbols and Hebrew writings.

Sassetta (Stefano di Giovanni). *Journey of the Magi.* c.1432. Tempera on wood, 8½ × 11⅝". The Metropolitan Museum of Art, New York City. In the Bible, it was the guiding star of Bethlehem that led the three kings to the newborn infant Jesus.

A stepped ziggurat at Ur (in present-day Iraq), possibly used for observing the stars by the ancient Mesopotamians (built c.3500 B.C.).

famed structures composed of stepped levels, may have been the platforms from which priests scanned the heavens. Dynasties and countries were the focus of predictions, not individual personal destinies. Prediction for national and worldwide events was later called mundane astrology in Greek times. Genethliacal (or natal) forecasting had not yet evolved. It was only in Hellenistic times, after Alexander the Great conquered the East, that personal horoscopes appeared; the oldest in existence were recorded during the last few centuries before Christ.

Several clusters of stars (constellations) that were near to the course of the sun (the ecliptic) were singled out as particularly important to prediction. Other stars that seemed to have erratic journeys rather than a fixed, regularized pattern of movement were thought to have been set on their eccentric courses by Anu, the supreme god inherited from the Sumerians. The Greeks later called them planets.

Apparently the only relationship between the positions of two planets that had significance to the Mesopotamians was close proximity (we call this "conjunction"). The extant records do not suggest the use of other mathematical angles (aspects) that became prominent in subsequent Greek astronomy-astrology. Nevertheless, Mesopotamian reports on the stars and calculations are extraordinary in light of the relatively rudimentary instrumentation and the limitations of the available mathematical methods. Some of the observations were even more accurate than the later Greek reckonings. The Mesopotamians assembled long lists of stars and could forecast with remarkable precision the timing of the appearance and disappearance of constellations, the apparent backward motions (retrograde) of the planets, their coming together in the same line of sight (conjunction), and the occurrence of the eclipses of the moon. Despite contrary claims, there is no evidence that they were so successful merely because the skies over

Mesopotamia were any clearer than the heavens over Egypt, Greece, or other lands.

Mesopotamian concepts were not static. They developed over the centuries, so that the inherited information contained in the *Enuma Anu Enlil* tablets, which were collected by Ashurbanipal in the seventh century B.C., received many additions in the subsequent years, especially in Hellenistic times. Berossus, a Babylonian priest of Alexander's time who emigrated to Greece, probably to one of the Ionian Islands, has often been credited as a potent influence in the spread of Mesopotamian astrology. It is also evident that the composite of Greek practices—such as personal horoscopes and divination—was also transmitted back to Mesopotamia, but the basis for astrology in the Western world and also in sectors in the East rests on Mesopotamia's contributions. Even well after the Hellenistic Greeks themselves had instituted birth-chart delineations, they still often referred to horoscopes as "Babylonian numbers."

Mesopotamian astrology also has associations with the seven-day week, which came from Babylonia and then through the Jewish people into Christian civilization. The names of the days arose from the astrological system of assigning a ruling planet to each of the twenty-four hours of the day, in an order based on the planets' distances from earth, as visualized by stargazers. Of course, the names of the days as now used in various Western languages are Greco-Roman and Teutonic in origin.

The title of each day was based on the planet ruling its first hour. Thus in Roman times the first hour that began the week was under Saturn, the next under Jupiter, and so on. Therefore the first day of the week was Saturn's (Saturday), the next was the Sun's (Sunday), then the Moon's (Monday), then Mars's (*Mardi* in French; Tuesday after the Norse god Tiu), Mercury's (*Mercredi* in French; Wednesday after Woden), Jupiter's (*Jeudi* in French; Thursday after Thor), and finally Venus's (*Vendredi* in French; Friday after Freya).

A nineteen-year cycle set in 383 B.C. by Kidinnu, the Babylonian astronomer, to synchronize the lunar and solar calendar years became the eventual basis for subsequent modifications and reforms of the Greek, Roman (Julian), and finally the Gregorian calendar that we now observe. Meton's calendar, which originated in 432 B.C. in Greece, actually preceded the Babylonian calendar and may have influenced the Babylonian calculations—although this is not established. The Hebrew calendar also used the sunset-to-sunset's limits of the day, marking the first appearance of the moon's crescent after sunset as the beginning of a month, as in Babylonia. The Hebrews inserted a thirteenth month irregularly, as did the Babylonians, to hold lunar and solar calendars together and thereby keep Passover constantly in the same season, in the month of Nisan, on the full moon after the spring equinox.

There is much dispute concerning the place of astrology in the history of the Jews. The Old Testament contains recitals that are clearly a mockery of astrologers, with Isaiah and Daniel, for instance, confounding the magicians of the court. Some passages unmistakably condemn the predictions of the neighboring Babylonians and Assyrians, particularly those referring to the pantheon of gods dwelling in the stars. Indeed, various prophets forecasted the destruction of the star worshipers.

Yet other references are seen by some as an acknowledgment that the stars govern human affairs under God's command and that eclipses portend wrathful punishments by God. In the Hellenistic period some synagogues were even decorated with signs of the zodiac, despite the traditional Jewish religious prohibition against the representation of living creatures. In the Middle Ages and the Renaissance the philosophic mysticism of the cabala took hold among segments of Jewish culture, for whom numerological-astrological practices were a prominent occult method.

In the New Testament, the Magi who visited Mary, Joseph, and the infant Jesus in the manger at Bethlehem were led there by a star. Many types of descriptions have been given to that sign in the sky: a conjunction of Jupiter with other planets; a comet; the "Star of Jacob" (a bright star in the constellation of Cassiopeia that appeared every few centuries to signify the birth of an heir to a queen). The Christian Church's attitude toward such speculations swung between acceptance and rejection.

Thus, although names later changed, methods varied, and purposes became modified, Mesopotamian star lore provided a foundation for virtually all Western and even some Eastern astrology.

The close agreement between ancient surviving Babylonian cuneiform texts and Chinese writings of later periods suggests a strong contribution from Mesopotamian star lore. For instance, some Babylonian mundane predictions associate the movement of Mars into certain areas with the occurrence of serious happenings: Mars in proximity to Venus with catastrophes; Mars near the Moon at an eclipse with events unfavorable to the ruler; Mercury and Venus close together with victory for the monarch. Chinese forecasts refer to the same planets, using their Chinese names but virtually paraphrasing the Babylonian predictions. (Evidently predictive astrology has been a permanent fixture in Chinese culture. Even if the estimates by travelers such as Marco Polo are exaggerated—he spoke of five thousand court astrologers—there must have been at least hundreds of them connected with the royal court and thousands among the common people. The continued popularity of astrology is attested to by the Communist government's efforts to prohibit its professional practice in the 1950s.)

Babylonian observations and interpretations of the

Zodiac figures on the ceiling of a chapel in the Hellenistic Egyptian temple of Hathor at Dendera. Third century B.C. (after Greek influence entered Egypt). Musée du Louvre, Paris.

heavens contributed to Indian astrology, although it has been difficult for scholars to assess the precise influences, especially since the datings of Indian writings have received differing evaluations. Apparently many of the transmissions came principally from Hellenistic Greece, after the fourth century B.C., which in turn were from the original sources in Mesopotamia. Although there are similarities between Indian and Western astrology, other characteristics seem to be purely Indian in origin and may well be from as early as the third millennium B.C.

Indeed, the Vedas, the hymns and epic writings, refer to those old beliefs and customs. The moon, for instance, may have been a central figure in the symbolism, rather than the sun. This is seen in the Lunar Mansions of Indian astrology (*nakshatras*), of which there are twenty-seven or twenty-eight. The Indian word comes from the Vedic for "bright star," the appearance of which at full moon is said to have marked the start of autumn, the beginning of the year in prehistoric times.

Yet the oldest actual astrological texts that summarize Indian astrology date to either the Hellenistic period of the fourth century B.C. or to much later times, after the Babylonian teachings had entered Greek astrological practices. Thus Mesopotamian star lore is the progenitor of most of the astrology in the East as well as in the West.

Egypt

Hieroglyphics and archaeology show that astronomical information was known to the ancient Egyptians for thousands of years before the Christian Era. Some scholars infer that a well-developed method of interpreting by stargazers was in effect very early in Egypt; however, the extent to which astrology was significant is in dispute. It is possible that much of what passes for antique Egyptian lore was actually a late importation from Mesopotamia or the result of even later romantic attributions by Hellenistic Greek writers. Mythical accounts actually written as late as 150 B.C. were believed by the Greeks and Romans to come from a very ancient legendary Egyptian ruler, Nechepso, or the priest Petosiris.

The picturing of animals in constellations does not necessarily mean that a zodiac, as we use the term, existed in ancient Egypt or that these representations played a part in what we now call astrology—that is, the prediction of events and the description of character traits according to configurations in the sky. It is true that the bull and the lion, zodiac signs of later Greek periods, were assigned in Egypt to two star clusters in the second millennium B.C. On the other hand, another Egyptian star figure was the crocodile, which does not appear in any other zodiac. Evidence is scant that the stars were used for any purposes other than time measurement and the anticipation of natural phenomena. The star Sirius (Sothis), for example, was of great importance, probably from very early times, for its first appearance in the sky coincided with the annual flooding of the Nile, an event of crucial significance to Egypt's agricultural economy. Specialists have deduced other astronomical connections with the orientation and construction of ancient temples and pyramids. The Great Pyramid of the second millennium B.C., for example, contains shafts that would have allowed the North Star at that time to be sighted from inside. The ancient Egyptians also noted that there were two different kinds of stars—the "indestructible" and the "never-weary," corresponding with the later division of fixed constellations and planets.

Three different kinds of annual calendars were gradually developed in Egypt and were all in use simultaneously: a lunar structure based on moon phases; a later, modified lunar system; and a solar division of the year into twelve months of thirty days each, with five additional days intercalated at the end of each year to keep the seasonal occurrences constant. This last system, because of its simplicity and regularity, was attractive to subsequent civilizations throughout the West.

Another Egyptian practice also became incorporated into later astronomy and astrology: the division of each day, from sunrise to sunset, into twelve parts (and of night darkness from sunset to sunrise into another twelve). This structure meant that the twenty-four segments were of varying lengths depending on the season. In summer, daylight and its corresponding twelve parts were longer; in winter, the reverse was true.

It was the Egyptian *decan,* however, that had the greatest impact on later Western astrology. It referred to the ten days between the appearance of different constellations in the sky, and it also was a method of dividing the nighttime hours. Each *decan* was governed by a separate deity. Much later, the Greeks used a similar method,

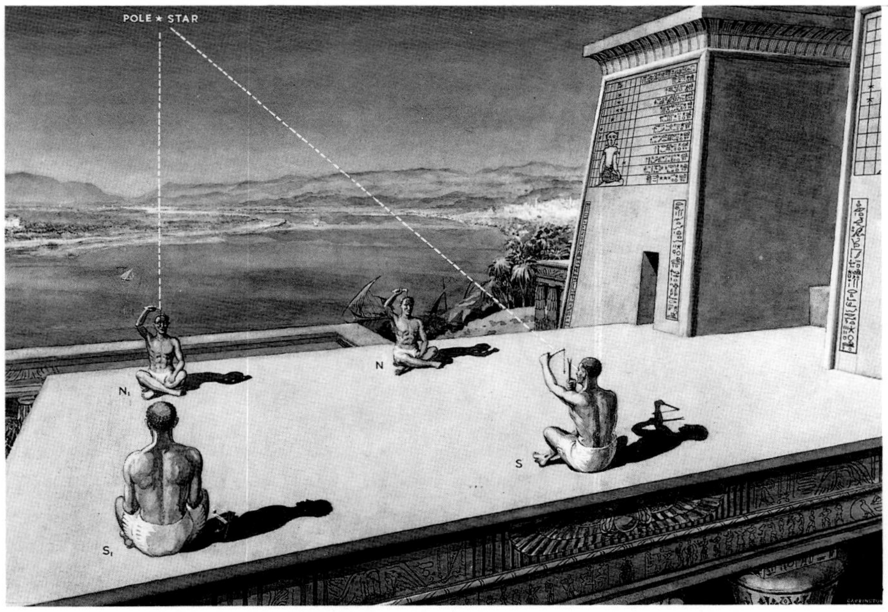

Measuring the angle of the pole star. On the face of the tower on the right is a table of the "hour-stars" dividing the night. The Science Museum, London.

An Egyptian portable shadow rod constructed before the eighth century B.C. for marking the hours during daylight. Bildarchiv, Preussischer Kulturbesitz, Berlin.

This ancient Egyptian view of the world shows the sky goddess Nut stretched over the universe; the horizon extends from her fingers to her toes; the earth, Geb, is the reclining dark figure at the bottom; the god of air, Shu, stands with upraised arms between Nut and Geb. Papyrus. Department of Antiquities, Cairo.

dividing each zodiac sign into three parts of ten degrees each and assigning a god to each segment. The Romans adopted the system and introduced the actual word *decan* (from the Greek *déka,* pertaining to ten). This Egyptian technique of assigning a god to each *decan* led to later cultures' establishing a deity for each hour and eventually to naming each day of the week after the god of the first hour.

By the sixth century B.C., a developed system of star lore was apparently in place. Evidently after the Persian conquest of Egypt in 525 B.C., Mesopotamian astrologers brought their practices to Egypt. To these methods were added Greek influences after Alexander the Great conquered Egypt in the fourth century B.C. According to tradition, the development of Babylonian-Greek astrology in Egypt was hastened by the teachings of Manetho, an Egyptian priest of the third century B.C. who was said to have obtained his knowledge from the Babylonians. Priests are also believed to have continued to be the official observers of the heavens, responsible for fixing the calendar, marking lucky and unlucky days, and forecasting.

Although the sum total of later information and ideas concerning the earth, stars, and universe was inherited from prehistoric cultures and the practices of Mesopotamians, Egyptians, and Greeks, the fundamental principles and techniques actually belonged to the Hellenistic period in Egypt after Alexander the Great's conquest in the fourth century B.C.

Greece

For our purposes we can classify Greek astrology into pre-Hellenistic (up to the fourth century B.C.) and Hellenistic (the fourth century B.C. and after) systems, but the accumulation of information and the development of concepts were gradual. No sudden signposts announced the beginnings of a new intellectual direction. Information and hypotheses about the makeup of the cosmos were transmitted from Homer (c.800 B.C.) to Hesiod (c.700 B.C.) to Thales of Miletus (c.585 B.C.) to the pre-Socratic philosophers (in the sixth to the fourth century B.C.) and to Plato (fourth century B.C.). The early Greeks seem to have derived their explanations from observed data and nonreligious speculations. In this sense they differed from the Mesopotamians and Egyptians. Yet, from our viewpoint, the speculation of Plato concerning the heavens, for instance, contains as much religiosity and mysticism as it does secular, material reasoning.

Greek scientific explanations are perhaps epitomized in a statement Ptolemy (A.D. 85–165) of Alexandria made in his *Syntaxis:* "We think that it is right to explain phenomena by the simplest possible hypotheses, provided that they do not conflict with the observations in any important way." Many Greek scientists accepted the reality of a globular earth although ordinary observation would have indicated that it was flat. Thus, thinking (reasoning from data) and observation (the collection of data), both of which are necessary to science, were practiced by the Greeks.

Pythagoras, who lived on Samos and then in Croton during the sixth century B.C., is a seminal figure in astrology (and also in numerology and medicine). The cosmology of Pythagoras and his followers proposed that there was a central fire in the universe about which all other bodies revolved. Some have seen in this arrangement a forerunner of a sun-centered system, but the central fire described by Pythagoras, and especially by his follower Philolaus, was circled not only by the earth, the five known planets, and the fixed star clusters, but also by the moon and the sun itself. Because these spheres together constituted only nine revolving systems and in Pythagorean philosophy the perfect number was ten, a tenth body, "a counter earth," was also believed to revolve about the mythical central fire. The Pythagorean visualization of the universe clearly was not a heliocentric cosmos. Astrology inherited some Pythagorean ideas in its measurements (four elements, three qualities, twelve signs, and twelve houses).

Before Alexander the Great's time there is virtually no evidence of the Greeks casting personal horoscopes—not even predicting historical events based on the arrangements of heavenly bodies, as had been practiced in Mesopotamian cultures. Indeed the type of charting and interpretation we now call the birth horoscope may have come into being only after Alexander's conquests of Western Asia in the late fourth century B.C. Even in the Babylonian regions the earliest birth horoscope dates from well after Alexander.

What is now meant by astrology may have evolved from the original star sightings for religious, calendric, agricultural, and political purposes in Mesopotamia into a more elaborate birth horoscopy in Hellenistic Alexandria and then may have been transmitted back again to Babylonia. How the information and its uses arose in or spread to India and China remain unclear, but some cross-fertilizations and modifications are evident. Astrological information was also dispersed from the "pagan" East to the Christian West through the mediation of Syriac, Hebrew, and Arabic translations of surviving ancient Greek and Latin manuscripts. It was within the precincts of the exceptional library and museum of ancient Alexandria that many of the great intellectual contributions of the past were stored and supplemented for hundreds of years. It was also here that the world's prominent scientists observed, speculated, experimented, and taught. Not every scientist of the time worked in Alexandria, but sooner or later most writings were obtained and sent to this center.

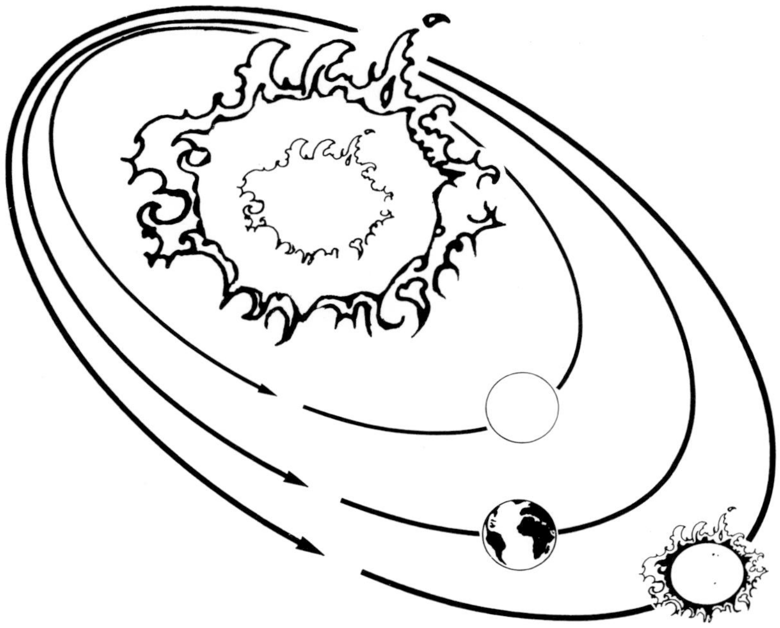

The Pythagorean concept of the cosmos proposed that there was a central fire around which all the planets, including the earth and also the sun, revolved.

Much of Western philosophy is said to have begun with Socrates, the great Greek thinker of the fourth century B.C. about whom we know chiefly through Plato, his pupil. Plato (429–347 B.C.), and therefore probably Socrates (469–399 B.C.), counseled that truth could be reached only through logical reasoning. Yet a mystical quality pervades the logistics of Platonic conceptions in the *Timaeus, Phaedrus,* and other works: the heavens, earth, and planets, matter and spirit, the divine and the material are all unified in one universal living soul. Spirit, however, is seen as separate from and beyond physical reality. To Plato, observations and measurement nevertheless are important in constructing a mathematical basis to the universe, for numbers, as in Pythagorean philosophy, are at the origin of all things. Each planet is believed to be in a transparent sphere. Each sphere rotates on its axis and moves in a spatial relationship to the adjacent spheres. Beyond are the fixed stars, which are embedded in a gigantic outer sphere. The whole structure revolves about the earth.

Eudoxus (c.390–340 B.C.), a contemporary of Plato's, and Callippus (n.330 B.C.), a student of Aristotle's, also used the same model of homocentric spheres revolving around the earth. Eudoxus suggested that each planet was enveloped in four spheres within spheres—three for the moon—thereby accounting for their fluctuating motions and positions. He differed from Plato, however, in that he was one of the earliest (some say the first) to construct purely mathematical explanations, devoid of mystical philosophy and metaphysics, for the observed mechanics of planetary motions.

Aristotle (384–322 B.C.), the pupil of Plato, generally did not subscribe to the mysticism of his teacher, although some might see in Aristotle's concepts merely a substitution of his own mysticism for Plato's. He synthesized what had gone before, and like Plato he too tried to fit observations into an hypothesized ideal model (to "save the phenomena"), but in contrast to Plato he assigned to animate and inanimate things separate realities. In Aristotle's two-tiered cosmos, one tier was the impermanent, decaying terrestrial world; the other was the permanent, incorruptible celestial harmony of the universe. Each functioned by different laws. The heavens were

The philosopher-scientists of ancient Greece and Rome, as visualized in a Roman mosaic discovered in Pompeii. Right to left: Zeno, founder of the Stoic School, Pythagoras, Epicurus, Socrates, Plato, and Theophrastus. Museo Nazionale, Naples.

eternal, with no beginning and no end. (This belief in a fundamental difference between the heavens and the earth was one of the tenets that allowed the Christian Church centuries later to accept Aristotelian philosophy.)

Aristotle accepted Euxodus's rotating system of transparent, crystalline spheres containing the stars and planets and its implied concept that the heavenly bodies and the space surrounding them were made up of a special "fifth essence," separate from the four basic elements of matter: air, water, fire, and earth. This fifth substance was "ether."

The conquests of Alexander the Great changed the political and cultural face of virtually the entire known world in the fourth century B.C. In Alexandria, the city named after him, personal astrological horoscopes became prominent.

Fig. 69 Aristote

Aristotle, Greek philosopher-scientist of the fourth century B.C., tutor of Alexander the Great, and worldwide intellectual authority for over two thousand years, had a theory of the universe that visualized levels of transparent, concentric spheres rotating around the earth.

In this detail from Raphael's fresco *The School of Athens* (1509–1510), Plato (left) is depicted pointing to heaven (spirit) and Aristotle is gesturing to the earth (the senses), thus epitomizing their different emphases. Stanza della Segnatura, Vatican, Rome.

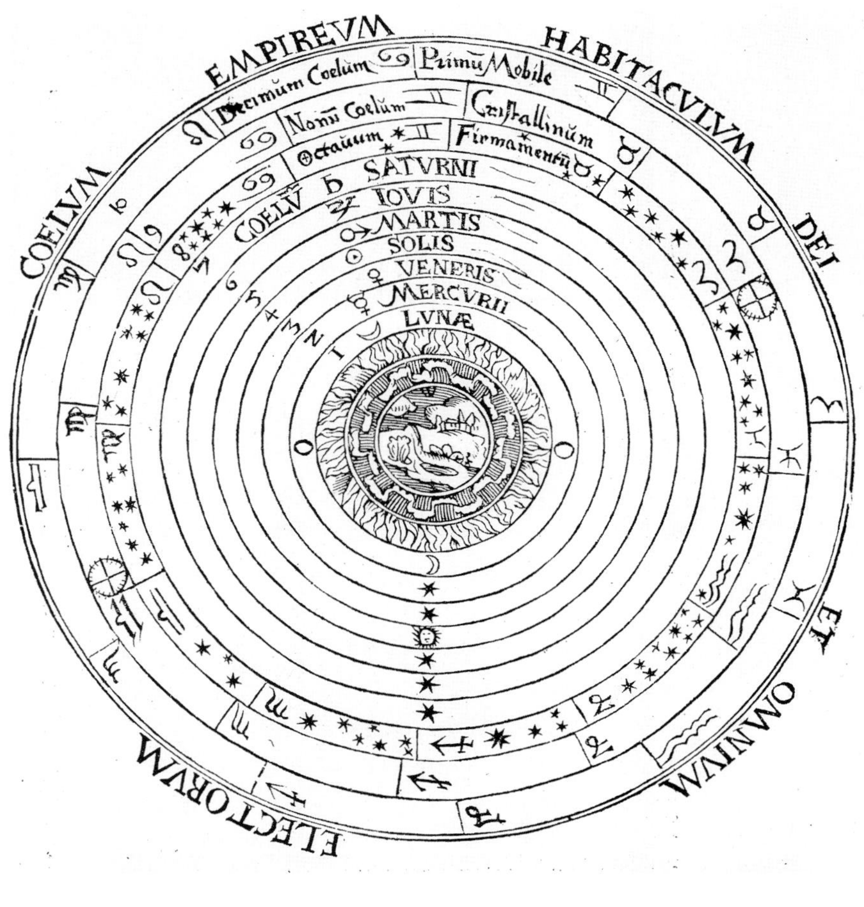

The Aristotelian concept of the universe as pictured in the *Cosmographia* (Antwerp, 1539) by Peter Apian, consists of ten concentric spheres, with the earth, sun, and moon in the innermost sphere and the "*Primum Mobile*" (that which moves all the other spheres) in the outermost.

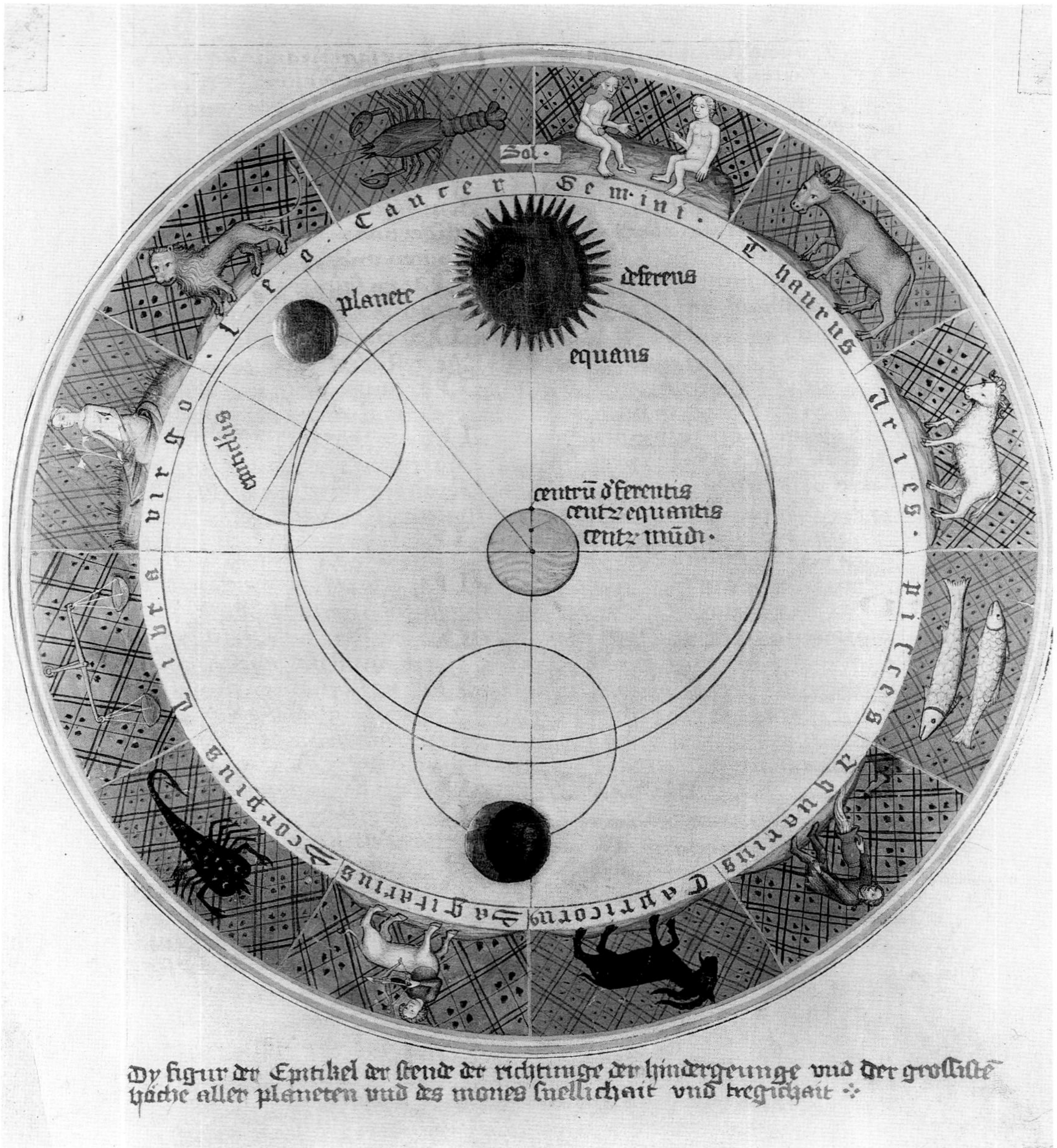

A Greek conception of the cosmos: earth is at the center orbited by the sun and also by the planets, which additionally revolve in epicycles, or small, lesser circles. On the periphery is the band of the zodiac signs representing the constellations. From *Sphaera Mundi,* a German manuscript written and illuminated in the first quarter of the fifteenth century. The Pierpont Morgan Library, New York City.

OPPOSITE: A diagram showing the precession of the equinoxes. In about 2000 B.C. the zodiac sign of Aries appeared beside the sun in springtime. By the Christian Era, because of the "wobble" of the earth's axis, Pisces—not Aries—would have been seen by an observer on earth (symbolized by the dot on the solid-line circumference) to be beside the sun in spring (the vernal equinox). The sun will seem to be "in" Aquarius in the next millennium and will continue this transition to a new zodiac sign about every 2,500 years.

The origin of the idea that all matter can be divided into four elements—water, air, fire, earth—is not known, but Empedocles (c.493–433 B.C.), a Greek scientist in Sicily in the fifth century B.C., has often been depicted as the codifier of the doctrine, although actually at least one hundred years before him it was already part of accepted thinking.

Thus, the teachings of Plato, Aristotle, and their disciples attempted to reconcile actual observations with theories of ideal astronomical motions in the sky. They placed the earth at the center of the universe and assigned to celestial phenomena certain effects on the physical earth and its inhabitants.

In those manuscripts accumulating in the library at Alexandria that can be classified as scientific, a very gradual but persistent shift toward the quantification of phenomena, rather than just their description, occurred as the mathematics of Euclid (c.300 B.C.), Apollonius of Perga (c.250–200 B.C.), and Archimedes (c.287–212 B.C.) were developed. Some of their works have direct bearing on astrology and astronomy, such as the hypotheses of epicycles used to explain the retrograde motions of some planets in the sky. Since planets seem to an observer on earth periodically to halt their movement in one direction and to reverse their path (go retrograde) before finally resuming their original journey, Apollonius reasoned that each planetary sphere rotates in a small circle (an epicycle) while the entire epicycle itself revolves around the earth. His ingenious model mathematically explained retrograde motions.

Four of the most significant contributors to our knowledge of the stars were Heraclides (388–315 B.C.), Aristarchus (300–250 B.C.), Eratosthenes (c.275–194 B.C.), and Hipparchus (c.190–125 B.C.). Heraclides concluded that although the large sky of stars is fixed, two of the planets, Mercury and Venus, circle around the sun, thereby explaining their seemingly erratic motions. Aristarchus of Samos (c.310–230 B.C.) stands out as a maverick, for he proposed a heliocentric cosmos—that is, a universe with the sun at the center and the planets, including the earth, revolving about that center. Our information about

Aristarchus comes from others, one of whom is Archimedes, the great mathematician and his younger contemporary. Aristarchus deduced his concept in order to account for the apparently peculiar planetary motions in the sky. His reasoning also led to the assumption that the panoply of stars beyond the sun, moon, and planets had to be much farther away than had been believed heretofore. Aristarchus also calculated the distances from the earth to the moon and the sun. Astronomers today can point to the inaccuracy of his results, but his errors are really so relatively small that his computation is an astonishing feat, especially in view of the limited information and instrumentation available then.

Another significant computational contribution in Alexandria was the measurement of the circumference of the earth by Eratosthenes, long before the largest portion of the earth had been mapped or was even known to the Greek and Roman civilizations. Eratosthenes, who was the director of the Alexandrian library, devised a remarkably original scheme to make the measurement. He figured that if one could determine the exact differences in the lengths of the

Precession of The Equinoxes

shadows cast by the sun at the same time in two different places, whose precise distance from each other was known, the total circumference of the earth's surface could be calculated by simple geometry, assuming that the globe was a regular sphere.

The two needed places were readily at hand. The city of Syene, where the sun was known to shine directly on the bottom of a particular well at high noon on the longest day of the year; and Alexandria, whose distance from Syene had been measured precisely. He needed only to measure the shadow that was cast in Alexandria, for there was none cast into the Syene well at midday. Everyone was aware of the rate of the sun's course across the sky, and so the calculation could be made without difficulty. The arithmetic yielded 25,000 miles (expressed in "stadia," a Greek unit of measurement), a minuscule difference of only 481 miles from our present value, which we have achieved by means of sophisticated instruments and voluminous direct observations.

About a century later, Hipparchus contributed three especially significant features to astronomical knowledge. One was his correction to within a second of accuracy of the time calendars bequeathed by the Mesopotamians. Second, he separated the sidereal year (the time for the sun to journey around all the zodiac star clusters) from the tropical year (the time for the sun to go through all the seasons). The differences are relatively small, but they are of considerable importance to calendars and to accuracy over large periods of time. The third contribution, for which he is probably best remembered, was his establishment of the "wobble" of the earth's rotation, called "the precession of the equinoxes." He may have derived this latter conclusion from a comparison between the pattern of stars recorded by the Mesopotamian ancients and the arrangements he was able to observe and catalog. Hipparchus ingeniously postulated that a gradual shifting in the earth's axis would explain the discrepancy.

These displacements have fundamental significance to the validity of astrology. For example, if the sun in Ptolemy's day, the second century A.D., was in one zodiac sign in April (the spring equinox) and this was different from its present April zodiac position in the twentieth century, then all the horoscopes that use the Sun-sign and the rising zodiac sign are off by about one zodiac sign. Most astrological systems still assign the same ancient and incorrect Sun-sign to the present-day native. In recognition of the actuality of the precession phenomenon, many astrologers label epochs according to the zodiac sign that contains the sun at springtime (the equinox). During some distant prehistoric period, the spring equinox occurred with the sun in Taurus, indicating a Taurean Age. In about 2000 B.C., it was in Aries; during the Christian Era, Pisces. In the near future, we will enter into the Age of Aquarius—as the opening song in the musical *Hair* proclaims.

ABOVE: An Etruscan augur (haruspice) reading the liver of an animal to make a prediction.

ABOVE RIGHT: A Roman coin from Spain, c.19 B.C., showing on one face Capricorn (the goat-fish symbol). This was probably the ascendant sign of Emperor Augustus, who is pictured on the coin's other face. The British Museum, London.

Although there had been an ancient Etruscan heritage of augury, the astrological system of predicting from birth only took hold near the beginning of the Hellenistic period, about 300 B.C., when other Eastern systems and philosophies were entering Roman consciousness.

To Romans, astrology, like some other cults that flourished in the empire, had always been clothed in an oriental or Greek aura. While this connection did have a certain mystical attractiveness, it also made it slightly suspect in some quarters. However, when the influential and entirely Roman encyclopedic writer Publius Nigidius Figulus (first century B.C.) fully endorsed astrology, it became even more acceptable. Figulus's contemporary Cicero was a fervent opponent of astrology, but the two reportedly maintained a close comradeship both personally and politically.

One of the reasons for the acceptance of astrology may have been the Roman propensity for pragmatic application of knowledge. The horoscopes seemed to give promise of predicting the future. One could better survive if one knew which nobles had the stars with them and which had unfavorable arrangements of heavenly bodies in their nativities. Concomitantly, to those in ruling positions, the horoscope was a tool of power by providing advance information. It was also a source of dread lest an adverse public forecast lead to the withdrawal of support by followers.

For example, Octavian (63 B.C.–A.D. 14), who defeated Marc Antony in 31 B.C. and was later hailed as Emperor Augustus, honored the astrologer Theagenes, who had correctly predicted Octavian's future career from his birth horoscope. Indeed the emperor had his own ascendant sign, Capricorn, struck on coins minted during his reign. Yet he also officially banned astrologers from Rome, possibly just because he believed in them and feared their influence. Nero (who was emperor of Rome from A.D. 54 to 68), too, had his own private astrologer, and it has been reported that he awaited the propitious astrological moment for assuming the emperorship. The young Septimus Severus (A.D. 145–211), long before he was emperor, is said to have finally chosen a wife from Syria because none of the horoscopes of the many other women he considered for marriage had favorable enough readings. He chose his Syrian bride because her astrological delineation showed that she would some day

Rome

During Rome's hegemony over the Western world, interest in astrology heightened. There was a sort of alternation between promotion and opposition, varying during both the Republic and the imperial era. Yet even at times when philosophic, political, and religious attitudes were antagonistic to astrology, the implicit acceptance of astrology's basic tenets was firm. Astrology's strong influences can be seen in the plethora of soothsayers who made forecasts by the stars and by the numerous writers who concerned themselves with its practices. The educated upper classes gave less credence to other forms of forecasting, but since astrology was based on the astronomical knowledge of the time and required computational precision, it was attractive and acceptable to most. Besides, Romans noted, Greek philosophers for centuries had acknowledged the notion that the stars influence human events.

A client consults a soothsayer in this wall painting from Pompeii. Museo Nazionale, Naples.

marry a man who would become a king, a prudent way of insuring his own eventual attainment. Emperor Tiberius (42 B.C.–A.D. 37) even executed astrologers who made political forecasts so that their readings would not be revealed. The story is told that one of these soothsayers, Thrasyllus, whom Tiberius planned to have murdered, predicted his own imminent violent death when the emperor asked him to read his own horoscope. Impressed by the honesty of Thrasyllus, Tiberius spared his life and trusted him thereafter. Some emperors embraced astrology if only

CLAUDIUS PTOLEMY,
Born at Pelusium, in Egypt Ano. Dom. 135.

A depiction of Claudius Ptolemy from *Nativities* by Placidus. Ptolemy, the second-century A.D. codifier of traditional astrology, is seen here with a diagrammatic wheel showing the standard aspects and zodiac symbols.

OPPOSITE: A mocking depiction of two Roman augurs laughing at each other, after a painting by Jean-Léon Gérôme.

because it enabled them to reinforce their own divinity. Whether true or not, these episodes and many others emphasize the popular hold that astrology had on the populace and on the rulers, even when tinged with disbelief. (Some Roman words show how deeply astrology had penetrated. For instance, *considerare,* rooted in *sidus* [star], literally means "to put together the stars." The English word *consider,* the French *considerer,* and the same word in other derivative languages all have the same root.)

Among the Roman philosophic attitudes toward astrology, one can array opposing camps. The proponents, or more accurately the acceptors, were exemplified by the Stoics. Their view that the universe was one inseparable unit cemented by fire, with the human body a manifestation of that fire, was in harmony with the teachings of astrology. Posidonius (c.135–50 B.C.) evidently was one of the strong protagonists of both Stoicism and astrology, although we know his ideas only through the writings of others. Among the other proponents was Marcus Manilius (first century A.D.), who wrote a literary poem that became a significant underpinning of the techniques and principles of astrology. The concept of "Zodiac Man," in which each bodily part is given a ruler from one of the twelve zodiac constellations, was subscribed to in the *Astronomica* of Manilius. This idea was probably in existence before, but Manilius's description became the fullest and most influential version. His works and the writings of Claudius Ptolemy became the main foundations for later contributions to astrological methodology.

On the other side of the debates about astrology stood the opponents, notably the Epicureans, followers of the philosopher Epicurus (c.342–270 B.C.). One of the non-Epicureans, Panaetius, in the second century B.C., although a Stoic himself, also saw no validity in astrologic principles. What particularly repelled the Epicureans was the relative absence of free will implied—at times even stated explicitly—in the birth horoscopes. The very idea that destiny was in the hands of stars or cosmic spirits was unacceptable to Epicurean philosophy. Scathing attacks were penned by the satirist Juvenal (c. A.D. 110), who ridiculed both astrology and astrologers.

The objections to astrology of Cicero (106–43 B.C.) were arrived at through more logical analysis. His *De Divinatione* opposed all divinations, but particularly astrology, establishing a series of arguments against each of its tenets. How many people were influenced by his reasoning is not known. However, the very nature and intensity of his arguments do suggest that astrology must have been widespread among Roman intellectuals, as well as among the less-educated—as can be seen by his references to astrology in Roman law.

Undoubtedly, there were more than these two segments of opinion. Many different gradations probably existed: outright espousal, guarded acceptance, neutrality, uncertain skepticism, and strong opposition.

Ptolemy

In the long history of astrology, probably the most significant writer has been Claudius Ptolemaeus (A.D. 85–165). There were indeed contemporaries of his who contributed to the subject, such as Vettius Valens, an influential authority on astrology who drew up widely read, detailed horoscopes, but none presented the ideas and methods with comparable clarity, comprehensiveness, and organization. Even the occasional revisionist (such as Robert

The Ptolemaic universe is pictured in this 1668 engraving by astronomer Andrew Cellarius. The earth is at the center, orbited by each of the seven planets, which are in turn surrounded by the oblique ring of zodiac figures. The British Library, London.

NETARUM
PLECTEN
GRAPHIA.
LE O
ARI ES
TAV RVS
GEME NI
PI SCES
ÆQVINOCTIALIS
FIRMAMENTVM STEL: LARVM FIXARVM SEDES.
Orbis Saturni
Via Iovis
Orbita Martis
Venus et Mercurius circa Solem
Terra
Luna
HYPOTHESIS BRAHEA.
in quâ centrum Lunæ et Firmamenti est Terra, reliquorum quinq; Planetarum Sol.

Newton, a contemporary astronomer and historian) who both denigrates Ptolemy's accuracy and intentions affirms his lasting influence. Present-day astrological structure is based essentially on the system that Ptolemy assembled, developed, and codified.

Ptolemy's main contributions to astrology and astronomy are to be found in his two great works, the *Mathematical Syntaxis* (later called the *Almagest*) and the *Tetrabiblos*. Despite the original suggestion by Aristarchus in the third century B.C. that the earth and at least some planets revolved around the sun, scientists, including Ptolemy, remained geocentric in their thinking. Nevertheless Otto Neugebauer, the twentieth-century historian of ancient science who deplored all astrology as a "wretched subject," noted that in order to read and to follow the astronomical writings of Copernicus and even of Kepler, one necessarily had to know and understand the *Almagest* of Ptolemy. Like many before him, Ptolemy labored to "save the appearances"—that is, to make his observations fit into hypothetical models in order to achieve an ideal construct of the universe. This led to marked errors, but his thinking was in keeping with the intellectual climate of the time, as opposed to modern scientific practice in which theory must conform to observation.

For Ptolemy, astronomy and astrology (terms as we use them today) were linked inextricably, as they had been since the beginnings of history, but his writings do seem to imply that astrology was a separate system of forecasting through a knowledge of astronomy. Most of Ptolemy's astrological principles are contained in the *Tetrabiblos* (A.D. 150). He proposed that the sun is of central importance to everything material on earth, animate and inanimate, including the seasons, productivity, and generation, and that the moon exerts an influence (for instance, on the tides and the biological cycles) distinct from the sun's. Further, he noted that the stars and planets cause changes on earth as they move across the sky. Ptolemy codified the geometric, angular relationships of planets and zodiac signs into a system of "aspects," which is still used today with few modifications, and he assigned particular meanings to each aspect. He believed that the stars, by their arrangements and properties, determine the mental and physical makeup of humans and that comets, eclipses, lightning, and other natural phenomena announce coming events on earth. Ptolemy's writings indicate that while some things are fixed and unchangeable ("primary causes") in human nature and events, much can be prevented or modified either by chance or human activity ("secondary causes").

There is evidence that the texts of Ptolemy recognized the actual, disparate dimensions of the observed constellations but nevertheless used the traditional typical zodiac with its twelve equal parts. (We do not know precisely when the method of dividing the sky into twelve "houses" first occurred. Before Ptolemy, by the time of Manilius in the first century A.D., the ecliptic had been divided into eight houses. The order of numbering by Manilius went clockwise. Later house systems, including Ptolemy's, were ordered in a counterclockwise direction.)

Indeed very little of the apparatus of modern astrology is absent from Ptolemy's works. The methods of traditional modern astrology are fundamentally a bequest from him.

Early Christian Era

By the beginning of the Christian Era, astrology already had a long history. (The Bible itself contains many references to celestial signs and omens, and in some translations of the New Testament from the original Greek, the three Magi were "astrologers.") Since Christian intellectual pioneers had to contend with varying and sometimes contradictory opinions among their own followers, the Church's attitudes toward astrology were ambivalent and continually changing.

Two of the philosophical systems in the forefront of early Christian thinking were Gnosticism and Neoplatonism, each of which affirmed the preeminence of free will over predestination. Gnostics, on the one hand, opposed astrological practices but acknowledged that the stars could control fate. The Gnostic aim was to reach through real knowledge the divine realm outside the material universe. Influences from the planets, which were material and physical, were inimical to the triumph of the divine spirit in humans and therefore had to, and could, be overcome. To the Neoplatonists, inheritors of the Platonic tradition, the stars were influential in both material and spiritual affairs, but they did not rule or determine fate. Free will enabled humans to use the configurations in the sky as signposts either to be followed or avoided. The writings of the founder, the Alexandrian Plotinus (A.D. 205–270), received varying interpretations by others. For instance, Porphyry (A.D. 232–305), Plotinus's contemporary, argued against the validity of astrology. A century later, Julius Firmicus Maternus asserted that an astrologer must live a life of virtue and serve as an interpreter between human souls and celestial beings.

The Christian Church continued to reflect ambivalent attitudes toward astrology through most of its subsequent history. An influential work presumed to be by the Alexandrian writer Clement (A.D. 150–211) summarizes the way in which apologists in the Church reconciled astrology with orthodox theology. The stars, Clement wrote, are an indication of the past, present, and the future but require much study and piety to be understood; free will, however, can change the behavior of persons and nations, even altering an astrologically perceived outcome.

Synesius of Cyrene, a bishop in the early fourth century, also proclaimed that astrology had a relationship to the higher mysticism in Christianity. Yet many other Church leaders strongly opposed astrological practices.

SIC AVGVSTINVS SACRIS SE TRADIDIT VT NON
MVTATVM SIBI ADHVC SENSERIT ESSE LOCVM

Saint Augustine (A.D. 354–430), the influential Christian theologian, at first was a proponent of astrology but later preached against what he considered to be its pernicious and heretical tenets. He is depicted next to an armillary sphere in this fresco (c.1480) by Sandro Botticelli in the church of the Ognissanti, Florence.

OVERLEAF: The personal horoscope of Iskandar, ruler of Shiraz (1409–1414), made from observations at the time of his birth (Monday, April 25, 1384), is detailed in this illuminated manuscript page dated to 1411. Wellcome Institute Library, London.

Tertullian (c. A.D. 160–250), for instance, inveighed vigorously against astrologers, magicians, and other diviners, whom he classified with pimps and criminals. In A.D. 325 Church leaders at the Council of Nicea officially condemned astrology. Several decades later, the Council of Laodicaea prohibited forecasting by astrologers (the *astrologi*), although other observers of the stars (the *mathematici*) apparently were not so condemned.

Astrology in Christian teaching was dealt a near-fatal blow by Saint Augustine (A.D. 354–430), who had a profound effect on Christian philosophy and activity. At first a believer in astrology, Augustine later rejected its principles and practices for both secular and theological reasons. He emphasized the importance of free will and the heretical ramifications inherent in astrological interpretations. Yet even Augustine's arguments were paradoxical. When the predictions and the analyses of astrologers turned out to be correct, he made the Devil responsible. Thus he acknowledged that astrology could make correct predictions—although only because of the evil work of magicians and the Devil.

Some historians view the subsequent few centuries in the West as being almost devoid of astrological practice. With learning confined to a very few people and with consistent theological opposition, there was also a lessening of available information on astrology-astronomy. However, the writings of some supporters of astrology, the functioning of an underground network of astrologers, and the universal propensity of people to glimpse into the future through occult systems allowed astrology to continue.

Islam

Astrology received a revivifying jolt as a result of the Arab conquests of Europe. Islam had spread to the West in the seventh century, traversing North Africa and reaching Spain about A.D. 710. After the conquests of the Mediterranean,

A painted illustration from a thirteenth-century astrological treatise by Albumasar, the ninth-century Islamic astronomer-astrologer. The Moon and Venus are in the zodiac sign of Cancer. Bibliothèque Nationale, Paris.

ancient Greek and Roman writings were discovered and translated by the Arabs, thence conveyed to a limited extent into Christian lands, and later returned in full measure to Western cultures, mainly during the Crusades.

There are ironies in this history. The great libraries at Alexandria contained Greek and Roman books originally considered heretical both by the Islamic conquerors and by Christian zealots centuries before them. At least twice therefore they were targets for destruction. Doubtless, some works were hidden or secretly saved each time. Later these same documents were the focus of study and expansion by Arabic writers, becoming the very basis for the intellectual glory of Islam during the Middle Ages. Thus, the Islamic enemies of Christendom, against whom the crusader armies moved, gave to the Christian West Arabic translations of the ancient pagan Greco-Roman contributions, which the Christian Church itself had opposed in its early years. These works were to be an important impetus to the Renaissance in Europe.

Among the preserved and translated books, there were treatises on astrology—notably Ptolemy's *Tetrabiblos* and *Almagest*. Such astronomical measurements and calculations from the past were consolidated and expanded by Arabic writers. The calculations and tables of the stars by al-Khwarizmi (c.780–850) became a much-used source throughout the Middle Ages. (Our own word *algorithm* is derived from his name.) Arabic writers (that is, those who wrote in Arabic whatever their national origins) reemphasized the four elements and four qualities. They also introduced new technical astrological methods still in use today, such as the *hyleg*, the Part of Fortune, and other properties of the horoscope, now known in Western astrology as "Arabic parts." Arabic astrologers employed horoscopes to answer questions directed at finding lost persons and objects, apprehending criminals, uncovering treasures, and resolving difficult decisions. This type of interrogatory astrology has similarities to today's horary astrology. Arabic astrologers were also much concerned with choosing the most propitious times for all types of activities (akin to our electional astrology), from great dynastic enterprises to the most insignificant endeavor. Delineating birth horoscopes (genethliacal, or natal, astrology) continued to be the basis of all astrological endeavors.

Arabic scientists, in their practice and teaching of alchemy, also made use of astrology. They applied astrological forecasting methods to the planting, harvesting, and preparing of plants for medicinal purposes. The association of certain planets and constellations with therapeutic benefits, as described by Galen, the ancient Greek medical authority, was affirmed and developed.

The Islamic world had three main intellectual centers: Baghdad, Cordova, and Cairo. In the eighth century al-Mansūr (709–775), caliph of Baghdad, founded an institution for teaching astrology (the House of Wisdom) in which Jacob ben Tarik, a Jew, played a prominent role. Harun al-Rashid, the caliph of Baghdad referred to in *The Arabian Nights*, and his grandson al-Mamun established an observatory where astronomical data were collected. Perhaps the earliest writers in Arabic on astronomy-astrology were the Jew called by the Arabic name Masha'allah (Messahala) and Abu-Ma'shar (Albumasar), both of whom were Baghdad residents in the ninth century. Their works were considered authoritative in the medieval period.

In the West, Spain became the seat of Islamic power and learning, especially through the teachings of scholars such as Avenzoar, Averroes, and Maimonides. Maimonides, another Jew who wrote in Arabic, lived in Cordova in the twelfth century. He became personal physician to Saladin, Egypt's ruler, after he fled from religious persecution in Cordova to the North African coast and then to Cairo. Maimonides accepted the notion that the stars influenced human affairs but expressed contempt for astrological practices and the magic of the occult. It was in Spain, too,

A Persian plate signed by Abd al-Wahid showing the twelve zodiac signs. A.D. 1563. Diameter 15″. Staatliche Museen, Berlin.

LEFT: The Islamic astronomer-astrologer Takiuddin in his observatory at Galata, from the Lokman *Sahinsahname* (1581). 14 × 5″. Université Kutuphanesi, Istanbul.

OPPOSITE: This leaf from an anthology of Persian poetry shows three scenes, each representing a personification of the Moon with a zodiac sign: Sagittarius (top), Capricorn (middle), and Aquarius (bottom). Mongol school. *Munis al-Ahrar.* 1341. Colors and gilt on paper, 8 × 5½″. The Metropolitan Museum of Art, New York City. The Cora Timken Burnett Collection, 1957.

A fourteenth-century rendering of the astrologer Albumasar, with the Roman poet Virgil (70–19 B.C.), supposedly foretelling the birth of the Christ Child, with Mary on the throne of Solomon. Jesus actually was born many centuries before Albumasar. Westphalian. Fourteenth century. Canvas on wood, 50×96″. Staatliche Museen, Berlin.

that the Toledo Tables, an influential astrological calendar, was completed about 1080. (It was later modified and named the Alphonsine Tables during Christian hegemony in the thirteenth century.)

From Cairo, Saladin (1137–1193) exerted his political, military, and intellectual force over the world of Islam. After Christian crusaders suffered devastating defeats at the hands of Saladin's armies they retreated from Egypt, but they brought back to Europe many of the ancient Greco-Roman works that had been preserved and translated by the scholars of Islam.

So closely associated with astrology were the Arabic writers, scientists, and medical practitioners in the minds of the medieval West that astrology commonly was referred to as "the method of the Arabs." Indeed, the term "judicial" astrology, still in use today, may have been derived from the Arabic root word *hkm,* meaning a learned person's declaration. *Ahkām* (or *hukm*) came to mean an authoritative statement. The contemporary historian Richard Lemay has suggested that John of Seville in the twelfth century translated the word in Latin as "judgments." Others later transformed "judgments" into "judges" (those who make judgments). Since the pronouncements of judges were "judicial," the system of astrology that made judgments and evaluations based on the stars became known as "judicial astrology."

The Later Medieval Period

In the Christian West astrology continued to have adherents and detractors, but always existed as an underground culture. Sporadic infusions from the intellectual world preserved by Islam, before and especially after the Crusades, also contributed to keeping astrology alive. In the tenth century the scholar Gerbert d'Aurillac became Pope Sylvester II (999–1003). He emphasized the sphericity of the earth and the universe and also subscribed to much of Aristotle's cosmology. As Christianity regained influence in Spain and the Muslim centers of Cordova, Toledo, and Seville declined, more and more Arabic manuscripts were translated into Latin. Gerard of Cremona (1114–1187) completed in Toledo voluminous Latin translations of Euclid, Apollonius, Ptolemy, Avicenna, and others. There were as well occasional works written on the cosmos, notably by William of Conches (eleventh century) and Bernard Silvestris (twelfth century). As the intellectual world took more and more notice, popular works also began to appear on astrology, some of which were closely tied to ancient magical ideas from Egypt and the East.

By the twelfth century treatises by respected philosophers, teachers, and theologians endorsed astrology as an acceptable subject. Rulers now consulted their astrologers on politics, war, public projects, and personal

RIGHT: The star mantle of Henry, Duke of Saxony and Bavaria (1129–1195), suggesting the importance attached to the stars by royal courts. Cathedral Treasury, Bamberg.

BELOW: A tenth-century manuscript page showing Christ (with his hand raised at the center) surrounded by the zodiac signs. At the corners are personifications of the four seasons. Bibliothèque Nationale, Paris.

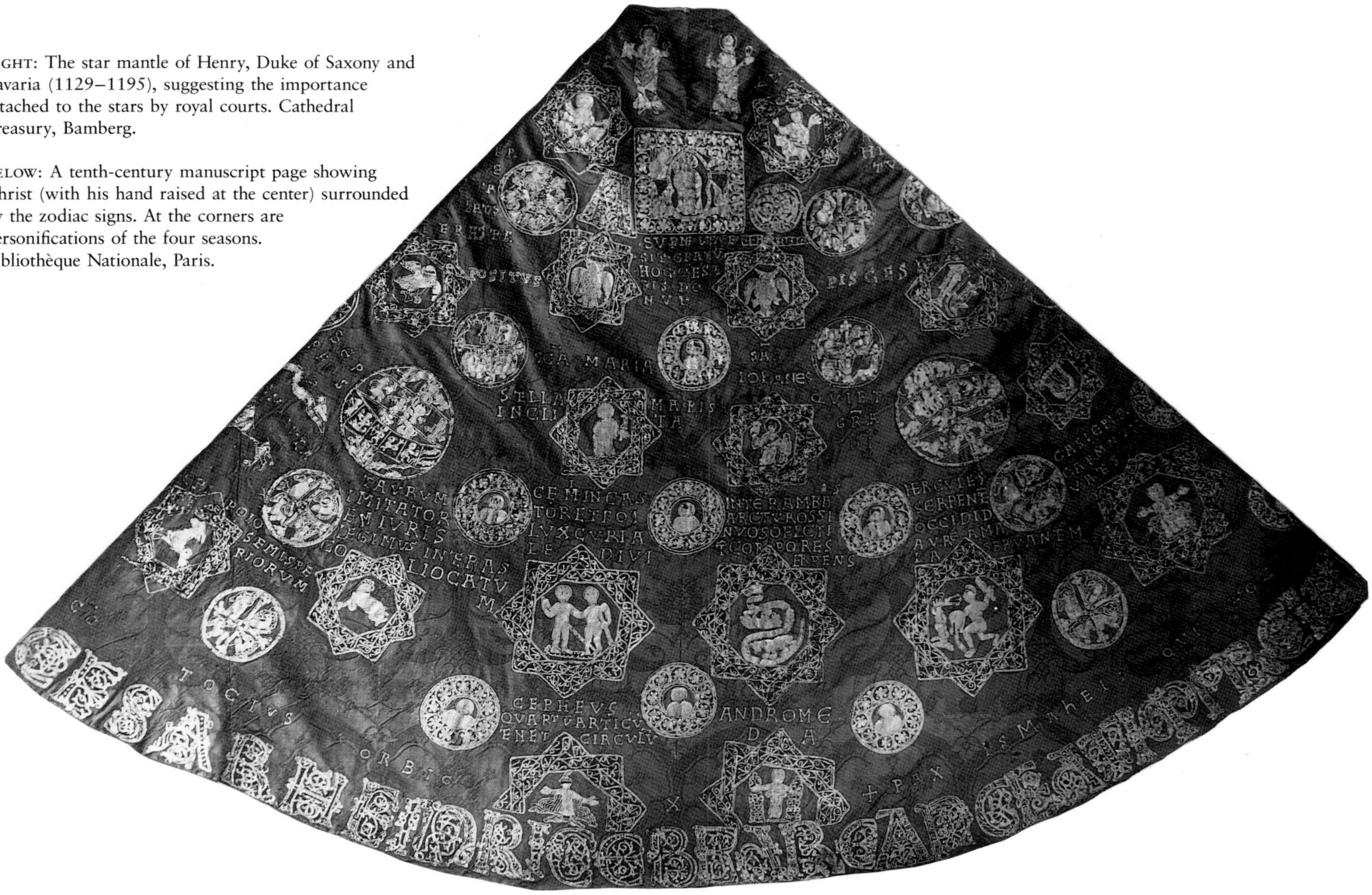

affairs. Upper-class parents had horoscopes drawn up for their children and for themselves. The populace read astrological almanacs and visited genuine astrologists as well as stargazing fakirs for advice on love, money, and health. Even domestic animals were diagnosed and treated according to the patterns of the stars.

Spurious books also began to appear that were purported to have been written by Aristotle. A particularly influential work was the pseudo-Aristotelian *Secret of Secrets.* The ancient Egyptian god Thoth was thought to have fathered other tracts on magic, alchemy, and also astrology.

The year 1186 became the focus of a dire prediction. Because a number of planets were assembled in conjunction in Libra (associated by astrologers with air), terrible calamities associated with the air were forecasted, such as storms and hurricanes that would devastate whole regions of the earth. Nothing of this kind happened but some claimed that various victories by the armies of Islam had been the disasters presaged.

Physicians were expected to be scholars of astrology, applying its techniques to diagnosis and to prognosis. There was a common medical saying, for example, "A doctor without astrology is like an eye without sight." A sickness caused by a preponderance of phlegm, the humor that was cool and moist, required a healing medication that was hot

A depiction of the Wife of Bath ("born under Taurus with Mars therein") from an illustrated fifteenth-century manuscript of Geoffrey Chaucer's *Canterbury Tales.* Henry Huntington Library, San Marino, California.

Astrologer casting a horoscope, from *Image of the World* by Gauthier de Metz. Thirteenth century. The British Library, London.

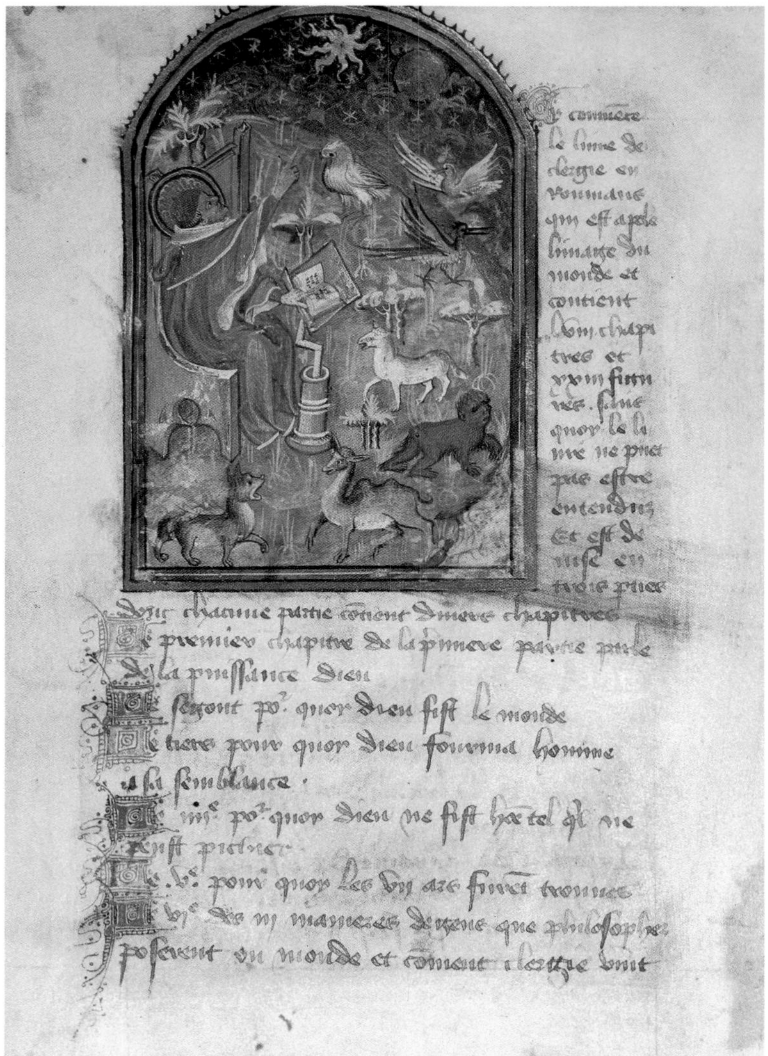

OPPOSITE BELOW LEFT: An astronomer holds an astrolabe in this illumination on vellum from the *Psalter of Blanche of Castille*. c.1200. Bibliothèque de l'Arsenal, Paris.

OPPOSITE BELOW RIGHT: A cleric or scholar studies the heavens, from *Image of the World* by Gauthier de Metz. Thirteenth century. The British Library, London.

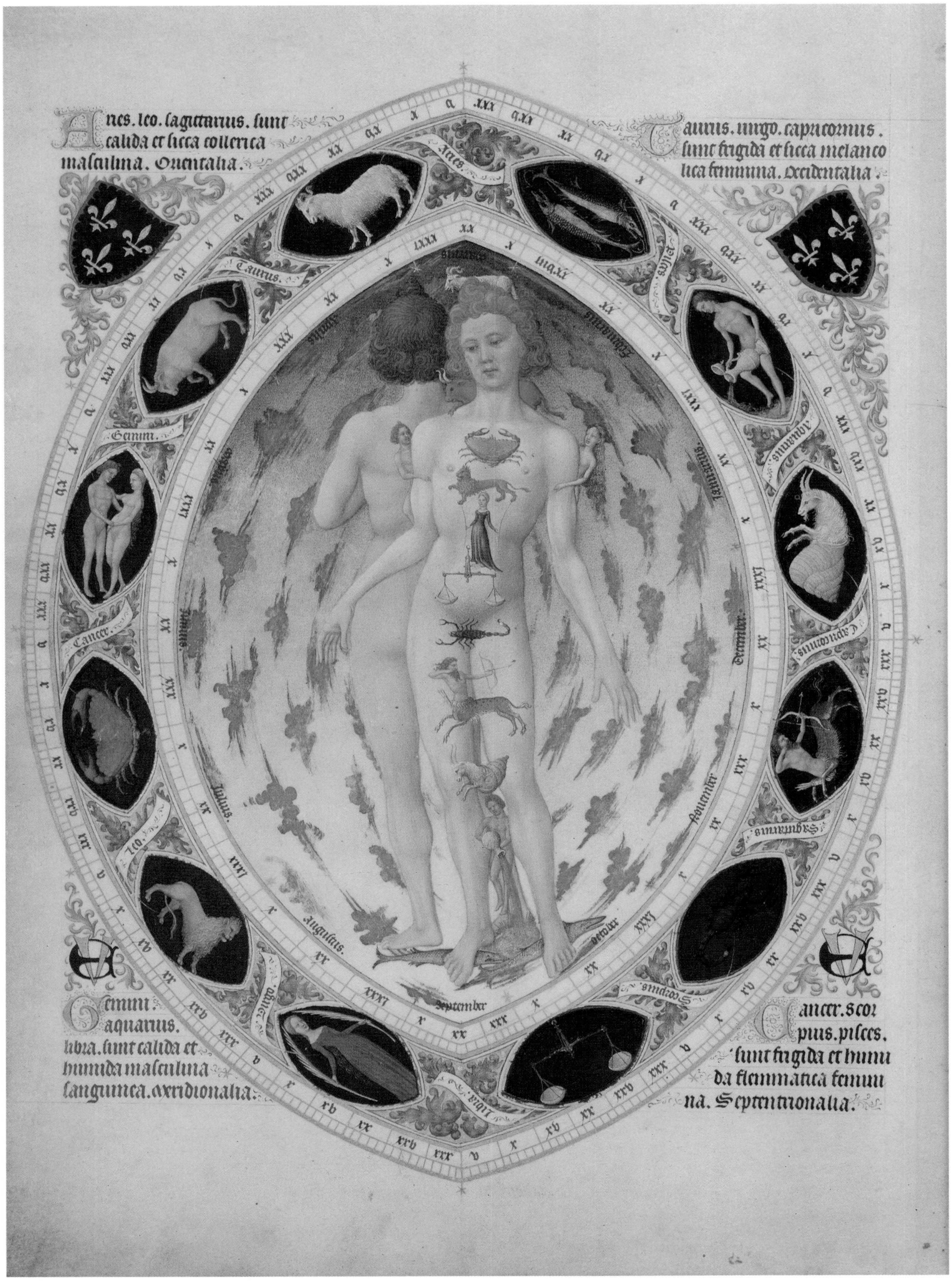

One of the more sophisticated renditions of the concept of Zodiac Man is seen in this example from the *Très Riches Heures* of the Duke of Berry. Each zodiac sign exercises influence over a specific body part. 1413–1416. Illumination on vellum. Musée Condé, Chantilly.

and dry and therefore had to be harvested and prepared when a fiery zodiac sign (Aries, Leo, or Sagittarius) was in ascendance and its ruling planet (Mars, Sun, or Jupiter) in favorable aspect. Each part of the body was under direct influence of one particular constellation in the zodiac. For instance a person born with the sun in Pisces might be expected to be susceptible to troubles with the feet; if in Gemini, chest diseases. It was widely accepted that there were connections between zodiac signs and parts of the body.

In *The Canterbury Tales* there is the "perfect physician" knowledgeable in the minutiae of astrological lore, which Chaucer himself obviously knew well. Some literary historians believe Chaucer's characterizations of the physician and the Wife of Bath were satirical, but whether written as ridicule or in seriousness, these poetic tales illustrate the prominence of astrology in the thinking of the time.

Universities gave astrology much attention in the curricula as a legitimate branch of knowledge. In Bologna, the site of one of the earliest universities, a department and a professorship of astrology were established in 1125. Robert Grosseteste (c.1175–1253), the first chancellor of Oxford University, assigned astrology high priority in scientific study, asserting that the arrangements of the constellations and planets were important to every human endeavor.

Numerous scholars and teachers at the forefront of intellectual thinking wrote on the subject. Some of them, such as John of Salisbury in the twelfth century, condemned astrology principally because its doctrines, if accepted, would supersede God's; others were opposed on rational, secular grounds. Yet the Dominican Albertus Magnus (1200–1280) fully accepted birth horoscopes as examples of applied science and saw no contradiction with Christian theology. The stars did affect the body and the will but the soul was exempt, he argued, retaining the power to make decisions and therefore to counter the compulsions created by the bodies in the sky. Saint Thomas Aquinas (1225–1274), whose philosophical teachings were popular in this era and became known as "Thomism," also gave legitimacy to astrological tenets, claiming they were in agreement with orthodox Christian views of the cosmos. He saw the stars as messengers between the angels and earthly affairs, thereby carrying out God's purposes. But, although he believed that the celestial bodies are the cause of all that happens on earth, he held that the mind can and does dominate the stars.

Roger Bacon (c.1220–1292) went even further, finding correspondences between the planets and Christian dogma. The Christian religion itself, he believed, was associated

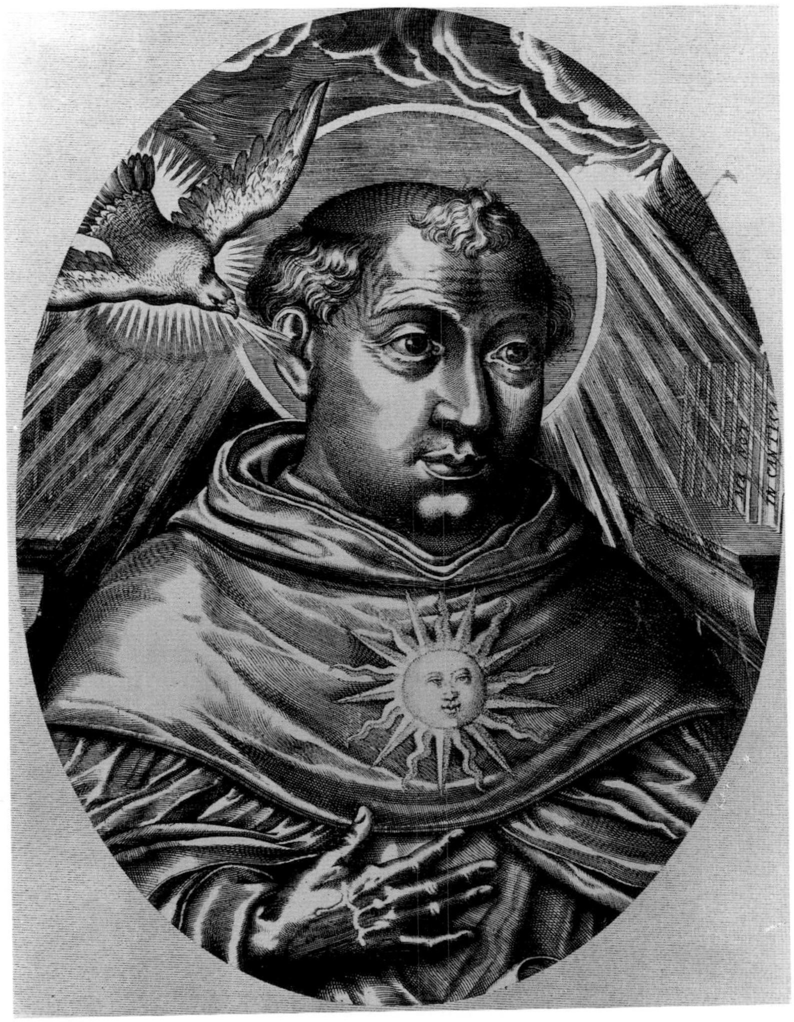

with Mercury, which signaled difficulties ahead. Along with his work in religion, astrology, and alchemy, he made intensive studies of the sciences—for instance optics and experimental chemistry. (Some say that his experiments enabled him to make gunpowder.) Yet his own Order of Saint Francis expelled him, and the Church imprisoned him for fourteen years and burned his major works because his philosophical views were considered heretical.

However, this harsh treatment did not equal the fate of Cecco d'Ascoli, who was burned at the stake about fifty years after Roger Bacon entered prison because he seemed to elevate astrology above God's decision. He asserted that Christ came to earth because the astrological arrangements were precisely correct for his epiphany. Among others whose favorable opinion of astrology incurred the disapproval of the Church was Arnald of Villanova, whom one medical historian deemed the best-known physician of his day.

The leading astrologer of the thirteenth century, whose dynamic personality, substantial learning, and high political position also made him one of the most famous occultists of his day, was Michael Scot. His knowledge was vast, extending from theology to medicine, philosophy, languages, and science. His scholarly translations of Aristotle from the Greek and of Averroes and Avicenna from the Arabic were

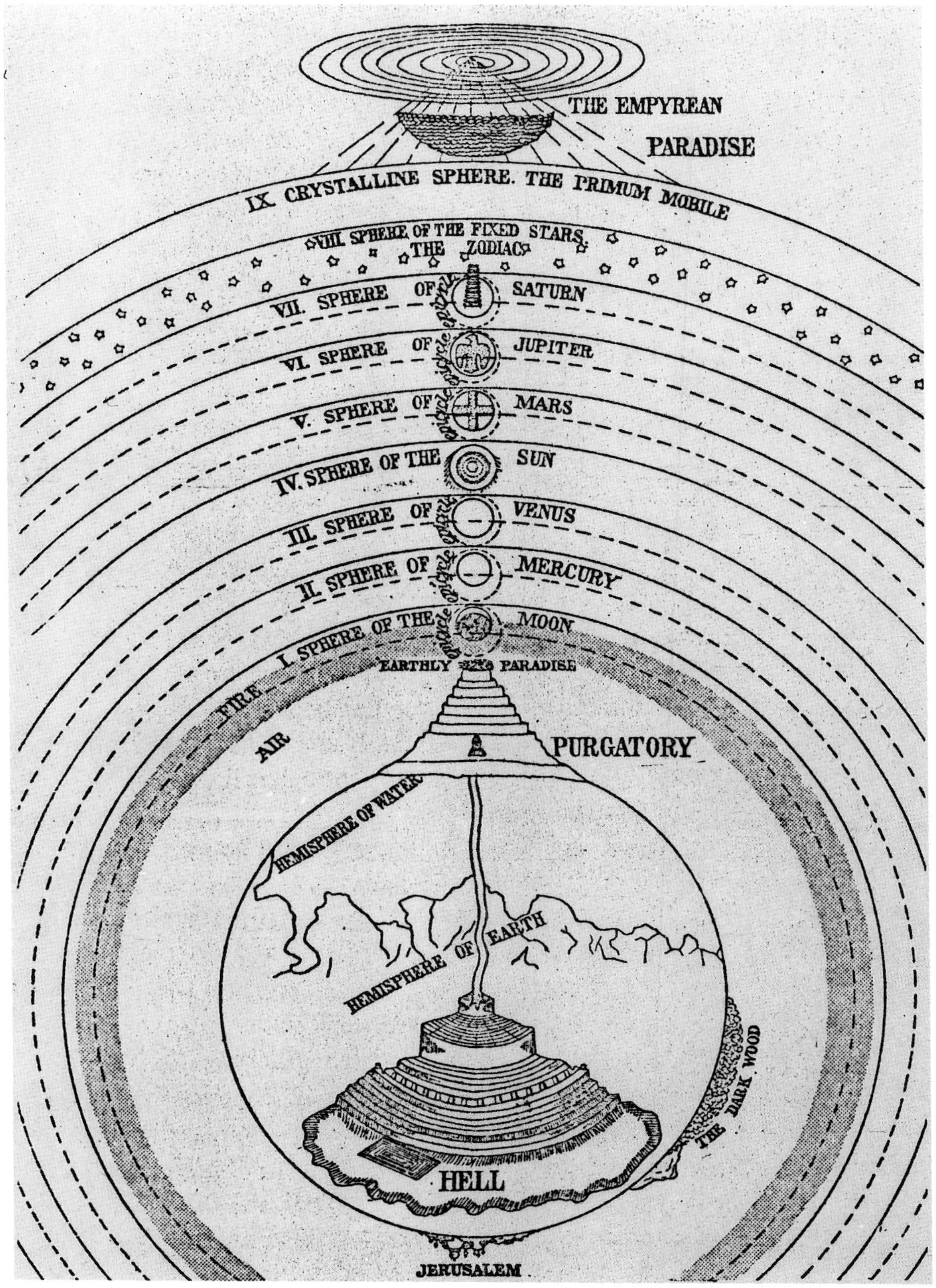

OPPOSITE BELOW: An illustration from a fifteenth-century Italian manuscript, showing Virgil leading Dante to Hell, where those who predict the future have their heads fixed backward as punishment for trying to usurp the power of God. The British Museum, London.

OPPOSITE ABOVE: Saint Thomas Aquinas (1225–1274) considered astrology to be in keeping with Christian concepts of the universe but emphasized that the mind could overcome the influence of the stars.

A diagram of Dante's conception of the structure of the universe, depicting the nether regions below the earth and the planets, stars, highest sphere (*Primum Mobile*), and Paradise. From *La Materia della Divina Commedia di Dante Alighieri*, by Michelangelo Cactani, 1855.

used by prominent teachers and students. He had entered religious orders, and the pope himself at one time offered him an archbishopric, which he declined. Later he fell from papal favor when he became the court astrologer to Frederick II of Sicily, an antagonist to the Holy See. His writings summarized and described virtually every magical system then in existence, though there is some question as to whether he actually subscribed to these practices or merely reported them.

The writings of Dante (1265–1321) offer a cosmology that elaborates on the structural version of the universe that was then generally accepted by the religious orthodox. Dante's cosmos rests on the basic Aristotelian system of concentric spheres with an outermost driving *primum mobile* by means of which God turns the heavens around the earth. Dante also depicted Purgatory and Hell as being below the earth, in a nether region where the spirits of the dead are collected. He placed some of the past's famous people there in idiosyncratic ways. For instance, all forecasters, including astrologers, had their heads fixed to face backward as punishment for predicting the future. (Avicenna, however, was not in Hell or in Purgatory but in Limbo—in recognition of his greatness despite the fact that he was a Muslim infidel.) Yet Dante appears to have known and given tacit recognition to astrology. Although he opposed its usurpation of Providence, he referred to its methods in delineating the character of persons, the course of dynasties, and the propitious times for enterprises.

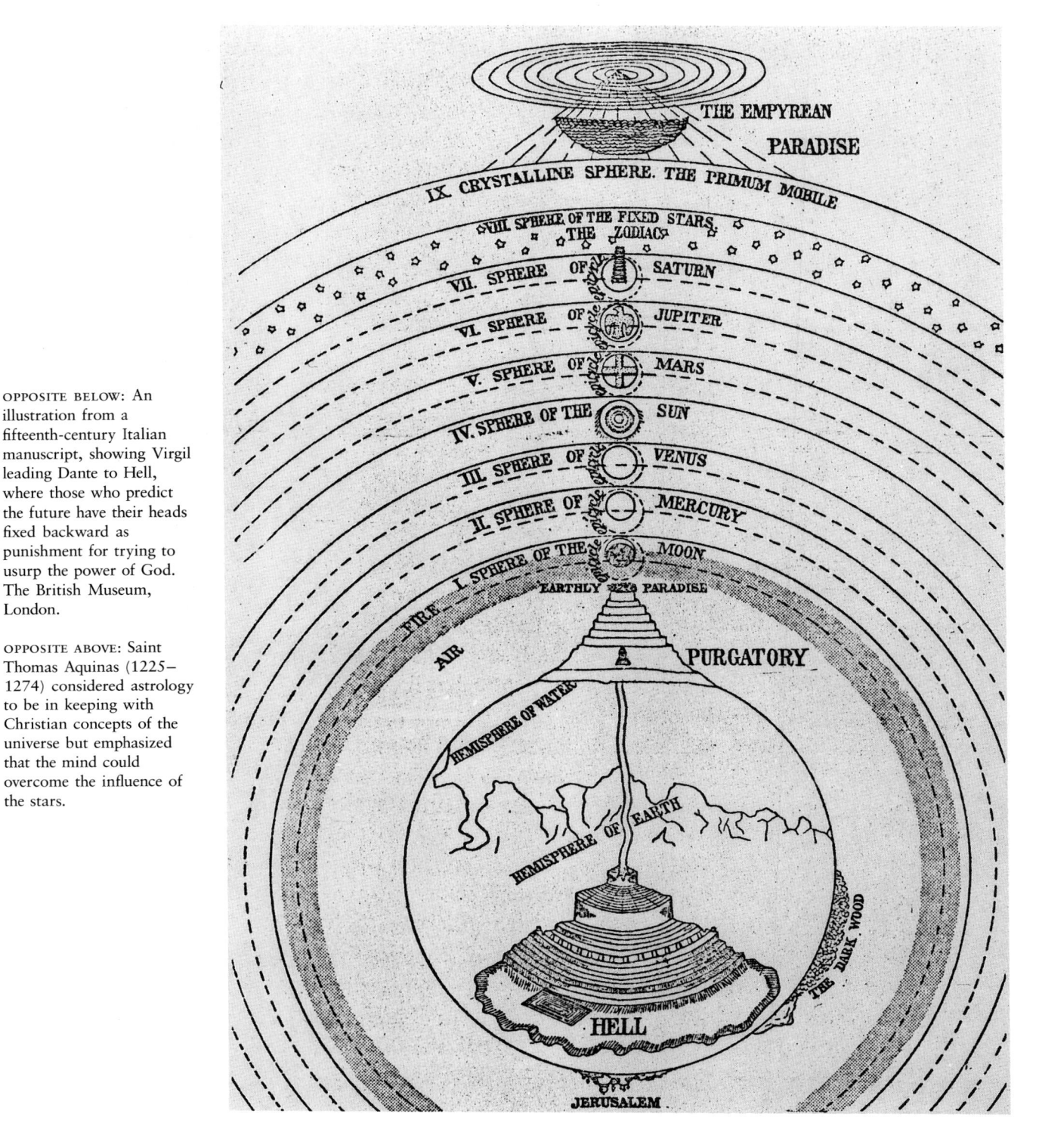

The twelve signs of the zodiac from an Italian book of hours. Left to right, top to bottom: Aries, Taurus, Gemini; Cancer, Leo, Virgo; Libra, Scorpio, Sagittarius; Capricorn, Aquarius, Pisces. c.1475. The Pierpont Morgan Library, New York City. William S. Glazier Collection.

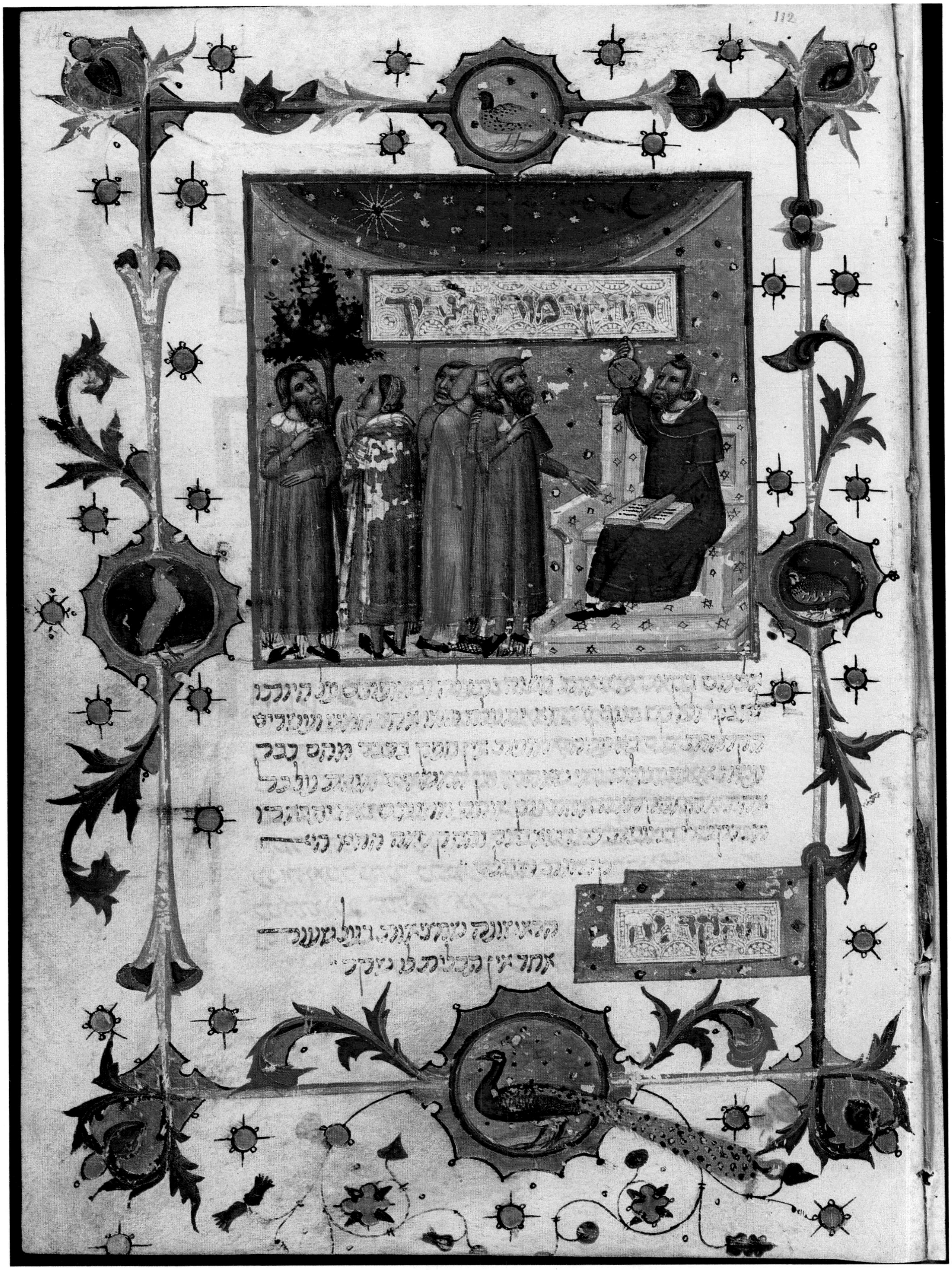

A teacher is seen instructing by means of an astrolabe in this illumination from Maimonides's *Guide to the Perplexed*, translated by Levi bar Isaac from an Arabic manuscript. 1348. The Royal Library, Copenhagen.

The Jacob's staff devices used in medieval and later times permitted measuring the angular distances between sky bodies, as shown on the left—and also the heights and distances of buildings. Nationalbibliothek, Vienna.

The Renaissance and After

The Renaissance witnessed a flowering of astrology as part of a general rise of interest in occultism. However, there were also notable reactions against occult practices, including astrology. By the seventeenth century, the influence of the detractors during the Renaissance had increased, but few thinkers cast aside astrology completely. Detractors often substituted their own dogma and mythology for the disdained doctrines, whereas occultists sometimes displayed the more openminded thinking now usually associated with scientists, thus indicating how difficult it is to assign labels to human thought and behavior.

Descriptions of the work of certain influential thinkers may illustrate paradoxes in rational science and mystical occultism of this era, at least in the light of our modern-day attitudes. Johann Müller (1436–1476), who called himself Regiomontanus (a Latin derivation from the name of his birthplace, Königsberg), combined in his work the study of astronomy and astrology. He published mathematical corrections of the authoritative Alphonsine Tables, and, together with his teacher and colleague George Purbach, contributed astronomical observations on various phenomena such as comets and eclipses, developed calendars and ephemerides, constructed measuring devices, and expanded the uses of trigonometry. Indeed, Pope Sixtus IV invited him to Rome to assist in modifying the astronomical calendar. At the same time, he performed as a practicing astrologer and expanded the astrological principles of Ptolemy, writing and lecturing all over Europe and adding his own sophisticated mathematical system of house division to astrological practice.

Cornelius Heinrich "Agrippa" von Nettesheim (1486–1535) forged a philosophy based on magic, science, and theology. His checkered career took him from being advisor to a king, physician to a royal court, historiographer to a queen, and honorary doctor of divinity at the University of Dole in Switzerland to becoming the inmate of a debtor's prison and a refugee from the Inquisition. Praised by the

Abbot Trithemius and the humanist scholar Erasmus, he was also denounced by many as a practitioner of the black arts. He engaged in alchemy but reported satirically that the only ounce of gold that he ever made was from another ounce of gold. He wrote extensively on magic, especially on the cabala. Some historians evaluate his works more as a compilation of the magical practices inherited from the past than as an endorsement of their use. Employed at one time as an astrologer, which he deemed essential to magic, he later ridiculed its doctrines.

And what is one to make of Philippus Bombastus von Hohenheim (1490–1541), a gigantic figure in the history of medicine? Paracelsus (the pretentious name he took to imply that he was like the great Roman encyclopedist Celsus) taught reliance on personal observation rather than on the dogma of authority, introduced the use of metallic compounds into medical therapy, and simplified the methods of using medications. Later, followers of his teachings were called "Paracelsians" in contradistinction and opposition to Galenists, those who adhered to Galens's complex therapy. Yet, Paracelsus's rational, pragmatic system included the mystical "archus" (an arcane vital force at the center of organs) and also the astrological concept that each part of the body is under the control of a specific constellation (Zodiac Man). Another felicitous irony is displayed by the contributions of the astrologer Torella, whose studies led him to seek a means of counteracting the malign influences of the planet Saturn, which he took to be the cause of syphilis. Since in astrology the planet Mercury is the proper moderator of Saturn, he chose the metallic substance Mercury for therapy. In fact, before the advent of antibiotics doctors discovered that Mercury compounds were one of the effective staples of treating syphilis. Perhaps the extent of the influence of astrology on Renaissance medicine can best be inferred from a great debate in 1437 at the University of Paris on the subject of which days were truly auspicious times for bloodletting.

The two outstanding persons who typified the contrasting attitudes in the Renaissance toward astrology were Marsillo Ficino and Pico della Mirandola. Although the two friends and associates differed sharply on astrology, they were both mystics. Some historians consider them the founders of the intellectual bulwark of Neoplatonic philosophy in Italy. Ficino believed in astrology, taught its doctrines, and cast horoscopes (for example the nativities of the families of Cosimo and Lorenzo de'Medici). He was only one of the astrologers employed by the Medicis. Catherine de'Medici, the queen of France, was also a strong advocate of astrology and magic, and the astrologer Luca Gaurico read correctly the natal chart of the young prince Giovanni de'Medici, predicting that he would one day become pope. On the other hand, Della Mirandola, who was the founder of Renaissance cabalism, made a clear distinction between astronomy and astrology and castigated

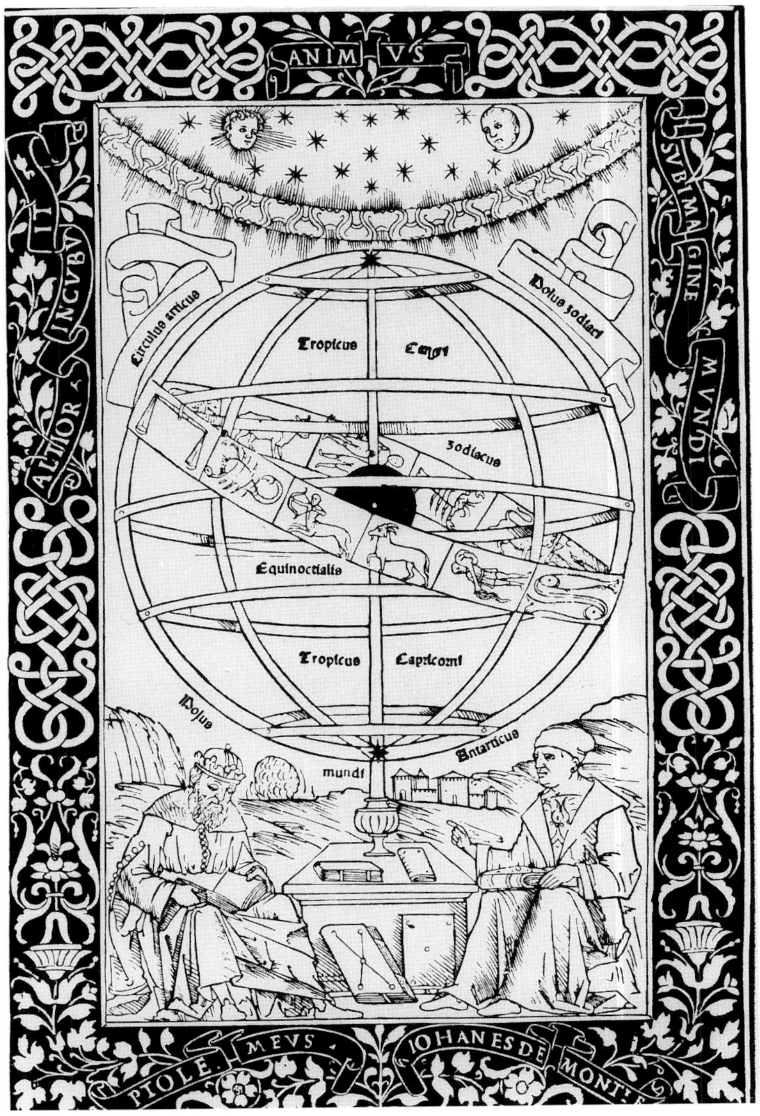

Frontispiece to the *Epitome of Ptolemy's Almagest* (Venice, 1496), a recapitulation of Ptolemy's *Cosmos* by Johann Müller (Regiomontanus), an astrologer who introduced his own mathematical division of the houses in astrology.

the latter's principles as a violation of Christian concepts. He also denigrated astrology's validity in prognostication on the basis of his own experience.

In the seventeenth century Placidus de Titis, an Italian Benedictine monk and mathematician, wrote a rebuttal to Della Mirandola's objections against astrology. In order to overcome the criticism that the house system in astrology was merely an abstraction with no basis in reality, Placidus devised his own house divisions according to the sun's observed course (the ecliptic). The Placidian system is still one of the most widely used today.

The Christian hierarchy continued to be ambivalent toward astrology. Some popes were strong opponents, Sixtus V and Urban VIII being notable examples. When astrologer Pierre de Lorrain forecasted the imminent death of Pope Paul II, he was imprisoned. Even when his forecast was seen to be correct, he was not pardoned. On the other hand, a long line of pontiffs either subscribed wholeheartedly to astrological principles or were benignly tolerant. Pope Alexander VI's astrologer was Torella; Sixtus IV enlisted the

A portrait of Paracelsus by Jan van Scorel. An innovative physician, alchemist, pharmacologist, and occultist, Paracelsus combined independent rationalist attitudes with mystical thinking. Musée du Louvre, Paris.

J'annonce vérité simplement et sans pompe,
Et mon présage vrai nullement ne me trompe.
Michel NOSTRADAMUS naquit à S.t Remy, petite Ville de Provence, le 14 du mois de décembre de l'an 1503, à l'heure de midi, il était fils de Jacques Nostradamus, Notaire Royal de cette Ville, et de Renée de S.t Remy-damoiselle; il était petit fils, tant paternel que maternel, de Médecins et Mathématiciens célèbres; il fut reçu Docteur en l'université de Montpellier dont il exerça la charge de professeur. Ce grand homme a vécu sous les régnes de Louis XII. François I.er Henry II. et Charles IX. dont il fut Médecin; il retourna à Salon, autre Ville de Provence, et y mourut en bon chrétien, après avoir été tourmenté par les gouttes qui, dégénérées en hydropisie, le suffoquèrent au bout de huit jours, ayant prédit l'heure et le jour de sa mort, qui arriva entre trois et quatre heures du matin, le 2 juillet 1566.
De la Fabrique de PELLERIN, Imprimeur-Libraire à ÉPINAL.

Rendering of Michel de Nostredame (Nostradamus), astrologer of the sixteenth century, whose predictions in verse have been interpreted by many as correct forecasts of numerous historical events. He became one of the most famous names in prophecy, though astrology does not appear in his forecasts. Collection Fritz Eichenberg.

help of Regiomontanus; Clement VII, like his friends the Medicis, fully accepted astrological predictions; Julius II is said to have chosen his coronation day according to the stars; and Paul III waited for astrally propitious times before scheduling his consistories—indeed he knighted his astrologer and made him a bishop.

Protestant clerics of the Reformation were no more consistent in their views of astrology than the Catholic hierarchy. Martin Luther, although opposed to astrology, wrote in the preface of an astrological work that signs in the stars "warn and threaten the godless lands and countries and have significance." Yet the staunch reformist John Calvin condemned astrology as foolish, devilish superstitious, and pernicious.

One of the earliest popular books to come off the press after the invention of printing was the *Kalendar and Compost of Shepherds,* appearing first in Paris in 1493. Its title was derived from the common belief that shepherds are

Pope Julius II (1443–1513), who engaged Michelangelo to paint the Sistine Chapel, selected the day for his official investiture on the basis of astrological advice. Raphael. *Mass of Bolsena* (detail). 1512. Fresco. Stanza d'Eliodoro, Vatican, Rome.

This painting by Aldo Dulazzi depicts a meeting called by Pope Gregory XIII in 1582 to reform the calendar; the Western and much of the Eastern worlds now operate according to the revisions that resulted. The astrological signs of Scorpio and Libra are being indicated by one of the scholars. Biblioteca Communale degli Intronati, Siena.

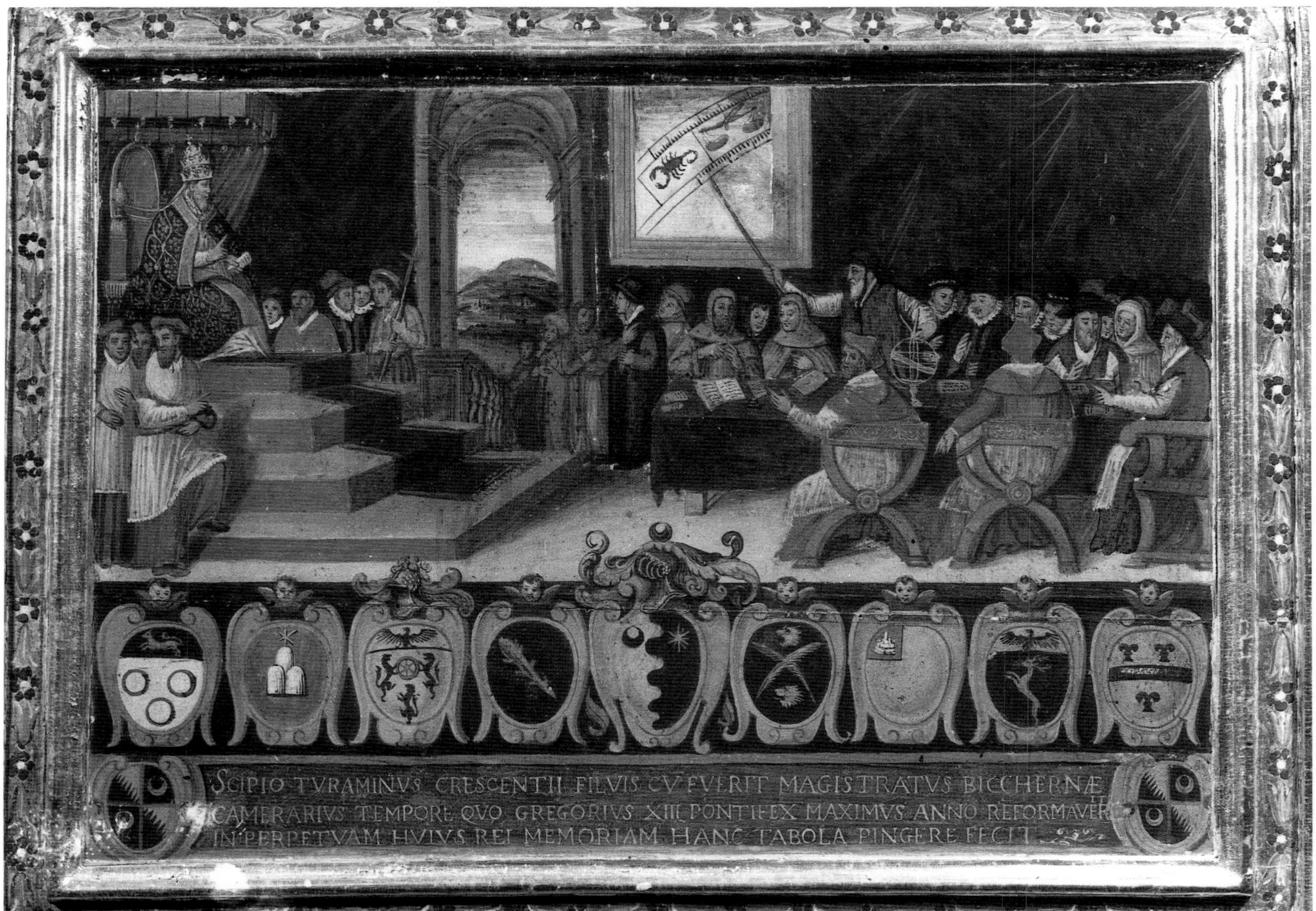

knowledgeable about the sky since they spend so much time under its wide expanse and need to know about weather. The *Kalendar* summarized traditional astrological beliefs of the time, such as the rule over each hour by specific planets, celestial connections to health, sickness, and treatment, and the association of people's physical appearances with their Sun-sign and ascending zodiac sign at birth. An avalanche of almanacs and calendars followed, offering astrological information and forecasts. A veritable craze for these popular pamphlets led Francis I (r.1514–1547) of France and others after him to ban these publications, but the evidence suggests that there was little or no slackening in their production or their consumption.

Astrology took hold in more than just popular culture. Michael Servetus (c.1500), the medical thinker who may have understood the process behind the circulation of the blood well before Harvey, believed in astrology. He was burned at the stake for his theological pronouncements, though not for his practice of astrology. Giordano Bruno, the philosopher and cosmologist, accepted astrology and also the Copernican concept of the earth revolving around the sun. He too was burned, not because of his astrological leanings, but rather for implying that a heliocentric universe caused him to doubt Christian teachings. Rabelais evidently believed in astrology, but in *Gargantua* and *Pantagruel* he ridiculed most occult methods of prediction.

ABOVE: A woodcut from Martin Luther's Bible (1543) depicting a version of the cosmos based on Ptolemy's system in the second century A.D. The Granger Collection, New York City.

Albrecht Dürer. *Celestial Map: Northern Hemisphere.* c.1515. National Gallery of Art, Rosenwald Collection. Washington, D.C. The map depicts the zodiac figures and other constellation symbols and portrays prominent astrologers in history: Aratus, Ptolemy, Arabus, and Manilius.

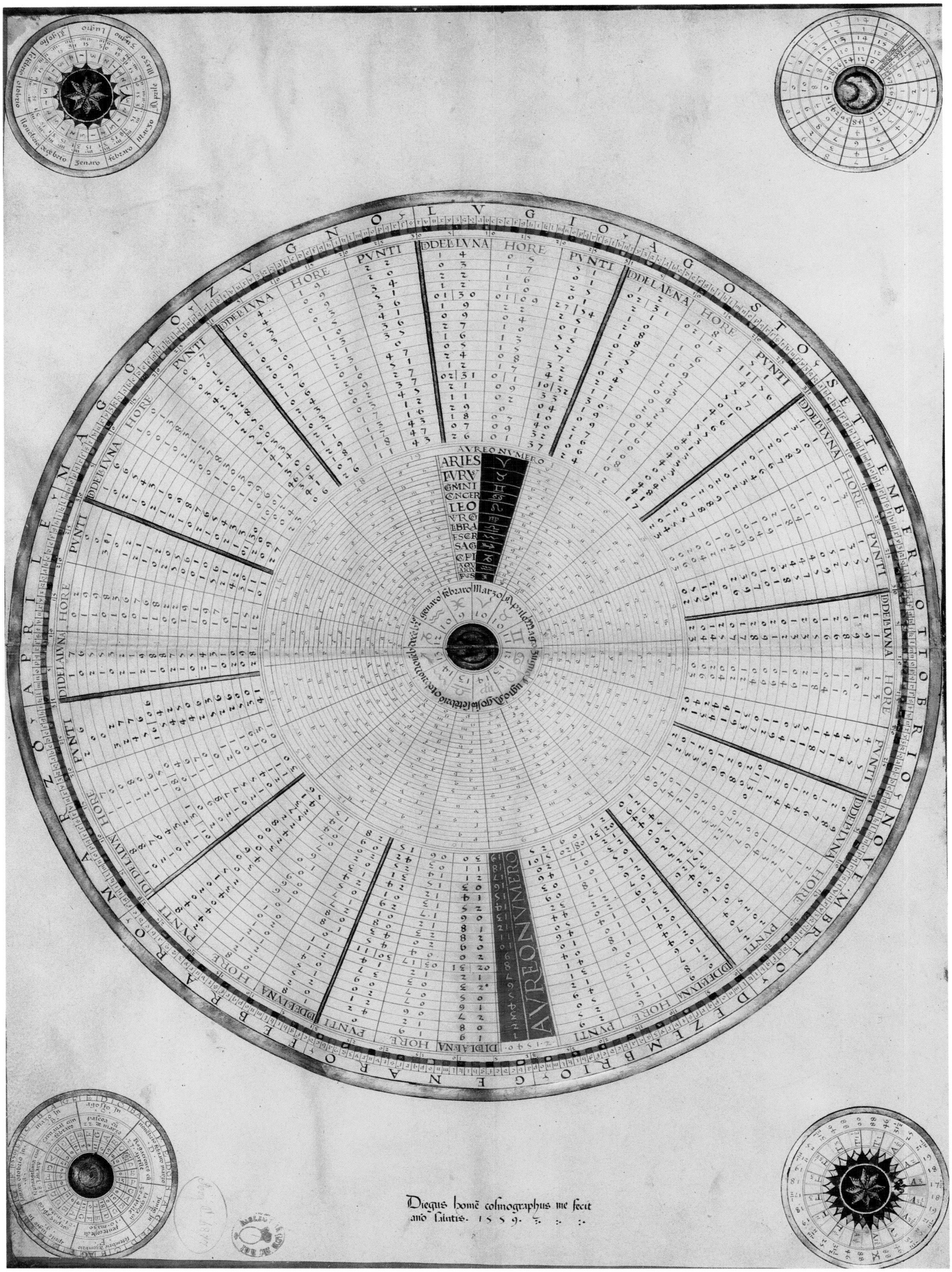

ABOVE: A perpetual calendar devised by the Portuguese Diegus Homé in 1559 for each nineteen-year cycle, after which the solar and lunar years repeat themselves. In the outer rings are the months and appearance dates of the new moon. The four corners contain significant dates, such as religious holidays. Bibliothèque Nationale, Paris.

OPPOSITE: The astronomical clock at Hampton Court Palace, constructed by astronomer Nicholas Kratzer for Henry VIII in 1540, a few years before the publication by Copernicus of his sun-centered system. Thus the earth is placed at the center, with moon, sun, and stars encircling; the clock shows the hour, day, and month, and the position of the sun in the zodiac. Hampton Court Palace, London.

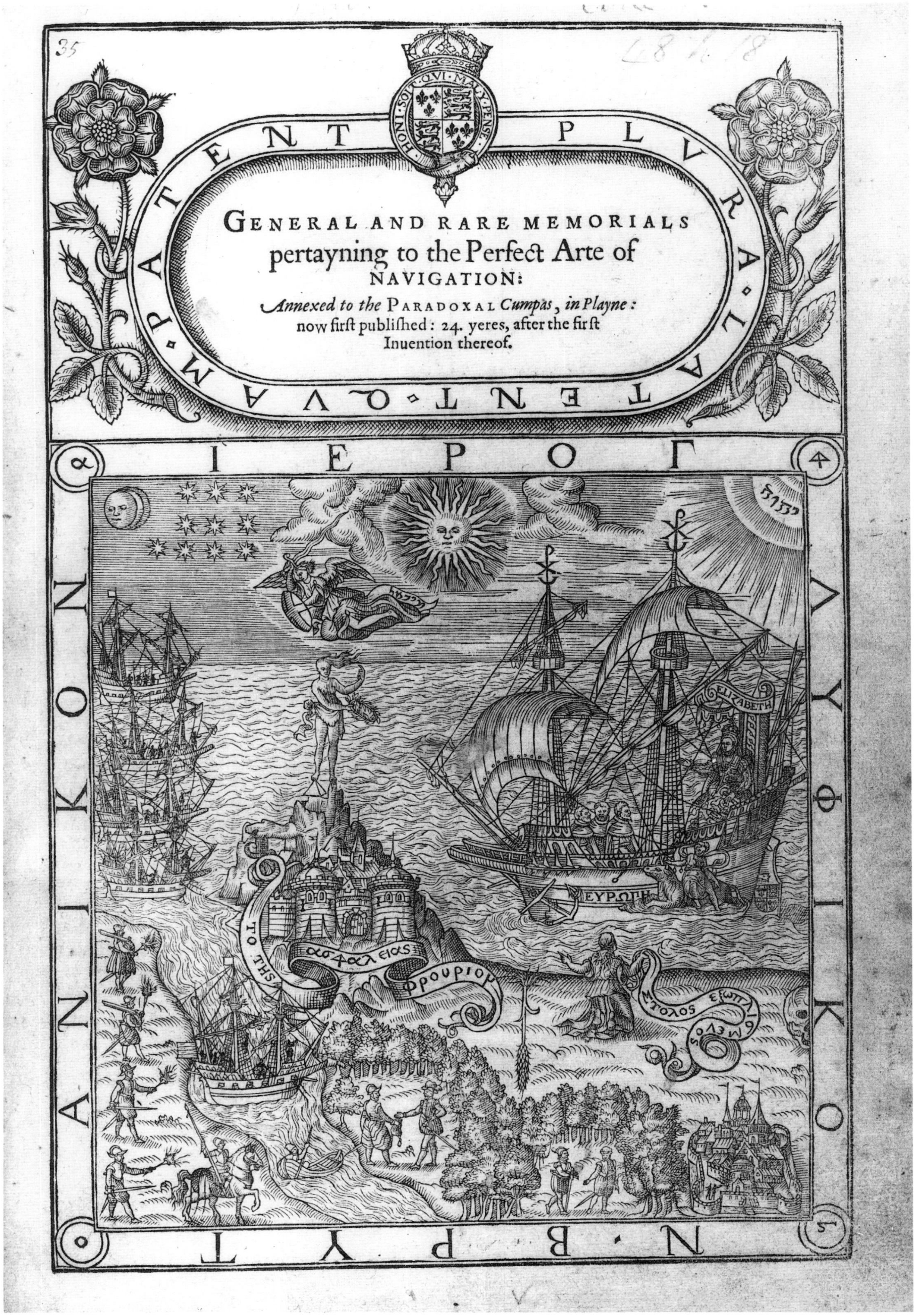

PATENT · PLURA · LATENT · QUAM ·

GENERAL AND RARE MEMORIALS
pertayning to the Perfect Arte of
NAVIGATION:
Annexed to the PARADOXAL *Cumpas, in Playne:*
now first publiſhed: 24. yeres, after the first
Inuention thereof.

OPPOSITE: The title page of *General and Rare Memorials,* a book on celestial navigation by John Dee, an advisor to Queen Elizabeth I. Dee was a highly competent mathematician and also a firm believer in astrology and other occult practices. 1577. The British Library, London.

An astrologer drawing up a horoscope, suggesting that astrologers used observation of the skies as well as calculations from charts (on the lectern) and a model of the globe (on the table). From Robert Fludd's *Utriusque Cosmi* (1617–1621). E. P. Goldschmidt & Co. Ltd., London.

In England, where the Renaissance came later than on the Continent, the same type of ambivalence existed, except that for a long time astrology seemed to be tainted by its foreign origins and associations. By the reign of Henry VIII, native astrologers were numerous enough to warrant people abandoning the foreign bias, but the strong doubts held by many in private were matched in public by a law in 1541 against sorcery, including astrology. The effect appears to have been minimal (astrology went underground), as members of the royalty and scholars continued to follow its principles. Elizabeth I, for one, honored and closely heeded her court astrologer, John Dee. An outstanding contributing mathematician, Dee was a sincere, practicing astrologer who is said to have calculated the astrologically auspicious day for the coronation of Elizabeth, at her own request.

Shakespeare's works also illustrate the prominence of concerns with the stars in Elizabethan times, but scholars are not in agreement on whether these passages were examples of acceptance by Shakespeare of starry influences or just common contemporary attitudes and figures of speech. The references to astrology that appear in his works are in concordance with the "moderate" opinion that gained ascendancy—belief in the influence of the stars but not in their dominion over humans:

Our remedies oft in ourselves do lie,
Which we ascribe to heaven. The fated sky
Gives us free scope, only doth backward pull
Our slow designs when we ourselves are dull.
—Hebra in *All's Well That Ends Well*
(act I, scene I)

Similarly, in *Julius Caesar* Cassius seems to deny all starry effects:

The fault, dear Brutus, is not in our stars
But in ourselves, that we are underlings.

Literary allusions to astrology in the Elizabethan period were numerous. Christopher Marlowe's plays include disparagement and ridicule. The diviner Agrippa von Nettesheim is said to have been the model for the foolish astrologer in Marlowe's *Faustus.* On the other hand, clergyman Robert Burton's writings showed enthusiasm for astrology, and the poet John Dryden was also a believer, even casting horoscopes himself. Sir Francis Bacon (1561–1626), influential court chamberlain, essayist, and philosopher of science, condemned astrology as "full of superstition" and marshaled his intellect against its predictive validity. Yet, he acknowledged an influence by the stars in some terrestrial events and human affairs.

An astronomical clock, attributed to Caspar Behain, displaying both the astronomical divisions of time and also the signs of the zodiac. 1568. Gilt-bronze and steel, 14½ × 8¼ × 5¾". The Metropolitan Museum of Art, New York City. Gift of J. Pierpont Morgan, 1917.

An illustration of a scene from the satirical poem *Hudibras* by Samuel Butler (1612–1680), which mocked astrology and astrologers. Sir William Fetter Douglas. *Hudibras and Ralph Visiting the Astrologer*. c.1856. Oil on canvas, 25½ × 42½". National Gallery of Scotland, Edinburgh.

BELOW: Horoscope chart of Louis XIV cast by his astrologer, J. B. Morin of Villefranche, from *Astrologia Gallica* (The Hague, 1661). Early horoscope diagrams were drawn in the shape of a square. Koninklijke Bibliotheek, Amsterdam.

Advances in astronomy at the end of the Renaissance brought more attention to the skies and led practitioners to improve on the uses of astrology by correcting some of its inaccuracies. Further support for astrology came from medical scholars, who subscribed to the significance of the stars in prognosis and treatment, and from natural scientists who affirmed the effects of the moon on tides and on minerals, such as selenite (its name is derived from the Latin for *moon*). But by the sixteenth century astronomy and astrology were assumed to be different disciplines.

European royal families continued to support astrologers but their patronage often depended on whether the astrologer's prediction was optimistic or pessimistic, not on whether it was accurate. Louis XIV of France is said to have hidden his astrologer, Jean-Baptiste Morin de Villefranche, in the royal bedchamber to allow a horoscope to be cast at the moment of birth of the offspring, the future king. Some even averred that the astrologer was also on hand to record the precise instant of impregnation.

William Lilly (1602–1681) became the best-known astrologer in England. His many successful forecasts gained

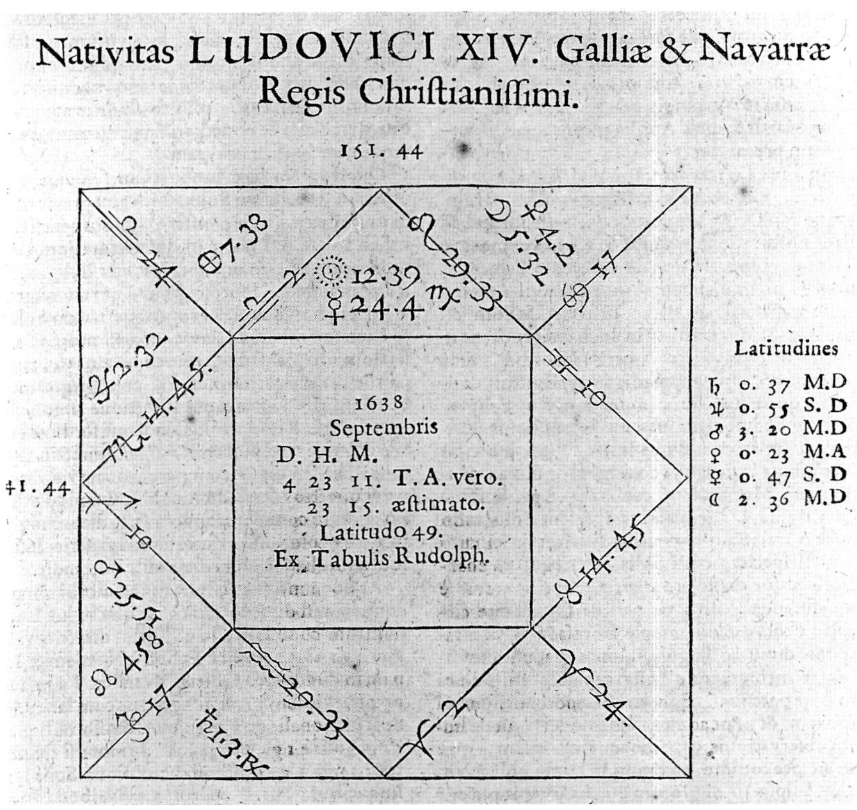

Richard Saunders (1613–1687) was an influential astrologer whose books were among the most widely read astrological theses in seventeenth-century England. Wellcome Institute Library, London.

ABOVE AND OPPOSITE ABOVE: William Lilly (1602–1681) was the best-known astrologer in England. He predicted the Great Fire of London in 1666 (right), among other events. He was brought before Parliament as a suspect when the catastrophe occurred. The British Museum, London.

him much popularity among the public. At least one of his predictions of unrest in the country, indicated by the presence of Saturn in the fifth house, was made after the English Civil War had already started. Jealous detractors among his fellow astrologers, including the Royalist George Wharton, were quick to depict him as a scoundrel and an imposter. When Lilly predicted in 1651 that there would be a great fire in London in 1666, he was brought before a committee of investigation for possible complicity after the event actually occurred. Lilly needed a friend at court. Elias Ashmole, after whom Oxford University's famous library is named, gave favorable representations on his behalf. Ashmole and Lilly's testimony convinced the courts of his innocence and further enhanced his reputation as an astrologer. Nevertheless, Samuel Butler lampooned William Lilly and astrology in his satirical poem *Hudibras*:

Knew when she (the moon) was in fittest mood,
For cutting corns or in letting blood,
When for anointing scabs and itches,
Or to the bum applying leeches . . .

In the seventeenth century, physician Sir Thomas Browne, who summarized the philosophic attitudes of the scientist toward religion, accepted the basics of astrology but not some of its claims. The Royal Society rejected astrology outright and considered it a denial of the true dominion of God. A particularly popular writer in seventeenth-century England, Nicholas Culpeper (1616–1654), linked the planets and constellations to all aspects of medicine. Since every disease, even each symptom, and all plants were under the influence of the celestial bodies according to Culpeper, the astrologic association of a herb had to be matched with the affected bodily part and to its ailment in order to achieve effective treatment. Culpeper's publications, used not only in England but also in other countries, were referred to well into the eighteenth and nineteenth centuries.

Astrology's acceptance and rejection were often related not only to the new scientific attitudes, but also to the political, theological, and sociological interplay of the time. According to one scholar's estimate, about one-third of all the families in England had bought at least one astrological publication before or during the war between the Royalists and the Parliamentarians.

After the restoration of Charles II, the opposing political forces differed in their attitudes. The upper class, the newly reinstalled aristocracy, associated astrology unfavorably with anti-Royalism, atheism, and lower social status. Yet the general impression among intellectuals was that the stars "impel but do not compel." Among the lower social and economic classes, faith in astrology remained steadfast.

Since the new spirit of rationalism and the astronomical findings seemed to upset previously accepted tenets, the astrologers themselves were split into separate divisions in attitudes.

In response to the new intellectual climate, the inheritors of astrological traditions, among them Joshua Childrey and Joshua Goad, tried to make their doctrines more acceptable as a rational discipline based upon correlating the careful observation of events and personalities with planetary arrangements.

However, even these reforming astrologers were divided in their aims. One group attempted to introduce scientific principles to accommodate the Copernican concept of the sun, rather than the earth, as the center of the solar system. Others went even further, casting off zodiac signs and other paraphernalia of traditional astrology, while retaining the basic tenets of celestial influence on human affairs. The astrologer John Gadbury typified the contending forces. His political and theological convictions gradually changed through the years from a conservative, Anglican position favorable toward standard astrology to more radical, Royalist, reforming attitudes (his critics called them downright Catholic), although he was consistently devoted to observing and evaluating statistical data, emphasizing the need for research into the validity of astrology. The second group of astrologers, of which John Partridge was a notable member, adhered to the original teachings of Aristotle and Ptolemy and condemned the new-fangled corruption of pure traditional doctrine.

Thus, in England within each of the intellectual segments—conservative and radical, Royalist and Parliamentarian, Anglican and Catholic, Tory and Whig—there were degrees of acceptance and rejection of

In this woodcut by Jost Amman (1695–1751), astrologers cast a newborn's horoscope from the arrangement of the stars in the sky. Ars Medica Collection, Philadelphia Museum of Art.

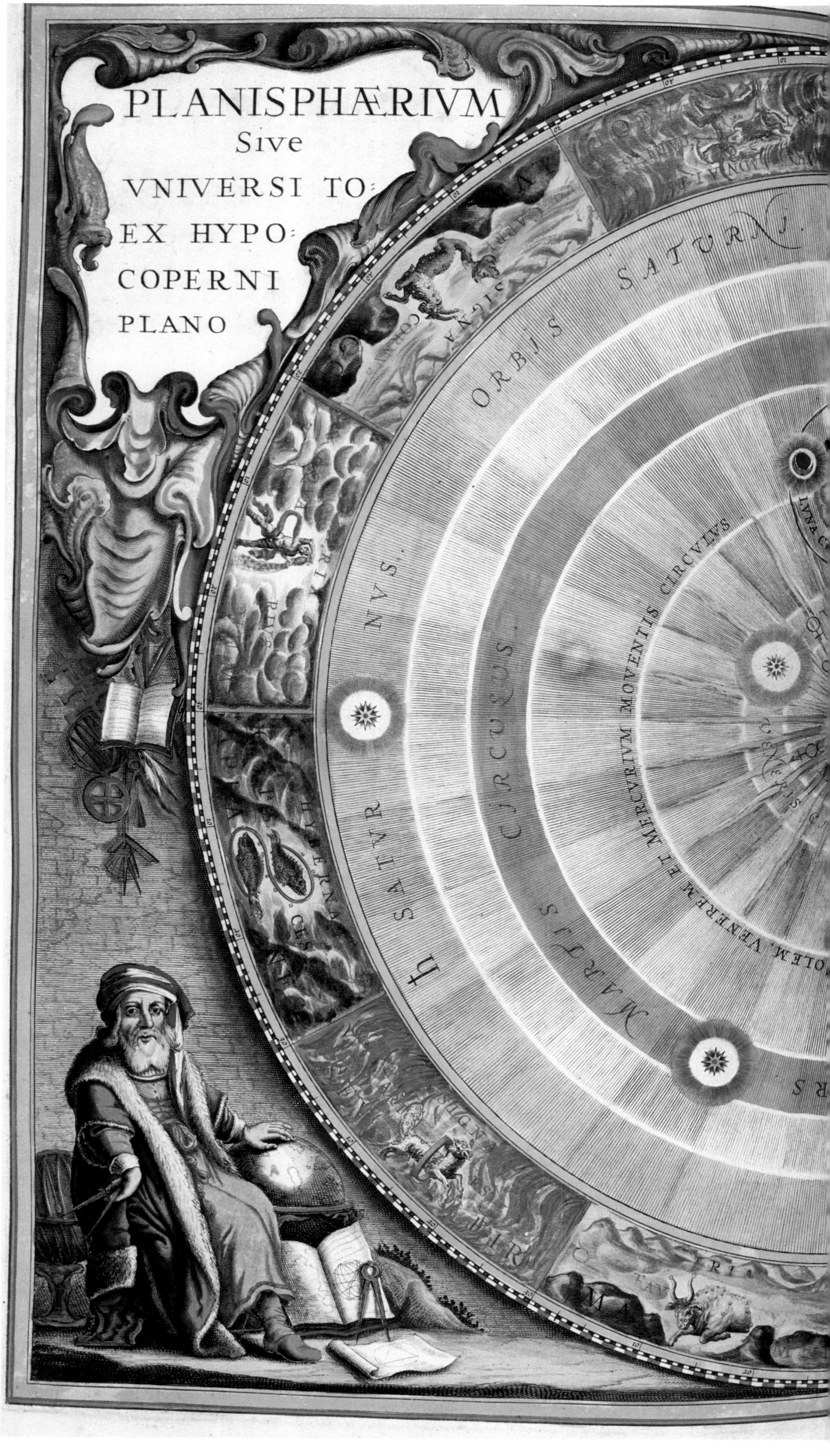

An illustration of the Copernican solar system, in which the planets revolve around the sun. Andrew Cellarius. Color engraving from the *Atlas Coelestis* (1660). The British Library, London.

COPERNICANVM
Systema
TIVS CREATI
THESI
CANA IN
EXHIBITVM.
IVPI
TER
Jovis Circulus
GLOBI SVBLVNARIS CVM LVNA ET QVATVOR ELEMENTIS

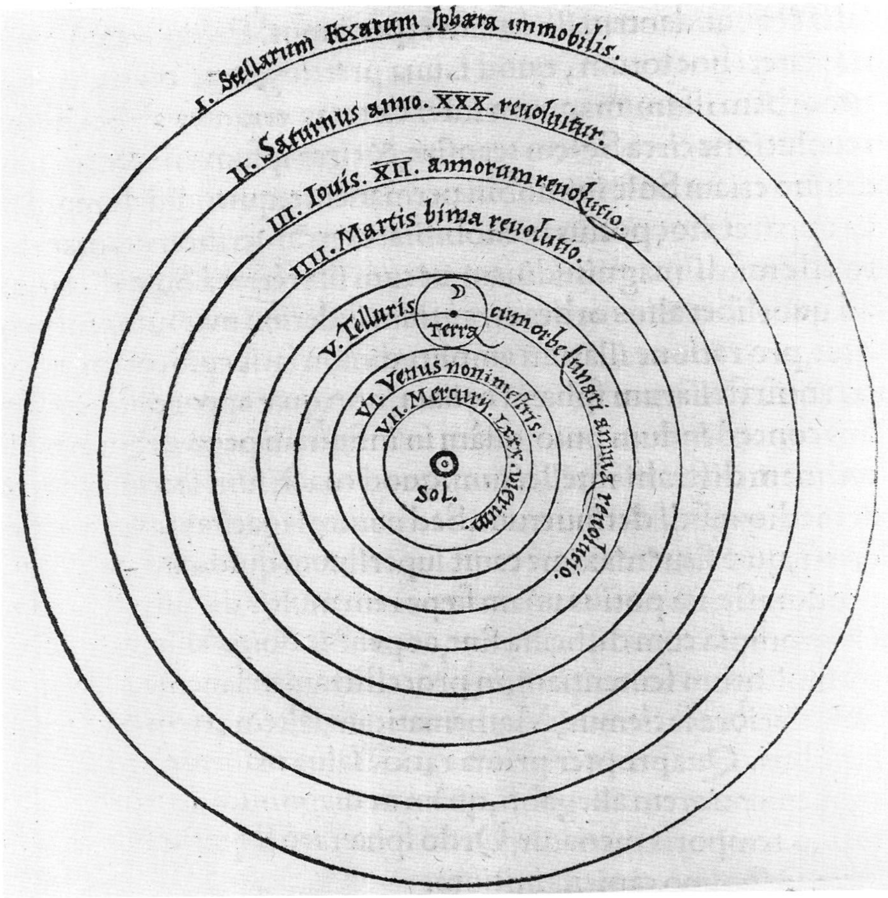

A view of the Copernican universe with the earth and the planets orbiting the sun, and the immobile stars in the outermost rim. Copernicus incorrectly assumed the orbits were circular. From the *De Revolutionibus Orbium Coelestium.* (Nuremberg, 1543.)

astrological laws and theories, which to some extent paralleled the political, religious, and social divisions of the society.

The Earth Revolves Around the Sun

At the root of astrology was the notion that the sun, moon, and planets revolve around the earth. Medieval and Renaissance observers, like people for thousands of years before them, also accepted a geocentric universe, even though in the sixth century B.C. Pythagoras had hypothesized that the earth moves and in the third century B.C. the Greek Aristarchus had actually formulated a universe with the sun at the center (an idea that had few supporters and hardly lasted through the lifetime of its originator).

In the mid-sixteenth century Nicolaus Copernicus (1473–1543) not only established the revolution of the earth but also started a revolution in thinking. The ideas he expressed were not widely accepted at first, and Copernicus himself delayed their publication for ten years—composing a type of abstract of his conclusions and then a longer work upon which the published volume was based. A possible reason for his caution was his reluctance to confront the Church, although no danger of chastisement ever seems to have been actually present. His report seemed to the scientists of the time and to the Church mainly a model of a more perfect cosmos rather than a description of the actual state of the universe. The traditionalists therefore saw no reason to oppose the model. Others, such as Galileo Galilei (1564–1642) and Johannes Kepler (1571–1630), were impressed by the observations and the reality of the conception. Another more likely explanation for Copernicus's hesitation is stated in his book—that the suggested heliocentric system would seem absurd to the populace and untenable to intellectuals. The Church's need for an annual calendar that established consistent religious holidays prompted Pope Paul III to favor the publication. The *De Revolutionibus Orbium Coelestium* was even dedicated to the pope. George Joachim Rheticus, a mathematician and friend of Copernicus's who edited and arranged for the printing, tried to make the treatise more palatable by including an introduction that employed astrological terms and tenets and also explicitly stated that the ideas in the book were suggestions rather than doctrines and that the conception was only one of several possible theories on the mechanism of the universe.

Because Copernicus visualized the orbits of the earth and planets to be circular rather than elliptical, a number of inaccuracies were contained in his proposed system, but his findings and calculations were astonishingly correct in view of the crudeness of the instrumentation and the necessary limitations in the methods available to him. For instance, he measured the movements of the stars by sighting their changing positions through slits cut into the walls of his house.

His monumental affirmation that the earth spins on an axis and also revolves around the sun, along with all the planets, was embraced by some mathematicians and

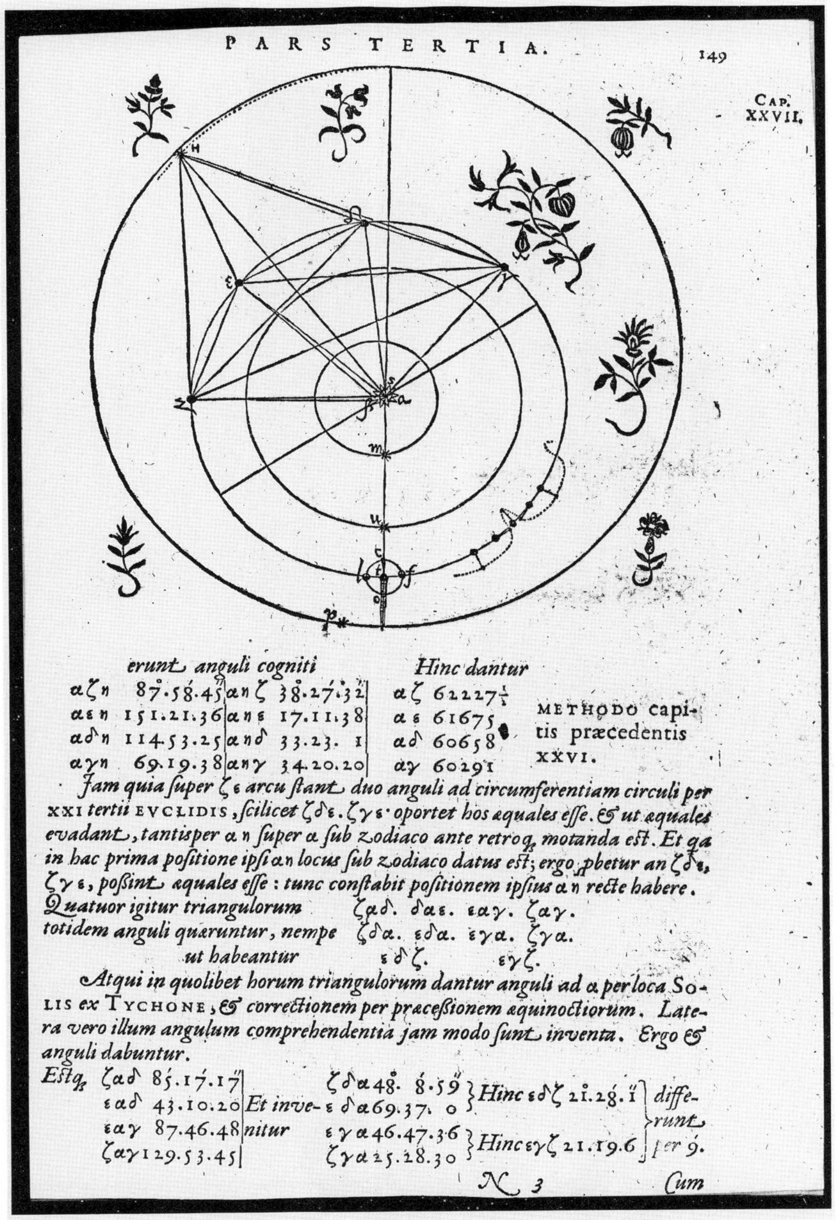

A drawing by Tycho Brahe of the planetary orbits, diagrammed on the basis of his observed data.

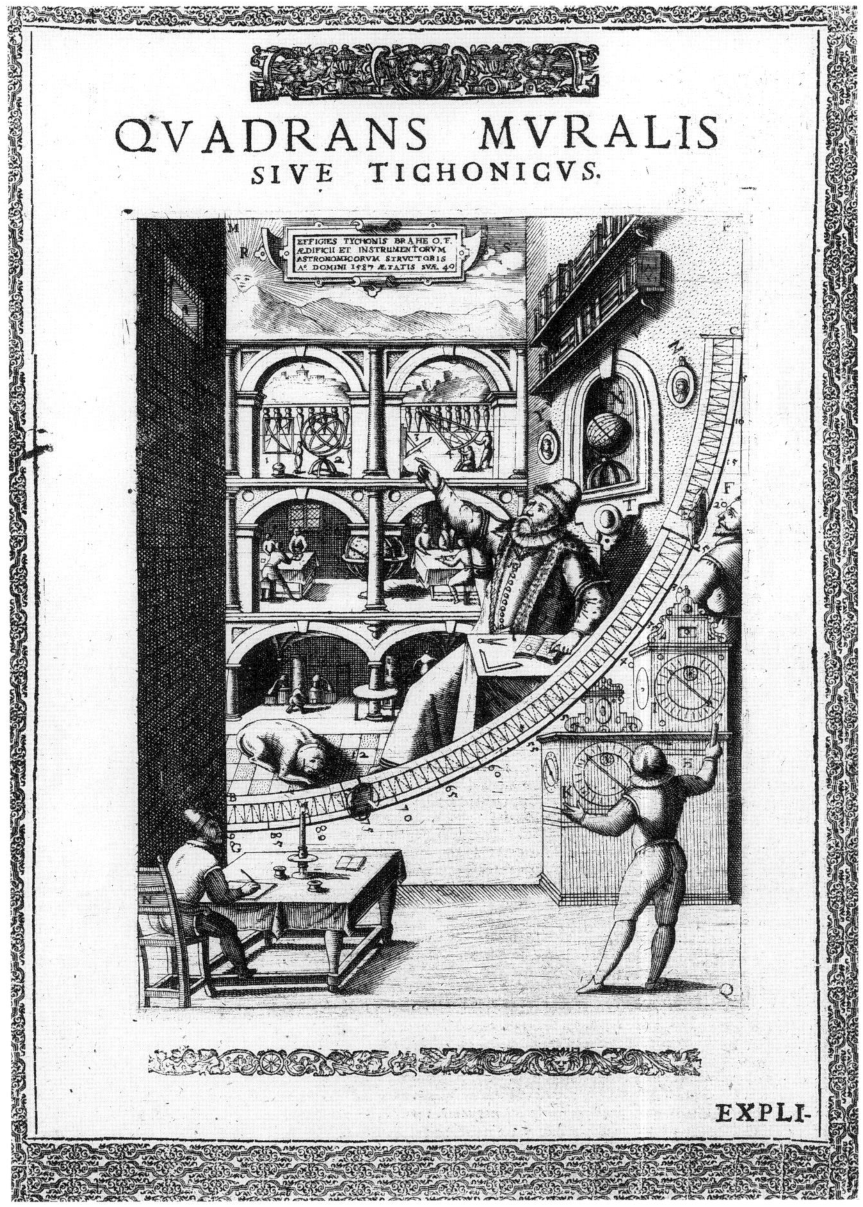

An imagined representation of Tycho Brahe in his observatory with assistants, instruments, and charts. From *Astronomiae, Wandsbek*, 1598. The New York Public Library. Astor, Lenox, and Tilden Foundations.

astronomers. On the other hand, many remained openly critical. Indeed, a hundred years later the Paris Observatory still proclaimed Copernicism as false. Even into the eighteenth century both geocentric and the heliocentric doctrines were taught together as two differing explanations of the mechanics of the universe in the universities of America. Not until early in the nineteenth century did the Catholic Church formally admit into its curriculum the notion of a sun-centered solar system.

Traditional astrologers, by contrast, adjusted rapidly to the new conception, for it did not bar them from continuing to believe that the planets and stars influence terrestrial behavior and human development. The new system was merely a mathematical and geometric way of explaining why the sky patterns changed each hour, day, and month. The angular relationships of the planets (the aspects) stayed the same. The zodiac remained as always. The theoretical division of the sky into houses had the same basis. Increasing observations and measurements advanced knowledge of the heavens but did not necessarily alter fundamental astrological concepts.

Ironically, Tycho Brahe (1546–1601), an adherent of traditional astrology who provided highly significant astronomical data upon which later astronomers, such as Kepler and Isaac Newton, were to base their own revolutionary contributions, was an opponent of Copernicism. His own exceptionally precise findings convinced him that the earth was at the center of the universe, that the sun was in orbit around the earth, and that the five known planets circled around the sun in a system of epicycles. To him, the Copernican theory was both foolish scientifically and false according to Scripture.

ATLAS COELESTIS;
seu
HARMONIA
MACROCOSMICA.

ABOVE: Heinrich Hansen. *Tycho Brahe's Observatory at Night*. National Historike Museum, Frederiksborg, Denmark. Brahe's observations became the basis for much of modern astrology and astronomy.

OPPOSITE: The frontispiece illustration to *Harmonica Macrocomicas* by Andrew Cellarius, picturing Tycho Brahe, Ptolemy, Saint Augustine, Copernicus, Galileo, and Cellarius (c.1660).

In addition to the development of precise instruments and detailed observations, Brahe introduced new information on the moon's course and explained for the first time the misleading appearances of celestial objects because of refraction by the atmosphere. Further, when he discovered and reported the sudden appearance of a new star (a nova or supernova) and placed it in the sphere of "fixed" stars, a region heretofore accepted as unchanging, he thoroughly overturned Aristotelian cosmology. Nevertheless, he was convinced of astrology's merits and drew horoscopes for the royal family of Denmark, who had him ensconced on an island where he could pursue his studies of the sky.

Brahe's contributions show that both observation and hypothesis are necessary to furthering knowledge. His theories on the structure of the solar system proved to be erroneous, but his observations enabled his pupil Kepler to derive by calculation and hypothesis the laws of planetary motion that became fundamental to all subsequent astronomy. Kepler accepted the heliocentric view of Copernicus but found it inconsistent with the accurate, detailed observations of Brahe because of Copernicus's incorrect conception that the orbits of planets are circular. When Kepler proposed that the orbits are elliptical, all facts fell into place. One may also recognize in the careers of Brahe and Kepler that observed facts may be explained and understood in different ways, depending on the spirit of the times and the individual beliefs of the interpreter.

Our present view of the solar system begins with Kepler's three laws, presented mathematically in formulas. Essentially their meaning is that (1) the planets all revolve around the sun in elliptical orbits; (2) each planet moves at varying speeds related to the shape and size of the orbit; (3) the time it takes for a planet to make one complete revolution about the sun has a proportional mathematical relationship to its distance from the sun. Like Pythagoras almost twenty-five hundred years earlier, Kepler also believed in the concept that the spinning and revolving bodies produce harmonious musical tones specific to their individual velocities.

Kepler's association with astrology has received differing evaluations. He certainly did state that astrology was the foolish daughter of the wise mother astronomy, but at a later time he acknowledged that experience had compelled him to believe in the effects of the constellations on human nature. He equated accepting the influence of the stars with believing in God's wisdom. Evidently he drew up horoscopes and composed astrological almanacs that made forecasts, principally, some say, for financial gain. On the other hand, he also advised those intellectuals who objected to astrology out of hand to separate the superstitious parts from its genuine elements. Since he also subscribed to the ancient adage that the stars impel but cannot compel, he used astrology to reveal tendencies and probabilities, allowing for humans to overcome deficiencies caused by the

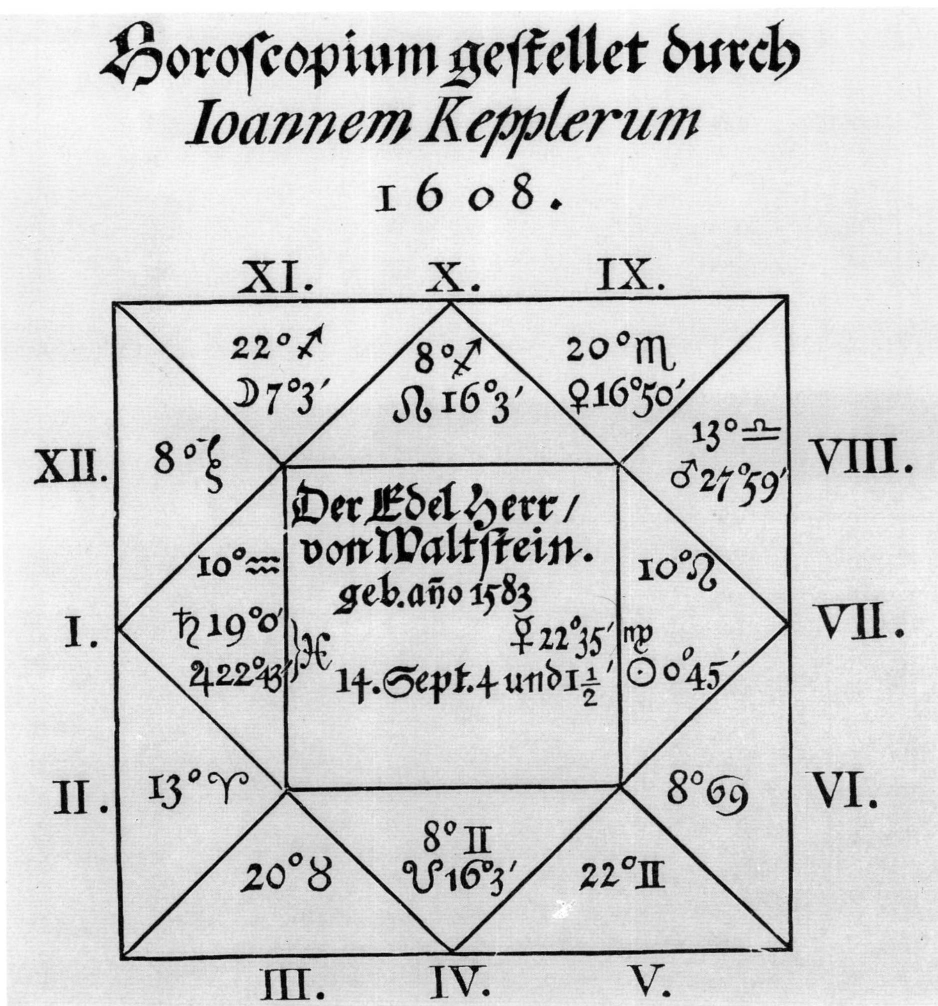

A horoscope constructed in 1608 by Johannes Kepler for Count Wallenstein, later Duke Albrecht von Wallenstein, from which Kepler is reputed to have predicted the future career of the count.

OPPOSITE: A mechanical model of Johannes Kepler's planetary system is shown in this woodcut from his *Mysterium Cosmo Graphicum* (Tübingen, 1596).

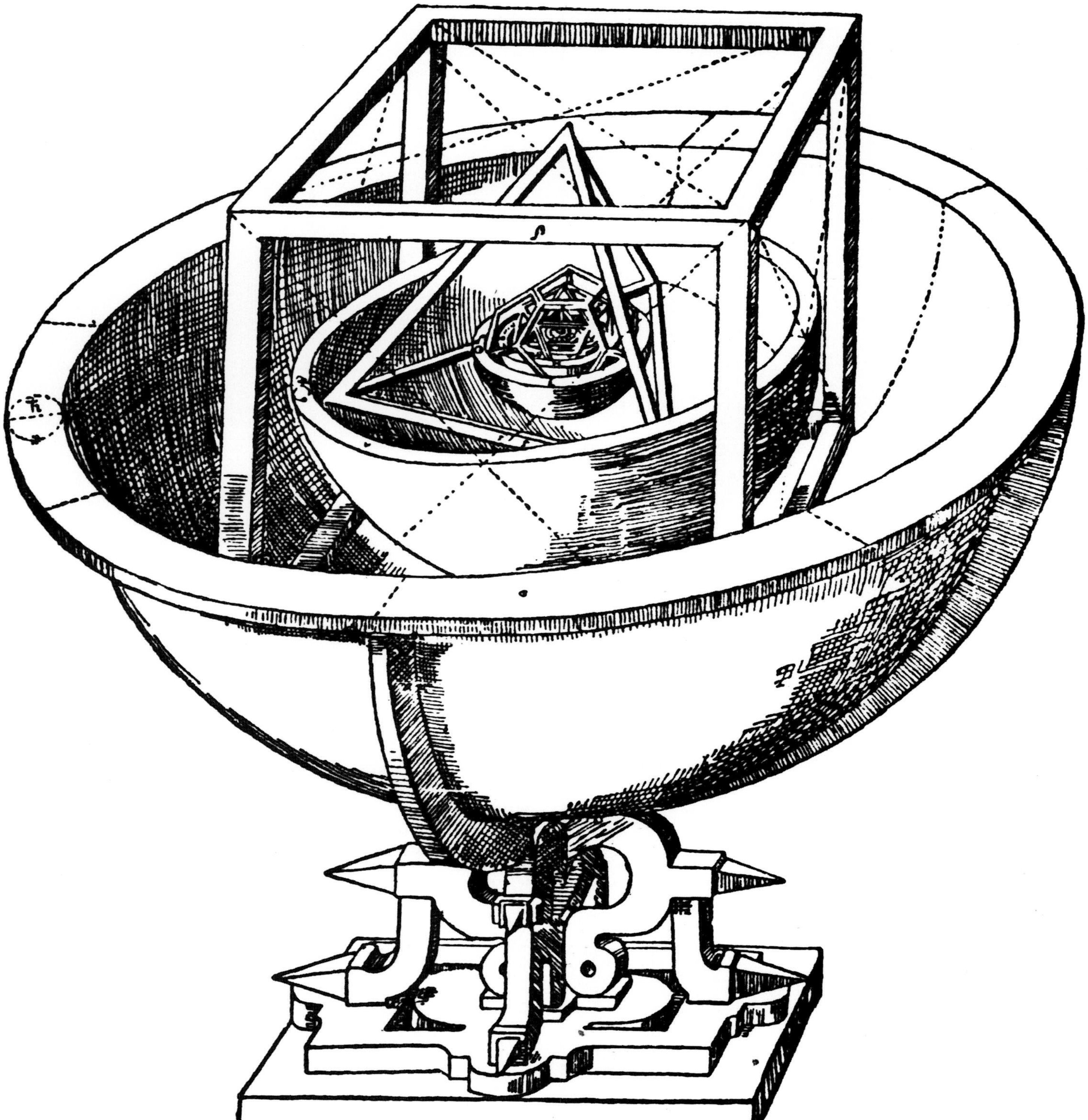

Robert Fleury. *Galileo Before the Holy Office.* 1847. Musée du Louvre, Paris.

OPPOSITE: A replica of the telescope used by Isaac Newton for his direct observations of the sky.

The title page to Isaac Newton's *Philosophiae Naturalis Principia Mathematica* (first issue, first edition, London, 1687), one of the most important milestones in science. The Library of Congress, Washington, D.C.

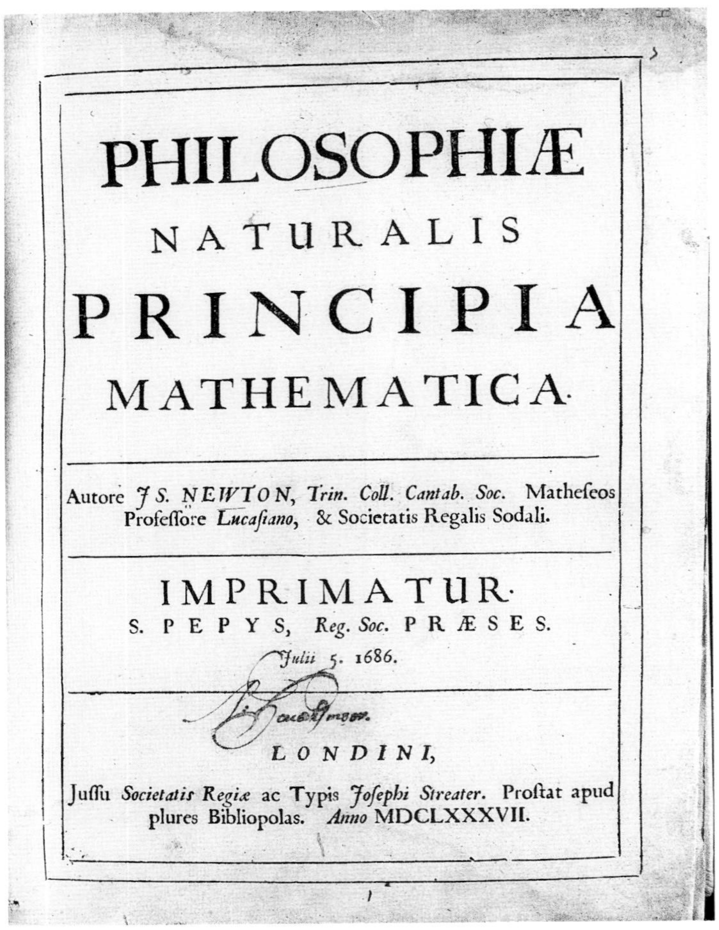

PHILOSOPHIÆ
NATURALIS
PRINCIPIA
MATHEMATICA.

Autore *J S.* NEWTON, *Trin. Coll. Cantab. Soc.* Mathefeos Profeffore *Lucafiano*, & Societatis Regalis Sodali.

IMPRIMATUR.
S. PEPYS, *Reg. Soc.* PRÆSES.
Julii 5. 1686.

LONDINI,

Juffu *Societatis Regiæ* ac Typis *Jofephi Streater*. Proftat apud plures Bibliopolas. *Anno* MDCLXXXVII.

stars and to redirect the stream of events predicted by astrological charts.

Galileo fully supported Copernicus's theory. He published observations that he made by means of a telescope, an instrument that he refined to a high degree of usefulness. He studied and flirted with astrology but eventually rejected it. His discoveries and reports confirmed the heliocentric solar system but also brought him into conflict with the Church. The Inquisition eventually limited his writings and exacted a public renunciation of his astronomical views.

The Eighteenth Century

Isaac Newton's career spanned the latter part of the seventeenth and the early eighteenth century and in some ways typified the characteristics of both periods. His *Principio,* first published in 1726, was a fitting extension of the contributions made by others in the seventeenth century. To Kepler's laws of planetary movement, Newton added the laws of motion, which explained and revealed the vast

ABOVE: A detail of the tapestry at Bayeux, France, depicting the events surrounding the conquest of England by William, Duke of Normandy, in 1066. A comet seen in the sky at the time of the battle cast fear into the Saxons and raised the Normans' hopes of victory. c.1070–1080. Musée de Peinture, Ancien Evêche, Bayeux.

LEFT: Portrait of Edmund Halley (1656–1742), whose observations and writings explained much about the heretofore little understood comets.

universe as a physical machine operating under the principles of mechanics. He recorded that every mass at rest or in the heavens continues at rest or in motion in a straight line unless changed by forces acting on it (the law of "inertia"); that alterations in the status of a mass are produced in mathematical proportion to the acting force; that every action has an equal opposing reaction; and that every mass attracts every other mass directly according to the densities of matter and inversely according to the square of the distance between the masses (law of gravity).

These mechanistic views were in keeping with the eighteenth-century scientist's tendency in other fields to bring "rationality" rather than mysticism to bear on explanations. In this "Age of Enlightenment" philosophers such as David Hume, René Descartes, John Locke, and others avoided occult and arcane religious doctrines. Yet Newton was both a groundbreaking mechanist and a religious-minded Neoplatonist who affirmed the wisdom of the scriptures. His physics became the bedrock for later astrophysics and much else in science; but Newton himself regarded his primary function to be illuminating the ways of the Creator of the Universe. His aim was to achieve personal salvation.

Edmund Halley, Newton's younger contemporary and supporter, was an astronomer who unequivocally characterized astrology as superstition. He also laid to rest the notion that comets (one of which has become famous as "Halley's Comet") were scientifically inexplicable phenomena in the heavens. Numerous characterizations of comets had been offered through the millenniums, but it was Halley who perceived and promulgated the basic principles of cometary motion.

Comets have always been considered significant by those who watch the sky and universally thought of as harbingers of events on earth. Fearful consequences were anticipated by most individual observers and most peoples for many centuries: for instance when a brilliant comet with

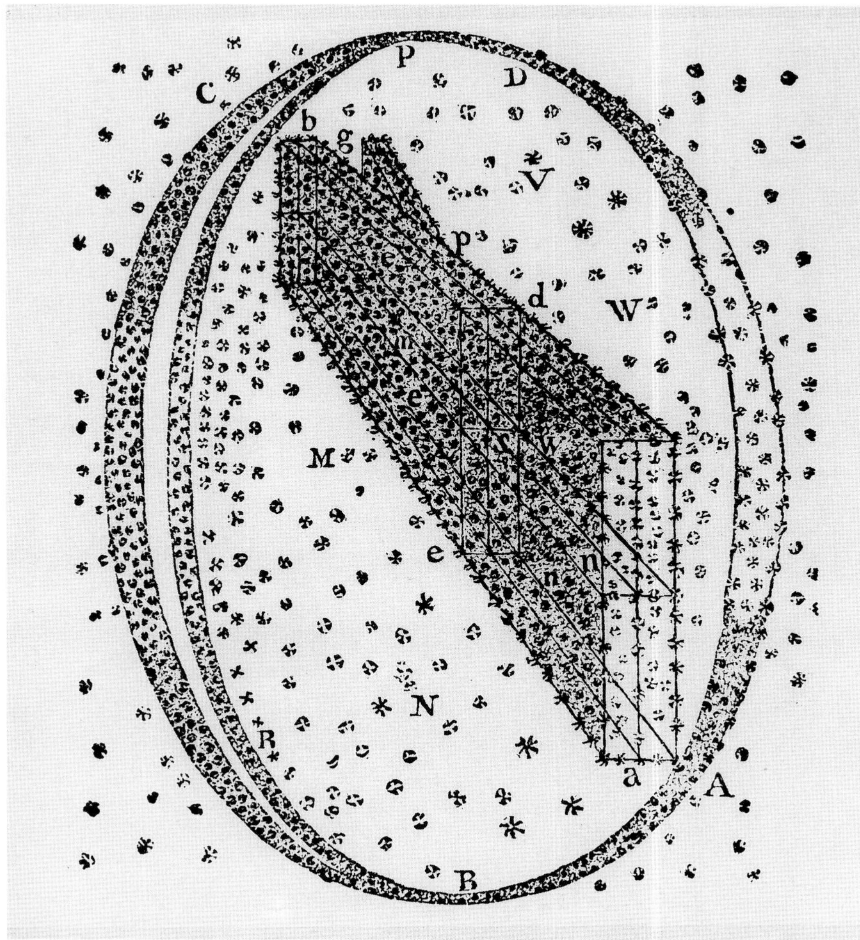

A diagram of the Milky Way, as visualized by Herschel, discoverer of Uranus, from the *Encyclopedia Londinensis* (London, c.1810).

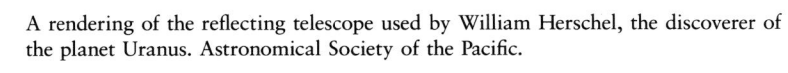

A rendering of the reflecting telescope used by William Herschel, the discoverer of the planet Uranus. Astronomical Society of the Pacific.

a bright tail appeared in 1066 during the Battle of Hastings, between the Norman William the Conqueror and the Anglo-Saxon King Harold of England, the invader is said to have hailed it as a sign of victory to come. The king, as the story goes, saw it as a prediction of disaster.

Another outstanding contribution in the eighteenth century, which became a significant but temporary setback to astrology, was the discovery in 1781 by William Herschel (1738–1822) of a brand new planet in the solar system. He wanted to name it "Georgium Sidus," after his monarch and patron George III. Others chose "Herschel," but it finally received the name Uranus, in keeping with the pantheon of Greco-Roman gods' names assigned to the other planets. Its symbol became an "H" for Herschel, with the addition of a planet suspended from the crossbar of the letter.

The discovery of this eighth planet upset astrology's ancient and sacred faith in the number seven and risked invalidating all the horoscopes that had been delineated for

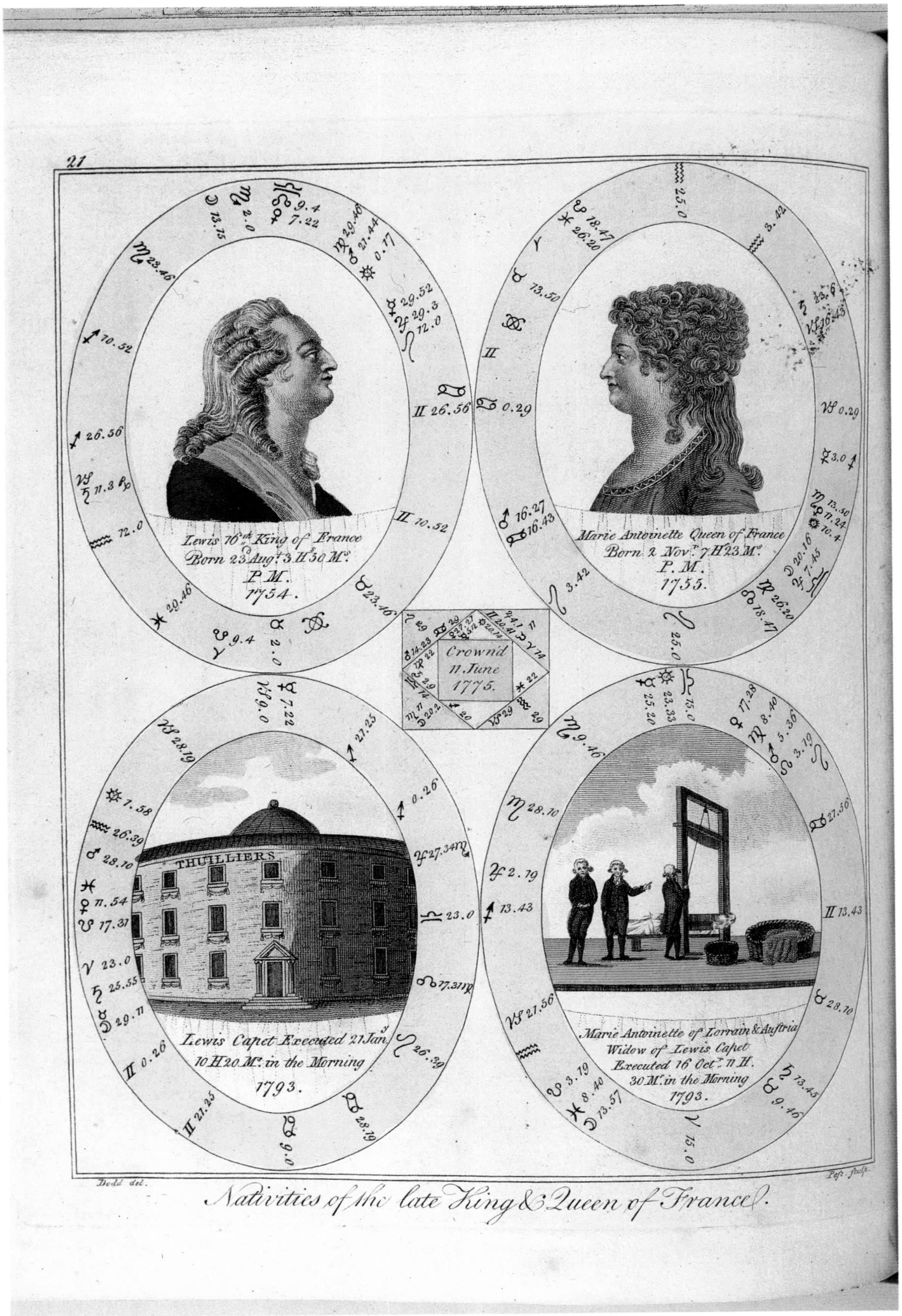

The horoscopes of Louis XVI, King of France, and Marie Antoinette, his Queen, both of whom were receptive to the practice of astrology. 1794.

OPPOSITE: Portrait of Giuseppe Balsamo (1743–1795), who took the name of Count de Cagliostro and hoodwinked people of high and low birth in several countries in his career as a magician, astrologer, and soothsayer. Wellcome Institute Library, London.

centuries without including Uranus. Astrologers however quickly adjusted to the new addition. They implicitly acknowledged the incompleteness of past readings and also pointed out that this did not overturn earlier interpretations but merely indicated that even better delineations could have been possible. Further, such a discovery simply made the new judgments of people and events more accurate. When the discoveries of Neptune and Pluto were reported in the twentieth century, they too were readily accepted into the family of astrological planets. The new planets, astrologers argued, were so much slower moving than the others that their effects on destiny were felt over longer periods of time, more in the nature of background effect than of specific influence. Thus horoscopes were refined and expanded, but the basic information remained unchanged.

Despite the willingness of astrologers to make accommodations, the new revelations about the universe, together with the general rationalistic intellectual atmosphere of the time, led to rejection of the tenets of astrology. Suspicion and sometimes contempt became more evident. Laurence Sterne, for example, poked fun at the methods of astrology in his novel *The Life and Opinions of Tristram Shandy*. Jonathan Swift concocted an elaborate and devastating hoax to mock astrology and to discredit one of its most famous and successful practitioners, who had written popular almanacs and drew up abundant astrological delineations under the pseudonym of "Partridge" (his family name was Hewson). Swift pretended to be a contending astrologer, "Isaac Bickerstaff," criticizing Partridge's skills in making predictions. Bickerstaff forecasted the death of Partridge himself on a specific date not far off. No sooner had the credulous readers of Bickerstaff taken the bait than Swift changed his pen name to Partridge too and wrote an answer to Bickerstaff after the prediction of death had passed uneventfully. As Partridge, Swift now castigated Bickerstaff for making an

erroneous prediction, bewailing the severe inconvenience caused by people taking his death for granted, including an undertaker who wanted his bill paid for having buried him. The final irony was that members of the Inquisition in Portugal were fooled too, burning the public predictions of Bickerstaff, who had also pretended to prophesy other deaths and calamities, in addition to the demise of Partridge.

Nevertheless astrology was far from moribund. Not only in cults and secret societies did it continue to flourish, it also showed its influences in public. William Denham's *Astro-Theology* was reprinted many times. Perhaps the most widely read book on the subject was the illustrated *Celestial Science of Astrology* (1790) by Ebenezer Sibly, a bona-fide surgeon who was a Fellow of the prestigious Royal Society. Furthermore, astrological language became part of conversation and literary works in many countries. For instance, the autobiography of Goethe began with the precise time and date of his birth along with the interpretation of his natal horoscope. Some astrologers continued to occupy important positions in royal courts. Both rulers and their subjects frequently based their decisions—whether in politics, travel, or love—on astrological portents.

Among the practicing astrologers of the eighteenth century, two colorful figures may be singled out because of the many stories told about them. Count Alessandro di Cagliostro (1743–1795; born Giuseppe Balsamo in Sicily) and the Comte de Saint Germain (?b.1710; whose real name is not precisely known) apparently bestowed their titles on themselves. Although each man independently developed his own reputation, they met up with each other, possibly in Sicily, formed a lasting friendship, traveled extensively together, and were mutually supportive. The elder of the two, Saint Germain, affected the manner of a mysterious seer and at one time took an enigmatic name, "Althotas." A practitioner of many of the occult arts, he may have been the instructor in astrology of his admiring devotee Cagliostro. Saint Germain's fame as a chiromancer also lasted well beyond his century. A secret agent of the King of France and an accepted visitor to other courts of Europe, he impressed people with his erudition and special gifts. Cagliostro's memoirs paid homage to Saint Germain and described him glowingly.

Cagliostro himself was even more flamboyant, and he was richly rewarded, even lionized, by European royalty and the upper classes. He practiced as both physician and astrologer in Rome, Venice, Naples, Sardinia, Paris, London, Spain, Persia, Arabia, Egypt, and the Island of Malta. All varieties of the occult were within Cagliostro's purview: alchemy, magical love potions, elixirs of youth, necromancy, and astrology. His personal magnetism coupled with the beauty of his wife were apparently irresistible charms that gained him considerable sums for his advice and predictions. These talents, however, also led him into unsavory practices, such as embezzlement, under the guise of manufacturing gold through alchemy, founding secret cults with erotic rites, claiming miraculous medical cures, and trickery in astrological forecasts. One of his schemes involved attempting to defraud the French royal court and its jewelers of a valuable diamond necklace, for which Cardinal de Rohan was his accomplice and also his dupe. Imprisoned in the Bastille, Cagliostro managed to prove his innocence, avoiding punishment as he had so many times before. His charmed life finally ended at the age of fifty-two at the hands of the Inquisition. He had fled to Rome after being briefly incarcerated in London and after an exposé of his nefarious activities was published in France. In Rome he could not seem to keep out of self-induced trouble. His attempt to set up another mystical sect in defiance of the Roman Catholic Church brought him before the Holy Examiners. He was executed after a prolonged inquiry, which lasted well over a year.

Serious students and practitioners of astrology look upon Saint Germain and Cagliostro as examples of the types of charlatans and rogues who have given astrologers a bad name. Indeed, the careers of these two point to the propensity of people—even those in high places—to believe in mystery and magic and to seek occult means of defeating fate.

The Nineteenth and Twentieth Centuries

Astrology blossomed in the nineteenth and twentieth centuries. Strikingly this occurred at the same time that significant advances in astronomy were proceeding and contempt for astrology by scientists was growing. The increasing efficiency of telescopes, which enabled William Herschel to see the planet Uranus in the eighteenth century, also helped astronomers in the next two centuries to confirm the presence of Neptune and Pluto. Because of a slight but definite eccentricity in the orbit of Uranus, noticed by astronomers and by mathematician Pierre de Laplace half a century after Herschel's discovery, telescopic researches sought these planets over the following two decades without success until the observations and calculations in 1846 by John J. Adams in England, U. J. Leverrier in France, and Johann Galle in Germany finally detected the faraway planet Neptune.

Relatively minor deviations from the expected orbital paths of Uranus and also of Saturn suggested to astronomers that still another unseen body was acting on Uranus and Saturn. The most persistent search for the proposed planet was undertaken by Percival Lowell in Arizona, who in 1905 was convinced by mathematical examinations of the courses of Uranus and Saturn that a "planet X," existing well beyond Neptune, was definitely responsible for the patterns of activity. Lowell kept taking serial photographs of the area of the universe he thought the planet was in, but he died in 1916 without having achieved his objective. The search was not taken up again until 1930, but this time a spot of light was detected on timed photographic plates, precisely as Lowell had calculated and proclaimed. Neptune and Pluto, along with Uranus, now occupy the list of astrological planets, with characteristics and rulerships assigned to them to match the ancient gods after whom they were named.

By the eighteenth century astronomers and astrologers were performing entirely separate functions, although up to then individuals had sometimes engaged in both practices. For centuries the two activities had actually been accepted as different types of endeavors—some had even detected in the writings of Eudoxus, in the fifth century B.C., and of Ptolemy, in the second century A.D., a recognition that studying and calculating the positions of the stars were entirely different from associating information with human nature and destiny—but by the eighteenth century the distinction between the two activities was clearly demarcated. Furthermore, in the nineteenth century the field of astrology began to contain within itself disparate practitioners: traditionalists, symbolists, mystics, statisticians, and psychologists.

Traditional Astrology

Among the traditional astrologers practicing in the nineteenth century, Julius Pfaff in Germany compiled what were essentially summaries of the teachings and commentaries of previous adepts through the centuries. In England, James Wilson developed an encyclopedic textbook based on the conventional doctrines of Ptolemy. Many others early in the century contributed works on the subject and practiced with considerable recognition. One of them, Lady Hester Lucy Stanhope, a niece of the English prime minister William Pitt the Younger, was consulted by people throughout the world at her retreat in Lebanon.

Astrological almanacs also began to appear, notably *The Horoscope of Napoleon III,* published by the German Johannes Karl Vogt (1808–1873), and *The Book of Fate* (author uncertain), which listed litanies of predictions. Another popular publication of the early nineteenth century was William Simmonite's *Meterologist and Medical Botany or Herbal Guide to Health*. By mid-century hundreds of newspapers in many countries contained daily horoscopes. Thousands of articles appeared in magazines, and there were enough books on astrology being published to fill the pages of bibliographic catalogs.

The two most famous astronomical almanacs of the nineteenth century were by two Englishmen, "Raphael" (1795–1832; Robert Cross Smith) and "Zadkiel" (b. 1795; Lieutenant Richard James Morrison). *Raphael's Almanac, Prophetic Messenger, and Weather Guide* became a best-seller and is still in print today. An acquaintance of William Blake's, Smith (Raphael) cast the poet's horoscope and collaborated with other prominent persons in the publication of pamphlets on predictions. After Smith died in 1832, others continued to update the famous almanac under the pseudonym. "Zadkiel," the name taken by Richard Morrison, an officer in the Royal Navy, founded an almanac in 1832 that became even more influential than Raphael's. *Zadkiel's Almanac* lasted for at least a century, under a succession of editors, one of whom, Alfred Pearce, authored books that gave instruction in traditional astrology and marshaled arguments in its defense. Morrison's prognostications were usually highly sophisticated, although he sometimes included advice on investments or on betting the horses. Morrison also authored a series of other publications on astrology and founded the Astro-Meteorological Society. His collaborator and partner in business ventures, Christopher Cooke, who was a lawyer, challenged the Parliamentary Vagrancy Act passed in 1824 (an extension of a 1736 law against witchcraft), which declared astrology illegal along with witchcraft and fortune-telling and under which prosecutions for forecasting by astrology are known to have been brought. Indeed, Sir Walter Scott in 1829 had changed the prospective plot of one of his novels in order to avoid what might have been construed as an affirmation of astrology.

In France, two traditionalists, Faucheux and Formalhaut, were responsible for awakening interest in astrology. However, there was not sufficient enthusiasm to support a cadre of professional astrologists. Most, if not all, of the leaders in astrology, including Paul Choisnard, Charles Nicoullaud, and Henri Selva, earned their living in other jobs. Nevertheless publications increased in number and remained popular into this century.

Although in the last two centuries practicing astrologers in the U.S. have numbered in the thousands, it is doubtful that more than a very few garnered enough compensation to be considered professionals. It is true that some have received substantial royalties from books and mail-order services, but the vast majority either have eked out a modest living or have engaged in astrological activities as a sideline. However, at least one of them, Evangeline Adams (1865–1932), not only succeeded in becoming rich but also was received as an advisor by famous persons from a variety of occupations: a king, an opera singer, a movie star, a financier. Arrested for fortune-telling in 1914, she was tried in court—by her own preference—and so confounded the judge by her erudition and especially by her correct delineation of a sample horoscope from a birth date that he had handed her (it turned out to be the judge's son) that he decided in her favor and announced that astrology was an exact science as Mrs. Jordan (Evangeline Adams) practiced it. She gave considerable popular respectability and credibility to the subject, but her methods, which followed the traditional systems, made no contribution to its academic standing or to the principles of astrology itself.

Symbolism and Mysticism

Symbolic rather than literal reliance upon conventional astrological teachings has also gained adherents over the past two centuries. Associations between astrology and biblical and scriptural works have been emphasized most notably in the twentieth century by Frances Rolleston, Carl Anderson, and Rosa Baughan (who also established links between methods of astrology and handreading).

Broad astrological symbolism has developed into more mystical attitudes and away from the conventional techniques of astrology. At the very beginning of the nineteenth century, Francis Barrett in England had heralded this departure in his embrace of occultist cabalistic notions. Although he subscribed to the influence of the stars over people, as have all the astrological mystics, he paid little attention to traditional methods of astrology. In nineteenth-century France, maverick astrologers, such as "Papus" and "Eliphas Lèvi" (Alphonse Louis Constant; whose *History of Magic* included a mysterious "astral light" and a variety of occult theories), also invented their own astrological interpretations. Others, such as "Paul Christian" (Christian Pitois), used astrological doctrines but mainly as underpinnings for their mystical divinations. This trend toward occultism was continued into the twentieth century by Alexandre Volguine in France, who deplored the growing tendency toward scientific methods. He proclaimed that the very strength of astrology lay in its transcendence of statistics and of the cold, soulless discipline of science.

Most occultists have continued to use at least some features of astrology. For instance Aleister Crowley (1875–1947), a founder of an occult society, the Hermetic Order of the Golden Dawn, included some elements of astrology in his teachings, but his main interests were the cabala, tarot cards, and other mystical methods. Philosophers of mysticism usually either accept the basic teachings of astrology outright, using the planets and the zodiac as symbols, or at least acknowledge that the stars play a role in determining the nature of a person.

In the United States, mysticism and astrology were institutionalized with the establishment of the Theosophical Society in 1874–1875 by Helena Blavatsky and Colonel Henry Steel Alcott. Although the founders had only a secondary interest in astrology, since their primary focus was studying psychic powers and comparative religions, they accepted astrological principles wholeheartedly, thereby helping astrology to be accepted as an intellectual pursuit. Especially effective in this respect were the vigorous efforts of Annie Besant, the forceful successor to Madame Blavatsky.

Many of those who became prominent as astrologers in the Western world had close connections with the theosophy movement. For instance, early in the twentieth century in Germany Hugo Vollrath's Theosophical Publishing House

BELOW: The title page of *The Astrologer of the Nineteenth Century* (London, 1825). Books on occult sciences were popular in the nineteenth century.

RIGHT: A colored aquatint and etching showing some events of 1832, from *The Prophetic Messenger* ("Justice"), a popular astrological almanac of the nineteenth century. c.1850. Wellcome Institute Library, London.

Spica
Sol Eclipsed
July 27th
1832.
Astra Regunt
homines.
Algol
Andromeda
Allah-il-all
Libertas
Vox
Populi
Vox
Dei
Justitia

became a principal printer of astrological works. By the end of World War I he had published numerous pamphlets and almanacs, and astrological societies were holding conventions throughout Germany.

In England, "Alan Leo" (1860–1917; William Frederick Allen), one of the most successful practicing astrologers and the publisher of astrological magazines and horoscopes, was an enthusiastic member of a theosophical group to which he had been introduced by his friend "Sepharial" (Walter Gorn Old). Sepharial was a highly popular writer himself, making many predictions for the stock market and horse racing, as Zadkiel had also done. Neither Zadkiel nor Sepharial ran afoul of the law, but Alan Leo was arrested, tried, and fined a small sum for fortune-telling.

Dane Rudhyar, an astrologer in the U.S. working after World War I, counseled astrologers to break from the traditions transmitted from Greece and Rome, especially the attempts to predict from horoscopes, which he equated with fortune-telling. He leaned toward psychological and intuitive uses of astrology (akin to Carl Jung's concepts) and favored esoteric astrology, where instinct reigns over natal delineation and mundane prediction.

The Theosophical Society also heightened interest generally in arcane philosophies and mystical societies all over the world. Rudolf Steiner (1861–1925), a strong supporter of theosophy in Germany who emigrated to the United States, in 1912 established his own brand of mystical philosophy, anthroposophy, and became a respected influential educator in fields outside his own private philosophy. Max Heindel, originally a theosophist and pupil of Steiner's, also came to the United States, where he wrote a number of popular books on astrology.

Mathematics and Statistics

Some groups and individual astrologers have turned their attention away from the mystical features of astrology and attempted to place traditional astrology on firm mathematical, empiric ground. In the late nineteenth century "Richard Garnett" (A. G. Trent) of the British Museum had been among the earliest astrologers to try scientifically to systematize horoscope readings. In France, Paul Choisnard continued this effort by offering statistics to justify the validity of astrology. In the twentieth century G. Lakhovsky applied new scientific information on electromagnetic waves in space to explain the effects of planetary movements on the physiology of humans. Similarly, Wilhelm Hartmann in 1950 argued that conventional astrology is based on the principles of physics. Carl Payne Tobey classified astrology as a branch of mathematics. Others have used astrology as a scientific method of predicting the weather.

In the 1950s Michel and Françoise Gauquelin examined in detail the association between people in particular professions and the presence of a specific planet in one sector of the sky at their birth. The Gauquelins tried to discover whether any pattern at birth was statistically significant concerning people's career choices. Among their conclusions was the finding that Mars was most often in one area of the sky at the birth of athletes and soldiers; Jupiter was the planet present for that of ministers. However, they did not presume to confirm or deny the doctrines, structure, or predictions of traditional astrology.

Psychology

Another direction in the development of astrology has been to emphasize its psychological implications. André Barbault was in the forefront of accenting Freudian principles to explain astrological symbols. His own reading of Sigmund Freud's horoscope received considerable prominence. The Swiss K. E. Krafft (1900–1945) established in Germany a school of thought he called "astrobiology," which linked astrology and psychological principles. He poked fun at elaborate systems of predictions and maintained that true delineations must include personal interviews in which psychological knowledge and insight can operate. Margaret Hone also insisted that astrologers must consult people's psychological perceptions directly to avoid "blind" horoscope readings, but otherwise her methods were in line with traditional astrology.

Carl Jung, an early follower of Freud's who later dissented from the mainstream of psychoanalysis, gave much support to astrology. He considered many of the occult traditions to be species-inherited patterns of thought, based on a true perception of reality buried in the unconscious, with astrology as one intuitive path to understanding fate. Second, he saw in the simultaneous occurrence of some events an acausal relationship, which was different from a scientific explanation but just as significant in meaning. This connecting principle he called "synchronicity." Astrologers and mystics have seen in this concept a justification for their systems, since according to Jung a physical or causal relationship in happenings does not have to be proved in order for a meaningful connection to be present. For example, science may require a clearly demonstrated effect on the newborn by the rising constellation (ascendant) of Gemini in order to accept an association with the child's cleverness or propensity for languages. But the astrologer, using Jung's theory, can state that the sky event and the baby's mental makeup are connected in fact, the absence of proof of a direct linkage notwithstanding.

Jung's comparison of the horoscopes of hundreds of married people revealed, among other things, that the conjunction of the husband's sun with the wife's moon occurred more often than statistical chance might suggest. This confirmed to astrologers the long-standing interpretation that this sun-moon aspect signifies a good marriage. Jung himself, however, did not consider his overall findings conclusive.

One of those who applied Jungian psychology to astrology was Walter Koch, who used Jung's terms of "introvert" and "extrovert" extensively in horoscope interpretations. He was one of the founders of the Cosmobiological Society but differed from the other members in that he promulgated his own method of house division as a modification of the Regiomontanus and Placidian systems, whereas cosmobiologists generally have removed the houses from their horoscope readings.

The original founder of cosmobiology, Reinhold Ebertin, in 1928 had attempted to overturn much of the accepted structure of astrology. He accented the groupings of planets and the ascendant zodiac sign, paying little attention to the other zodiac divisions and omitting the houses altogether. His methods followed those of Uranian astrology (methods developed after the discovery of Uranus), an approach developed in the 1920s by the Germans Alfred Witte and Friedrich Sieggrun.

Uranian astrology is only one of several new methods introduced in the twentieth century. Some systems are based on heliocentric rather than geocentric charts. Nevertheless the traditional astrological structure, as inherited over thousands of years, remains the overwhelming choice of astrologers all over the world.

Combinations of Astrology, Mysticism, Mathematics, and Psychology

A number of astrologers have integrated elements of symbolism, mathematics, mysticism, and psychology into various astrological methods. Marc Edmund Jones (1888–1980), an American Protestant minister, established a society for the purposes of research and instruction in astrology, which he termed "Sabian Assembly," after the medieval Islamic Sabians who saw the parts of the cosmos as symbols of reality.

His protégé Charles Jayne, Jr., subscribed to Jones's general views and applied precise mathematical methodology. He tried to give astrology an acceptable academic standing, urging astrologers to avoid commercialism and the trappings of the fortune-teller. For Jayne, the cycles of the positions of the five outer planets were related to historical events. Comets, among other phenomena, were signals of upheavals in earthly affairs. He edited one of the first—perhaps the earliest—international journals devoted to astrological investigations. He advocated scientific inquiry in his Association for Research and Cosmecology, founded in 1970.

Among contemporary astrologers, Robert Hand has proposed a combination of the mechanistic and the esoteric features. Basically a traditionalist, he derives his ideas from symbolism, mysticism, psychology, and mathematics. Rupert Gleadow's emphasis on the psychological uses of astrology also gives considerable attention to its historical development.

It is the contention of Fred Gettings, a modern historian of astrology, that there were always two simultaneous but different astrological attitudes, which sometimes merged: the "esoteric," looking to the stars for their mystical and symbolic meanings; the "exoteric," focused on the concrete natal and predictive uses.

Opponents

In the nineteenth and twentieth centuries, astrology has had its detractors. Otto Neugebauer, an authoritative scholar of ancient history, especially of astronomy and astrology, deplored having to deal with the latter subject at all in order to understand the history of astronomy. Another historian of astrology, Auguste Bouché-LeClercq, considered its practice a waste of time. To Carl von Bezold, Bart Bok, Franz Boll, Roger Culver, Franz Cumont, Richard Eisler, Martin Gardener, Philip Ianna, Lawrence Jerome, Fritz Saxl, Aby Warburg, and many others who have written on the subject, astrology has no validity and is a regrettable cloud over rational thinking. Two of the most emphatic antagonists are the Committee for the Scientific Investigation of Claims of the Paranormal and *The Humanist Journal,* which issued a manifesto against the claims of astrology.

Nevertheless, astrology continues to occupy millions of people who are readers of newspaper horoscopes, magazine articles, books, and pamphlets. Surveys consistently show that at least two-thirds of the people in the Western world know their Sun-signs and a large proportion believe in the validity of astrology. The number of people who actually consult astrologers is not known, but thousands of practitioners all over the world advise clients in public and private, indeed even in the 1980s in the White House, we are led to believe.

The reliance on astrological advisers is far more common in the East than in Western countries. However, after the communist revolution in China, astrology was banned, and in the U.S.S.R. it is frowned upon except for a few attempts to link it with weather prediction. However, in 1988 an astrology column regularly appeared in a widely read Moscow newspaper. Still illegal in some countries as a type of fortune-telling, the practice of astrology has nevertheless very rarely led to arrests. The notable cases of Alan Leo in London and Evangeline Adams in New York have already been mentioned.

The literature of virtually all countries contains stories, poems, and essays about astrology. Astrologers increasingly have banded together in organizations, which sponsor courses of instruction, require examinations for certification, and promote high ethical standards. Moreover, astrology is part of many occult teachings, so that its influence is even wider than might be apparent.

Technique of Astrology

The positions of particular constellations of stars and the planets as viewed from the earth are the basic armature of astrology. Of the millions of constellations of stars only twelve specific ones are employed in astrology. Each of these twelve constellations (the zodiac) appears to remain in the same location—as if they are "beside" the sun—for about a month. Astrologically and astronomically speaking, the sun is "in" that sign (the Sun-sign). The zodiac constellations are actually billions of miles distant from the sun, the earth, and each other, but in our line of sight the Sun-sign appears to be within the sun's region. Just before or at sunrise, the constellation at the extreme eastern part of the horizon is called the ascendant zodiac sign (the "rising" sign). The position of this constellation varies with the time of day. The yearly course of the sun through the zodiac, as it appears to us on earth, is called the "ecliptic."

The ancients noticed early that some individual stars are not always in the same regular relationship to other stars or to the sun. These "eccentrics," or "wanderers," are now called planets. Because the sun and moon also have their own motions, they too were classified as planets by the ancients and given the added title of "luminaries" in recognition of their brightness, which illuminates the earth's surface.

Actually, each star in a constellation is itself a sun, creating its own light, just as our own sun does. The moon and planets shine only when reflecting light from our sun, but in astrology Sun and Moon are classified with the planets because of their individualistic motions in the sky and their changing relationship to each other. (*Sun* and *Moon,* like the other planets, are capitalized when used in an astrological context.) The word *star* has come to mean both types of shining bodies in the sky—the planets and the suns comprising the constellations. However, astrologers

OPPOSITE: Astrologers observing the stars from the summit of Mount Athos, from a fifteenth-century Bohemian illuminated manuscript of *The Travels of Sir John Mandeville.* The observers are using astrolabes and other instruments to sight and measure positions, while their colleagues record and calculate. The British Library, London.

Jan Vermeer. *The Astronomer.* 1668. Oil on canvas, 19⅝ × 17⅞". Private collection. The astronomer is shown studying the globe on which personifications of the starry constellations can be seen.

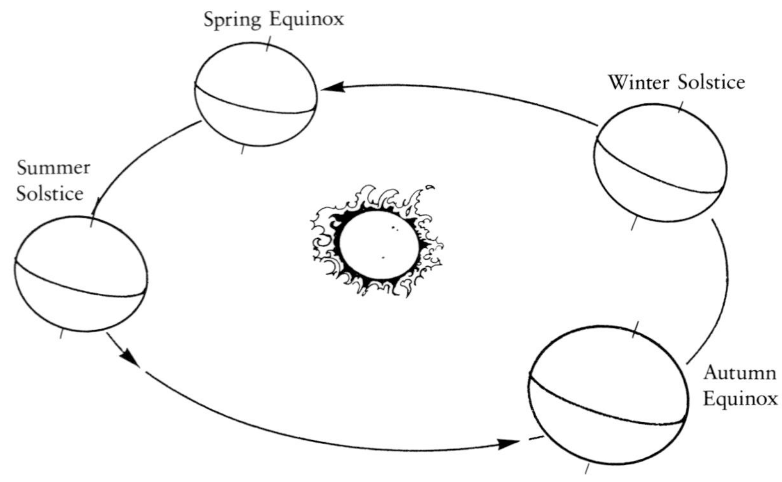

The Seasons

The Seasons. As the earth, tilted on its axis, revolves around the sun, the different parts of the globe receive varying amounts of sunlight. On the left (June, July, August), the northern hemisphere is tilted toward the sun; at the lower right (September, October, November), both northern and southern hemispheres receive equal amounts; at the right (December, January, February), the southern hemisphere is closer to the sun than is the northern hemisphere; at the top left (March, April, May), the earth is again equally illuminated.

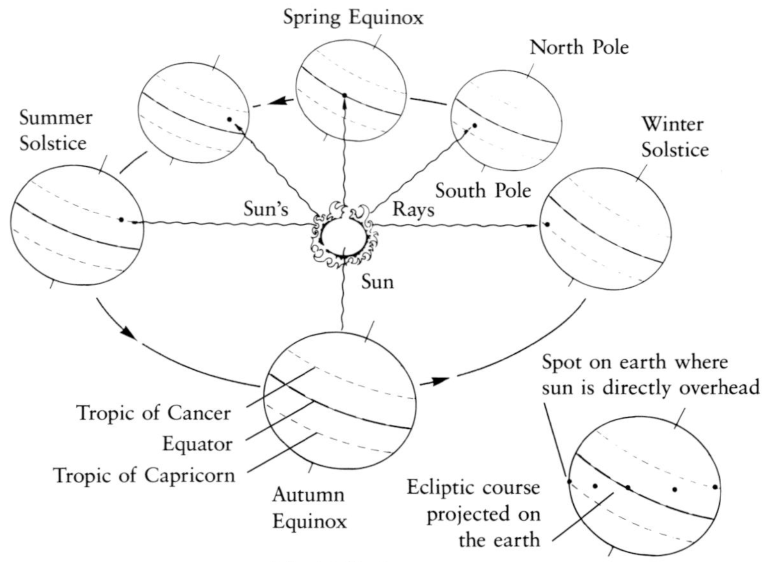

The Ecliptic

Diagram of the spot on earth where the sun is directly overhead—a position that changes through the year, depending on the revolution of the earth around the sun and the obliquity of the earth's axis. The diagram at the lower right plots this apparent path of the sun (the ecliptic) around the earth.

plot and read a diagrammatic wheel rather than the stars themselves, whose actual positions have been followed and checked for thousands of years.

There is also another highly important part of the structure of traditional astrology, the theoretical mathematical divisions of the sky into twelve sectors, or "houses." Of the many house systems, only about a half-dozen are in general use. In each system, the houses of the sky do not change position. When the earth revolves along its orbit, the entire band of zodiac signs appears to shift gradually, from month to month, through the year, but the houses, the geometric divisions of the sky into sectors, remain fixed.

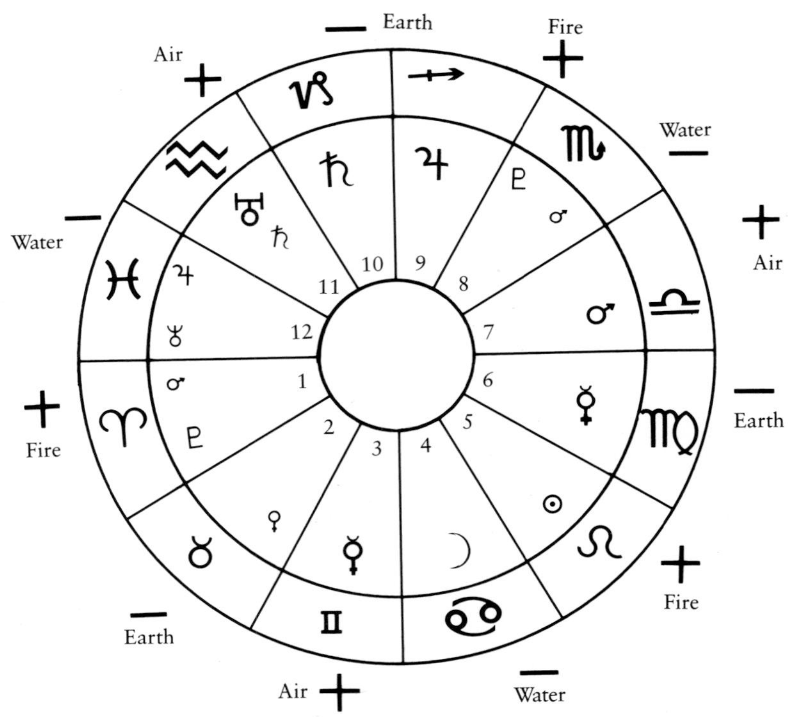

Horoscope Wheel

Horoscope wheel showing the zodiac signs with the planets that rule each of them, their polarities, and the houses. The elements of the signs (the triplicity) are: fire for Aries, Leo, Sagittarius; earth for Taurus, Virgo, Capricorn; air for Gemini, Libra, Aquarius; water for Cancer, Scorpio, Pisces.

The arrangement of the planets, signs, and houses at the birth of a person (the "native") is the basis for the horoscope, which is usually represented as a circle or a wheel. The beginning boundary of each house and each zodiac sign on the diagrammatic wheel is called its "cusp." Distances in degrees of separation of the planets on the horoscope chart from each other and from the house cusps are called "aspects"—as for instance conjunction (within 5 degrees), opposition (180 degrees), square (90 degrees), sextile (60 degrees), and trine (120 degrees). These aspects represent the angles of separation between two bodies in the sky, as viewed by an observer on earth.

The placement of the planets governs the traits of a person. The zodiac signs indicate how these characteristics reveal themselves. The houses are the areas of life's activities, in which the influences of planets and signs are manifested. Thus, the planets say *what;* the signs show *how;* the houses tell *where.* By rough analogy, musicians' talents are the planets. The performing instruments are the zodiac signs. The types of musical compositions played are the houses. The interrelationships among players in an orchestra are the aspects.

Usually, the various astrological parts are plotted on a circle that is divided into twelve equal segments; 30° is allotted for each zodiac sign. On this horoscope circle, the zodiac signs are indicated by their respective symbols together with a notation in degrees of their location on the circle, since the boundaries of the signs do not necessarily coincide with those of the houses. Each planet, represented by its symbol, is inserted within a house's borders, accompanied by a notation of its precise location in the zodiac sign. These values in degrees and minutes are found in an astronomical table, the Ephemeris. Astrological computer services now perform all these functions and send a completed diagram containing all the symbols and numbers in their proper places.

The Planets

There are ten astrological planets: Sun, Moon, Mercury, Venus, Mars, Jupiter, Saturn, Uranus, Neptune, and Pluto. Each symbolizes a lexicon of favorable and unfavorable traits, but traditionally several of the planets used to be designated as beneficent (Sun, Moon, Jupiter), while others were considered more likely to represent malefic influences (Mars and Saturn). Mercury's characteristics have the potential to be desirable or undesirable. Opinions have not yet formed fully on how to categorize the three more recently discovered planets, Uranus, Neptune, and Pluto. Indeed, modern astrologers tend to avoid classifying any of the planets as definitively favorable or unfavorable. Instead, the polarized properties now give way to more integrated concepts, with the features of each planet modified or even determined by its position on the horoscope chart and its relationship to zodiac signs and the other planets.

In astrological parlance, there is a tendency to speak of a "Solar person," a "Jupiterian," or a "Venusian" as someone who presumably has the characteristics represented by the respective planet. Of course, few people possess all or even most of the features represented by a planet. The actual reading of a horoscope (the delineation) must take into account the positions on the chart of all the planets, signs, and other astrological data. Furthermore, the traditional association of physical attributes with planets and zodiac signs generally has not been continued into contemporary times. Although some astrologers today do subscribe to the principle, others merely take note of the planetary correspondences when the physical makeup of a person strikingly fits the traditional association.

The faster-moving planets remain in a zodiac sign from the perspective of a person on earth for relatively short periods: Moon (two and a half days), Mercury (approximately fifteen days), Venus (approximately twenty days), Sun (approximately one month), Mars (approximately one and one-half months). Thus their influence over persons and events continually changes. The effects of the slower-moving bodies (Jupiter, Saturn, and especially Uranus, Neptune, and Pluto) are usually more long-term.

In astrology, each planet "rules" one or more zodiac signs—generally the cluster with similar propensities. For example, Mars typifies energy and action. It governs the zodiac sign Aries, which invokes the energetic force of enthusiasm. When in the sign of Libra, which has the opposite tendencies of balance and calm, Mars is said to be in "detriment." Each planet also has two other special positions in the signs: "exaltation," where it is enhanced; "fall," where its negative features are increased. When a planet is in a sign where it is neither the ruler nor in detriment, exaltation, or fall, it is termed a "peregrine" planet. Its influence there is weaker or ambivalent.

Each planet revolves continuously about the sun, each at its own specific rate and in its own elliptical orbit, but when viewed in the sky from the earth, a planet may sometimes seem to alter its speed and its course—even appearing to stop its forward motion and to begin to go backward, an illusion caused by the differing rate of revolution of each planet when compared to the earth's. During such a time the planet is called "retrograde." To astrologers, this retrograde direction lessens the impact of the planet's influence or may even increase the planet's negative features.

Certain relationships between planets are believed to have special significance. Mercury, for instance, never appears to be more than twenty-eight degrees from the Sun. Therefore the angular relationships (aspects) of Mercury and the Sun are either in conjunction (that is, very close) or there is no aspect involved at all.

Planets have their natural domiciles, the houses, mathematical divisions of the sky used by astrologers. When in its compatible house, a planet's features are apt to be manifested harmoniously, provided there are no other signs or planets positioned to exert counteracting influences. A planet at the "top" of the chart—that is, near the vertical meridian, or *Medium Coeli*—is often interpreted to suggest the ultimate result of the person's choices and actions, where the "chickens come home to roost," or the "landing field."

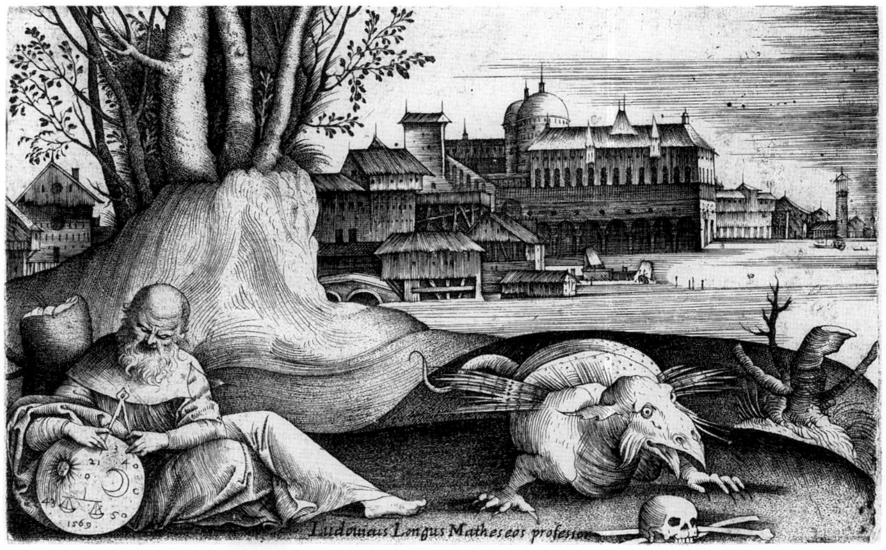

An astrologer is making measurements on a disc containing numerals and symbols of the Sun, Moon, and zodiac sign of Libra (the scales) in this engraving of 1569 by Giulio Campagnola. New York Public Library.

Joseph Cornell. *Sun Box*. c.1955. Painted wood, metals, cork, 7¾ × 12⅞". Collection Mr. and Mrs. B. H. Friedman, New York City.

A drawing by Joseph of Ulm, c.1404, showing the Moon goddess with crescent horn and various activities under the influences of the Moon. University Library, Tübingen, Germany.

A detail of Fernando Gallego's fresco from the library vault of the University of Salamanca. 1493–1506. Mercury is on his chariot, pulled by birds. The wheels show the two zodiac signs ruled by Mercury: Gemini and Virgo.

Mars is shown with the two zodiac signs that he rules, Aries and Scorpio, and surrounded by military activity. Miniature from the *De Sphaera* manuscript. Fifteenth century. Biblioteca Estense, Modena, Italy.

Sun

☉

Symbol: spirit (circle) with person at the center (dot).
Day of the week: Sunday. Hours of the day: 8th, 15th, 18th, 22nd.
Takes one year to move through all the zodiac signs, spending about a month in each sign.

The Sun is the most powerful of the planets, as it is the most important heavenly body to those on earth, for in effect all life depends on its presence. The Sun gives to the native the characteristics of the zodiac sign in which it appears at birth in the horoscope. This particular zodiac sign is known as the native's "Sun-sign." Indeed, the usual reader of astrological items in newspapers considers the Sun-sign virtually the be-all and end-all of the horoscope. One may frequently hear expressed, "I am a Libra; what is your sign?" As influential as this imprint of the Sun is, astrologers weigh this feature as only one of the several equally significant properties of the horoscope. The Sun heightens the characteristics of the particular sign in which it is placed, or, contrarily, it can lessen, blunt, or even change the zodiac sign's impact. Energy, life force, and will are commonly associated with the Sun. It brings creativity and concentration to bear. The "Solar" personality is affable, generous, and fair but also adventuresome, ideally suited to positions of leadership. The Sun's light is self-generated. Therefore it typifies self-awareness and self-expression.

The Sun is especially relevant to the young adult years (ages twenty to thirty), when people's energies are said to be in full power. As would be expected, it is the ruling planet of the fiery zodiac sign Leo, which symbolizes ego and self-expression, and is the natural resident of House V, the area concerned with creativity and adventure.

The negative features associated with the Sun are those that exaggerate its generally positive qualities—"too much of a good thing." These are pride, arrogance, tyranny, and overconfidence. The affable nature then can become uncooperative, unfair, rash, and prone to gambling.

Moon

☽

Symbol: experience and feeling or soul (crescent).
Day of the week: Monday. Hours of the day: 2nd, 9th, 16th, 23rd.
Takes approximately 28 days to move through each of the zodiac signs; spending about 2½ days in each sign.

In ancient Mesopotamia, the Moon, Sin, was masculine and even more powerful than Shamash, the Sun-god. He was not only a higher deity but also more inscrutable. In Greek mythology the Moon-god was Selene, a sister of Helios. The Moon has continued to be considered female.

The Moon's purview includes the fluidity of life, the rhythms of nature and of humans, emotions, and health. The sea, long voyages, and the body's fluids and their elaborating organs are believed to be under the influence of the Moon. The subconscious mind is also under lunar influence, and our term *lunacy* refers to the belief that the Moon (especially when full or at its new appearance) affects the sanity of stable humans and sets off the unstable.

Dreaminess fits the Moon's personality, and dreams themselves are especially likely to be fulfilled when the Moon is in the zodiac signs of Taurus, Leo, Scorpio, and Aquarius. The time of infancy, sometimes also early adulthood, is governed by this planet. Thus, domesticity can be expected to be included under lunar activity. Indeed, House IV, the natural residence of the Moon, is concerned with the home environment, land, and also beginnings—areas of life involved in changes. The Moon rules the watery sign of Cancer.

Since each planet and sign has negatives in addition to positives, the Moon's influence can also lead to the very opposites of its constructive features: poor, instead of sharp, memory; prejudice rather than open-mindedness; uncertain attachments. Some characteristics may be exaggerated, thus leading to hypersensitivity, inconsistency, self-indulgence, or extremes of dreaminess.

Mercury

☿

Symbol: Soul (crescent) over spirit (circle) and matter (cross).
Day of the week: Wednesday (French: *mercredi.* Norse for Mercury: *Woden*).
Hours of the day: 3rd, 10th, 17th, 24th.
Takes approximately 88 days to move through all the zodiac signs; spending about 15 days in each sign.

The Babylonians referred to this planet as Nabu, god of the intellect and the mythical inventor of writing, the son of Marduk, who was the chief god of the pantheon. In Greece he was Hermes, messenger of the gods and patron of commerce, speech, and communication. The Roman Mercury had the same qualities as the Greek Hermes, but more noticeable were his swiftness, friendliness, and mischievousness.

Whereas the Moon influences the subconscious, Mercury affects the functioning of the conscious mind. Logical, analytical, and innovative, the Mercurial person is adept at mental gymnastics, close reasoning, and didactic organization. As the patron of communication, Mercury governs words, both spoken and written.

Both male and female qualities are combined in this planet's influence. Mercury therefore resonates with such dual characteristics as serving and being served, achieving and yet trying to do too much, acquiring and transmitting information, creating for the general good but also potentially engaging in clever crookedness. Our term "mercurial" suggests wide swings and changes in emotions, although the behavior is apt to be modulated by a tendency to aloofness or by the tact inherent in high adaptability. From these traits, it is obvious that the Mercury person excels in endeavors requiring special skill in communication, such as art and music.

Mercury rules Gemini, and the planet and the zodiac sign have many obvious correlations. Mercury is also considered by some to be the ruler of the Virgo sign.

The body parts assigned to Mercury are the lungs, central nervous system, upper extremities, and organs involved in locomotion. Ages from four to fourteen (childhood to puberty) are under Mercury's sway. The planet is also associated with sibling relationships. Its natural Houses are III—communication, expression, short journeys, and siblings—and VI—services, health, and hygiene.

Venus

♀

Symbol: matter (cross) surmounted by spirit (circle), meaning ideals and practicality.
Day of the week: Friday (French: *Vendredi.* Norse for Venus: *Freya*).
Hours of the day: 4th, 11th, 18th.
Takes approximately 22 days to move through all the zodiac signs; spending about 2 days in each sign, except when in retrograde.

In Babylonia, the goddess Ishtar was the third in the triumvirate that also included Sin (Moon) and Shamash (Sun). She could be both kind and cruel. Love and eroticism were her dominion. Her descendants, Aphrodite in Greece and Venus in Rome, were also concerned chiefly with love. In astrology this planet is less concerned with physical passion than with emotional attachment. Its glyph has come to signify the female in science and art.

Love, beauty, and harmony are the principal areas influenced by Venus. Love also implies affection, romance, gentleness, pleasure, and marriage. Under beauty are grace, taste, charm, artistic performance, personal adornment, and decoration. The practical aspects of personal relationships, notably in money matters, also slips into this category. Harmony includes a sense of beneficence in social behavior.

Adolescence is the chronological period under Venus's special influence. Lovers are under its aegis. She rules Taurus and Libra—the one earthy, the other balanced. Her houses are II (possessions and money) and VII (relationships, friends, and enemies in one's surroundings). The female sex organs, skin, intestines, and veins come under Venus too.

When carried to extremes, the Venus-motivated person can be self-indulgent, weak when female and effeminate when male. The traits that Venus can show if placed unfavorably in the horoscope are miserliness, boorishness, and inconstancy.

Mars

♂

Symbol: spirit (circle) and matter (arrowlike cross), meaning practicality over ideals.
Day of the week: Tuesday (French: *Mardi.* Norse for Mars: *Tiu*).
Hours of the day: 5th, 12th, 19th.
Takes 22 months to move through all the zodiac signs; spending about 45 days in each sign, except when in retrograde.

The Babylonian god was Nergal, god of war; in Greece, Ares; in Rome, Mars. This inherited picture is of a vigorous, brutal figure; yet the Egyptian counterpart, Horus, was a benign and healing god. Modern astrology chooses less of the hateful traits and more of the pleasant features of this planet. Nevertheless astrologers generally consider Mars a malefic planet, although, of course, its ultimate effects are related more to its association with other planets and its position in the zodiac rather than to its unmodified traits.

Energy and action are the outstanding features. Furthermore, the initiative of Mars encourages embarkation on enterprises. The sexual drive is strong. The head muscles, blood, and sex organs are in Mars's province. Mars's energy can also produce leaders and sportsmen. The Mars outlook allows incisive decisions, manipulations, and sharpness of perception. The person over the age of thirty in full maturity is influenced by Mars. It influences leaders of households.

Mars rules Aries and Scorpio. Its natural domiciles are House I, which covers health and appearance and House VIII, which covers war, taxes, debts, possessions of others, and death.

Mars is indeed considered a malefic planet when unmodified by the steadying influences of other planets and parts. An array of unappealing tendencies must be guarded against, such as selfishness, jealousy, impatience, hostility, destructiveness, brutality, boastfulness, and thievery.

Jupiter

♃

Symbol: matter (cross) with soul (crescent), meaning engagement and self.
Day of the week: Thursday (French: *Jeudi.* Norse for Jupiter: *Thor*).
Hours of the day: 6th, 13th, 20th.
Takes approximately 12 years to move through all the zodiac signs, spending about one year in each sign.

Although Shamash (the Sun god) and Sin (the Moon god) were supreme beings in ancient Mesopotamian culture, Marduk, the counterpart of Jupiter, was more the "flesh-and-blood" deity and became the principal god related to humans. He was in charge of the councils of the gods and was held to be the wisest. Zeus in Greece and Jupiter (Jove) in Rome were his analogues. His benevolence and justice, however, were more in evidence in Mesopotamia than in Greece and Rome.

This planet has all the attributes that go with expansiveness and generosity: cheerfulness (joviality), friendliness, truthfulness. Jupiter also protects the rights of others and shows compassion toward those in trouble. Indeed, this most virtuous of planets fittingly carries with it the heights of good fortune. Events and people almost seem to combine for the purpose of fulfilling ambitions (which the Jupiterian can possess in full measure). Wisdom and leadership are ever in evidence.

The mature years reaching into old age, from fifty to sixty, are under Jupiter's patronage. The signs of Sagittarius and Pisces are ruled by Jupiter and receive its qualities when in favorable relationship. Both the positive shining features and the negative dark sides of Jupiter are suggested in the two houses with which Jupiter is associated: House IX is the area of philosophy, education, long journeys, communication, and religion—all appropriately the areas in which Jupiter excels. But House XII is also Jupiter's abode, where the occult, secrecy, hidden enemies, and criminal activity are located.

When carried to extreme, generosity can become impracticality and expansiveness can lead to gambling compulsion, drinking, and carelessness. The wise, fatherly figure can become dogmatic, overly ambitious, and boring. Moreover, as in all the traits of the planets and signs, the opposing tendencies always lurk in the unconscious and require recognition and regulation. Deceit, indolence, greed, and depression may take hold unless looked for and controlled.

The Jupiterian character is best directed to the professions, religious positions, or organized philanthropy. The body organs assigned to Jupiter are the thighs, arms, arteries, stomach, liver, and sometimes the lungs. Father figures and uncles and aunts are considered to be in Jupiter's province.

Saturn

♄

Symbol: matter (cross) over soul (crescent), meaning practicality over soul.
Day of the week: Saturday.
Hours of the day: 7th, 14th, 21st.
Takes almost 30 years to move through all the zodiac signs, spending about 2½ years in each sign.

Until the late eighteenth century, Saturn was the last and farthest from the earth of the known seven planets—in a sense, the "highest" planetary globe. To the ancients, it was sometimes considered the most powerful. In 1781, when Herschel discovered Uranus, the uniqueness of Saturn diminished, but it was still looked upon as the possessor of coldness, slowness, and aloof strength.

In Babylon, Saturn was Ninib (also called Niurta),

The Hausbuch Master. *The Planet Venus.* c.1475. Engraving, $9\frac{1}{8} \times 5\frac{5}{8}$". The equestrienne Venus is shown with the scales (Libra), the zodiac sign that she rules. Below are activities under her dominion. Rijksmuseum, Amsterdam.

Jupiter is seen ruling over the occupations, social ranks, customs, and costumes in his domain. Miniature from the *Boke of Astronomy.* Late fifteenth century. The Bodleian Library, Oxford.

SATVRNVS
Saturno huomini tardi et rei produce
Rubbaduri et buxiardi et assasini
Villani et uili et senza alchuna luce
Pastori et zoppi et simili meschini

Saturn with Aquarius and Capricorn, the two zodiac signs that he influences, together with activities in his domain. Page from the *De Sphaera* manuscript. Fifteenth century. Biblioteca Estense, Modena, Italy.

A drawing by Jan Harmensz Müller (1571–1628) of Neptune with his trident and horses. Pen with dark brown ink, brown wash, heightened with white on light brown paper, 16¾ × 11½″. Yale University Art Gallery, New Haven. Everett V. Meeks Fund.

OPPOSITE LEFT: William Herschel, who discovered the planet Uranus in 1781.

OPPOSITE RIGHT: Percival Lowell (1855–1916), who was convinced in 1905 that a ninth planet—Pluto—was present, but only after his death were his observations and calculations confirmed.

often associated with war but also with steadiness. Greek mythology identified the planet with the Titan chief, Cronus, who castrated his father, Uranus. As an irony of symbolic history, Uranus was finally avenged through being discovered by Herschel and thereby lessening the special significance of Saturn, who thereafter was no longer the last and highest planet.

Many malefic, undesirable traits have been assigned to this planet in the past, especially in medieval times, in contrast to the admirable features of Jupiter. It has also been erroneously associated with Chronos, Father Time, a confusion with Cronus, the Greek ancestor of the Roman Saturn.

The early evaluations of Saturn as a dreadful sphere in the sky have given way to more acceptable, even praiseworthy features. To some astrologers, Saturn limits and directs the excesses of the other planets, producing genius in conjunction with Jupiter, adding philosophy to the Sun, and generally exerting a steadying influence, much as did Ninib in ancient Babylon.

Thus, steadiness is its outstanding property. The discipline of self-control, the property of defining the boundaries of a focus, and pragmatism in perception are associated with Saturn's wisdom and strategy. Persistence is a second quality. Alongside are caution and sobriety. Conservative, traditional, authoritative values are in ascendancy. Thus, the traits given to Saturn often fit the executive, with his or her steadiness and persistence.

To fit the image of Father Time (this association seems to remain despite its incorrectness) and the slow, cautious, wise traditionalist, old age belongs to Saturn. Saturn rules Capricorn and Aquarius and is linked with House X, of paternal and public positions, and House XI, of aspirations and friendships.

The basic structure of the body in its skeleton is considered to be under Saturn's influence, especially the knees. The skin derivatives, notably the teeth, also are attached to this planet. These assignments are appropriate to the traditional visual picture of a bent, dry-skinned, edentulous, hobbling old man.

The extremes of its traits are narrowness, selfishness, rigidity, coldness, ponderousness, austerity, and fearfulness. Pessimism, guilt, and envy come from extreme self-focus. Mistrust, falseness, and malice must be guarded against. Generally, dire characteristics are not considered when this planet is summarized today.

Uranus

♅

Symbol: the initial of its discoverer (*H* for

Herschel) with the new planet suspended from it. Takes 84 years to move through all the zodiac signs, spending seven years in each sign.

Uranus, Neptune, and Pluto have no counterparts in the Babylonian pantheon. Uranus in Greek mythology was the Heavens overhanging all, when Chaos finally dissolved into Mother-Earth and Father-Sky. The planet was at first called Herschel after its discoverer, then "Georgium Sinus," in honor of the English monarch George III. Finally the name of the Greco-Roman god was assigned.

Herschel's discovery in 1781 affected the heretofore magical number of seven planets. Astrologers, however, adjusted to the new inhabitant of the sky, as they did later when Neptune and Pluto were added to the wanderers through the zodiac. Indeed, at least one astrologer has used the previously unknown existence of Uranus as an explanation of the errors in delineations and predictions of the past. Uranus has also given its name to a newly developed astrological methodology, the Uranian system.

Because Uranus is slow moving, as are the two other outer planets, its influence is generally believed to be exerted in concert with the faster spheres. Events that involve a marked change result from Uranian influence. This includes reform, revolution, and the acquisition of independence, but also implied are group action and the appearance on the scene of anything unexpected, including accidents and disasters. The Uranian mind, which seeks out technology and innovation, also possesses intuition, creativity, and originality and has a bent toward science and the pursuit of truth in other fields. The occult is often placed in this category, as is astrology itself in its intuitive aspects. The Uranian attitude displays tolerance for new ideas and for strange and unconventional concepts. Uranian traits favor someone who is an inventor, entrepreneur, scientist, and investigator in any field of endeavor.

The smaller blood vessels and the ankles are governed by Uranus according to some lexicons.

Uranus has been crowned by some as the ruler of Aquarius and Capricorn, the same two zodiac signs that are also under Saturn. Uranus rules House XI (aspirations and friends).

The dangers of the Uranian influence lie in extremes: violence, universal rebelliousness, tactlessness, irresponsibility, and outrageous eccentricity. By focusing on the actions of a group, there is a tendency to turn away from the needs of the individual person and toward intellectual concerns without feeling.

Neptune

♆

Symbol: sea (trident) over matter (cross), or soul (crescent) over matter (cross).
Takes approximately 165 years to move through all the signs, spending about 14 years in each sign.

The planet Neptune was not discovered until 1846. Moreover, the irascible Greco-Roman god of the sea whose name was given to it by its discoverers (Poseidon in Greece; Neptune in Rome) is considered by some astrologers to be inappropriate to many of this planet's characteristics. To others, the association with water is correct and the sign over which it rules, Pisces, certainly is in keeping with water symbolism. Yet the influences that the planet exerts in astrology are subtle, spiritual, and intangible, quite different in character from the Greek divinity. There is still a difference of opinion on its most acceptable relationship.

Nebulousness with all its implications is a description of the planet's traits. Fantasy, which is involved in creativity, aesthetics, and abstractions, is also a prominent concern of Neptune. Music and drama are considered Neptunian. Hidden things fit the planet's pattern. Whatever is secret, seclusive, mystical, and meditative is assigned here. Its natural domicile is House XII (hidden enemies, the occult, crime, secrecy).

One can readily see that appropriate occupations include teaching, because of the ideals and values in this profession; the arts, notably music, poetry, drama; the occult; undercover activities; and jobs that bring contact with the sea or other bodies of water.

The extremes of Neptune are dangerous. Dreaminess can become diffuseness, uncertainty, depression, and withdrawal from reality. Sensitivity may increase to hypersensitivity. Propensity for secret things may show as deviousness and untrustworthiness. Concern with the abstract can end in delusion.

Pluto

♇

Symbol: the initials of its discoverer (*P.L.* for Percival Lowell and for the first letters of the planet) or spirit (circle) over soul (crescent) with matter (cross) underlying all, meaning that depths (cross) and heights (circle) are transcended by experience (crescent).
Takes 248 years to move through all the zodiac signs, spending about 24 years in each sign.

Pluto was the Roman name for Hades, the Greek god of the underworld. This name was assigned in 1930 when the planet was discovered as a revolving body in

the farthest reaches of the known solar system. If the discovery of the previously undetected Uranus and Neptune were upsetting to the traditional astrological structure, Pluto was even more disturbing, since it takes about twenty years to go through one sign, four or five human lifetimes to visit all of the zodiac. But just as the other two planets became integrated into astrological thinking, so did Pluto. Some astrologers, in anticipation of further discoveries, have postulated that there are planets in the solar system beyond Pluto and have already assigned names and have even defined traits.

The slower a planet's movement in the sky, the less the effect on the individual nature and life course. Therefore this planet is most significant in mass activities and long-term influences. Perhaps for the same reason, technology that has to do with large-scale size or performance is also under its purview. For example, transportation applies here. In extension of the concern with masses, leadership over countries, groups, gangs, and large-sized holdings is in the realm of Pluto. Astrologers have also assigned the planet to signify renewal, thus involving regeneration; reversal of form; the ends and beginnings of actions, events, and ideas. Pluto's effects are usually gradual rather than sudden.

Attached to the symbolism of the mythological deity are the underworld, the unexpected, the hidden or buried (such as contained energy), deficiencies, inheritances, taxes, and insurance against casualty and death. In addition to both death and regeneration, the planet is associated with gradual changes in moods and feelings. Some have also seen in Pluto a sexuality that is unconventional, but magnetic.

Its rulerships are still in dispute. Most listings place it in Scorpio; some in Aries too; others indicate Pisces instead of Aries. Its houses are I for self, appearance, and bodily health, and VIII for death, taxes, debts, and the possessions of others.

Pluto's qualities are consonant with executive positions, political leadership, and insurance. Also appropriate is psychiatry, probing the hidden recesses of the mind, searching the undiscovered past, or exploring.

The combination of leadership and mass involvement can draw those under Pluto's influence into fanaticism, dictatorship, and destruction. There are dangers of treason and secret cabals. Excessive focus on the impersonal to the exclusion of more intimate and personal aspects is also a risk.

The Zodiac

In traditional astrology today, there are twelve zodiac signs, roughly equivalent to twelve particular star clusters in the sky. Each zodiac division is considered to be 30 degrees in dimension and to lie approximately 8 degrees on either side of the path of the sun (the ecliptic), forming together with the other zodiac signs a celestial band. The 30-degree divisions are arbitrary in that the starry constellations themselves are of differing sizes as viewed from the earth.

The *tropical* zodiac system measures a year of twelve months traveled by the sun through the seasons, starting with the zero point of Aries as the beginning of the vernal (spring) equinox. (Of course, it is actually the earth that is moving around the sun against the backdrop of the zodiac constellations and the sun that appears to be moving in our view on earth.) Although this point has shifted slowly through many centuries (the "precession of the equinoxes") so that now the onset of the spring equinox is really well into the cluster of Pisces and no longer in Aries, most Western astrologers still use Aries as the reference point.

The *sidereal* zodiac system measures a year as the precise time it takes for the sun to move through all the star constellations. Most Hindu and a few Western astrologers use the sidereal system. The two zodiac structures, tropical and sidereal, are slightly different ways of measuring; they coincided some time near the start of the Christian Era and will coincide again in about 25,800 years. Meanwhile, about every 2,200 years the tropical zodiacal beginning of the spring season will have shifted a full zodiac sign along the zodiac wheel (reaching Aquarius in about A.D. 2150; Capricorn in A.D. 4300, etc.).

ABOVE: Francesco del Cossa. *Zodiac Sign of Taurus* (detail). c.1469. Fresco. East Wall, Palazzo Schifanoia, Sala dei Mesi, Ferrara.

OPPOSITE: Aries, from *The Jamnapattra of Prince Navanibal Singh*. Nineteenth century. Colors on paper. The British Library, London.

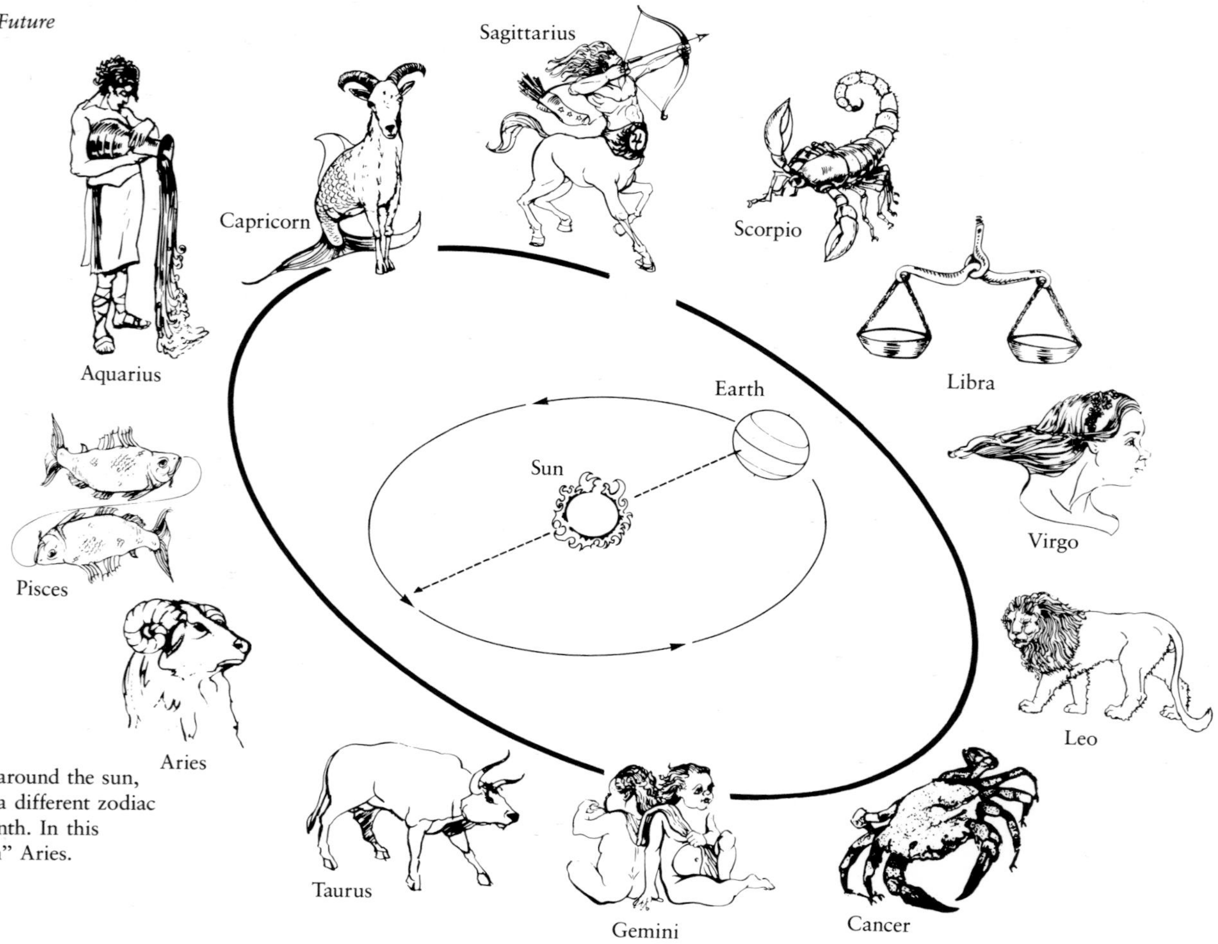

As the earth revolves around the sun, the sun "enters" into a different zodiac constellation each month. In this diagram the sun is "in" Aries.

At the top of the astrological diagrammatic circle of zodiac signs is the MC point (*Medium Coeli,* or midheaven), at the bottom, the IC (*Imum Coeli,* or bottom of the sky). The ascendant point is at the east (left) on the diagram; the descendant at the west (right). The circle may be visualized as if the observer were at a northern position looking from the bottom of the wheel southward to the top of the wheel. Thus the bottom half of the horoscope wheel is its northern hemisphere.

Since the ten planets revolve around the sun in orbits that are all in virtually the same plane, they each move entirely along the zodiac band, some changing their positions rapidly (Moon, Sun, Mercury, Venus, and Mars), others moving more slowly (Jupiter and Saturn), and three very much more slowly (Uranus, Neptune, and Pluto).

While the planets convey their symbolic traits to all creatures on earth, the zodiac signs indicate how those characteristics are manifested. When the Sun is in a zodiac sign at someone's birth (the "Sun-sign"), the characteristics associated with that sign are among the most important contributions to the person's psychological and physical makeup.

As the earth spins (rotates) on its axis, a different zodiac sign appears (rises) on the eastern horizon every few hours, varying in duration in different parts of the earth. This zodiac sign on the eastern rim, called the "ascendant," is at least as important to delineation as is the Sun-sign.

The signs are classified into several categories, paralleling the ancient divisions of all matter into elements, qualities, and polarities. There are three signs (every fourth sign around the horoscope circle) that are associated with the element fire (Aries, Leo, Sagittarius, indicating outgoing behavior); three with earth (Taurus, Virgo, Capricorn, indicating care and detail); three with air (Gemini, Libra, Aquarius, indicating intellect); and three with water (Cancer, Scorpio, Pisces, indicating emotion). These categorizations of groups of three are called the Triplicity. The three fiery signs are sometimes also termed the "fiery trygon," referring to the triangle formed on the horoscope diagrammatic wheel by lines connecting Aries, Leo, and Sagittarius.

The four zodiac signs at each axis on the horoscope circle are considered to be of "cardinal" or initiating quality (Aries, Cancer, Libra, Capricorn). The four adjacent signs—counting counter-clockwise—are "fixed" or firm (Taurus, Leo, Scorpio, Aquarius). The subsequent signs are "mutable" or adaptable (Gemini, Virgo, Sagittarius, Pisces). Each of the qualities thus contains four signs, the Quadriplicity.

In addition, alternating around the circle, the signs are either positive or negative (in earlier times, masculine and feminine). Aries is of positive polarity; Taurus negative; Gemini positive, and so on, with Pisces, the last on the circle, negative.

As indicated in the preceding section on the planets, each zodiac sign is "ruled" by at least one planet, which usually has traits that resemble those associated with the sign and that are thereby reinforced when the planet is in its ruled sign. Further, each planet is enhanced (in "exaltation"), depressed (in "detriment"), or diminished (in "fall"), depending on the particular zodiac sign in which it is present.

Aries

♈

The Ram (March 20 or 21–April 20)
Quality: Cardinal
Element: Fire
Polarity: Positive

Aries is usually listed as the first sign of the zodiac, for in ancient Mesopotamia the solar year in the northern hemisphere began with the sun rising in Aries, the onset of spring; in ancient Egypt the sun-god Ra was associated with the same constellation. We now call this beginning in late March the vernal equinox.

Energetic force is the hallmark of Aries. Enthusiasm, activity, ardor, initiative, courage, and adventure are its outstanding properties. These characteristics can produce leadership, ambition, physical powers, and achievement. Expectedly, it is symbolically connected with House I, where self is the area of focus. Another property of Aries that is not always emphasized is the positive quality of sharpness and high-mindedness. Courage in the service of a lofty principle can produce nobility of character and manner.

Generally, Aries is said to confer propitious characteristics when its planetary rulers exert a favorable influence there, but destructive traits when too strongly accented by the Sun and Mars. One ruler is Mars, whose traits coincide thoroughly with those of Aries. The relatively new planet Pluto has occasionally also been given dominion over the sign. As might be surmised, the Sun is exalted in Aries. Venus, with its almost opposite traits, is in detriment and may be overwhelmed and transformed into negative features while in Aries. Some consider this combination a source of conflict; others applaud Venus's moderating influence. Similarly, Saturn, which is in fall in Aries, can be considered an influence for good or evil depending on other points in the horoscope chart.

Adverse influences on Aries by the planetary arrangements in a particular horoscope can result in exaggerations and misdirections of its forceful energies: impetuosity, impatience, aggressiveness, egotism, and sensuality in the direction of ruthless domineering.

In intimate relationships, the unmodified Ariean needs a mate who is tolerant and resilient enough to bend rather than break; the emotional needs and drives need warm response, not rejection, for the Ariean has a tendency to be inconstant, falling in and out of love, prompted more by burnout than by fickleness.

Taurus

♉

The Bull (April 21-24–May 20-21)
Quality: Fixed
Element: Earth
Polarity: Negative

The glyph of the horns over the face of a full moon has been variously interpreted to be either a bull or a cow. In a Babylonian myth, the goddess Ishtar, rejected in love by the epic hero Gilgamesh, persuaded the god of the sky to have him destroyed by the heavenly bull. In expiation, the bull thereafter had to pull a plough in the heavens through eternity.

In the mythology of ancient Greece, Zeus in the form of a snow-white bull carried away Europa on his back. The early representations of the bull figure show only the front parts because, some say, the remainder were beneath the sea during the journey. At least one influential Roman astrologer saw this zodiac symbol as an ox, because generally the sign has been associated with more bovine than taurine traits. Yet, beneath the external placidity of a Taurus can lie the assertiveness that when provoked becomes bull-like in furor, slow to arouse but unrestrained in intensity.

Taurus was considered a highly important constellation in the earliest civilizations, and from 4000 B.C. until approximately 1700 B.C., when Aries became the rising sign of spring, it was the first sign marking the vernal equinox.

Patience, practicality, firmness, and possessiveness are the outstanding associated traits. The patient person is usually stable, tranquil, diligent, obedient, thorough, reticent, and slow to anger. But this does not affect the natural sense of humor. Following rather than leading is preferred. Firmness is seen in tenacity, endurance, loyalty, and the perseverance that ensures the paying of debts and obligations. The possessiveness of Taurus, which extends to material things and people, also brings with it affection and focus on family.

Usually agreeable, gentle, unselfish, and unmindful of ordinary slights, the personality symbolized by Taurus nevertheless has the potential to become ferocious if pushed to the limits of patience. There is also always the danger of stubborn rigidity and indolence when patience and firmness become too extreme. Taureans try to avoid uncomfortable situations. Practicality can also mean lack of imagination and ambition. The possessive must guard against jealousy, gluttony, and materialism.

Taurus is ruled by Venus, which can intensify a person's sense of beauty, harmony, and gentleness. The emotionality of the Moon, which is exalted in Taurus, may give Taurus more imaginative perspective. As would be expected, Mars is incompatible and therefore in detriment in this sign, presaging conflict between the opposing natures. Uranus is said to be in fall here also, and both the planet and the sign may show their negative features.

Gemini

♊

The Twins (May 22–June 21)
Quality: Mutable
Element: Air
Polarity: Positive

From earliest times, stargazers have visualized two human forms in this constellation: most often two brothers, but sometimes a boy and a girl. Hindus see in it the Mithuna; in the Vedas it is described as representing the two Asvin horsemen; South African bushmen, on the other hand, see two women. In China this star cluster came to symbolize the two basic forces in the universe, yin and yang. In the West, the Latin term *Gemini* became the constellation's title, as Castor and Pollux, twin sons of Jupiter (the Dioscuri sons of Zeus in Greece), were considered to be the figures represented in the sky. Because these two demigods in Greek legend aided the Argonauts during a destructive storm, they became patrons of seagoing people. The glow sometimes seen on the rigging of a ship during lightning and thunder ("Saint Elmo's fire") has also led to the twins' association with electricity. The favor of Castor and Pollux was also sought in war, possibly because of their famed prowess in fighting, in which they instructed Hercules. Evidently the word *Gemini* began to be used as a mild expletive quite early in classical times. "By Jiminy" is said to derive from "O Gemeni" or "O Gemony."

Under the headings of communication, intellect, and change, one can classify virtually all the influences assigned to this constellation. Communication assumes talking, writing, and teaching. Intellect includes judgment, logic, studies, absorption of facts, and mental acuity. Change covers rapidity of action, affinity for the new in ideas and activity, flexibility, travel, ambition to move ahead, and versatility.

The planet Mercury, with essentially the same characteristics as those given to the zodiac sign of Gemini, is the ruler. Jupiter, which rules Sagittarius, is in detriment in Gemini. Furthermore, the dark underside of Jupiter may be exposed by Gemini's influence. (It may be remembered that in the Greek myths it was the Olympian monarch Jupiter himself who lost faith in humans and punished Prometheus for bringing them fire.) On the other hand, Jupiter and Gemini can so interact that the blend of Jovian high principles and the intellectual quickness of Gemini can produce a well-rounded, fascinating, and benign personality. Mercury in Gemini can also exert an additional favorable influence by adding entertainment and humor to a love relationship.

The interplay of Gemini with most of the planets yields a quickening of action and of thought. The Moon and Neptune, however, are apt to lose some sensitivity. Of course this can also be beneficial to those who are hypersensitive or emotional.

The Gemini native is apt to have a good disposition and courteous manner, to be articulate and undismayed by criticism, and to display quickness of mind and resourcefulness. But sometimes these very attributes can be undesirably exaggerated. Gemini needs to guard against verbosity, nervousness, indecision, superficiality, craftiness, selfishness, effeteness, and fickleness.

Cancer

♋

The Crab (June 22–July 22)
Quality: Cardinal
Element: Water
Polarity: Negative

From very early times this constellation was known as the crab, lobster, or crayfish, although at first it was considered to be a tortoise by the Mesopotamians, and Egyptians of the second millennium saw it as a sacred beetle. This cluster of stars is relatively inconspicuous with rather a muted degree of luminescence. Occasionally it has even been associated with darkness. The Chaldeans of Babylonia and the Platonists of Greece believed it to represent the portal or gate through which souls left Heaven to enter the bodies of the newborn.

In Greek and Roman mythology it was Juno (Hera) who lifted the lowly crab into the heavens after Hercules crushed it for having nipped his toes while he was fighting. Its glyph in Greece and Rome was probably always meant to represent the crab, although

ABOVE: Francesco del Cossa. *Zodiac sign of Gemini* (detail). c.1469. Fresco. East Wall, Palazzo Schifanoia. Sala dei Mesi, Ferrara.

RIGHT: Zodiac sign of Cancer (the Crab). Illuminated manuscript page, *June* (June 22–July 22), from *The Hours of the Duchess of Burgundy*. c.1450. Vellum. Musée Condé, Chantilly.

OPPOSITE: Villard de Honnecourt. *Lion and Porcupine*. Bibliothèque Nationale, Paris.

another possibility is that it derived from the two asses who in Greek legend participated in the struggle between the gods and the Titans in the early formation of the universe. Some have even seen it as a symbol for female breasts.

Emotion is Cancer's main identifying property. Understanding and care for others are its outstanding beneficent traits. The feelings associated with it are apt to be tender love, either maternal or paternal. This attribute tends to bring with it protectiveness, patience, patriotism, loyalty, and conservatism. Domesticity, dietary interests, and ownership are attractions. The Cancerian is also apt to be intuitive rather than logical. Quiet, soft, and sensitive inside, like the crab, the Cancerian has a hard shell that allows it to be tenacious, resistant, and also protective.

The only zodiac sign ruled by the Moon is Cancer. The Moon and Cancer when together generally intensify the more favorable traits in each other, although immaturity and excessive reliance on the home and family must be kept in mind. A person's breasts, stomach, and body fluids are influenced by this sign.

Venus in Cancer also brings out warmth and tenderness. Jupiter, which is exalted in this constellation, contributes to the security of the native and the concern for others that is characteristic of the planet and the sign. Neptune and possibly Pluto are also said to have favorable connotations in Cancer. Mercury may have some of its intellectuality lessened, but its detachment enhances sensitivity and memory. The aggressiveness of Mars may yield some of its vigor, but this can now be directed toward other concerns. The emotional warmth of the domestic scene may be cooled somewhat by Saturn. Uranus may introduce rebelliousness. On the other hand, extreme independence may be kept within bounds by Saturn in Cancer.

The characteristics associated with Cancer often create occupational difficulties with people: reticence can be misinterpreted as aloofness. Yet, in the proper job environment the loyal, considerate person may shine. The fitting business activities are those where friendliness and quiet perception are useful. Intuition can lead to high success, whether in broad policy or in choosing people.

Moodiness, hypersensitivity, passivity, and insecurity—virtually the same weaknesses that can be shown by the Moon—are dangers. Behavior can be "crabby." Cancer and its ruler, the Moon, need to be directed away from emotional instability.

Leo

♌

The Lion (July 22 or 23–August 22 or 23)
Quality: Fixed
Element: Fire
Polarity: Positive

In Egypt, this constellation was thought to be the site of the sun's rising at the beginning of creation, and it signified the brightness and hotness of the sun. A legendary explanation assigns the appearance of the great sphinx to a combination of the body of Leo and the head of Virgo—which is the succeeding sign in the zodiac. Some of the stars of Leo in Egyptian times, when the constellation was considered to contain fewer stars than are in the modern cluster, were perceived to form a knife (in Mesopotamia it was a scimitar; elsewhere later a sickle). Throughout antiquity and into contemporary periods, the Sun and Leo have been closely associated.

Energy typifies Leo—and its ruler, the Sun. This characteristic is expressed in enthusiasm, leadership, lordliness, ambition, conscientiousness, and intensity. Almost as an extension of this drive is the expansiveness shown in generosity, pleasure seeking, and affection for children. The native displays a sunny disposition, courage, and confidence; broad-mindedness in offering and receiving ideas, optimism, and a flair for the dramatic and the artistic. As a fixed sign, Leo is noteworthy for its firmness of purpose and performance.

Leo resembles Aries in its energetic, outgoing traits, but whereas Aries is self-aware, Leo is actually

focused on self. Aries thrives on competing with others; Leo brooks no competition. Aries (of cardinal quality) initiates and achieves. Leo (a fixed sign) carries through and completes. They both are quick-tempered, but Aries cools faster.

Just as the Sun would be expected to be Leo's ruler, to which it renders enhanced dignity, Saturn, Mercury, and a cool customer like Uranus are in detriment or fall when in Leo. Uranus can be lifted to superior feelings and actions, but these can be in the direction of either nobility or arrogance. While Mercury can have its communicative capabilities further expanded it can also become pompous and garrulous when in Leo. Although Saturn is also in an unfavorable conflicting climate in Leo, there is the chance of warming up the Saturnine gloom. The Moon's interests are broadened toward creativity and the pursuit of enjoyment. Venus also is stimulated toward expressions of affection and enhanced in its search for pleasure. Mars can be so intensified in command that its excessive energies must be controlled. Leo enables Jupiter to give full vent to warmth, generosity, and the display of feelings. Neptune's idealism can be expanded to wider fields.

Obvious dangers lurk in the sunny, expansive Leo personality: arrogance, tyranny, grandiosity, vanity, even the hubris for which the ancient Greek gods dealt out severe punishment. The expansive person can become reckless and perpetually ostentatious. A flaring temper can smolder destructively, turning a generous nature toward resentment. Occasionally, like the morning after an excess, the extremes of energy can be followed by a period of sloth. The firmness and determination need a full measure of generosity and broad-mindedness to prevent the development of a prickly personality.

Virgo

♍

The Virgin (August 23–September 22)
Quality: Mutable
Element: Earth
Polarity: Negative

This constellation has always been recognized as a maiden, usually associated with fertility, the harvest, and innocence. (The Chinese at first saw the star cluster as a bird's tail, later as a "frigid maiden.") The figure may have been the Isis of Egyptian mythology, Ishtar of Mesopotamia, Ashtoreth or Astarte of biblical times, and Aphrodite or Ceres of Greece. In northern parts of the world and in the Middle East, India, and Persia, its representation was commonly a single female figure holding a stalk of wheat, a staff, or a scale. The origin of the present glyph has been variously assigned: the letters M.V. might stand for the Virgin Mary, the first three letters of a title in Greek, or a diagram of the wing of Ishtar.

Virgo is ever patient, with the capability of dealing with the minutest details. Perfection is the ultimate goal. But good sense, coolness, and practicality inform Virgo's attitudes and decisions to the point of its appearing limited. Health is an interest, especially nutrition. Virgo's earthiness, however, also encompasses the solid foundations of intellect. The mixture of patience and practicality give to mental activities the analytical qualities of discrimination in a sane, forthright direction.

The Virgo native has self-confidence, but, in contrast to the native of Leo, for example, is also both willing and eager to be self-analytical, to seek imperfections. Idealism accompanies Virgo's activities, so that service to others becomes a fundamental asset. As a helpful, modest, precise, efficient member of a team, Virgo excels in a position below the very top.

In view of these characteristics, it would be difficult to anticipate that Mercury is the ruler. It is adaptable, as is Virgo, and its airy classification also includes intellectuality, but the planet soars while the zodiac sign of Virgo is earthbound. The ego of Mercury looks to speed ahead rather than to tarry for discovering faults. Virgo is apt to be quiet, patient, and pragmatic; Mercury can be communicative, mobile, and quixotic. It is said that when in the sign of Virgo, Mercury is modified in the direction of good sense and more sober reflection.

The Moon's imagination is prevented from breaking into dreaminess and is allowed to focus when the planet is in Virgo. Saturn in Virgo is energized to

Zodiac sign of Virgo from an astrological treatise based on Albumasar. c.1403 A.D. Illumination on vellum, 9⅝ × 7″. The Pierpont Morgan Library, New York City.

OPPOSITE ABOVE: Zodiac sign of Libra from *The Ascension of Propitious Stars and Sources of Sovereignty* by Matali al-sa'ada wa manabi 'al-Siyada. Turkish. 1582. Illumination on polished paper, 10⅞ × 7″. The Pierpont Morgan Library, New York City.

OPPOSITE BELOW: Zodiac sign of Scorpio by the Rohan Master in *Les Grandes Heures* of the Duke of Rohan. c.1418. Illumination on vellum, 10 × 7″. Bibliothèque Nationale, Paris.

be analytical. The combination of Saturn and Virgo can lead to intensive application of thought and action, so that great contributions can be achieved. Uranus too may be prompted to use its originality for feasible goals. Pluto in Virgo is influenced to give time and attention to individuals rather than to masses.

Apparently the other planets can be adversely affected, although there is a possible beneficial side as well. Mars may be so distracted by details that nothing can be accomplished. But Mars may also become more involved in service to others. Jupiter's expansiveness can be markedly constricted. Its generosity, on the other hand, can be kept to sensible levels. The struggle between the nebulousness of Neptune and the earthy practicality of Virgo can cause destructive conflict or may result in an efficiency not otherwise likely.

The intestinal tract is the particular area of the body under Virgo's sign. It is said that Virgo's tendency to hold back can be associated with constipation. The patience and orderliness can turn the Virgo native into a "Craig's Wife"—compulsive to the exclusion of affection. Modesty can become extreme shyness, introversion, and nervous decline. The larger picture can be sacrificed to the hypercritical smaller focus. The propensity for service and helping others must be differentiated from servility.

Libra

♎

The Scales (September 21-24–October 20-23)
Quality: Cardinal
Element: Air
Polarity: Positive

Libra may well have received its name and symbol in early Chaldean times, although a variety of other representations followed. Generally, this cluster is seen as either a yoke, beam (for weighing), scales, or claws (from Scorpio the adjacent constellation). It lies on the autumn equinox, at a time when night and day are equal in duration.

One view of its origins as an astrological symbol is that the Romans were responsible for adding Libra to the eleven signs that had comprised the zodiac previously. Julius Caesar even claimed to have invented it as a separate part of the zodiac. Early Greek astronomers, Hyginus, Aratus, Eratosthenes, Hipparchus, and others considered this group of stars to be the claws of the constellation Scorpio. As the scales or as a scale beam it was part of ancient Hebrew and Indian sky cultures. The Chinese eventually named it the "celestial balance" after having at first called it the "star of longevity."

The glyphic symbol is said to show a balance beam, although early Mesopotamians may have seen it as a lamp, related later to the Great Lamp, the lighthouse at Alexandria that was one of the seven wonders of the ancient world.

The symbol of the scales typifies the balance in Libra's nature. The attitude tends to be nonpartisan, recognizing both sides of an argument, avoiding extremes. Neatness and order—but with less compulsion than Virgo—allow Libra to do well in organizing abstract ideas, thus emphasizing a second trait, intellectuality. Subtle meanings are clear to Libra. The mind is capable of hard work and can be applied intensively to specific endeavors. Interrelationships among people are a strong feature of Libra. The personality is agreeable, kind, gently warm, and often displays a sparkling wit. Marriage and long-standing close relationships are eagerly sought.

Venus is a fitting ruler, with its warm affection and gentleness. The more desirable traits of the planet Venus and the sign Libra are enhanced when they are together. A seemingly strange circumstance is that the traditional gloomy, plodding Saturn is in exaltation in Libra. Actually, Saturn is prodded to be more outwardly oriented and its pessimism more balanced, while Libra is pushed farther into relationships and responsibilities.

The Moon is reinforced in its harmonious effects and Libra is given more emotional latitude. Mercury, prompted to become engaged more purposefully, contributes its own expressiveness to Libra. As would be expected, Jupiter is further strengthened in its fairness and yet is given more balance to its generosity and expansiveness. Libra directs the originality of Uranus into the arts. Mars is likely to find difficulties when in Libra, where it is in detriment. But in some circumstances, the effects of Martian roughness can be smoothed over to allow better personal relationships. The idealism of Neptune can be led to focus on the attainment of peace. Pluto, the slowest moving of the known planets, was in Libra from about 1970 to 1984, and some have seen the planet's influences manifested in the frequent divorces and remarriages during this time. Pluto has now moved toward Scorpio, a sign that it rules. The kidneys, hips, back, and internal glands are under Libran dominion.

Scorpio

♏

The Scorpion or Claws (October 20-24–November 20-22)
Quality: Fixed
Element: Water
Polarity: Negative

Scorpio is one of the most ancient of the signs and a member of the earliest zodiac, which consisted of only six constellations. Different images have at times been assigned, as for instance an eagle or a snake crowned by a diadem, in earliest Egypt. However, the zodiac on the ceiling of the temple of Dendera contains a scorpion. In China, the "Blue Dragon," the "Great Fire," "Divine Temple," and the "Hare" were names given to this figure until the sixteenth century, when the title of "Celestial Scorpion" was adopted. In Mesopotamia a stinger was the usual nomenclature, although some have translated the cuneiform tablets to mean a "double sword."

The Greeks and Romans consistently saw a scorpion in the star cluster, but sometimes their astronomers referred to it as the "Great Beast" or the "Great Sign." In mythology it was the scorpion who slew the formidable giant Orion and caused the horses of Apollo to bolt. The very ancient temples of Greece were supposed to have been built to point to the bright Antares, a brilliant star in Scorpio at the spring equinox. Explosions of supernovae have been seen many times in the vicinity of Scorpio, adding a measure of power and destruction to its malign impression.

Of all the constellations in the traditional zodiac, this group of stars is farthest away from the ecliptic

band marking the sun's positions through the year. Indeed, for only nine days of the year does the sun actually appear in any portion of Scorpio, although it is considered in astrology to remain in this zodiac sign for a month, since the sun appears to be near although not actually in Scorpio.

Scorpio is a fixed sign whose traits are firmness and single-mindedness, within which is a strong coloring of aggression. Nothing is superficial in Scorpio, for a relentless penetration informs its thoroughness, courage, strength, stamina, and resourcefulness. Things below the surface are its focus. With its doggedness there are also strong moral principles.

In keeping with its persistent intensity of emotion, labeled by many as passionate, sexual, and magnetic, the drives are highly personal, fueled by a curiosity that is more intuitive than analytical. The personality is said to be dignified, with leadership charisma, and yet sensitive. Like other fixed signs, the tendency is to keep intensity in check but when awakened or stimulated, a mesmerizing characteristic may emerge.

In some respects Scorpio is anomalous. For instance, the other two watery signs show passivity, whereas Scorpio is fiery and aggressive. Its negative polarity also seems to be at odds with its aggressive vigor. One explanation given is that Scorpio's aggression fights back only when challenged.

Mars has been the traditional ruler, capable of being brought to passionate and ambitious heights when in Scorpio. A hostile, forceful nature ordinarily kept within useful bounds may be prompted to explode into resentful, persistent, and destructive acts. Since the discovery of Pluto, this planet has become a second and even more significant ruler, aiding Scorpio's nature with more feeling and purpose.

The Moon is in fall here, yet much of the Moon's passivity and repression may be directed into activity and open expression. Venus finds its warm affection so intensified as to be consuming and destructive, but at the same time the Venusian can be strengthened, abandoning frivolity in favor of lasting attitudes and emotions.

Mercury may find its versatility and objectivity circumscribed. Its ability to communicate can be enhanced by passion though words may be more barbed. Jupiter becomes more perceptive and enthusiastic, but Saturn may lead to exaggerated stubbornness and caution to the point of inaction. The individualism of Uranus, which is exalted in Scorpio, can be intensified. The ideals and the formless ideas of Neptune may receive a dose of passion and direction. Mystical and mysterious endeavors attract Scorpio—whether in the occult or in philosophy.

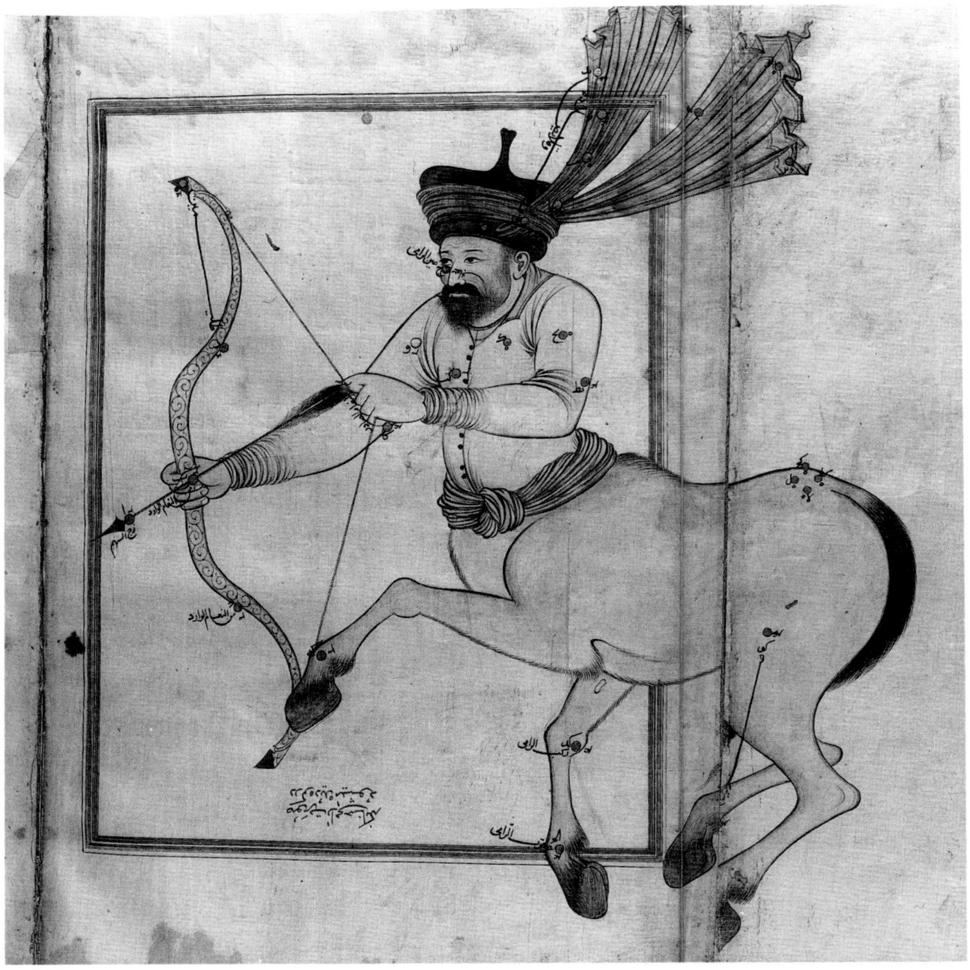

Zodiac sign of Sagittarius from *Book of Stars ar* *Constellations* o Abd al-Rahman Sufi. 1690. Illumination on $9\frac{1}{2} \times 15\frac{3}{4}$". Spe Collection. The New York Publi Library. Astor, Lenox, and Tild Foundations.

Sagittarius

♐

The Archer (November 23–December 21)
Quality: Mutable
Element: Fire
Polarity: Positive

An archer has most often been assigned to this constellation. Probably it was in Mesopotamia that the association originated, though the cuneiform tablets also appear to give other names, such as "Giant War King" and "Shining Face of the City." The bow, drawer of the arrow, and bowstretcher, however, were more prominent assignments. To ancient Egyptians, too, these stars seemed to form images connected with archery.

The Greeks and Romans preserved the idea of the archer, and Sagittary became the common name for the constellation. The glyph is a symbol of an arrow and bow. The archer in the heaven was almost always shown aiming at the nearby zodiac sign of Scorpio.

In India and other cultures the cluster is seen as a horse or a horseman. The half-man–half-horse picture gradually became the norm. In Chinese astronomy a portion of Sagittarius was once grouped with the Virgo, Libra, and Scorpio star clusters as part of the huge overall zodiac sign known as the "Blue Dragon," and some observers merged it with the equivalent of Capricorn. But the earliest representation in China was that of a tiger, only becoming the man-horse under Western missionary influence.

To the Greeks and Romans, Sagittarius was the mythological Centaur, son of Cronus the Titan, teacher of Apollo, Diana, and Asclepius. Sometimes, the man-horse in the sky was a less noble and more aggressive satyr, but for the most part a more benign symbolism prevailed, so that Sagittarius in traditional astrology is characterized by expansiveness, adaptability, and thoughtfulness. Together these traits make its natives friendly people, leaders, and useful partners.

Good luck, good humor, and good will all seem to arise from the expansive nature. Some have claimed that the hottest part of a burning flame is typical of Sagittarius, as distinguished from the other two fiery signs: Aries with its initiating heat and Leo with its glare. A propensity for adventure, independence, leadership, joviality, and vigorous physical activity is also prominent in Sagittarius. Enthusiasm and optimism are the keynotes.

The half-man–half-horse combination ensures adaptability (a characteristic of mutable signs) possessing both the perceptive intelligence of the human and the runaway rashness of the equine (the Sagittarian is interested in fact in all animals). When these two traits are merged harmoniously, the Sagittarian can move ahead into new ventures while maintaining prudence. Just as Chiron, the centaur, was knowledgeable, wise, and generous, Sagittarius is thoughtful, aims at moral truths, and perceives the essentials among a morass of ideas, though the interests and views are apt to be broad rather than detailed.

Jovial, expansive Jupiter is the ruler, capable of actions with the highest motivation when in Sagittarius. The Moon can also become more expressive and free. Venus may be more outspoken in its affectionate feelings and less inhibited in relationships. Usually, Mars also does well in Sagittarius. Although the energies of the planet Mars and the sign Sagittarius together may get out of hand, the tendency is to pursue adventure in a useful direction.

The broad vision of Sagittarius may either widen the constricted horizons of Saturn or add confusion to Saturn's usual concern with details. Neptune is in exaltation in Sagittarius, enhanced in its idealism and energized in its mysticism but more expressively optimistic in its tone. When Pluto gets to Sagittarius, near the middle of the twenty-first century, it may be prompted to be more benign, to release its energies in a more gradual, less explosive fashion. Mercury is in detriment, in danger of losing attention to details, overenthusiastic in verbal expression yet communicating less. Conversely, its adaptability may actually be improved and its understanding widened.

The spirited Sagittarian personality can go to excess in gluttony, gambling, tempestuousness, and recklessness. The high-mindedness may degenerate into self-righteousness, hypercriticism, and pomposity. The deep thinker must guard against becoming opinionated. Adaptability must not be allowed to end as a lack of commitment and fecklessness. The thighs and hips are ruled by Sagittarius, possibly because of an association with horseback riding and mobility.

Capricorn

♑

The Goat (December 22–January 20)
Quality: Cardinal
Element: Earth
Polarity: Negative

For most of its history, the goat or ibex has been this constellation's symbol. In ancient Egypt some representations show an ibis-headed man riding on a goat. The appearance of this constellation also marked the time of the rising of the star Sirius, which coincided with the Nile flooding. Sirius and Isis were often synonymous.

In ancient Greece, the horned goat was sometimes linked with Pan, the goat-footed, half-perfected creature. But it was also seen symbolically as a sea-goat, goat-fish, ocean storm, or even rainmaker. Sometimes Capricorn was even looked upon as Neptune's child.

In ancient Mesopotamia, a connection between Capricorn and the sea was made quite early and manifested in figures of the goat or ibex with the tail of a fish. Ea, god of the oceans and usually shown as a fish, was also sometimes represented in goat form.

In India, although a goatlike figure or an antelope was a common indicator of the constellation, there were also combinations of goat and fish, goat and hippopotamus, or fish alone. Some oriental myths relate the nursing of the sun-god by a goat, a tale similar to the later Western legend of the infant Jupiter (Zeus) being nurtured on the milk of the she-goat Amaltea. In China, the ox or bull eventually became the goat-fish, probably as a result of Western influence.

One may wonder at how this earthy sign's character corresponds with these amphibious representations. A possible answer might be that Capricorn encompasses the entire earth, in which both land and water are essential components. In Greek mystical philosophy, Capricorn also represented the gateway to the gods through which the souls of the deceased passed on their ascent into the stars, just as Cancer was the gate of men, the passageway for souls from the starry heavens to enter the bodies of people at their birth.

This constellation has been variously evaluated as fortunate and unfortunate: lucky because this "mansion of kings" was the ascendant sign of two great, popular Roman emperors, Augustus and Vespasian; unlucky as it is associated with storms at sea. The glyph may arise from the first two letters of the Greek word for goat, from the curled tail of the animal, or from the entire figure of a fish-tailed ungulate.

Traditional astrology assigns to Capricorn the traits that may be summarized broadly as practical and reliable, but under these two headings there is a considerable variety of manifestations. Common sense, discipline, decisiveness, and efficiency are the expected concomitants.

Although reliability clearly includes self-control, prudence, and fairness, it also signifies self-denial for the greater good, as long as the result is also obviously useful and effective. No false idealism or romantic heroism! Capricorn tends to preserve traditional values and ceremonies, needing social acceptance and recognition. It responds to father figures and is prone to be authoritative itself.

The mind's journey may be deliberate, and even slow, but it also is subtle and courageous, possessed of dignity in its expression. Initiating projects is inherent in this sign's cardinal quality but the plans are usually well thought out beforehand. Fun can well be a part of Capricorn's sociability, although it may tend to be purposefully linked to what is acceptable. Jokes about oneself take precedence over mocking others. Playfulness is apt to be restrained rather than exuberant. Friendship can be deep and enduring, formed principally with principled people.

Saturn rules Capricorn, heightening its own caution and pragmatism. Mercury, too, may become more serious and cautious. The emotional attachments of Venus tend toward the practical, and the display of emotion is more prudent. In Capricorn, the Moon, another emotional planet, is in detriment, restricted in its imagination, defensive, and perhaps uncomfortable in relying on itself. Jupiter is also said to be adversely affected; its generosity may be constricted. However, bringing Jupiter down to earth can make its interests more practical and thereby in the end more effective and rewarding.

Mars, however, is exalted. The surging aggression is directed toward worthwhile ends, its ambitions guided into useful channels. The intuitive thinking of Uranus may have to become more methodical and its individualism more socially oriented. (Some think that Uranus is a co-ruler together with Saturn.) Neptune has just entered Sagittarius and will not reach Capricorn for a long time. Pluto will not meet the sign of Capricorn until well into the twenty-first century.

In affections, reticence is common at first, giving way gradually to excitement and even passion. Capricorn is faithful and committed through good and bad times. A suitable mate is demonstrative and yet patient, matching Capricorn's steadfastness.

When the nature of Capricorn is carried to extremes, the pragmatism may evolve into crass materialism and callousness. Caution may end as timidity. The reliability may be overblown to severity and stiffness. All these have to be prevented from showing in the outward personality. In Capricorn's dominion are the skin and bones—especially of the knees.

Capricorn is seen in this painted tile—showing the goat-fish origins of this zodiac sign—from the ceiling of the synagogue at Dura Europos. Third century A.D. Musée du Louvre, Paris.

Aquarius

♒

The Water Carrier (January 21–February 19)
Quality: Fixed
Element: Air
Polarity: Positive

Curiously, Aquarius is classified as an airy sign (along with Gemini and Libra) and yet has been associated with water images virtually throughout its history. A human figure pouring water, along with variations and derivatives, is its symbol in most cultures. In ancient Egypt it was the Lord of the Canals in some translations of the hieroglyphics, possibly because the Nile was fully flooded when the Sun was in this sign. Mesopotamia saw it as rain because of its coincidence with the month of January, and also as the "Sea." Even in early Babylonia the representation was a man pouring out water from a container. In ancient India it was once thought of as a god of storms. In ancient China, Pisces, Aquarius, Capricorn, and a segment of Sagittarius once formed the giant constellation known as the "Dark Warrior."

Greek terms also gave this sign watery connotation. In Rome it was shown as a bright plumed bird epitomizing the month of Juno (Hera in Greek), whose symbol was the peacock, or as a goose, which was also sacred to the powerful Olympian queen. At other times, the sky figure had strong associations with water, a water container, or a water pourer. The Arabians, who balked at showing a human figure because of religious prohibitions, formed a bucket or a wine jar out of the cluster.

How then to reconcile an air sign with so much water? Even the traditional diagram of Aquarius has been traced by some to the Egyptian hieroglyph for water. One explanation for the symbol by astrologists is that the winds of the air blow upon the water, ruffling its surface into waves. Alternatively, the poured water is said to bestow on mankind the needed element of intuitive intelligence, "watering" the streams of human progress.

The traits of Aquarius are clearly those of the air element, especially its intellectuality. Detached, thoughtful, inventive—even experimental—the Aquarian is full of ideas. The psyche is continually active, perceptive, and creative. The mind is usually directed toward the organization and goals of society. Even mathematical and scientific endeavors maintain a larger view of ultimate effects on the mass of people. The world's needs and benefits rather than those of the individual's occupy attention.

Although the Aquarian is fair, the firmness of a fixed sign is manifested in resistance to any detour or opposition. The determination that is part of a fixed sign shows itself as independence. In contrast to Taurus, Leo, and Scorpio (the other fixed signs), the individualism is nonconforming, stubbornly in opposition to the demands of tradition and conservatism. Aquarius, however, is committed and loyal to the course that has been set.

The traditional ruler is Saturn, also oriented toward group concerns, but the planet's unswerving rigidity can be made more flexible to make room for the radical and unconventional ideas that Aquarius may bring. In turn, Aquarius can receive Saturn's patience and organization. Most astrologers now designate Uranus as the ruler or a co-ruler. They see similarities between the planet and the sign in the innovative views and intellectual detachment that are short on personal feeling and long on broad concepts.

Mercury is in exaltation in Aquarius. The interest in science and invention is mutually stimulating. Expansiveness and compassion of Jupiter are also enhanced. Mars is prompted to direct its energies into more socially beneficial paths. The Sun itself is said to be in detriment—cooling its energy but also prompting it to project its light and heat further outside itself. The Moon may develop conflicts, being uncomfortable in this unemotional and untraditional atmosphere. Yet it is less restricted here than when in Capricorn, and its feelings may be made more objective. Venus, too, may find its artistic judgments more flexible and its affections less ardent. Neptune has a long way to go before getting through Sagittarius and Capricorn. Perhaps when it is in Aquarius, scientific imagination may be broadened. Pluto is too far away for speculation at this moment.

There is danger of eccentricity, perverseness, fickleness, and disruption. The head may so predominate over heart that coldness may result. Love of mankind in general may contrast with callousness toward individual people. Aquarians do especially well in technology, research, invention, social work, progressive politics, and urban planning. Aquarius is given dominion over the circulation of the blood, especially in the smaller blood vessels, and also over the ankles.

Pisces

♓

The Fishes (February 20–March 20)
Quality: Mutable
Element: Water
Polarity: Negative

Fishes have always been Pisces's symbol as either one or two figures. One Hellenistic legend told of how Aphrodite and Eros hid from the monster Typhon by jumping into the Euphrates as fishes, with their tails bound together to prevent separating. One Arabic commentator inferred that only one fish was the original name, which agrees with the opinion of Eratosthenes, the Greek scientist of the third century B.C. who suggested that the prototype was a Syrian goddess from whom the term "Great Fish" was derived. The double form may have come from the Babylonian practice of adding an extra month to the calendar at this time of year every six years in order to make up for the missing 5 days in their 360-day year so that it would coincide with the solar year of 365 days. The connection with water may also have come from the coincidence of the rainy season in some parts of the world with the presence of the sun in this constellation. The Aztecs for instance called the cluster "Water." The Chinese named the Pisces cluster the "Pig," but the eventual term became "Two Fishes."

The two fishes face in different directions. The conjunctions of Jupiter and Saturn in Pisces in the year A.D. 747 gave some later commentators (the astronomer Kepler was one of them) the idea that these stars were the Star of Bethlehem, which guided the Magi to the site of the Nativity. Subsequent findings and events have altered this view—particularly after the assignment of a different date to the birth of Jesus. But the Christian Era and the zodiac sign of Pisces have commonly been linked. Some rabbinic writings at one time also placed a conjunction of planets in Pisces previous to the birth of Moses and also anticipated another meeting of planets in this sign to mark the further arrival of the Messiah.

The universal closeness of Pisces to the idea of water has given it the strong astrological significance of emotionality. Included are the traditional attributes of sensitivity, gentleness, imagination, compassion, and intuition. The subconscious and repressed secret desires play a role in the Piscean makeup. Self-criticism is always lurking. As a member of the mutable quadriplicity, this sign possesses adaptability and concomitant versatility, flexibility, and the gift of imitation. The ability to cope with almost any situation, sometimes through shrewdness, carries with it the price of inner turmoil, but usually without ruffling the cool exterior.

A Piscean propensity is to help others, sometimes in a modest, self-effacing way. Aquarius, as we have seen, has a conscious ego that identifies with a group or a social organization. Pisces is more likely to focus on one or more individual members of the group.

Traditionally Jupiter rules Pisces, coinciding with the benevolence, generosity, and nobility of character in the sign. Pisces lends sensitivity to Jupiter's expansiveness. In turn, the optimism and knack of finding good luck can add cheerfulness and a note of confidence. Since the mid-nineteenth century, however, Neptune has become at least a coruler, heightening the intuition and sensitivity of the sign. Neptune in turn becomes more mystical. The planet and sign together add to creativity.

The Moon, resembling the sign in its emotionality and imagination, may be led to unreality and fantasy but it can instead be raised to a high level of intuition and perception. There is a possible danger in unrealistic attachments or affections. Mercury is in fall in Pisces, apt to become hazy in its mental processes and uncertain and formless in its own versatile activities. On the other hand, if the intuition and compassion of Pisces are added to the conscious cleverness of Mercury the result can be salutary.

Venus is exalted here. Sensitive artistry, understanding affection, aesthetics in thought and action can result. Mars, in some ways the opposite of Pisces, may be benefited by the tempering of its aggressive energy, the softening of its attack, and the guiding of activity into worthwhile pursuits. Of course, Mars can be deprived of its vigor if Piscean influence is too extreme. The inner directed focus of Pisces may be weighted into gloom by Saturn but the uneasy emotionality can be given stability. The intuition of Pisces lends effectiveness to Saturn's persistence. Cautious Saturn may be able to perceive more acutely the obstructions ahead and thereby achieve its goals more quickly.

Innovative breakthroughs are possible when Uranus finds itself in this constellation. As the intuitive thinking of both the planet and the sign are enhanced, the cool detachment of Uranus may be given the added dimension of feeling. Slow Pluto is too remote in position to consider. The feet, endocrine secretions, and body fluids are given the symbol of Pisces in the charts of the Zodiac Man.

Emotionality must be kept within bounds lest it become neuroticism. Indecisiveness is an ever-present danger. Self-blame may reach the depths of self-pity and despair. Pisces must guard against excessive guilt, shyness, and hypersensitivity. Receptivity must not be allowed to deteriorate into inaction. Cheerful surroundings and unstressful situations are needed, since negativity from surroundings is easily absorbed.

Pisces's flexibility allows fulfillment in many different types of occupations, but the creative, mystical, and imaginative are usually the most desired.

OPPOSITE: Zodiac sign of Aquarius from an Italian book of hours. Vellum. c.1475. The Pierpont Morgan Library, New York City. William S. Glazier Collection.

RIGHT: Zodiac sign of Pisces, from a stained glass window in Chartres Cathedral, France. Thirteenth century.

Houses

Astrologers divide the sky into twelve separate sectors, the houses, for the purpose of indicating the areas of life in which the influences of the planets and signs are manifested.

The houses are created by spherical geometric calculation, they are not visible divisions in the sky. While the planets and zodiac signs move continuously, the house system stays stable—it is the framework through which the other parts of the horoscope move. The horizontal axis of the horoscope wheel represents the horizon, and the zodiac signs noted there are the actual constellations that would be located at either side of the horizon at the time for which the chart is cast. The vertical axis represents a line that runs through the earth from the heavens above one hemisphere to the bottom of the other. The top of the vertical axis is called the midheaven (the *Medium Coeli*, or MC) and represents the point on the ecliptic above us; the bottom point is called the *Imum Coeli*, or IC. About two dozen different systems of house construction have developed over the past two thousand years. Several historians of astrology believe that there were originally eight segments, but there are now twelve houses in most systems.

Astrologers who employ houses consider them essential to delineation in order to perceive more accurately the dissimilarities among persons who have similar birth charts. Different times of birth, even for twins, and different places of birth can put the planets and zodiac signs into different houses. Moreover, in any one house each person may choose to focus more on one area of activity than on others. One identical twin may be involved in sports and the other in business speculation—both of which lie in House V. The resulting interactions of each person with his or her line of endeavor (within a house) modify thought, action, and destiny. Thus, although two people may have the identical configuration of planets, signs, and houses, one of them may end up as a ne'er-do-well but cheerful, immature sportsman and the other as a rich, moody, unhappy business tycoon.

Roughly speaking, the dominion assigned to each house conforms to the properties of the zodiac sign with which the house is primarily associated. In the Equal House system, for example, this association can be seen on the horoscope wheel at the time of the vernal equinox, when the boundaries of Aries and of House I are the same. At that time Taurus would coincide with House II, Gemini with House III, and so on through the twelve signs and houses. The elements and qualities assigned to the zodiac signs are also held by the houses. In addition, the location of each house on the wheel is significant. The common direction used in numbering the houses on a chart is counter-clockwise. Houses I, IV, VII, and X, whose beginning boundaries (cusps) are at the horizon axis (east-west on the chart) or at the meridian (the vertical line) are termed "angular." They are associated with personal affairs. When there are planets in these houses, dynamic astrological qualities are intensified. Houses II, V, VIII, XI, following the angular houses, are called "succedent" and are the repository of potentials. Planets here are apt to signify stability in life's situations. Houses III, VI, IX, XII are called "cadent" and emphasize dependent activities. Planets in a cadent house often suggest a tendency to passivity but also to adjustability.

The contemporary astrologer R. W. Holden prefers to categorize the many systems of house division according to whether they are based on divisions of the ecliptic or of space or time. Larousse's encyclopedia, for example, tabulates the methods as: direct division of the ecliptic, projected division of the ecliptic, division based on axial rotation of the earth, or topocentric division based on the precise location of a person's birth. There are of course other methods, too.

There are limitations attributed to each house method, and some astrologers do not employ any house system at all, but the majority consider them important. Kepler, the astronomer and astrologer of the seventeenth century, and others found them either misleading or unwarranted. The Gauquelins divide the celestial sphere into thirty-six sectors. Modern astrologers Cyrus Fagan and G. Allen have used an eight-house division numbered clockwise. Most of the current systems of division are illustrated here.

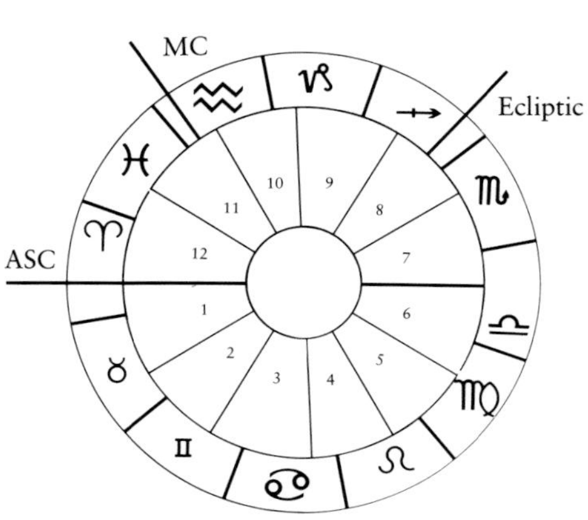

Equal House System

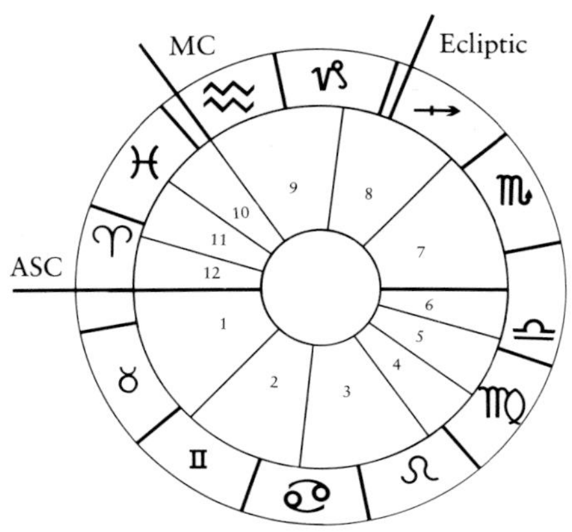

Porphyry Method

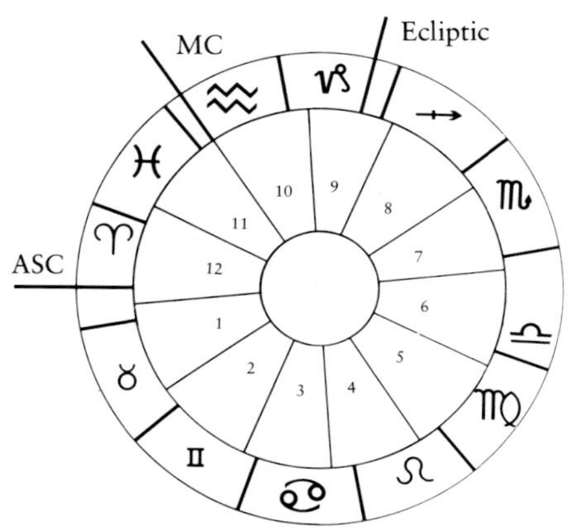

Mid-Heaven House Method

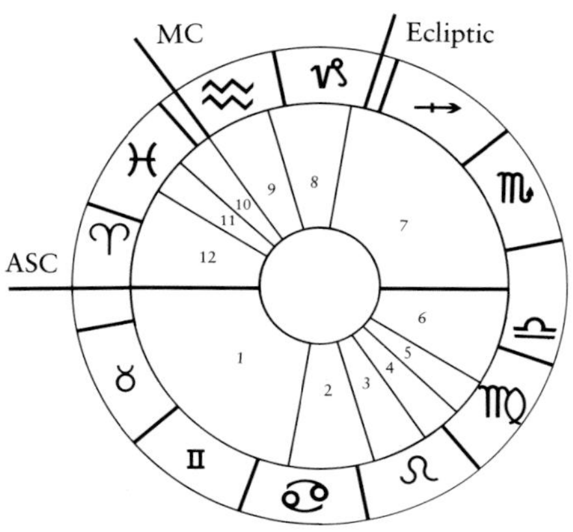

Campanus Method

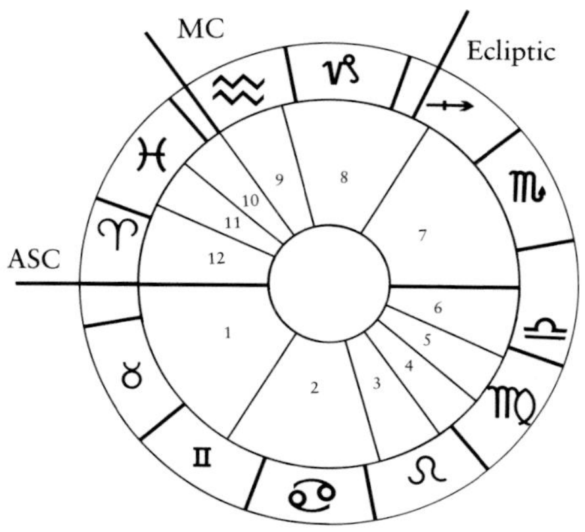

Regiomontanus Method

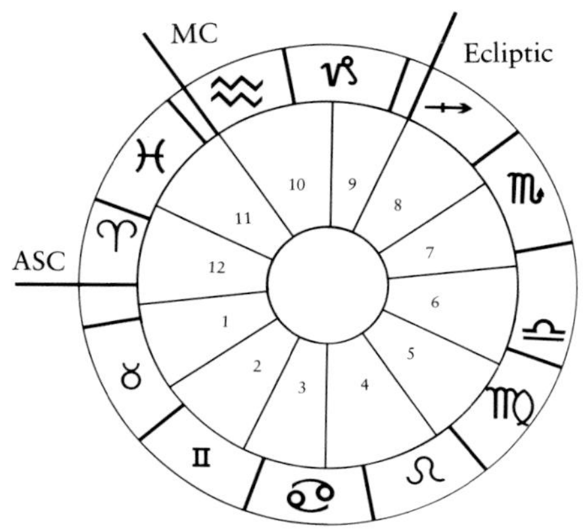

Morinus Method

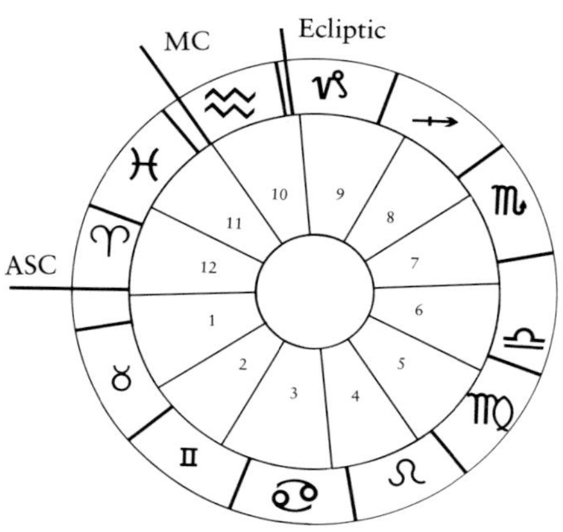

Axial Rotation Method

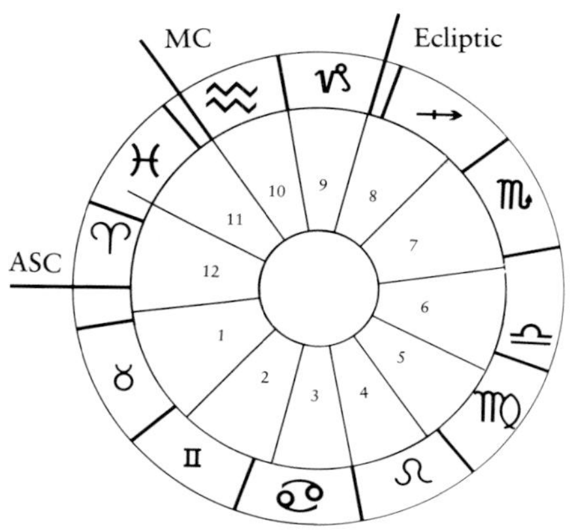

Zenith Method

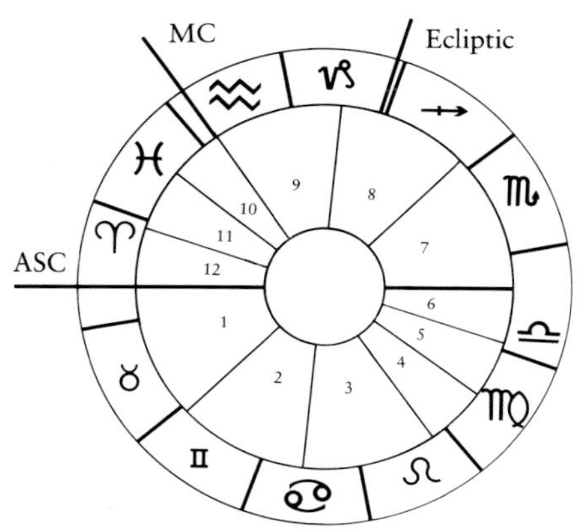

Alcabitius Method

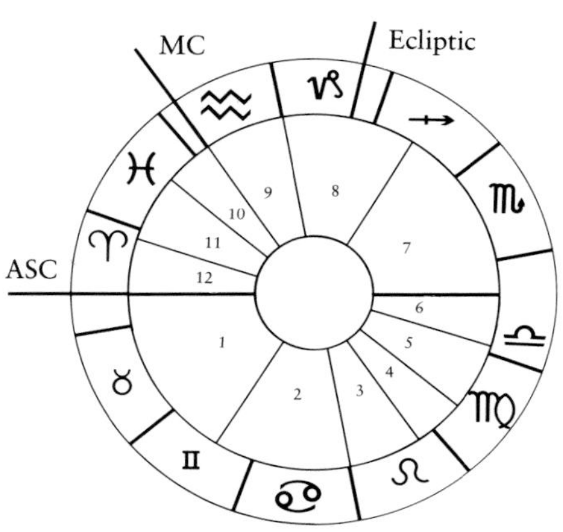

Placidus Method

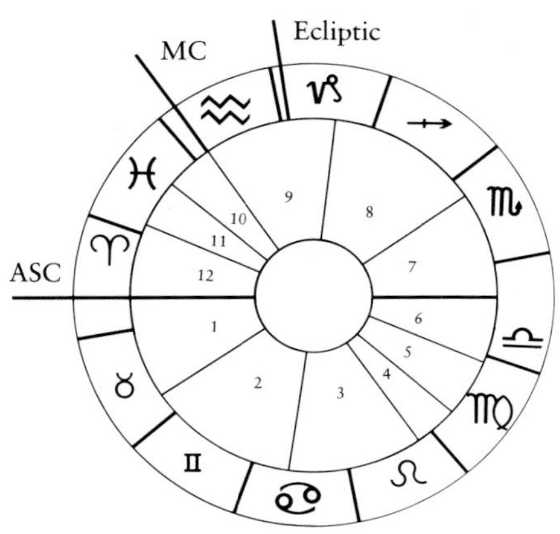

Birthplace Method

Examples of eleven of the standard house divisions, illustrating the great variety of relationships among the houses, the *Medium Coeli*, and the *Imum Coeli*.

The Houses

House I
Personality and Self

Chart location: angular
Element: fire (self-involvement)
Quality: cardinal (initiating activities)

Areas of Life
Personality: the impression we give to others, physical appearance, outward behavior, and disposition.
Self: self-fulfillment and self-image, health and vitality.

Effects on the Planets
Clustering of planets here indicates strong self-expression in projection of personality.

Primary Zodiac Sign
Aries (and therefore the ruler is Mars)

House II
Possessions, Heredity, Social Status

Chart location: succedent to House I
Element: earth (substance)
Quality: fixed (substantive items)

Areas of Life
Things and attachment to things, valuables, values.
Money and finances: Liquid assets, personal debts and obligations.

Effects of the Planets
Clustering of planets in this house indicates much interest in things and money.

Primary Zodiac Sign
Taurus (and therefore the ruler is Venus)

House III
Family, Communications

Chart location: cadent to House IV
Element: air (relationships)
Quality: mutable (adaptability)

Areas of Life
Immediate surroundings: brothers, sisters, cousins, uncles, aunts, nephews, nieces, early schooling, neighbors.
Communications: letters, books, transportation, trips to near places, and lecturing.

Effects of the Planets
Clustering of planets indicates many activities in the areas covered by House III.

Primary Zodiac Sign
Gemini (and therefore the ruler is Mercury)

House IV
Home, Beginnings, Endings, Private Life

Chart location: angular
Element: water (sensitivity)
Quality: cardinal (initiating activities)

Areas of Life
Beginnings: early influences, parents, domestic surroundings, community, houses, land, sea, heredity and family history.
Endings: old age, post-maturity activities, decline in power, termination of a career.
Privacy: personal affairs, intimate matters.

Effects of the Planets
Clustering of planets emphasizes attachment to family, to close friends, immediate surroundings, sense of security.

Primary Zodiac Sign
Cancer (and therefore the ruler is the Moon)

House V
Creativity and Love Given

Chart location: succedent to House IV
Element: fire (self-involvement)
Quality: fixed (substantive items)

Areas of Life
Creativity: new enterprises including risk and speculation, games of chance, original research, writing, artistic endeavors.
Pleasures: children, love affairs, pets and toys, sports, vacations, theater.

Effects of the Planets
Clustering indicates heightened focus on the areas in this house.

Primary Zodiac Sign
Leo (and therefore the ruler is the Sun)

House VI
Service and Health

Chart location: cadent to House VII
Element: earth (substance)
Quality: mutable (adaptability)

Areas of Life
Service: employment, servants, secondary positions, menial chores, working techniques.
Health: mild sickness, preventive medicine, maintenance of physical and mental fitness, food.

Effects of the Planets
Clustering suggests an intensive focus on hard work, fitness, and practicality.

Primary Zodiac Sign
Virgo (and therefore the ruler is Mercury)

House VII
Others, Partners, Competition

Chart location: angular
Element: air (relationships)
Quality: cardinal (initiating activities)

Areas of Life
Partnership: marriage, legal attachments, business associations.
Competition: opponents, competitors, lawsuits, public relations, advisory and judgmental activities, war, treaties.

Effects of the Planets
Clustering indicates a need for association with many others.

Primary Zodiac Sign
Libra (and therefore the ruler is Venus)

House VIII
Death and Regeneration

Chart location: succedent to House VII
Element: water (sensitivity)
Quality: fixed (substantive items)

Areas of Life
Death: inheritance, legacies, transfer and sharing of possessions, insurance, crime.
Regeneration: new endeavors, transformations, birth of people and ideas, sexuality, finances of others, business and commercial endeavors, psychological process (insight).
The occult: spirituality, spiritualism, inner drives, arcane endeavors.

Effects of the Planets
Clustering signifies possible crises, upheavals, and rebirth.

Primary Zodiac Sign
Scorpio (and therefore the ruler is Mars). Pluto is now assigned to House VIII.

House IX
Philosophy, Religion, Journeys

Chart location: cadent to House X
Element: fire (self-involvement)
Quality: mutable (adaptability)

Areas of Life
Philosophy and religion: intellectual innovation, forecasting, publishing, higher education, language,

The Planets

	Rules Over	*Exalted In*	*Detriment In*	*Fall In*
Sun ☉	Leo ♌	Aries	Aquarius	Libra
Moon ☽	Cancer ♋	Taurus	Capricorn	Scorpio
Mercury ☿	Gemini ♊ Virgo ♍	?Aquarius	Sagittarius	Pisces ?Leo
Venus ♀	Taurus ♉ Libra ♎	Pisces	Aries Scorpio	Virgo
Mars ♂	Aries ♈ Scorpio ♏	Capricorn	Libra Taurus	Cancer
Jupiter ♃	Sagittarius ♐ Pisces ♓	Cancer	Gemini Virgo	Capricorn
Saturn ♄	Capricorn ♑ Aquarius ♒	Libra	Cancer Leo	Aries
Uranus ♅	Aquarius ♒ ?Capricorn ♑	Scorpio	?Leo Cancer	Taurus
Neptune ♆	Pisces ♓ ?Sagittarius♐	?Leo ?Cancer	?Virgo ?Gemini	?Aquarius ?Capricorn
Pluto ♇⯓	Scorpio ♏ ?Aries ♈	?Aquarius ?Pisces	Taurus ?Libra	?Leo ?Virgo

The Zodiac Signs

House	*Zodiac Sign*	*Ruler*	*Quality Quadriplicity*	*Element Triplicity*	*Polarity*
I	*Aries* ♈	Mars ♂	Cardinal	Fire	+
II	*Taurus* ♉	Venus ♀	Fixed	Earth	–
III	*Gemini* ♊	Mercury ☿	Mutable	Air	+
IV	*Cancer* ♋	Moon ☽	Cardinal	Water	–
V	*Leo* ♌	Sun ☉	Fixed	Fire	+
VI	*Virgo* ♍	Mercury ☿	Mutable	Earth	–
VII	*Libra* ♎	Venus ♀	Cardinal	Air	+
VIII	*Scorpio* ♏	Mars ♂ Pluto ♇⯓	Fixed	Water	–
IX	*Sagittarius* ♐	Jupiter ♃	Mutable	Fire	+
X	*Capricorn* ♌	Saturn ♄	Cardinal	Earth	–
XI	*Aquarius* ♒	Uranus ♅ Saturn ♄	Fixed	Air	+
XII	*Pisces* ♓	Jupiter ♃ Neptune ♆	Mutable	Water	–

Tables of planets and zodiac signs.

religious principles and meanings, dreams.
Journeys of body and mind: travel to strange terrains, foreign people and cultures, relatives by marriage.

Effects of the Planets
Clustering suggests a propensity to travel and study and an interest in religion and law.

Primary Zodiac Sign
Sagittarius (and therefore the ruler is Jupiter)

House X
Public Life

Chart location: angular
Element: earth (substance)
Quality: cardinal (initiating activities)

Areas of Life
Career: occupation, reputation, social status, ambitions, honors, business.
Authorities: employers or supervisors, government, parenthood.

Effects of the Planets
Clustering suggests a drive to reach the top, to attain a position of power and influence.

Primary Zodiac Sign
Capricorn (and therefore the ruler is Saturn)

House XI
Love Received

Chart location: succedent to House X
Element: air (relationships)
Quality: fixed (substantive items)

Areas of Life
Friends: companions, altruistic endeavors, groups, professional societies, and business combines.
Aspirations: cherished goals, usually in conformity with larger principles.

Effects of the Planets
Clustering suggests much concern with friends and groups.

Primary Zodiac Sign
Aquarius (and therefore the rulers are Saturn and Uranus)

House XII
The Subconscious and Confinement

Chart location: cadent to House I
Element: water (sensitivity)
Quality: mutable (adaptability)

Areas of Life
Subconscious: frustrations, secret fears, hidden strengths, mental health, mysticism.
Confinement: incarceration, restraint, exile, disgrace, lawsuits, severe illness.
Good works: charities and social service, institutions (schools, hospitals). Traditionally, this house has been the repository of virtually all the undesirable troubles of life. Much attention has been given in recent years to how to act in these areas by using the favorable features of the horoscope chart, to anticipate the perils, and to manage the risks so that reward and security can be grasped. Good works, charities, and social services are therefore an integral part of House XII.

Effects of the Planets
Clustering signifies crises and also difficulties to be resolved.

Primary Zodiac Sign
Pisces (and therefore the rulers are Jupiter and Neptune)

Aspects

The planets affect each other's powers of influence when there are certain angular relationships among them. These relationships, or aspects, on the horoscope chart represent the degree of their closeness to each other in the sky as viewed from the earth. Thus, if the Moon is seen on some night nearly directly overhead and at the same time the observer looks toward the western or eastern horizon and notices the planet Venus just above the rim of the earth, the Moon and Venus would be considered to be at a right angle to each other. On the horoscope chart such a relationship is expressed in degrees. In this case, the Moon and Venus are approximately ninety degrees apart, known as a "square" aspect.

The aspects traditionally considered to be especially important are conjunction (0 degrees); opposition (180 degrees); square (90 degrees); trine (120 degrees); and sextile (60 degrees).

Each of the principal aspects exerts itself in either "easy," beneficent (sextile and trine) or "difficult," unfavorable (opposition and square) ways. A conjunction can suggest "easy" or "unfavorable" situations depending on the planets involved.

Because two planets are rarely in exact aspect to one another, a certain amount of leeway (the orb) is allowed: about 5 degrees in either direction. Thus, two planets are considered in a trine aspect (120 degrees) if they are located anywhere within a distance of between 115 and 125 degrees on the horoscope wheel from each other. The "tighter" the orb, however, the greater the influence of the aspect is supposed to be. (The sextile is sometimes restricted to a smaller orb than the other major aspects.)

The influence of the aspects also depends on the nature of the planets involved. Those with clashing characteristics (the Moon and Mars; Venus and Saturn) heighten difficult aspects; those with similar traits (such as Venus and the Moon) lessen them. On the other hand, two planets with compatible features in an "easy" aspect may be too much of a good thing: for example, the Moon in trine (120 degrees) with Venus might make the native imprudent or overly sensitive.

A number of "minor" aspects are also held to be significant: in particular, the semisquare (45 degrees), the sesquiquadrate (135 degrees), and semisextile (30 degrees), as well as the quintile, biquintile, septile, octile, and quincunx. The orb permitted with these aspects is usually 2 degrees or less.

Astrologers usually avoid assigning a cut-and-dried evaluation to planets in difficult aspects, preferring instead to indicate potential difficulty and emphasizing the need for resolution. Likewise, planets in "easy" relationships run the risk of complacency; while those with more conflicting links can create a tension that leads to high achievement.

Conjunctions (0 degrees): Variable influence ☌

Planets in conjunction affect each other according to their degree of compatibility. Traditionally, beneficial effects are assigned to conjunctions among the Sun, Moon, Mercury, Venus, and Jupiter. (The Sun, Mercury, and Venus, which are always relatively close to one another as viewed from earth, are often in conjunction.)

Any combination of planets in conjunction can be favorable if this aspect leads the native to a course of thinking or action capitalizing on the features of the planets involved—or one of guarding against potentially destructive influences. The Sun (ego, energy) in conjunction with Venus (emotion, affection) is apt to enhance a warm disposition; on the other hand, when in conjunction with Saturn (difficulties, delays), a more negative effect is likely. When the Sun is in conjunction with the Moon (subjectivity), the influence may run in either direction: amplifying the Moon's sensitivity or giving the Sun's light and heat a touch of the lunar imagination.

Opposition (180 degrees): Difficult ☍

Here, conflicts are to be expected and unfavorable traits are heightened, particularly in the context of relationships with others. For instance, the Moon in opposition to Mars creates a tension between inner-directed sensitivity (Moon) and tendencies toward brashness and extroversion (Mars). When the Moon is in opposition to Jupiter, a planet with which it is usually compatible, the expansive nature of Jupiter may become contracted while negative lunar tendencies may become exaggerated by Jupiterian grandiosity—leading to dogmatism and even to a penchant for gambling. With the Moon in opposition to Mercury, two planets with a neutral relationship, the native may be affected either by lunar hypersensitivity or Mercurial shiftlessness.

Nonetheless, a balance can be achieved if the inherent conflict is recognized, acted upon with energy, and used constructively.

Trine (120 degrees): Easy △

Planets' favorable qualities are enhanced in this relationship, bringing harmony and fusion. Venus in trine with Jupiter—

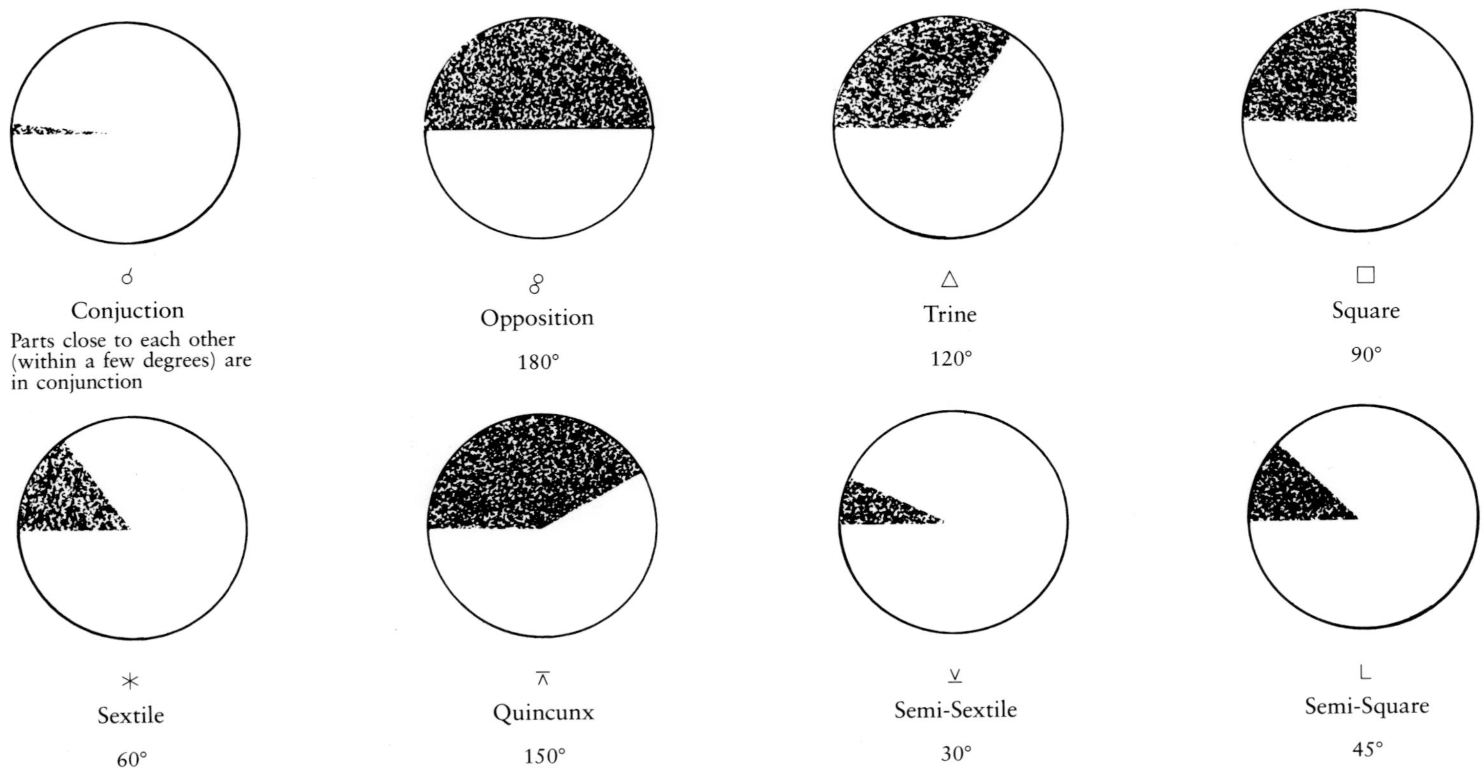

The aspects with their symbols. Top row, left to right: conjunction, opposition, trine, square. Bottom row, left to right: sextile, quincunx, semisextile, semisquare.

two particularly compatible planets—accent friendliness, good taste, and the absence of envy. The incompatible natures of Venus and Saturn (a planet that signifies discipline and structure, as well as difficulties) are mutually rewarded, leading the ardent Venus into more pragmatic but lasting affectionate attachments and adding a measure of warmth to cool, analytical Saturn.

On the other hand, a potential weakness in trine aspects is a tendency toward a false sense of security, which may persuade the native to remain passive in the face of problems that require urgent attention.

Square (90 degrees): Difficult □

Turmoil, resistance, and upheaval are indicated when two planets are in square with each other. Incompatible planets, such as Mars and Uranus, have a tendency to create destructiveness, seeking change but arriving at no purposeful course of action. The aggressive Mars in square with Jupiter, with which it is usually agreeable, can pervert Jupiter's impartiality and be pressed by Jupiterian grandiosity into greed. (Again, recognizing these trends, more constructive paths can be pursued: for example, the acquisitiveness and partiality indicated by the Jupiter-Mars square could be turned to advocational pursuits, to a career in finance, or to collecting.)

Sextile (60 degrees): Easy ⚹

The significance of the sextile aspect is similar to the trine, but its influence is not as strong; favorable results require more drive. In a sextile aspect the agreeable relationship of the Moon with Uranus enables imagination and judgment to mingle, making sensitivity more overt and giving lunar dreaminess more focus. Mars and Saturn, usually incompatible, combine to allow Martian vigor to energize Saturn's analytic tendencies, while giving structure and purpose to the recklessness of Mars.

Minor Aspects

Opinions diverge on how the remaining aspects should be classified. Some hold quincunx (150 degrees) to be easy, but others see it as having difficult or indeterminate effects, with one planet dominating the other.

Semisextile (30 degrees) has a mildly favorable connotation, as semisquare (45 degrees) and sesquiquadrate (135 degrees) are held by many to be mildly stressful. On the other hand, strong influences are sometimes assigned to these lesser angular relationships.

Grand Trine

The grand trine aspect is formed when three planets are each in trine (120 degrees) with each other. In order for this arrangement to occur on a chart, each of the three planets will often be in a sign that is of the same element (fire, earth, air, or water). Although trine aspects signify an "easy" combination of traits of the planets in these relationships, the grand trine can indicate a surfeit of the characteristics of one element over the others, thereby creating imbalance in the personality.

ثاني وجه
من ثاني وجه
قال صاحب الكتاب ابو معشر صاحب هذا الطالع يكون اسمر اللون يعلوه حمرة حسن الراي غليظ

ABOVE: Jupiter is in the sign of Scorpio in the harvest month of October, and the complete zodiac wheel surrounds the scene in this Flemish tapestry. c.1525. The Metropolitan Museum of Art, New York City. Bequest of Mrs. August D. Juilliard. 1916.

OPPOSITE: The planets Moon and Jupiter in the zodiac sign of Sagittarius, from a thirteenth-century Arabic manuscript illustrating an astrological treatise by Albumasar of the ninth century. Illumination on vellum, 11⅜ × 9¾″. Bibliothèque Nationale, Paris.

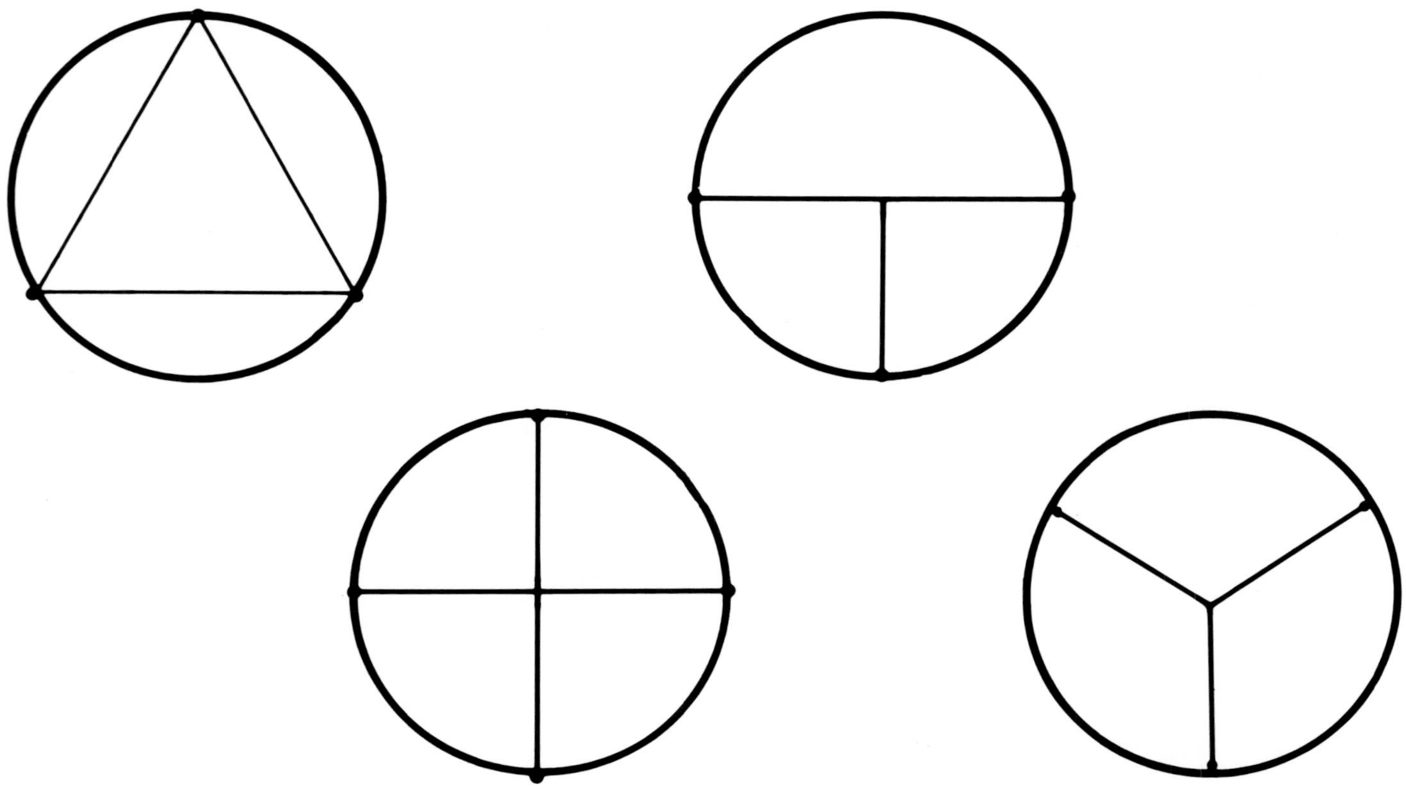

Special aspect arrangements of the planets. Top: grand trine, T-cross, bottom: grand cross, yod.

T-Cross
In the T-cross, two planets are in opposition to each other while a third is in square to the other two. The planet squaring the other two is intensely influenced by the others.

Grand Cross
In this aspect each of four planets is in opposition with one of the other planets and in square with two others. This combination powerfully magnifies the interrelationships of the planets.

The Yod
The yod (named after the Hebrew letter and symbolic of the finger or hand of fate) is an aspect that occurs when three planets form a Y on the horoscope circle with the planet at the foot of the Y in quincunx (150 degrees) with each of the other two. The zodiac sign and house in which the planet at the foot of the Y lies indicate the probable flow of the native's destiny.

Other Configurations

There are some other aspects, as for instance the grand quintile and the kite, which signify heightened power of one or more planets in the configuration, but these are not often used by astrologers.

Parallels
Two other aspects may be mentioned, the parallels and antiscia. Two planets are in parallel when they are the same number of degrees north (or south) of the celestial equator. If one planet is north and the other is south of the equator by the same number of degrees, they are contraparallel—that is, on opposite sides of the equatorial plane. A parallel is supposed to have the same inference as a conjunction; the contraparallel is similar to opposition.

Many horoscope charts designate these relationships, or the calculations can be arrived at by complex mathematical figuring. These two aspects are actually "declinations," a more precise astronomical term referring to their degrees of latitude. For the purposes of delineating a chart, one may simply accept their placement without necessarily examining the astronomical derivation.

Antiscion (also called Solstice Point)
Another arithmetic group of aspects, the antiscia, achieved prominence in Arabic astrology. They are aspects formed by two planets equidistant on the chart from a solstice zodiac sign (Cancer or Capricorn). The calculations involve either the most northern zodiac sign, Cancer (at 0 degrees), which is the summer solstice, or Capricorn (at 0 degrees), the winter solstice. When the cusp of either Cancer or Capricorn is midway (at midpoint) between two planets, then those planets are in antiscion to each other. The aspect is said to heighten the characteristics of each of the planets. To some, in the Uranian system of astrology, for example, an antiscion is also present when the zodiac sign is Aries, but the cusp of that sign represents an equinox not a solstice.

Other Points on the Horoscope Wheel

Ascendant
Among the most significant and influential points in the horoscope is the ascendant, the zodiac sign at the moment of birth that is located at the most easterly point—the eastern, or sunrise, horizon (corresponding to the cusp of the first house in most systems of house designation). Many perceive the ascendant to be more important than the Sun-sign. Indeed, in some historical periods, the word "horoscope" (from the Greek word for "hour watcher") referred mainly to calculating the ascendant's position, the zodiac star cluster that appeared first above the horizon. The phrase "Taurus rising," for example, meant that the easternmost point on the horoscope wheel fell within the borders of Taurus at the person's birth.

As a mark of the very first moment when the fully formed newborn enters the world beyond the womb, the ascendant symbolizes the type of impression that the person makes on others: his or her personality as perceived by the world. (Some propose that the moment of conception, not the birth, is the true time for assigning the ascendant.)

The ascendant exerts influence on all parts of the horoscope. The standard planetary ruler of the ascendant is considered by many to be the ruler of the entire chart, no matter what other sign the planets may be occupying. For instance, if the native has Taurus rising, and the Sun is in Libra (making Libra the Sun-sign), Venus, as the ruler of the ascendant (Taurus), remains the most powerful determinator among the planets on the wheel.

Midheaven
Midheaven in Latin is *Medium Coeli* (MC), "the middle of the sky." It is the tip of the upper meridian, where the ecliptic and the vertical meridian intersect, marking the sun in the sky at noon. Of course, this is only for the northern hemisphere. In the southern hemisphere, the situation is reversed, with the MC then becoming the "bottom of the sky," the IC. The sun does not reach the very top of the sky at noon in most locations, and its highest point varies with the season of the year. The actual uppermost spot directly overhead, as viewed from any one place on earth, is termed the "zenith." The noonday sun may be north or south of this "zenith," depending on how far one is from the equator. The midheaven is the cusp of House X in some systems but by no means in all. The MC and the IC form a vertical axis on most horoscope charts.

The midheaven indicates goals and the extent to which others perceive these goals to have been attained—in essence, the native's public status. Planets in aspect to, or very near, this point—especially if it is the ruling planet of the chart—are considered prime effectors of career choices. The zodiac sign here at the top of the chart also announces the area of achievement.

A demonstration of the midpoint aspect, formed when a planet is in a position that is approximately an equal angular distance between two other planets.

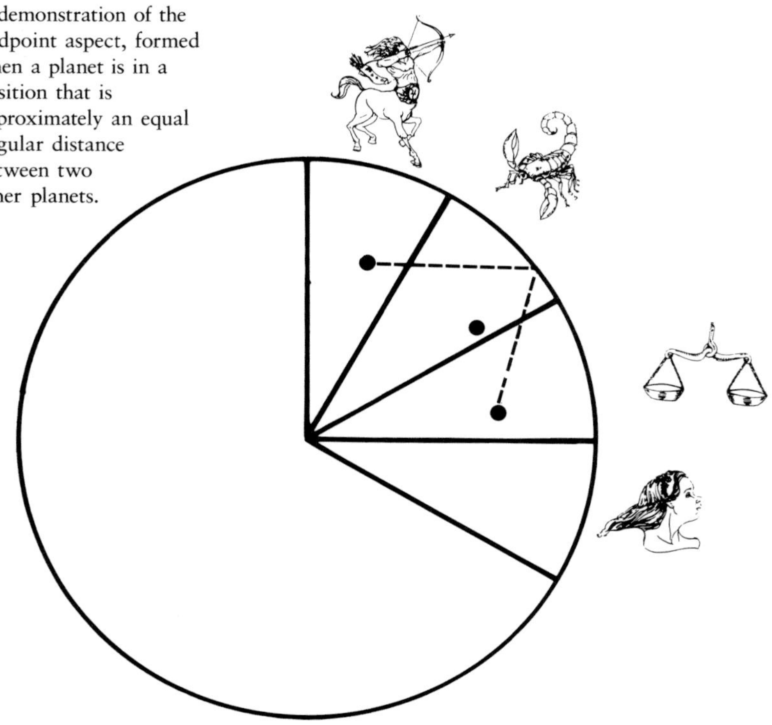

Midpoint
This aspect is formed when a planet is in a position that is approximately an equal distance between two other planets, linking all three together, even if there is no other aspect between them. The central planet may signify an extraordinary event or relationship involving the two planets that it joins. Some astrologers place particular emphasis on the midpoints.

Nodes
Nodes are the points of intersection between the orbits of two planets. Since each planet revolves in a roughly elliptical pattern, the orbits will intersect over time in at least two points. For the most part, only the Moon's nodes are important to traditional astrology. The Moon's path actually crosses the path of the planet earth as it revolves around its parent body. However, when the Moon is viewed from earth, it appears to intersect the projected path of the Sun (the ecliptic).

Where the Moon crosses the ecliptic moving north, the north, or ascending, node is signified. When crossing as it goes south, the Moon passes the south, or descending, node. Because a solar eclipse or a lunar eclipse occurs when the new moon or the full moon is very near one of the nodal points, the nodes have been likened to a dragon swallowing the Sun or the Moon. Thus, the north node is often called "dragon's head" (*Caput Draconis*) and the south, "dragon's tail" (*Cauda Draconis*). The two symbols are ☊ for head; ☋ for tail.

There is no precise meaning assigned to the Moon's nodes. Ancient astrologers looked upon the north node as beneficial; the south as harmful. Those who subscribe to reincarnation give to the north node undeveloped qualities from former lifetimes that need exposure. They assign to the south node a representation of unfavorable characteristics from the past that require removal by conduct in the present.

Modern astrologers usually invest the north node with the formation of associations and a giving of self; the south node with separating connections and even a dissatisfaction with self.

Arabian Parts

Many of the features on a horoscope that are considered significant by some are given scant or no attention by others. However, the Part of Fortune is one of the many lesser points that appears often in delineations. It is a member of a group of mathematically derived spots, "Arabian parts," that have no planetary, zodiac, house, or angle representation. The general formula is an equation based on the celestial longitude of the ascendant plus the longitude of the Moon minus the longitude of the Sun, which equals the Part of Fortune. A variety of interpretations is given to this point depending on which signs and planets form aspects to it, but its implications are good luck and favorable outcomes. Its symbol is ⊗.

Although titled "Arabian," the origins of these hypothetical points go back several centuries before Christ, much earlier than the times of Arabic astrology. The *hyleg*, however, is an Arabian part that is actually Persian in origin. It is another hypothetical mathematical place on the chart that is supposed to indicate the time of death—or, conversely, the length of life. Modern horoscopes rarely contain this point on the chart.

Predictive Methods

Predictions in astrology may be made by several methods. The first and foremost is to consult the natal horoscope chart, in which the arrangement of stars and planets suggests tendencies that lie ahead. Astrologers today usually refrain from directly forecasting specific happenings and personal involvements. Instead, they indicate where danger lies, personal weaknesses that must be overcome, and the strengths and talents that should be developed.

Since character is the key to destiny, the natal horoscope is itself a prediction, as observed by Zipporah Dobyns, a modern astrologer. Indeed, even those mechanisms used in astrology for looking ahead are all based on the birth chart.

More specific systems calculate the future arrangements in the heavens in order to draw conclusions about likely happenings and the most favorable and unfavorable circumstances. These methods aim at answering questions about future events, finding appropriate times for action, and evaluating the types of relationships that are apt to be beneficial.

Mechanisms of Astrological Prediction

Two of the most frequently used charting methods are secondary progressions and transits.

Progressions

A commonly employed astrological method is the "day-for-year" progressed chart, which is drawn by calculating each day of a person's life as if it were one year. Thus, if the date to be studied is twenty years after the person's birth date, the arrangements of the planets and signs twenty days after the birth date are charted and compared with the natal horoscope. These positions are easily obtained nowadays from an astronomical ephemeris. Formerly astrologers had to make complicated calculations in order to arrive at the progressed arrangements.

After obtaining the diagram, the progressed and the natal wheels are compared. This enables the astrologer to see the relationship of the progressed planets to the planets on the birth horoscope. Day-for-year progression is sometimes called "secondary progression" or "secondary direction." (There are also progressions in which one day after the native's birth is considered equivalent to a month; still others, tertiary progressions, in which each month is equivalent to a year.)

Progression methods are based on the revolutions of the planets around the Sun. The predictive mechanism that relies on the apparent daily motion of the planets, as seen over the twenty-four hours when the earth rotates on its own axis, is the system of directions. Thus, "primary" direction technique calculates a degree ahead on the chart as a year, whereas "secondary" progressions use days or months instead of degrees.

The symbolic principle behind the progressions and directions is that the makeup of a person or group of people is closely related to the movements of the heavenly bodies before birth and after birth. These motions and changes are connected to the orbits of revolution of the earth and the planets, the daily rotation of the earth on its axis, and the relationships among all the bodies and stars in the heavens.

Here are a few examples of how a progressed chart, no matter how it is arrived at, can be interpreted:

If the Sun on a progressed chart is in conjunction to the Moon on the natal chart, a time of change is signaled.

Favorable aspects, such as trine and sextile, suggest successful enterprises. Unfavorable aspects (square and opposition) indicate the possibility of domestic tensions.

The progressed Sun in any aspect to Mercury may announce a communication or a literary or monetary event, with the type of aspect suggesting its favorable or difficult nature.

The progressed Sun in an aspect to the natal ascendant indicates strong personal development. If the aspects are easy, a fuller understanding and development of one's own makeup and talents can be expected. If the aspects are difficult, personal conflicts are apt to lie ahead.

Transits

In the predictive method of transits, the chart is drawn for the specific date in the future that is chosen for analysis. In a manner similar to the interpretation of progressions, the transited planets are evaluated according to their relationship to the natal planets.

In general, the faster-moving planets—Moon, Mercury, Venus, and Mars—remain in any one position a relatively short time. For instance, the Moon changes position within hours. Any one transit of Venus (its specific place on the chart) is present for about two days. By contrast, the slower planets—Saturn, Uranus, Neptune, and Pluto—stay much longer in their transit relationships to the natal planets. The more planets there are in transit aspects, the greater chance there is for many significant events.

For example, Jupiter in transit to natal Neptune provokes greater attention to philosophical or spiritual concerns, when the aspect is favorable. A difficult aspect warns against indecisiveness, dreaminess, and fanciful flights of thought and action. Jupiter in transit to natal Jupiter means that all the characteristics of Jupiter are likely to be emphasized. The zodiac signs and houses in which the two Jupiters are placed show further the expected positive and negative trends ahead. Generally, they are expected to be happy, successful events.

Usually the slower-moving planets are supposed to have more significance than the faster, inner planets in both the progressed and transited charts, when compared with the birth horoscope.

Purposes of Prediction

The three main purposes for which any of the predictive systems are constructed may be classified as electional, horary, and synastry.

Electional Astrology

Electional astrology is used to help the questioner choose the most favorable time for an action already decided upon: a journey, starting a business, entering a negotiation. In a sense, the astrologer is actually looking for favorable transits. He or she studies the arrangements of planets and signs ahead, within the time frame that the client has set for the contemplated activity, in order to discover a transit chart showing a preponderance of favorable planetary aspects to the natal planets and an absence of difficult aspects.

For instance, if the charts of transits in the weeks or months ahead were to reveal squares and oppositions of Saturn to the client's natal Sun, Moon, or ascendant sign, the likely advice would be that the client should wait for more favorable arrangements before beginning the projected undertaking. On the other hand, if the ephemeris shows arrangements in which Jupiter is in conjunction or trine to the Sun, Moon, or the ascendant, that time may be considered excellent for moving ahead in travel or a new enterprise.

Horary Astrology

In horary astrology, the questioner asks whether a particular course of action is wise. The exact arrangement of the planets and signs is plotted for the precise time at which the question is asked. This horoscope is then examined for its favorable and unfavorable characteristics, as far as the questioner's contemplated action is concerned.

The questioner is required to have a possible action in view. The question has to concern something material, not a thought or opinion. The same question cannot be asked at a different time. The request must be very specific to the person—not whether a game will be won but rather whether the petitioner should play in that game. It is not a future outcome but a particular course of action that is sought. Horary astrology also assumes that the direction of all things will remain as they are unless the questioner changes that direction by acting—the advisability of which he or she asks from horary astrology. To give an example, the question asked might be: "Shall I go into the publishing venture?"

Several tenets are operative in interpreting the chart:

1. The Moon has prime significance. When the Moon makes no aspects at all to other planets, it is termed "void of course," and no action should be taken. That is not the case here.

2. An approaching aspect of the Moon has a bearing on the start of the enterprise, with the easy or difficult nature of the aspect a determining factor regarding the advisability of beginning the venture at that time. A separating aspect of the Moon suggests the possible outcome of the enterprise.

In the diagram (page 130) the Moon is approaching a sextile aspect with Jupiter, usually expressed as ☽20♎✱♃24♐, which means that Moon is at 20 degrees in Libra and in sextile with Jupiter at 24 degrees in Sagittarius. This arrangement signifies that favorable circumstances are near.

3. Favorable Moon aspects to the Sun (for instance,

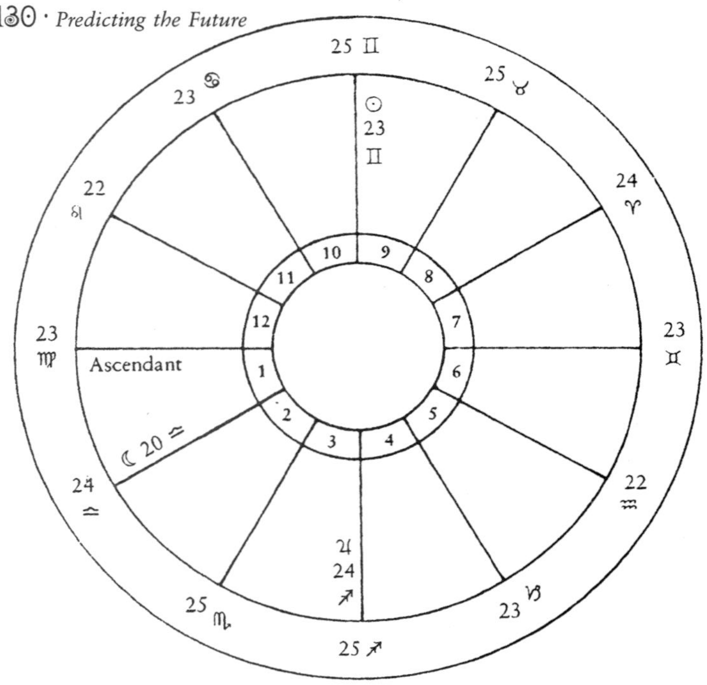

Horary Chart

trine) indicate that the questioner should go ahead. An unfavorable square aspect gives a negative answer. In the diagram, the Sun at 23 degrees Gemini is trine to the Moon at 20 degrees Libra (☉23♊△☽20♎), which suggests that the questioner should go ahead.

4. Aspects of the Moon to the other planets (not on this diagram) also show what to do, depending on the type of aspect and the area governed by the planet. The Moon's aspects to Mercury would give clues on communication-related questions; to Venus, on art and love; to Mars, on violence, excitement, and energy. An aspect to Jupiter tells whether to proceed with optimism or guard against overconfidence. Saturn urges caution and a slow start, or even no start. Uranus forecasts an unexpected event. Neptune can label an action illusory and deceptive or it may approve an imaginative course, depending on the aspect. The Moon in square to Pluto warns against an illegality or a "ripoff"; in trine, it predicts that hidden matters will be part of the enterprise. The sextile aspect of the Moon to Jupiter suggests optimism.

5. The location of the ascendant's cusp at the time the person poses his or her question is another significant feature. If it is within three degrees of the easternmost point on the chart, the contemplated action may be too early, but a position in the last three degrees suggests that it is too late. In the diagram, the easternmost point is at 23 degrees Virgo, which is the ascendant zodiac sign in this chart, and therefore the time is neither too late (as it would be at 27 degrees Virgo or higher) nor too early (if it were at 3 degrees Virgo or closer).

6. The planets' positions in the houses are also important. House I stands for the self, so that the particular planet present there gives a clue to the suitability of the person's psychological state for the endeavor being considered. For example, Saturn in House I would reveal that the person's frame of mind is unsuited to the action he is considering undertaking. The Sun in this house signifies the questioner's attitude is enthusiastic. The Moon suggests moodiness; Mercury, nervousness; Venus and Jupiter, a sunny, optimistic approach; Uranus, uncertainty; Neptune, unrealistic evaluation; Pluto, with major redirection of one's purposes.

The areas of life covered by each house are emphasized or deemphasized depending on which planets are there. For an answer to a financial question, House II is to be especially scrutinized; House VII is to be observed for marriage and partnership issues. If a house is empty of planets, the astrologer looks to see where the natural ruler of that house is placed and draws inferences from its position. The diagram indicates that Jupiter is in House III, communication, and therefore gives a favorable signal for a publishing venture. The Sun is in House IX, career, another good omen.

7. The astrologer may find the horoscope wheel either unclear or confused by contradictory features. The chart then is deemed unreadable, and the question cannot be answered.

Of course, before a conclusion can be reached, the entire chart with all the planets and parts has to be studied.

Synastry

The comparison of the horoscopes of two or more persons is called synastry (meaning "stars together"). Usually the questions concern marriage, business, or children. What type of person should I marry? What problems are likely to occur in the future between my child and me? What is the basis for the difficulties in our present relationship?

The birth horoscopes are first studied to develop an astrological description of each person. The two charts are then compared.

The characteristics examined for comparison are Sun-signs, ascendants (rising zodiac signs), midheavens (MCs), and the signs and planets in House VII, of marriage and partnership.

Professional astrologers generally deplore the decisions based merely on the classification of compatible and incompatible Sun-signs. Of far more influence are the relationships between the Sun-sign of one party and the ascendant sign of the other. If they are close in position, a consonance of attitudes is suggested. If they are in opposition ("at opposite ends of the pole"), the significance can be unfavorable, but it is more likely to presage a good fit, with each person supplying what the other lacks. This is similar to the conventional maxim that a union between the light-haired and the dark-haired is salutary. A trine or a sextile between the Sun-sign of one and the ascendant of the other strongly implies harmony.

However, even when two Sun-signs belong to the accepted compatible categories, if the Sun-sign of one and

POSITE: Skeletonized
ary chart of the
mple used in the
. Only the Sun,
on, Jupiter, the
iac signs, and the
ses are shown on
horoscope circle
ted for the precise
ment when the
stion was asked,
all I join the
lishing venture?"

Personification of planets—shown upright in their ruling signs, upside-down in the opposite sign (in detriment). Top left: Saturn in Capricorn and in detriment in Cancer. Bottom left: Mars in Aries and in detriment in Libra. Top right: unidentified planet in Libra and in detriment in Aries(?), Capricorn(?). Bottom right: Moon in Cancer and in detriment in Capricorn. *Planets and Signs in Conjunction* from the *Ascension of Propitious Stars and the Sources of Sovereignty* by Matali al-sa'ada wa-manabi 'al-Siyada. Turkish. 1582. Illumination on polished paper. The Pierpont Morgan Library, New York City.

the ascendant of the other are in square or semisextile, trouble is believed to be brewing. Tenseness is to be anticipated and has to be dealt with.

Another prime indicator is the relationship between the ascendant sign of one and the midheaven sign of the other. If they are the same or in easy aspect to each other, virtually all negative influences are looked upon as being softened. The same favorable outlook accompanies a good aspect to midheaven by Jupiter, Venus, and sometimes the Moon.

Generally, two people whose Suns are in adjacent zodiac signs (in semisextile) are considered at risk of incompatibility unless there are also mitigating factors in the rest of the chart.

In addition, if one person's Sun-sign or ascendant sign has the same traditional ruling planet as the other's Sun-sign or ascendant sign, even if the other factors are negative, satisfactory adjustment between the two people is likely. For instance, someone with the Sun-sign in Capricorn can do very well with a supposedly incompatible Aquarian, because the ruler of both signs, Saturn, is the same. The conventionalism of one and the untraditional orientation of the other can merge to achieve lasting harmony. The same types of blendings can occur between Taurus and Libra (Venus is their ruler) or between Aries and Scorpio (Mars).

Usually it is only when virtually all of the planetary aspects, angles, and Sun-signs are unfavorable that an astrologer will read the portents as a bad omen for the union. Modern synastry advises against absolute negative generalizations, suggesting instead a summary of the possible difficult factors that should be recognized and overcome.

Other Mechanisms of Prediction

There are also a number of other mathematical mechanisms used to construct charts that are compared with the natal horoscope. A sampling of the many methods includes:

Solar arc: charts the distance moved by the Sun in the day-for-year progression chart. This calculation is then used to arrive at the progressed ascendant or other properties on the chart.

Solar return: the chart drawn for the moment of the Sun's return to its precise original position at birth. Often this time does not coincide with the birthday, and the planets, signs, and other points on the chart are usually different from the natal arrangement.

Converse progression: the chart is arrived at by calculating through the day-for-year method but going backward in days or years before birth.

Uranian system of prediction: employs a 90-degree instead of a 360-degree wheel. It emphasizes the midpoints between planets and other astrological parts, certain specific aspects between planets, and eight hypothetical undiscovered planets.

Delineation

All of the astrologer's information on planets, zodiac signs, houses, aspects, and other parts of a horoscope chart are directed toward one eventual goal: delineation, the reading of the meanings contained in the diagrammed configurations.

An astrologer may formulate one or several predetermined programs to examine a chart, depending on the features displayed in any one horoscope. The outline that we will use to delineate a particular horoscope is listed here as a guide rather than a rigid system. The procedure may in fact vary considerably according to how a reading develops.

I General Features
- A. Shape
- B. Singleton planets
- C. Stellium of planets
- D. Special configurations
- E. Absence of planets in house groups
- F. Intercepted signs

II Angles
- A. Ascendant sign
- B. Descendant sign
- C. *Medium Coeli,* or midheaven (top of the chart)
- D. *Imum Coeli* (bottom of the chart)

III The Four Elements, Three Qualities, and Two Polarities
- A. Their accent or absence
- B. Their qualities
- C. Polarity

IV Planets in the Signs and Houses
- A. The ruling planet (the planet ruling the ascendant sign)
- B. Sun-sign
- C. Moon
- D. Prime mover (planet rising just before the Sun; also called "planet in oriental appearance")
- E. Planets in mutual reception
- F. Retrograde planets
- G. Planets near the cusp
- H. Absence of planets from signs and houses
- I. Position of each planet: (1) in the signs and houses; (2) disposition (rulership, exaltation, detriment, fall); (3) aspects and lack of aspects

V Other Points
- A. Nodes of the Moon
- B. Part of Fortune
- C. Other parts

General Features

Just as we may size up a new acquaintance on first meeting by dress, face, physique, gestures, and voice, we may also receive an overall impression of a horoscope by its general appearance. And just as we learn more about the personal makeup of our new acquaintance, so can we also fill in the meanings on a horoscope by closer scrutiny of the chart's details.

1. Emphasis on a Hemisphere

A concentration of planets in the northern (bottom) half of the chart signifies that private interests and activities predominate. A southern (top half; "above the horizon") concentration indicates that public appearance and activities are primary. If the eastern half (on the left) has the majority of planets, emphasis is placed on the querent's choices and courses of action. The western half suggests that other people are influential in the native's destiny. A lack of planets in any hemisphere indicates that the characteristics of those areas figure weakly or not at all in the person's activities.

2. Emphasis on Particular Signs and Houses

If two opposite signs or two groups of signs between them contain all or almost all of the planets, the native is likely to be able to see both sides of questions and to entertain two major interests. It is also significant if the concentrations fill adjacent houses. For instance, if House VIII and House IX have many planets in them, there is a strong inclination to the philosophical and occult. Of course, clustering of planets in one sign or house signals a special emphasis on those particular traits or activities, and a widely dispersed placement of planets throughout the chart is a mark of many areas of focus, commitment, or potential.

Singleton

When one planet stands out in one section of the chart, isolated from all the other planets, that planet's character, natural zodiac sign, disposition, and other features receive special attention in the delineation.

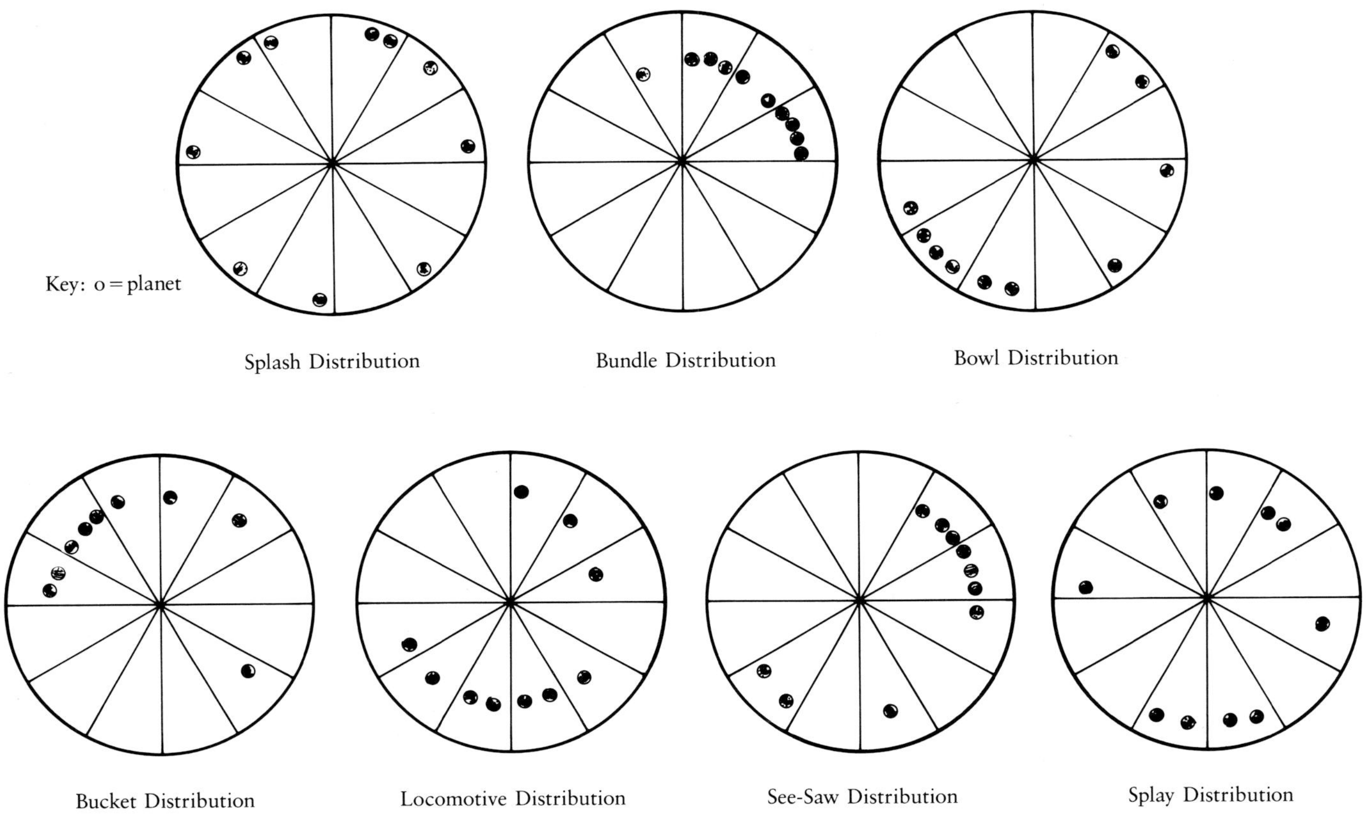

Various overall distributions of the planets on the horoscope wheel based loosely on the classification of Marc Edmund Jones: splash = multiple interests; bowl = circumscribed involvement; bucket = accent on one or two areas; see-saw = shifting emphasis; locomotive (four adjacent houses unoccupied) = driving disposition; splay = independence.

Stellium
The occurrence of four or more planets in one sign gives added influence to that sign.

Special Configurations
The grand trine, T-cross, and other arrangements and groupings may be readily apparent to the delineator.

Absence of Planets in House Groups
This can mean that particular areas of life are not entered with energy or interest. Angular houses (I, IV, VII, X) include activities that are oriented to the present. Succedent houses (II, V, VIII, XI) contain future directions. Cadent houses (III, VI, IX, XII) deal with past influences. Presumably, since a lack of planets in all the houses of any one group depicts difficulty in dealing with those areas, the native is advised to give special attention to the potential problems. For instance, a person whose chart has no planets in cadent houses needs reminding that past experience should teach us to avoid the same mistakes.

Intercepted Signs
When a zodiac sign does not cross or reach the borders (cusps) of any house, it is termed "intercepted" (summarized in the introduction to the zodiac section). The symbol of the sign is then usually placed on the perimeter of the horoscope circle at the house in which it resides, but no degrees of its location are stated, in contradistinction to the other signs on the wheel—except for its opposite zodiac sign on the opposite side of the wheel, which will also be intercepted. Thus if Taurus is intercepted, then so will Scorpio be intercepted.

The influence exerted by this intercepted zodiac sign through its ruling planet, wherever it may be located, and by whatever planets find themselves in this intercepted sign is seriously diminished. If Gemini is in an intercepted position, then its ruling planet Mercury is considered by some to be subservient to whichever planet is the ruler of the house in which Gemini is contained. If that house is XI, for example, the natural domicile of Saturn, Mercury's tendencies to delve into a multitude of interests would be markedly restrained by the methodical constraints of Saturn.

Ascendant Sign ("Rising Sign")
The zodiac sign at the extreme easternmost part of the chart is the ascendant. Some weight this feature as one of the most significant properties of the horoscope because it is the most specific point of the chart and sets up the rest of the placements. The ruling planet of the ascendant is commonly labeled the ruling planet of the chart. The traits of this planet, the ascendant sign itself, the Sun-sign, the Moon's position, and the midheaven (*Medium Coeli*) sign are believed by many astrologers to constitute the most potent

ABOVE: A Jain cosmological chart. Paint on cloth. Wellcome Institute Library, London.

OPPOSITE: The Sun is in the zodiac sign, Leo, that he rules in this Indian miniature on paper. Seventeenth or eighteenth century. The Pierpont Morgan Library, New York City.

influences in the delineation, signaling the personality shown by the native, especially concerning his or her future direction.

Descendant Sign
The zodiac sign at the western end of the chart is directly opposite the ascendant sign and marks the likelihood of how outside influences will affect personality and behavior.

Medium Coeli/Midheaven (Top of the Chart)
The zodiac sign and planets at the top of the chart indicate the extent of public recognition and the culmination—favorable or unfavorable—of the native's past actions. The traits of the zodiac sign in this location are emphasized by its position at midheaven.

Imum Coeli (Bottom of the Chart)
The nature of the person's most private feelings, aspirations, and deeds are signaled by the planets and sign at the IC.

Elements: Fire, Earth, Air, Water
The distribution of planets in each of the three zodiac signs (the triplicity) that constitute an element is looked at by the astrologer to see if there is an accent on one or more elements with their corresponding characteristics or if there is an absence of planets from the signs of one of the elements.

Qualities: Cardinal, Fixed, Mutable
What is the distribution of planets in each of the four zodiac signs (the quadriplicity) that constitutes a quality?

Polarity
A concentration of planets in positive signs signifies an active, open attitude. A gathering of planets in negative signs indicates receptivity, reactive behavior, or covert actions.

Ruling Planet of the Chart
The planet that is the accepted ruler of the ascendant sign gives a clue to the attachments and meanings in the native's life. All the other planets in aspect to the ruler act as helpers or modifiers. Of course, the ascendant sign's ruling planet may be in any of the other signs. When the ascendant's ruler, however, is its own domicile in the rising zodiac sign, all of the meanings of both the sign and the planet are enlarged and intensified.

Sun-Sign
The Sun-sign is not necessarily the most important part of the reading. However, it does have substantial significance, although by itself it would merely be one clue. However, other features might instead lessen, blunt, or even change the Sun's impact.

Moon
Some astrologers look especially to the Moon, after the Sun and the ascendant sign, as having particular significance in delineation. Whereas the Sun announces the ego, the Moon reveals the subconscious and emotion.

Prime Mover (also called "Planet in Oriental Appearance")
The planet that rises over the eastern horizon, the easternmost point on the wheel just ahead of the Sun, is the prime mover. It may be far away on the chart from the Sun, but it is still the prime mover. Since the Sun moves clockwise, from east to west, on the astrological wheel, the planet most nearly west of the Sun can be designated as this prime mover, or "planet in oriental appearance." It signifies basic motivation, coloring a person's actions.

Planets in Mutual Reception
When the ruling planets of two zodiac signs are each in the other's sign, they are in mutual reception. All of the favorable features of each planet are enhanced by the other. For instance, if the Sun is in Aquarius (one of whose rulers is Uranus) and Uranus is in Leo (the Sun's territory), the originality and independence of Uranus and the will and energy of the Sun become predominant, even though the position of these two planets put them in an opposition aspect.

Retrograde Planets
The "backward" motion of the retrograde planets weakens the impact or turns the energy inward.

Planets near the Cusp
The closer that a planet is to the cusp, the beginning boundary of a sign, counting counterclockwise from the easternmost point, the more influential is that planet.

Absence of Planets from Signs and Houses
Just as empty houses in the horoscope deemphasize their areas of life's activities, so does the absence of planets from one or more signs lessen the importance of those signs.

Position of Each Planet
Before ending the reading of a chart, each planet is examined in order to glean information from its location in the signs and houses; whether it is in a ruling position, exaltation, detriment, or fall, as well as its aspects to other planets, signs, and points.

Other Points

Individual astrologers may refer to any number of other points on a horoscope chart. The most frequently used are the nodes of the Moon and the "Part of Fortune." All the other features summarized in the previous sections—and more—may be a source of added information.

Medical Astrology

Those who follow the system of astrological medicine rely on the ancient concept that all things are composed of four elements: fire, water, air, and earth—each modified by any of the four qualities (hot, cold, dry, moist). The body's state of health is held to be the resultant balance of the four humors: blood, which is an airy humor, moist and hot; phlegm, which is watery, moist and cold; black bile, which is earthy, dry and cold; yellow bile, which is fiery, hot and dry. Diseases are classified under various combinations of the humors. A preponderance of one humor over the others brings about imbalance and illness.

In addition, as in medieval times, each zodiac sign is assigned to a part of the body. Thus, diseases of the head belong to Aries, the neck and shoulders to Taurus, the chest and arms to Gemini, and so on down the body to Pisces for the feet.

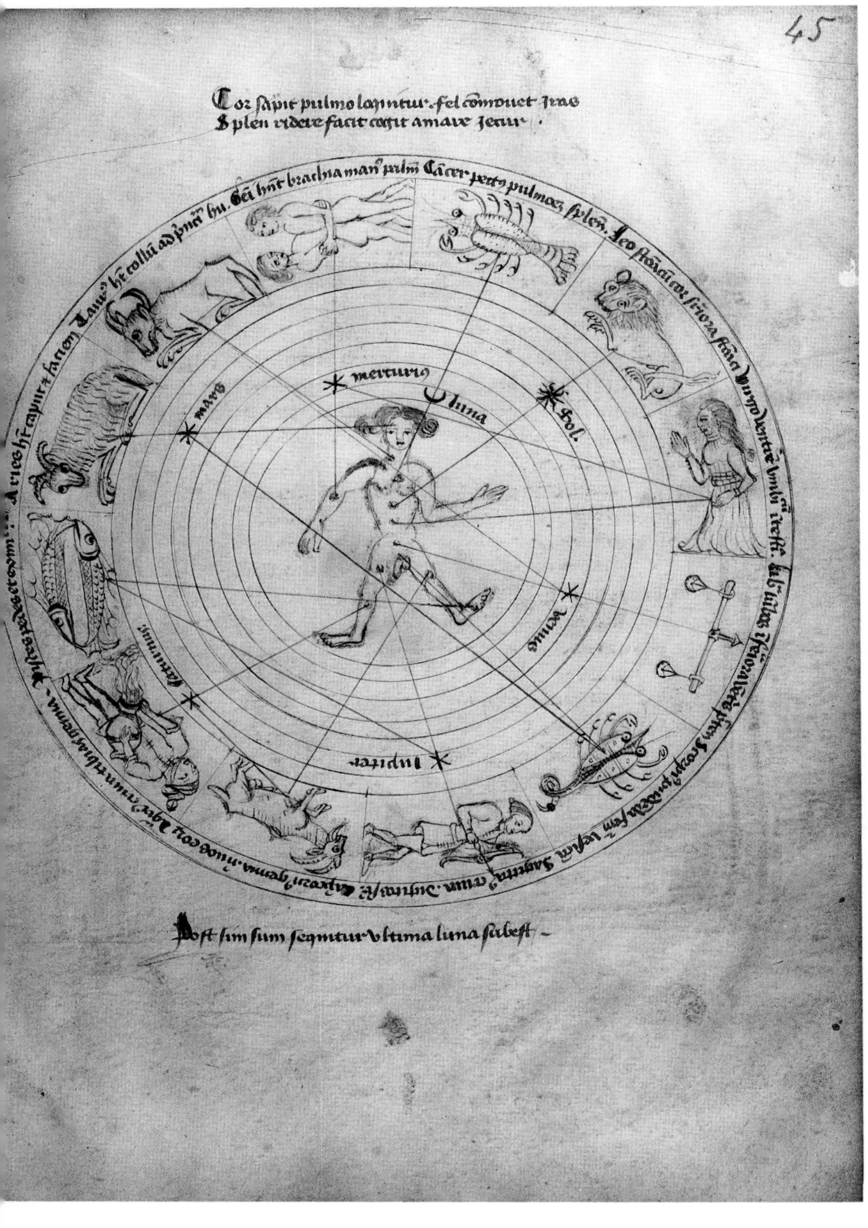

A Zodiac Man schematic, in which the figure represents the earth, and the planets and the zodiac signs are assigned to specific body parts. Unidentified manuscript. c.1400. Bibliothèque Nationale, Paris.

Every illness, as in centuries past, is also under a planet's influence, so that therapeutic drugs are chosen from the group ruled by a planet that is astrologically opposed to the planet superintending the illness. For example, diseases associated with Mars are high fevers, elevated blood pressure, hemorrhaging, inflammation, swellings, and sores. They have to be counteracted by medications under Saturn, the antagonist of Mars and therefore antipyretic (against fever), sedative, styptic, astringent, and anti-inflammatory: aconite, aspen, barley, belladonna, cannabis, flaxseed, henbane, oak, thistle, tea, antimony, and hemlock. These classifications were part of many ancient herbals. Some of the remedies were under several planetary rulerships. For instance, thistle, which was supposed to be Saturnian and consequently acted against Mars's illnesses, was also under Mars and therefore not opposed to Martian sickness. Peppermint was attached to Jupiter, as well as to Mars. Oak was both Saturnian and Jupiterian. The explanation given for these apparent inconsistencies was that these substances could also act therapeutically by the principle of sympathetic influence.

Prognosis too is linked to the stars. For instance, when Moon is in the zodiac sign of Capricorn, lowered vigor and emotional decline is to be expected. An illness is apt to have a benign course when the Sun is in House VIII. This house, the domicile of death and termination, in antique times could suggest the type of death, depending on which planets were there in the person's birth horoscope. Neptune, for instance, would warn of the danger of drowning in the future; Mars, death by violence; Mercury, lung disease; Uranus, explosive catastrophe. Jupiter's presence on the other hand was a highly favorable omen and signaled a long life.

The tremendous influence of astrology on medicine in the past can be inferred from the great 1437 debate (mentioned above) at the University of Paris on the subject of auspicious times for bloodletting. Also, a century earlier, in 1348, the medical faculty of Paris made a public prediction of an imminent medical disaster based on the conjunction of Mars, Jupiter, and Saturn in Aquarius several years before. Indeed this pronouncement was considered prophetic when the bubonic plague broke out not long after.

As understanding of physiology and the causes of diseases expanded, especially in the nineteenth and twentieth centuries, physicians abandoned these concepts. Even among astrologers today, only an occasional adept still subscribes to treatment by these ancient tenets. However, some astrologers do rely on the standard predictive techniques of astrology, such as the natal horoscope and the progressed and transited charts, to evaluate the course and prognosis of an illness.

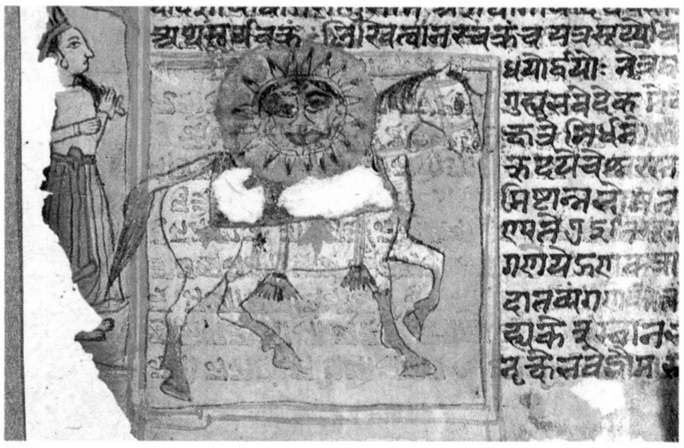

Indian

Just as there are several Western astrological systems, Hindu theory and practice also recognize a number of different methods. Some of the Indian techniques resemble Western astrology.

For instance, the favorable character of the Indian equivalents of Jupiter, Venus, and the Moon and the unfavorable nature of Mars and Saturn are retained. Mercury can be either fortunate or unfortunate in keeping with the changeable properties of this planet in Greco-Roman astrology. As in the West, the planets determine basic character and the twelve zodiac signs indicate how the person's traits are applied. The houses are also incorporated into the Indian system, although the strongest influence is exerted in the middle of the house rather than at the cusp as in Western astrology.

However, Indian astrological techniques differ from most of the Western varieties in several ways, a few of which may be summarized. For example, Hindu systems are based on the sidereal zodiac, which represents the actual positions of the star clusters in the sky rather than the unchanging zodiac of the West. Predictions of happenings—mundane and individual—are the principal focus, not the

Representations of the nine planets, from the *Lagnacandrikā* by Kāsīnātha, a Sanskrit work on natal astrology. Seventeenth or eighteenth century. Clockwise from top left: the Sun (Sūrya); the Moon (Candra); Mars (Bhauma); Mercury (Bhudha); Jupiter (Brhaspati); Venus (Sukra); Saturn (Sani); Ketu (body of the demon); Saimhikeya, considered the ninth planet, responsible for comets; Rahu, head of the demon Saimhikeya, seizes the sun and moon and causes eclipses. Courtesy Wellcome Institute Library, London.

Astrology

personal characteristics of the native. Greater emphasis is placed on the nodes of the Moon, especially the north node. Two planets are considered to be in conjunction if they are in the same zodiac sign; in Western astrology the two planets have to be much closer, anywhere from two to eight degrees. When planets are within one degree of each other on the Indian charts, they are assumed to be in a planetary battle, with supremacy assigned to the planet closest to the eastern point on the chart, counting in a clockwise direction (Western measurements are made counterclockwise on the horoscope diagram). Indian methods also emphasize the dominion over the months of pregnancy by different planets. For example, Venus rules the first month and the Moon presides over the ninth.

Furthermore, the life of each person is divided into separate periods, with a special influence exerted by a specific planet assigned to each period. Most importantly, the doctrine of reincarnation (karma) permeates Indian astrology as it does virtually all Hindu philosophy. The horoscope can reveal the stage of a person's soul on its way to nirvana, the ultimate and highest state of existence.

Chinese Astrology—

Rat
November 22–December 21. Yang
Positive: ambitious, self-assured
Negative: irascible
Fixed element: water

Ox
December 22–January 20. Yin
Positive: patient, inspirational
Negative: rash
Fixed element: water

Tiger
January 21–February 19. Yang
Positive: protective, ardent
Negative: rebellious
Fixed element: wood

Rabbit
February 20–March 20. Yin
Positive: talented, peacemaking
Negative: pedantic
Fixed element: wood

Dragon
March 21–April 19. Yang
Positive: passionate, fashionable
Negative: impractical
Fixed element: wood

Snake
April 20–May 20. Yin
Positive: self-controlled, conventional
Negative: vain
Fixed element: fire

Month Animal Symbols

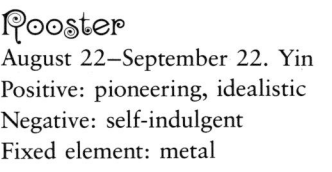

Horse
May 21–June 21. Yang
Positive: sexually attractive, perceptive
Negative: self-doubting
Fixed element: fire

Sheep
June 22–July 21. Yin
Positive: artistic, trustworthy
Negative: indecisive
Fixed element: fire

Monkey
July 22–August 21. Yang
Positive: intelligent, versatile
Negative: unscrupulous
Fixed element: metal

Rooster
August 22–September 22. Yin
Positive: pioneering, idealistic
Negative: self-indulgent
Fixed element: metal

Dog
September 23–October 22. Yang
Positive: ethical, social
Negative: tactless
Fixed element: metal

Pig
October 23–November 21. Yin
Positive: chivalrous, unpretentious
Negative: superficial
Fixed element: water

The animal symbols of the Chinese zodiac. Clockwise from top center: snake, horse, sheep, monkey, rooster, dog, pig, rat, ox, tiger, rabbit, dragon.

The twelve animal signs of the Chinese zodiac are shown on this carved jade plate in white nephrite, which was presented to Emperor Ch'ien-lung (r.1736–1795) as a birthday gift. On the reverse side are trigrams of the *I Ching*. Width 12". Museum of Natural History, New York City.

Chinese Astrology

Chinese astrological tenets and practices form a complex but logical structure, which can only briefly be summarized here.

Chinese cosmology and philosophy are unique. For thousands of years, the duality of yang (male) and yin (female) principles and the predominance of the number five in classifying virtually everything—elements, seasons, colors, flavors, virtues, social duties, organs of the body, emotions—also has been extended to the five divisions of the sky: Sun, Moon, Earth, stars, and constellations. In ancient times, the polar star rather than the Sun was the central point about which all others revolved.

Chinese astrology today uses twelve animal figures and five elements. The horoscope depends on the year, hour, and month of birth—and also in some systems, the day of birth according to the Chinese calendar. These are the "four pillars of fate."

The Animal Figures

Each year is associated with one of the twelve signs (also called "Earth Branches") in rotation, so that every twelve years the cycle begins again. The animal figures (with some possible variations) are: Rat, Ox (or Bull, Cow, or Water Buffalo), Tiger, Rabbit (or Hare or Cat), Dragon, Snake, Horse, Sheep (or Goat), Monkey, Rooster, Dog, and Pig (or Boar). The animals display specific characteristics.

The five elements—wood, fire, metal, water, and earth—are each assigned to a zodiac sign for two years, so that while it takes twelve years for the cycle of zodiac signs to start over again, the five elements repeat every ten years and therefore over time are not always attached to the same animal sign.

Each of the twelve months of the year also has an animal symbol. Since the Chinese calendar is lunar, the beginning day of each year is different. The New Year, the *Lap Chun,* starts with the second new moon after the winter solstice. One month every three years is lengthened by thirty days, in order to put the Chinese lunar reckonings in agreement with the solar astronomical relationships and thus keep the seasons in their proper places. Thus, the Chinese "leap year," occurring every three years, is thirty days longer than other years. In Western cultures, which use a solar calendar, one day has to be added every four years—during the Western "leap years"—to maintain accurate astronomical arrangements.

The Chinese year begins in late January or early or mid-February. Some "years" may have two New Years or none. For instance, when the New Moon after the winter solstice occurs after February 5 and the following lunar year starts before the fifth day of February, there is no New Year. That year is correspondingly termed to be "blind" (and therefore inappropriate for partnerships, domestic and commercial). If the New Moon that begins one lunar year shows itself after February 5 and also before the next February 5 the following year, then there are two New Years (very auspicious).

There are twenty-eight lunar mansions to mark the days of each lunar month. In addition, the twenty-four hours in a day are divided into twelve two-hour segments with each of the zodiac animals also ruling two hours, beginning with the Rat at 11 P.M. and ending with the Pig at 9 P.M. to 11 P.M. the following day. The animal in dominion over the hour of a person's birth is thus "in ascendance" (similar to the ascendant sign in the Western system), adding its traits to the animal symbol of that year. The hour animal points to the native's inner personality, which harbors the characteristics that strive to make themselves known.

As the universe is divided into the duality of the yang and the yin, so are the years and also the twelve animal symbols, in alternation around the Chinese zodiac circle: Rat is yang; Ox is yin; Tiger, yang; Rabbit, yin; and so on to the last figures of Dog, yang, and Pig, yin. Six of the symbols are yang and six, yin. This arrangement also pairs each figure with the one following in a yin-yang combination. Together, the partners represent an area of life, a "house." These Chinese astrological groupings are quite different from the Western houses, for they are not actual divisions of the sky but rather linkages to represent the yang and yin parts of existence.

The compatibilities among the animal types depend on their relative positions on the zodiac diagrammatic circle. In Western astrological parlance, the figures in trine to each other (120 degrees) are apt to have good and easy relationships. Those in opposition (180 degrees) or square (90 degrees) tend to be incompatible.

Thus, Ox, Snake, and Rooster; Tiger, Horse, and Dog—produce compatible triads. But Ox, Sheep, Dragon; Tiger, Monkey, Snake, and Pig—are in incompatible relationships. In folklore and among some social groups, a few of these interpretations are not always held to strictly. "Tiger people," especially females, may be viewed with suspicion generally. Rooster and Snake, although clearly compatible in position on the circle, are often believed to be in disharmony. On the other hand, Rabbit and Snake are usually considered a felicitous linkage although they do not fit the standard pattern.

The planets also participate in the division into yang and yin. Sun is yang, Moon is yin, Jupiter is yang, Venus is yin, Mars is yang, Mercury is yin, Saturn is yang.

Chinese Astrology

Animal Signs and their Years

Rat	1900	1912	1924	1936	1948	1960	1972	1984
	1996	2008	2020	2032	2044			
Ox	1901	1913	1925	1937	1949	1961	1973	1985
	1997	2009	2021	2033	2045			
Tiger	1902	1914	1926	1938	1950	1962	1974	1986
	1998	2010	2022	2034	2046			
Rabbit	1903	1915	1927	1939	1951	1963	1975	1987
	1999	2011	2023	2035	2047			
Dragon	1904	1916	1928	1940	1952	1964	1976	1988
	2000	2012	2024	2036	2048			
Snake	1905	1917	1929	1941	1953	1965	1977	1989
	2001	2013	2025	2037	2049			
Horse	1906	1918	1930	1942	1954	1966	1978	1990
	2002	2014	2026	2038	2050			
Sheep	1907	1919	1931	1943	1955	1967	1979	1991
	2003	2015	2027	2039	2051			
Monkey	1908	1920	1932	1944	1956	1968	1980	1992
	2004	2016	2028	2040	2052			
Rooster	1909	1921	1933	1945	1957	1969	1981	1993
	2005	2017	2029	2041	2053			
Dog	1910	1922	1934	1946	1958	1970	1982	1994
	2006	2018	2030	2042	2054			
Pig	1911	1923	1935	1947	1959	1971	1983	1995
	2007	2019	2031	2043	2055			

The Elements

The five elements are wood, fire, earth, metal, and water. Each rules for two years. Every ten years the cycle begins again. Therefore, each of the five elements has a changing relationship to the animal zodiac signs. Over the two years, the element's positive features alternate with the negative. For example, January 28, 1960–February 14, 1961, a year of the Rat, is controlled by metal in its positive phase. February 15, 1961–February 4, 1962, an Ox year, is under metal in its negative classification.

Each animal sign also has a fixed element, independent of the element that is in ascendance in any of the years. Thus each animal symbol has two element annotations: (1) the year's element, positive or negative, different in each year; (2) the fixed element and polarity always attached to that animal.

WOOD
Positive: cooperative
Negative: imprudent

FIRE
Positive: self-assured
Negative: dominating

EARTH
Positive: organized
Negative: unimaginative

METAL
Positive: persevering
Negative: obstinate

WATER
Positive: persuasive
Negative: passive

Example of the actual dates of each year according to the Chinese calendar, showing the animal associations, yin-yang assignments, elements, and positive-negative polarity.

Rat	February 10, 1948, to January 28, 1949	yang	Earth	(+)
Ox	January 29, 1949, to February 16, 1950	yin	Earth	(−)
Tiger	February 17, 1950, to February 5, 1951	yang	Metal	(+)
Rabbit	February 6, 1951, to January 26, 1952	yin	Metal	(−)
Dragon	January 27, 1952, to February 13, 1953	yang	Water	(+)
Snake	February 14, 1953, to February 2, 1954	yin	Water	(−)
Horse	February 3, 1954, to January 23, 1955	yang	Wood	(+)
Sheep	January 24, 1955, to February 11, 1956	yin	Wood	(−)
Monkey	February 12, 1956, to January 30, 1957	yang	Fire	(+)
Rooster	January 31, 1957, to February 17, 1958	yin	Fire	(−)
Dog	February 18, 1958, to February 7, 1959	yang	Earth	(+)
Pig	February 8, 1959, to January 27, 1960	yin	Earth	(−)

Sample Reading in Chinese Astrology

To illustrate how the apparatus of Chinese astrology may be used to delineate a horoscope, let us take the example of a young woman born on January 12, 1949, at 11:30 A.M. Consulting the tables of precise datings of the years, in order to determine her birth year's animal and element symbols, we find that this person's date of birth fell between February 10, 1948, and January 28, 1949. Although in Western terms, her birth year was 1949, the Chinese New Year had begun in 1948 on February 10 and ended after her birthday, on January 28, 1949, so that she belonged to the Rat year, under yang influence, with the year's element, earth, positive in polarity. In traditional Western astrology, January 12 is under the Sun-sign of Capricorn. In the Chinese system, her birth month is the Ox, of yin principle, as seen in the table for lunar month symbols. The hour of birth (11:30 A.M.) is ruled by the Horse, a yang figure, with fire its fixed element. However, the fixed, permanent element associated with the Rat is water.

This horoscope therefore has as its chief parts:

Animal symbol of the birth year = Rat, yang for that year.

Element of that particular birth year = Earth, yang (+) for that year.

Fixed element always associated with that animal symbol = Water.

Animal symbol of the lunar month of birth = Ox, yin.

Fixed element associated with the Ox sign = Water.

Animal sign of the hour of birth = Horse, yang in classification.

Fixed element of Horse symbol = Fire.

The traits for the Rat are self-assurance and self-disciplined features, which are emphasized further by the earth element of that year. This woman is organized, prudent, and has a forward outlook. Since this was a positively polarized year, she will be likely to avoid altogether or at least overcome tendencies to irascibility, inconstancy, and self-indulgence. The fixed element water associated with the Rat symbol suggests that she will be able to persuade and stimulate others. Her charming behavior will be embellished by compassion and intuitive understanding. The danger of the water element is in becoming too compliant, dependent, and passive.

Her lunar month of the Ox enhances her soothing, inspirational abilities. On the yang side she may have creativity and an outgoing nature, but the yin side imparted by the Ox prevents her from being too ambitious (Rat, yang) and impatient. The water features of the Rat fixed element are increased by the Ox's fixed element, also water, so that communication, sensitivity, and perseverance become the outstanding features.

The symbol of the hour of birth (Horse) indicates what lies inside. She would like to be sexually attractive and needs popularity. Her charm, which the Rat year imparts, is just what she is glad to possess. Her agreeable outward personality, however, conceals the Horse's fierce independence and compulsion to express inner needs.

A Chinese astrologer at work. c.1750. Medallion, brocaded satin, polychrome silk on cream ground, Diameter 25″. Los Angeles County Museum of Art.

She can do well enough with people of intelligence (Monkey), cleverness, enthusiasm, and talent, especially if they are as curious and articulate as she. She may even get to rely on the Monkey's ability to simplify what seems to be complex situations. An Ox person could also become her close friend. Its trustworthiness and steadfastness would be a strong support to her. The Dragon's sense of fashion and fastidiousness are similar to her own and she is apt to embrace that type of lively and exciting personality. Although she would be highly compatible with a Dragon, male or female, her basic honesty and forthrightness will not tolerate any negative features of the Dragon—such as the pursuit of evil ways. She is likely also to be intolerant of any self-righteousness, overconfidence, or false aspects in the Dragon personality.

The years ahead that are governed by Rat, Monkey, or Dragon are most likely to give rewards both romantically and monetarily. During Horse, Rabbit, and Rooster years, she should act cautiously. Still, if this native avoids risky ventures (Horse) and imprudence in domestic affairs (Rabbit) and limits activities to reasonable boundaries (Rooster), she can actually benefit in those years from conservation of money, health, and energies.

Horoscope of Colette

As an example of how the delineation process works, we shall read the horoscope of a famous woman who became one of France's greatest writers, Sidonie-Gabrielle Colette (born January 28, 1873, at 10 P.M. in southern France). First we will interpret her birth chart, searching for the potentialities and hazards displayed there. Then we will examine what might have been predicted for a particular year by her progressed horoscope and also her transiting planets, two of the better-known methods of astrological prediction. This is only my reading, based on the methods of various astrologers. Others may wish to draw different meanings or to see other configurations.

General Features

The first step is to look at the distribution of the planets on Colette's natal chart. Is there a concentration of planets in any half of the circle: eastern or western; bottom hemisphere or upper half? Six planets are present in the northern (bottom) half and four are in the southern (upper), an almost equal distribution, but with a slight preponderance in the northern half, suggesting a subjective life or homebound activity, in contrast to outside functioning. Does this fit our native? After all, Colette had experience as a performer and was in contact with many people. Yet, all her writing and her principal, all-encompassing focus was at home.

What about planets in the eastern and western hemispheres? Here there is a more noticeable difference. Seven of ten planets on the western side signifies opportunities and fulfillments dependent on other people entering situations rather than creating them. Finally, the chart should be examined to see whether there is a single planet standing apart from all the others—a singleton, which would alert us to an influence exceeding the importance of any of the other planets on the chart. However, no singleton is present here.

Clusterings

How are the planets clustered in the signs? We have just recognized that seven are in the western hemisphere and only three are in the eastern, but which zodiac signs hold these planets? Colette has two planets in Capricorn, two in Aquarius, and one each in Pisces, Aries, and Taurus; in the eastern half, two are in Leo and one in Scorpio.

The clustering of four planets in the two signs of Capricorn and Aquarius is entirely contained within House IV, the boundaries of which include portions of both zodiac signs (the last ten degrees of Capricorn and the first twelve degrees of Aquarius). Hard work and ambition are shown by Capricorn. Aquarius symbolizes unconventional, even bohemian, behavior. House IV (the area of home) suggests here too that Colette was home-oriented. Indeed, her domicile was her place of work and where, during one period of her life, almost all of her time was spent. For instance, she loved to write while in bed, and although her conduct was indeed against the conventions of the times, she

A photograph of Colette, the internationally famous French writer (born January 28, 1873, at 10 P.M.). When she was born the Sun was in Aquarius, with Libra rising as her ascendant sign.

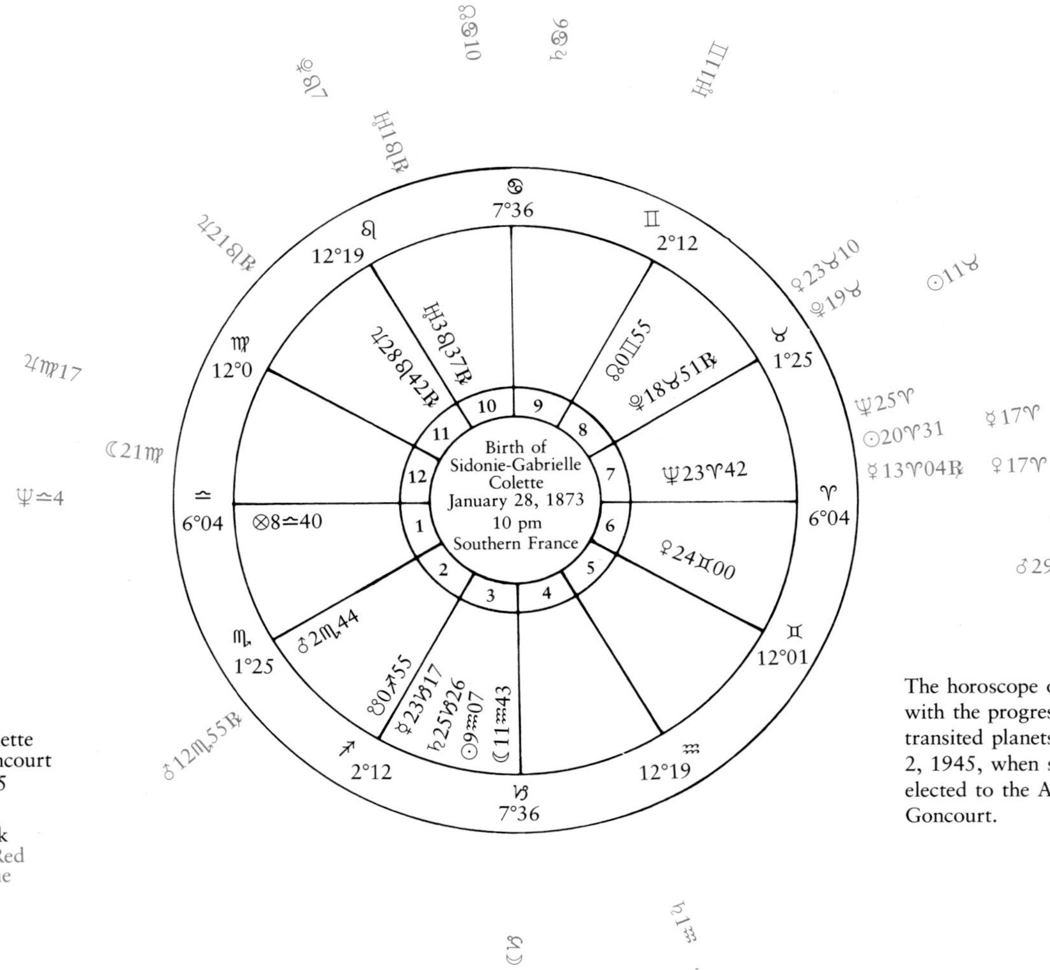

Election of Colette
to Académie Goncourt
May 2, 1945

Natal = Black
Progressed = Red
Transit = Blue

The horoscope of Colette, with the progressed and transited planets for May 2, 1945, when she was elected to the Académie Goncourt.

was very private. House IV also deals with real estate—and Colette certainly bought and sold several homes.

Retrograde Planets
We note too that the chart has several planets in retrograde (labeled R^X^): Pluto retrograde is in House VIII; Uranus in X; Jupiter in XI. Retrograde movement is supposed to indicate an emphasis on the subjective side of the planet's traits. Jupiter retrograde here might mean that the subject's religion and philosophy (Jupiterian areas) are very personal—not in the general mold. Of course, this is also in keeping with the behavior of unconventionality announced by the presence of planets in Aquarius.

Ascendant
At the eastern angle—the ascendant—Libra is the rising sign, indicating that although the native may be a highly independent person, she does not relish being alone. She needs and seeks partnership. This is not the horoscope of a loner. The ascendant, Libra, will be referred to again later, for it colors the significance of other influences on the chart.

Imum Coeli
At the bottom of the wheel, the IC, stands Capricorn, suggesting that the subject's nature is fundamentally serious and diligent. It can also suggest that the parents were relatively old when the native was born, but we do not happen to know whether this was true or false.

Descendant
The descendant on the House VII cusp is Aries. House VII is a place of partnership. Since the ascendant, Libra, is a sign of "we" rather than "I," and Aries suggests leadership, one might conclude that this person looks to a partner for leadership. If the situation were reversed, with Aries the ascendant and Libra the descendant, the native might seek a relationship in which she would be the dominant partner.

Midheaven
On the midheaven, Cancer usually suggests a strong family quality—clearly not a focus of Colette's writing. Cancer does however often signify a concern with women and the female in life and work. Some have considered Colette's books particularly geared to women, for women are the principal characters in her writings. Men are significant only in how they affect or are affected by women. Since she wrote specifically from the woman's perspective, a delineator might see a consonance between Cancer at midheaven and her female orientation.

Elements
The distribution among elements here is virtually even. Two planets are in an air sign (Aquarius), two in water (Pisces and Scorpio), three in fire (Aries and Leo), and three in earth (Taurus and Capricorn). If there had been a concentration of four or five in air, emotional detachment and rationalization would tend to prevail; in water, it would be intuition and feeling; in fire, expression and enthusiasm; in earth, practicality and sensuousness. Instead the balance of elements is in keeping with Colette's rationality and practicality mingled with sensitivity and expressiveness.

Qualities
Fixed signs are noticeably prominent on this chart. Six of

ten planets are in the fixed signs (two in Aquarius, two in Leo, one in Taurus, one in Scorpio). The cardinal signs contain three planets (Aries one, Capricorn two, Libra and Cancer none). The mutable sign of Pisces has one planet, and there are none in Gemini, Virgo, or Sagittarius, the other mutable signs. The main quality here therefore is a tendency toward regularity and perseverance—sometimes rigidity. Colette was indeed almost unswerving in her devotion to her writing. Every day for a predetermined number of hours, she labored, virtually never straying from her fixed schedule.

Polarity

Signs are also classified as positive and negative. Colette has five planets in the positive signs (air and fire) and five in the negative signs (earth and water), showing a balance between the rational and aggressive (positive) and the intuitive and receptive (negative). Some astrologers could interpret this arrangement differently, concluding that this distribution heralded conflict between these opposing traits.

Sun and Moon

On this chart, the Sun is in Aquarius, in keeping with Colette's unconventional attitudes. This chart also has the Moon in Aquarius, accenting the libertine influence. When the Sun and Moon are in the same sign and the same degree (conjunction), the Moon astronomically is in the "New Moon" phase, suggesting extreme subjectivity and specialization. The Sun is ego. The Moon is emotion. These two planets in conjunction suggest a virtual embrace of both intellectuality and emotionality.

Uranus

Our next search will be for the position of Uranus, the planet considered to be the ruler of Aquarius (the Sun-sign). We find it in Leo and, most significantly, in opposition to the Sun and Moon in Aquarius, thereby making even more critical and dramatic the quality of nonconformity and individualism. An opposition aspect adds tension to the planets involved. This person's chart therefore shows she might have difficulty in fitting into society's molds.

Mutual Reception (Sun and Uranus)

Other features of Uranus might also be pointed to, including its opposition to the Sun. Uranus is in the Sun's home sign of Leo. This special relationship in which two planets are in each other's sign is called "mutual reception." The Sun-Uranus opposition, ordinarily detrimental, is now combined favorably and made less intense by the mutual reception. Creativity, the self, individualism, expression of will, and the intellect are especially heightened.

Prime Mover (Planet in Oriental Appearance)

The Moon may be closest to the Sun on this chart, but the planet that rose just before the Sun is Saturn, which is therefore the prime mover since the Sun and the planets move clockwise on the circle. Saturn is just ahead of the Sun, having made the clockwise tour from the easternmost point on the circle around to the bottom of the chart. As the prime mover, Saturn's characteristics are revealed: thoroughness and conscientiousness. This is in keeping with the emphasis on the quality of fixity (six of ten planets are in fixed sign) in her horoscope.

Mars and the T-Square

Mars, standing somewhat alone and separated from the other planets, is in Scorpio, in a clear square (90 degrees) with the Sun and the Moon. But it is also in square (90 degrees) to Uranus. This makes a T-square: Sun-Moon and Uranus in opposition, and Mars in square to Uranus and also to Sun-Moon. Sun-Moon and Uranus spell out individualism and nonconformity. Mars, the ruler of—and located in—the sign of Scorpio, at the bottom tip of the T-square, contributes its passionate energy, as well as its energetic sexuality. Thus we have the planets in Leo (romance), Aquarius (unconventionality), and Scorpio (passion) strongly related and perhaps declaring an unconventional sexuality. Indeed Colette went through a period of homosexuality and also conceived a child before marriage.

Mars in House II

Being part of a T-square, which signifies tension, Mars may announce by its presence in House II the importance of money, suggesting that financial issues are critical in this person's life—and indeed they were. Colette needed the aggression of Mars to fight for proper remuneration for her work.

Since Mars in Scorpio (in House II) is in square to the planets Sun and Moon in Aquarius (in House IV) and also in aspect to Uranus up in Leo (in House X), one can read this arrangement as a conflict among the three Houses: X of career, IV of home security, and II of money. As Colette once noted: "I've just received a letter in which he [Lucien Saglio] refuses to pay me the price he promised for serialization [one of her books]. Losing money is less important than losing a friend."

Ascendant Influence

An astrologer might at this point reiterate the importance of the rising sign, the ascendant Libra, which colors all Colette's relationships. Although almost everything she did had personal ramifications, and as an Aquarian (the Sun in Aquarius), her friendships tended toward the intellectual rather than the intimate, yet Libra, as the rising sign, dictated an attachment to others. Colette's professional relationships were indeed virtually never free from some type of personal involvement with the other party.

Mercury
Mercury's position at the bottom angle (IC) gives added weight to this planet's significance. The outstanding trait of Mercury is communication. Writers and speakers are especially favored.

We also note that Mercury is in House IV. This house is concerned with home, parents, beginnings, and also the end of life. Colette was induced to write by her family and she wrote virtually to the end of her life. Mercury in the sign of Capricorn points to pragmatism. Mercury's money and calculation merge into Capricorn's practicality. She may have written out of compulsion, but she actively sought remuneration and recognition.

Mercury-Saturn
One cannot look at the glyph for Mercury on this wheel without seeing immediately adjacent the planet Saturn in close conjunction. This could show that Colette's writing talent remained with her into her old age (Saturn). Colette certainly had artistic longevity.

The virtual union of Mercury with Saturn usually has an even more important association. It is supposed to describe a methodical, laborious type of performance, whereas Colette had the reputation of composing speedily, producing her works in rapid fashion. However, she once wrote in a letter: "If I didn't work so slowly, with so much caution and circumspection, I could visit you oftener. But I am so made that an hour's pleasure undoes the rest of my day."

Apparently she was a dedicated and workmanlike performer. Evidently she accomplished much, not because she was fast, but rather because she was so intense in application, as befits the conjunction of Saturn with Mercury.

Saturn
We have already mentioned that Saturn can instill longevity into talent. It can also add limitations, even inhibition. How might this containment of Mercury's communication have shown itself in Colette? The very compulsion of Saturn can give the feeling of never being finished, never being secure in accomplishment, never believing that one is quite ready. Having received the great honor of election to the Belgian Academy, Colette nevertheless revealed her uncertainty in a letter: "Fine. But I'm already turning green with fear at the thought of delivering my speech, scheduled for next January."

Saturn as Final Dispositor
Saturn in its angular position and in House IV gives added weight to seriousness and dedication in work. In sextile (60 degrees) to Venus, Saturn might represent her affectionate relationships with people of widely different ages. The trine (120 degrees) of Saturn with Pluto in Taurus suggests a slowly evolving financial state and considerable interest in monetary resources, particularly property. Being in its own sign of Capricorn and near the IC, Saturn is "the final dispositor" and thus carries special weight. It may have been the one feature that kept the strong Aquarian influences and the disruptive square aspects among Mars, Uranus, Sun, and Moon from damaging Colette's ability to accomplish anything concrete.

Venus
Some astrologers would have started the chart's analysis with Venus as the first planet because it is the ruler of the ascendant sign, Libra. Venus is not in its own sign of Libra, but instead is in House VI in Pisces, where it is normally exalted.

House VI covers the areas of health and work. The presence of the planetary ruler of the chart (in this case Venus because it is the ruler of the ascendant, Libra) in House VI means a significant concern with both health and work. Colette is supposed to have had problems with health, notably arthritis and a respiratory condition, which an astrologer might attribute to Mercury (chest) in Capricorn (bones and joints), but she did live to a ripe old age. More significantly, work was the central definition of her life, and the presence of her chart ruler, Venus, in Pisces, the sign of imagination, in House VI of work, fits this compulsion.

A sextile aspect (approximately 60 degrees) is present between Venus and the conjunction of Mercury and Saturn. This usually favorable relationship might be interpreted as an attention to beauty (Venus) in the art of writing (Mercury) arrived at by methodical concentration (Saturn). Venus's associations also announce a high degree of artistry. As the chart ruler, because it is the normal ruler of the ascendant sign of Libra, Venus intensifies originality by being present in Pisces, a sign of imagination.

Jupiter
Jupiter is in Leo in House XI and is one of the three retrograde planets in this horoscope, emphasizing subjectivity. House XI deals with hopes and also with one's friends. Mingling the sign of Leo (creativity) with the house of friends, one would look for friendships among creative people, and so there were—artists, writers, performers. The presence of Jupiter in the sign also announces a "show-biz" quality, and indeed Colette spent a number of years on the stage.

Uranus
Uranus is part of a T-square, involving also the Sun and Mars, and therefore a harbinger of tensions. Uranus additionally is an especially potent influence because it is "elevated" in this horoscope—at the highest position of any of the other planets—signaling heightened nonconformity. We have already examined Uranus's square with Mars.

Pluto
Pluto is in Taurus in House VIII. At the time that Colette was born Pluto had not yet been discovered, but in hindsight we can examine its supposed effects. House VIII is traditionally associated with Scorpio, and therefore is ruled by both Mars and Pluto. This house includes death, regeneration, and legacies (that is, other people's money). Pluto in House VIII would imply a strong preoccupation with death, but we have no confirming information on this subject. Perhaps the category of inheritances and other people's money can be related to Colette's activities in seeking funds for child support from the father of her child.

Neptune
Neptune has been saved for last because it illustrates a number of ways in which aspects can be utilized for delineation.

Neptune by itself signifies romanticism and a lack of prudent discrimination, but one must additionally consider the zodiac sign of Aries, in which Neptune finds itself. Mars is the traditional ruler of Aries; Mars and Aries together have to do with identity and self-assertion. This activist propensity can overcome Neptune's dreaminess and imprudence, although Colette did surrender to her first husband's domination.

How this combination might fit Colette may be perceived in the very significant square aspect of Neptune to both Mercury (innovative communication) and Saturn (anxiety, ill health). This could refer to writing under a pseudonym. For instance, the square aspect to Mercury could imply some kind of deception, but there is no evidence that Colette ever did this. What did happen, however, was that her first husband substituted his own name for hers on her early works—with her acquiescence.

Moreover, we always have to keep in mind the clues given by the ascendant sign and the concentration of planets. In this instance we may recall that Libra is the ascendant sign and the concentration is westerly oriented. *Other* people are thus symbolized. Here fraud was committed by others. The deception of name substitution (and incidentally also of philandering) by her first husband as signified by Neptune in House VII also meshes well with the accent on the acts of others.

The square configuration of Neptune to the planets in House IV, especially Mercury and Saturn, is in a "tight," virtually orbless 90-degree aspect. House IV speaks of home, family, and marriage (her first husband was a friend of the family). Saturn is connected with age (he was many years older than she).

Neptune also trines Jupiter, which is in Leo in House XI of friends. Her circle of friends indeed was wide and important to her life and work.

Other Points
The Part of Fortune (⊕) is near the ascendant sign's cusp at 8 degrees of Libra. (This horoscope point results from a mathematical calculation involving the longitudes of the ascendant sign, the Moon, and the Sun.) In keeping with the other features in this horoscope, good fortune and favorable outcomes in Colette's path through life were the result of other people's help—as signaled by the position of the Part of Fortune in Libra, the sign covering relationships with others. Of course, the Part of Fortune here in House I (self) also suggests that she could be successful when she relied on herself.

The Moon's nodes (north and south) mark the two intersections of the Moon's orbit with the apparent path of the Sun (the ecliptic). The south node usually implies dissatisfactions and a separating of connections. Here in House II the south node indicates a frustration in terms of earning potential because it is in House II of money and resources. Its presence in Sagittarius suggests also uncertainty concerning recognition.

The north node, the symbol of forming connections, is in House VIII of others' resources. It may refer to Colette's linkages with people who had substantial holdings.

Afterword
One of the values of a horoscope lies in the numerous details and nuances that one can find on the chart. None of us is so simplistically constructed that a few words or even paragraphs can sum up our personalities, drives, and potential. Perhaps it is better to recognize that the information conveyed in this delineation fits the complex nature of a human being. At least we have been able to obtain a view of Colette as illustrated by her horoscope and some idea of how one may analyze a person's astrological design.

Colette's Horoscope in Prediction

Having delineated Colette's natal horoscope chart, we may now use two of the most common methods of prediction to see what could have been predicted for May 2, 1945, when Colette was elected to the Académie Goncourt, a prestigious recognition of her literary talents.

Secondary Progression
A progressed chart is drawn by calculating each day after birth as if it were one year. Colette was born on January 28, 1873. The horoscope wheel for the progressed year of 1945, 72 years after her birth, is derived by examining the positions of the planets 72 days after her birth. The progressed planets' positions are then compared with the planets in Colette's natal horoscope.

Some astrologers might look at the progressed chart by itself and infer that progressed Sun in trine to progressed

Jupiter affirms the occurrence of a happy, lucky event. Jupiter is also in Leo in both the natal and progressed charts, suggesting recognition by the outside world. Progressed and also natal Jupiter in House XI indicates the achievement of a goal.

But let us compare the progressed and natal charts. Progressed Venus is in trine (120 degrees) to natal Mercury and in sextile (60 degrees) to natal Venus. Thus, an outstanding feature of this progressed chart is the involvement of Mercury. Something to do with a communications-related event is signaled. Here it is a literary happening. Venus in aspect to Mercury suggests its fortunate characteristic, and even progressed Venus in sextile to natal Venus indicates enhancement or the addition of performance in something to do with the arts.

The outer planets have moved little in the intervening period between the two charts. Progressed Uranus has passed beyond a square (90 degrees) to natal Mars in Scorpio and therefore is not significant. Neptune and Pluto are virtually unchanged in relation to the natal arrangement. All three move too slowly to be significant here.

Progressed Sun in Aries in House VII, competitive activity, of the natal chart fits with the winning of a competition.

Transits

In the transit system of prediction, the actual positions of the planets and signs of the date concerned (in this instance, May 2, 1945) are read from the astronomical ephemeris. These planetary arrangements are then compared with the configurations in the natal horoscope.

Sun to Moon

There is a square aspect between transiting Sun and natal Moon suggesting mixed emotions, with the elation of the Sun coloring the sadness of the Moon. In examining these charts in hindsight, an astrologer might simply state that this Sun-Moon arrangement fits no known interplay or circumstance connected with the event. On the other hand, the pattern might seem to reflect perhaps elation at the literary recognition but also self-doubt of worthiness.

Mercury and Venus to North Node

Transiting Mercury and Venus are in semisquare (45 degrees) to the natal node in Gemini. The Mercury-node aspect suggests some general coming together (north node) on the subject of communication (Mercury and also Gemini). Here it was a literary convention. The Venus-node relationship announces a pleasant, even celebratory, atmosphere.

Uranus to Moon

The natal Moon in Aquarius is also being trined by the slow-moving transiting Uranus. One might see in this circumstance Colette's reception by literary officialdom, for Uranus the planet and Aquarius the sign both deal with groups. As an "Aquarian" (the natal Sun in Aquarius), Colette was likely to be associated with or favorably related to groups of this kind. What of the planet Uranus in trine to the planet Moon? This may reflect issues of self-expression, unexpected happenings, or emotional relationships. Whether an astrologer would relate this combination to the sudden death of a female friend earlier in that year is conjectural.

Jupiter

Transiting Jupiter (in Virgo) is in semisquare (45 degrees) to natal Mars. Transiting Mars (almost at the end of Pisces) is in a quincunx (150 degrees) aspect to natal Jupiter (near the end of Leo). Thus, these two planets do seem to be linked twice. Together they proclaim a successful activity—but rewarded with renown rather than money.

Neptune

Transiting Neptune hits the ascendant in two ways: it conjuncts (although some might say the orb is too wide) the natal ascendant, Libra, and is also in an aspect on the transit chart. This may have to do with helping or nursing someone who is ill. The "otherness" characteristic of Libra indicates that the Neptunian feature of illness is someone else's rather than the native's. Along with the Moon in Aquarius, this someone else may have been a female friend.

Pluto

Transiting Pluto does make an aspect of some sort with the natal Venus (sesquisquare of 135 degrees). This aspect could signify the loss of someone, involvement with investments and inheritances, or a deeply passionate physical affair. Yet none of those conditions appear to apply to Colette at the time of her election into the Académie Goncourt.

Saturn

If transiting Saturn were to be in aspect to natal Venus, it might indicate a separation; to the natal Sun it could suggest much activity or a problem with a father figure. However we see none of these arrangements. What does stand out as an obvious feature is the position of transiting Saturn at the very top—at the midheaven—of the natal chart. Saturn in House X (career) usually speaks of achievements. Saturn here at the end of House IX, but at the very top of the chart, announces the ultimate result of life work, either the culmination or the failure: in full public display the person will be receiving either rewards or blame. Here Colette was reaching the apex of her literary stardom.

In general, the progressed horoscope for this date presages a literary event. The transits show the culmination of a career.

Evaluation

Presentations of conflicting arguments on the validity of astrology are themselves rarely without bias. It is of course understandable that few persons by now are free of an opinion as to whether astrology is a valid, useful study and occupation or is at best a delusion contradicted by the facts of science.

Arguments for Astrology

Astrology is a discipline with origins as ancient as the first civilizations and has lasted through the millenniums. It has become modified according to the knowledge and attitudes of the times, but it espouses and uses a fundamental truth—that the earth and its inhabitants are linked to and interrelated with the universe.

As science itself has delved into the nature of the cosmos, more and more effects on terrestrial events are seen to derive from the celestial bodies. Sun-spots influence weather and the functioning of animate and inanimate things, either directly or indirectly; cosmic rays affect living cells and their genetic material; electromagnetic waves fill the earth's atmosphere and the void beyond; gravity is a fundamental force acting on every galaxy from extraordinary distances; there are doubtless many other energies and mechanisms that remain to be discovered.

Furthermore, many types of animals are impelled to take long journeys (sometimes all at the same time in all parts of the globe), apparently stimulated by the alternation of light and darkness. These migrations were not understood until relatively recently, when the phenomenon was elucidated and given the name "photoperiodism." Some of these same creatures navigate incredible distances, apparently to the same spot, scientists aver, by relying on the arrangement of the stars.

Through many centuries of observing correlations between the traits of people and the positions of planets and stars, astrologers have compiled a system of understanding the ways that the celestial macrocosm is related to the earthly microcosm and its inhabitants. Twelve basic types of human makeup, corresponding to the constellations of the zodiac band in the sky, are merely the substrata of astrology. The ten known planets (the Sun and Moon are included among these wandering bodies), by means of their interrelationships and according to their positions and movements through the star clusters, produce an infinite variety of possible personalities. Thus, astrologers decry the simplistic, instant horoscopes of newspapers and magazines. Professional astrologers of integrity discover combinations of traits, strengths, tendencies, and weaknesses that are announced by the configuration of the planets and stars at the instant of a person's birth.

Even if it were later shown that people's personalities and their horoscope delineations were merely coincidences, these associations would still have significance. Acausal relationships, termed "synchronicity" by Carl Jung, are meaningful. In science itself explanations for the repeated association of two findings have often remained hidden for epochs or have never been found at all. Later they may be discovered to be causally related to each other—or they may each be dependent on still another series of phenomena. Astrological claims to correlations may one day be more clearly shown to have been correct. If not scientifically proved now, they are not necessarily less valid—just as in science.

Moreover, astrologers claim that, mechanisms and explanations aside, astrological techniques of delineation do work successfully. Astrologers and their clients all over the world have attested to astrology's usefulness for many centuries. In the 1950s, Michel and Françoise Gauquelin, without any preconceived conclusions, proved through thorough, rigid statistical examination the proposition that the positions of planets have correlation with the career propensities of people. Outstanding athletes, for instance, are more likely to be born at a time when Mars is in certain sectors of the sky; politicians, when Jupiter has particular positions. Surveys by others have repeatedly shown a high correlation between astrological principles and character traits.

There are other universal truths in astrology. For instance, scientists are fond of pointing to the fundamental materials—rocks, minerals, and chemicals—that constitute the planets and the earth, as well as the inhabitants. The stars in the constellations are concentrations of gases with the same thermonuclear processes that are in the Sun. Astrologers accept and even emphasize that these indentifications support the concept that the heavens and the earth form a unity. The macrocosm and the microcosm interact with each other.

It is certainly true that the horoscope diagram contains a plethora of information because humans themselves are so complex. The interpretations of any one astrologer may differ from another's for there is an art as well as a science in diagnosis. No bona-fide astrologer claims to be infallible. All should, and many do, reexamine their conclusions in the light of subsequent events. "Did I give sufficient weight to the position of Saturn on that chart?" "Clearly, I overlooked the complicating presence of Uranus alongside the other planets in that sign and house." Physicians and other professionals engage in the same type of exercise. As for predictions, the astrologers' forecasts based on personal horoscopes are certainly no worse than those of economists. The correctness of economic forecasts depends on whether the public, businesses, and governments act as the economists anticipate. In astrology, the course of future events depends upon how the person deals with the strengths and weaknesses shown on the birth chart.

Present-day astrologers have concluded that the influences of the planets and the zodiac signs impel but do not compel. They suggest tendencies, not inevitabilities. The predictive methods merely institutionalize the projections of an individual's world and perceptions on the basis of the tendencies set at birth.

In addition, all is not explained by materiality. Even the universe of the astronomers does not explain or even address the questions of what force began it all. How did the first black hole get there? Our infancy in the understanding of mechanisms and causes should suggest that the future may well explain and validate what can only be suspected now—including the teachings of astrology.

Astrology can encourage people to seek out their strengths and weaknesses. It enables the clients to discuss problems with someone else—especially a person who offers to help in dealing with fears, uncertainties, desires, and misfortunes. People would not continue to return to astrologers for counsel if they were not receiving useful information. Professional astrologers have learned to be excellent students of human nature, as the recipients of self-revelations. They are also able to detect significant, although hidden, emotional disturbances and to steer people to the appropriate medical professional. The birth chart shows the astrologer where to look for the potential psychological dangers in a person's makeup and thereby help him or her to forestall trouble. At the very worst—even if one were to deny all validity to astrology—no harm is done and much good can result.

Finally, some of the most intense critics of astrology have little knowledge of it. Very few, perhaps hardly any, can construct or read a horoscope. The same bias for which they denounce astrologers is shown by the critics themselves. Having first decided that astrological principles and practices are contemptible, they have made no effort to become instructed in its techniques. William Herschel, the founder of modern astronomy, drew horoscopes. Isaac Newton was also a believer. He saw no contradiction between astrology and astronomy. That most scientists today do not accept astrology is not an argument against astrological principles: medicine and science are filled with examples of truth ultimately outliving unpopular ideas.

Arguments Against Astrology

Astrology still uses theories inherited from the past, when knowledge of the skies was limited. It is understandable that ancient peoples saw the reddish tint of Mars as a harbinger of war, the fast-moving Mercury as a synonym for rapid progress, the slowness of Saturn as the symbol of deliberation, but to continue these associations by analogy is a perpetuation of ignorance. To assign to a bright morning star the attributes of the goddess Venus is merely a continuation of antique religious assumptions. Indeed, modern astrologers themselves do not regard the planets or the moon and the sun as the abodes of gods. Yet they continue the tradition of looking upon the same planets in the same way.

As new planets were discovered in the solar system, astrology attached to them governance over human traits, which their arbitrarily designated names signified in ancient mythology (Uranus, Neptune, Pluto). The presence of these hitherto unrecognized celestial bodies, now incorporated into the system of astrology, means that all the horoscopes before the eighteenth century and also before the mid-nineteenth century were deficient because no account had been taken of the influences of these planets. If an additional planet is discovered in the future, would that not again seriously alter all horoscopes now being cast?

Whatever may be the symbolism of the planets and constellations in the sky, they are so far away that their rays, waves, or other hypothetical vibrations are minuscule. For instance, moving from a standing to a sitting position has a larger gravitational effect than that imparted by the largest planet in the sky. Electromagnetic forces and the vibrations generated within the earth itself exceed by an enormous figure all the radiation from the eight planets. The strength of the electromagnetic waves from a light bulb in the room where a child is born is greater than that of all the celestial bodies—except the sun. The newborn's traits and tendencies therefore cannot be caused or conditioned by the stars.

The zodiac signs are the constellations providing the visual background to the path of the sun through the year (the ecliptic). It is a band of only a relatively few stars out of the approximately five thousand visible stars in the heavens. Astrology assigns prime importance to the effects of these twelve groups although there are millions or billions of others that are near enough to exert an equal or even stronger influence on those on earth. Moreover, some of the brightest stars are outside of the zodiac band and yet are emitting more energy than those within.

One of the most vulnerable targets in astrology is the concept of the houses. These are abstract sectors of the celestial sphere, each of which is supposed to encompass a different area of life's activities. In addition to demonstrating that neither the concept nor the technique has any basis in astronomy or physics, critics show that the dozens of varied methods of house division result in entirely different horoscopes for the same person.

The aspects of the planets present a similar problem. Astrological conjunctions and angular degrees of separation of the planets from one another are merely visual illusions. Two bodies in the sky may be millions of miles away from each other and yet to the observer on earth they may appear to be close together (in conjunction). Furthermore, why does a 90-degree angle between planets as visualized on earth mean one thing and a 120-degree angle signify something else? No physical or biological evidence exists for these claims.

Astrology rarely (some say never) has tested its own validity. Even Carl Jung, whom astrologers look to as a supporter, found his comparisons of horoscopes of couples inconclusive. Despite the stated claims by astrologers that valid testing has proved the truth of astrological principles, the only reports that have the stamp of objectivity are the studies of Michel and Françoise Gauquelin, and their methods have been questioned. Any association between the planets and people's careers is hardly larger than might occur by chance. Moreover, the Gauquelins clearly stated that their work did not confirm the tenets of astrology.

A most damaging argument against the validity of astrology arises from the placement of the zodiac signs according to writings codified by Ptolemy in the second century A.D. As mentioned before, a "wobble" in the earth's rotation has moved these star clusters into a different position than where they were almost twenty centuries earlier. This astronomical phenomenon, the "precession of the equinoxes," was first reported by Hipparchus in the second century B.C. The result is that the zodiac sign in front of which the sun has shone for thousands of years in the spring is not Aries, held by astrology to be the Sun-sign of persons born between March 21 and April 21, but instead actually Pisces. Thus someone born on April 10 is not actually of Aries but rather of Pisces, two signs that could hardly be more dissimilar in symbolism. The same error exists for all the other zodiac signs; they are each about one sign away from the assignment made in astrology. All of the horoscope delineations using the traditional Sun-sign and ascendant sign positions are therefore false.

There are so many features on a horoscope chart that virtually any combination of aspects and configurations can be found to conform to a person or event. Those characteristics that fit the person can be selected while ignoring or reformulating the inappropriate features. Further, astrologers can and do reinterpret their charts if subsequent happenings are not in keeping with the original evaluation. If five out of ten predictions come true, the gullible think that they have witnessed extraordinarily successful predictions. Yet, guesswork might come up with the same percentage. Actually, astrological predictions are often correct fewer than fifty percent of the time. It is the one or two successful ones that create a stir.

The possible social harm of astrology is twofold. In the first place, the astrologer may not be competent to detect a disturbance in a client and may give advice contrary to the actual psychological needs. Astrologers are not trained to be psychological advisers. There is also the danger that the irrational in a person may be unwittingly intensified.

But there is another harm to society. The beliefs engendered by occult practices draw people away from rational, critical thinking. It is this same kind of mystical association that led in the past to belief in witches, accompanying mass hysteria, and the resultant persecutions and burnings. Thus astrology is psychologically dangerous and socially harmful.

For these and other reasons critics scoff at astrology's pretensions to scientific standing, and virtually no modern astronomers subscribe to astrology. Its theories and laws are occult and metaphysical. Astrologers employ numbers, but they resemble the medieval activity of estimating the number of angels that can stand on the head of a pin, not the mathematical uses of science. Astrology relies on belief—even against reason—rather than reevaluation, experimental analyses, and abandoning unsubstantiated doctrine, all of which are the methods of rational science. Scientific facts and theories are subject to possible disproof. The focus in science is always on discovering whether conclusions are incorrect. Such a critique is almost absent from astrology.

Rebuttals

For Astrology

Opponents of astrology are quick to accept the statements by Michel and Françoise Gauquelin that their results give no support to astrology, but the same antagonists refuse to acknowledge the findings by the Gauquelins when they seem to confirm relationships of Mars and Jupiter with the choice of careers. This type of evaluation by scientists is highly prejudicial—accepting only those results that fit set opinions but rejecting the same data when they are contrary.

The correlations between planetary sky positions and careers are shown to be statistically correct through the rigorous, unbiased testings of the Gauquelins. Whatever may be the extent of these associations, their significance is even higher than appears, for many people are in careers that they are not suited for. Choice is the result of ability, circumstance, and competing motivations. Therefore, any correlation at all that is greater than chance is even more important than is shown in the figures.

Against Astrology

The methods of the Gauquelins in which they compare the configurations in the sky at birth with the subsequent careers of the people studied are seriously flawed in design. But even if their results were statistically accurate, the correlations between the sky and the careers are so

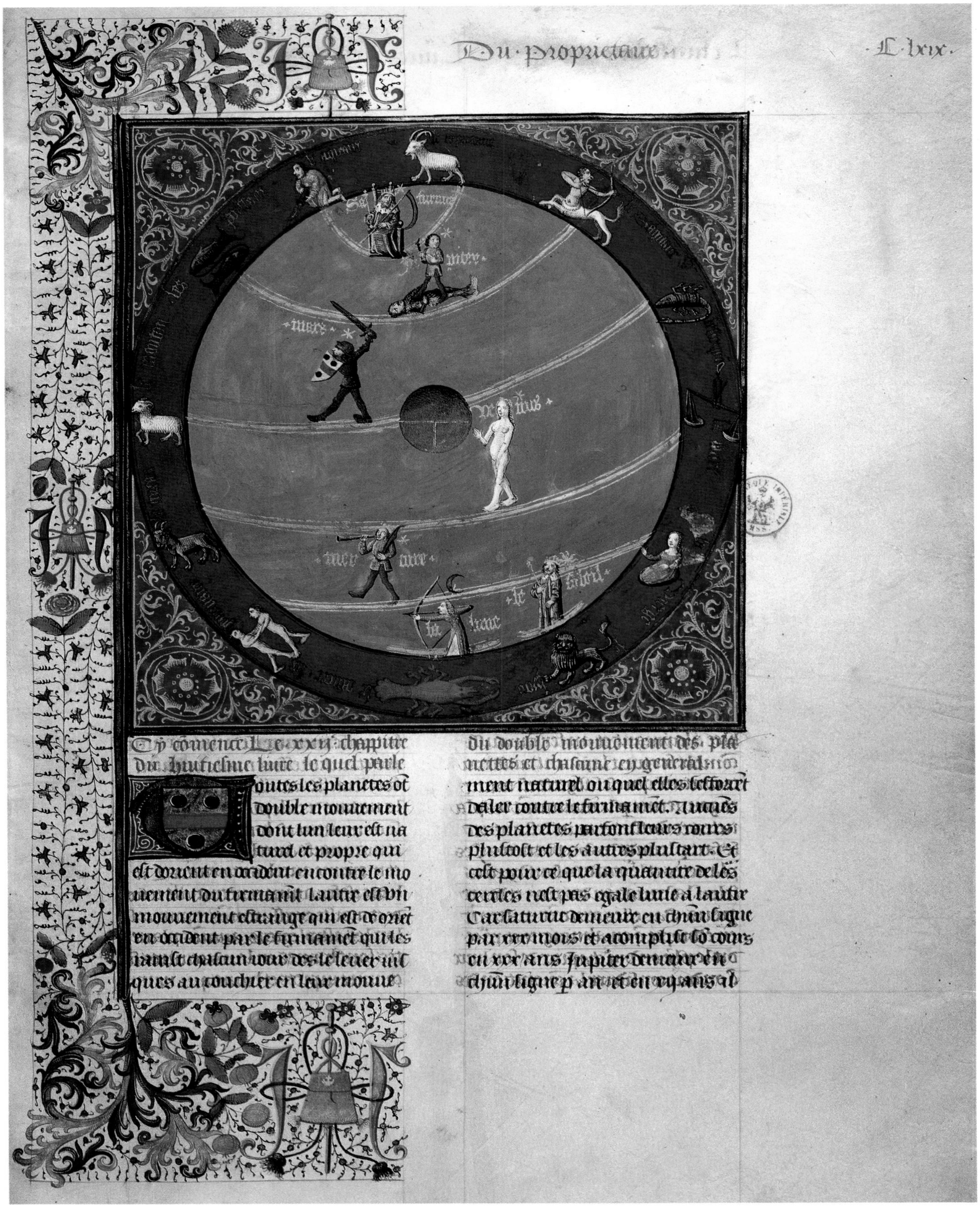

A page from the fifteenth-century French manuscript *Liber de Proprieratibus* by Bartholomeus Anglicus, depicting personifications of the twelve zodiac signs and their rulers, the seven known planets. Evard d'Espinques. Illumination on vellum, 20 × 11″. Bibliothèque Nationale, Paris.

relatively small that they give astrology no confirmation. The investigators themselves, who maintain that their studies and their mathematics are statistically valid, found no support for the teachings of astrology.

Conclusion

We end on the same note that we sounded at the beginning of this chapter. Astrological principles and practices have been followed for thousands of years. At the same time, strong objections to their validity and usefulness are held by virtually the entire scientific community. This presentation is but a brief summary of the history, apparatus, and attitudes of astrology and astrologers as a subject of widespread interest in almost all countries of the world.

Numerology

Numerology

Number marks the time and day,
It counts my wealth and age,
It tells my speed, my height and weight,
Number is my gauge.

The basis of numerology is the reduction of a person's date of birth and name to a single whole numbers, which represent particular qualities. By understanding the inner meanings of the numbers the numerologist can describe a person's character and thereby suggest the likely future course of the person's life.

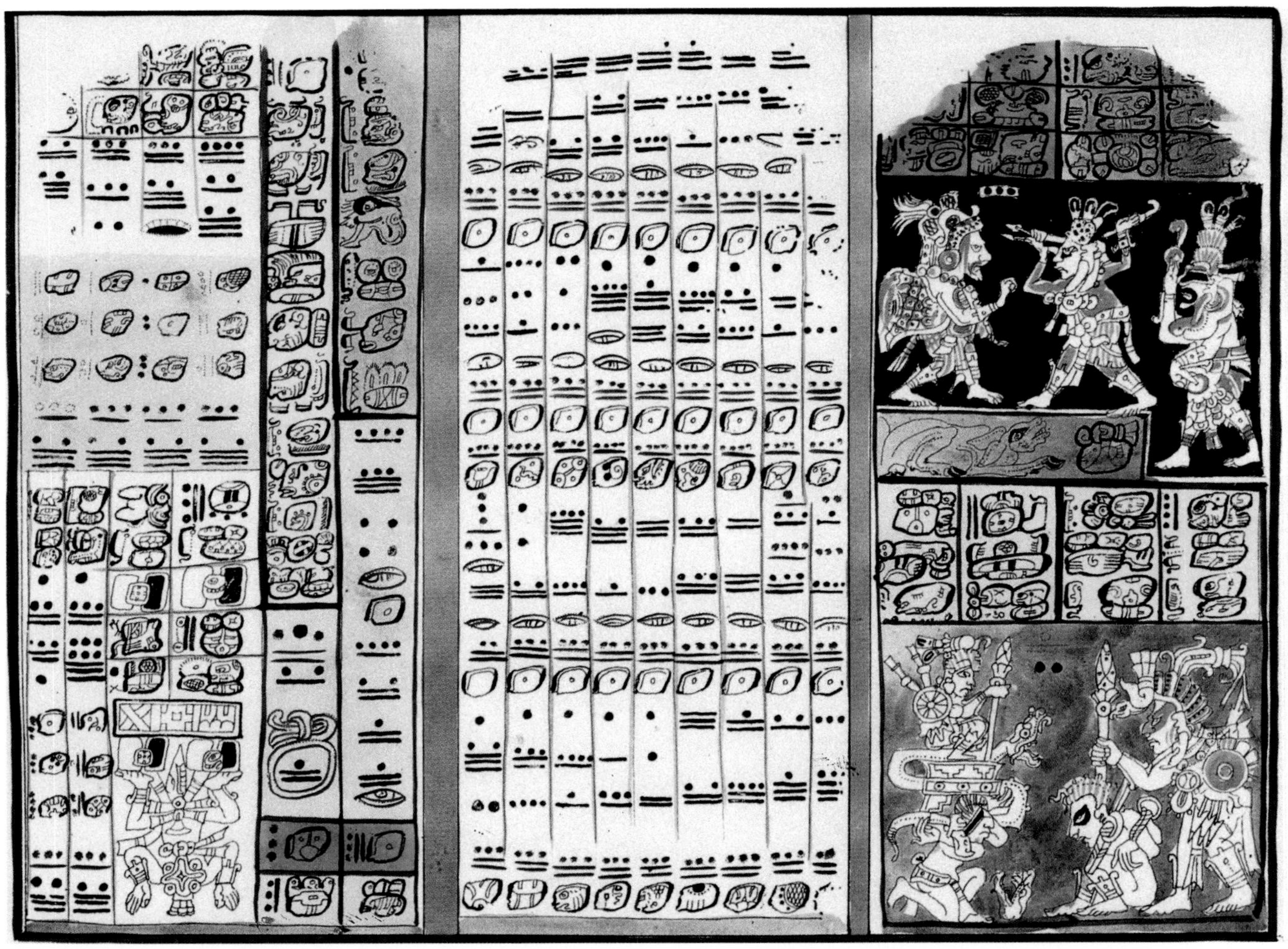

ABOVE: Numerical notations from the Pre-Columbian Dresden Codex, c. A.D. 1100. The Mayans used a zero in their mathematical system, well before the West received the concept from India.

OPPOSITE: A Sumerian tablet in cuneiform writing recording the distribution of rations. 2040 B.C. Library of Congress, Washington, D.C.

History

Modern numerology is a composite of contributions from ancient Babylonia, the teachings of Pythagoras and his disciples in sixth-century B.C. Greece, astrological philosophy from Hellenistic Alexandria, early Christian mysticism, the occultism of the medieval Gnostics, and the belief systems of adherents to the cabala in the late Middle Ages.

Throughout history numbers have been used in various ways. They were developed early for counting and measuring things. In ancient Egypt, the enumeration of objects and the construction of buildings necessitated a counting system, and artifacts indicate that the number of assembled humans or animals could be recorded early. Some scholars believe this capability was a demonstration of the beginning of abstract number concepts.

CLOCKWISE FROM TOP LEFT: Boethius, Plato, Pythagoras, and Nicomachus from a twelfth-century manuscript of Boethius's *De Arithmetica de Musica.* The four philosophers are seen showing relationships between mathematics and sound and harmony. Vellum, 11½ × 8″. Syndics of Cambridge University Library.

Distinctly abstract concepts of counting and mathematics were very much in evidence in ancient Mesopotamia, especially Babylonia. From 2000 B.C. to 1200 B.C., sophisticated, precise calculations involving a kind of algebra were developed. Their sexigesimal mathematics, with six and multiples of six as the base, gave us our sixty-second, sixty-minute clock, to use only one example. The Babylonians could manipulate numbers by methods that even resemble the modern system of quadratic equations. However, these processes were in essence a computational arithmetic.

The Babylonians attached to some numerals special meanings, which were the forerunners of the mystical attributions later given to numbers in sixth-century B.C. Greece. Numbers that were divisible into whole numbers by many other numbers were believed to have magical powers—as for instance the number twelve, which can be divided by one, two, three, four, and six. Yet the introduction of this type of abstract numerical magic contained only the glimmerings of a philosophy of numbers. The principal Babylonian connection to occult numerology was through astrological practices transmitted to the West, in which such concepts as the twelve divisions of the zodiac, the seven planets, and other numerical associations had special significance.

Pythagoras

It was in Greece in the sixth century B.C. that the principal ideas of mystical numerology began. The philosopher Pythagoras and his disciples saw numbers as the foundation not only of the world but also of the actual cosmos itself. In an admixture of geometry, arithmetic, religion, and philosophy, Pythagorean principles held that all things, ideas, and feelings are fundamentally related to the first ten numbers.

What is known of Pythagoras has been gleaned from writings by his disciples and later commentators. He is supposed to have traveled to Mesopotamia and Egypt, where he acquired some of his ideas. But so fragmentary is the biographical information and so eager were the Greeks of that time to attribute their intellectual origins to the East, that few firm facts can be established. Even Aristotle, who was writing less than a hundred years after Pythagoras's death, used the term "so-called Pythagoreans" to describe his predecessor's followers. Evidently Pythagoras was born on the island of Samos in the Aegean Sea, promulgated and taught a philosophy, fell out with the local ruler, and fled to Crotona on the southern coast of Italy. There he founded a mystical brotherhood, exercised considerable influence

Orpheus playing his lyre. The perfection of Orpheus's harmonies was considered to have spiritual and healing values by the Pythagoreans. Bronze Etruscan mirror. Fourth century B.C. Museum of Fine Arts, Boston. Francis Barlett Fund.

under the patronage of the ruler, but was forced to flee once again during a period of political turmoil, presumably ending his days in Metapontum, much farther east on the Italian coast. The teachings of the Pythagoreans may have been partly responsible for their changes in fortune both on Samos and in Crotona, but it is just as probable that purely political involvements were the significant cause.

What were the doctrines of Pythagoras and his followers that had such profound effect on later philosophies, medicine, and mathematics? They may be summarized under four main headings: numbers, the soul, ethics, and ritual.

1. Numbers. The Pythagorean axiom was "number is all"—in substance as well as symbol. Of course this attempt to find a single origin for all life resembles the teachings of philosophers before and after Pythagoras. The sixth-century B.C. Greek philosopher Thales of Miletus considered water to be the fundamental element in all things. Others saw the universe as composed essentially of fire, air, or indivisible particles. Today's scientific thinking places energy at the core. To Pythagoras all aspects of nature revealed numerical relationships. Legend has it that his ideas were inspired by the sounds he heard plucked on strings. He observed that octaves, fifths, and fourths in music could be defined by numerical relationships, and he postulated that every sphere in the universe revolves around a central fire, each at its own velocity and distance from the earth, producing sounds in harmony, or what he called the "music of the spheres." He also concluded that a person's character and actions could be attributed to numbers representing the mind, marriage, justice, and other abstractions and that odd and even numerals mirror the paired opposites of nature in balance—a duality similar to the yang and yin of Chinese philosophy.

Pythagorean mathematics was based on geometry. A *point,* (expressed as 1) flows into *line* (2), which sweeps into a *plane,* or *surface* (3); this in turn becomes a *solid* (4). The sacred oath of the secret society of the Pythagorean brotherhood was made on the tetractys—a geometric figure produced by pebbles laid in a triangular shape: ten stones are laid in four rows, with four at the base (∴̈). From this configuration were derived other designs involving more

OPPOSITE: Pythagoras (left center) and members of the School of Athens, including the Muslim philosopher Averroes, are shown presumably calculating or philosophizing on the universe. Raphael. *School of Athens* (detail). 1510–1511. Fresco. Stanza della Segnatura, Vatican, Rome.

RIGHT: Two Roman ivory counters showing Roman numerals VII (thumb and two fingers) and VI (thumb and one finger). First century A.D. Diameter 1″. British Museum, London.

pebbles and further relationships among numbers. When a triangle was drawn whose sides were in a special association, the Pythagorean theorem resulted: the sum of the squares of the sides of a right-angled triangle equals the square of the hypotenuse (the diagonal). This relationship was considered an essential truth; proof of the enduring, fundamental power of numbers. Many other mathematical and geometric connections were also part of Pythagorean teaching, which focused especially on the proportions of triangles, circles, solids, and rectilinear forms. The six-pointed star of interlocking triangles (✡) was the symbol used by the members of the brotherhood for identification.

2. *The Soul.* Pythagorean theory also suggested that each living creature has a soul, which comes from and is attuned to the stars. The soul of one person can transmigrate into the living body of another (metempsychosis) and can be released from the flesh (a type of reincarnation).

3. *Ethics.* Pythagoreans established an ethical system, complete with prohibitions. For example, no blood should ever be shed, and no flesh should be eaten. The reasons for the interdiction by the brotherhood of some foods and practices are not well understood, but physical and spiritual health was a goal to be sought diligently. Music was one of their methods of healing. It may be that the concept of "critical days" in later Greek and medieval medicine came from Pythagorean ideas, as did the idea that certain numbered days in a period of illness mark the time of crisis.

4. *Ritual.* A panoply of rites and rituals evidently occupied the Pythagoreans. The disciples continued the principles and practices after Pythagoras. It was through their writings that Plato later was exposed to the doctrines.

Two different streams of followers developed after Pythagoras's death: the Acusmatici, who emphasized the behavior and ethics inherent in the philosophy; and the Mathematici, who were chiefly concerned with geometry, music, and astronomy. Although their focuses were different, both groups adhered to the same basic doctrines. The Pythagorean brotherhood virtually disappeared at the end of the fourth century B.C., but its influence was present in later philosophies and mathematical systems. During the fourth century B.C., Euclid's mathematical theories demonstrated significant similarities to the geometric conclusions of the Pythagoreans, but it was Plato (c. 428–348 B.C.), among the post-Pythagorean philosophers, whose ideas most closely resembled Pythagorean mysticism.

Plato

Plato founded the Academy, whose members debated virtually all intellectual subjects, including politics, science, and religion. The study of numbers was one of the primary topics—especially numerical representations of abstract qualities such as beauty and truth. Like Pythagoras, Plato believed that numbers—and also ideas—exist as entities by themselves. Humans may discover or observe them but they do not originate or invent them. The Platonists believed that all properties and qualities (for instance, colors, tastes, and sounds) are received by the senses, but numbers could only be perceived by meditation and mental processes and therefore exist independently.

Rome

In the last centuries of the Roman Empire numerous religious and philosophical systems were permeated with Pythagorean teachings. Priestly functions commonly included astronomical, astrological, and predictive activities, each of which placed great emphasis on numbers. One of the highly influential Neo-Pythagoreans, the first-century A.D. Roman encyclopedist and supporter of astrology Nigidus Figulus, elaborated on the spiritual aspects of numerology. Plutarch also endorsed Pythagoreanism. Much of the writings in subsequent centuries on numbers as mystical symbols relied on a basic treatise in Greek, the second-century A.D. *Introduction to Arithmetic,* in which the Neo-Pythagorean Nicomachus classified the nature of numbers and their relationships.

Early Christian Era

Early Christian sects embraced both astrology and numerology in various ways. To the Gnostics, whose influence lasted several centuries, specific numbers were part of the makeup of the cosmos. Simon Magus, the purported originator of the movement at the time of Jesus, accented the linkage between numbers and mysticism. For instance, the 12 zodiac signs were considered to be symbolic of evil; the 36 *decans*, a counterbalance of good; the 7 planets controlled fate; there were 7 spiritual fundamentals; the year's 365 days were composed of 12 months of 30 days each plus 5 inserted mystical days, in keeping with the 5 planets remaining after subtracting the 2 luminaries of Sun and Moon.

Another of the early Christian sects, the Manichaeans—an offshoot of the Persian Zoroastrians—gave special attention to the number 2, which to them symbolized the presence of two distinct godheads, one presiding over light and one over darkness. Five was also a sacred number. Thus the various sects saw numbers as the basis and the actuality of existence. In medieval Europe, these schemas of the universe were incorporated into some of the doctrines of the cabala, the Hebrew occult system of the late Middle Ages.

The early Church fathers strongly opposed and condemned the teachings of the Christian Gnostics and the other quasi-religious and philosophical sects. However, the principle that numbers have spiritual significance was accepted rather than challenged.

The works of Philo Judaeus (c.30 B.C.–A.D. 40), a devout Jew who analyzed numerical implications in the Scriptures, served as a standard for later treatises by Church leaders. He found numerical significance in line after line of his interpretations of the Bible. Philo thus was one of the earliest Neoplatonists of the Christian Era.

By the second century A.D., attaching numbers from 1 to 10 to letters in Hebrew, Greek, and Roman alphabets had come into vogue as an expression of mystical meanings. The assignment of number values to letters, names, and words was followed from then until contemporary times. This numerological process is now called "gematria." Although the name-number methodology began in Alexandria, it became widespread, and many Neoplatonists, such as Iamblichus of fourth-century Syria, propagated combinations of Pythagoreanism, Platonism, and the mystical numeration of names. Many made use of passages in the Bible to affirm the importance that God gave to the numbers of things: number of commandments, plagues, psalms, and days of the Flood and of Creation.

Saint Augustine (A.D. 353–420), through his personal conduct and theological reasoning, became the Church's model of a person who traveled the path from heresy to orthodoxy. In his influential writings he wrote that numbers are the universal language offered by the deity to humans, a confirmation of the truth of Christian teachings. Just as the Pythagoreans had proposed, Augustine too believed that everything has numerical relationships; it is up to the mind itself to seek and penetrate their mysteries or else to have them revealed by divine grace. Augustine's reverential attitude toward numbers lent his imprimatur to numerology as an acceptable aid to interpreting the sacred writings. He and other church fathers drew upon pagan methodology but Christianized the meanings.

After Saint Augustine, numerological scrutiny of the Scriptures, especially the New Testament, maintained this "transcendental arithmetic." Numbers such as 3 (the Trinity) and 12 (the apostles) assumed special significance. Saint Isadore of Seville (570–636) compiled a dictionary of the numbers that appear directly or indirectly in the Hebrew and Christian bibles. Saint Thomas Aquinas (1225–1274) derived concepts about numbers from Aristotle, and Dante Alighieri (1265–1321) in his *Divine Comedy* made numerous references to the mystical meanings of specific numerals.

Islam

When Islam spread throughout the Middle East, Africa, and Spain, Greek mathematics, including geometry, was maintained, investigated, and ultimately retransmitted to the West. The word *algebra* is said to have come from the Arabic treatise *Al-jabr w'al muqabalah.* The written symbols for numbers used over much of the world are called "Arabic numerals." The Arabs apparently introduced the zero (*sifr* in Arabic), although others claim that it began in India first. The mystical teachings of Pythagoreanism also appeared in Arabic writings, and particular emphasis was

A medieval translation into Latin of Arabic numerals used in a calculation. Princeton University Library, Princeton.

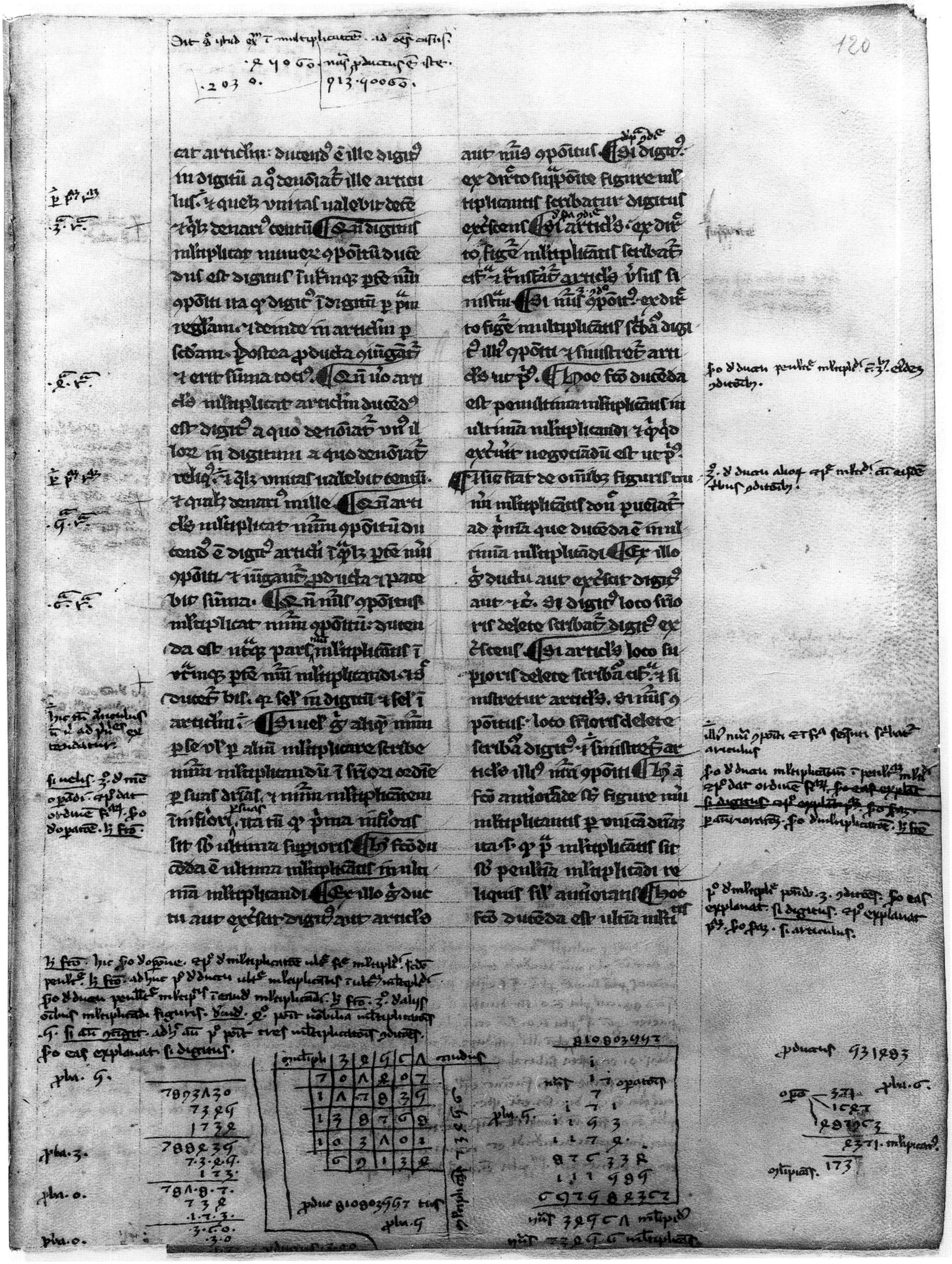

A thirteenth-century mathematical table from an Armenian manuscript. Walters Art Gallery, Baltimore.

given to specific numerals (notably seven) in ceremonies, myths, and literature. The numbers ten and twelve were also held to be lucky. For instance, the circumstances of the birth of Suleiman the Magnificent, ruler of the Ottoman Empire, were considered highly auspicious, for he was the tenth descendant of Osman, founder of the dynasty, and took office in the tenth century after the flight of Mohammed. That he became the twelfth sultan was an additional sign of his good fortune.

Although scholars differ on the precise line of bequest, the numerology of the followers of the legendary al-Geber, looked upon as the founder of the alchemy of Islam, had derivations from Pythagorean, Platonic, and Aristotelian writings. For example, number seventeen, to which the Pythagoreans gave special significance, was at the very basis of all Geberian alchemy, indicating the equilibrium in nature. It may also be mentioned that the Greek alphabet has seventeen consonants and seven vowels (another highly valued number in Pythagorean numerical philosophy).

The Reformation

By the time of the Protestant Reformation in the sixteenth century, the principal tenets of numerology were for the most part in place, and the secular arithmetic of computation, geometry, and algebra were still not widely seen as disciplines separate from the use of numerals for mystical purposes. John Napier (1550–1617), for example, a Scottish mathematician who invented logarithms and was an innovator in the use of the decimal system, also practiced the gematrial methods of linking occult meanings to numbers and names. His numerological studies determined that the pope was an Antichrist—a type of intellectual exercise that was much in favor. The Revelation of Saint John, a New Testament book, referred to 666 as the "number of that man" who was the Satanic Beast. Protestant and Catholic numerologists competed in deriving the dreaded number from the names of leaders of the opposing church. The projected date of the end of the world (Napier believed it was to be sometime between 1688 and 1700) was supposed to coincide with the reappearance of Jesus after the Antichrist had been destroyed.

The Renaissance

Attacks on some of the occult systems occurred during the Renaissance. Galileo, for instance, after being interested at first in astrology abandoned it completely. There is no evidence that he concerned himself at all with numerology. Giordano Bruno (1548–1600), a Churchman, is often cited as another who turned his back on the occult. Yet Bruno's numerology was based on pure Pythagorean mysticism, not on the Christian methods of reading significance into numbers in the Scriptures, as Augustine, Aquinas, and other Church fathers had done.

From time to time, reactions to occult numerology,

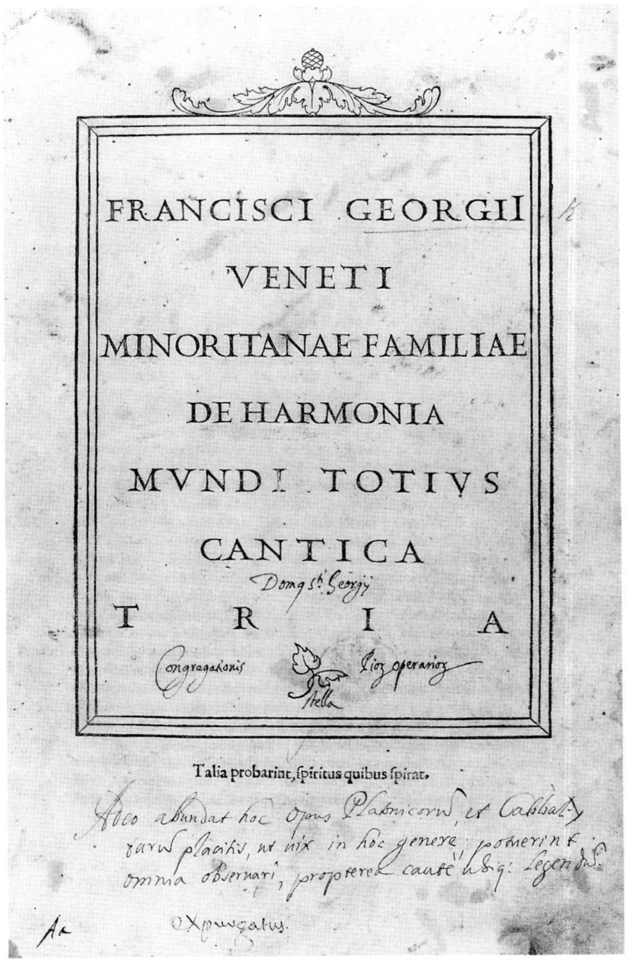

Title page from the Neo-Platonist *De Harmonia Mundi*, by Francesco Giorgi, 1525. The Venetian author of this cabalistic document emphasized the harmonies to be found in the universe. Church censors noted on the title page that the book was to be read with caution. BELOW: a French translation (1578) of the same manuscript in which the numerological associations of the heavens, the sky, and the earth are described. The British Library, London.

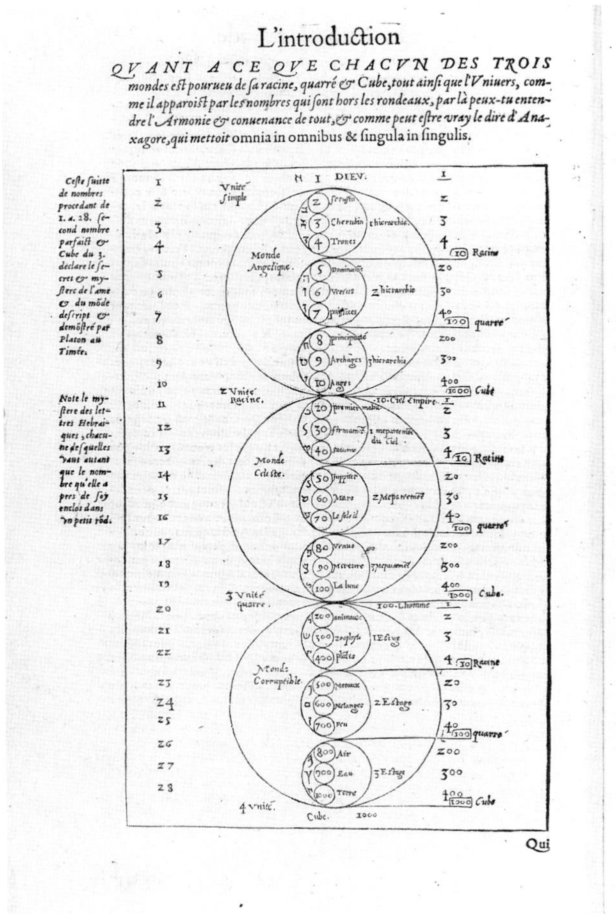

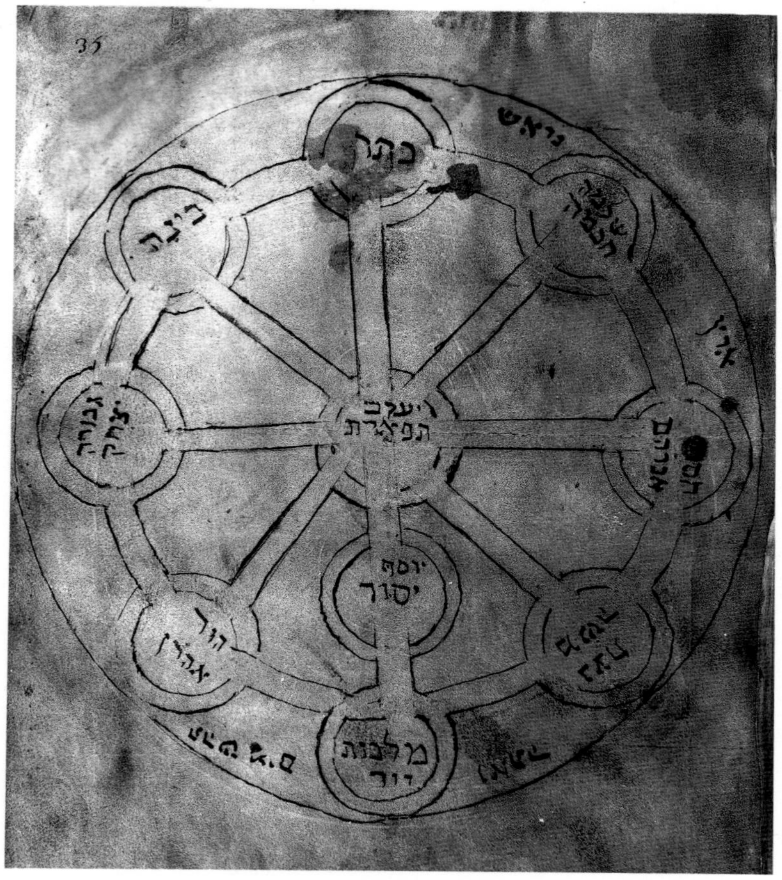

A circular scheme of the cabala from a medieval Hebrew manuscript. Bibliothèque Nationale, Paris.

Title page of *Doctor Faustus* by Christopher Marlowe (1620), showing the magician Dr. Faustus within a magical circle with symbols of the zodiac signs and planets and discoursing with the devil. The British Library, London.

both on the Continent and in England, brought into disfavor some highly placed persons who had dabbled in astrology and mysticism. Mostly the oppositions to occult practices in royal courts were responses to unfavorable predictions, charges of undue influence on the monarch by the practitioners, or accusations of communication with the devil.

The Cabala

Significant developments in numerological doctrines came from the cabala. The cabala is a complex, highly developed system of philosophy and theology. It has a long history involving many commentators. The actual dates of cabalism as a developed methodology are uncertain. Some claim that the core philosophy is in the Hebrew biblical books themselves, especially Prophets (Nebhium), Writings (Kehubim), and even the Torah (the five books of Moses in the Old Testament). The angels transmitted the words of God to Adam; he to Noah; thence to Abraham, to Moses, and to all humankind.

The cabala was formed from several intellectual approaches, of which the most prominent were Gnosticism and Neoplatonism. All three seek to reach God through intellectual probings, although the deity is considered to be unknowable and even unimaginable. One of the ancient precursors of the cabala was Jewish mysticism of the first and second centuries. During the Renaissance, elements of Gnosticism, Neoplatonism, Neopythagoreanism, Hebrew cabalism, and Hermeticism (the secret mystical teachings believed to have been composed and transmitted by the ancient occultist Hermes Trismegistus) were combined into a Christian cabalism.

The word *cabala,* based on the Hebrew *quibbel,* meaning to "receive," signifies doctrines that have been handed down by oral tradition and later committed to writing. It assumes that in order to be comprehended guidance is required by enlightened teachers instructed in their secrets. The power of the cabala is to be used only for achieving understanding of the godhead and for personal betterment—not for magical, destructive, or selfish purposes. Of course, various magicians and adepts have claimed to draw upon its secrets to perform miraculous feats. The legendary tale of the Golem, a statue, is one of those stories. The Golem was built by a learned rabbi of a small, Jewish village in the Middle Ages. He infused it with temporary life through occult symbols from the cabala in order to smite the persecuting local Christian rulers and thereby deliver the oppressed community.

The features of the cabala that pertain to numerology include the ten nodes of the Tree of Life, the twenty-two paths connecting them, and the esoteric meanings of the Hebrew alphabet. The system stimulated numerous commentaries, but the three fundamental works are the *Sepher Yetzirah* (Book of Creation, or Book of Formation),

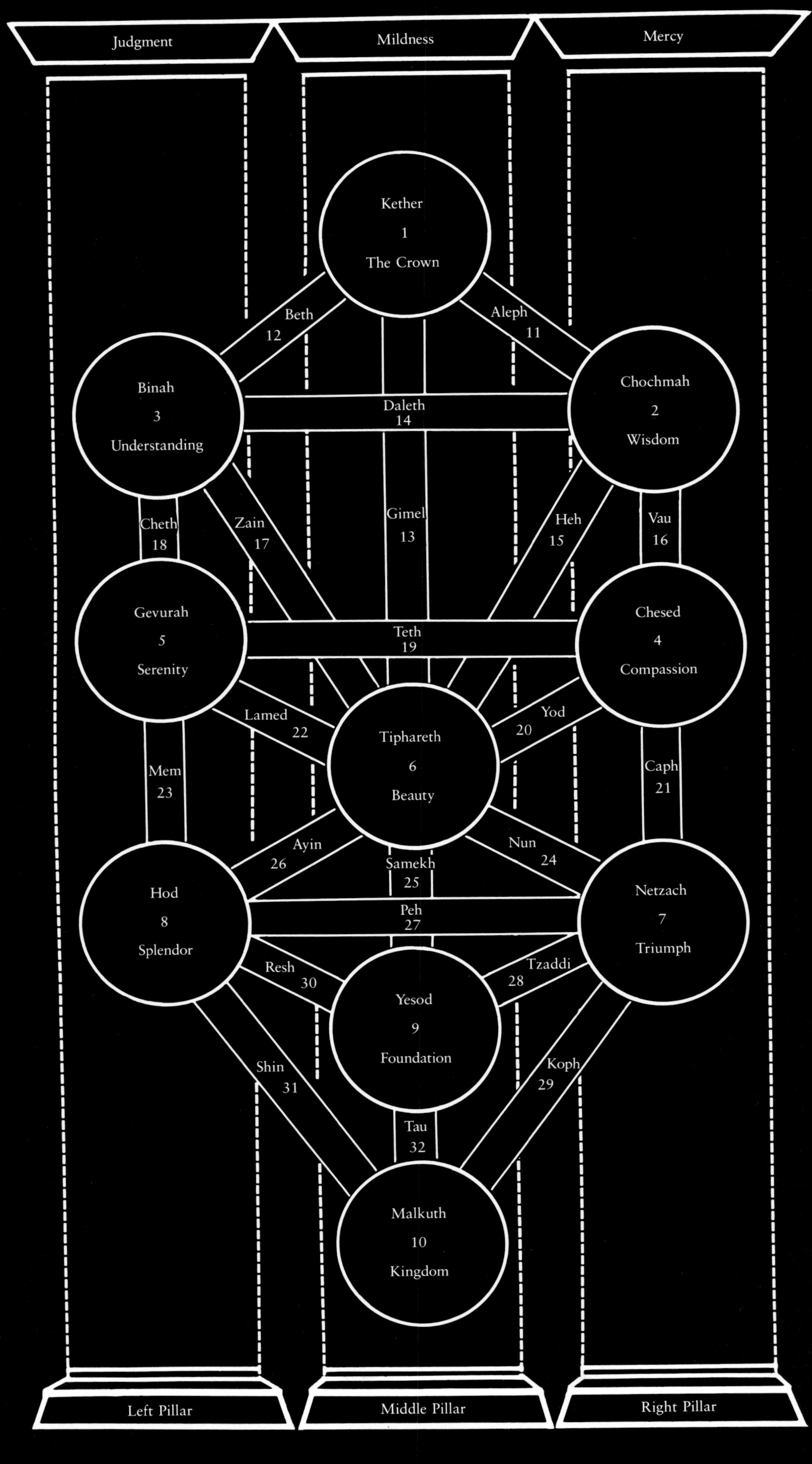

Sephiroth Tree (Cabala)

the *Sepher Bahir* (Book of Clarity), and the *Zohar* (Book of Splendor or Brightness).

The *Sepher Yetzirah* was written down between the third century and the sixth century A.D. Based on earlier Hebrew traditions, it links the creation of the universe, the Hebrew alphabet, and numerals, which are also Hebrew letters. All things—indeed the cosmos itself—are related to the first ten numbers. The Eternal One, "En Soph," indicates his existence by means of ten Sephiroth ("Emanations" or "Intelligences"). These ten, together with the twenty-two letters of the Hebrew alphabet, form thirty-two paths to wisdom. Some claim that the actual analysis of words and names through the assignment of numerical values and meanings to the letters may have begun in the second century A.D., but the precise origins are unresolved.

In the *Sepher Bahir,* written in southern France in the twelfth century, the Sephiroth are also referred to in terms of "Light." The arrangement of the ten Sephiroth and the twenty-two letters on the Tree of Life may have also begun in this treatise. The *Zohar* is probably the most influential of the basic works. Although legend had it that a mythical Simon ben Jochai wrote the text in the second century A.D., modern scholarship considers it a thirteenth-century compilation of the cabalistic philosophy of the time by one Moses de Leon.

The Tree of Life, which is detailed in the *Zohar,* is a diagram of ten stations or "nodes," the Sephiroth, which are usually represented as circles or spheres, connected to each other by twenty-two lines or roads, the "paths." Each of the ten Sephiroth (the singular word is *Sephirah*) is assigned a Hebrew letter, name, and number and stands for a specific moral concept. God is above and outside the Tree, the En Soph (the Boundless, the Eternal) from whom emanate the Sephiroth, beginning with the higher, spiritual attributes (starting at Kether, the Crown, number 1) and proceeding to the lower and more earthly (Malkuth, the Kingdom, number 10 at the bottom). By meditating on life's meanings, humans strive to ascend in graduated steps from the lowest Sephirah to the highest in an effort to comprehend the deity.

Faust in His Study. A magician, possibly Dr. Faustus, the archetypical magician and cabalist, pictured by Rembrandt in 1652, observing the image of magical symbols that he has conjured up. 1652. Etching on oatmeal paper. Museum of Fine Arts, Boston. Gift of Miss Ellen Bullard.

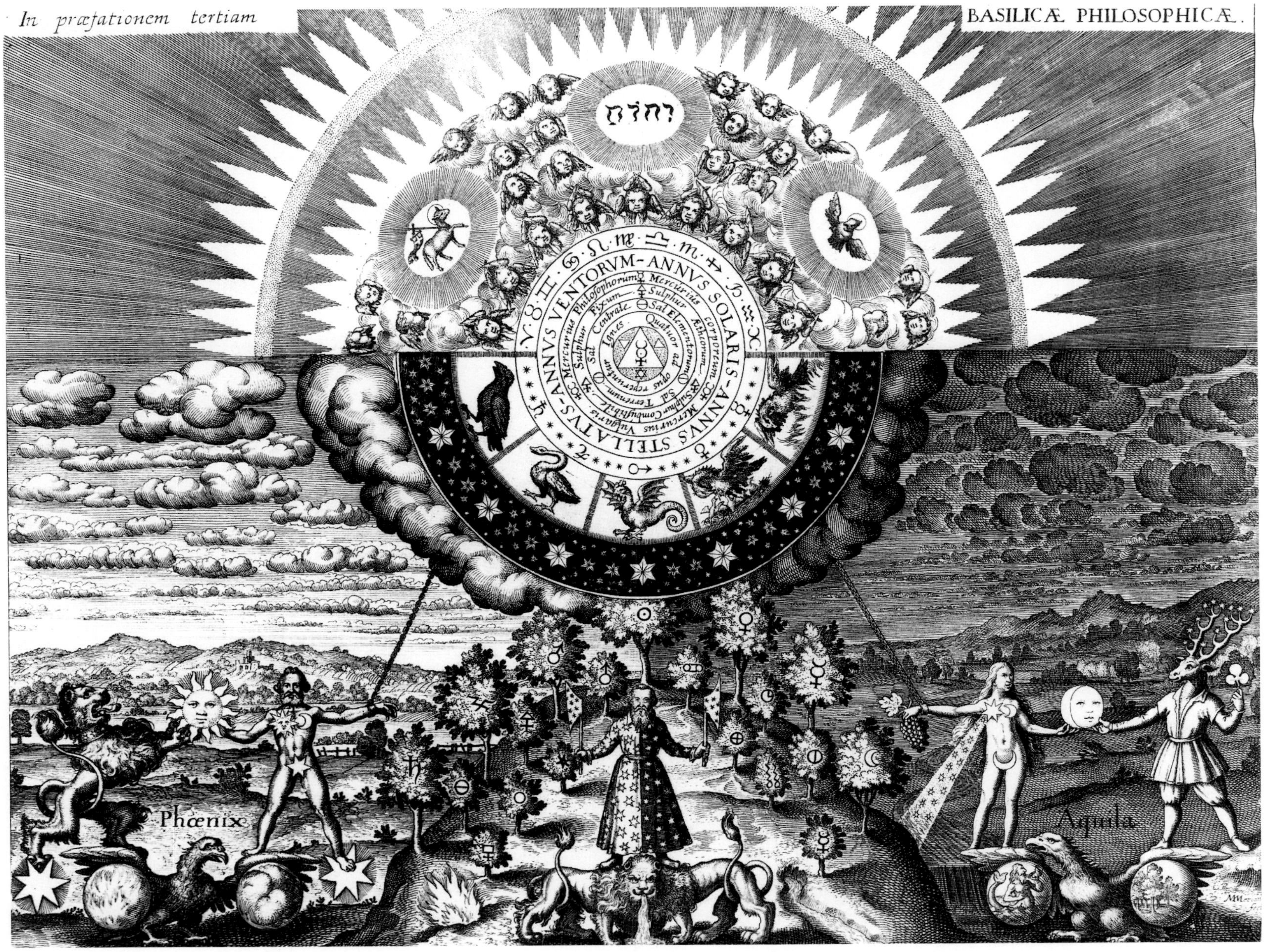

An allegory of the microcosm (the earth and its inhabitants) and the macrocosm (the cosmos), from Johann Mylius's *Opus Medico* (Frankfurt, 1618).

The twenty-two Paths between the Sephiroth are each assigned a number, from 11 to 32. The figures on the Tree resulting from these combinations have been classified in a variety of ways: in the vertical row of Sephiroth on the right, 2, 4, 7 are masculine and comprise the Pillar of Mercy, or Form; on the left, 3, 5, 8, are the feminine Pillar of Judgment, or Force; the middle four, 1, 6, 9, and 10 are the Pillar of Mildness.

The upper triangle formed by 1, 2, and 3 (Crown, Wisdom, and Intelligence) represents the Intellect; 4, 5, and 6 are Morality and Ethics; 7, 8, 9 are Materiality—with 10 as the bottom station, from which humans must start their ascent. The nodes and paths have also been apportioned among the three regions of the Soul (for the upper triangle), Mind (nodes 4, 5, 6, 7, 8), and Instincts (10). There are obvious associations between the structure of the cabala and other occult systems, such as the twenty-two cards of the Lesser Arcana.

The doctrines of the cabala have had significant connections to the contemplations of the Hasidic movement; from the sixteenth century until well into the eighteenth century, the cabala was also at the center of most forms of Jewish mystical thought.

Christian cabalism applied the Hebrew alphabet, through gematria (assigning esoteric meanings to numbers and letters) and other mystical doctrines from the cabala, to affirm Jesus as the Divine Son and representative of God on earth. The Renaissance period saw a special emphasis on cabalism in Florence, where a ruling prince, Cosimo de' Medici, even engaged Marsilio Ficino to translate a newly discovered cabalistic manuscript, the *Hermetica,* purported to have been written by Hermes Trismegistus. Giovanni Pico della Mirandola, the head of the Medici academy, found in the awesome tetragrammaton (the four Hebrew letters of the name of Jehovah), proof that Jesus was God. By adding to *Yod* (standing for Fire), *He* (for Water), *Vau*

I. SPIGEL DER KVNST VND NATVR.
NATVR
KVNST
Cabala vnd die Alchymei,
Geben dir die hochste artzney.
Dar Zu auch den weißen Stein,
In dem das fundament allein,
Ligt, wie fur augen zu sehn ist,
In disen figurn zu der frist.
Ach Gott hilf das wir danckbar sei,
Fur diese Gab so hoch vnd rein.
Wem du nun auf thuts hertz vnd sin,
Der da volkomen ist hierin.
Zu bereitten hie Dises Werck,
Dem sey gegeben alle Sterck.
PRIMA MATERIA.
VLTIMA MATERIA
HEISS
TRVCKEN
KALT
FEVCHT
T R I V
ZOT
L
PHILOSOPHIÆ
ERDT.
ASTRONOMIÆ.
WASER.
ALCHIMÆ.
LVFFT.
VIRTVTES.
FEVER.
SVLPHVR
WISMATT.
VITRIOL.
ANTIMONIVM.
Raphael Custodis. sculpsit.
Stephan Michelspacher Ex.

OPPOSITE: An illustration from the *Cabala, Speculum Artis* (Augsburg, 1658) by M. Michelspacher, containing pictorial examples of the four elements, alchemical processes, the cabala, and astrology. Wellcome Institute Library, London.

RIGHT: The celestial ladder depicted in Ramon Lull's *De Nova Logica* (1512). Lull was a prominent cabalist. This scene symbolizes the harmonious interrelationships of the world. The British Library, London.

BELOW: An illustration from *Liber de Gentili et Tribus Sapientibus* (1721–1742) by Ramon Lull, depicting a cabalistic complex of virtues, symbols, and philosophies of the past. The Warburg Institute, London.

(for Air), and *He* (for Earth), an additional Hebrew letter, *Shin,* to indicate the fifth element, Spirit, he derived the resulting name *YHSHVH,* spelled Jeheshua, the Hebrew for Jesus—God's presence on Earth.

In the subsequent decades and centuries, numerous commentators and translators added to the growing lore of the cabala. The abbot Johannes Trimethius, patron of Agrippa von Nettesheim (whose writings are discussed in the chapter on astrology) developed a lexicon of numerals and letters including their mystical meanings. John Dee, the influential mathematician, astrologer, and adviser to Queen Elizabeth I, also promoted the cabala. His significance in the history of numerology is that the course of his influence mirrored the changing fortunes of occultism. At first in high repute and a close favorite of the queen's, he later fell precipitously out of favor at the same time as occult systems began to be regarded as intellectually silly or diabolically unsavory. Today the word *cabal* has come to mean a secret group engaged in intrigue and conspiracy.

A particularly strong supporter of Christian cabalism, Robert Fludd, took the Hermetic writings, as resurrected by Cosimo de'Medici and others, at face value, thereby emphasizing a mysterious Egyptian connection. He also pictorialized a universe that could account for good and bad without having to implicate God as the creator of the evil. Johannes Kepler, the pioneering seventeenth-century astronomer, engaged in heated controversies with Fludd on cosmology and harmonics. Fludd supported occult uses of numbers as part of his philosophy. Kepler saw in numbers a distinction between their mathematical explanations of phenomena and their symbolism of abstract meanings, which he too believed in. Although they both relied heavily on the Bible for supporting evidence, Kepler concluded that the world was planned and constructed by God according to the measuring properties of numerals, whereas Fludd considered the entire composite of natural and supernatural things to be integrated through the mystery of numbers, a belief similar to that of the Pythagoreans.

A portrait of Robert Fludd, a highly influential physician and cabalist whose spiritual views clashed with Johannes Kepler's scientific thinking. From the *Philosophia Sacra et Vere Christiana Seu Metereologica Cosmica* (1626). Houghton Library, Harvard University, Cambridge, Massachusetts.

Later Centuries

Many commentators and adepts in the succeeding centuries used the Christian cabala in their applications of occult systems. Although numerology played a role in their concepts, it was not the primary focus. In the nineteenth and twentieth centuries there have been a host of occult writings in which number symbolism figures prominently; but the cabala and the tarot lie at the heart of those philosophies and practices. An example is the work of Alphonse Louis Constant (he even took on a Hebrew pseudonym, Eliphas Lèvi), who developed a grand schema of occultism embracing the cabala, tarot, astrology, and numerology. Among the founders of one occult group, the Golden Dawn, Westcott, Woodman, and Mathers interwove the gematria into their teachings, although it was not the primary focus. Aleister Crowley, the widely known leader of the order, entitled one of his books *777.* Yet number mysticism was more in service to, rather than in explanation of, the fundamental ideas of his theosophy. The tarot and the cabala, not numerology, were at the center of his principles.

Advocates of numerology in the twentieth century often combine the cabala, the tarot, and numerological practices, which modern occult writers see as intricately linked. To take only a few examples: Paul Foster Case makes connections between the Hebrew alphabet and tarot cards; Mouni Sadhu uses Hebrew letters, the tarot, and numerology for divination; Dion Fortune draws on the cabala and numerology in her philosophy; Robert Wang's main treatise considers together the tarot, cabala, and numerology; books by Richard Cavendish describe connections among virtually all the occult systems, of which numerology is one part. Although the original primordial numbers of Pythagoras have been modified in meaning and expanded in significance, the ancient Pythagorean number symbolism remains the essential frame of modern numerology.

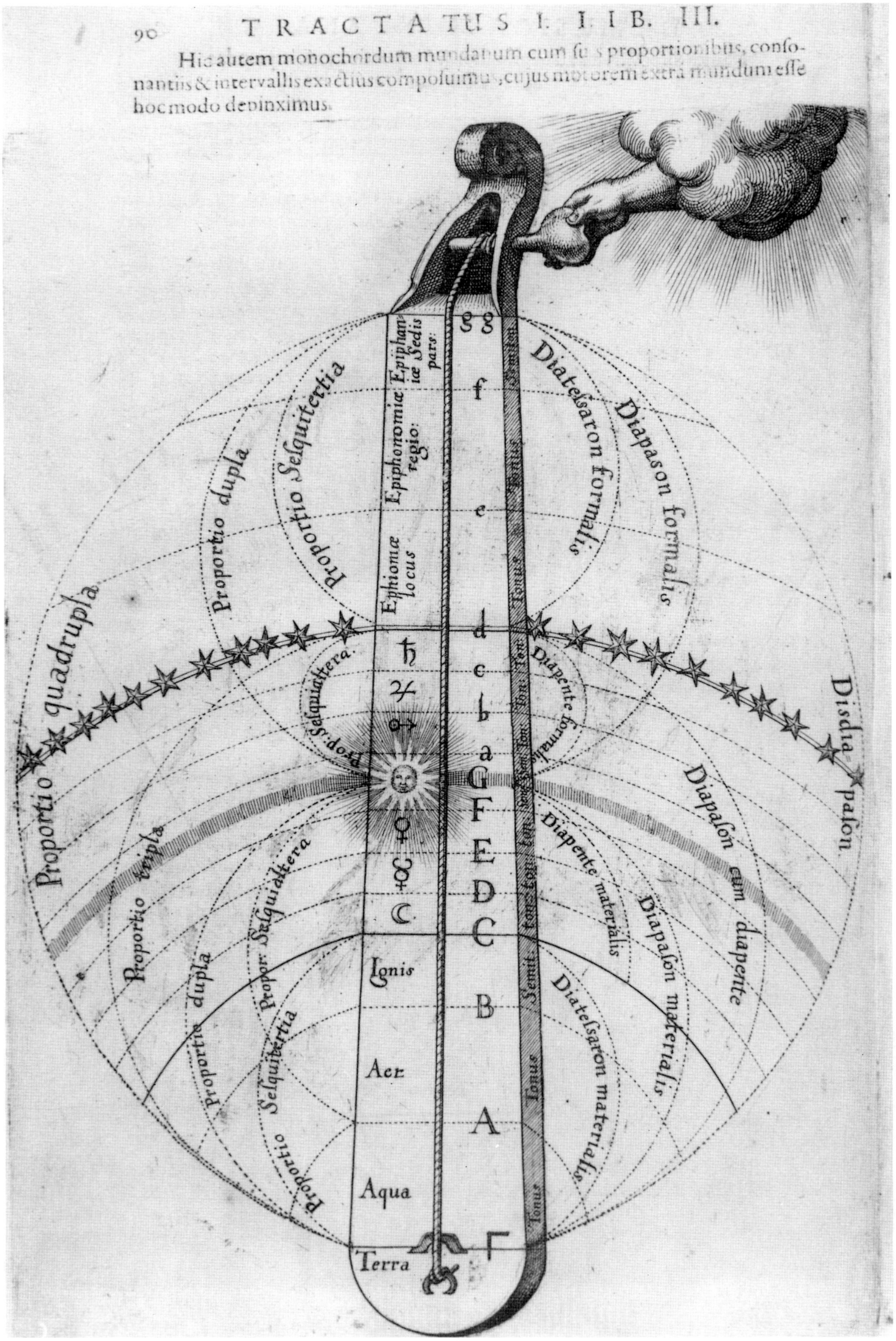

According to Robert Fludd, all planets, the sky, numbers, substances, letters, and humans were part of an ordained unitary harmony, a monochord. *Utriusque Cosmi.* c.1617. Department of Special Collections, Library, University of Chicago.

The association between the macrocosm (the universe) and the microcosm (the individual person). Title page of Robert Fludd's *Utriusque Cosmi*. Department of Special Collections, Library, University of Chicago.

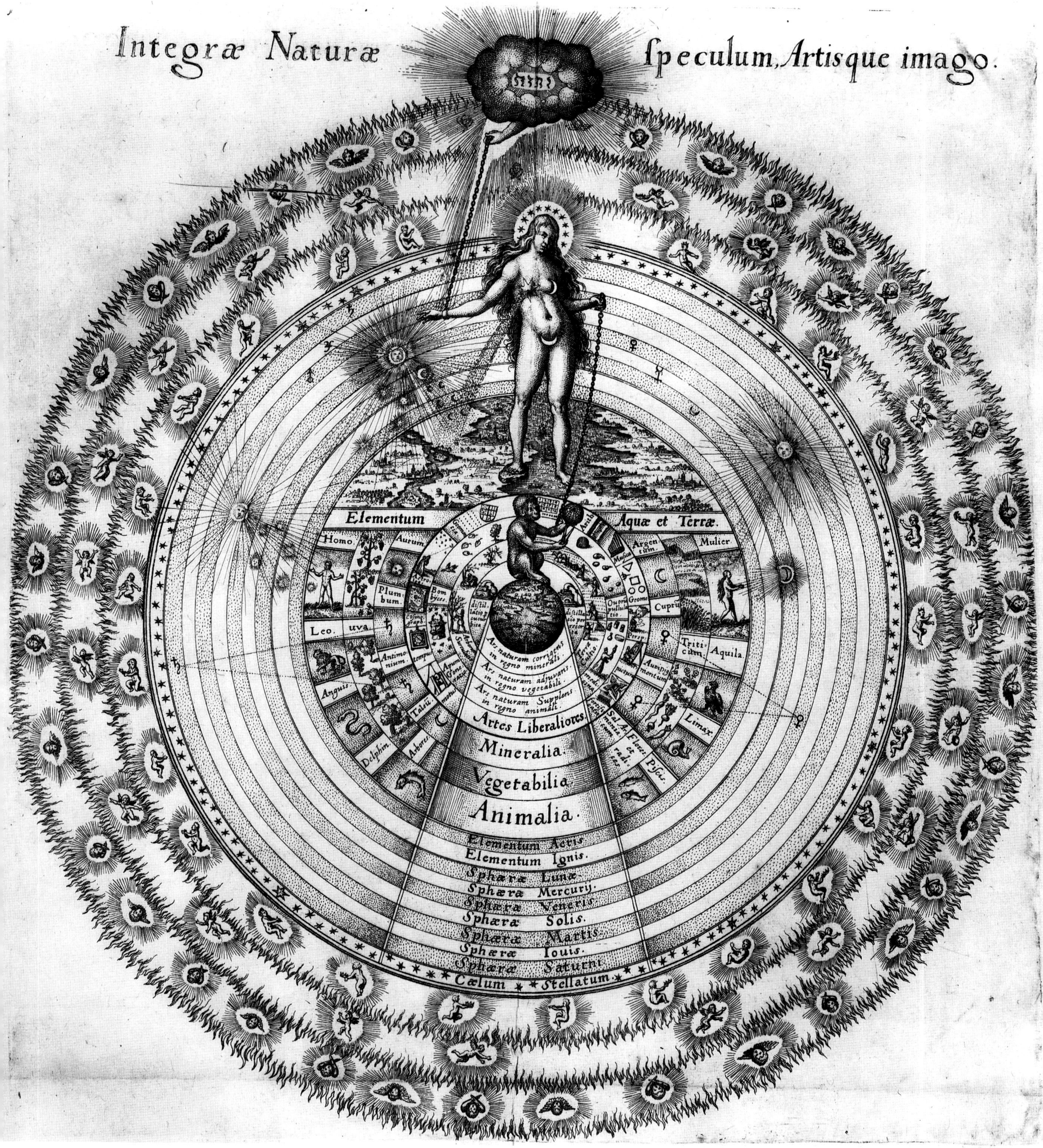

The universe according to Robert Fludd's *Utriusque Cosmi* (c.1617). The world of the elements separated from the heavens and the skies. God (symbolized by the Hebrew letters at the top) controls nature (the woman) who controls earth and people (the monkey). Houghton Library, Harvard University, Cambridge, Massachusetts.

Technique of Numerology

In numerology, the assignment of a number to any name, birthday, or date is arrived at by simple calculation.

The Birth Number is the sum of the position of the month in the annual calendar (January is 1, February is 2, etc.—for numbers above 10, the two digits are added together; 12 becomes 1 plus 2) plus the day of the month plus each digit in the date of the year (1945 becomes 1+9+4+5). Thus, a birthday of May 28, 1912, is computed as 5 (May)+2+8 (the 28th day)+1+9+1+2 (the year 1912). The total sum of that birth date is 28. Since all numbers in numerology, with a few exceptions, are reduced to a single digit between 1 and 9, the sum of 28 is computed as 2+8=10. Ten then becomes 1+0=1. The person born on May 28, 1912, therefore has a Birth Number of 1. (The exceptions to this final computation are master numbers, which have special significance in some systems and consequently are not reduced. The special numerals that are usually designated as masters are 11 and 22, sometimes 33, rarely 44, and a few others.)

Names are similarly put into numerals. For instance, in modern numerology each letter in Western languages such as English, French, German, Italian, Spanish, and the Scandinavian tongues is assigned a number according to its position in the alphabet. In English, the assignments are:

1	2	3	4	5	6	7	8	9
A	B	C	D	E	F	G	H	I
J	K	L	M	N	O	P	Q	R
S	T	U	V	W	X	Y	Z	

In the Spanish language, one method of assignment is:

1	2	3	4	5	6	7	8	9	
A	B	C	D	E	F	G	H	I	
J		L	M	N	O	P	Q	R	
S	T	U	V		X	Y	Z		(and RR)
	CH				LL				

For Italian:

1	2	3	4	5	6	7	8	9
A	B	C	D	E	F	G	H	I
		L	M	N	O	P	Q	R
S	T	U	V				Z	

Every person is named at birth. He or she therefore has a particular number personality. However, the person may change names and become clothed in different numbers at different times. For instance, after marriage, the new last name may be substituted for the maiden name, or both may be used. The letters in the various names may add up to quite different numbers for the same person. Each of us therefore may be a multiple numerological personality. For example, Henry Cabot Lodge by numerological computation was a 7. However, if he were known as Henry Lodge, with his middle name eliminated completely, then the letters would add up to 59, which is adjusted to 14 and then to 5.

Of course, the Birth Number, sometimes also referred to as the Life Path, Path of Destiny, or the Personal Lesson number, always remains the same, for it is the sum of all the numbers in one's date of birth.

Number One

To numerologists, number 1 contains the characteristics of a leader. As a superachiever, 1 may be compensating for deep-seated uncertainty. Reluctant to seem weak and wavering, a person whose Birth Number is 1 can be afraid that a compromise would appear to be weakness or a defect in the self-image of strength and decisiveness. When leadership is recognized by others, number 1 can be generous but, when challenged or rejected, can become domineering, unreasonable, irascible, or else withdrawn, unsociable, and moody. This number does best when acting alone even if positioned at the forefront of the crowd.

Although potentially a constructive originator, 1 must guard against foolish schemes and narrow vision. Advanced ideas can conflict with accepted conventions. Number 1 should ride freely on the positive traits while always guarding against exaggerations.

BACKGROUND NOTES

The Pythagoreans saw the number 1 as representing the unity of all, the godly spirit in everything. It was the active essence—as contrasted with the passive principle manifested in number 2.

Since 1 generates all other numbers, it is the beginning of numeration and is present in all numbers. Any value multiplied by 1 remains the same. To the Pythagoreans therefore it was both no number and every number.

Virtually all cultures have sought unity among the parts of the cosmos. Even in the twentieth century, Einstein looked for a unified field theory, and physicists, chemists, and biologists find the same foundations in the basic structure of animate creatures and inanimate substances. Number 1 therefore implies both spirit and substance.

Number Two

The outstanding characteristics of 2 are associating well with others, forming firm friendships, and being universally liked. In any group, this type of person is apt to be the peacemaker. This number actually needs partners, companions, and a lively social milieu.

In enterprises, here is a team player, loyal to the organization and yet sensitive to the problems of the individual colleague. He or she takes few chances and performs with conscientiousness. The top positions are not sought, and yet 2 can be so suited to defusing anger, acting fairly, and lifting morale, that a high executive role may result. Moreover, although innovation and bold strategy may be absent, prudent judgment, analytical perception, and the ability to see all sides of an issue may result in a capacity for policy making.

Sensitivity and understanding may lead such a person into the pictorial arts. To compensate for self-deprecation, number 2 may be attracted to the theater, where a person can submerge his or her own personality in the character being played.

The virtue of adaptability may become exaggerated into self-effacement. Unless the inherent tendency to yield to every pressure and to fail to assert one's rights is overcome, this personality can end up as a "doormat," a nonentity, colorless in ideas and expression, a friend to all but an admired companion to none. The reluctance to enter wholeheartedly into a project can lead to an unnecessary focus on picayune details.

Number 2 has to learn to expand the natural skills of friendliness, diplomacy, fairness, and judgment; take the chance of being unequivocal; be willing to act alone; keep uppermost a positive self-image.

BACKGROUND NOTES

In the teachings of Pythagoras, number 2, the dyad, was the passive aspect and therefore represented matter, as differentiated from spirit. It also signified the principle of opposites, the existence of differences in nature. Number 1 was both unity and an entity itself. Number 2 was less clear-cut, without sharp, recognizable boundaries.

The Pythagoreans paired all the contraries in the cosmos as a function of 2:

odd	even
good	evil
one	many
limited	unlimited
right	left
masculine	feminine
light	dark
straight	crooked
motionless	moving
square	rectangle

With undefined boundaries and two sides to each characteristic, the Pythagorean 2 represented uncertainty and therefore opinion rather than fact.

TOP: Number 1 resides in the words *printemps* (French) and *primavera* (Italian and Spanish) and is associated with beginnings, symbolized by springtime. Sandro Botticelli. *The Rite of Spring.* 1478. Panel painting, 80 × 124″. Galleria degli Uffizi, Florence.

ABOVE: The creatures of the earth entered Noah's ark two by two, in keeping with the duality of nature and the partnership signaled by number 2. Edward Hicks. *Noah's Ark.* 1826. Oil on canvas, 32½ × 41½″. Philadelphia Museum of Art. Bequest of Charles C. Willis.

RIGHT: Number 3 represents a trinity in theology, human endeavor, and nature. Peter Paul Rubens. *The Three Graces.* 1639–1640. Oil on wood, 87 × 71½″. The Prado, Madrid.

The balance in nature symbolized by number 4 was emphasized in the concept of the four humors of ancient and medieval medicine. Here two of the humors are shown: on the right, sanguine (blood), and on the left, melancholic (black bile).

Along with 1, 2 was also almost a nonnumber, for it was the link between 1 and the other numbers. Thus, 3 was virtually the first numeral.

Number Three

The keynote of this number is expression in all forms, especially in speech, writing, and the arts. Moreover, many different fields of interest attract this personality. The tendency is to be involved in too many projects to permit any single enterprise to be completed. When required to adhere to a single line of endeavor, 3 is apt to become bored. Nonconformist, 3 prefers to look at accepted ideas and practices in a new light, offering fresh insights and innovative principles. However, it is the overall concept rather than the detail that holds the attention. Self-expression is also seen in fulsome affection, which 3 desires to give as well as to receive. Radiant good cheer sometimes can be extended to the extremes of silliness and practical jokes. The need to be in the midst of social activity enables such a person to be a good host or hostess, but it can also lead to disgruntlement and jealousy if the person feels left out.

Number 3s would be well advised to engage in a single enterprise at a time rather than in many and to carry through before switching paths; to be patient with themselves and with others.

BACKGROUND NOTES

The first number to refer to many things in the development of counting may well have been 3—as distinguished from 1 and 2. Aristotle, as late as the fourth century B.C., believed that 3 was a surrogate word for "all."

The union of 1 and 2 forms 3, the triad, standing for the world in Pythagorean concepts. The human family was also symbolized by 3 (father, mother, and child). Since 2 was the first even number and 3 the first odd number, 5 became the figure for marriage. But 1 (the self) plus 2 (together) also suggested that 3 was another kind of union and an entity in itself.

The idea of a divine Trinity in Christian theology had earlier counterparts in many cultures and in the ancient Greco-Roman divisions of heaven (ruled over by Zeus, or Jupiter), the ocean (ruled over by Poseidon, or Neptune), and the underworld (ruled over by Hades, or Pluto).

Number 3 figures prominently in Judaeo-Christian culture. God has three names according to the Psalms. Three angels visited Abraham. God called to Samuel three times. Jesus remained entombed for three days before rising.

At one time, people thought of nature as having only three seasons, spring, summer, winter. The day, especially in ancient Egypt, originally was marked by morning, noon, and sunset. Even today we use the expression "morning, noon, and night" to indicate the entire gamut of a day.

The highest degree of anything has often been announced by three appearances: the Greek astronomer Eratosthenes used the metaphor of cleansing oneself three times to free the mind. In many fairy tales three wishes appear. Even in sports, for instance in the American game of baseball, three strikes by the batter retire him (he has had enough opportunities to hit the ball). In science, confirmation of a finding or a theory requires more than just one repetition. At least two more agreements for a total of three are usually needed. In *Alice in Wonderland,* the reciter states baldly, in "The Hunting of the Snark," "What I say three times is true."

Number Four

Solidity, reliability, and integrity are the shining attributes of this number. Full effort is spent in performing the tasks at hand. Number 4 is organized, thorough, and unswerving in getting work finished. Number 3 may develop brilliant ideas or insightful plans, but 4 pursues them and can end by being far more productive than an undisciplined 3. Conventional behavior and attitudes are usual but in the desire to set and follow the rules, 4 can become resistant to and even rebellious against any attempts to alter the pattern that has been established. This type of firmness can therefore end in bitter quarrels.

Everybody can rely completely on 4 to adhere strictly to ethical principals. The desire to be completely honest, however, may produce tactlessness. Indeed, the extremes that must be guarded against are pedantry and humorlessness. The person who is not willing ever to bend may be so self-righteous and stubborn that he or she becomes tiresome.

Number 4 must try to maintain the qualities of fairness, honesty, and perseverance but also to lighten up, avoid forcing ideas on others, and take a broader, more tolerant view.

BACKGROUND NOTES

To Pythagoras, number 4, the tetrad, was the number of balance, the makeup of nature. Throughout Greco-Roman times and well into recent centuries, there were four basic elements (fire, water, air, earth), each with four qualities (hot, cold, dry, moist), and in conformity with four humors comprising the bodily structure and function (blood, yellow bile, black bile, phlegm). Even today physicists classify nature into four basic forces.

Numbers 4 and 7 had close associations. Of course the moon and therefore the month involved both numbers: four weeks of seven days each; twenty-eight lunar mansions; twenty-eight constellations.

It may also be that 4 and 9 were rivals for one of the abstractions of Pythagorean theory, Justice. These two numbers are the only squares (2×2 and 3×3) among the first ten numbers (if we leave out number 1). The Pythagoreans made the choice of 4 (and the square shape) rather than 9 to stand for the fairness implied in Justice (and also in Brotherhood). We have continued to use the terms "square deal," "on the square," "square-fisted," "square-jawed." The Egyptians also gave prominence to 4 in representations. The pillars of the world for instance were four in number. The Judaeo-Christian God is named by a combination of four Hebrew consonants—*Yod, He, Vau, He.* Jehovah created the sky bodies on the fourth day. The four Christian apostles (John, Luke, Matthew, Mark) had their four representations (Eagle, Bull, Angel, Lion), matching in a sense the early concepts of the division of all matter into four essentials. The macrocosm has usually been assumed in number 4—four winds, four directions and points (east, west, north, south).

Numerologically speaking, when a number is multiplied by 10, that is, has a 0 added, its significance is heightened. The enhancement of 4 ($4 \times 10 = 40$) was important in various cultures. The duration of the world after the Exodus, according to the Book of Kings, is supposed to be a total of four periods of one hundred and twenty years (40×3). In ancient Mesopotamia the forty days when the constellation of the Pleiades was missing in the sky were a time of rain and storm. At the end, the change was celebrated, on their reappearance, as a restoration of freedom.

Number 5 contains the trait of expression in words, as is symbolized in this Hebrew word introducing the five books of Moses (the Torah). Bibliothèque Nationale, Paris.

Number Five

An unfettered mind and expressive tongue typify the traits of number 5. Freedom to pursue varied interests, goals, and places is essential. Sparkle, wit, and unconventional attitudes create a charming, magnetic, optimistic personality. Of course, there is the danger of insincerity, sarcasm, and the need to shock rather than to deliver solid substance. Number 5 is drawn to new things and is enamored of change but it can be organized in these pursuits. However, in 5 the sense of order is a means to an end rather than the main focus, as it is in 4. The variety of skills of course can lead nowhere and the very daring intellect may end with rashness. Discipline is needed.

Number 5 has to let the mind run free and adapt to change, but it must not be allowed to be buffeted by every wind. The 5 person needs to stay awhile to learn, to rein in the tendency to mock others, to use charm for constructive ends.

BACKGROUND NOTES

Early counting systems may have been based on the five digits of each human hand and foot. The term for 5 has sometimes been "one hand"; for 10, "two hands." (Whether this perception led eventually to the decimal system is by no means certain.) In Chinese philosophy, medicine, and magic, number 5 is prominent. There are five colors, five tastes, five virtues, five elements (in contradistinction to the Western idea of four elements). To Fire, Water, Earth, and Air was added Wood, a Chinese fundamental. The bodily organs were also divided into five groups. Indeed virtually all human endeavors and nature's possessions were collated into five categories in ancient Chinese culture.

Among the Greeks, categorization by 5s was a rival to grouping by 4s: five senses, five essences, five zones, five divisions of living things. The material world itself was signified by number 5. Indeed the fifth essence by medieval times had come to mean the highest degree or the essential ingredient. Our term "quintessence" indicates the significance of the number 5 of former times.

The Roman naming of months and of sons singled out 5 especially. Originally, after the months of Maius and Junius (these were the third and fourth months at one time, for March began the year), the months thereafter, contributed the names Quintilis (fifth), Sextilis (sixth), Septembris (seventh), Octobris (eighth), Novembris (ninth), Decembris (tenth).

Number Six

This number stands for the pillars of family and community, the advisor to all, the generous arbiter of disputes. Adverse to quarrels, number 6 craves and creates harmony and beauty. As with number 2, friendship is an outstanding trait but the attachment is often deeper and more lasting. In partnership, however, 6 is apt to end as the more dominant member. Yet power and position are sought for security rather than control. Loyal to a fault, 6 expects corresponding commitment. If carried to the extreme, these demands can lead to suspicion and secretiveness when full affection is not shown.

The desire to be the rock on which others can stand may turn 6's traits into perfectionism. Worry may be ever present. Such a person must guard against a martyr complex.

Six tries to maintain ideals but should stay within reasonable bounds and recognize that not everybody has to have the same principles.

BACKGROUND NOTES

Pythagoras considered number 6 to signal perfection. It is the first number whose divisors (1, 2, and 3) when added together equal that number; when multiplied together they also yield the same number.

Philo Judaeus at the beginning of the Christian Era asserted that creation had to take six days because it is the most perfect and productive of all numbers. Saint Augustine came to the same conclusion that God had created all things in six days just because that number represents perfection, rather than because the Lord finished his work in six days.

As a mathematical rival of 5 in its ancient meaning of marriage, 6 is the female number of marriage. It is the product of 3, the first accepted odd number, and 2, the first even number, whereas 5 is the sum of these two. Indeed 6 is reached by the addition of the fundamental first three numbers—1, 2, and 3. Pythagorean theory also recognized that there are six plane geometric figures.

An exceptional symbolism involving number 6 was the numerological analysis in the Revelation of Saint John. A passage tells how to recognize the Antichrist, the Beast of Satan, the most despicable

666, the medieval "number of the Beast of Evil" or the anti-Christ, would have probably led to panic if it had appeared in a high place in the medieval world. Photograph by David Berman.

Numerologically speaking, Paul Klee's name is a number 6. The search for beauty and harmony is a characteristic of number 6 and therefore also applies in general to art and artists. Photograph of Paul Klee. 1939. Collection Felix Klee, Basel.

person in the world. By converting the letters of a name to their corresponding numbers—the standard mechanics of numerology—Revelation marked 666 as the number of the Beast. The two-horned Devil Beast, states verse 18, is perceivable by an understanding mind, for the number of that man who is the Beast is "six hundred threescore and six."

Thomas Aquinas himself also participated in that numerological exercise. Indeed, in the headlong rush to brand theological opponents with the hateful number, some manipulated the name of Pope Leo X to yield 666. Similarly, defenders of the Vatican distorted Martin Luther's name to produce 666. This type of "beasting" was repeated over and over in order to pin the label on an enemy. As with the Pope and Luther, the mechanics necessary to fit the names into the number were often so devious and ludicrous that virtually any name or birth date could have been made to conform.

This stigmatizing of 6, which the Pythagoreans had dubbed a perfect number and which has become highly moral in modern numerology, may have arisen from several sources. In Latin, 6 is *sex*. Egyptian *seshemu* is sexual congress in meaning and hieroglyphic symbol. Arabic and Persian mystics used a similar word to express eroticism. Even the Middle Eastern fairy tale of the secret mountain, in which the magic phrase is "Open Sesame," may have been referring to similar terminology. Some have even equated the secret cave in that charmed mountain with the uterus. Whatever the line of derivation may have been, 6, sex, and sin were at times all closely associated in medieval lore and some Christian mysticism. But the earlier meanings of purpose, responsibility, and security have eventually triumphed.

Number Seven

Seven has usually been considered a lucky number. It marked the end of the creation process when God rested and was satisfied with the result. At one time, 7 meant ill fortune rather than good luck, perhaps just because on the

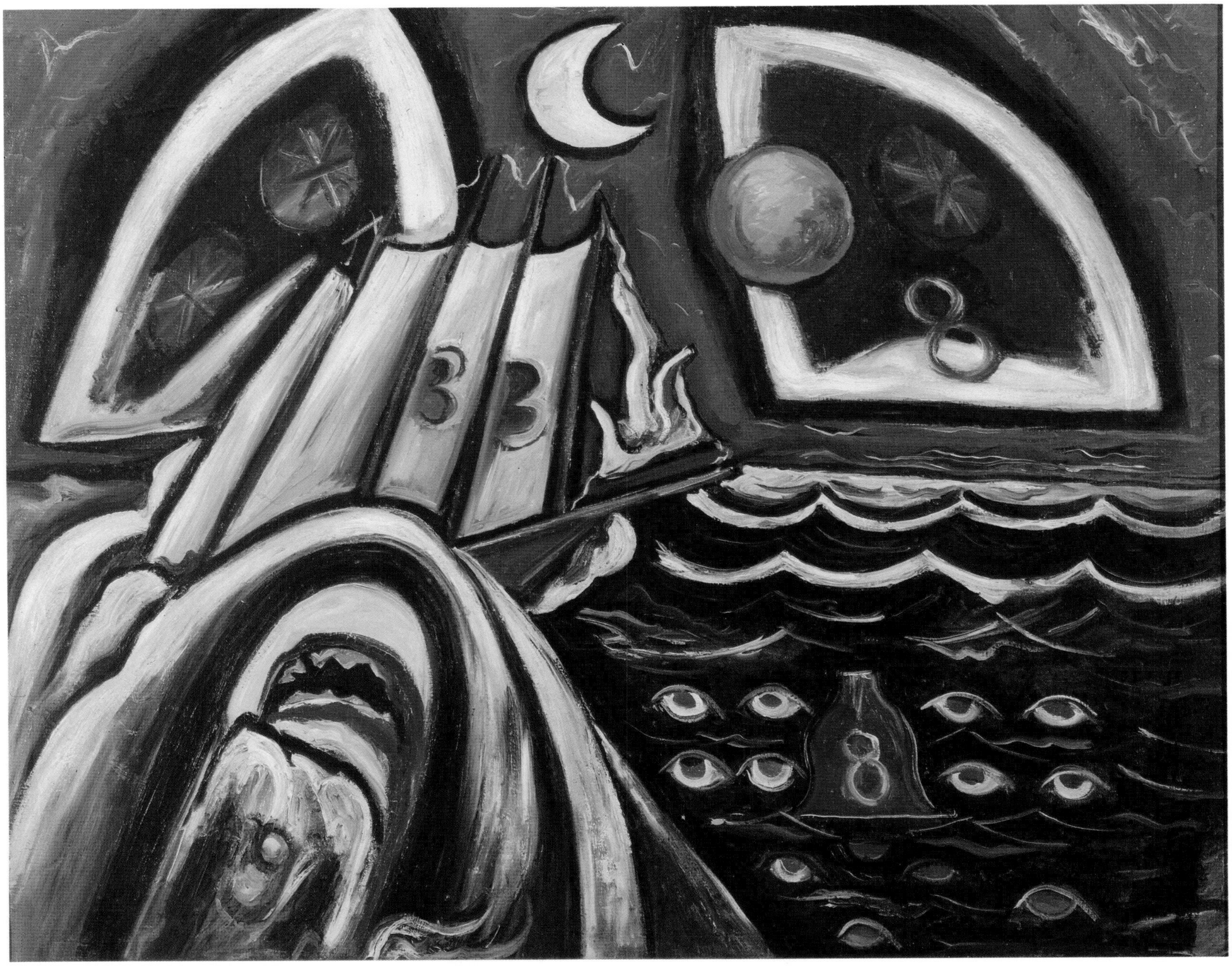

OPPOSITE: The seven liberal arts fit the characteristics of a 7's erudition and understanding. *The Seven Liberal Arts* from *Hortus Deliciarum* by the abbess of Herrade de Landsberg. Twelfth century. Bibliothèque et Cabinet des Estampes, Strasbourg, France.

ABOVE: Marsden Hartley. *Eight Bells Folly: Memorial for Hart Crane.* 1933. Oil on canvas, 31⅝ × 39⅜". University Gallery, Minnesota.

seventh day all activity was forbidden and every enterprise was to be avoided. Even in early Mesopotamian times, special days of the month that had unfortunate significance were multiples of 7. For instance, the forty-ninth day (7 × 7) after the beginning of the previous month was especially ominous. However, wisdom and contentment are most often associated with this number.

But the perceptiveness and understanding of a 7 person, along with studiousness and erudition, can appear as pedantry and humorlessness. Contentment may be interpreted as smugness, and the combination of an analytical mind, intuitive capability, and quiet behavior may lead to observation rather than participation, to eccentric reclusiveness rather than involved friendliness. The thinker must not become a dreamer. The exceptional intellect and broad idealism need the friendliness of others.

Seven has to let abilities shine forth rather than remain hidden; analysis is best accepted when accompanied by expression of sympathy and affection; contemplation should be followed by action.

BACKGROUND NOTES

In Pythagorean numerology, 7 had the unique significance of wisdom and self-containment. This number was unrelated to any of the solid figures—each of which had an assigned number. In a sense, therefore, 7 generated itself. Only seven moving sky bodies were known at that time—Sun, Moon, Mars, Venus, Mercury, Jupiter, Saturn. For a long time there were seven accepted stars in each of the several constellations that were important to seafarers. That there were seven planets, and only seven, was satisfying, for it signified a consistency in the order of destiny. Indeed, one of the objections to Galileo's discovery of the moons of Jupiter was that it upset the comfortable established system of seven heavenly bodies.

As mentioned in the segment on the number 4, 7 and 4 had relationships with each other. The four winds of Mesopotamia were expanded to seven. The week as a unit of seven days came into use in the first century A.D. in Alexandria. The ziggurat towers of ancient Babylon had either three or four stories—which add up to 7. Each of the seven steps had seven colors. The goddess Ishtar passed through seven gates.

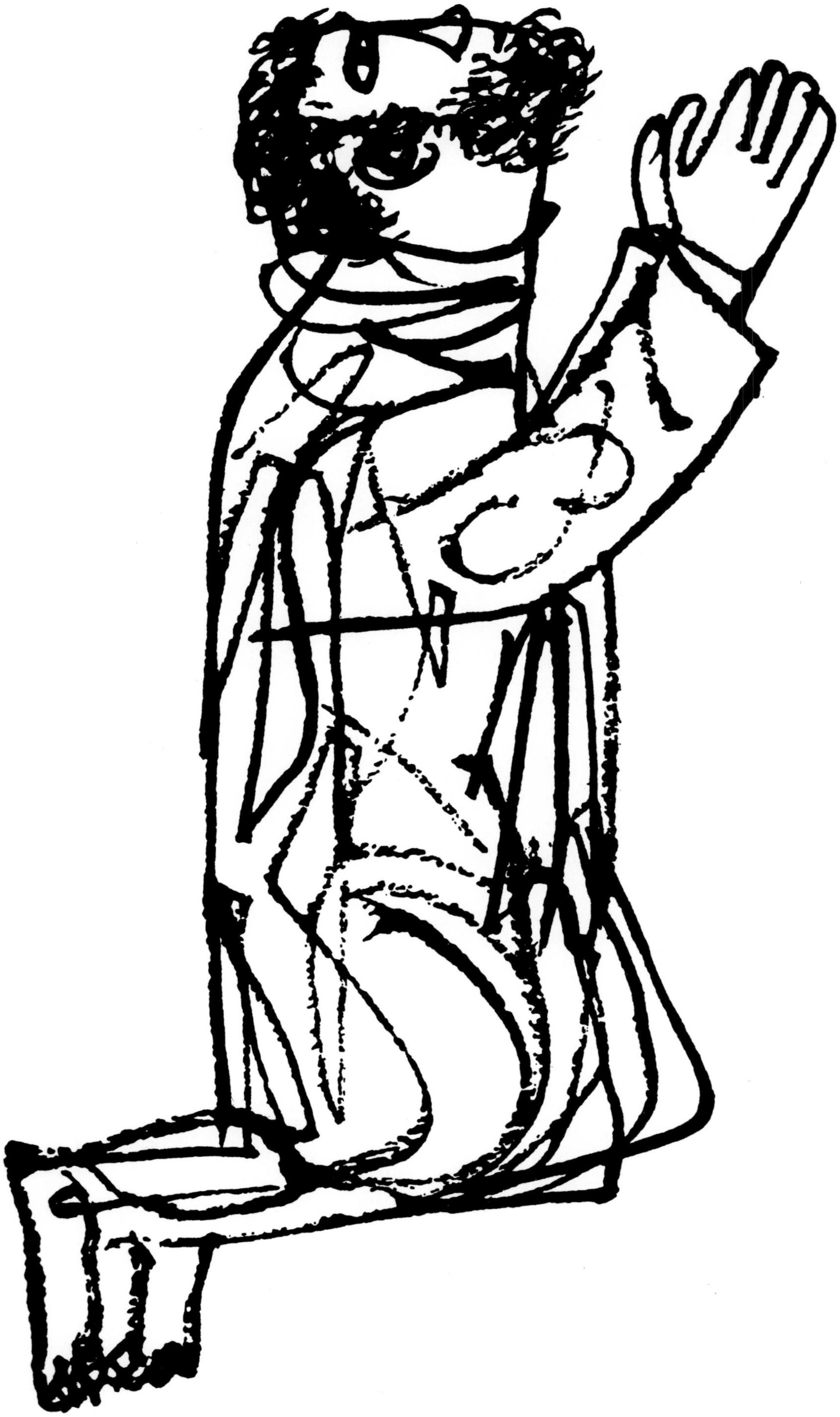

The number 9 is often associated with spirituality and the highest level of morality before perfection itself, symbolized by 10. *Prayer* by Ben Shahn.

Religious associations in other cultures were also strongly associated with this number. The Hebrew candlestick has seven branches. The leprosy of Naaman in the Bible was cured by immersion in the Jordan seven times. Dante described seven levels of purgatory, which fit into later concepts of the seven steps to perfection. "Seventh Heaven" has come to mean the highest bliss just below the ultimate paradise.

Arabic writings contain a host of references to 7: seven great leaders from Adam to Muhammad; seven repetitions of magical formulas; seven degrees of Hell; seven journeys of Sinbad the Sailor; seven regions of the earth; seven seas; seven divisions of the arts; seven verses for completion of a poem.

Of course, folklore, literature, and customs are replete with accents on 7. There are seven openings in the head—two eyes, two nostrils, two ears, and one mouth. The seven wonders of the ancient world were a model of marvels. Shakespeare described the seven ages of man. Ancient and medieval medicine held particular days of an illness to be critical, when either resolution or decline would result. The seventh day was one of those special times. Indeed, 7 itself was sometimes imbued with a sense of time. In the gambling game of craps, 7 is central for its appearance signals either a win or a loss, depending upon how the player has placed the bet.

Number Eight

Number 8 reaps the harvest. Power and position are used in order to be productive and achieve financial gain, not for the sake of the power itself. However, the tendency to be dictatorial and authoritarian must be guarded against. Although material rewards are the goal, ideals and principles often lie unperceived underneath. Large philanthropic enterprises may be an objective, often stimulated by the observance of unfair treatment of others' needs and rights. Inspiring confidence and aware of the incentives that can drive people, number 8 falls easily into positions of authority. He or she is bold and adventuresome and correspondingly often successful but may also taste failure instead, because extremes are part of this personality.

The dual nature of the number stands for other opposites besides success and failure: destruction and regeneration; disappointment and promise; practicality and generosity. The paradox is further emphasized in the numeral itself. Upright, it is the two circles of self-containment and its arithmetic quantity is a doubling of 4, the number that is "down to earth." Yet, on its side, 8 is the mathematical sign for infinity, a reminder of boundlessness and eternity.

The 8 personality must learn to exert control over self, not just others; choose a mate and companions who can add intellect, art, and spice; slow up and taste, instead of rushing ahead single-mindedly.

BACKGROUND NOTES

Sanctity has enveloped this number from early times. The four Hebrew letters standing for Jehovah—in Hebrew they are consonants—*Yod, He, Vau, He,* are the tenth, fifth, sixth, and fifth letters in the alphabet. These numbers add up to 26 $(10+5+6+5)$, which numerologically is 8 $(2+6)$. Furthermore the last letter in the alphabet is the twenty-sixth, also therefore an 8 $(2+6)$.

The sacred covenant between God and the Jews was the circumcision—on the eighth day after birth. Eight also meant the second beginning of humankind after the Flood. Since there were only eight persons in Noah's ark, the subsequent makeup of the earth's population came from those eight people. The new world of humans was far better in God's eyes than that of the past but it was not as perfect as the original creation in six days. After seven years of famine in the biblical story of Joseph, the eighth year began a period of plenty. To sanctify a place as holy, eight days of sacrifice or ceremony were required. In Pythagorean geometric mathematics, 8 stood for the first cube, and because its surfaces numbered 6 (the perfect number), it was also a perfect structure. Numbers 7 and 8 were often linked in number philosophies, since 7 was the highest and the most that could be expected before the ultimate 8.

In the ancient lore of several cultures, there were seven steps to perfection before the eighth, Paradise, was reached. The Neoplatonists postulated a journey after death by the soul through each of the seven planets (Sun, Moon, Mercury, Venus, Mars, Jupiter, Saturn) in order to return the traits originally received from each sky body before the spirit could attain the eighth level of heaven.

Number Nine

Number 9 is regarded as particularly special. By whatever number it is multiplied, the product ends in the same number 9, using the numerological method. For example: $2\times9=18=1+8=9$; $3\times9=27=2+7=9$; $85\times9=765=7+6+5=18=1+8=9$. Perhaps of even greater mathematical significance, when any single-digit number (that is from 1 through 9) is added to 9, the resulting figure by numerology remains that same number. For instance, $1+9=10=1+0=1$; $2+9=11=1+1=2$; $3+9=12=1+2=3$; $4+9=13=1+3=4$.

Therefore, the 9 outward personality, inner drive, and life path in numerology can be like any other number's. It is a chameleon, allowing the coloration and characteristics of other numbers to be taken on—through choice. Thus, influenced sufficiently and motivated enough, 9 can direct the self according to circumstances, in keeping with its numerological characteristic. Yet its basic features remain: universality, intellect, and emotion. Generally 9s are broadminded, altruistic, and far-seeing, but the extremes of naiveté, unreality, and vulnerability can be dangers.

Wisdom coupled with wide knowledge permits a 9 to perceive the essential nature of persons and events not readily apparent to others. That talent for quick insight is apt to lead to impulsive action rather than deliberate behavior. Moreover, the tendency to take the long view may cause immediate concerns to be overlooked.

Although the impression given may be of coolness, actually compassionate feelings are strong and affection is needed in return. The 9 person seeks admiration and recognition rather than material rewards.

Advice to number 9 people is to see the individual trees not just the forest; to consider material needs of others in addition to the cosmic view; to follow their own vision but to keep their sights on the local path.

BACKGROUND NOTES

Universality has long been implied by this number. Whereas number 1 was considered as already in all numbers and therefore virtually not a number to the Pythagoreans, 9 was capable of becoming all numbers and yet remained the same. Since 10 was completion, 9 was not quite the end. It symbolized the last defect before perfection. As the last of the single-digit numbers of which everything was composed, it signified a broad worldview.

It also was used to express a long duration and exceptional power. For nine years Troy was besieged and Odysseus wandered. In medieval times, 3 times the Trinity made 9 even more potent than 3. The symbolic meanings in number 3 thus were heightened, that is, were multiplied into 9, while the unique universality of 9 itself was maintained.

Number Ten

The End and A New Beginning

Number 10 had great significance in Pythagorean times, but modern numerological principles usually separate every double-digit number into two. Thus 10 is $1+0=1$. Those who look upon 10 as a separate number may assign to it honesty and also ambition; the vision to find and the worldliness to grasp opportunity.

It is the end of all and yet the beginning again. It represents totality and therefore perfection itself. Even today, we use the phrase "on a scale of ten" when we evaluate a person, a thing, or an action.

This number has had many associations. In astrology, three decans of ten degrees make up each zodiac sign. Greek mathematicians saw that all of the planar and solid figures together comprised ten types. So important was 10 to the concept of perfection that the Pythagoreans postulated a tenth body, a "Counter-Earth," in order to fulfill the theoretical requirement of ten heavenly bodies (Sun, Moon, five planets, Earth, and a central fire around which the others revolved equal only nine units). In Mesopotamia, the tenth day was significant for religious practices. Multiples of ten figured in the one hundred days of the flooding of the Nile in Egypt. There are ten plagues in the Bible and God is reported to have issued various warnings ten times. There are the Ten Commandments, and today when ten males gather together in Jewish observances (a "minyan") various religious ceremonies can be performed.

All numbers are in 10, which is also 1 numerologically. It is the end of the first 10

numbered series and therefore the measure of completeness.

Number Eleven
Revelation

The numbe 11 suggests unusual talents, particularly insight, and even more perceptivity than 9. This type of person may be inspired to start a new movement or introduce an original concept. He or she does not easily form a partnership but on the other hand is not a loner. Once a relationship is made there is intense commitment to one mate or companion. Discrimination and selectivity are the characteristics. Selfishness, aloofness, and fanaticism are dangers. The leadership and originality of 1 are enhanced so that 11 is virtually an inspired prophet, illuminating the road ahead.

Number 11 must not be overwhelmed by dreams or be too zealous in espousing his or her own cause. Balanced discernment is needed with receptivity to the ideas of others. The 11 person should keep to a lower key (to resemble 2, which is the sum of 1 + 1) and yet maintain creativity and individuality, as a double of the power manifested by 1.

Since 11 is beyond 10, it has been held to represent transgression beyond the Ten Commandments. This unfavorable connotation is balanced by the implication of insight beyond the norm, the ability to go beyond completed measurements.

Number Twenty-Two
Integration

The Hebrew language—which some cabalists assume was the tongue used by God to create the world and to communicate with humans—contains twenty-two letters. The number therefore is inspired. It implies power and prophecy. However, as the relative of 4 (2×2), 22 also signals the substance of reality; concern with the environment and material resources, but not money itself.

Involvement in the earth's possessions can lead to an altruistic devotion to the betterment of humankind. Practicality and control can achieve high productivity. In the most favorable sense, 22 integrates the individual with the whole of society. It can make dreams come true.

Number Thirty-Three
Harmony

Those who consider 33 as one of the separate master numbers, rather than as a 6 ($3 + 3$), place harmony, service, and sympathy as its hallmarks.

OPPOSITE: Perfection and its quest are implied in number 10, the beginning and end of all other numbers. Robert Campin. *Saint Barbara*. 1438. Panel, 39¾ × 18½″. The Prado, Madrid.

ABOVE: Number 13 has lucky and unlucky connotations: lucky because of the association with maturation in the Jewish tradition; unlucky because of the thirteen persons present at Jesus's last Passover feast before the Crucifixion. Leonardo da Vinci. *Last Supper*. 1495–1497/98. Fresco. Refectory, Santa Maria delle Grazie, Milan.

This number's importance is stressed in various ways. For example, the highest degree in the Masonic order is the thirty-third. The expressiveness exemplified by number 3 (in this instance 33 is 3 doubled) and the purposefulness of 6 (as the sum of 3 + 3) can combine to produce revolutionary attitudes and a challenge to authority. However, this dissident person achieves the goals of lifting the oppressed, helping those in need, and preserving peace by persuasion, good cheer, and friendship, rather than by confrontation and destruction. One must avoid being overbearing and the opposite, surrendering one's principles.

Numbers Twelve and Thirteen

A few words may be said about the numbers 12 and 13, although for the most part they do not stand by themselves but instead become 3 (1 + 2) and 4 (1 + 3).

Number 12 has been of considerable significance virtually throughout human history. For instance, the months of the year, the signs of the zodiac, the purported tribes of Israel, the number of apostles, and other associations of this arithmetic number, including the term "dozens," have figured prominently through the centuries. In medieval times, 12 had mythical religious implications and was even given as the number of Christ. Just as 7 was sacred because it was formed by the first true odd number 3, standing for the Trinity, and the even number of the 4 apostles, who also mirrored the basic elements of nature, so also was 12 a sanctified numeral (3 × 4). Universality as an abstraction was also symbolized by 12, for 4 was materiality and 3 spirituality.

Number 13 has been considered both unlucky and lucky. Its unfortunate connotation, such as "13 at the table," has been ascribed by a few scholars to the Last Supper, the meeting of Christ and his disciples, a total of 13, which was to be followed by the trial of Jesus and the Crucifixion. Similarly, whatever went beyond the 12 apostles had sinful meanings. Even witchery has been assigned. Others have offered a variety of other explanations for the unlucky 13.

Yet 13 is also the age when a Jewish youth attains manhood in the sight of God, responsible from then on for his transgressions and also for his good works, becoming a "son of duty," and correspondingly a son of good deeds, Bar Mitzvah. In early India and also in Pre-Columbian America, celestial space was a combination of horizontal and vertical dimensions, yielding 13 spatial components that encompassed the universe. To the early Aryans of Asia, 13 lunarians, not 12, comprised the year. From these standpoints, 13 was a good rather than unfortunate omen.

Of course a host of other numbers is variously evaluated by different numerologists. We have dealt here only with the basic ten and a few of the additional numerals.

Evaluations of partnerships between any two of the numbers can be made in a similar manner. The purpose to be kept in mind is to educate the participants on how to connect in fruitful and rewarding ways. The point that numerology emphasizes is that if the advantageous and disadvantageous aspects of each number are recognized, whether in personality or life's directions, even those with numbers basically unsuited to each other can do far better than the compatible numbers whose unfavorable tendencies are unperceived or ignored.

Principles of Interpretation

Among the single-digit numbers to which dates and names are reduced, the most important ones for numerological interpretations are derived from the full date of birth (known as the Birth Number, Life Path, or Path of Destiny), the name given at birth (Personal Number), the vowels in the birth name (Inner Drive or Soul Urge), and the consonants in the name (called the Outer Personality by some, the Passive Nature by others, and the Potential by still others). Additional numbers often used are the birth day, the birth month, and a host of combinations involving parts or all of the dates and names. Differing relative emphases are placed by numerologists on these numbers, but all agree that the Birth Number and the Personal Number are the most important.

Birth Number
(Life Path)

The Birth Number is formed by adding together all the numbers of the date of birth and reducing them to a single digit—except when it is a master number (11 or 22).

Some prefer to reduce each part of the date and then add together the single-digit numbers thus obtained. This latter method of listing sometimes can result in a master number showing up before reduction that might be missed in a straight addition of all the numbers. For example, February 1, 1934, yields $2+1+1+9+3+4=20=2+0=2$. But first reducing each part: February $=2$; day $=1$; year $=1+9+3+4=17=1+7=8$. The sum is then $2+1+8=11$, yielding a master number missed in the previous addition system. Of course, if the master number 11 were further reduced, it would be $1+1=2$, the same number again, but these special master numbers are often used intact. (On the other hand, the method of first reducing the parts of the date can also miss a master number that the ordinary addition of all the numerals would reveal.)

The Birth Number signals the direction that lies ahead. However, the number represents the impetus but not necessarily the ultimate journey, for numerology recognizes the influence played by an individual's decisions, teaching that if someone is aware of the likely path suggested by his nature, that person can either continue or alter direction, avoiding or compensating for the negative and making the most of the favorable features.

Birth Day

The Life Path obtained from the full date of birth is sometimes modified by the significance of the day in the month that a person is born. For instance, an example of May 28, 1912, with a Life Path number of 1, is further supported by the 28th day $(2+8=10=1)$. Here the value of the Life Path 1 is reinforced by the 1 of the Birth Day. But if the day of birth had been the fourth of the month, conscientiousness, strict integrity, and efficiency would have given organization and limitation to any rash, unrealistic, or acquisitive aspects. Extravagant tendencies would be more likely to be circumscribed.

Birth Name Number
(Personal Number)

All the vowels and consonants together form the Personal Number, indicating a person's full makeup, the sum of inner forces, outer display, and total potential.

However, a person may be born with one name, be nicknamed another, choose a third, or be known by a fourth. He or she may have received several names at birth and may drop one or more. An initial may be used for one of the names or the person may be known entirely by one of the names. And upon marriage a woman may continue to employ her maiden name or substitute the married name, or have both maiden and married names together.

For instance, Lenore Robinson (with a Personal Number of 4) is known to all, even herself, as just Leni, without any last name. Her Personal Number then would be considered 22, for 3 (L) + 5 (E) + 5 (N) + 9 (I) = 22. This master number may be the principal key to her attitudes and feelings, rather than 4.

The Vowels

The vowels in Lenore Robinson yield 5 (E) + 6 (O) + 5 (E) + 6 (O) + 9 (I) + 6 (O) = 37 = 3 + 7 = 10 = 1. This sum is known as the Inner Drive or Soul Urge. It represents the drives that are the bases of a person's attitudes. For Lenore Robinson, 1 signifies the urge to lead, to give play to originality. While adhering strictly to the conscientiousness and originality that her Personal Number 4 announces, she cherishes underneath the ambition and the individuality to take a chance and to forge ahead boldly.

(Some letters of the English alphabet, particularly Y, are looked upon as either a vowel or a consonant. For example, used directly after A or O, Y is a vowel; but directly before a vowel, Y can be considered a consonant. This possible versatility can change the total number value of the vowels or the consonants, depending on how the numerologist classifies the letter.)

The Consonants

Numerologists are not universally agreed on the significance of the consonants. To many, outward personality is announced by the sum of the consonants. To others, this number represents the undriven nature, the quiet part of the person, even unrealized potential. The individual numerologist thus determines how the characteristics of the number will be interpreted. For instance, it may be that to the world Lenore Robinson, a 3 in consonants, sparkles with good cheer, self-expression, and affection—but she may have insecurities.

Personal Year

Clearly many different aspects of the same person can be found in an examination of the numbers. Indeed, there are also a great many uses to which the numbers can be put. Some systems through complicated assignments choose days, months, and even hours that are in harmony or disharmony with a particular person's Personal Number (Birth Name Number).

The Personal Year, sometimes also called the

Year Lesson, is relied upon to evaluate the chances for good or bad fortune in the current year or in any future time. The sum of a person's month of birth and day of birth plus the year being examined yields the Personal Year number for the year chosen. For instance, if one wished to know what was ahead in 1988 for someone born on May 28, 1912, 5 (the birth month of May) is added to 2 + 8 (the 28th) + 1 + 9 + 8 + 8 (the sum of the digits in the year 1988) to yield a total of 41 = 4 + 1 = 5. This is the Personal Year number of the year 1988 for the person born on May 28 of any year.

We saw that the Life Path or Birth Number of this person (which uses the month, day, *and* year of birth) is 5 + 2 + 8 + 1 + 9 + 1 + 2 (May 28, 1912) = 28 = 2 + 8 = 10 = 1 + 0 = 1. The Life Path of 1 and the Personal Year of 5 can then be matched to see how they will mix in 1988. Number 1 as the Life Path is apt to do best in 1988 in communications and in the pursuit of any change in the offing, whether in people, business, money, or activities. However, the unfavorable 5 properties suggest there are dangers to be kept in mind and avoided: rashness, waste, and inconsistency. This 5 Personal Year would appear to be suited especially to entertainment, commerce, and teaching for the 1 person's enterprising, executive, creative, and communicative skills.

Personal Month

The Personal Month number is obtained by the addition of the Personal Year number (just described) plus whatever month one is asking about in that year. Continuing our example of the person with a birth date of May 28, 1912 (Life Path of 1), and a Personal Year number of 5 in 1988, the number for August 1988 would be 5 (the Personal Year) + 8 (August is the eighth month) = 13 = 1 + 3 = 4.

An interpreter could say that although new endeavors and bold ventures, notably in the communicative fields, are especially suited to this person in 1988—as sketched in the preceding paragraphs on the Personal Year—August in 1988 is a time for caution. The 4 Personal Month number tells the person to be sure to attend to details, maintain full integrity, and be conscientious. The month of August might best mark the point in 1988 to slow the pace, to reexamine what has been done, and to set up pragmatic, realistic goals in the remaining months of the year.

Many other days, weeks, and even hours in any year ahead or in the current year are assigned a number based on calculations similar to those for the birth month and day. Usually the hour from midnight to 1 A.M. is assigned to 1, 1 A.M. to 2 A.M. to 2, etc., until the 8th to 9th hour, which is assigned number 9. The next hour, from 9 A.M. to 10 A.M., is 1 again, and so forth.

Other Modifying Numbers

There are also many other methods for deriving other significant numbers. For instance, the combined value of the first and last letters of a person's first name may have special significance apart from other number assignments. Also, in names with an odd number of letters, the letter in the middle may be seen as an added key to personality, a clue to the central core of the person's makeup. For example, William might suggest that the value of 3, in the middle letter L, lies ready to be realized, even though the Personal Number (Birth Name Number) of William is 7.

Numerologists also derive numbers from a variety of other additions and subtractions—using names, birth months, days, and years—to arrive at myriad interpretations and forecasts. Years in cycles of 3, 9, and 12 are supplied to each person according to special calculations for the purpose of evaluating an entire lifespan. Another system finds numerological meaning in each 27-year-span. From birth to about age 27, the significant operative number is obtained by subtracting the day of birth from the month of birth. The number controlling the next approximately 27 years is found by subtracting the birth year from the day of birth. The remainder of life is influenced by the qualities of the number derived from subtracting the birth year from the birth month. These represent the significant numbers for each cluster or cycle of years in a person's lifetime and summarize the challenges that he or she must face up to. These challenge numbers are further manipulated to reveal an unchanging, ever-present number by subtracting the number for the second 27-year cycle from the first 27-year-cycle number.

Missing Numbers

In a listing of all the reduced numerals for the full name, the vowels, the consonants, and the date of birth, several numbers from 1 to 9 will probably not be present for any one person. These missing numbers are held to represent those characteristics that the person lacks. The numerologist therefore may point to these absent numbers as representing traits and endeavors that the person should try to add in order to enlarge and enrich his existence. Some mystics deem that these traits are related to actions and attitudes of a person's past lives.

Compatibilities

Numerologists look for compatibilities between two people with different number values. For instance, the leadership personality of number 1 is eminently suited to the passive, receptive number 2; 3 and 5 are in perfect harmony, adding together the self-expression of 3 and the freedom of 5. On the other hand, 7 and 4 may be incompatible because the bold, creative, energetic bent of 7 wars with the conservative, down-to-earth, and patient tendencies of 4. But numerology recognizes that someone whose name adds up to any particular number, for instance 6, may be quite different in personality from another 6 person because of the different mixes of the positive and negative features. Since each number has favorable and unfavorable properties, the strengths inherent in any two numbers may be blended to produce a superb team effort and the dangers can be nullified by identifying and subduing them, but even the most suitable pair of numbers may be in utter mutual opposition if the negative features are allowed free rein.

Here are a few examples of how the strong qualities can be enhanced and the potential weaknesses adjusted to achieve a firmly cemented relationship and a productive goal:

1 with 2: the initiative of 1 and the friendliness of 2 can combine to produce highly effective teamwork. Let the cooperative nature of 2 mollify the headstrong bossiness of 1. In return, number 1 with its originality and courage can lead 2 out of apathy and shyness.

1 with 3: the self-expression and versatility of 3 can carry the creativity of 1 into channels acceptable to others. Each must control impulsiveness and diffuseness.

1 with 4: finance and business enterprise can be thoroughly successful when the originality of 1 is added to the organization and conscientiousness of 4. Number 4 must not weigh down 1's expansiveness with rigid narrowness. Number 1 has to guard against upsetting the prudent, orderly actions of 4 with rash, unrealistic decisions. The incorruptible integrity of 4 can turn 1 away from greedy and grasping paths. Number 1 can inject a touch of expansiveness into the overly prudent, strait-laced outlook of 4.

1 with 5: this combination of eloquence, wit, and persuasiveness that is possessed by 5, mingled with the originality, boldness, and aspirations of 1, can form an irresistible duo. But the dangers are competitiveness and too much individuality. Number 5, with its adaptability and broad-mindedness, can handle possible frictions better than 1. On the other hand, 1 can prevent 5 from straying into frivolity and superficiality through determined, serious leadership. Number 1 can also give more purpose to the shifting interests of 5.

1 with 6: the feeling for the arts and the intellect in 6 can give roundness and warmth to the ambitious strivings of 1. The imagination and investigative mind of 1 may expand the single-mindedness of 6 and discourage timidity. The individuality and demands of 1 must be curtailed; 6 has to become more open.

1, 2, 3 HURRA
12

Sample Reading

In the chapter on astrology, the horoscope of the writer Colette was the basis for our sample delineation. Let us see how a numerologist might view the same person.

Colette's full name at birth on January 28, 1873, was Sidonie-Gabrielle Colette. Her mother's special nickname for her was "Minet-Chéri." But Colette was the eventual name under which she wrote and became famous. By examining each of these appellations numerologically, we can obtain clues to certain characteristics:

SIDONIE	GABRIELLE	COLETTE
1946595	712995335	3635225
(=39)	(=44)	(=26)
3+9=12=3	4+4=8	2+6=8

The sums of her names yields 3+8+8=19=1+9=10 =1. Thus her Birth Name Number is 1.

Colette was a person of action and originality. She was self-reliant and aspiring. Yet as the unfavorable properties of the number shows, she was often withdrawn and a loner. Colette certainly was all of these and moreover was a perfectionist in her writing.

Her outward personality, as others saw her, was announced by the sum of the consonants in her name (1+4+5+7+2+9+3+3+3+3+2+2=44=8). When she became famous, her financial position certainly suggested a pragmatism in line with a number 8 nature. But as the summary of the number 8 suggests, underneath material concerns lay ideals and principles that Colette maintained steadfastly. Her devotion to artistic excellence and her fierce loyalty to friends were in keeping with the number 8 traits resting beneath the materialistic shell.

Her vowels add up to 11, a master number, reemphasizing the hidden idealism that was under wraps in 8. Indeed her unusual talents, insightful writing, and intuition are also indicated by the inner drive of 11. Advice offered to her by a numerologist would include keeping a low profile and yet maintaining creativity and individuality. Colette managed for the most part to behave as if she followed those suggestions. Of course, there was a particular occasion, for instance, early in her career in 1906, when she shocked people with her suggestive dancing and a presumed sexual affair with a woman friend. In that respect, she was true then and later to the boldness, extravagant rashness, and self-assured individualism of her Birth Name Number.

The suitable mates for a number 1 are supposed to be steady but without rigid adherence to accepted norms. Colette's first husband, Henri Gauthier-Villar, also a number 1, fit these requirements in some ways. However, the unfavorable characteristics of his Birth Name Number predominated, and he tyrannized her, becoming the opposite of what she needed. He was commanding, self-assured, enterprising, and practical. Negative features, however, were abundant—selfishness, greed, and unfairness. "Willy," the name by which he was called by everyone, even himself, has a 9 value. Here too, he displayed all the unappealing traits, restricting Colette and taking the credit for her creations. Just as a 9 can assume a variety of guises and appear to be all things to all people, Willy both charmed people and used them for his own benefit.

On the other hand, the man Colette later married, Maurice Goudeket, a 5, had all the favorable traits that she needed.

MAURICE	GOUDEKET
4139935	76345252
(=34)	(=34)
3+4=7	3+4=7

14=1+4=5

He was disciplined but his orderly mind embraced Colette's free spirit. He was in tune with her unconventionality. Unrestrictive, responsive, romantic, adaptable, and intellectual—the very characteristics suitable to the spouse of a number 1—Goudeket was her perfect soul mate. In some respects, he had the same makeup that Colette's mother invested her with when she referred to her in endearment as "Minet-Chéri" (a 5 name).

In 1926, after having written either under a pseudonym or as a coauthor, although she had always been the sole creator, Colette publicly acknowledged all her books, notably the very popular novels about the character Claudine, and from then on she was known as Colette. The numerical sum of those letters is 8 (3+6+3+5+2+2+5= 26=8). Significantly, that year of acknowledgment, 1926, was a Personal Year number for Colette of 1, thus

George Grosz. *Republican Automatons.* 1920. Watercolor, 23⅝ × 18⅝″. Collection, The Museum of Modern Art, New York City. Advisory Committee Fund.

Robert Indiana. *The Beware-Danger American Dream #4*. 1963. Oil on canvas, 102 × 102″. Hirshhorn Museum and Sculpture Garden, Washington, D.C.

Numbers serve as they are used: here it is for the predictive art of gambling. Jacob Lawrence. *Dominoes*. 1958. Tempera on gesso, 24 × 20″. Private Collection.

reaffirming the individuality and creativity that her Birth Name Number had indicated.

The meaning of the number 8, the numerical value for the name Colette, suggests that such a person reaps the harvest from the seeds sown. Colette did indeed finally achieve rewards for her endeavors and continued to be productive. As her Soul Urge (vowels) number 11 also shows, she always maintained ideals and principles—reacting openly and fearlessly to unfair practices and criticism of others. She bore out the paradox of 8—a free spirit, unconventional, and independently creative, yet practical and down to earth.

Let us return to her date of birth: January 28, 1873. The numerals together form 3 $(1+2+8+1+8+7+3=30=3+0=3)$. At birth, therefore, she had the potential to be engaged in forms of expression. She did indeed make the most of that talent, as one of the great writers of France. Even her early indulgences in dancing fits into this type of destiny. Innovation is inherent in this number but so is diffuseness. Colette may have recognized this propensity, for she disciplined herself to work compulsively. Her first husband, "Willy" Gauthier-Villar, of course had virtually locked her up to write incessantly for his own advantage, but Colette evidently slipped into the role herself and even when she married Goudeket and was free to do as she wished, she seems to have acted as if she were overcompensating for undisciplined leanings. Orderliness and mastery of her craft were uppermost. "Not happiness but work should be the goal," she stated.

Her birth on the 28th day of the month yields $2+8=10=1+0=1$. Colette's Life Path number, 1, was emphasized as she had the same number for her Birth Name Number. Action, originality, individualism, and ambition were confirmed. She moved in all of those directions.

We can further illustrate the techniques of numerology by choosing some dates in her career that were highly significant. What might the numbers have predicted?

Colette's crowning honor was her recognition by the Académie Royale de Langue et de Litterature Française in 1936. Her Personal Number for that year was 1 (January, her month of birth, is 1) + 2 + 8 (the 28th day of the month) + 1 + 9 + 3 + 6 (the year 1936) = 30 = 3. If a numerologist had been asked during her childhood or early youth what was in store for 1936 he could have suggested that a 3 Personal Year number meant some happening linked to expression. Number 3 is considered particularly compatible with number 1 (Colette's Birth Name Number) and therefore is likely to presage a happy circumstance. The forecaster might have suggested that as far as her future occupation was concerned, that year would mark an activity associated with politics, teaching, executive position, theater, writing, music, or public relations. For Colette, it was a literary event—the winning of a highly coveted award.

Colette, the acclaimed French author, was named Sidonie-Gabrielle Colette at her birth on January 28, 1873. The numerical significance of her name, birth date, and date of election into the Académie Goncourt in 1945 is summarized in this chapter, for comparison with the astrological delineation of her natal horoscope in the chapter on astrology.

Although it would probably not have been foreseen, as it turned out, the number 3 of the event and the 1 of her Birth Name number combined to show her nonconformist independence. To receive the citation, she appeared in sandals with toenails brightly polished in red—a most unconventional dress. Of course one might also say that this particular display was an example of the extravagance of number 1, even the silliness of number 3.

Curiously, the other noteworthy recognition, election into the elite Académie Goncourt, perhaps the ultimate prize for a French author, was also in a Personal Year of 3: 1 (January, her month of birth) + 2 + 8 (28th day of the month of her birth) + 1 + 9 + 4 + 5 (1945, the year of the award) = 30 = 3. Here again, an outstanding involvement with expression, as a contributor or recipient, might have been signaled.

Apparently the meanings of 3 and 1 (and of course 11 too) were continually seen in her life. Even when she died on August 3, 1954, the Personal Year number was also 3. Her burial became a subject for much writing in the newspapers, since the church forbade a funeral service at L'Église Saint-Roche. Graham Greene, a devout Catholic himself, openly criticized the cardinal's decision. A full state ceremony followed and interment was in the Pére Lachaise Cemetery, reserved for the country's honored citizens. Although her death had been quiet and peaceful, 1 and 3 continued to operate to make her a literary, unconventional cause célèbre.

Evaluation

Modern defenders of numerology emphasize that numbers play an important role in virtually all the activities of our lives: dates, social-security numbers, telephone numbers, and many other measurements identify us to ourselves and to others. The ancient Pythagoreans concluded that the cosmos of heavenly bodies, the earth, its creatures, and its objects form a single unit, of which the fundamental connections can be expressed by numbers. The assignment of abstract spiritual meanings to each of the basic numbers continues today because the validity of the associations in the minds and experiences of people in all walks of life has been confirmed. The connections between Hebrew letters and numbers are still used by Hasidic sects to formulate profound truths. The more scientists learn about the universe, the more they find that numbers are at the basis of all things. Space, energy, matter, sight, and sound can be expressed by mathematical and geometrical relationships.

The mechanism by which numerical values exert their influences on us is not known, but increasingly we are discovering the heretofore unsuspected forces acting from other bodies in the universe and existing within each atom in all substances around us. Some numerologists postulate that vibrations are inherent in each number. Others remain uncommitted to any specific explanation. All, however, accept the ancient Pythagorean principles as valid.

Numerologists teach that names and dates of birth reveal character and behavior. Detractors might argue that we often become what we and others expect of us. Reducing a name or date of birth to one of the nine primary numbers encourages each person to become whatever that number signifies, as long as we believe in its significance, but that set of circumstances is in no way a proof of the truth of numerology. However, numerology's supporters point out that this argument by the objectors actually affirms the beneficial influence of numerology, even if it were true that its tenets are not factual. The use of the associations between letters of the alphabet and their corresponding numbers has been a workable method for understanding the observed influences of names and numbers on people, even if they are merely living up to what the numbers are supposed to signify. This reliance on a useful, although as-yet unproved, hypothesis, say the supporters, is standard scientific methodology.

On the other hand, say the opponents, although the world is indeed full of numbers and statistics, statistical evaluations have not been applied to the significance of numbers as indicators of human traits, behavior, and events. It is unreasonable in principle and undemonstrated by testing that only the first nine numbers (and an additional few more in some systems) are a rational basis for perceiving psychological makeup, drives, behavior, destiny, and events—in short, all human thoughts, fears, and actions. Numerologists arbitrarily combine the basic nine numbers in many combinations to accommodate the virtually endless varieties of experiences and happenings. The letters in the whole name, the vowels alone, and the consonants taken separately may each produce a different numerical sum. The numerologist thus can find support for any type of makeup and destiny, no matter what the number. Numerologists reply that the very diversity of possible meanings in names and numbers fits the complexity of humans. The basic nine numbers are merely the fundamental building blocks, just as physicists use the four basic forces in the universe to explain energy and matter.

In short, detractors look upon numerology as number nonsense; whereas its practitioners see a useful application of ancient principles that have lasted for twenty-five hundred years.

Number 5 was the marriage number and also symbolized sparkle to the Pythagoreans of sixth-century B.C. Greece. Charles Henry Demuth. *"I Saw the Figure 5 in Gold."* 1928. Oil on composition board, 36 × 29¾". The Metropolitan Museum of Art, New York City. Alfred Stieglitz Collection, 1949.

Tarot

The Sun and Judgment, Greater Arcana cards from a tarot deck made for Cardinal Sforza in Cremona, 1484. Illumination on cardboard. The Pierpont Morgan Library, New York City.

Tarot

I saw them coming from afar,
Along the roads and into town,
Through schools and stores, to church and bar,
In working shirts, in cap and gown;
Haphazardly, they'd go or stay,
But finally all fell in line;
Then as they passed, each turned my way
—And every face was mine.

Allegories are stories in which the characters and happenings can stand for people, events, and abstract ideas. Virtually every culture on the five continents has its share of allegories. Examples in English and American literature are Edmund Spenser's *Faerie Queene* and Edgar Allan Poe's *Masque of the Red Death*. The process of reading tarot cards is similar to constructing an allegory about the person for whom the divination is being performed. A forecast is developed through the allegorical meanings represented by the picture on each card. At the outset of the reading, one card is chosen to stand for the petitioner; a number of other cards are placed in a standardized, traditional arrangement. The reader offers interpretations based on the relationships among the cards in answer to a question posed by the petitioner.

Composition of the Tarot Deck

The modern tarot consists of two virtually separate packs of cards: the Greater (Major) Arcana of twenty-two cards and the Lesser (Minor) Arcana of fifty-six cards (a few decks have only fifty-two). Some authorities believe that only the Greater Arcana is proper for divination; others see the Lesser as an essential addition. A very few tarot readers use only sixteen individual cards, called the "court cards," from the Lesser Arcana. Generally the Greater Arcana cards are held to be of more significance wherever they appear in an arrangement chosen for divination.

Greater Arcana

Each card in the Greater Arcana has a number, except for the Fool, which is either unnumbered or assigned the number 0. In some modern decks, the Fool is the first card; in others, the last; in a few it is placed next to last, between the cards for Judgment and the World. There are also variations in listings of the other cards.

0	Fool (or Madman)	XI	Strength
I	Magician (or Juggler)	XII	Hanged Man
II	High Priestess (or Female Pope)	XIII	Death
		XIV	Temperance
III	Empress (or Queen)	XV	Devil
IV	Emperor (or King)	XVI	Tower (or Thunderbolt)
V	Hierophant (or Pope)		
VI	Lovers	XVII	Star
VII	Chariot	XVIII	Moon
VIII	Justice	XIX	Sun
IX	Hermit	XX	Judgment
X	Wheel of Fortune	XXI	World (or Universe)

Lesser Arcana

The Lesser Arcana is made up of fifty-six cards in four divisions (the suits). Each suit has four court cards (king, queen, knight, and page) and a numbered series from 1 (ace) to 10.

The modern deck of fifty-two playing cards used in bridge, poker, rummy, and other games is probably the descendant of the Lesser Arcana, but its composition is not the same as the tarot's, although some perform divination with ordinary playing cards too. The knight is no longer in the game deck. (Some think that it was actually the page, not the knight, that was dropped. Others regard the jack as the combination of both the knight and the page and indicate that the queen may not have been in the earliest decks.) The joker may originate with the Fool of the Greater Arcana.

The four suits of the Lesser Arcana may represent divisions of feudal society in medieval times: swords (shown on the cards as spades, piques, epées) represent the military; cups (hearts, chalices, or goblets), the clergy; pentacles (diamonds or coins), the merchant class; wands (clubs, staves, scepters, batons, or cudgels), the peasantry.

The four court cards in each suit probably symbolize personages in the ruling royal medieval household: the king (or lord of the castle or manor); the queen (or lady of the court); the knight (or courtier); and the page (or knave, servant, or yeoman of the nobles). Several well-known historical figures sometimes were directly identified with the images on the court cards. In certain decks, the king of cups might represent Charlemagne; the queen of cups, Isabelle of Bavaria; the knave of wands, Hector of Galard. In some French decks such royal analogies were modified in the eighteenth century to conform to antiroyalist sentiments after the revolution. Even in recent times, caricatures of public figures may be found in a few decks. Often it is only the court cards of the Lesser Arcana that contain an image, but sometimes other cards in the Lesser Arcana may also depict persons and objects.

The Lesser Arcana may well have a different heritage from the Greater Arcana and may have begun earlier and been used exclusively for gaming, but the origins of both decks are unclear. At various times, the ordinary numbered cards by themselves have been used for divination and to answer questions in the manner of an oracle, by means of a great variety of arrangements.

History

The beginnings of the tarot are obscure. Indeed, the origins of all cards, whether for playing, divination, instruction, or religious symbolism, are uncertain. Furthermore, it is not clear if the Lesser Arcana antedated or followed the Greater Arcana. It is probable that the original functions of the tarot were for a card game rather than for prediction. Certainly, the card game of "tarock" (from the Italian *tarocchi*) was in existence at least from the fifteenth century well into the twentieth century. Sigmund Freud, for one, was particularly fond of the game of tarock, which he played often with friends.

The very name itself, *tarot,* is not understood. In the eighteenth century the occultist Antoine Court de Gébelin suggested that the tarot was a relic from ancient Egypt. He believed *tar* (an Egyptian word for "road") and *ro* (suggesting "royal") were the progenitors of the name. Alternatively, in the nineteenth century Eliphas Lèvi (Alphonse Louis Constant), a cabalist who trained for the Catholic priesthood, assigned Jewish origins to the tarot, surmising that there was a Judaeo-Christian history to the word. Some believe the Latin word *rota* (a circle) was the etymological antecedent of *tarot.*

The Taro river region in northern Italy, where early tarot decks began to appear in the fourteenth century, has also been considered an ancestor of the name, as has *Tarotée,* a French term used to describe crisscrossing patterns that decorate the backs of many early playing cards. Small dots forming a spiral on the borders of some cards have been referred to in Italian as *tarocchi* or in French as *tares* (or *tarau* or *tarots*). According to the contemporary historian Michael Dummett, tarot cards were first documented in Ferrara in 1442. They flourished thereafter as *carte da trionfi,* an Italian game of trumps. *"Triumphe"* was a card game in fifteenth-century France, and "trump games," such as whist, were popular in England and Spain in the sixteenth century. In late sixteenth-century France, cardmakers themselves called their guild an organization of *tarotiers.*

Many legends surround the origins of the tarot. One story suggests that the symbols on tarot cards came from pictures in a chamber of the pyramids and played a role in initiation rituals in ancient Egypt. Indeed, de Gébelin classified the suits as representatives of Egyptian castes. In this mythical attribution, the novitiate was shown the sum of mankind's wisdom as depicted in the images that later became the illustrations on the tarot cards, especially on the Greater Arcana. To the Egyptophiles, the tarot is actually the Book of Thoth, the godly giver of all knowledge. Others have suggested that the four suits of the Lesser Arcana are connected to Christian iconography, deriving their identities from the sacred chalice, the lance of Longinus that pierced Jesus, the sword of David, and the dish used at the Last Supper. There is also a claim that the suits came from the four mythic Celtic "treasures": the cauldron of Dagda, the spear of Lug, the sword of Nuada, and the stone of Fal.

More substantial conjectures attribute the beginnings of cards for gaming or any other purposes to Korea, China, India, or the Arab world. Ancient Korean divination by casting arrows may be related to the later representations of arrows on the backs of Korean playing cards. Playing cards apparently were mentioned in tenth-century A.D. China, not long after the invention of paper, and Chinese paper money seems to have begun at about the same time. Did they both start together, with the money itself that was involved in gaming later becoming represented by its surrogates, the cards, much as chips stand for money in the gambling of today? Or was it vice versa, with the cards used first for gambling and then for money? One tale relates that the first playing cards were made for the amusement of the concubine of Emperor S'Eun-Ho, the ruler of China in the twelfth century A.D. Decks of Hindu playing cards have ten suits, conforming to the ten avatars of Vishnu, but when these associations arose is not known. There is also an Indian card-related game called "Four Kings," which may go back to the fifth century as a prototype of modern chess. A Muslim game appearing no earlier than the middle ages became known in Italy in the fourteenth century as "*naib,*" from which is derived the Spanish word for playing cards, *naipes.* It is noteworthy too that the Hebrew word *naibi* means magic or sorcery.

The Christian crusaders have sometimes been credited with bringing to the West the cards of their Muslim adversaries. However, that estimate would place the appearance of cards in Europe no later than the thirteenth century, the time of the last crusades, whereas the first mention of cards does not occur until at least a century later. The Saracens themselves could also have brought *naipes* into Spain and Italy, but the dates of the Muslim penetration of southern Europe and the presence of playing cards in those countries do not coincide.

Another common suggestion taps gypsies as the conveyers of cards to Europe; but this is also at odds with the facts, for cards were known in the West well before the arrival of gypsies from India in the fifteenth century. There are many other farfetched legends and fanciful conjectures pointing to different countries and centuries for the beginnings of cards.

The very first Western descriptions of cards may have been in a German work and in a French verse early in the fourteenth century, but these assignments are in dispute. A presumed reference to cards in a regulation issued in the fourteenth century by the Spanish King Alphonso XI of Castile has been challenged in subsequent scholarship. However, the generally accepted and verifiable existence of cards does date to the latter part of the fourteenth century. In whatever manner they may have been introduced and wherever they came from, cards apparently were first recognized and recorded in present-day Germany, Italy, Luxembourg, France, and Spain between 1377 and 1387. Before then, writers whose works dealt with the activities of daily life made no mention of cards for gaming, occult dealings, or other purposes. Furthermore, although there were prohibitions issued from time to time against games of chance during the thirteenth and fourteenth centuries, references to card playing were not made until 1397. Once present, however, cards multiplied in types and uses, and their proliferation coincided with the development of printing techniques.

Representations on cards were usually related to the purposes to which the cards were put at various times: amusement, gambling, divination, satire, propaganda, and instruction in the arts, sciences, morals, religion, politics, commerce, philosophy, history, geography, grammar, music, and arithmetic. It is said that the young Louis XIV received his lessons from Cardinal Mazarin by means of card decks. Particularly after de Gébelin's work in the eighteenth century, tarot decks became especially associated with divination. The figures and decorations of cards were thus created to fit prevailing sentiments and attitudes. For example, Egyptian motifs, classical Greek deities and heroes, and fashionable political personages, philosophers, and writers were represented from time to time.

The fourteenth-century German friar Johannes, who is considered by many to have written the first comments about the presence of cards in Europe, looked upon the images as transmitting worthwhile lessons to nobles and peasants. The ruling groups could be stimulated to fulfill their social obligations and the lower classes could learn the ordered structure of society, with every person aware of his or her proper place. On the other hand, the established churches—Catholic, Jewish, Muslim—were often opposed to all cards, including the tarot, although occasionally a different moral evaluation was given to the Lesser Arcana playing cards (sometimes permissible) as distinguished from

OVERLEAF: Goldschmidt tarot cards from a mid–fifteenth-century deck. Left to right, top row: five of clubs, ace of cups, the Sun, Death (or ace of swords). Left to right, bottom row: the Pope, the Emperor, the Fool, the Queen in prayer. Deutsches Spielkarten-Museun, Leinfelden, West Germany.

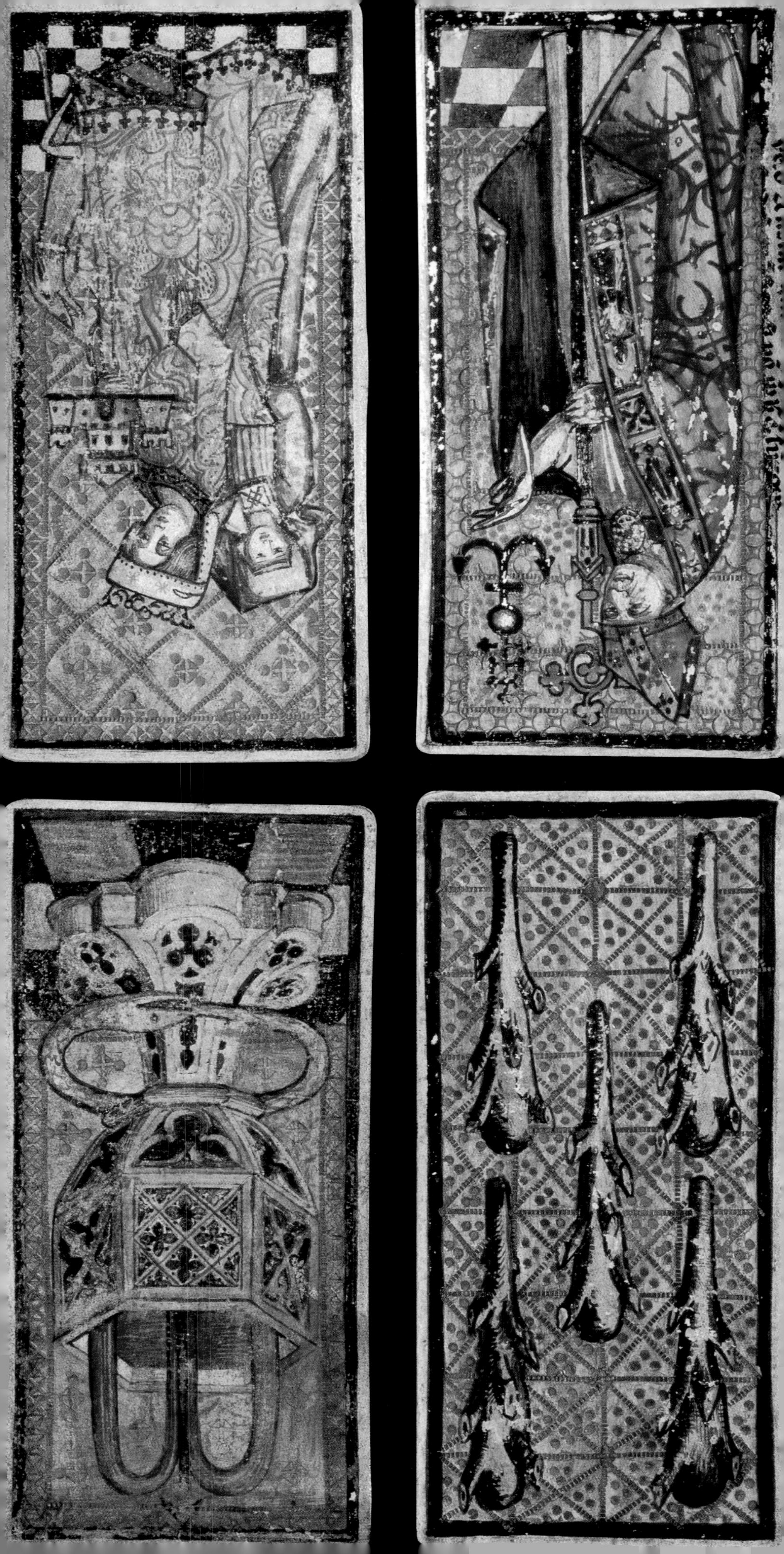

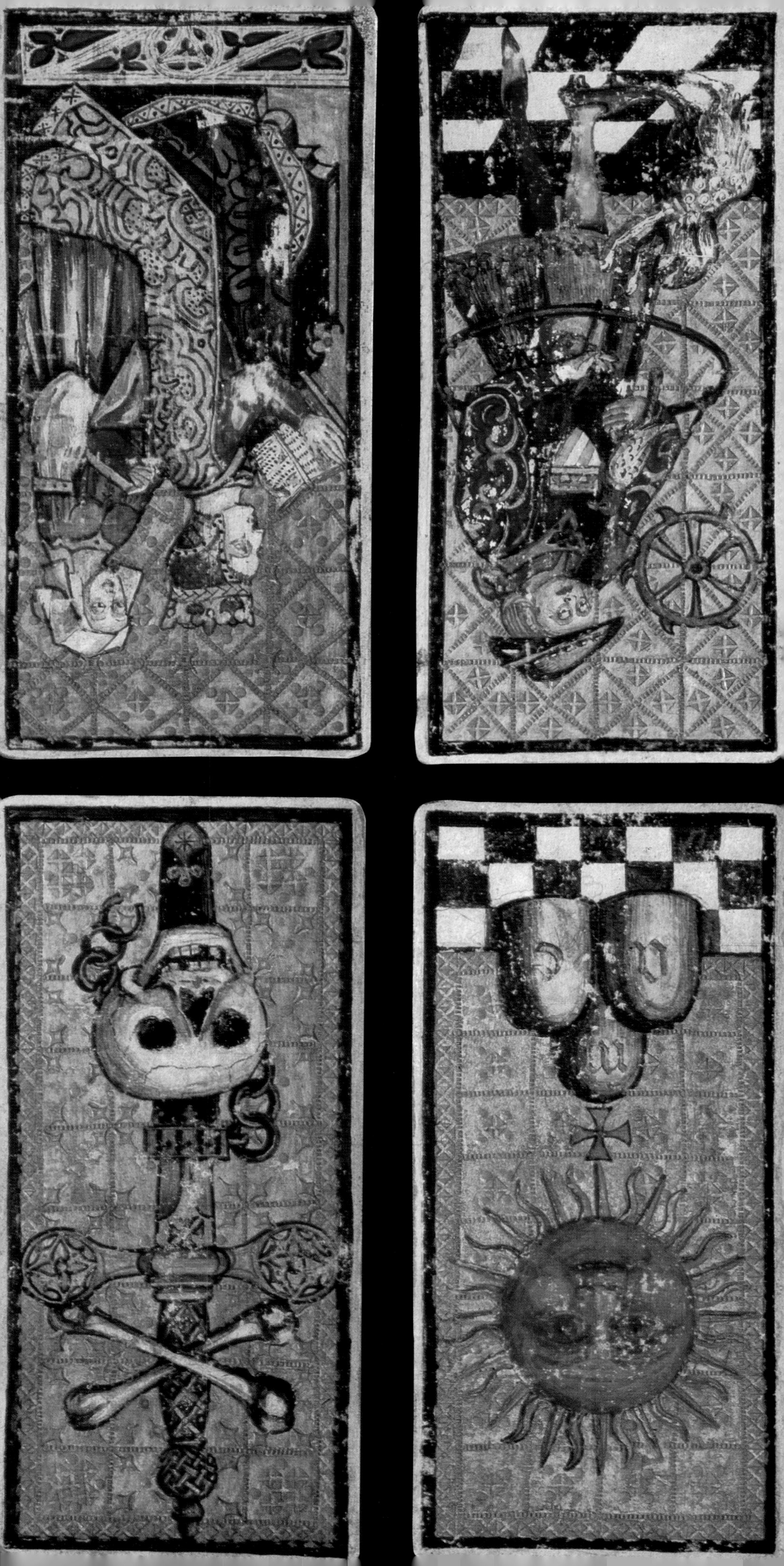

Knight and page from a *tarocchi* deck, c.1496, drawing by Albrecht Dürer. The British Museum, London.

the Greater Arcana (whose images were considered to be sacrilegious). By and large, the "devil's picture book," as the tarot and cards in general were called, was condemned by both Catholic and Protestant clergymen as a distraction from religious contemplation and the duties of existence. Of course, all divination is anathema to formal religion because such practices presuppose a predestined pattern of the future, placing them outside God's grace through good works.

Early Decks

A brief review of a few famous tarot decks indicates how the packs developed and how varied they became. Designers, illustrators, and publishing companies have produced hoards of diverse decks through the centuries, many of which are still in use, and the two different card groups that make up a tarot deck—the Greater Arcana trumps and the Lesser Arcana court and numbered cards—have undergone numerous modifications in terms of symbols, their order of placement in the deck, and the numbers of cards in a deck. Some of the major trumps in the early decks have since been dropped; others have been added or substituted. There are also differences of opinion as to where and when specific decks originated and how they are related to each other, but what we can deduce from the development of the cards is itself a summary of the history of the tarot phenomenon.

Two types of decks in use today, the Venetian-Lombardi and Marseilles packs, are regarded as bearing an authentic resemblance to the earliest European tarot decks. There is some evidence that the original decks were painted by Jacquemin Gringonneur for Charles VI of France in the late fourteenth century, but many historians think they are actually of Venetian origin; the cards in the Bibliothèque Nationale attributed to Gringonneur apparently date to the late fifteenth century. A deck published by Claude Burdell in the eighteenth century is said to be based on the early decks and is called by some the Classic Tarot. It was created originally as a series of wood-block prints and also is known as the Tarot of Marseilles.

Bologna, an active center of tarot-card making and playing from the fifteenth century on, has been credited as the place of origin of two early tarot decks—one from the fifteenth century attributed to Prince François Fibbia of Pisa; a second from the seventeenth century by the artist Giuseppe Maria Mitelli. There are sixty-two Fibbia cards with twenty-two Greater Arcana images and forty Lesser Arcana cards, but without any 2s, 3s, 4s, or 5s. Mitelli's deck had two popes, perhaps to replace the female pope with a second bearded vicar. Substitutions also appear in later Bolognese tarot decks, such as a mallet-wielding man replacing the Hanged Man.

A fifteenth-century pack of fifty tarot cards incorrectly attributed to the artist Andrea Mantegna and still incorrectly identified as the "Carti di Baldini," but now believed to be the work of a Ferrara artist, Parrasio Michele, was evidently made principally for instruction. The images personify figures and symbols from all classes of society and from mythology, the sciences, virtues, and astrology.

Among the best known of the early cards are those referred to as the Visconti or Visconti-Sforza group, which some scholars consider to be among the earliest extant tarot images. They were painted for Francesco, first Sforza duke of Milan, who succeeded Filippo Maria Visconti in 1450. The decks are for the most part incomplete, varying from seventy-four cards in the Pierpont Morgan Library in New York City and the Accademia Carrara in Bergamo to sixty-seven in the Yale University collection, forty-eight in the Brera Gallery of Milan, thirteen in the Montreal Museum of Fine Arts, six in the Museo Fournier, four in the Victoria and Albert Museum in London, and one card only in various other repositories in Italy, London, and the United States.

Apparently these elaborate tarot decks were painted for special occasions, marking royal betrothals, weddings, accessions to rulership, or other similar noteworthy events, and the presence of the heraldic devices of the Visconti, Sforza, and Savoy families (Francesco's son married Bona of Savoy) on various cards of the packs has been one form of evidence for their place and time of origin. But there are still questions about who designed and painted the figures. The name of Bonifacio Bembo of Cremona has given way in recent years to Francesco Zavattari as the artist of at least one pack of these cards.

Another famous deck, the Minchiate-Florentine Tarot, probably came into existence in the sixteenth century or the seventeenth century. There are ninety-seven cards (forty-one Greater and fifty-six Lesser Arcana cards in four suits). A Pope card is absent, but four virtues, four elements, and twelve zodiac images are added. A Sicilian pack, introduced from the mainland in the seventeenth century, replaced the Pope, Popessa, Devil, and Judgment cards with the Beggar, Constancy, Ship, and Jupiter cards. In the eighteenth century German decks began to appear displaying a mélange of motifs that included representations of literary characters, animals, hunting scenes, monsters, and even images of faraway lands.

Later Decks

By the late nineteenth century the tarot was especially associated with occult traditions. Members of secret orders have often been tarot practitioners—Freemasons, Rosicrucians, Knights Templars, theosophists, followers of the Golden Dawn, and others. In general, adepts of mystical systems have usually linked their iconography to ancient writings, such as the Bible, the Egyptian Book of Thoth, Greco-Roman arcane doctrines, Hindu mythology, Gnostic principles, and the cabala. Virtually all occult groups subscribe to the proposition that the ancients held the key to the universe of the spirit; that these principles resided in secret doctrines, which were either hidden deliberately from the populace or were too abstruse to be comprehended except by those who could perceive their meanings through study, contemplation, or psychic powers. The tarot, such groups believe, symbolized these principles and its iconography was directly derived from specific ancient sources.

The French occultist Antoine Court de Gébelin (1725–1784) had a profound effect on the use of the tarot, attributing the origins of the cards to ancient Egypt. (Although in his time Egyptian hieroglyphics had not yet been deciphered. The Rosetta Stone, now considered the key to ancient Egypt's written language, was not discovered until 1799, fifteen years after de Gébelin had died.) He postulated in his formidable study of the occult, *Le Monde Primitif* (1781), that the tarot was the visual representation of Egyptian thought and metaphysics. As a result of his influence, images on tarot decks have often assumed a

distinctly Egyptian flavor. He also altered some of the meanings of particular cards. For instance, he turned the Hanged Man upright and retitled the card "Prudence."

Alliette, a Parisian wigmaker and follower of de Gébelin's principles in the late eighteenth century, tried to create a unified system of divination by dreams, cabalism, horoscopes, alchemy, palmistry, magic, and cards. He also attempted to account for the various origins of the cards by asserting that the tarot was created by seventeen magi about two centuries after the "Great Flood" under the direction of the Greek god Hermes Trismegistus, the archetypal magician of occultism. Alliette, who chose to reverse the letters of his name and be called Etteilla, originated an entirely new tarot deck, rearranging the order of the cards and totally changing the images.

The French nineteenth-century occultist Eliphas Lèvi also linked the cabala with the tarot, but he condemned Etteilla as a preacher of false doctrines. Lèvi saw a significant connection between the twenty-two cards of the Greater Arcana, the twenty-two chapters of the Book of Revelation, and the twenty-two letters of the Hebrew alphabet. He assigned Jewish origins to the tarot, later extending tarot iconography to Christianity. He believed that the four suits symbolize the tetragrammaton, the four holy letters of God's name in Hebrew. To him, the ten numbered cards were in harmony with the ten cabalistic aspects of God. In his writings, Lèvi implied that he was in the process of reconstructing the tarot, but evidently he never did actually produce his own version.

Modern Decks

The nineteenth and twentieth centuries witnessed a diversity of modifications and innovations in the tarot's images and purposes. De Gébelin's version of the history of the tarot was re-created in a spate of decks. French occultist Paul Christian (Jean-Baptiste Pitois), strongly impressed by the writings of both de Gébelin and Eliphas Lèvi, elaborated on the concept of an Egyptian origin of the tarot in constructing his own deck. It was Pitois who proclaimed in the 1860s that the tarot cards descended from the secret pictures on the walls of the "Great Pyramid," which summarized the totality of human wisdom and which were known only to the priests of Egypt. He claimed to have reached this conclusion from reading the work of Iamblichus, a fourth-century A.D. Neoplatonist.

One of the most widely used decks has been the Egyptian-flavored tarot that was designed in the late nineteenth century by the Swiss hypnotist Oswald Wirth. He introduced his version of the tarot trumps as they had been described in de Gébelin's writings and issued *Le Tarot des Imagiers du Moyen Age* as the manual for his deck. Wirth's mentor, the Marquis Stanislas de Guaita, was a magician, spiritualist, and devoted follower of Eliphas Lèvi's teachings. Many subsequent tarot cards by other designers

OPPOSITE: A card from a German deck, c.1440, that superficially resembles a tarot card but was actually used for an entirely different purpose, presenting a story of falconry. This has been identified as the queen of falcons, from the pack of Princely Hunting Cards of Ambras. Kunsthistorisches Museum, Vienna.

ABOVE LEFT: Knight of swords, a court card, from a late fifteenth-century tarot deck, showing a wounded knight huddled over his horse, holding a sword, symbol of the sword suit in the Lesser Arcana. 100×45″. Museo Biblioteca & Archivio di Bassano del Grappa.

ABOVE RIGHT: The Fool, a Greater Arcana card from the French Gringonneur deck, fifteenth-century type. The Fool wears a cap with the ears of an ass and holds a necklace of outsize beads.

Personification of Mars from an eighteenth-century Mantegna *tarocchi* deck, an example of the tarot being associated with astrology. Biblioteca Vaticana, Rome.

Euterpe, muse of music and lyric poetry, depicted on a Mantegna *tarocchi* card of the eighteenth century. Biblioteca Vaticana, Rome.

and publishers were principally variations on the basic images in the Wirth pack.

Wirth's tarot deck was the subject of *Le Tarot des Bohémiens* in 1889 by Papus (the physician Gerard Encausse), another disciple of Lèvi's doctrines, who relied heavily on his clairvoyant powers in making medical diagnoses. He was also a member of the cabalistic order of the Rose-Cross that had been created by the Marquis de Guaita. Papus founded his own sect in order to propound the divinatory methods of the cabala and numerology. Among his writings on the occult was *Le Tarot Divinatoire,* published in 1909. The illustrations in his books show marked changes from Wirth's original cards, although they retain much of the Egyptian character, blending features of Wirth's deck with some of the Etteilla pack's pictures. Numerological and cabalistic meanings are attached to each card.

The Hebrew tetragrammaton of the cabala is prominent in Papus's analyses of the tarot. For instance, the suit of wands and the court cards' kings belong to the Hebrew letter *Yod;* cups and queens to *He;* swords and knights to *Vau;* pentacles and knaves to the second *He.* As Eliphas Lèvi had taught, the ten numbered cards of the Lesser Arcana were the Sephiroth stations on the cabalistic "Tree of Life" and the twenty-two Greater Arcana cards were related to the twenty-two letters of the Hebrew alphabet.

One of the most significant influences on the depictions, mechanics, and interpretations of the tarot was the international occult group, the Hermetic Order of the Golden Dawn, a society founded in 1888 that was the spiritual heir to Lèvi's basic doctrines. Although Lèvi's specifics were often markedly changed in different ways by various members, the fundamental associations between the tarot and the cabala remained. The Golden Dawn blended virtually every occult system, including the tarot, into their numerous methods of mystical divination. Many of the subsequent contributors to the tarot had a connection to the

"Misero," numbered 1 at the bottom, an uncommon representation of the Fool card. Here the figure is an old man rather than a youth, but the staff and the dogs at his feet are standard inclusions. Bibliothèque Nationale, Paris.

Astrologia, muse of astrology, from a Mantegna *tarocchi* deck, probably used for instruction rather than divination. Bibliothèque Nationale, Paris.

Golden Dawn—notably, Mathers, Waite, Case, and Crowley.

Samuel Liddell Mathers (who later changed his name to MacGregor Mathers to emphasize his Scottish ancestry) was a founder of a branch of the Golden Dawn in England. He composed a booklet, *The Tarot, Its Occult Signification, Use for Fortune-Telling, and Method of Play,* in 1888, a year before the publications of Oswald Wirth and Papus. Although no specific deck is attributed to Mathers, others designed pictures based on his writings, and Mathers himself originated spreads of the cards for interpretation that bear his name as MacGregor Mathers I, II, and III. In assigning his own evaluation of the abstract qualities in the Greater Arcana, he rearranged the standard order of a few of the cards. Unable to interest his brother-in-law the philosopher Henri Bergson in the teachings of the Golden Dawn, Mathers also failed to hold his own dominant position in the brotherhood that he had founded; he was expelled in 1900.

The tarot images conceived by the Englishman Arthur Edward Waite (1857–1942) and designed and painted by the American Pamela Colman Smith, which have come to be known as either the Waite-Smith (for its designer and painter) or the Waite-Rider (for its first publisher) deck, are now widely used. *The Pictorial Key to the Tarot* of 1910 is Waite's book-long treatise on the meanings and uses of these pictures. Waite was an early—and perhaps even the first—adepts to endow each of the numbered cards in the Lesser Arcana with human figures, instead of only the suit symbols of swords, cups, batons, and pentacles. Many modern practitioners have been attracted to the Waite deck, either as originally drawn or in its later modifications.

Although Waite subscribed to links between the tarot and the cabala, as Lèvi had advocated before him, he was critical and even contemptuous of the interpretations by other writers on the tarot—especially Papus, whom he singled out for ridicule. He rejected previous recitations of

Cards from the Golden Dawn's tarot deck. Left to right: king of cups, queen of cups, the Universe, and Judgment.

the tarot's history and saw its ancestry in arcane systems, such as alchemy, masonry, the Rosicrucians, and unrevealed ancient doctrines.

The Celtic origin of the four suits, Waite's idea, was taken up by Jessie Weston in *From Ritual to Romance.* Robert Graves, the scholar of ancient history and mythology, also saw a correspondence between the twenty-two letters of a Celtic alphabet and the twenty-two Greater Arcana figures. And the great Irish poet W. B. Yeats embraced the tarot's Celtic sources wholeheartedly. Yeats became an important participant in the Golden Dawn and at one time headed one of its factions. His constant companion was a tarot deck, from which he derived ideas, flights of fancy, and a view of the unified "Soul of the World." (T. S. Eliot also referred to the tarot in "The Waste Land," but whereas Yeats was a thorough adept, Eliot, by his own admission, knew little of the tarot's makeup and meanings. In Eliot's poem, his character Madame Sostris divines from cards, but only three of the five cards mentioned are bona fide members of the tarot.)

In the first half of the twentieth century, Aleister Crowley may have made the most spectacular claims of the Golden Dawn members. He was dubbed by some "The Wickedest Man on Earth," a title that he seemed to relish rather than resent. The epithet may have arisen in large measure because he portrayed himself as the Antichrist, the Beast 666, the number in Revelation derived by numerology. He claimed to be the incarnation of Eliphas Lèvi. Crowley designed a tarot deck that was painted by Lady Frieda Harris, and these cards were the subject of his treatise on the Book of Thoth, in which he supported the Egyptian connections.

A later tarot deck by Zain (Elbert Benjamine) also attributed the tarot to ancient Egypt. On Zain's cards, every person, object, and structure is Egyptian. Crowley's Book of Thoth deck, however, bears virtually no resemblance to any other tarot. (It has been described as having erotic symbolism.) All of the packs introduced by members of the Golden Dawn—by Mathers, Waite, Case, Crowley, and others—were supposed to have been based on the secret teachings of the tarot available only to the "inner order" of the society.

Currently in circulation there is a great variety of tarot decks. For example, a relatively recent deck of tarot cards issued by U. S. Games Systems, Inc., and created by Robert Wang in consultation with Israel Regardie, claims to be the original tarot as taught by the Golden Dawn and explained by MacGregor Mathers for the inner circle of the order. The *Encyclopedia of Tarot* by Stuart R. Kaplan depicts and summarizes virtually every type of tarot of the past and present. The very obscurity of the tarot's origins has contributed to its mystique and encouraged a wide variety of interpretations and meanings. However, no matter which deck is used, the imagination of the reader, rather than the actual pictures, and the intuitive perceptions of the interpreter, not the rules, are the important features in tarot divination.

Technique of Tarot

Greater Arcana

The Greater Arcana cards bear images symbolizing officials of secular and religious ranks, lesser members of society, abstract concepts, allegorical figures, personifications of objects, or even astronomical representations. The Greater Arcana cards are often referred to in English as the *trumps; atutti* in Italian; *atous* in French. The word may have come from the Italian *trionfi,* with the implication that these cards have superior value.

The following outline summarizes some of the Greater Arcana's principal images (to indicate how varied they can be) and lists their more common divinatory meanings. There are so many different and often contradictory cabalistic and numerological assignments given to the cards and their images that only a smattering of the linkages can be mentioned. Although no uniformity exists for images, occult associations, and interpretations among the numerous decks, the condensation that follows is a composite synthesis of many of the systems in use.

The pictures on each card differ among the various decks—either markedly or at times only in minor respects. Some of these differences will be mentioned as each card is described. Yet, despite the variety in details, the basic meanings remain the same—with a few exceptions—no matter which deck is used or which arrangement of the cards is chosen. Of course, as will be explained in the section on reading the cards, each diviner interprets in an individual way.

O *The Fool* (or Madman)
(French: *Le Mat.* Italian: *Il Matto.* German: *Der Narr.*)
Fate and fortune, past and future

Images in Various Decks
A bearded or clean-shaven young man. He wears a court jester's cap or a cap with a red feather or wreath and a collar of gay design or with bells. He carries a stick in his left hand, which is balanced over the right shoulder with a bundle or pouch on it and a pole or wand in his right hand. A dog is at his heels or biting his leg.

Meanings
Thoughtlessness, immaturity, irrationality (but also passion and infatuation); insecurity, extravagance; initiative, spontaneity.
Reversed meanings: danger of inertia, apathy, hesitation, instability.

Advice when this card is last in the spread: avoid extravagance; resist temptation; move ahead, but with caution.

I *The Magician* (or Juggler)
(French: *Le Bateleur.* Italian: *Il Bagatto.* German: *Der Gaukler.*)
Willpower, search for knowledge

Images in Various Decks
A man (sometimes with a beard) standing or sitting at a table that contains paraphernalia, including a knife, cup, coins, thimble, juggling objects, and other items. He wears a hat with a wide brim in the shape of the symbol for infinity (the lemniscate). When the head is bare, the symbol may hover over it. The magician may wear a belt; when present it may be narrow or with a sinuous serpentine pattern. In his left hand he holds a wand, sometimes with knobbed ends, which some adepts consider to be a phallic symbol. His right hand is usually free and pointing downward. Sometimes he holds a small sphere or ball.

Meanings
Originality, wisdom, imagination, rationality and emotion combined; self-reliance, willpower, resourcefulness, intellectual strength; skill, guile, scientific understanding, psychic powers, versatility.
Reversed meanings: danger of deceit, bewilderment, mental instability; suspension of activity.

Advice when this card is last in the spread: use talent for constructive ends; fulfillment depends on initiative.

II *The High Priestess* (or Female Pope)
(French: *La Papesse.* Italian: *La Papessa.* German: *Die Päpstin.*)
Hidden knowledge, prophecy

Images in Various Decks
A female wearing a headdress, the triple-tiered crown of the papacy. A veil or flowering headdress may also be present. Some decks have substituted Egyptian diadems or a crescent moon. She holds a scroll or book in one or both hands. (A flower or butterfly may be present instead.) She is seated on a throne; two pillars or curtains are behind her. Occasionally this card has instead a male, bearded pope in addition to the pope on card V, but most often the image is a woman in papal robes.

This latter depiction was probably based on a false rumor circulated in the late thirteenth century that a female pope, Joan, disguised as a man, succeeded Leo IV in the ninth century. The story even had the popess becoming pregnant. However, her supposed reign would have had to supersede that of the genuine Pope Benedict III, who came to office less than two months after Leo IV died (before the fictitious female pope was supposed to have gained election). Possibly to abandon the falsehood and yet to retain the card, a clearly male pope was substituted in some decks. But the significance of a female clerical leader remained in the interpretation.

Another basis for the card may lie in the story of Guglielma, the woman founder of the Guglielmites of Bohemia, a religious sect of the thirteenth century. In the fourteenth century a Sister Manfreda was selected as the female leader ("pope") by the Guglielmites. For this heresy, she was burned by the Church.

The Greco-Roman Juno (Hera) has replaced the priestess in some decks, with the classic goddess standing in front of her symbol, the peacock.

Meanings
Wisdom, intellect; mystery, hidden knowledge, intuition, the occult; serenity, balance, dualism of spirit and matter, the female gender (the Priestess signifies intellect and mind, as the Empress signifies feeling and body).
Reversed meanings: danger of ignorance, conceit, superficiality, uncontrolled passion, undesirable influence of the opposite sex.

Advice when this card is last in the spread: fulfill intellectual drives; add some emotional involvement to activities, but resist domination by the opposite sex.

III *The Empress* (or Earth Mother or Queen)
(French: *L'Impératrice* or *Grand Mère.* Italian: *L'Imperatrice.* German: *Die Herrscherin.*)
Achievement, fulfillment, understanding

Images in Various Decks
A regal woman, who has a halo of nine stars and the wings of an angel, holds a scepter in her left hand, indicating dominion over earthly things. In her right hand she holds a shield, often golden with an emblem of an eagle on it. The shield may carry the astrological symbol for Venus. She wears a flowing gown, which some see as indicating pregnancy. Sometimes a red heart adorns her neckline, signifying warmth and affection. She has a cross, indicating spirituality, and underfoot has a crescent moon (emotion) and a pomegranate (fertility). Some cards also include a sheaf of wheat, the symbol of the earth goddess Demeter (Ceres) of Greco-Roman mythology. In the background there is sometimes a waterfall (representing the subconscious) or merely a natural landscape.

Meanings
Fruitfulness, accomplishment, initiative; practicality, orderliness, decisiveness,

feminine influence; inspiration, understanding, harmony, pleasure, protectiveness.
Reversed meanings: danger of disharmony, overprotectiveness, lack of achievement, imprudence.

Advice when this card is last in the spread: shower others with largesse.

IV *The Emperor* (or King)

(French: *L'Empereur*. Italian: *L'Imperatore*. German: *Der Herrscher*.)
Power, independence, protection

Images in Various Decks
A mature man, implying solidity and substance, usually with a mustache or beard and wearing an unspectacular crown or helmet, suggesting conviction in his high position. In some decks a six-pointed helmet is supposed to represent the six-pointed star, which has occult significance. A yellow color, when present, announces spirituality. The man's robe is sometimes ornamented, sometimes simple. In his right hand he holds a scepter or similar symbol. In his left hand he may hold a green orb (world dominion). Below or at the side of the hand is a shield with the eagle emblem of authority. One leg is crossed, suggesting to some that the legs form the astrological symbol of Jupiter. To others the posture is one of unworried ease, announcing the security that comes from unthreatened authority. This relaxed attitude is confirmed in the casual position of the left hand at the belt. From a neck ribbon is suspended an amulet, usually in the shape of a circle (power). His throne may have armrests with rams' heads, perhaps of astrological significance. The cube shape of the seat in some images is seen to represent basic matter. The background is usually simple or a stark, rocky terrain.

Meanings
Power, achievement, wealth, orderliness, self-confidence; male influence, patriarchy, brotherhood, vigor, protection; intellect over instinct; fairness, decisiveness.
Reversed meanings: danger of ineffectiveness, indecision, emotionality, subservience.

Advice when this card is last in the spread: adhere to the principles of fairness but guard against inflexibility.

V *The Hierophant* (or Pope)

(French: *Le Pape*. Italian: *Il Papa*. German: *Der Papst*.)
Tradition, advice, morality

Images in Various Decks
An elderly man who often has a full mustache and a beard. Generally assumed to represent the pope. The figure symbolizes the papacy or else a religious or spiritual leader. In some decks the figure may be related to the Egyptian god Osiris. In a few decks, the figure is actually Jupiter, with his thunderbolt and an eagle. The man has a crown of three levels, for spirit, mind, and body. In his left hand, he has a staff or scepter with a triple cross, reiterating the significance of divine spirit, human thought, and earthly matter. Usually two fingers of his right hand are held up, an ancient gesture of blessing and also of the universality of dualism, a sign used as far back as ancient Egypt. The right hand across his chest may have one finger pointing up, possibly to suggest silence. He wears gloves, symbolizing honesty (the avoidance of contamination), and carries a key, sometimes two. They may be the keys to the kingdom of heaven, to spirit and matter, or to astrology and the tarot. *Pontifex*, the Latin name for the pope, means a bridge between the spirit and the senses; the sacred and profane. In the foreground are two kneeling figures. They may be dressed as cardinals or novitiates. His throne often has two columns behind to signify the choices possessed by free will—that is, to obey or disobey.

Meanings
Tradition, form over substance, orderliness, tendency toward inflexibility; kindness, generosity, justice; inspiration, spiritual leadership; passivity.
Reversed meanings: danger of folly, impotence, vulnerability, unkindness, unconventionality.

Advice when this card is last in the spread: spread largesse with passion but prudence; face the new and relinquish the outdated.

VI *The Lover* (or Lovers)

(French: *L'Amoureaux*. Italian: *Gli Amanti*. German: *Die Liebenden*.)
Choice, marriage, partnership

Images in Various Decks
This card is said to recall the mythological judgment of Paris, who had to choose among Hera, Athena, and Aphrodite. It represents combinations of lovers, male and female: one male with two females (the choice between virtue and vice), or two males and one female (lover, bride, and priest, resembling a marriage, or merely lovers and an observer). Sometimes there are several couples in a dance or in an embrace to represent courtship. One or two angels are shown on a cloud, in the sun, with a nimbus, or on a pedestal. The angels may be blindfolded; often with bow and arrow aimed at the middle lover, which may be an image of Vice. Some decks show only a Venus bathing with handmaidens and a blindfolded Cupid on the shore.

Meanings
Decision, choice between good and evil, between mind and body; affection, friendship, engagement and marriage.
Reversed meanings: danger of deceit, frustration, poor judgment.

Advice when this card is last in the spread: be decisive, no choice is free of fault; be cautious and guard against immoral influence; aim at truth.

VII *The Chariot*

(French: *Le Chariot*. Italian: *Il Carro*. German: *Der Wagen*.)
Conflict and triumph

Images in Various Decks
A chariot, wagon, or cart, possibly the chariot of Osiris or Ezekiel or Mars, or the throne of God. Some cards have the chariot decorated with male and female genital symbols. The chariot's driver is a male warrior with armor, or a female, clothed or unclothed. A crown may be worn by the driver, who also carries a scepter, sword, ax, or orb. There are two white horses or a white sphinx and a black sphinx. The animals pull the chariot in opposite directions. There are no reins. In the background are columns, a canopy, or a walled city. There may also be a dog accompanying the chariot.

Meanings
Conflict, adversity, confusion, revenge; triumph, spiritual and material success, rewarding travel, attention to detail.
Reversed meanings: danger of defeat, last-minute losses, avoidance of reality.

Advice when this card is last in the spread: savor success but mix it with realism; take care lest triumph end in defeat; control rash impulses; keep a balanced mind.

VIII *Justice*

(French: *La Justice*. Italian: *La Giustizia*. German: *Die Gerechtigkeit*.)
Fairness and balance

Images in Various Decks
A female with a resolute but benign and clear expression, wearing either a crown or a simple cap and sitting on or standing by a throne. She wears flowing robes or armor and holds in her left hand scales or a double-edged sword. In the background are two pillars, representing the positive and the negative; strength and integrity.

Meanings
Fairness, righteousness, virtue, honor, purity; balance, reasonableness.
Reversed meanings: danger of prejudice, bigotry, severity, intolerance, falseness.

Advice when this card is last in the spread: decide your own destiny; do not be dominated by fate; resist temptation; be cautious before decisions.
The number of this card is not the same in all decks: it sometimes changes place with card XI (Fortitude). It also may have a different position in a few other tarot packs.

IX *The Hermit* (or Beggar)

(French: *L'Ermite*. Italian: *L'Eremita*. German: *Der Weise*.)
Wisdom and enlightenment

Images in Various Decks
An elderly bearded man—a hunchback in some decks—sometimes with a snake (which when swallowing its own tail is a symbol of the perpetuity of change and a later derivative of

Chronos, or Time). The man has a voluminous cloak, often hooded (implying hidden knowledge) and carries a lantern (illumination and contemplation), often lit or containing a star (sometimes it is an hourglass), and a walking stick or crutch used as support (assistance, search).

Meanings
Enlightenment, secret knowledge, counsel; contemplation, introspection.
Reversed meanings: danger of unwarranted delay or unwise haste, immaturity, treason, lack of objectivity.

Advice when this card is last in the spread: seek understanding; plan ahead; use knowledge for useful ends; share wisdom.

X *The Wheel of Fortune*
(French: *La Roue de Fortune*. Italian: *La Rota di Fortuna*. German: *Das Glücksrad.*)
Fate, change

Images in Various Decks
The images on this card are frequently modified—in keeping with the meaning of the card itself, which emphasizes changes in destiny. A turning wheel is shown, perhaps in a wooden frame, at the edge of a cliff, on a vessel in the water, on the back of an elderly bearded, white-robed man who is on all fours, or suspended in the sky. The figures on the wheel might be three monkeys, ascending, descending, and at the top, or a youth ascending ("I shall reign"), a mature man descending ("I have reigned"), and an elderly man on all fours ("I am without a reign"). Many other combinations are also possible.

Meanings
Fortune, good or bad; culmination of unexpected events, opportunity.
Reversed meanings: danger of bad luck, failure, inconsistency, ignoring opportunity.

Advice when this card is last in the spread: be patient, for the wheel always turns; be humble in the presence of good fortune, the wheel keeps turning; seize opportunity and thereby do not succumb to fate.

XI *Strength* (or Fortitude)
(French: *La Force*. Italian: *La Forza*. German: *Die Kraft.*)
Courage and conviction

Images in Various Decks
The figure may be Hercules wrestling with or clubbing a lion, or, more usually, a woman is either pulling a lion's jaws apart or holding them shut (symbolizing love over brute force). The lion may be replaced by a column being broken by either a woman or by Hercules. The woman wears a broad-brimmed hat like the magician's in card I. The infinity symbol may be represented by the shape of the hat brim or by the lemniscate diagram itself.

Meanings
Strength, courage, endurance; conviction, confidence; will over desire.
Reversed meanings: danger of fear, faithlessness, impotence, indifference, uncertainty.

Advice when this card is last in the spread: face challenges and danger with courage and conviction; keep strength under control; use strength for reconciliation.

XII *The Hanged Man*
(French: *Le Pendu*. Italian: *L'Apesso*. German: *Der Gehängte.*)
Transition, adaptability

Images in Various Decks
A man hanging upside down. In only one deck (de Gébelin) the man is upright and the card is called "Prudence." The structure from which he hangs may be a gallows, two trees, or a cross. One or both feet are tied by a rope from which the man is suspended. One leg may be bent or crossed over the other in the shape of the number 4. His hands are either held behind the back or they hold sacks of coins. There may be no sacks, but then the coins fall from the pockets of the upside-down man. Apparently, to be hung upside down was one type of punishment for debtors.

Meanings
Transition, renunciation, sacrifice; readjustment, regeneration.
Reversed meanings: danger of ego fixation, unwillingness to change.

Advice when this card is last in the spread: renew spirit and purpose; right wrongs committed; contemplate change.

XIII *Death*
(French: *La Mort*. Italian: *La Morte*. German: *Der Tod.*)
Transformation

Images in Various Decks
A skeleton (universal image of death), which may be male or female, sometimes seen wearing armor, is shown with a scythe, used by the skeleton to cut down all life around. This symbolizes the finiteness of life and the sameness of all humans. In one deck the scythe is absent and a mounted figure holds a banner. In some decks, the skeleton is mounted on a horse. A white scarf may be worn by the skeleton. The background landscape is covered by the corpses and body parts of kings, popes, and common people. New growing plants are sometimes depicted.

Meanings
Endings, dissolution of attachments and restrictions, loss of wealth, a clearing away of past failures; beginnings, new attachments, triumph of the spirit.
Reversed meanings: stagnation, inertia, escape.

Advice when this card is last in the spread: all material things are impermanent; break the chains of the old and embark on the new. Tarot readers usually give a more favorable than unfavorable significance to this card since it announces embarkation on something new. It represents the slaying of ego to prepare for harmony ahead.

XIV *Temperance* (or Balance)
(French: *La Tempérance*. Italian: *La Temperanza*. German: *Die Mässigkeit.*)
Moderation

Images in Various Decks
The card shows a woman or angel possibly with one foot placed cautiously in a stream while the other foot remains securely on the shore. The woman pours liquid from one jug to another. Some consider the fluid to be water; others, wine. It is the symbolic essence of life. The symbolism strongly resembles that of the astrological sign Aquarius.

Meanings
(When this card appears after the Death card, it emphasizes rebirth.) Moderation, calmness, mercy, parental significance; self-restraint, accommodation, easy relationships with others.
Reversed meanings: danger of conflict, discord, hostility, impatience.

Advice when this card is last in the spread: pursue goals slightly beyond easy reach lest too little be achieved; avoid too many projects at once.

XV *The Devil*
(French: *Le Diable*. Italian: *Il Diavolo*. German: *Der Teufel.*)
Frustration, fear, caution
(This card is absent from some decks.)

Images in Various Decks
The card has a demon, horned or wearing a helmet sprouting antlers like a Celtic god. The demon may be winged and is usually animal-footed or entirely goatlike, with resemblances to Pan or to Mithra, the Eastern fire-cult figure. The demon carries an unlit torch (signifying the absence of enlightenment) or a sword or pitchfork. A pedestal often loosely holds the figure, whose right hand is usually raised to indicate magic or destruction. The mark of Saturn may be on the palm. Two additional horned devils or a man and a woman may be on either side of the pedestal. Freemason or alchemical motifs may also be present.

OVERLEAF: Reproductions of the twenty-two Greater Arcana cards from a Marseilles tarot deck, probably of the late fifteenth century. Bibliothèque Nationale, Paris.

LE MAT
THE FOOL
I
LE BATELEUR
THE MAGICIAN
II
LA PAPESSE
THE HIGH PRIESTESS
III
L'IMPÉRATRICE
THE EMPRESS
IIII
L'EMPEREUR
THE EMPEROR
V
LE PAPE
THE POPE
VI
L'AMOUREUX
THE LOVER
VII
LE CHARIOT
THE CHARIOT
VIII
LA JUSTICE
JUSTICE
VIIII
L'HERMITE
THE HERMIT
X
LA ROUE DE FORTUNE
THE WHEEL OF FORTUNE

XI
LA FORCE
FORCE
XII
LE PENDU
THE HANGED MAN
XIII
LA MORT
DEATH
XIIII
TEMPÉRANCE
TEMPERANCE
XV
LE DIABLE
THE DEVIL
XVI
LA MAISON DIEU
THE TOWER OF DESTRUCTION
XVII
L'ÉTOILE
THE STAR
XVIII
LA LUNE
THE MOON
XVIIII
LE SOLEIL
THE SUN
XX
LE JUGEMENT
JUDGEMENT
XXI
LE MONDE
THE WORLD

Meanings

Self-indulgence, ill-temper, unethical behavior, mockery of others, violence; subservience, self-imposed bondage; frustration, inefficiency.

Reversed meanings: liberation, respite, dissolution of a relationship, understanding, enlightenment, triumph over fears.

Advice when this card is last in the spread: exercise caution; aim at removing restraints; turn thoughts outward rather than inward.

XVI *The Tower*

(or Tower of Babel or House of God)
(French: *La Maison de Dieu*. Italian: *La Torre*. German: *Das Haus Gottes*.)
Inspiration and punishment

Images in Various Decks

The card has a tower in the shape of a crown with bricks falling off. The rooftop is separating from the base (break with the past). There are three small openings in the tower (signifying a limited view). Lightning is striking (a sudden, powerful event), and flames are spreading along one wall. Sometimes the sun is shining vigorously (fire from the sky is punishing the builders). A man and woman are falling from the tower, suggesting a new direction in life. Sometimes it is a naked woman emerging from a doorway followed by a man.

Meanings

Sudden change, abandonment of old ideas and past relationships; search for hidden knowledge, inspiration, arrogant pride.

Reversed meanings: resistance to change, ineffectiveness, confinement, dullness.

Advice when this card is last in the spread: embrace new ideas; move into new attitudes and surroundings with bravery; avoid hubris as the arrogance of pride brings punishment.

XVII *The Star* (or Stars)

(French: *L'Étoile*. Italian: *Le Stelle*. German: *Die Gestirne*.)
Hope, even without possessions

Images in Various Decks

The card bears a maiden, sometimes crowned, usually naked, and either kneeling or standing. Her hands may be held in prayer, and she is by a pool (the waters of life). She holds a container, out of which liquid is being poured (new ideas coming forth; rejuvenation). A large star sometimes surrounded by seven smaller stars is in the sky, in keeping with the ancient astrological principle of seven planets revolving about earth. The star is often equated with the Star of Bethlehem that guided the Magi carrying gifts for the Christ Child. There is a tree (promise) in the background and a falcon or ibis, standing for the soul or the intellect, or a dove, recalling the bird who announced to Noah that the deluge was over and land had appeared.

Meanings

Hope, opportunity, insight, fulfillment, optimism and action; enjoyment, spiritual and intellectual attachment; healing.

Reversed meanings: danger of despair, doubt, narrowness, rigidity, indifference.

Advice when this card is last in the spread: have faith and trust in what lies ahead; express feelings; act with confidence; no destruction is final.

XVIII *The Moon*

(French: *La Lune*. Italian: *La Luna*. German: *Der Mond*.)
Warning, uncertainty

Images in Various Decks

The moon is seen shining full or in a crescent, and two dogs are baying at it (the hounds of Diana?). A crayfish or crab is crawling out of the earth's waters. Sometimes the goddess Diana is shown with the crescent moon in one hand and a broken bowl in the other. In other decks a man with a stringed instrument serenading a girl on a balcony or astrologers observing the sky might be shown. In the background are towers, suggesting outside influences.

Meanings

Deception, prejudice, envy, fickleness, slander; danger, caution, secret enemies, insecurity, imagination.

Reversed meanings: minor deceptions and danger, easy rewards, triumph over evil influences.

Advice when this card is last in the spread: appearances can be deceiving; do not aim unrealistically at an unattainable goal.

XIX *The Sun*

(French: *Le Soleil*. Italian: *Il Sole*. German: *Die Sonne*.)
Growth, attainment, youthful spirit

Images in Various Decks

The sun is shown, or sunflowers carried sometimes by a little angel on a cloud. Alternatively, the sun god Helios (precursor of Apollo) driving a chariot drawn by white horses or Icarus falling from the sky are depicted. Other decks show two children touching (indicating contentment), almost naked (indicating that there is nothing to hide), or a blonde woman walking or spinning (one of the Fates?), or simply two lovers. In the background there is a red, yellow, and blue brick wall enclosing a garden. There might be a scorpion in the sky (this is not astrologically associated with the sun but with Shamash, the Mesopotamian sun god, who was guarded by scorpions).

Meanings

(The sun means expansion; the moon, card XVIII, emotion; star, card XVII, insight.)

Contentment, affection, friendship, freedom, acceptance; triumph, health, riches.

Reversed meanings: danger of dissatisfaction, unhappiness, poor relationships, uncertainty, deceit, phobia.

Advice when this card is last in the spread: take satisfaction in joyful freedom, health, and material possessions but do not become smug or careless lest the seeds of self-destruction escape detection; spread goodwill.

XX *Judgment*

(French: *Le Jugement*. Italian: *L'Angelo*. German: *Das Weltgericht*.)
Atonement and resurrection

Images in Various Decks

One or two angels on a cloud blowing a trumpet announcing Judgment Day are shown with a godlike figure holding a sword. Below, there are nude people, sometimes shrouded, or mummified figures arising from a grave, coffin, or tomb. There is also a flag, usually emblazoned with a cross.

Meanings

Atonement, forgiveness, accountability; rejuvenation, liberation, will, improvement.

Reversed meanings: punishment or reward; the results of past actions.

Advice when this card is last in the spread: reevaluate present and past behavior; reconsider one's influence over others; take a new, praiseworthy direction.

XXI *The World* (or Universe)

(French: *Le Monde*. Italian: *Il Mondo*. German: *Die Welt*.)
Synthesis, completion

Images in Various Decks

This card often has a nude female, in a variety of possible poses, wearing a loose narrow band of drapery, usually holding an arrow and a crown. Another type of image is a clothed female holding a scepter and orb and standing on a sphere, within which are walled cities, castles, and mountains resting on stylized waves. Jupiter with a thunderbolt may replace the woman. He is usually accompanied by his eagle, young girls, and prostrate soldiers. Further alternatives include two naked cherubs holding a sphere containing a castle, the sky, and the sea. An oval wreath (Nature) of green, yellow, red, or blue, often encloses the various figures. In the four corners of the picture are the symbols of the four elements and four evangelists with their representations: air (an angel symbolizing Matthew); water (an eagle symbolizing John); earth (a bull symbolizing Luke); fire (a lion symbolizing Mark).

Meanings

Completion (as the last card it has the implication of the end of a journey); perfection, material success, arrival; awareness, knowledge of the world, mastery over environment.

Reversed meanings: incompleteness, imperfection, failure, immobilization.

Advice when this card is last in the spread: attainment is only a beginning; material success is incomplete without spiritual awareness.

Lesser Arcana

Swords (spades, shields, leaves)
This suit generally implies danger ahead. It is the suit of disputes and movement, the struggle to resolve the conflict between spirit and matter.

Favorable significance: courage, strength, initiative, accomplishment, leadership.

Unfavorable significance: misfortune, loss, overriding ambition.

King of Swords

Images
Signify dominion (a serious dark-haired man).
Meanings
Action; determination, force, originality; authority, justice, experience; law, engineering, medicine.
Reversed meanings: self-focus, doggedness leading to defeat, cruelty, perversity, danger, lack of purpose.

General advice: keep to a steady course; avoid diffuseness, but be flexible.

Queen of Swords

Images
Signify capability, resplendence, femininity (a dark-haired woman).
Meanings
Perceptiveness, keenness, subtlety, accuracy, versatility, skill in diplomacy; fortitude, strength in the face of misfortune, generosity, self-assurance.
Reversed meanings: sadness, widowhood, loneliness, separation, deceit, malice, unreliability.

General advice: maintain fortitude; be generous; cast off malice.

Knight of Swords

Images
Signify extravagance and romanticism (a young man).
Meanings
Bravery, chivalry; skill, shrewdness, alertness, diplomacy.
Reversed meanings: rashness, conceit, simplicity.

General advice: meet opposition head-on but use persuasion and shrewdness rather than force.

Page of Swords

Images
Signify deception and discretion (a youth).
Meanings
Detection of the concealed, secret agency, insight; vigilance, discretion, alertness.
Reversed meanings: sloth, envy, impotence, deceit, hypocrisy.

General advice: be alert, forthright, and active; use discretion but not deceit.

Ten of Swords

Meanings
Low state, grief, confinement, disappointment, anguish.
Reversed meanings: liberation, reward, temporary benefit, acceptance.

General advice: recognize the low point; anticipate, expect, and plan for coming success.

Nine of Swords

Meanings
(Highly unfavorable. Said to be the most ominous sign in the deck.)
Misfortune, suffering, anxiety, disappointment.
Reversed meanings (also unfavorable, but less intensely so): suspicion, slander, shame, timidity.

General advice: accept misfortune, wait out troubles, bend and be ready to snap back.

Eight of Swords

Meanings
Danger, hidden enemies, confinement, censure, calumny; conflict, crisis, adversity.
Reversed meanings: favorable

General advice: plan painstakingly to overcome difficulties; recognize them and determine to triumph.

Seven of Swords

Meanings
Hope, planning, foresight, confidence; weaknesses probed, opposition confronted.
Reversed meanings: quarrel, uncertainty, loquaciousness, need for advice.

General advice: avoid quarrels; move ahead.

Six of Swords

Meanings
Travel, change from present conditions; expediency, anxiety overcome, opposition met; planning.
Reversed meanings: opposition, unwelcome offer, insolubility.

General advice: persevere until problem is entirely solved or until all the difficulties are overcome.

Five of Swords

Meanings
Triumph or loss, resolution depends upon prudence and self-control; either success or dishonor, either conquest or defeat.
Reversed meanings: indecision, new difficulties, treachery.

General advice: overcome pride, reassess realistically, recognize possible treachery by associates.

Four of Swords

Meanings
Recuperation, respite, seclusion; delay, strategic retreat, caution.
Reversed meanings: abandonment, exile, cowardice, jealousy, financial difficulty, social demands.

General advice: utilize withdrawal to replenish; be prudent without showing cowardice.

Three of Swords

Meanings
Separations, travel, dispersion, absence; conflict, destruction of the outmoded.
Reversed meanings: enmity, argument, disorder.

General advice: anticipate misfortune by leaving the outdated and making way for the new.

Two of Swords

Meanings
Balance, harmony, affection, friendship, equilibrium; change, loss, removal, truce, calm after the storm.
Reversed meanings: deceit, disloyalty, dishonor, treachery, but opportunity is at hand.

General advice: use affection, friendship, and balance to deal with separation and loss; take action.

Ace of Swords

Meanings
Justice, liberation, thoughtfulness, punishment for wrongs; triumph, strength through adversity.
Reversed meanings: destruction, misuse of force, fear, unfairness, excessive zeal.

General advice: anticipate success; preserve humility; act fairly.

Cups (hearts, chalices, flowers)
The most favorable suit. The suit of emotion and love.

Favorable significance: love, emotion, relaxation, peace.

Unfavorable significance: excessive sensuality, flattery.

King of Cups

Images
Signify confidence, relaxation, peace.
Meanings
Reliability, honesty yet diplomacy, steadiness, respect more than affection; kindness, generosity, peace; learning, professions, arts, sciences.
Reversed meanings: hastiness, injustice, cunning, self-serving attitude.

General advice: aim at affection in addition to respect; avoid hasty decisions; be generous.

Queen of Cups

Images
Signify practicality and warmth, maturity.
Meanings
Affection, warmth, enjoyment, devotion, honesty, fairness; practicality, implementation of ideas; foresight, intuition, imagination, poetry.
Reversed meanings: dishonesty, perversity, lack of realism, inconstancy, unreliability, unfairness.

General advice: use devotion, fairness, good humor, and pragmatism to implement dreams.

Knight of Cups

Images
Signify adventure, extreme youth.
Meanings
Opportunity, new ideas, proposals, challenges, dreams; persuasiveness, artistry.
Reversed meanings: poor judgment, delusion, boredom, cunning, fraud.

General advice: do not let opportunity slip by; maintain high principles; avoid delusions.

Page of Cups

Images
Signify quiet reliability, an aesthete.
Meanings
Loyalty, friendship, obedience to authority; contemplation, foresight; talent, artistry; birth of a child.
Reversed meanings: superficiality, diffuseness, selfishness, flattery.

General advice: cherish friendship; be generous; avoid diffuseness; resist flattery.

Ten of Cups

Meanings
Domestic tranquility, personal order, contentment; reputation, honor, fulfillment.
Reversed meanings: conflict, family disruption, disorder, pettiness.

General advice: taste the rewards of the quiet, honorable life.

KING OF SWORDS
QUEEN OF SWORDS
KNIGHT OF SWORDS
PAGE OF SWORDS
KING OF CVPS
QVEEN OF CVPS
CAVALIER OF CVPS
VALET OF CVPS
KING of WANDS
QUEEN of WANDS.
KNIGHT of WANDS.
PAGE of WANDS.
KING OF PENTACLES
QUEEN OF PENTACLES
KNIGHT OF PENTACLES
PAGE OF PENTACLES

Nine of Cups

Meanings
Fulfillment, success, abundance; stability, mental and physical well-being.
Reversed meanings: error, loss, misplaced trust, obstruction, complacency.

General advice: enjoy success without complacency.

Eight of Cups

Meanings
Disillusionment, interruption of plans, the turning away from relationships; timidity, self-deprecation, restlessness.
Reversed meanings: joy, celebration, pursuit of new goals.

General advice: do not abandon present relationships too early; celebrate when the new way is clear.

Seven of Cups

Meanings
Reexamination of goals and motives; illusions, dreams, self-delusion, unrealistic goals; mysticism.
Reversed meanings: broken promises, inaction, practicality.

General advice: examine one's path realistically; reflection should be followed by action.

Six of Cups

Meanings
Memories, nostalgia; trust, belief in others.
Reversed meanings: the future, coming events, new plans.

General advice: build new plans on past events; place trust only after realistic appraisal.

Five of Cups

Meanings
Union, loose affiliation, abnormal jealousy; imperfection, indecision, worry, loss.
Reversed meanings: reunion, inheritance, return of the lost or separated.

General advice: redirect energies and actions; take a stand; strengthen relationship or separate.

Four of Cups

Meanings
Satisfaction, apex of goal reached, enjoyment of circumstance, smugness; postponement, resistance to the new.
Reversed meanings: excess, new information, new relationships.

General advice: enjoy arrival but do not tarry; move ahead.

Three of Cups

Meanings
Fruition, attainment of emotional goals, marriage, maternity, comfort, harmony, healing.
Reversed meanings: overabundance, sensuousness without emotion, rashness, lack of appreciation, selfishness.

General advice: savor present circumstances; avoid impetuosity; add feeling to enterprises.

Two of Cups

Meanings
Reconciliation, understanding, cooperation, agreement, strong union, friendship.
Reversed meanings: misunderstanding, callousness, disunion, betrayal, separation.

General advice: attend to relationships; promote harmony; give sympathy.

Ace of Cups

Meanings
Growth, creativity, productivity, abundance, marriage; optimism, faith, fulfillment.
Reversed meanings: failure, inertia, faithlessness, instability, pessimism.

General advice: share joy with others; guard against inertia and deceit.

Wands (clubs, rods, batons, staves, scepters, acorns)
The suit of business, career, and free choice between the demands of work and personal fulfillment; talent.

Favorable significance: growth, invention, energy, work.

Unfavorable significance: opposition, failure, materialism.

King of Wands

Images
Signify strength and paternalism.
Meanings
Paternalism, maturity, wisdom, strength, tradition, sense of humor; honesty, conscientiousness, justice, loyalty.
Reversed meanings: despotism, bias, rigidity, narrowness, lack of feeling.

General advice: be decisive but wear authority lightly.

Queen of Wands

Images
Signify grace and practicality.
Meanings
Chastity, loyalty, self-control, tradition, love of nature (like Diana); practicality, understanding, perceptiveness, material things, business.
Reversed meanings: faithlessness, volatile temperament, vanity, domination, jealousy.

General advice: rule by charm not force; maintain poise in the face of opposition; direct attention to others not self.

Knight of Wands

Images
Signify alertness to danger.
Meanings
Separation, flight, departure, loss; advance, support.
Reversed meanings: disruption, discord.

General advice: advance alertly to meet the foe; act in anticipation of support from others.

Page of Wands

Images
Signify a bearer of messages.
Meanings
Service, dissemination of information, enthusiasm, loyalty, trust, consistency.
Reversed meanings: misinformation, slander, betrayal, inconsistency.

General advice: spread good tidings but avoid misinformation.

Ten of Wands

Meanings
Victory, triumph by force, power, drive to succeed; honor, unexpected good fortune, security.
Reversed meanings: oppression, obstinacy, deceit, separation.

General advice: use force to achieve, not to overpower.

Nine of Wands

Meanings
Difficulty, hidden opposition, delay; discipline, compromise.
Reversed meanings: rigidity, suspicion, obstinacy.

General advice: exert self-discipline; pause to plan for the new, not to remain stagnant.

Eight of Wands

Meanings
Activity, enthusiasm, travel, initiative, swift advance; opportunity, cooperation, understanding.
Reverse meanings: dissipation of energy, rashness, quarrel, delay, envy.

General advice: take advantage of favorable opportunities; avoid impetuosity.

Seven of Wands

Meanings
Resolution, opposition overcome, triumph through personal determination; gain, business success.
Reversed meanings: anxiety, hesitation, embarrassment.

General advice: move to overcome obstacles. Be courageous in the face of competition.

Six of Wands

Meanings
Diplomacy, success through negotiation, temporary delay; hope, partnership.
Reversed meanings: prolonged delay, fear, suspicion.

General advice: expect the best despite temporary delay; use others to fulfill one's hopes.

Five of Wands

Meanings
Struggle, stalled drives, conflict, trial; eventual satisfaction of goals, opportunity near.
Reversed meanings: danger, fraud, unnecessary litigation.

General advice: use cleverness to bypass opposition; avoid direct conflict.

Four of Wands

Meanings
Inspiration, originality, mental acuteness, intellect; respite, repose, pause, true love.
Reversed meanings: timidity, unreality, withdrawal, delay.

General advice: maintain confidence in one's own ideas; pause to reflect before advancing.

Reproductions of Lesser Arcana court cards: king, queen, knight, page of the four suits (swords, cups, wands, pentacles or coins). Examples from four different decks. Top row: swords, from the Morgan-Greer deck. Second row: cups, from the Papus deck. Third row: wands, from the Waite-Rider deck. Bottom row: pentacles (coins), from the Aquarian deck. U.S. Games Systems, Inc., New York.

Cards from Aleister Crowley's Thoth tarot deck. Left to right: Fool, knight of wands, Hermit, queen of wands, ace of cups.

Three of Wands

Meanings
Conviction, enterprise, business success, useful partnership, fruition of plans, realization of dreams.
Reversed meanings: deception by others, change of plans.

General advice: move ahead with expectation of success but keep plans flexible.

Two of Wands

Meanings
Achievement, rule over others, determination, abundant reward; wisdom, high principles, maturity, courage.
Reversed meanings: self-doubt, excessive pride, unexpected trouble.

General advice: maintain high principles; avoid both self-doubt and excessive pride.

Ace of Wands

Meanings
Beginnings, initiative, rejuvenation, new endeavors; inspiration, artistic perception, emotional ease.
Reversed meanings: anxiety, disruption, interruption of plans.

General advice: start afresh; be of good cheer; make new plans.

Pentacles (diamonds, coins, disks, bells)
The suit of money and material things; the outcome of the conflict between spirit and matter.

Favorable significance: comfort, possessions, stability, business.

Unfavorable significance: materialism, struggle.

King of Pentacles

Images
Signify experience, confidence, maturity.
Meanings
Practicality, business acumen, caution, skill, experience, confidence, intelligence without intellectuality; patience, terseness, conservatism.
Reversed meanings: temper, crassness, avarice, materialism, vengefulness, gambling.

General advice: maintain patience; restrain temper; add spirituality to materiality.

Queen of Pentacles

Images
Signify prosperity and generosity.
Meanings
Well-being, prosperity, luxury, good sense, security; generosity, compassion, affection, responsibility.
Reversed meanings: stinginess, narrowness, materialism, suspicion.

General advice: broaden outlook; add intellect to interests.

Knight of Pentacles

Images
Signify perseverance.
Meanings
Patience, efficiency, order, responsibility, persistence; practical action rather than abstract principles.
Reversed meanings: resistance, carelessness, smugness, sloth.

General advice: avoid complacency; lighten up.

Page of Pentacles

Images
Signify nobility.
Meanings
Concentration, scholarship, knowledge, diligence, organization, thrift; communication, effective expression, good news.
Reversed meanings: fussiness, pomposity, waste, selfishness, bad news.

General advice: add good humor to good work; avoid arrogance.

Ten of Pentacles

Meanings
Inheritance, ancestry, tradition, home, safety, prosperity.

ABOVE: Cards from the Napoleon tarot deck. Left to right: *Le Mat* (Fool), *Reine des Epées* (queen of swords), *Roi des Deniers* (king of coins or pentacles), *Roi des Coupes* (king of cups), *Roi des Epées* (king of swords), *La Roue de Fortune* (Wheel of Fortune).

OVERLEAF: Lesser Arcana "pip" cards: ace, 2, 3, 4, 5, 6, 7, 8, 9, 10 of the four suits (swords, cups, wands, pentacles). Examples from four different decks. Top two rows: swords, from the Etteilla deck. Bottom two rows: cups, from the Cagliostro deck. Facing page, top two rows: wands (clubs), from a Marseilles deck. Bottom two rows: pentacles (coins), from an Egyptian-style deck.

Reversed meanings: loss, disruption, risk, gambling, reliance on others.

General advice: do not rely only on what others give.

Nine of Pentacles

Meanings
Success, well-being, popularity, wealth; prudence, order, administration, foresight.
Reversed meanings: deceit, short-term security, loss by robbery.

General advice: try new enterprises; do not rely too much on good fortune.

Eight of Pentacles

Meanings
Craft, learning, training, achievement through skills; long-term goals, effort, virtue, candor, partnership or marriage.
Reversed meanings: sloth, hypocrisy, short-term success.

General advice: take the long view for lasting success.

Seven of Pentacles

Meanings
Gain, money, progress, determination; effort, productivity.
Reversed meanings: danger of loss or disappointment, worry, calumny.

General advice: overcome indolence; large rewards will come through perseverance.

Six of Pentacles

Meanings
Balance, business soundness; charity, kindness; reward, honor, gifts, support.
Reversed meanings: waste, loss, debt, selfishness.

General advice: balance gains and losses; share generously and receive bountifully.

Five of Pentacles

Meanings
Adversity, danger of loss, worry, temporary termination of money.
Reversed meanings: rigidity, danger of disharmony, but eventual love.

General advice: anticipate trouble; seek help from others; try a new pathway.

Four of Pentacles

Meanings
Materialism, emphasis on money and possessions, possible loss of money; enterprise, start of a large endeavor, successful negotiation.
Reversed meanings: obstacles, possible betrayal, delay, miserliness.

General advice: expect obstacles; prevail through negotiation.

Three of Pentacles

Meanings
Prestige, artistic activity, gain; initiative, timely effort.
Reversed meanings: quarrel, resistance to advice, mediocrity.

General advice: seek the proper timing for full efforts; aim higher.

Two of Pentacles

Meanings
Change, new ventures, travel, new attachments, temporary opposition.
Reversed meanings: lack of discipline, shortsightedness, inconsistency.

General advice: inject optimism into activities; anticipate good news; look ahead.

Ace of Pentacles

Meanings
Prosperity, successful business, new enterprises, contentment, comfort, gain.
Reversed meanings: undeserved reward, danger of greed, lack of imagination.

General advice: be grateful for good fortune; avoid smugness.

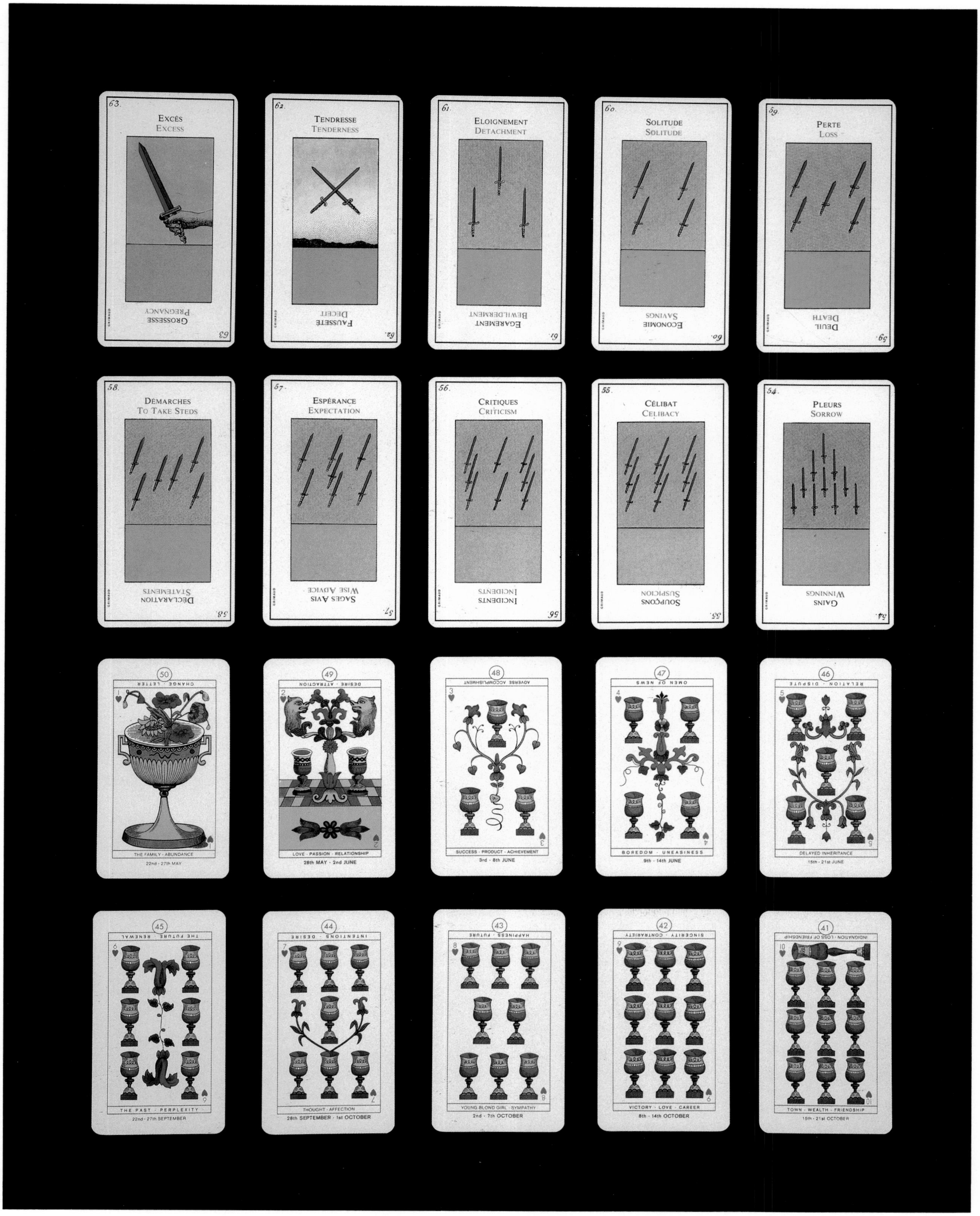
63. Excès Excess / Grossesse Pregnancy
62. Tendresse Tenderness / Fausseté Deceit
61. Eloignement Detachment / Egarement Bewilderment
60. Solitude Solitude / Economie Savings
59. Perte Loss / Deuil Death
58. Démarches To Take Steds / Déclaration Statements
57. Espérance Expectation / Sages Avis Wise Advice
56. Critiques Criticism / Incidents Incidents
55. Célibat Celibacy / Soupçons Suspicion
54. Pleurs Sorrow / Gains Winnings
50 CHANGE · LETTER / THE FAMILY · ABUNDANCE 22nd - 27th MAY
49 DESIRE · ATTRACTION / LOVE · PASSION · RELATIONSHIP 28th MAY - 2nd JUNE
48 ADVERSE ACCOMPLISHMENT / SUCCESS · PRODUCT · ACHIEVEMENT 3rd - 8th JUNE
47 OMEN OF NEWS / BOREDOM · UNEASINESS 9th - 14th JUNE
46 RELATION · DISPUTE / DELAYED INHERITANCE 15th - 21st JUNE
45 THE FUTURE · RENEWAL / THE PAST · PERPLEXITY 22nd - 27th SEPTEMBER
44 INTENTIONS · DESIRE / THOUGHT · AFFECTION 28th SEPTEMBER - 1st OCTOBER
43 HAPPINESS · FUTURE / YOUNG BLOND GIRL · SYMPATHY 2nd - 7th OCTOBER
42 SINCERITY · CONTRARIETY / VICTORY · LOVE · CAREER 8th - 14th OCTOBER
41 INDIGNATION · LOSS OF FRIENDSHIP / TOWN · WEALTH · FRIENDSHIP 15th - 21st OCTOBER

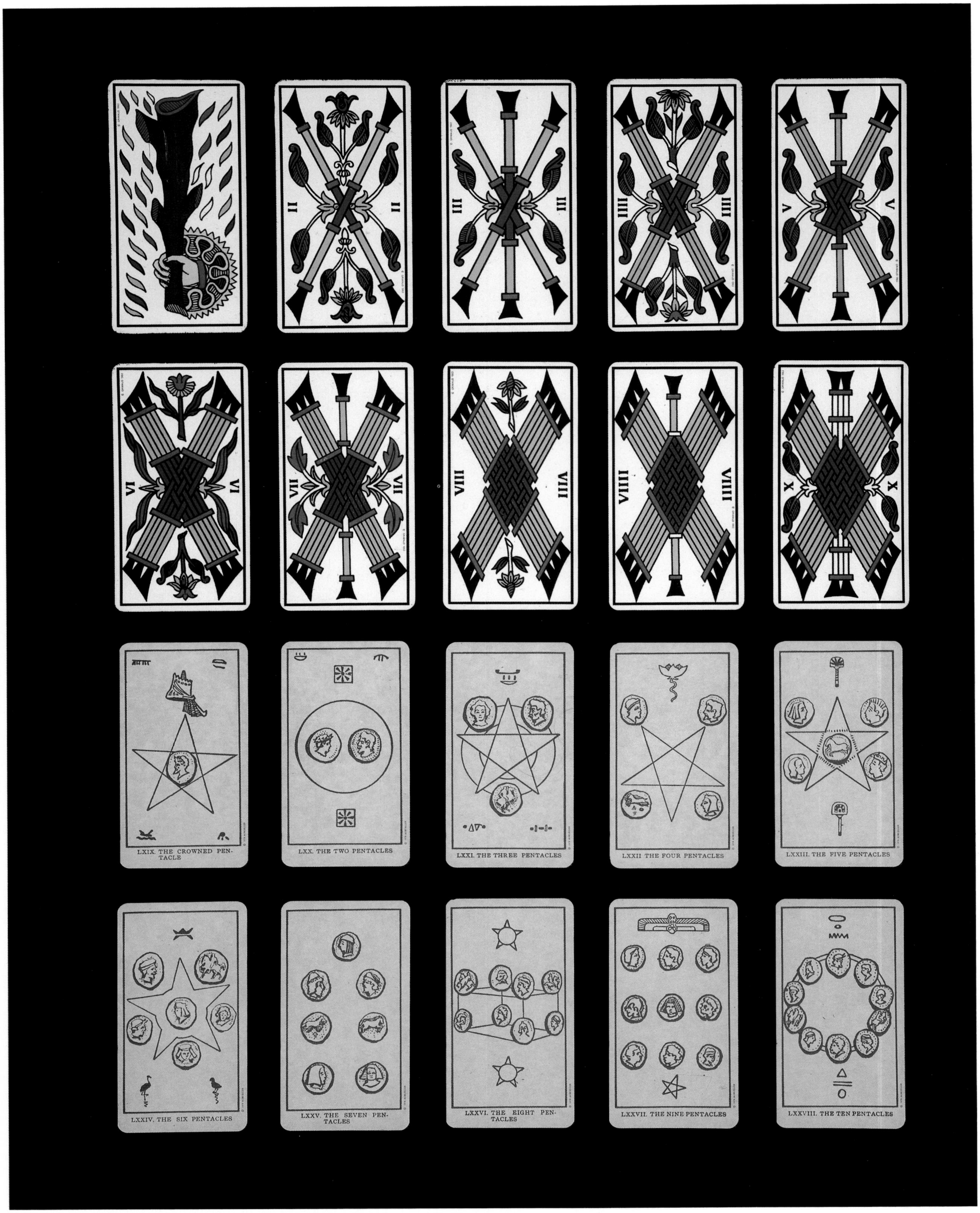
II
III
IIII
V
VI
VII
VIII
VIIII
X
LXIX. THE CROWNED PENTACLE
LXX. THE TWO PENTACLES
LXXI. THE THREE PENTACLES
LXXII THE FOUR PENTACLES
LXXIII. THE FIVE PENTACLES
LXXIV. THE SIX PENTACLES
LXXV. THE SEVEN PENTACLES
LXXVI. THE EIGHT PENTACLES
LXXVII. THE NINE PENTACLES
LXXVIII. THE TEN PENTACLES

Reading The Cards

Principles

To read the tarot cards—that is to say, to answer the questions posed by a petitioner—any number of card arrangements may be chosen. (Some of the many layouts are summarized in the following section on the spreads.) The substance of a reading derived from one spread may differ from the conclusions reached by using a different arrangement. Furthermore, the way an interpretation proceeds depends on who is doing the reading—the querent or a tarot diviner. Some tarot experts insist that most people should not use the cards to answer their own questions because they are not apt to be objective about themselves; the kinds of serious limitations inherent in psychological self-analysis apply also to tarot divining. Other tarot followers see consulting the cards as a method of probing subconscious desires and motivations—something one can only do for oneself.

The outside diviner, unlike a psychiatrist, has only silent cards and operates without the benefits of the free associations that patients express during psychoanalysis. Nevertheless, many well-informed tarot practitioners find reading the cards an effective method of reaching the roots of doubts and strivings and therefore a source of solutions to problems. Professional tarot readers believe that they can perceive in the cards themselves the thoughts that the client has imparted to them when concentrating on the arrangements. The ritual and atmosphere of preparation open the mind of the petitioner to the interpretations and insights of the performer.

Authorities differ on the meanings of some of the cards. Yet at least a few general principles can be said to apply to all tarot methods. First, the images are clues or triggers to intuition and perception. They are not necessarily to be taken as literal representations. Yet the Empress, for instance, is commonly considered to indicate influence by a woman; the Lovers often signifies a forthcoming marriage, engagement, or love relationship. Second, the meaning of a card depends in large measure on the position of the card in the spread. To take the ten-card Celtic cross spread as an example, Temperance in the No. 1 position may announce that the questioner is being prudent in his or her concern for the present predicament or that the person is feeling confident and capable. On the other hand, in the No. 2 place, where influences are signified, the same card may signify overcautiousness. As the No. 4 card, representing the more distant past, Temperance calls for self-control and the ability to appreciate one's own talents.

Meanings also depend on whether a card is upright or upside down (reversed). In general, an upright card enhances the probabilities of the image's positive features. The reversed figure stresses the special need to recognize the unfavorable aspects. In a few instances, the reversed picture enhances the positive rather than the negative features. The Devil is such an example. The upright meaning includes bondage and frustration, whereas upside down it announces liberation, respite, or enlightenment. Thus, when a card is upside down or inverted the meanings are altered—sometimes in direct opposition to the upright significance; sometimes merely different from the regular meaning.

Reversed images also usually indicate that dangers lie ahead. The reversed Magician suggests that since opposition is likely to occur to cleverness and existing plans of action, activities should be suspended, at least temporarily. The Sun, with its normally open, bright outlook, injects deceit when in a reversed position. An upright Hermit is a sign of introspection; reversed, it means lack of objectivity. The reversed Chariot can warn that plans are in danger of failing. Upright in the No. 10 position, it forecasts a resolution of problems; reversed in the same position, the card presages the chance of failure.

Nevertheless, whether upright or reversed, the image offers general advice that takes into consideration both the positive and the negative characteristics of the card. It is just that the upright card enhances the favorable aspects and the reversed stresses the dangers.

Tarot Preparation

One of the principles to which virtually all adepts subscribe is that the tarot must be approached with seriousness and concentration. Both the reader and the petitioner must clear their minds of all extraneous thoughts except the matter at hand. Some even go so far as to advise a preceding period of abstinence, especially for the diviner. Consuming alcohol and stimulating drugs or drinks is forbidden before and during the session.

A rigorous system of shuffling, stacking, and turning over the cards must be followed no matter which layout is used. The methods of sorting the cards vary widely, but they all have in common a prearranged order of procedure. However, shuffling, preparing, and spreading out the cards and assigning their meanings are simply an armature on which each tarot diviner builds his or her own personal structure of interpretation. Since all parts of the ritual have the objectives of discovering the psychological bases for problems and providing a means for finding solutions, each reader may modify a standard method and layout according to individual preferences and the demands of a particular reading. Tarot performance is considered both methodological and intuitive.

The same questions should not be asked over and over again (as in questioning the *I Ching,* where similar proscriptions apply). When not in use, the cards themselves should not be handled by many people, but almost exclusively by the diviner. Some advise wrapping the cards in silk or a similar material for storage in a special receptacle.

Preparing The Cards: The Shuffle

The questioner and the reader sit opposite each other across a table with a dark or neutral covering that permits viewing without glare; clear but soft lighting—daylight or artificial—is necessary. Some advise the petitioner and the diviner to face East and West; others suggest North and South.

The reader prepares the cards first. One method is to arrange the Greater Arcana deck in sequence from I to XXI, placing the Fool between Judgment and the World. The Lesser Arcana cards can be similarly placed in order, ascending from the ace through the numbers and court cards. The Lesser Arcana deck may be either placed on top of the Greater Arcana or kept separate until the two decks are mingled in a shuffle. In one method, the decks are picked up at random without the cards being placed in any order. No matter how the deck is prepared, the shuffle must be thorough.

When the combined decks are used, the cards may be divided, after shuffling, into two or more stacks, each of which is shuffled separately again. A stack is usually placed facedown before and after the shuffling. For setting out the spread, the reader requests the questioner to choose one of the stacks into which the deck has been divided. The other cards are set aside.

One method cuts the deck into four packs, of which one will be used to divine occupation and career; the second is for marriage and love matters; the third, disputes and litigation; the fourth, money and possessions. The cards to be distributed in a spread are taken from the pack that best fits the area of the querent's petition to the tarot. (Sometimes the four different piles may be labeled according to the tetragrammaton of the cabala, I, H, V, or H, with each stack corresponding to the overall mystical meaning of the Hebrew letter to which it has been assigned.) Alternatively, instead of four packs, the shuffled deck may be divided into twelve, with each pack referring to one of the twelve houses of astrology; or to one of the twelve zodiac signs.

The diviner usually shuffles the cards first or merely arranges them and then either hands the cards to the querent directly or places them in a stack or stacks, facedown, on the table. The client then shuffles them deliberately, carefully, and thoughtfully. This ritual is considered a way of clearing the mind and also of transferring the mental processes or vibrations of the client to the cards, from which the reader will be able to divine what is going on inside the person's mind.

Riffling the deck with the fingers or shuffling hand-over-hand are both acceptable methods. The person doing the shuffling may be instructed to turn the cards every which way, so that a combination of upright and reversed images will result. Whether all the cards are kept together or separated into two, four, or more stacks, the shuffling mechanics are held to be far less important than the concentration level thereby achieved by the shuffler—especially the petitioner—on the problem and the inquiry to be made. During the shuffling, many tarot readers ask the client to repeat out loud the question to be asked.

The Placement

When the shuffling is completed, the tarotist picks up each facedown card, turns it up from right to left, or left to right, thus maintaining its face precisely as the shuffler had left it, and places it in the pattern that was chosen beforehand: Celtic cross, horseshoe, circular, royal, etc. A card is considered to be upright as it faces the diviner—not the petitioner. On the other hand, some tarot writers state that the card images are upright or inverted as they face the seeker, not the reader; that the position of the cards in the spread is according to the querent's view, not the diviner's. Commonly, the turned-up cards are left as they are, upright or reversed, although at least one authority advises the reader actually to turn some of the cards around if all or too many are in an upside-down position. This "meddling" is frowned upon by most. Each layout has its own ritual during the alignment. Once the spread has been placed, the remaining cards are set aside.

In many spreads one card is designated to represent the querent. This may be done by assigning the first card picked for the layout, by asking the questioner to decide which of the images he or she would like to have as the "stand-in," or by selecting a Greater or Lesser Arcana card that has some resemblance to the questioner's station, occupation, or personality. This representative is termed the significator. Generally a court card is preferred (king, queen, knight, or page). Often the kings and knights are chosen by men; the queens and pages by women. Alternatively, married querents may be represented by kings or queens; the unmarried by knights or pages. The Magician sometimes serves for a male; the High Priestess for a female; the Sun for anyone of either sex and any age.

Interpretation

When most of the cards in a spread that is using a combined, full deck are from the Greater Arcana, the meanings of these cards are of added significance. Also, if only one Greater Arcana image is present and the remainder in the layout are from the Lesser Arcana deck, then that one card is assigned a particularly strong influence in the reading. The same increased significance is attached to a single upright or reversed image in an arrangement.

A preponderance (more than four cards out of ten) of any particular suit among the cards in a spread adds a special emphasis, depending on the suit:

Swords: danger ahead
Cups: pleasure and productivity
Wands: energy and growth
Pentacles: possessions and materiality

A card lying between two cards of the same suit is considered to be of importance; between two different suits, it is weakened or lessened in its impact. The suits are also classified by compatibility: swords are friendly to cups and wands and when adjacent may exercise influences on each other. Swords, however, are unfriendly to pentacles; as are cups to wands. They are detractions when preceding or following each other.

The presence of several cards (three or more) of a particular type from the Lesser Arcana signifies specific meanings:

Aces: power and attainment
Kings: contacts with the powerful
Queens: influential friends
Knights: rapid movement of events
Pages: fresh ideas and youthful associations
Tens: major business activity
Nines: increased involvements
Eights: travel and change
Sevens: uncertain arrangements
Sixes: satisfactions and rewards
Fives: conflicts heightened and resolved
Fours: calm determination
Threes: perseverance through danger
Twos: reorganization and assembly

Thus, the significance of a card depends on several factors: its basic, assigned meaning; whether it is upright or inverted; its placement in the spread; its position before or after the cards on either side; the concentration of suits; and the categories of other cards in the layout.

The Spreads

Some layouts employ only cards of the Greater Arcana; others combine the Greater and Lesser decks; still others include both the Greater and Lesser decks but retain only certain key cards from the Lesser Arcana.

Celtic Cross

One of the most common layouts is the so-called Celtic cross. Apparently it is not derived from the Celts, but the arrangement does bear some resemblance to a Celtic cross. The entire deck of seventy-eight cards may be used, or only the twenty-two cards of the Greater Arcana, or a combination of the twenty-two cards plus six court cards and four aces. Traditionally, the spread comprises ten cards,

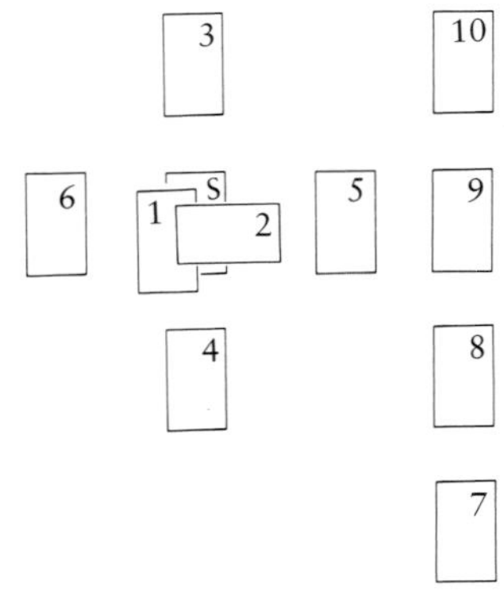

but a few authorities have preferred a total of nine or eleven, with accompanying modifications in the layout.

As the diviner lifts, turns over, and places the shuffled cards in the Celtic cross, he or she states out loud for the first card, "This is your present condition," meaning that the card stands for the person seeking the advice. If a separate significator has already been chosen, it is set down first, faceup, in the No. 1 position, and the first card from the deck is placed on top of it (without hiding it completely). The diviner then states, "This covers you."

The second card from the deck is accompanied by the words "This crosses you," as it is laid across the first card. The third card is positioned above the first two, "This crowns you"; the fourth is often put below, "This is beneath you"; the fifth is to the right of the first card, "This is behind you"; and the sixth is to the left, "This is before you." Some interpreters interchange the meanings and positions of the fourth and fifth cards, with the fourth placed instead to the right ("behind you") and the fifth below ("beneath you"). Furthermore, others reverse the meanings just described for the left- and right-positioned cards—using the right for the future and left for the past. These first six cards suggest the main influences leading to the answer.

The next four cards are laid in a vertical column to the right of the central group, beginning at the bottom with the seventh card, "This is you," or "This answers you." This card also stands for the questioner but now in a state of understanding that has advanced past that of the first card or the significator card. The eighth card indicates, "This is your home," or "This gives you strength"; the ninth is accompanied by the words "This is your hope and fear," or "This tells what is inside you." The last card calls forth, "This is the outcome." The phraseology may vary from diviner to diviner, but the general implications are the same. There are also some differences among tarotists on the relationships of some of the cards to each other, but the general categories remain approximately the same.

There are varying opinions as to what constitutes the traditional meaning of each position in this spread. Nevertheless, even if the assignments differ, the same categories are covered in the overall reading, and tarot performers are unanimous in seeing the card images as stimulators to ideas not as strict determinants. We offer the following assignments:

Position 1: the present situation. It summarizes the questioner and his or her present attitude and circumstances

Position 2: influences acting on the person at present, especially obstacles the person faces

Position 3: the actual goal or ultimate wish of the querent, if it were only possible

Position 4: the long past, the basis for forming the person's attitudes and actions

Position 5: recent happenings and outside influences

Position 6: the likely forces ahead that will exert influence; relationships with others in the future

Position 7: the nature of the questioner, the view of self; the beginning of a train of events of a clue that will lead to the eventual resolution of the problem

Position 8: the impact of immediate surroundings, particularly the home

Position 9: the inner emotional life, that which lies beneath the surface; hopes, desires, fears

Position 10: the likely outcome or resolution

Horseshoe Spread

The horseshoe spread may involve a limited number of cards or be quite extensive. The simpler form often serves either to answer a specific question or to give a short reading. The layout is an elongated ellipse resembling a horseshoe, with the open end most often toward the reader. As in the other spreads, the position of each card refers to a particular part of the petitioner's life.

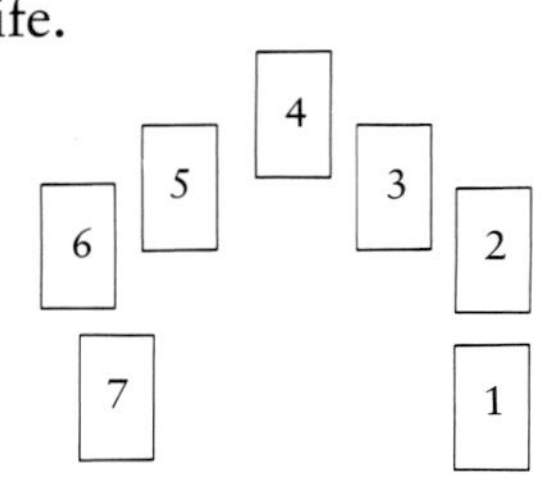

Position 1: past influences

Position 2: present influences

Position 3: the future or the subconscious

Position 4: prudent action

Position 5: other people

Position 6: obstacles ahead or action to take against them

Position 7: probable outcome

Another version of the horseshoe spread consists of ten or twelve cards in a similar semicircular pattern. Assignments to each of the ten or twelve positions are similar to those delivered with the Celtic cross.

For the extensive horseshoe spread a complete deck of seventy-eight cards is divided into six separate piles by an elaborate procedure: the top card of the complete, shuffled deck is removed and placed face down to start stack A; the next two cards of the full deck begin a second stack, B. This process is continued between the two stacks until A contains twenty-six cards and B has fifty-two. Stack B is then subdivided into piles C and D by the same method until stack B disappears altogether. Stack D is then subdivided into E and F. This leaves only A (twenty-six cards), C (eighteen cards), E (twelve cards), and F (twenty-two cards).

The spread is then laid out by picking consecutively, one by one, all the cards from pile A, then from C, then from E, until the fifty-six cards are placed in three separate, parallel (concentric) horseshoes. The remaining unused (F) cards are set aside. One horseshoe contains twenty-six cards from pile A, the second horseshoe eighteen cards from stack C, and the third horseshoe has twelve cards from stack E. The reading is performed by combining the meanings of the first and last card of each horseshoe and progressing up the horseshoe until all the cards are interpreted. Each horseshoe is read separately. The reading from this elaborate diagram can become a veritable allegorical novel of ideas, happenings, and predictions—formed entirely by the perceptions of the diviner.

Numerous other layouts are also in use. However, the principles of interpretation are similar. In whichever arrangement the cards are placed, the reader assigns a card or group of cards to the present situation, past influences and associations, future influences, goals and aspirations, underlying doubts, attitudes that are recommended, favorable actions to be taken, and the likely outcome.

In the following spreads, the methods of shuffling and the ritual of choosing the cards differ widely but their general principles are similar to those summarized earlier.

Royal Spread

Fifty-four cards are chosen from a full deck of seventy-eight; twenty-two Greater Arcana and thirty-two Lesser Arcana, of which sixteen are court cards, four are aces, and twelve are numbered cards (either twos, threes, or fours). These are read in pairs or groups in as many different ways as there are diviners.

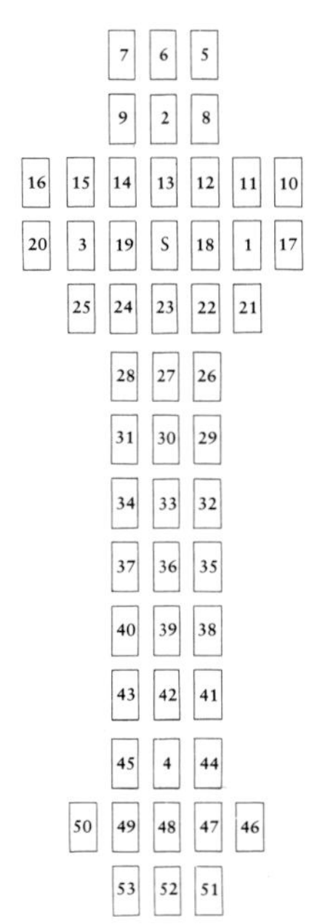

Circular Spread

Thirteen cards are chosen from a full deck of seventy-eight cards. Twelve refer to events in a coming month. The significator is mingled in the deck and may or may not

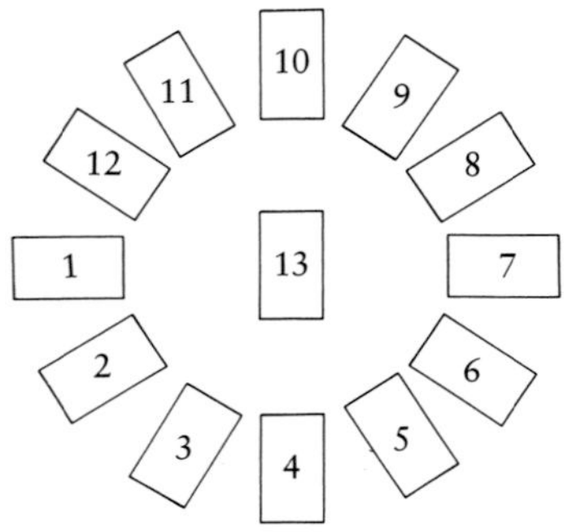

appear in the layout. The thirteenth card is read first and indicates the general circumstances that will prevail in the year ahead.

Seven-Card Spread

A pack of thirty-three cards, including the twenty-two cards of the Greater Arcana and eleven cards from the Lesser Arcana are used for this spread. Seven cards are selected from the shuffled pack and laid out in a row. Two represent the past; three the present; two the future. This spread can

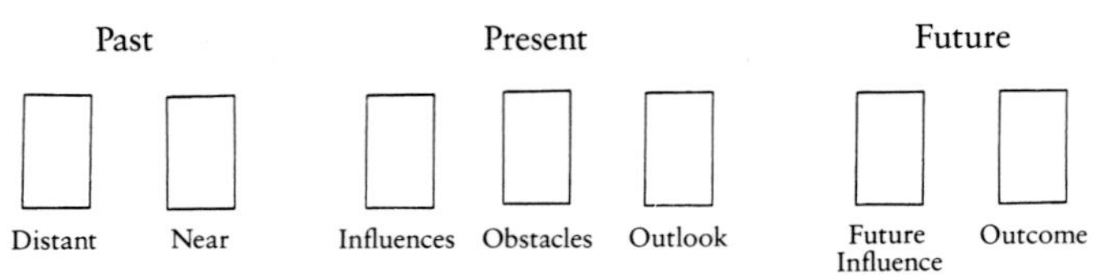

also be used to give an affirmative or negative response to a single question. Four reversed cards means "no" or a delayed "yes"; more than four reversed cards means a strong "no"; four upright cards means a strong "yes."

Seventh-Card Spread

From the full deck a significator is chosen (usually a court card) and then twenty-one cards are selected by repeatedly counting off and discarding six cards from the full deck and placing the seventh on the table until there are three rows of

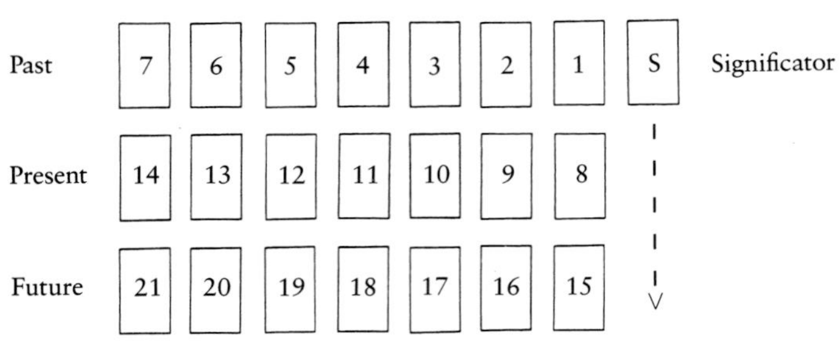

seven cards each. The meanings to the querent are influenced by the interpretation of the cards in each row—beside which the significator is placed as each of these cards is read. One row represents the past; the second is for the present; the third suggests the future.

A Gypsy Spread

This is one of the many different kinds of arrangements given the title "Gypsy spread." A pack of forty-two cards is formed from twenty Lesser Arcana cards chosen at random and combined with the full Greater Arcana deck. The cards are divided into six stacks of seven cards each, from which the rows are laid out. The cards in each row are read from right to left. Each row has an overall application:

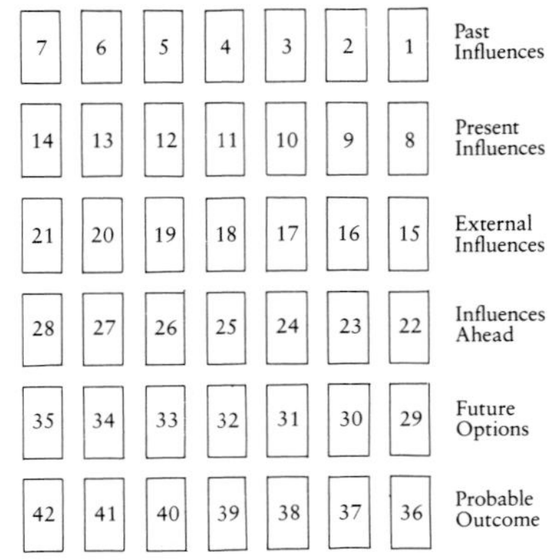

Row 1: past influences
Row 2: present influences
Row 3: outside influences
Row 4: influences ahead
Row 5: future options
Row 6: probable outcome

Short Papus Spread

This spread consists of seven cards—four from the Lesser Arcana and three from the Greater Arcana. The four Lesser cards are picked from the top of a shuffled Lesser Arcana deck. The three Greater Arcana cards to be used in the spread are chosen from a stack of seven cards randomly selected from the Greater Arcana. The Lesser four are laid in a "cross," then the Greater three are placed inside them.

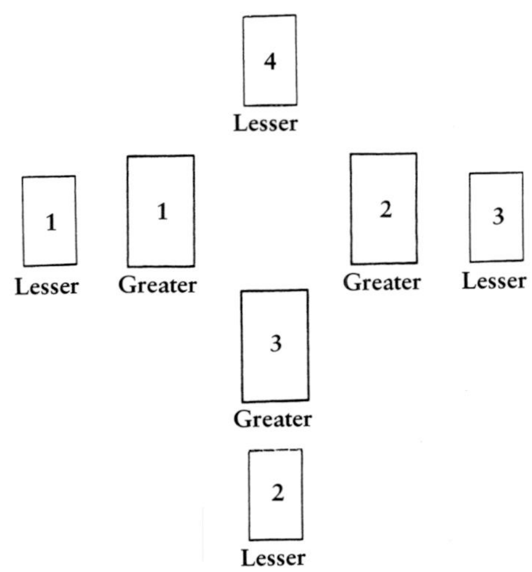

Lesser Arcana card 1: beginnings
Lesser Arcana card 2: culmination
Lesser Arcana card 3: obstructions
Lesser Arcana card 4: stalemate
Greater Arcana card 1: past factors in the present situation

Greater Arcana card 2: present factors influencing present situation

Greater Arcana card 3: eventual determining influences

Seven-Point Star Spread
Just as the circular spread projects events in the months of the year ahead, the seven-point star indicates what is likely to be faced in the coming week.

Seven cards (from the Greater or Lesser packs or from the full combined deck) are placed in a star shape with the significator in the center. Each position is assigned a day; and the significator modifies each of the cards:

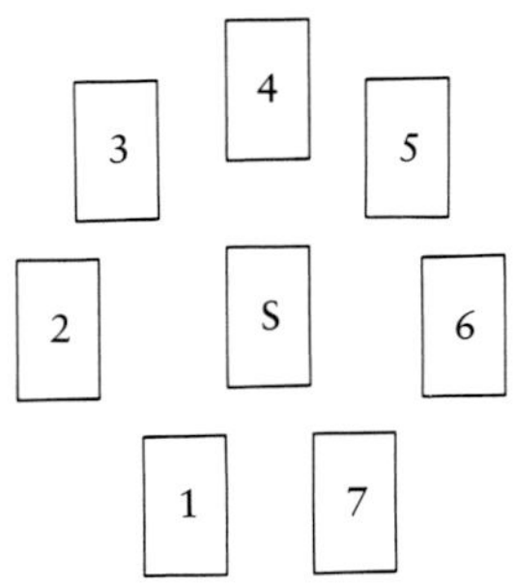

Position 4: Sunday
Position 1: Monday
Position 5: Tuesday
Position 2: Wednesday
Position 6: Thursday
Position 3: Friday
Position 7: Saturday

Tree of Life Spread
Seventy random cards are placed in stacks of ten cards each (from Greater and Lesser decks). The significator is chosen

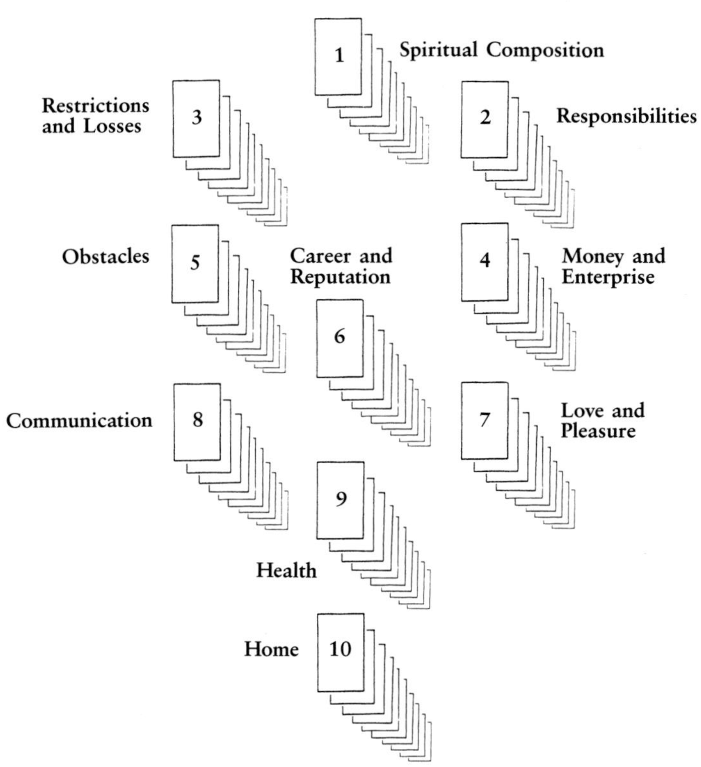

but left in the deck among the cards picked by chance to construct the cabalistic tree design. The ten Sephiroth of the cabala correspond to the ten piles of seven cards each. If the significator is found in one of the stacks, that stack is considered especially important. All seven cards in each of the ten positions are read to apply to the area of life signified by the assigned stations.

Stack 1: spiritual composition
Stack 2: responsibilities
Stack 3: restrictions and losses
Stack 4: money and enterprise
Stack 5: obstacles
Stack 6: career and reputation
Stack 7: love and pleasure
Stack 8: communication
Stack 9: health
Stack 10: home

Areas of Life Spread
Forty-eight cards from the combined decks are divided into twelve stacks of four cards each. The cards in each stack are interpreted according to the area of life that is assigned to that stack:

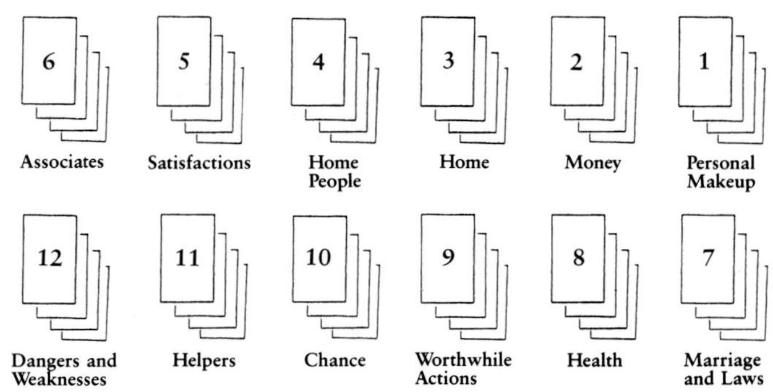

Stack 1: personal makeup
Stack 2: money
Stack 3: home physical surroundings
Stack 4: home people
Stack 5: satisfactions
Stack 6: associates
Stack 7: marriage and laws
Stack 8: health
Stack 9: worthwhile actions
Stack 10: chance
Stack 11: helpers
Stack 12: dangers to anticipate and weaknesses to be overcome

Sample Readings

The following summaries are merely two samples of how one diviner might interpret the cards. Of course, others may see very different meanings in each image, according to the significance they attach to the location of a card in the spread.

First Reading: The Question

Our first example is a reading given for N. T., a lawyer who looked to the tarot as just one method of helping to prepare him for the future: "Let's see what the cards tell me. Nothing else seems to convince me of what I should do." N. T., the petitioner, voiced his difficulty in trying to decide whether to continue practicing law on his own or whether to take on a different assignment—as a salaried counsel for a private insurance company. The dilemma sprang from his ambivalence toward the increasing strains of private practice and the possible financial diminutions ahead, as he was getting older and costs were rising. On the other hand, he was afraid of losing independence as a paid employee and also of lessening his income. Private practice might still bring the rewards, challenges, and ego satisfactions that had been his for many years; yet in a full-time job, he would be free from the demands and physical burdens of private practice and would have measurable security and regularized activity.

The Spread (Celtic Cross)

After cutting, shuffling, and preparing the cards, the diviner chose to lay out ten cards in the form of a Celtic cross. The querent had selected the king of wands as his significator. This choice must be kept in mind when the interpretations are made.

The arrangement places the Greater Arcana's Chariot as the first card to cover the significator. The reader considers this position to indicate the present situation saying, "This covers you." The second card is the five of pentacles, signifying immediate influences and difficulties ("This crosses you"). The third, the Sun, represents the ultimate goals ("This crowns you"). The fourth, the king of swords, stands for the distant past, the early life ("This is beneath you"). The fifth, the two of pentacles, suggests the recent past ("This is behind you"). The sixth, the Lovers, divines the future ("This is before you"). The seventh, the six of swords, represents present concerns ("This answers you"). The eighth, the queen of cups, is indicative of domestic surroundings ("This is your home"). The ninth, the Emperor reversed, reveals subconscious inner concerns ("This is your hope and fear"). The tenth, the Tower, represents the eventual outcome. ("This is the outcome").

The Interpretation

Thus, there is no predominance of any one suit, and the Greater and Lesser Arcana are approximately evenly divided, emphasizing, if anything, the divided attitudes of the petitioner. Only one card is reversed, the Emperor. In general, therefore, a relatively positive outlook is to be anticipated, but the very fact that there is only one card turned backward has added significance. A reversed Emperor, especially in the subconscious position, points to an all-pervasive indecisiveness and ineffectuality, a clear characteristic of this person and a danger always to be guarded against. Indeed it may suggest that no matter how the eventual outcome is announced by the last (tenth) card, subservience and hesitancy will probably always be the dragon that this querent must slay.

The Significator: King of Wands (Clubs)

Chosen by the querent himself, the significator is the king of wands. This suit is associated with initiative and strong drive. It is, however, more representative of the person's desired image of himself—and perhaps even his public posture—than of his actual character. It is therefore a clue to what this man wishes to be. The king of wands is strong, honest, and humorous, all probably virtues that the petitioner admires, although the other cards may indeed reveal a different nature. It also suggests that the person is

The Celtic cross layout for the first sample reading, using reproductions from a Marseilles deck in the Bibliothèque Nationale, Paris: king of clubs (significator); Chariot (card no. 1); five of pentacles or coins (card no. 2); Sun (card no. 3); king of swords (card no. 4); two of pentacles (card no. 5); Lovers (card no. 6); eight of cups (card no. 7); queen of cups (card no. 8); Emperor reversed (card no. 9); Tower (card no. 10). U.S. Games Systems, Inc., New York.

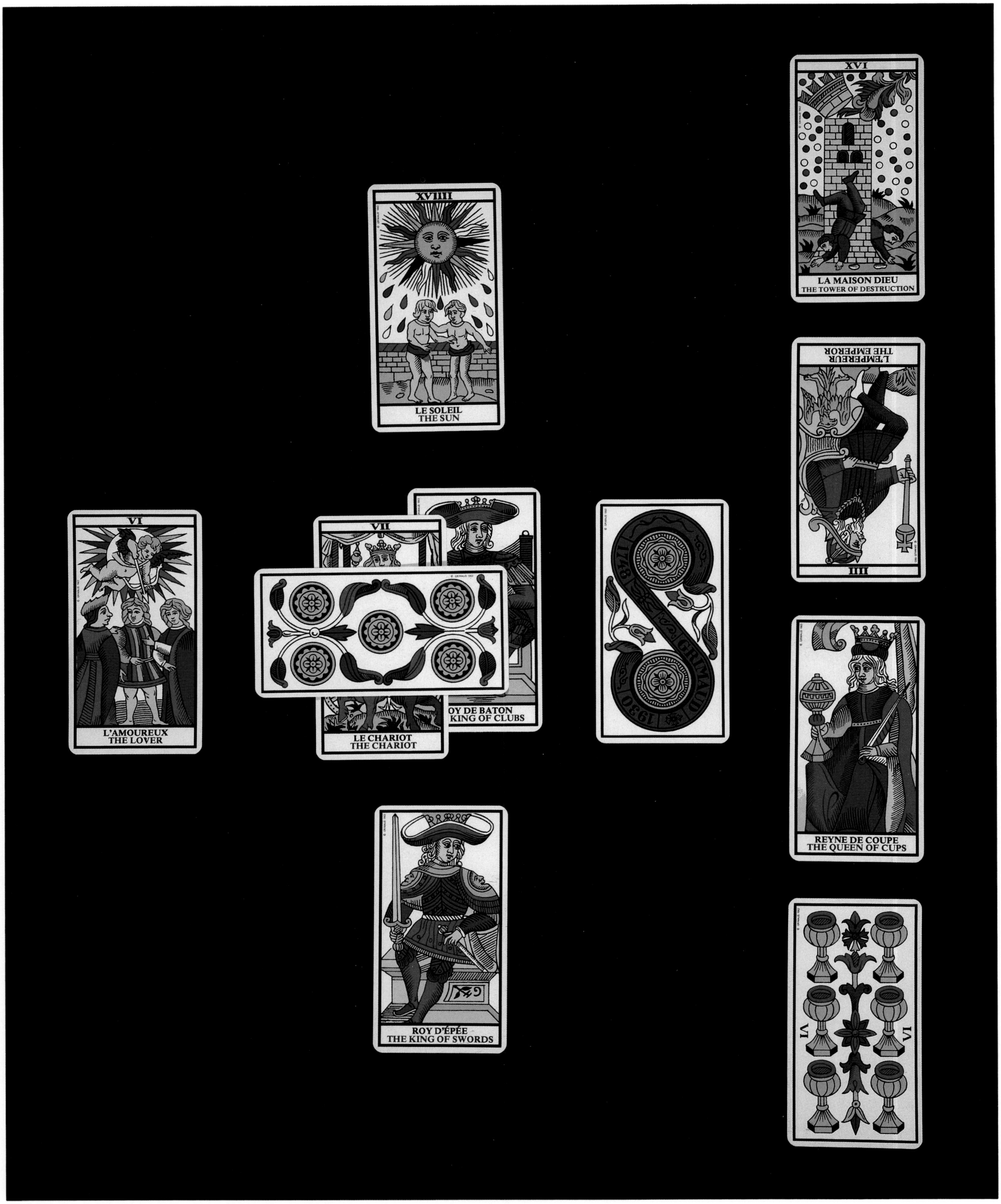
XVIIII
LE SOLEIL
THE SUN
XVI
LA MAISON DIEU
THE TOWER OF DESTRUCTION
L'EMPEREUR
THE EMPEROR
IIII
VI
L'AMOUREUX
THE LOVER
VII
LE CHARIOT
THE CHARIOT
ROY DE BATON
KING OF CLUBS
1748
GRIMAUD
1930
REYNE DE COUPE
THE QUEEN OF CUPS
ROY D'ÉPÉE
THE KING OF SWORDS
VI
VI

an able performer and probably a fatherly figure on whom clients can rely. Thus a tarot reader might conclude that the characteristics of this significator constitute the type of man the petitioner would like to appear to be.

Position 1, Present Situation: The Chariot
The card covering the significator is the Chariot. The image suggests conflict, in keeping with the statements of the petitioner at the beginning. Pulled in two directions, the Chariot is immobilized. Yet the driver would like it to move toward material success. The Chariot also implies great attention to detail. The petitioner probably is a thorough performer. His present uncertainty is all the more uncomfortable.

Position 2, Immediate Influence: Five of Pentacles (Coins)
Money matters signified by the suit of coins are the primary influence motivating the need for a decision. The card meanings refer to possible loss in income and termination of employment—in this case a possible diminution in practice.

Position 3, Ultimate Goals: The Sun
Just as the significator is an idealized version of the actual self, the Sun in the third position marks an unrealistic, extravagant goal of triumphant accomplishment and riches. It would be better for this person to aim at the other goals suggested by the card, such as the contentment that comes from affection, friendship, shared enjoyment, and acceptance.

Position 4, Distant Past: King of Swords (Spades)
According to this card the questioner in his early life was probably under the domination of a male figure, possibly his father. Authority, control, and even inflexibility exercised by that parent may have repressed the person and have engendered self-doubts, insecurity, and uncertainty. The king of swords may also represent other similar domineering superiors: a teacher or head of a department in which the querent served.

Position 5, Recent Past: Two of Pentacles (Coins)
The issue of money is again alluded to in the symbolism of this card's suit. Financial considerations have been prominent recently and also swings of mood, lack of purpose, and obstacles, probably due to elevated costs and reduced earnings. These concerns have led to the present search for a possible solution and new ventures. Seeking financial gain is a highly useful step in the right direction. Optimism is needed to replace the anxiety of the present.

Position 6, Future Influences: The Lovers
The person has to expect that eventually he must make a decisive choice. This card suggests that monetary rewards should be balanced against emotional satisfactions. The querent has to realize that whatever happens and however he decides, no choice is free from fault. The way ahead is never certain, nor is his—but acting with clear purpose can bring harmony, optimism, and emancipation from past uncertainty.

Position 7, Present Personal Status: Six of Swords (Spades)
The present unquiet, heavy heart is now becoming stimulated and lightened by the realization that expediency instead of unrealistic goals must be the keynote. One has to move away from present conditions, keeping in mind that pragmatism and dispassionate analysis rather than anxious longings should be uppermost priorities.

Position 8, Home and Immediate Influences: Queen of Cups (Hearts)
This card announces that warmth, affection, honesty, and enjoyment prevail in the immediate surroundings. These advantages should be emphasized and shared. The optimism at home can be infused into the attitudes outside.

Position 9, Subconscious Drives: The Emperor—Reversed
This is the only reversed card in the spread and therefore should be examined especially closely. Here the backward image suggests that beneath the significator's open pose of paternalism and strength lies the danger of weakness, subservience, and ineffectuality. Indeed, this man's present difficulty in deciding what to do may spring from the inner trends, possibly conditioned by the lowered self-esteem that he felt as a result of being controlled and overpowered by his father during childhood and by his superiors in the practice of his profession.

Position 10, Possible Outcome: The Tower
The Tower signals a break with the past. A final resolution of the problem will probably bring with it renewed confidence. The person can be encouraged to try something different and to enter into the new prospective activity in expectation of receiving the benefits of emotional ease and financial certainty, although it may be at a reduced level. However, the practicality of the six of swords, which is the seventh card and indicates changed awareness and gives an answer to the present ("This answers you"), might prompt the diviner to ask whether it would be feasible to continue private practice at a reduced level while starting the salaried position on a part-time basis. This would provide the continued ego satisfaction that comes with continuing to advise people and at the same time the chance to evaluate the new activity for a possible permanent commitment in the future.

Second Reading: The Question

The petitioner is an attractive young woman in her late thirties who is discouraged about her personal life. She has a responsible job as an editor, which she likes and in which she works very hard and demonstrates exceptional skill. However, her relatively modest salary keeps her in financial difficulties. She has had several love affairs in the past and one particularly intense union had broken up in the past year, followed by depression and even despair, but her emotions are now virtually fully dissipated. She sees herself getting older, still monetarily insecure, and without a man: "What should I do?" she asks. "What is likely to happen?"

The Spread (Horseshoe)

A significator is not usually chosen for this spread. After the shuffling and preparation of the deck, seven cards are placed in a horseshoe shape with the open end toward the reader. Counting counterclockwise and starting at the lower right, the cards are: ten of cups reversed (past influences); eight of cups (present influences); the Emperor (future); the Hanged Man (action); four of pentacles reversed (influence of others); the Hermit (obstacles); six of wands (probable outcome).

The Interpretation

Position 1, Past Influences: Ten of Cups—Reversed
This card in this position suggests that the person's early life was probably surrounded by disruption and conflict. Perhaps a divorce or separation in the family was part of the environment. In view of the querent's statements concerning her problem, the reversed card may indicate that deep feelings of insecurity were present possibly because of an actual domestic upheaval or merely a perceived uncertainty in the attitudes of her parents.

Position 2, Present Influences: Eight of Cups
Aimlessness and disillusionment, even self-deprecation, are represented by this card. Something or some person highly thought of has lost value. This could fit the loss of the beloved partner as reported by the petitioner, but it also implies that a new objective, personal or material, is under consideration.

Position 3, Future: The Emperor
The Emperor represents power, strength, self-confidence, and possible wealth. Therefore it must announce that this type of mature protective husband or partner is likely to come upon the scene—especially if the person actually seeks that kind of man. His maturity and stability are what she needs. The image could also apply to the questioner herself by advising her to exercise mind over emotion in the future and to be receptive to counsel, which in actuality is a mark of self-confidence.

Position 4, Action: The Hanged Man
In his interpretation of the tarot, Court de Gébelin had turned the image of the Hanged Man upright and designated the card's meaning and title to be Prudence. Although others have not perpetuated the suggested change, the basic symbolism de Gébelin assigned to the card has usually been adhered to. Transition and a pause for evaluation are the common indications, which are apt to result in prudent action. Here, then, the counsel is to readjust to present conditions, renew one's spirit, and consider change without rushing off hastily. Don't leave the job unless another more rewarding opportunity is in the offing. On a personal level, plan on how to meet and mingle with people of substantial purpose; with men and women, not boys and girls. Every new acquaintance of that nature will lead to others.

Position 5, Influence of Others: Four of Pentacles—Reversed
Here the warning is that one must expect obstructions by others. With the Hanged Man in mind, negotiation is the advisable method rather than confrontation. This card upright or reversed also suggests the start of a major endeavor, and its suit suggests the enterprise is likely to involve money.

Position 6, Obstacles: The Hermit
The previous card announced difficulties produced by other people. The Hermit, in the position in the spread that shows obstacles, should alert the reader and the questioner to one of the chief problems in this young woman—her own attitudes. The Hermit's self-absorption and introspection can lead to a loner's behavior. Is it possible that the person has created her own difficulties, both on the job and in her personal life? The knowledge and ideas that the Hermit symbolizes—and which the young woman evidently possesses in her work as an editor—must also be applied to her performance outside herself. Her focus should be external not introverted. The meaning of the previous cards in the spread is all falling into place. Reevaluation of self and situation must be for the purpose of taking prudent action, not for contemplation.

Position 7, Probable Outcome: Six of Wands
There is every expectation that her hard work and conscientiousness will lead to achievement. Fulfillment will come from involvement with others, a characteristic of this card. Delay is temporary. The divinatory advice of the card is to look outward, move forward, and use diplomacy. All of these counsels were already anticipated in the previous cards. Optimistic probabilities are therefore especially strong.

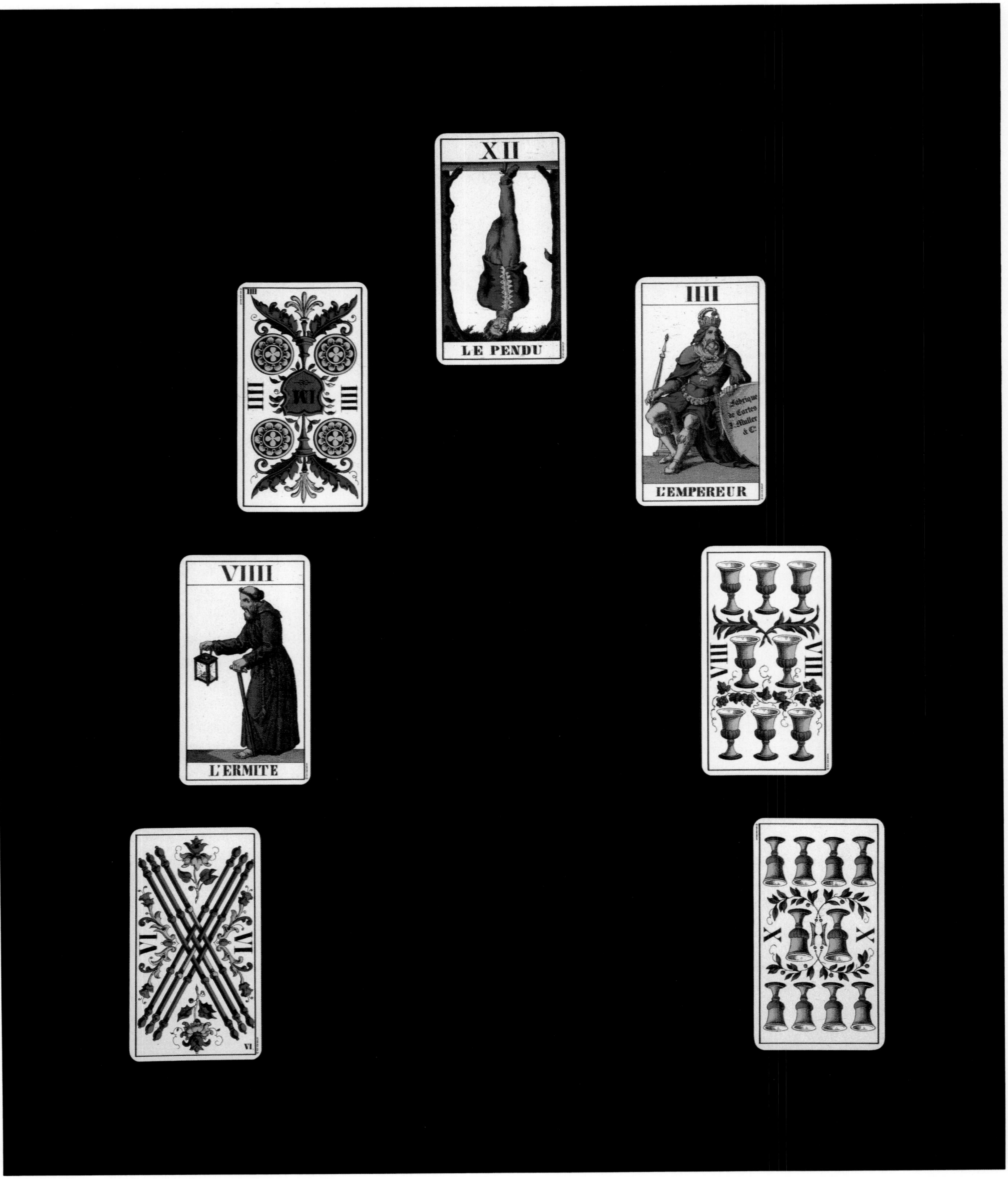
XII
LE PENDU
IIII
L'EMPEREUR
Fabrique de Cartes J. Müller & Cie
VIIII
L'ERMITE
VIII
VI
X

OPPOSITE: Sample horseshoe layout for the second sample reading, using the I. J. J. Swiss deck cards: ten of cups reversed (card no. 1); eight of cups (card no. 2); Emperor (card no. 3); Hanged Man (card no. 4); four of coins reversed (card no. 5); Hermit (card no. 6); six of wands (card no. 7). U.S. Games Systems, Inc., New York.

Cards from the Visconti Sforza deck. Left to right: three of cups, Popess, Hermit, page of pentacles, two of cups.

Evaluation

There are those who claim that intense concentration by the querent transfers thoughts into the tarot images, thereby enabling the diviner to read the cards and ascertain the past history, present condition, and future directions that lie in the psyche of the petitioner. Since this idea is a belief, not a fact, it cannot be evaluated. Others see the process of preparing the deck and focusing on the ritual of arrangement as a means of allowing the querent and the diviner to clear their minds of extraneous considerations so that both of the participants can address the problem that is concerning the petitioner. The pictures stimulate and trigger perceptions and lead to applicable solutions. Still other practitioners look upon the tarot as an opportunity to face difficulties with the confidence that comes from the feeling that someone else (the diviner) or some outside spiritual mechanism (the tarot) will point to the correct direction.

Just as Carl Jung viewed the *I Ching* as opening a door to the subconscious, tarot reading enables the petitioner to visualize symbolically the conflicts, fears, and hidden desires that might otherwise not be understood. Thus, the tarot may be either a mystical experience, a psychological journey, or a stimulus to reevaluate current problems systematically.

If astrology, handreading, and numerology are considered by their proponents to be methods composed mainly of laws, regulations, and calculations, with intuition playing a lesser role; if the *I Ching,* dreams, and tea-leaf reading are involved chiefly with personal insight; then the tarot stands somewhere between the two groups, using both intuition and rules in approximately equal measures.

Advisors or diviners who employ occult methods of any kind generally have learned to perceive in their clients or to elicit from their statements clues to psychological makeup, weaknesses and strengths, hopes and fears; in short, to discover what it is that the person wishes to hear. Sometimes they can also examine, together with the petitioner, the basis for present problems, the options available, and the prudent way of proceeding. In these instances, they act in much the same way that a sympathetic, wise friend would give counsel. Here the card layouts and illustrations are a basis for carrying on a personal discussion under the atmosphere of objectivity. Someone who might recoil from an intimate probe is often totally unresistant to and even fully cooperative with what seems to be the impersonal analysis of cards on a table before them.

The dangers seen by detractors of the tarot are that the reader may not be wise or objective or understanding; that the usefulness of a tarot reading depends entirely upon the skill and intention of the diviner with respect to the person asking for advice; that the cards are meaningless, for the same spread can be interpreted in as many ways as there are performers; even that the assignments of card positions to categories such as the present, past, future, immediate surroundings, and other areas of life are varied and sometimes contradictory.

A reading of the cards by the questioner himself or herself rather than a diviner is far more acceptable to the detractors. It is similar to formulating a decision while whittling a stick, painting a wall, watching a game, or taking a walk. The person will see in the images what he or she wants to see or has been afraid to see. This employment of the tarot, however, is a far cry from the organized, systematized, conventional divination by an adept for a client.

Tarot reading remains a scientifically untested system for helping people to make decisions or for anticipating the future. It is also an immensely popular endeavor to which many subscribe as a useful, readily available stimulus for making up their minds.

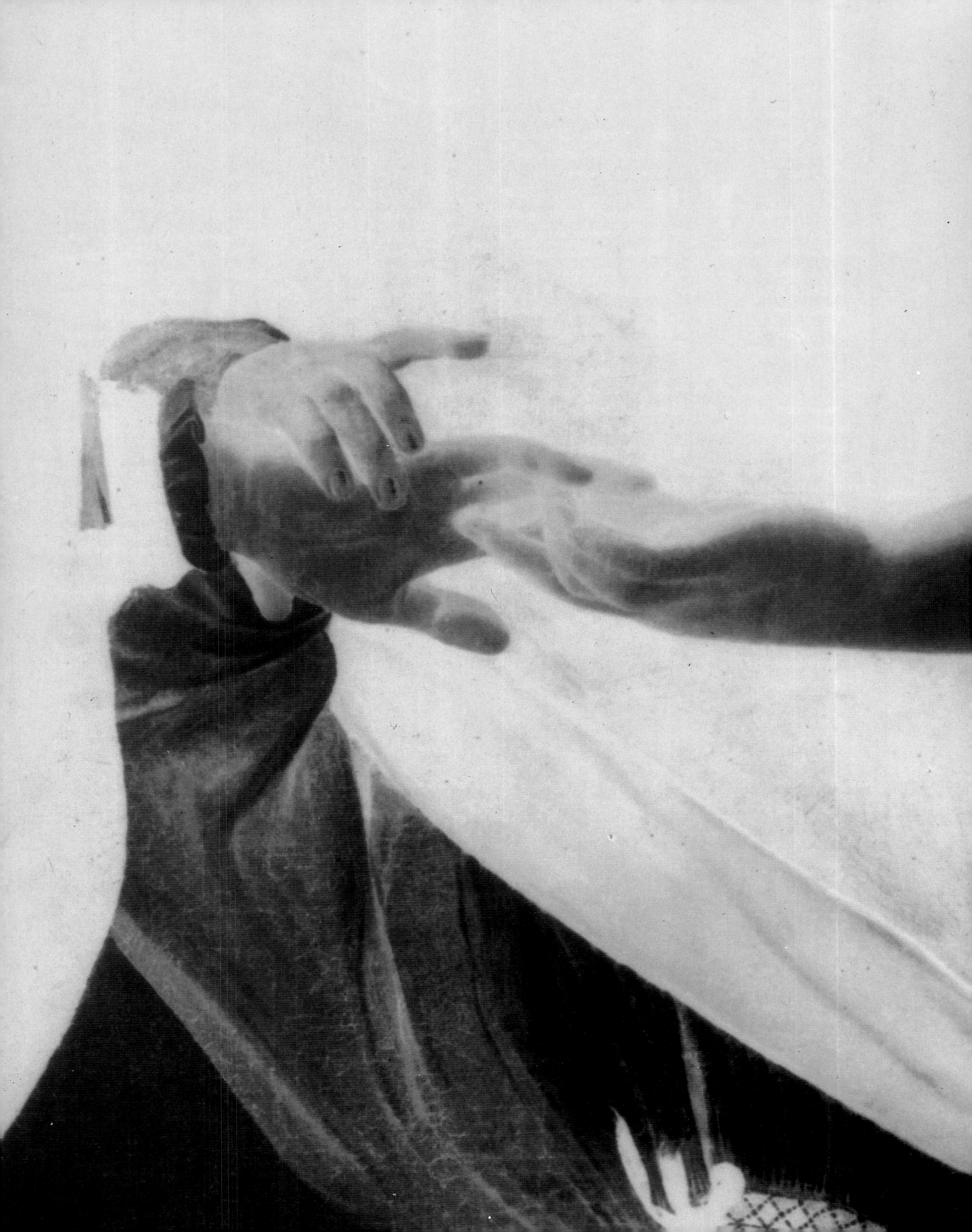

Handreading

Caravaggio. *The Fortune-Teller.* Late 1590s. Oil on canvas, $39 \times 51\frac{1}{2}$". Musée du Louvre, Paris.

Handreading

Hand me down my handled cane,
It helps me handle walking pain;
Its handy grip, its handsome band,
I keep beside me close at hand.

The hand has figured prominently in the evolution and history of humans. Indeed, the structure and function of hands are among the notable features distinguishing human beings from "lower" animals. The hand is also a significant symbol in many cultural contexts. Hand gestures and postures are part of our everyday existence and often are a basis for judging personality: a firm handshake conveys confidence and reliability; a limp hand suggests ineffectuality. (Of course, anyone can practice and learn how to shake hands in a desired manner, so that an estimate of character by this means has a high chance of being misinformed. Yet, the very act of modifying a grasp and thus affecting opinions may itself change that individual's view of himself or herself, reinforce the new impression, and thereby alter the person's behavior.)

We also cannot help observing the general appearance of hands, how they are held, the neatness of the nails, the length and contours of the fingers. We have a tendency to see in long, shapely fingers the delicacy of a craftsman or the skill of a surgeon, although this association is not borne out by the facts. Indeed, a renowned surgeon-anatomist was once approached by his beginning students who questioned him in dismay because they had noticed that some of the most admired surgical operators had ungainly or crooked or even slightly unsteady hands. "A good surgeon," he answered, "operates with his head, not his hands." However, many chirologists (those who study hands) have linked square, short-fingered hands with minds that lean to manual arts. Others suggest that the very shape of the hand itself may have actually nudged the person's thinking in a certain direction. Beautiful fingers, for example, may stimulate their possessors to display rather than to perform; knobby digits may provoke their owners into work.

But is there an association between mental makeup and the features of the hand—the general contours, mounts, valleys, and creases? Does the personality suggested by the map of the hand also indicate likely activities and future events? We do not propose in this chapter to offer answers. Instead, we will describe the centuries-old techniques and interpretations of handreading, without regard to their validity. Of course, differences in practices have always existed—as they do now—but we believe that our presentation is a fair sample of the widespread and accepted methods of divination by examining the hand.

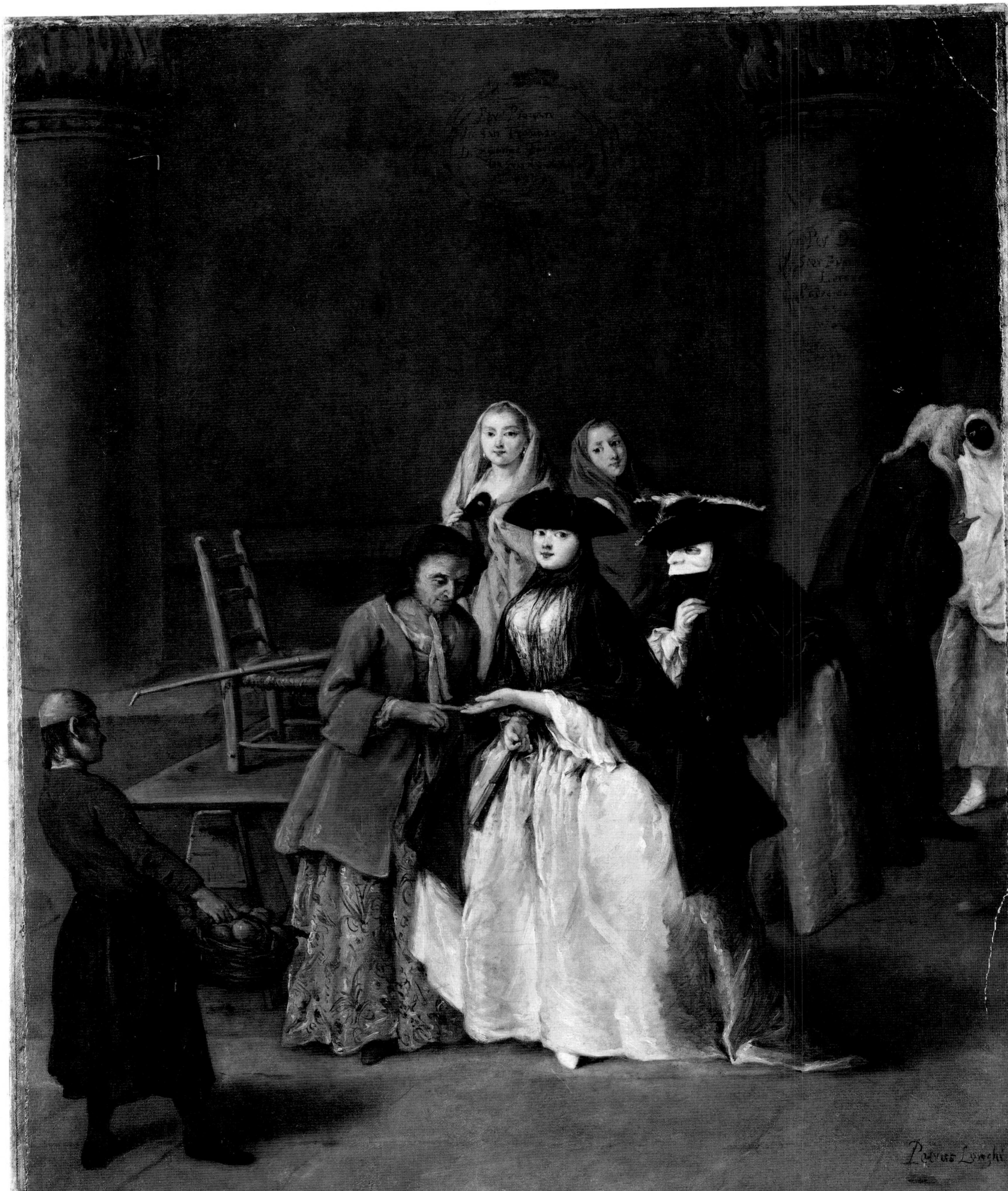

History

It is not known when humans first began to seek clues to character and destiny by studying their hands. People today in underdeveloped societies often attribute particular characteristics, such as a single line across the palm (now referred to as the "simian" line), to someone with an unusual character trait, or else they might observe an unusually large thumb on a forceful person. Consciously or unconsciously, they have thereupon associated traits with the hand's features, and early humans may have done the same.

Similarly, in today's technologically advanced cultures, some scientific writings have genetically linked particular shapes and line patterns on hands to specific mental aberrations and birth defects. However, these are not the same palm configurations that have been classified by divinatory palm readers.

Apparently, prehistoric humans did attach special significance to hands, drawing hands on cave walls, some even with parts of fingers missing. Often, the hand

ABOVE: A Chinese clay seal with the impression of a thumbprint probably used as an identifying mark. Before the third century B.C. The Field Museum of Natural History, Chicago.

OPPOSITE: Pietro Longhi. *In the House of a Diviner.* c.1751. Oil on canvas, 23¾ × 19″. The National Gallery, London.

representations are more realistic than the accompanying human figures and faces. In addition, in the incised swirls and whorls on the runes and rocks of mounts and caves, some observers have noted patterns similar to human fingerprints. But whether these drawings have ritual or more trivial meanings is not known.

The Bible

The Old Testament is filled with allusions to the special significance of hands and fingers, although none are specifically linked to prediction by handreading. "This is the finger of God," the magicians of Pharaoh are supposed to have said when defeated in magical display by Moses and Aaron. Indeed, God's hands—as in the old spiritual hymn "He Has the Whole World in His Hands"—have long been symbolic of the power to favor or condemn. Ezekiel was touched by God's hand and thereby was under His guidance. The "good hand of his God" is referred to by

OPPOSITE: Incised markings from Newgrange prehistoric site, County Meath, Ireland. These large markings resemble human fingerprints, but their actual significance is unknown.

BELOW: Michelangelo, *Ezekiel.* 1508–1512. Fresco. Sistine Chapel, Vatican, Rome. The hand is a significant symbol in the Bible and in religious art. In the Book of Ezekiel, God told the prophet Ezekiel to hold in his hand two sticks, one to represent the land of Judah, the other Israel. God promised, "They shall become one in thine hand, and I shall make the two lands into one nation" (Ezekiel 7:17).

Ezra. Contrarily, God said, "I will turn my hand against Ekiron." Saint Paul predicted that God would blind him for a season with His hand, and the Psalms plead, "Why withdrawest Thou Thy hand?"

Instances of humans sealing bargains and making pledges with their hands occur throughout the Bible. Identification by the hands apparently was so strong that when Jacob, disguised as Esau by a covering of animal skins over his hands, came before blind Isaac, the old patriarch mused, "The voice is Jacob's but the hands are those of Esau." Evidently more convinced by the simulated hairy hands of Esau than the actual voice of Jacob, Isaac gave the dissimulating Jacob his blessing of inheritance.

ABOVE: G. Flinck. *The Legacy of Isaac.* Oil on canvas, 50 × 80″. Rikjsmuseum, Amsterdam. Isaac, deceived by the simulated roughness on the hands of Jacob into thinking they are Esau's, awards him the inheritance.

OPPOSITE: Michelangelo. *The Creation of Adam.* 1508–1512. Fresco. Sistine Chapel, Vatican, Rome. The transmission of life is symbolized here passing from the finger of God to the finger of Adam.

RIGHT: By tradition, the Buddha's hand is said to have shown the past and future to those enlightened enough to understand its symbols. The lines, symbols, and Sanskrit writings on the Indian diagram of the Buddha's palm relate significant messages. Collection Fritz Eichenberg.

BELOW: Scene from an illuminated Bengali manuscript, the *Gandāvyūha*. Eleventh–twelfth century A.D. As is common in many cultures, the hands, not the faces, display the attitude and feeling of the two figures. Ink and color on palm-leaf, 21⅞ × 2″. The Cleveland Museum of Art. J. H. Wade Collection.

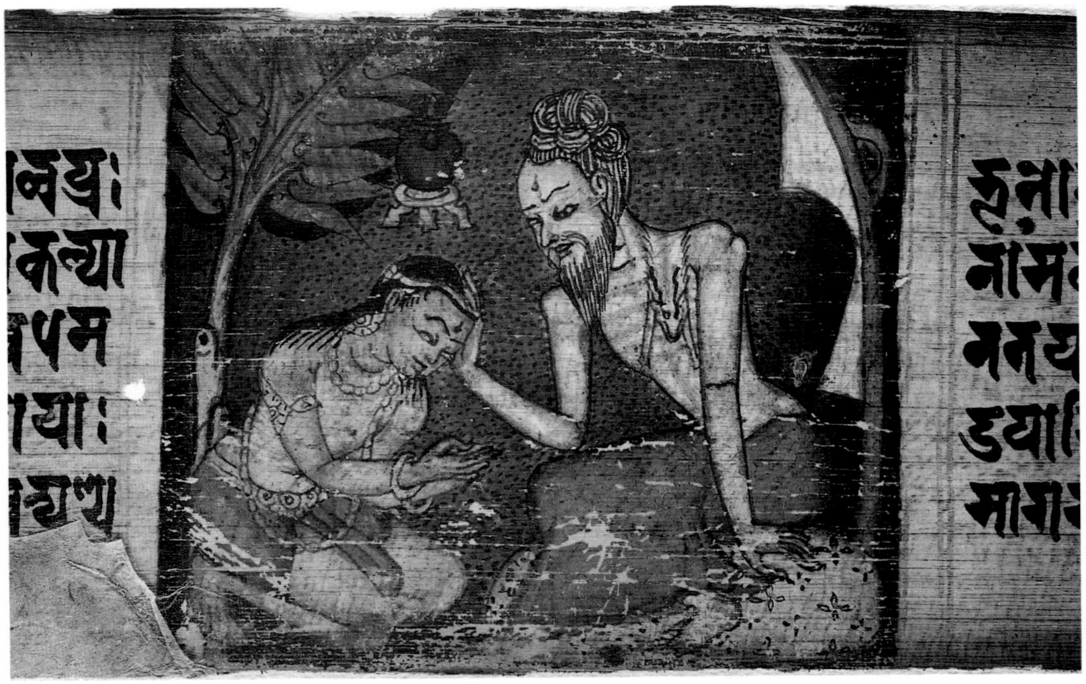

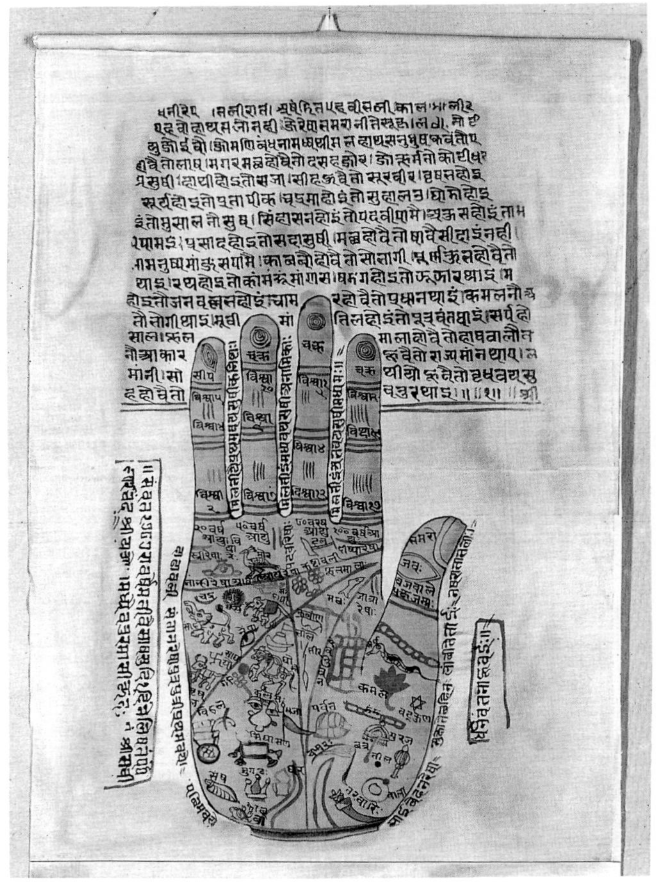

East Indian version of the significant parts of the palm, from *Brhatsāmudrikāsastra* (Bombay: Gangavisnu Srirsnadāsa, 1906). Wellcome Institute Library, London.

Nataraja, a manifestation of the Hindu god Siva, danced the cosmic dance of creation, in which the universe became a manifestation of the light reflected from his many limbs. This Indian eleventh-century copper statue is one indication that the gestural magic of hands can be symbolically powerful in many cultures. Height 43⅞″. The Cleveland Museum of Art.

Mesopotamia and Egypt

The evidence is scant that in Mesopotamia handreading was used for forecasting. However, in hepatoscopy (examining the liver of sacrificed animals in order to discover whether a sick patient would live or die), priests assigned special significance to various signs seen on the organs, such as a circle (good omen), square (protective meaning), triangle (favorable implication). These same designations have since been applied to handreading. Similar meanings are also maintained in the symbols of various cultures (for instance among Arabs and Persians). It does not appear that the reading of hands played a major part in Egyptian prophecy. Yet, we do know that two raised fingers, which in modern times implies blessing, good fortune, or divine involvement, also had favorable meanings in ancient Egypt.

The earliest references to actual prediction by looking at the body areas, including the hands, may be in ancient Indian writings. The sacred Vedic scriptures of about 1500 B.C. mention the significance of the palm. The *Anga Vidya* speaks of gods having special marks on their palms, notably Vishnu's in his incarnation as Krishna. Skanda is said to have been the god of palmistry and of astrology. Thus, since its beginnings handreading may have been associated with astrology. Legend also has it that the Buddha's glorious future was shown at his birth by signs on his feet; on his palm the marks of the entire universe were present. By the first century B.C., we know there was an accepted tradition of palmistry in India because the laws of Manu, the Indian precepts of moral and legal behavior (codified about 700–600 B.C.), decry dishonest practices by some handreaders. In about the ninth century A.D. the *Sardulakarnavadana,* a well-known Buddhist tale written many centuries earlier, had chapters added to it that dealt with various omens, including the signs seen on the palm. However, the earliest full-scale extant Sanskrit work on physiognomy and palmistry was not composed until the twelfth century A.D. Palmistry in its Indian forms continues to be practiced to this day. The Western tradition, while it has similarities with the Indian methods, is more the product of the Greco-Roman period.

It was not until Greek times that divination by the reading of hands was developed into a system. The term *chiromancy* is derived from the Greek words *chiro,* "hand" —from Chiron, the centaur who instructed Asclepius, the demigod of healing—and *mancy,* "divination".

Much of the writing on handreading that has been attributed to various Greek authors is considered by most scholars to be spurious, having actually been composed in late medieval times, many centuries after the supposed authors had died. For instance, a much-quoted treatise long attributed to Aristotle, *Cyromancia Aristotelis,* was actually a fifteenth-century text originating in Germany.

However, Aristotle did write about the significance of

An Egyptian two-finger amulet, a sign of good luck, probably limestone. Late Dynastic period. Length 3⅞". The Norbert Schimmel Collection, New York.

hands, among other body parts, specifically attaching meaning to the lines of the palm. In *Historia Animalium,* Aristotle stated: "The inner part of the hand is termed the palm and is fleshy and divided by joints or lines; in the case of long-lived people by one or two extending right across, in the case of the short-lived by two not so extending." Aristotle's *Problemata* contains almost the same words: "Why is it that men are very long-lived who have a cut across the palm?"

These passages appear to be referring to what we now call the "Head" and "Heart" lines, although other scholars have interpreted Aristotle's description to mean the modern palmists' "Life" (or "Vitality") line. In either case, it does seem clear that Aristotle assigned predictive meanings to the lines but only in incidental statements and not in a treatise on the subject.

An appealing legend, though entirely undocumented, concerns the purported reading of Aristotle's hand by a chiromancer who reported seeing a number of highly unflattering characteristics in the philosopher's palm. Incensed by this display of bad taste and—in their eyes—downright falsehood, the audience of students berated the professed handreader. Aristotle is supposed to have stayed their criticisms, stating simply that the very weaknesses that the palmist saw were indeed the same deficiencies against which he had been struggling all his life.

Aristotle's pupil, Alexander the Great, is also said to have consulted fortune-tellers, including palmists, and his swordmakers are reported to have included gypsies, who have been associated with various fortune-telling practices, including palmistry.

In the third century B.C., the Alexandrian scientist and philosopher Melampus wrote about movements of the body, including hands, but there is no information on how he viewed fingers and palms in relation to character and destiny. Galen, the great physician and medical authority in the second century A.D., included hands as a subject among his voluminous writings, but no evidence exists that he attempted forecasting or even character delineation on the basis of handreading.

Chiromancy was very much a part of the social mores in Greece and also in Rome. Juvenal avers, almost contemptuously, that upper-class women sought out astrologers and the lower-class used handreaders to while away their hours. Cicero, though a member of the college of augurs, nevertheless ridiculed as superstitious both hand-reading and astrology.

In palmistry, Greek and Roman gods have become associated with the parts of the hand: Venus (Aphrodite) with the thumb and the elevation at the base; Jupiter (Zeus), the index finger; Saturn, the long middle finger; Apollo, the ring finger; Mercury (Hermes), the little finger. These associations have continued to contemporary times. Evidently, no Greek or Latin codifications of chiromancy

Jean-Léon Gérôme. *Hail Caesar: We Who Are About to Die, Salute You.* 1859. Oil on canvas, 36⅝ × 57¼". Yale University Art Gallery, New Haven. Gift of C. Buxton Love, Jr. It is commonly stated that the victor in Roman gladiatorial combat appealed to the crowd to decide the fate of his victim. It is erroneously thought that "thumbs up" suggested mercy and "thumbs down" meant "finish him off." Although the sign language in this painting is not quite so graphic, explicit messages conveyed by hands—as in the salute—are universally understood.

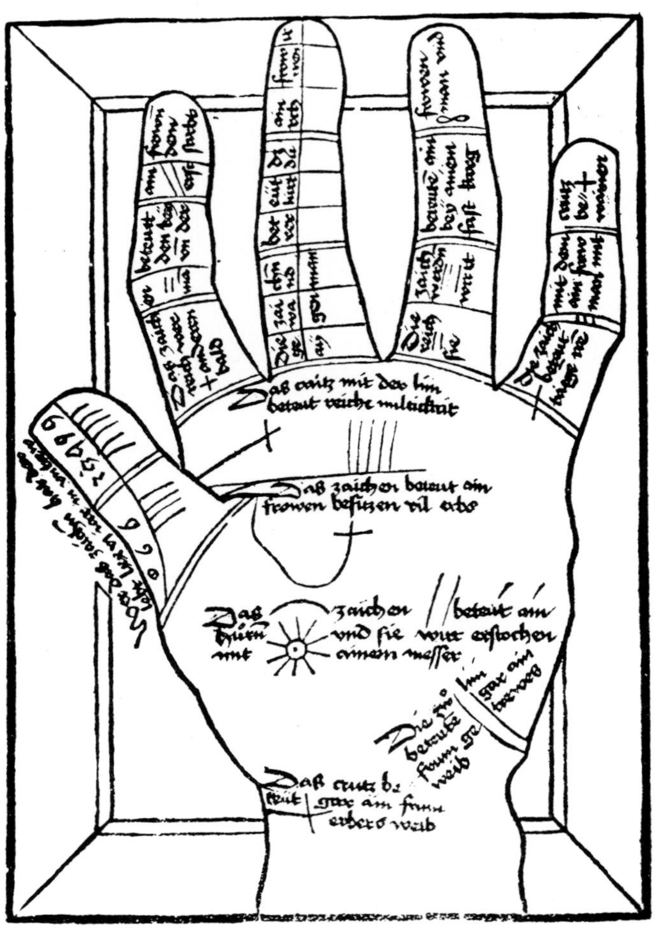

have survived from classical times, although there were numbers of references to such early works during the Byzantine and medieval periods.

In the Early Christian era, chiromancy, along with astrology, was ambivalently received by the Church. Thomas Aquinas had much to say against occult practices, but he did not disapprove of chiromancy. Other theologians did condemn it. Among the public at large and even among scholars, handreading was looked at sometimes as being more sound than other divinations; others accepted astrology but not palmistry. Arabic writers (that is, those Arabs, Persians, Christians, Jews, and others who wrote in Arabic) usually paid some attention to handreading. For instance, the famous and influential *Canon* by the Persian encyclopedist Ibn Sina (Avicenna) of the eleventh century discusses the significance of hand shapes. But it is chiefly astrology that occupies most of the treatises on prediction.

In twelfth- and thirteenth-century Europe, increasing numbers of manuscripts codified the lines of the palm with personality traits, future events, and medical conditions. Among others, Michael Scot, magician and astrologer to Frederick II, king of the Two Sicilies and Holy Roman Emperor, wrote on physiognomy, which included chiromancy. Notable people were believed to have consulted handreaders. Thomas Becket, confidant, advisor, and later clerical opponent of Henry II, is said to have frequented handreaders. There were detractors, too. John of Salisbury, the English ecclesiastic, believed that no truths could be deduced from the hand's wrinkles.

One of the early full treatises on chiromancy was by Johannes Hartlieb in 1448, *Buch von der Hand* (issued as *Die Kunst Chiromantia des Hartlieb* in 1470), which described in detail the predictive and medical ramifications of more than twenty pairs of hands. (This work under different guises, translations, and modifications was also assigned to Aristotle, one among the many spurious pseudo-Aristotelian books.) Some have termed Hartlieb's text the first full-scale book on palmistry, although an even more extensive work in English by John Methan may have been compiled before 1450.

ABOVE LEFT: A fourteenth- or fifteenth-century ink rubbing from the so-called Bogomil tomb sculpture in present-day Yugoslavia. Special prominence has been given to the hands, evidently the most important anatomical feature of the figure.

LEFT: A diagram of important parts of the hand from a 1475 German book on chiromancy. Many of the assignments of meanings to palm lines and fingers differ from modern interpretations. The two lines on the outside heel of the hand evidently are associated with marriage, whereas in modern palmistry the lines of marriage are much closer to the base of the fifth finger. New York Public Library.

OPPOSITE: The dedication of the Vivian Bible, showing a presentation of the Bible to Charles the Bold. c.845. 19½ × 13⅝″. Bibliothèque Nationale, Paris. Many types of hand gestures—from supplication to offering, with the hand of God over all—are portrayed in this early Christian scene.

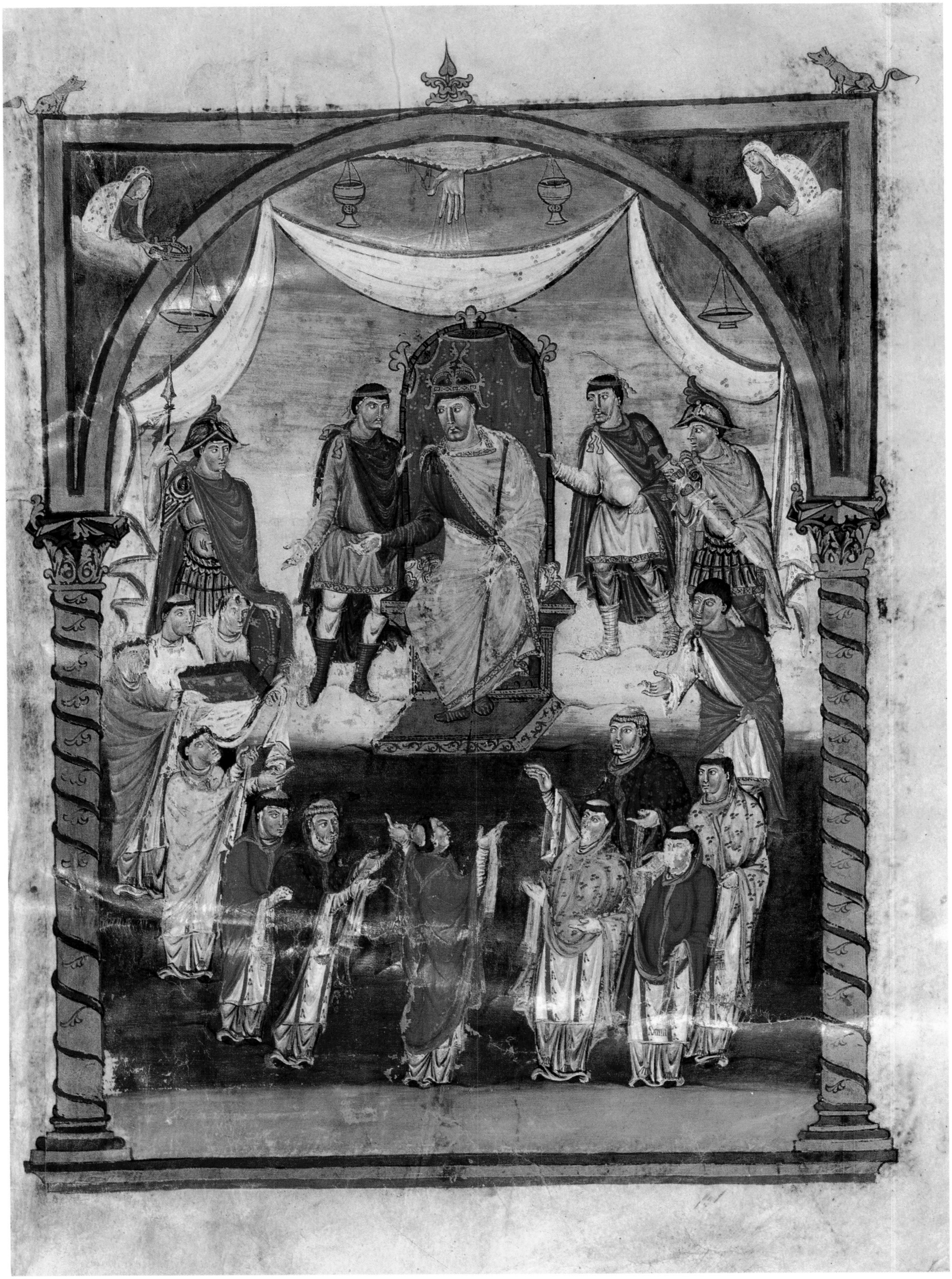

In the Middle Ages, the association of gypsies with fortune-telling, especially palmistry, was widely accepted. Indeed, palmistry, tasseography, and tarot-card reading are the principal divinatory methods universally linked with gypsies. In gypsy lore, the hand apparently had particular symbolic significance, especially the thumb. The beginnings of this diverse entity of people are still in dispute, but most studies agree that India was the probable region of their origin. Wandering from place to place, from country to country, either by choice or necessity, they were hounded and feared because of their seemingly strange customs, including their presumed ability to foretell and even to influence people's futures. The gypsies in turn may have encouraged belief in their supernatural gifts in order to ensure a livelihood and to afford a measure of protection against being molested. Female gypsies, almost never males, were the fortune-tellers. (Gypsies may also have contributed to the idea that the devil could be kept at bay by displaying silver and the sign of the cross. Thus Satan could be barred from the future if the gypsy handreader were to have her own palm "crossed with silver," preferably in the form of a silver coin.)

Anonymous (German). *The Hand as the Mirror of Salvation.* 1446. Colored woodcut. National Gallery of Art, Washington, D.C. Rosenwald Collection.

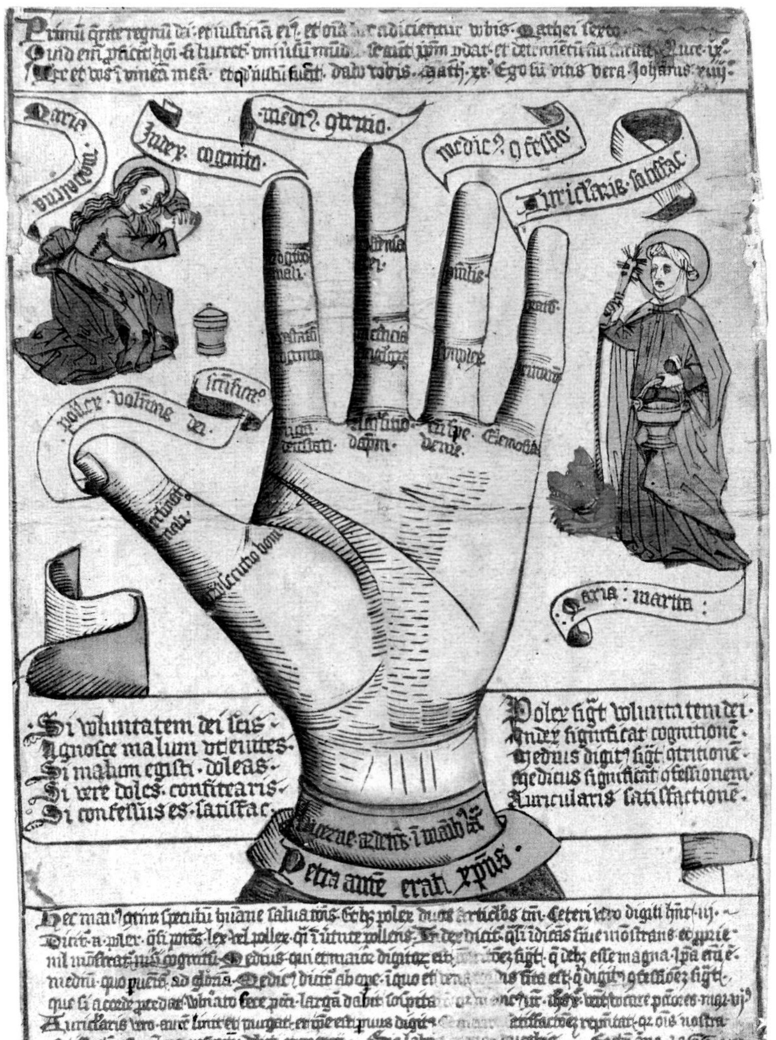

Alessandro Achillini (1463–?1512), an anatomist and practicing physician, was one of those who wrote on the association between medicine and the lines and shapes of the hand. Wellcome Institute Library, London.

Throughout the medieval period, a close correspondence was seen between stars in the heavens (macrocosm) and the events and makeup of humans on earth (microcosm). Palmistry may well have had associations with astrology very early in history, but it was in the Middle Ages and early Renaissance that the planetary and zodiacal connections to the fingers and palm became especially noticeable.

Medieval medicine relied extensively on astrological omens, and contemporary Arabic medical writings were filled with starry allusions, but chiromancy seems not to have been a part of Arabic medical practices (with a few exceptions—as for instance in works by the ninth-century philosopher-scientist al-Kindi). On the other hand, in the Christian West, Andreas Corvus (Barthelemy Cocles) in 1497 published an influential treatise on handreading that explicitly advised practitioners of medicine to apply its tenets. Physicians were also contributing to the literature on medical chiromancy. Among them were the Italian Giovanni della Porta, who was both a physician and a physicist, and Alexander Achillinus, an anatomist and practicing physician.

Astrological characteristics were assigned to the lines and mounts of the hand but the designations differed from scholar to scholar. For instance, Life, Fate, Head, and Heart lines as now placed in palmistry were not assigned the same locations by Renaissance writers. Also, the close association of the palm lines with the internal body organs, which was common then, is not emphasized in today's chiromantic practices.

Furthermore, whereas the modern handreader is usually careful to speak of "tendencies" rather than actual traits, of "hazards" rather than actual future events, the chiromancer of earlier times summed up character in definitive terms and predicted, often in ominous phrases, evil fortunes and disasters ahead. The reader and the client both saw the certainties of fate foreshadowed in the hand. While dire prophecies by any means had a strong likelihood of fulfillment in those times of almost continual upheaval, rampant epidemics, and general uncertainties, it is nevertheless remarkable that chiromancers were willing to take the chance of prophesying disaster, for throughout history the bearer of evil tidings has always been in danger. Thus it was, for instance, with Antioco Tiberto, one of the earliest chiromancers of the Renaissance, who was assassinated by order of the local ruler to whom he had predicted banishment and impoverishment.

One of several well-known sixteenth-century compilations of chiromancy was the *Opus Mathematicum* of Johannes Taisnier in 1562. Perhaps the most widely read and influential writings on palmistry of the mid-sixteenth century were by John Indagine, a Carthusian monk. A probable reason for their popularity was the author's engaging style, in contrast to the dry, pedantic phraseology of contemporary scholarly works. Modern palmistry uses much the same system of planetary rulerships over the elevations on the palm that Indagine described: the thumb is ruled by Venus, the index finger by Jupiter, the middle finger by Saturn, the ring finger by the Sun (Apollo), and the "pinky" by Mercury.

Paracelsus, a teacher, writer, and medical innovator of sixteenth-century Germany, deviated from the scholarly custom of using Latin and Greek, preferring to compose his numerous reports in the vernacular. His brilliant perceptions exerted profound influence on medical thinking and practices—and were taken up by generations of medical followers known as "Paracelsians"—but his iconoclasm and personal invective earned him considerable enmity. Despite his attempts to break with the past, his ideas often agreed with various ancient doctrines. For example, he embraced wholeheartedly the belief that mystical-spiritual forces in the universe penetrate the body and are manifested in the contours and features of the hands.

Jerome Cardan was another physician of the time who, like Paracelsus, engaged in both mystic and scientific pursuits. His system of palmistry assigned the mount at the base of the thumb to Mars (we now call this fleshy eminence Venus) and the elevation under the little finger to Venus (which in modern times is named for Mercury). Palm markings, such as spots and dots of color, came in for special attention. Cardan wrote that he observed on his own palm the appearance of a red mark that later became bloody, coinciding with the sentencing and execution of his son for murder.

Alongside the brilliant scientific and medical experiments of the seventeenth century, chiromancy, concomitantly with astrology, continued to be popular. While William Harvey, a physician, was proving his theories about the circulation of the blood and thereby—in the judgment of many historians—heralding the advent of modern medicine, it was another physician, John Rothman, who linked astrology more securely with palmistry and drew up a set of specific rules for palm reading.

Also among those who made significant contributions to palmistry in this century was the chiromancer Richard

Engraved frontispiece to Johann Rothman's *Art of Divining* (*Keiponanti'a*), published in London in 1652. The lines of the mind (*mensa*), life (*vitalis*), fate (*saturnia*), and girdle of Venus (*cingula veneris*) are shown, among others. The mounts and plains with their astrological symbols are also included—Venus, Jupiter, Apollo (Sun), Mercury, and Moon—with assignments similar to those given today. Wellcome Institute Library, London.

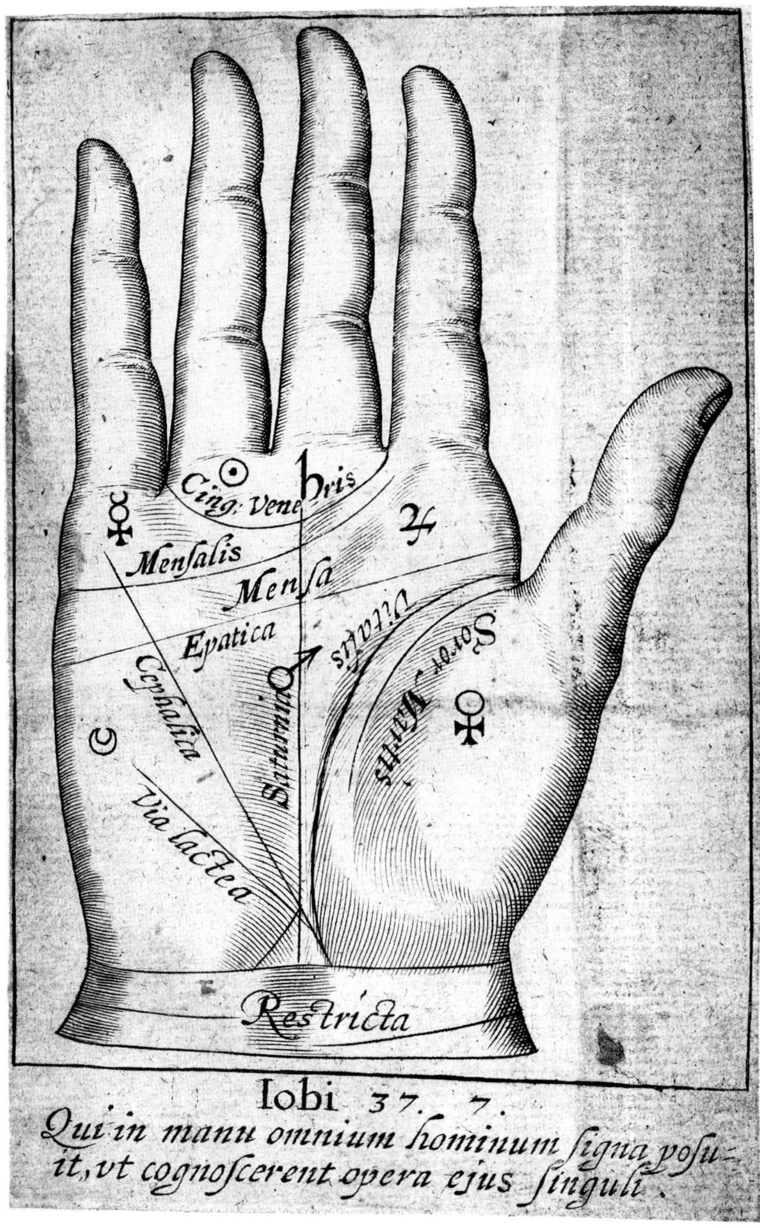

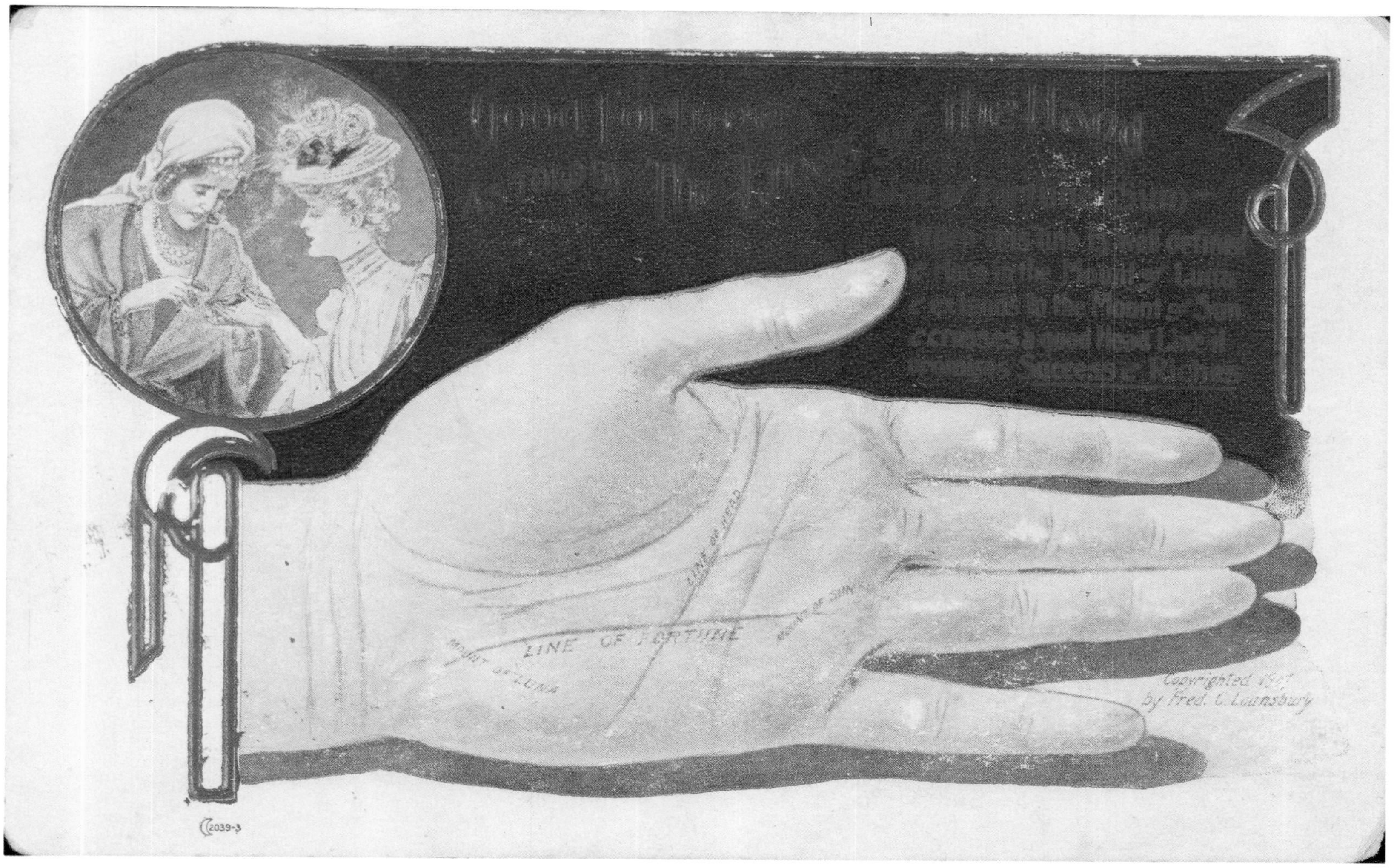

BELOW: The principal lines and mounts of the palm, together with the ages along the Life line, as diagrammed by the chirologist Alphonse Desbarolles in his *Mystères de la Main, Révélations Complètes* (Paris, 1859).

ABOVE: A postcard of the late nineteenth century with a diagram of the principal lines of the hand used in palmistry. Collection of Dr. and Mrs. Theodore Robinson, Richboro, Pennsylvania.

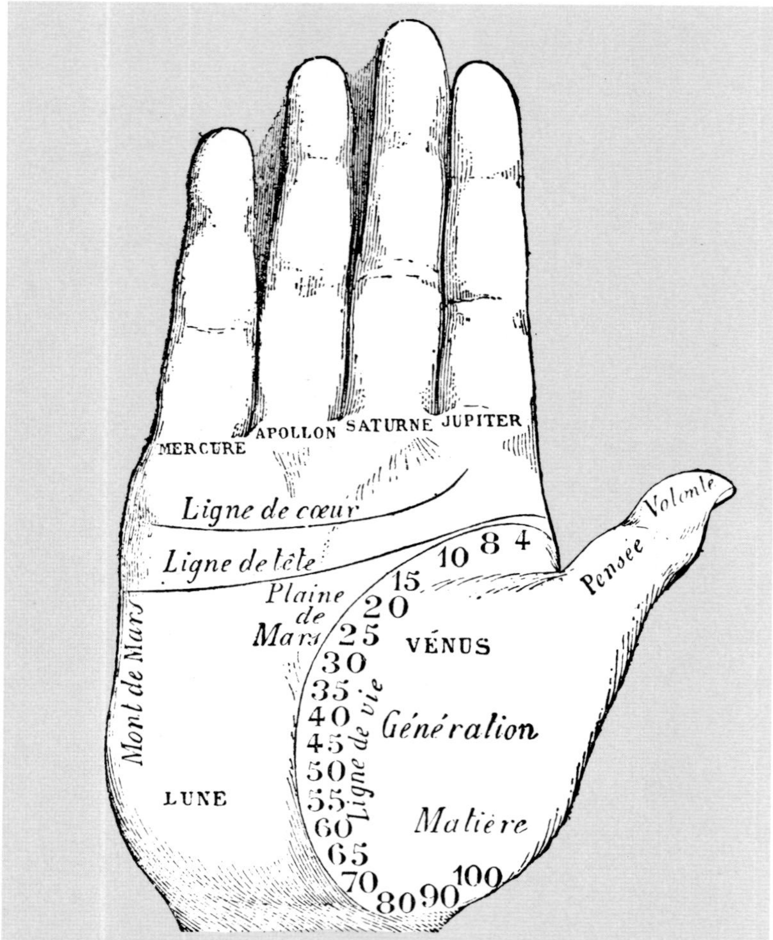

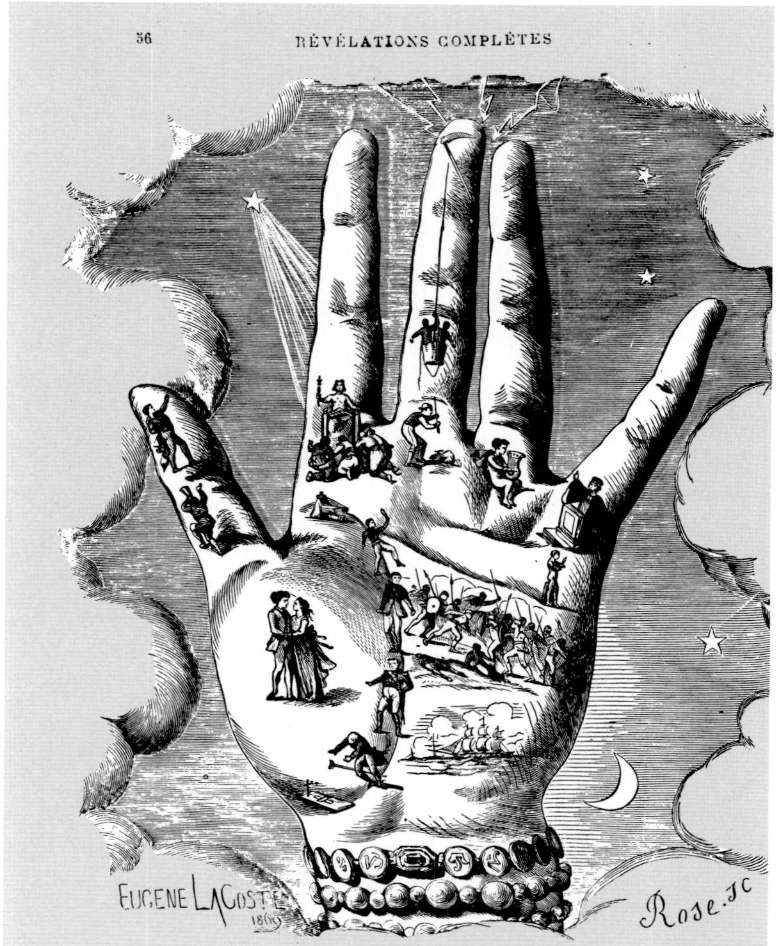

Saunders. He accented the special markings and lesser lines of the hand as signals of dreadful future happenings—such as death by fire, drowning, and hanging. The cleric Johannes Praetorius bolstered the acceptance of handreading by invoking the Bible's support. Universities included chiromancy in their curriculums, and individual physicians, notably the mystic Robert Fludd, proffered their own versions of the lines and elevations of the hand. Jean-Baptiste Belot also had a pronounced effect on chiromancy, for he codified the association of the signs of the zodiac with the fingers and their segments. The palm of the hand, in Belot's summation, was a startling complex of lines, markings, and regions, each with its own special significance.

The eighteenth century, often termed the "Age of Enlightenment," was a period when astrology and chiromancy were in general abeyance in both study and practice. However, there was at least one highly influential treatise that included opinions on the meaning of the hand, *Physiognomische Fragments* by Johann Lavater, a four-volume study of the connections between appearance and character in which the author determined, "If all men are not identical in character and training, then the hand is a specific characteristic of the particular person to whom it belongs."

In the nineteenth century hand studies and interpretation received considerable scientific attention. The anatomical writings of the English physician Charles Bell included extensive descriptions of the structure and functions of the hand as a whole and of all its parts. Bell's concerns were scientific anatomy and physiology, but he also looked upon the hand as the most important cultural instrument of the human brain. He showed no interest in the association of personal traits with hand features, but he seemed to express sympathy with the strivings of palmists to discover in the hand a clue to a person's character.

Carl Gustav Carus, royal physician of Saxony, also considered the hand to be an example of each person's individuality, fashioned through evolution as an indicator of inner nature. N. Vaschide, a member of the French Academy of Sciences, tried to apply scientific methods to handreading. Joseph Aszalay, another member of the academy, classified hands into four main types to correspond with personality traits.

Dr. C. G. CARUS,
Hof- und Medicinalrath,
Sr. Majestät des Königs von Sachsen Leibarzt.

Carl Gustav Carus (1789–1869), a prominent physician and romanticist of Saxony, believed that the hand revealed the unique character and inner nature of humans and that its features reflected the course of evolution. Wellcome Institute Library, London.

OPPOSITE BELOW RIGHT: A representation of astrological and palmistry associations, using personifications of the domains of the planets: the lecturer on the Mercury mount; harpist on the Apollo mount; handworker on Saturn; a ruler on Jupiter; a loving couple on Venus; a display of will on the tip of the thumb; the observer on the bottom phalanx; warriors in battle on the Plain of Mars; sailing vessels at sea on the Lunar mount; the progress of life from youth through maturity, age, and death on the Life line. From Desbarolles's *Mystères de la Main*.

RIGHT: Francis Galton (1822–1911), "father of modern genetics," classified fingerprints and patterns of lines on the hand, but his interest was in biological heritage, not in possible associations between the hand's features and character.

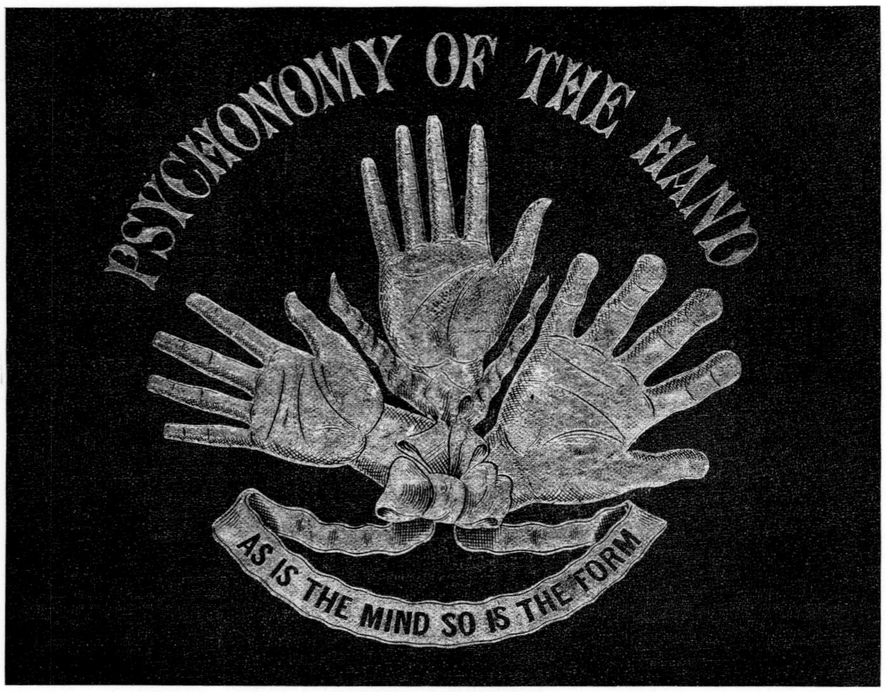

The front cover of *The Psychonomy of the Hand* by Richard Beamish (London, 1864). Psychonomy (psychological laws of the hand), a term coined by the author, implies a close connection between the mental makeup and the hand of a person. Wellcome Institute Library, London.

Bell, Carus, Vaschide, and Aszalay placed no credence in fortune-telling by the hand but their contributions to a philosophy of hand types was significant. Stanislas D'Arpentigny, a French army captain who also rejected predictive assumptions, drew on his own observations of thousands of people to conclude that the hand gives a clear indication of the character and the likely performance of its possessor. He organized hands according to contours, finger lengths and shapes, nail appearance, color, and skin texture. Many of the later classifications by palmists have employed D'Arpentigny's listings.

Adolphe Desbarrolles, a friend of D'Arpentigny's, denied that any special powers are needed to read hands. Instead he established what he termed a rational palmistry system based roughly on D'Arpentigny's classification but which also included the lines and elevations of the palm as significant features. Through his defined, organized method of interpretation of each feature of the hand, Desbarrolles argued that any student—without special gifts—could outline character and future tendencies. However, he also believed that the fingers received cosmic emanations, conducted to them by the nerves through the hand, into the body, and up to the brain. He subscribed to the ancient idea that fluids in nerves were the conductive mechanism: "The complicated system of nerves acts as a network of telegraph wires in transmitting from fingertips to cerebellum, the ever-traveling fluid." The principles of Desbarrolles impressed Balzac and Alexandre Dumas, who wrote the introduction to *Les Mystères de la Main* of 1859. Desbarrolles was also the handreader of Napoleon III, Empress Eugénie, and even Pope Leo XIII.

An outstanding example of palmistry's influence in the nineteenth century may be seen in the career of the chiromancer Mlle Normand, whose writings suggest that the Empress Josephine and Napoleon Bonaparte consulted her regularly. The accuracy of her drawings of the hands of both of these clients may be factual or fanciful, but there seems little doubt that Napoleon accepted both chiromancy and astrology, regardless of how much reliance he placed on them to affect his decisions.

One cannot help noticing in Normand's drawings that Napoleon's ring finger (Apollo) is longer than his index finger (Jupiter). As will be seen in the section on technique, the Jupiter finger coincides with fame, power, and achievement; the Apollo finger with artistry. Palmists would expect the opposite relationship to have existed between the two digits in Napoleon's hands. Indeed, an extra long or large index finger is often referred to as the "forefinger of Napoleon." Was Mlle Normand incorrect in her drawing and therefore a fabricator? Was she correct and Napoleon an example of the unreliability of palmistry? Or was the Jupiter finger not a sign of power in her lexicon?

The story is often repeated that when Mlle Normand reported to Napoleon that she saw in his hand the impending, though as yet only contemplated, divorce from Josephine, he had her incarcerated temporarily lest she break the news prematurely. Of course, this does not prove either that Mlle Normand was prescient or that the emperor was a believer.

Another name widely associated with handreading is that of the self-styled Count Louis Hamon, whose pseudonym, Cheiro (after the Greek root for "hand"), clearly represented him as a chiromancer but whose activities extended beyond palmistry to astrology, numerology, and other divinatory techniques. Cheiro became an influential personage among the gypsies. He is said to have been elected their leader, a position that he voluntarily relinquished. Writings actually by him and by others attributed to him contain didactic statements on the significance of the features of the hand. This type of detailed instruction has been further developed by Fred Gettings, a modern writer on chiromancy, who has divided the hand into zones of astrological influence, incorporating not only the planets and zodiac signs but also the qualities (cardinal, fixed, and mutable) and the elements (fire, air, earth, water) that are used in astrological classification.

In the twentieth century, attempts have been made to find correlations between features of the hand and medical conditions—such as diseases, mental aberrations, and inherited functional deficiencies. Charlotte Wolff, Ruth Achs, and Rita Harper are among those who have published the results of their investigations. Perhaps the progenitor of these studies was Julius Spier, who sought in the hand clues to inherited mental and emotional characteristics. For many years, he made direct and follow-up observations on people of all ages with the ultimate goal of completing an encyclopedic report on the hands of children, adults, and the mentally abnormal. Although he finished only a portion of the report, his student, Herta Levi, arranged for its publication after his death and appended a section of her own on the hands of the mentally diseased, using the methods of her mentor.

Spier was careful to acknowledge that intuition played a significant role in his handreadings but asserted that this intuitive faculty could be developed through the personal experience of looking for the association of various personalities with the features seen in their hands. He condemned forecasting as illegitimate and sometimes harmful. His aim was to find in the hand tendencies inherited from a person's forebears in order to allow that person to guard against innate weaknesses and to develop inherited strengths and talents. However, his work had little or no influence on the medical psychiatric profession. Indeed, Carl Jung's introduction to Spier's *The Hands of Children* is a complaint against the "contemptible treatment and defamation of these ancient arts [chiromancy and astrology]."

One feature of the hand that has occupied the medical and legal communities is the fingerprint. Dermatoglyphics is the scientific study of the patterns of ridges on the fingertips and on the palm. Actual fingerprints on clay from earliest times do exist. These may have been a type of identification or merely accidental markings incidental to molding a clay object when wet. Some of these artifacts go back thousands of years. Fingerprints were certainly used as authentications on written documents throughout history.

In the nineteenth century, Francis Galton (1822–1911), sometimes referred to as the father of human genetics, observed in fingerprint patterns the principles of inherited characteristics of the individual and their correlation with racial heritage. It may be that one pattern of ridges is statistically more common among the people of a particular national origin or race (this very term has become increasingly difficult to define) but not enough to allow identification of the ethnological heritage of any individual person. However, each fingerprint's uniqueness is genetically determined. It seems to have been chiefly William Herschel and Henry Faulds (they disputed each other's claims of priority), whose classifications became the standards of practical, positive identifications for each person. However, a treatise in 1823 and other publications describing nine different types of prints by J. L. Purkinje may actually have been the first scientific studies.

None of these works deals with character analysis, but as more people became aware of fingerprints as features unique to each person's hands, chiromantists added them to their interpretive systems. Generally, they recognized three main patterns, each associated with a specific group of

M. C. Escher. *Hand with Reflecting Globe*. 1900. Lithograph, 12½ × 8⅜″. National Gallery of Art, Washington, D.C. Rosenwald Collection. A common association between the artist or artisan and the hand is emphasized in this self-portrait by the famed surrealist.

personality features: the whorl, the loop, and the arch. At least one palmist uses fingerprints alone to make analyses and predictions, but the large majority of handreaders today consider the fingerprint simply as a modifier of the characteristics indicated by the shape and size of the finger itself.

In 1943 Harold Cummins and Charles Midloo published an in-depth study of fingerprints, palms, and soles, subtitled *An Introduction to Dermatoglyphics*. It examined exhaustively the history, comparative anatomy, anthropology, and biology of hands and soles. However, it is a treatise entirely outside the realm of handreading. Nowhere is there the slightest implication that the creases, ridges, or surface structures on the hand have any association with character or personality.

Thus the hand has been a subject of special interest to anthropologists, writers, anatomists, physicians, physiologists, fortune-tellers, mystics, and occultists—from prehistoric humans and ancient prophets of religion to the geneticists and handreaders of today.

Wilson began to study Luigi's palm, tracing the life-lines, heart-lines, head-lines and so on, and noting carefully their relations with the cob-web of finer and more delicate marks and lines that enmeshed them on all sides; he felt of the fleshy cushion at the base of the thumb, and noted its shape; he felt of the fleshy side of the hand between the wrist and the base of the little finger, and noted its shape also; he painstakingly examined the fingers, observing their forms, proportions, and natural manner of disposing themselves when in repose. All this process was watched by the three spectators with absorbing interest, their heads bent together over Luigi's palm, and nobody disturbing the stillness with a word. Wilson now entered upon a close survey of the palm again, and his revelation began.

—Mark Twain, *Pudd'nhead Wilson*

ABOVE: Piero Della Vecchia (1603–1678). *The Fortune-Teller and the Soldier.* Oil on canvas. The soldier appears to be worried as the chiromancer examines his hand. Wellcome Institute Library, London.

OPPOSITE: Reading the palm, after a model probably designed by J. C. Wilhelm Beyer. c. 1765–1770. Ceramic, painted in enamel colors and gilding, 8 × 5½″ (width of base). Victoria and Albert Museum, London.

General Technique

A variety of words has been assigned to handreading. Each can be given a narrow definition: *chiromancy*—divination by observing the hand; *chirology*—study of the hand, especially the meanings conveyed; *chirognomy*—knowledge of the hand, notably its size, shape, and gestures; *chirosophy*—interpretation of the hand (wisdom of the hand); *palmistry*—divination by reading the lines and elevations of the palm. Now each of the terms has come to signify judging personality and future tendencies by examining the various parts of the hand, although there are subtle differences of meaning among them.

Most handreaders size up a person's appearance, manner, expression, voice, and other attributes and then focus on the hands themselves. (But those aspects of handreading that relate to intuition, ESP, and other skills of the observer are not the concerns of this chapter.) The features of the hand that readers examine are: hand type; finger size, shape, and nails; elevations (mounts) and valleys (plains); lines of the palm; markings on the mounts and plains; fingerprints; and gestures and posture of the hands.

Presumed differences in significance between the right and left hands are not universally agreed to by palmists. To some, the left hand of women should be read and the right of men. Others reverse the process. Many insist on studying both hands. Most readers believe that for right-handed people the left hand manifests inherited characteristics; the right shows what has been achieved with that heritage and vice versa for left-handed people. (In this chapter we will use the left hand for readings almost exclusively.)

The reading process requires studying all the features and parts of the hand at the same time. Palmists consider all the divisions of the hand to be interrelated and interdependent.

Hand Types

Overall hand size is measured by palmists along the back of the hand, from the tip of the long middle finger to the level of the wristbone prominence located on the outside of the arm (whose anatomical name is the ulnar styloid). The average length is seven to seven and one-quarter inches in women; seven and one-quarter to seven and one-half in men. When much longer, the person is judged to prefer details to performance and to have a tendency to moodiness. People with smaller hands are more likely to have imaginative attitudes and to have a tendency to impracticality.

The shape of the palm is also significant. It is usually indicated as long or short, wide or narrow, depending on its proportions. Since the fingers sometimes have a "high takeoff" from the palm, they appear shorter when looked at from the palm side than they actually are when measured along the back side from the large knuckle to the tip of the finger.

Thinness of hand or fingers suggests nervousness and, in extreme cases, timidity. Thickness indicates sensuousness, even sensuality. Firmness points to purpose and balance but also to excessive discipline, which might be a hazard. The person with soft hands is easy-going but can be lazy and uncertain. Knobs (bulges of the joints) refer to concentrating abilities, which can be carried to single-mindedness. Smoothness of contour reveals intuitive makeup and artistic interest, with impulsiveness to be guarded against. Thus, palmists see in these features positive qualities but possible dangers as well.

Chiromancers determine if a hand is long-fingered by noting that when the fingers are bent toward the palm at the first and the second joints, the tip of at least one finger can reach close to the wrist. When the farthest that can be reached is the middle of the Venus mount, then the hand can be considered short-fingered relative to the palm length. Long fingers accent the intellect; relatively long palms favor the emotions. The more square the digit, the more practical the person's outlook is likely to be.

All these anatomic appearances must be added to and blended with other features that one finds in a finger or palm. We have used a classification that recognizes seven basic types, as designated by D'Arpentigny in the nineteenth century.

Fingers

The features of the fingers that are of particular interest to handreaders are their lengths and thicknesses, the prominence of the joints and knuckles, and the shape of the nails. Determination of whether the composite (overall) length of the fingers of a hand are long or short is relative to the length of the back of the hand: equal to, longer than, or shorter than the hand's length from large knuckle to wristbone. But each of the fingers also has to be compared with the other fingers as seen from the palm side to classify it as average, long, or short.

Short fingers are possessed by people who have broad ideas and can plan ahead. While perceiving the kernel of importance in a project, the short-fingered are apt to have little concern for details. Impulsive and restless with limited drive, they may have difficulty concentrating, so that the grand idea may never be implemented.

Long fingers signify focus on details. A project once begun will be adhered to until completed. This persistence may actually miss recognition of the large picture, so that the minutiae may become the principal purpose.

Smooth joints are associated with perceptiveness, intuition, and quickness. A focus on self-involvement can lead to vanity and lack of self-analysis. Knobby joints indicate analysis, patience, and skepticism, but pedantry must be guarded against. The presence of knots on two joints of the same finger is considered a sign of creative talent. A knobby base joint signals orderliness. Waist-shaped (contracting) phalanges suggest diligence, tact, and curiosity.

The base phalanx is associated with the application of the ideas and drives symbolized by that particular finger. The middle phalanx represents the degree of intellect and balance. The fingertip signifies emotions.

A pointed tip indicates the presence of mysticism and intuition, with a preference for fine things and also whimsy. A conic (rounded) finger end is associated with artistry and gentility with a preference for elegance. A square tip favors practicality and productivity, with preference for crafts and business. A spatulate end signifies physical activity and restlessness, with a preference for mechanical things and travel.

The degree of prominence of the mount at the base of a finger can modify the characteristics symbolized by the finger itself. For instance, a high Jupiter mount below a short index finger can lessen the tendency of self-effacement and introduce a measure of will and drive. High-set fingers on the hand indicate less influence by the mounts.

Hand Classifications

Broad Type

The palm is wide: the length from the base of the middle finger to the first bracelet at the wrist is equal to or less than the width across the palm (across the bases of all four fingers).
The fingers are short: measurement from the tip of the middle finger to the knuckle on the back of the hand is less than the length from the knuckle to the wristbone.

Elemental (materialistic)
Palm: wide with few lines.
Fingers: short and broad.
Nails: short and broad.

Attitudes: practical, conservative, materialistic.
Personality: aura of power, steadfastness.
Emotions: intense; can be sensual.
Suitable occupations: physical pursuits, manual endeavors, mechanics.
Money and business: cautious.
Interests and hobbies: food, drink, physical activities.
Negatives (dangers): resistance to the new, irritability, slowness.

Square (orderly)
Palm: square (width the same at wrist and at base of fingers).
Fingers: nearly the same lengths.
Nails: short and square-shaped.

Attitudes: practical, methodical, determined, honest, orthodox.
Personality: sincere, unselfish.
Emotions: undemonstrative but devoted, constant in attachment.
Suitable occupations: those that require perseverance rather than brilliance; also politics, law, business, teaching, medicine, science.
Money and business: ability to succeed in undertakings.
Interests and hobbies: any activity that is serious rather than flippant.
Negatives (dangers): stubbornness, suspicion of what is not understood, coldness, stiffness.

Spatulate (active)
Palm: broader at one end, either at the wrist or base of fingers (shovel-shaped, spatulate).
Fingers: wide and flat at the tips.
Nails: often shovel-shaped like the palm.

Attitudes: ambitious, independent, inventive, versatile, creative, nonconformist.
Personality: self-confident, brilliant, resilient.
Emotions: head over heart, not easily committed.
Suitable occupations: engineering, science, creative arts.
Money and business: perceptive, shrewd.
Interests and hobbies: intellectual pursuits, puzzles, challenging activities.
Negatives (dangers): unsteadiness, tendency to be a "show-off," unscrupulousness, loneliness.

Hand Types

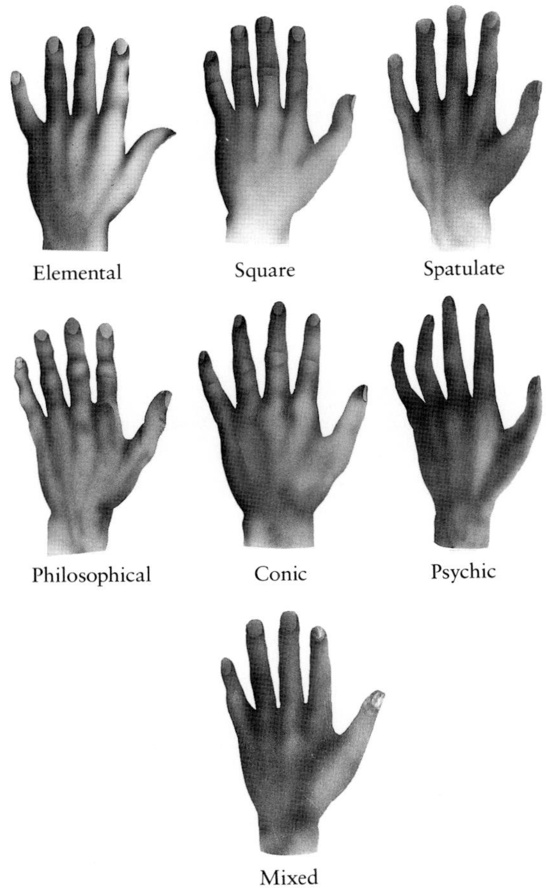

The palm is long or narrow. The length from the base of the middle finger to the wrist is clearly longer than the width of the palm.
The fingers are long: the measurement from the tip of the middle finger to the knuckle is longer than the length from the knuckle to the wrist bone.

Philosophic (analytical)
Palm: elongated, often thin.
Fingers: thin, knotty joints, square tips.
Nails: long.

Attitudes: imaginative, intuitive, spiritual, original.
Personality: studious, perceptive, serious.
Emotions: held in reserve but sustained when committed.
Suitable occupations: creative arts, science, teaching.
Money and business: little interest in money or finance.
Interests and hobbies: the obscure, arcane, and abstract.
Negatives (dangers): impracticality, loneliness, impoverishment.

Conic (skillful)
Palm: tapered toward base of fingers.
Fingers: also tapered with slightly rounded tips.
Nails: long.

Attitudes: creative, talented, quick in perception, honest, unprejudiced.
Personality: sparkling, witty, generous.
Emotions: sensitive, sympathetic, deeply committed.
Suitable occupations: creative and performing arts.
Money and business: potentially clever.
Interests and hobbies: luxuries and social affairs.
Negatives (dangers): impatience, superficiality, inconsistence, sloth.

Psychic (idealistic)
Palm: narrow.
Fingers: taper evenly, graceful looking.
Nails: long.

Attitudes: trusting, gentle, kind, uncritical, tolerant.
Personality: warm, generous, good-humored.
Emotions: empathetic, outgoing.
Suitable occupations: social work, arts, counseling.
Money and business: observant of broad objectives.
Interests and hobbies: metaphysics, occult, philosophy.
Negatives (dangers): dreaminess, impracticality, vulnerability.

Mixed Type (versatile)

Palm, fingers, and nails do not match each other or are unclassifiable in type.

Attitudes: adaptable, quick of thought, original.
Personality: charming, agreeable, witty, persuasive.
Emotions: expressed easily but self-protective.
Suitable occupations: virtually any endeavor; especially suited to selling.
Money and business: innovative, flexible.
Interests and hobbies: activities that offer excitement.
Negatives (dangers): restlessness, inconstancy, resistance to disagreeable tasks.

Finger Classification

Thumb

Signifies vitality, energy, management of fate

Overall length
Long (tip reaches above the halfway mark on the base phalanx of the index finger): intellectuality, sensitivity, forcefulness, sometimes subtlety
Short (tip is below the halfway mark on the base phalanx of the index finger): materialism

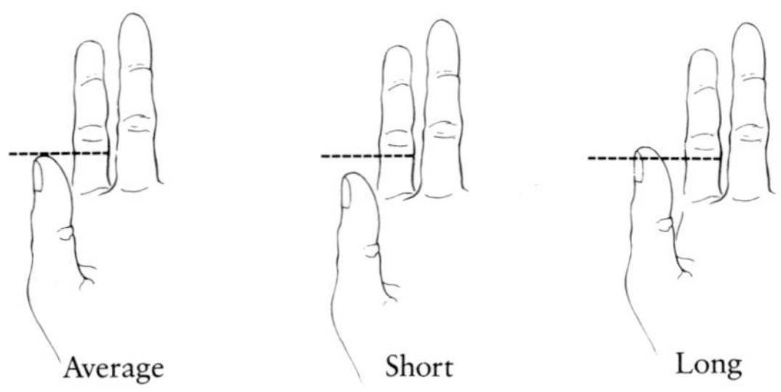

Overall shape
Large: drive, determination, positive values, bossiness
Small: instinctive decisions, use of others, hastiness
High set (close to base of index finger): intellectuality
Low set (far from base of index finger): physicality

Relationship to hand
Proportionate in size: balance
Disproportionately large or small: domination by the thumb's characteristics over the features shown by the palm.

Posture (average posture is if the thumb is held at a 45- to 60-degree angle to inner palm edge)
Held close (less than 45 degrees): secretiveness, self-protectiveness, frugality
Held wide (greater than 60 degrees): expansiveness, fearlessness, generosity, open-mindedness
Held midway (45 to 60 degrees): moderation, resourcefulness
Held inside fingers: uncertainty
Held locked to other thumb: self-concern
Held bent forward: tendency to self-effacement and withdrawal

Flexibility
Stiff (resists bending back): self-control, reserve, stubbornness
Flexible (can be bent back): accommodation, sympathy, danger of uncertainty and extravagance

Tip Phalanx
Signifies will

Length
Long: persistence, will power, danger of stubbornness
Short: diminished perseverance, danger of planning but not performing

Thickness
Thick: strong will, danger of tyranny
Thin: more pliant, danger of diffuseness

Shape
Spatulate: energy, strong opinions (on large thumb, can increase forcefulness; on small thumb, can decrease forcefulness), danger of impatience and domineering behavior
Square: persuasiveness, practicality (on large thumb, can heighten practical drives; on small thumb, can lessen prudence), danger of boorishness
Conic (rounded): expressiveness, enthusiasm (on large thumb, increased focus; on small thumb, less practicality), danger of uncontrolled temper
Pointed: idealism, impulsiveness (on large thumb, more pragmatism; on small thumb, more dreaminess), danger of ineffectuality

Base Phalanx
Signifies reasoning

Length (compared to tip phalanx)
Long: reason over action, danger of inaction
Short: logic a less prominent feature, danger of acting too hastily
Equal: balance, can make decision and act on it

Thickness
Thick: self-control, caution, danger of obstinacy
Thin: emotionality, danger of hastiness and indecision

Shape
Waisted: quickness, tact, danger of deviousness

Index Finger

(or Jupiter finger; at its base is the Jupiter mount)

Signifies ambition, pride, self-assertion

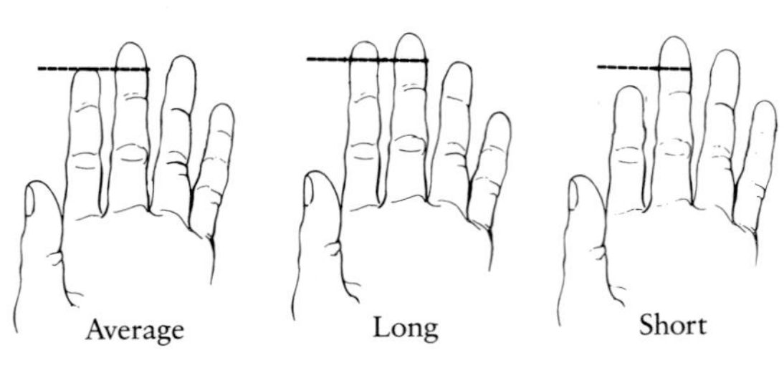

Overall length
Long (nearly the same length or even with Saturn finger): enhanced drive
Medium: (reaching to middle of tip phalanx of middle—Saturn—finger): reasonable will to achieve
Short: less drive

Overall shape
Straight: talent for observation
Curved to middle finger: self-possession
Curved to thumb side of hand: militance and assertiveness
Thick: sensuousness
Thin: strictness

Tip Phalanx
Length
Long: heightened ambition, intuition
Short: less ambition, skepticism

Thickness
Thick: tendency to sensuousness mixed with mysticism
Thin: tendency to firmness with danger of rigidity

Shape
Spatulate tip: practicality, inventiveness, interest in animals, travel, danger of bigotry
Square tip: regularity, punctuality, constancy, danger of resistance to the new
Conic (rounded) tip: artistry, intuition, nonconformism, danger of unreality, indulgence
Pointed tip: inspiration, idealism, mysticism, danger of unreality, indulgence

Middle Phalanx
Length
Long: ambition in practical terms
Short: less practical

Thickness
Thick: aims directed to material success
Thin: aims directed to nonmaterial achievement

Base Phalanx
Length
Long: recognition a primary concern
Short: recognition secondary

Thickness
Thick: sensuousness
Thin: interest in mind, not body

Middle Finger

(or Saturn finger; at its base is the Saturn mount; separates the active from the passive side of the hand)

Signifies sobriety, skepticism, curiosity, balance

Overall length
Long: intellect accented, status quo preferred, tendency to mysticism, loneliness
Medium: mixture of intellect and imagination
Short: intuition, reduced rationality

Overall shape
Straight: intuition, danger of dogmatism
Curved toward index finger: intellectual achievement
Curved toward ring finger: aesthetic achievement
Thick: thoughtfulness, sobriety, danger of aggression
Thin: spirituality, danger of pessimism

Tip Phalanx
Length
Long: perseverance
Short: acceptance

Thickness
Thick: roughness
Thin: callousness

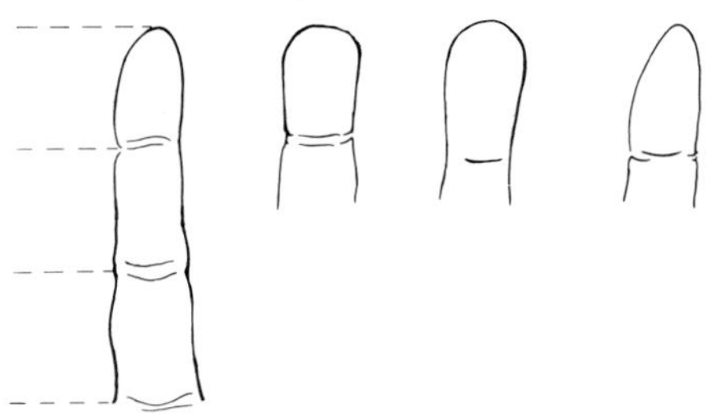

Shape
Spatulate tip: sobriety, danger of depression
Square tip: strictly moral, danger of pettiness
Conic (rounded) tip: more cheerful than sober, danger of rashness
Pointed tip: intuition, danger of lack of initiative

Middle Phalanx
Length
Long: rationality
Short: logic less important

Thickness
Thick: practicality
Thin: inquisitiveness

Base Phalanx
Length
Long: frugality
Short: sociability

Thickness
Thick: self-interest
Thin: curiosity

Ring Finger

(or Apollo finger; at its base is the Apollo mount; is on the passive side of the hand)

Signifies artistry, need for recognition

Overall length
Long: exceptional taste, heightened need for attention
Medium (about the same length as index finger): good taste, well-balanced needs
Short: preference for privacy, little focus on beauty

Overall shape
Straight: systematic, traditional
Curved toward little finger: inclined to seek monetary rewards
Curved toward middle finger: self-discipline in the arts; adds style to scholarly pursuits
Thick: accent on display
Thin: intellectual approach to art

Tip Phalanx
Length
Long: color sense, devotion to aesthetics and form
Short: less concern for aesthetic principles

Thickness
Thick: sensuousness
Thin: spirituality

Shape
Spatulate: inventiveness, danger of fantasizing
Square: technical ability, danger of pedantry
Conic (rounded): gentleness, danger of foolishness
Pointed: metaphysical and mystical, danger of hypersensitivity

Middle Phalanx
Length
Long: logic in art and technique
Short: less consistency in art and technique

Thickness
Thick: pragmatism
Thin: conciseness

Base Phalanx
Length
Long: self-centered focus
Short: less self-concern

Thickness
Thick: flamboyance
Thin: subtlety

Little Finger

(or Mercury finger; at its base is the Mercury mount; is on the extreme of the passive side of the hand)

Signifies tact, verbal expression, practicality, agility

Overall length
Long: tact, poise, perseverance
Medium (reaches to crease of tip of ring finger): balance in expression and perception
Short: perceptiveness, outspokenness, limited concentration

Overall shape
Straight: reserve
Curved toward ring finger: artistry in business adds practicality to art
Curved toward outside of hand: less expressive of ideas
Thick: expressiveness
Thin: endeavor

Tip Phalanx
Length
Long: capabilities in medicine, law, communications
Short: aptness for business pursuits

Thickness
Thick: indelicacy
Thin: elegance in expression

Shape
Spatulate: strong physical skills, danger of unscrupulousness
Square: professionalism, danger of intellect ruling emotions
Conic (rounded): eloquence, danger of verbosity
Pointed: intuitive, danger of lack of judgment

Middle Phalanx
Length
Long: business interests
Short: business concerns secondary

Thickness
Thick: aptitude for complexity
Thin: preference for simplicity

Base Phalanx
Length
Long: capable of devious reasoning
Short: preference for straightforward reasoning

Thickness
Thick: focus on material returns
Thin: interest in efficiency more than money

Nails

The nails' characteristics are read as modifications or additions to the other features of the finger, especially the tip.

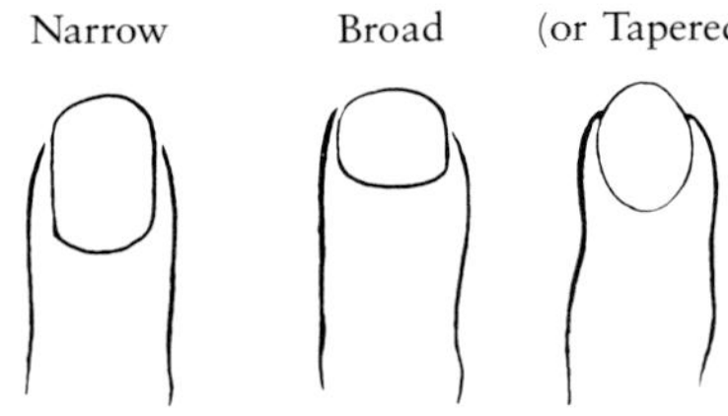

Shape
Broad: activist, steadfast, danger of hyperactivity, irritability, and negativism
Narrow: emphasis on the mind, psychic, danger of lack of feeling
Tapered toward base (filbert-shaped): candid

Length
Long: modesty, tact, danger of shyness and lack of discrimination
Short: criticism, curiosity, danger of hypercriticism and pugnacity

Moons (white portion at nail base)
Large: activism
Small or absent: passivity

Mounts and Plains

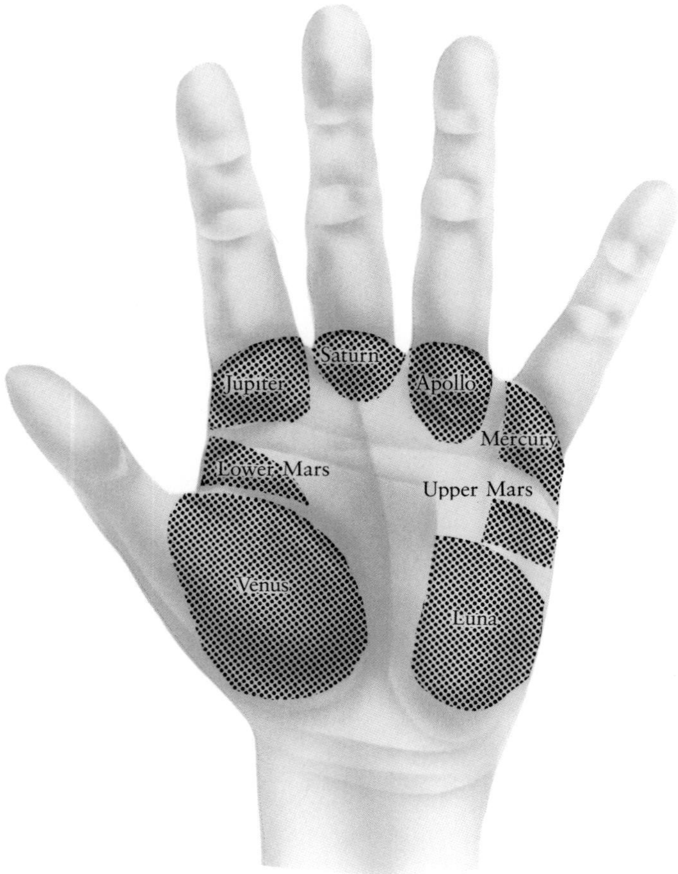

Mounts on the Palm

Although the size and shape of the hand are considered highly significant, when one refers to reading the hand it is the palm rather than the hand shape that is usually first called to mind ("palmistry")—that is, the interpretation of the mounts and lines on the palm according to their features and arrangement. In virtually all codifications of palmistry, astrological allusions are usually offered. Thus, the principal elevations (mounts) are named Jupiter (the area just beyond the junction of the index finger and the palm); Saturn (at the base of the long finger); Apollo (the ring-finger elevation); Mercury (at the base of smallest finger); Venus (the large, fleshy pad beyond the thumb extending toward the center of the palm and wrist); Luna (the palmar prominence on the outer side of the hand opposite Venus); and Mars (consists of two parts: the pad just above Venus on the thumb side of the hand—Lower, or Inner, Mars—and the elevation below Mercury—Upper, or Outer, Mars—

MOUNTS	**JUPITER**	**SATURN**	**APOLLO**	**MERCURY**
Symbolism	King god, justice, jovialty, ambition, pride	Cronos, father of Jupiter, loss of supremacy	Sun God—patron of arts, artistry	Messenger god–intermediary, cleverness
General Attributes	Just, intellectually curious, expansive	Wise, conforming, restrained	Creative, daring, appreciative of beauty	Expressive, practical, talented in medical sciences
Personality and Attitudes	Orderly, ethical, naturally elegant, charismatic	Authoritarian, perservering, inner-directed, controlled	Charming, tasteful, persuasive	Articulate, versatile, reliable
Emotional Features	Displays affection, faithful, high expectations of others	Undemonstrative, faithful, prudent in attachments	Needs admiration, needs to admire others, aesthetically sensitive	Needs devotion more than admiration, intellectual rather than emotional, admires discretion
Occupational Suitability	Positions of trust, public appearance and performance, home-oriented activities, diplomacy	Investigation and science-related work, medicine	Creative arts, decorative arts, sales, music in creation and performance	Business, publishing, medicine and nursing, sports, finance
Money and Business	Able to achieve position, generous, principled	Prudent, frugal, able to attain wealth	Innovative, generous, expansive	Astute investor, clever planner, venturesome
Hobbies and Interests	Food and entertainment	Probing endeavors (e.g., philosophy)	The arts, social activities	Children and their world, writing
Negatives	Overconfidence, pomposity, drinking, overindulgence, tyranny	Moodiness, violence and envy, dullness, perverseness, becoming a "loner"	Fickleness, gaudiness, effeteness, excessive gambling, conceit	Duplicity, dishonesty, greed, diffuseness, verbosity

on the outer side of the hand). The size of each mount and its position in relation to the adjacent mounts and lines of the palm indicate the extent of influence exerted by that mount.

The Plain of Mars lies in the center of the palm, a relatively flat surface approximately bounded by the mounts at the bases of the fingers, the Luna and Upper Mars mounts on the outside of the palm, and the Venus and Lower Mars on the inside. When the Plain of Mars is fleshy, a vigorous and positive temperament is signaled. A markedly hollowed-out Plain of Mars goes with a retreating, negative, ineffectual tendency. A gradually curved surface, neither dominated by the surrounding mounts nor equaling their elevation, fits an equable, balanced nature.

Each of the eight mounts signifies specific qualities in a person's character and life direction.

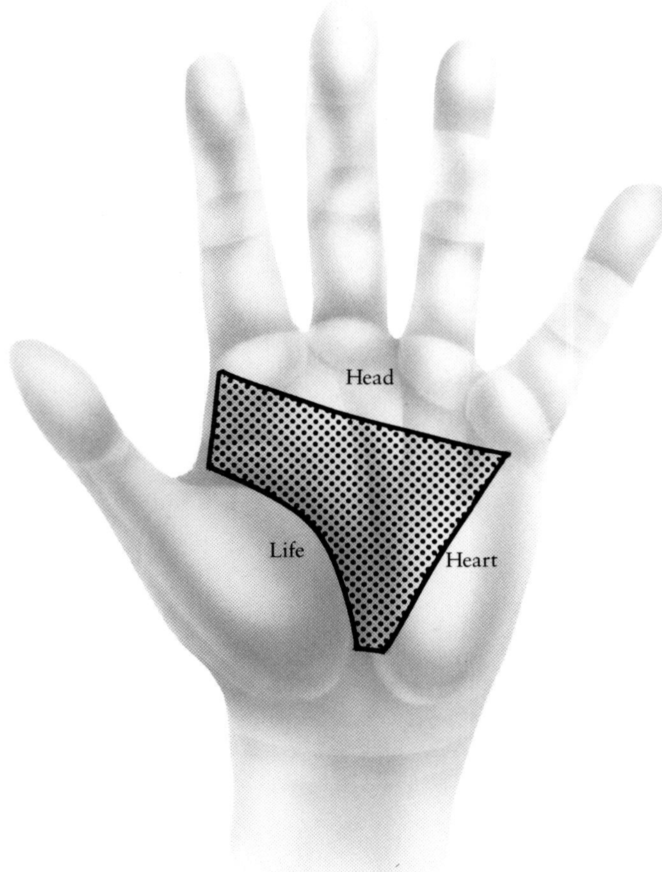

The Plain of Mars

VENUS Goddess of love, beauty, laughter, sentiment	**LUNA** Ancient goddess once supreme, imagination, emotion	**OUTER (Upper) MARS** God of power and war, resistance	**INNER (Lower) MARS** God of war and power, aggressiveness
Warm and affectionate, vital, peaceloving	Imaginative, introspective, love of travel	Passive but firm, skillfull, considerate	Self-assertive, independent, impulsive
Candid, outgoing, spontaneous, sexually attractive	Dreamy, unpredictable, creative, love of privacy	Courageous, principled, constructive, steadfast	Energetic, demonstrative, courageous, leading
Passionate, intense in attachments, attracted to the demonstrative	Cool-natured but likes to woo, attracted to the undemanding	Faithful, slow to arouse, intense	Passionate, seeks the responsive, attached to the strong
Arts, entertainment, public relations, catering	Creative arts, music, business activities, mysticism, literature, psychiatry	Demanding work, professions, crafts	Heavy industry, litigation, military
Money for use not accumulation, generous, public interest	Imaginative rather than materialistic, easily satisfied, effective in advertising	Conservative, patient	Expansive, generous, venturesome
Social work and philanthropy, parties and clothes	Travel and water activities, theater and music, the occult	Intellectual pursuits, social work, sports	Physical activities
Tactlessness, carelessness, irresponsibility, promiscuity, lack of discipline	Hypersensitivity, selfishness, instability, secretiveness, inconstancy	Stubbornness, single mindedness, unreasonable	Destructiveness, cruelty, overindulgence, profligacy

Palm Lines

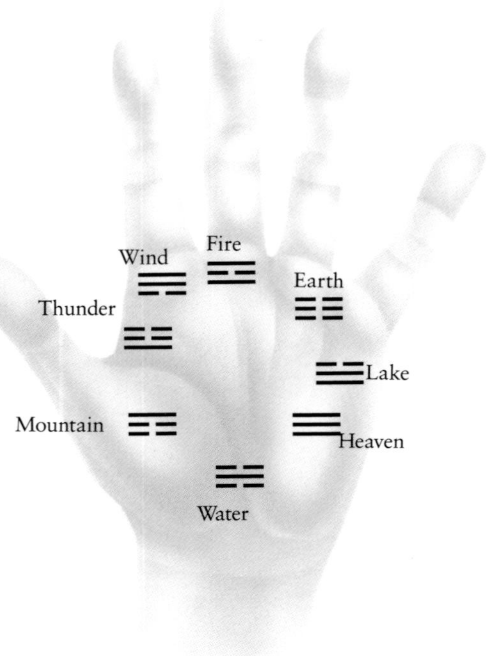

Association of the Trigrams and Areas of the Palm

Chinese Palmistry

Chinese methods of palmistry, presumed to be over two thousand years old, divide the palm into eight basic regions to correspond with the trigrams of the *I Ching*. The significance of each of these areas differs from the meaning of the similar region in Western handreading, although some chiromancers have tried to link the two systems.

For instance, the trigram *Sun,* which is in the same location as the Jupiter mount in Western palmistry, governs the mind and material outlook. This association can be considered closely related to the just attitude and high position influenced by the Jupiter elevation. In a similar way, the Chinese place on the upper part of Venus the trigram *Chên,* concerned with lightning, energy, and movement, elements that seem to have correlations with Lower Mars (signifying energy and aggression).

However, *Tui* (symbolizing domesticity) does not match its counterpart Luna (travel), although there is some concurrence in that both the Chinese area and Luna are governed by the watery sign of the moon. *Li* (brightness, fire, and fame) differs markedly from the restraint and sobriety of the Saturn area; *K'un* (yielding, giving, female principle), lying between the fourth and fifth fingers seems unrelated to the artistry and versatility of the Apollo and Mercury mounts; *Kên,* symbolizing the hardness and stillness of a mountain, hardly resembles the outgoing warmth and spontaneity of Venus; *Chien* (fatherhood and creativity) seems far from the emotionality and introspection of Luna; *K'an* is placed in the hollow between Venus and Luna, where no Western mount or region is designated.

The part of the hand that is given the most attention by handreaders is the palm, with its creases (lines), hills (mounts), and valleys (plains). Indeed, "palmistry" is the term most commonly applied to the process of examining the hand to determine character and predict the future. The most prominent features of the palm for these purposes are its lines, of which the principal ones are Life (Vitality), Head (Mind), Heart (Emotion), Fate (Saturn), and Art and Fame (Apollo, Sun).

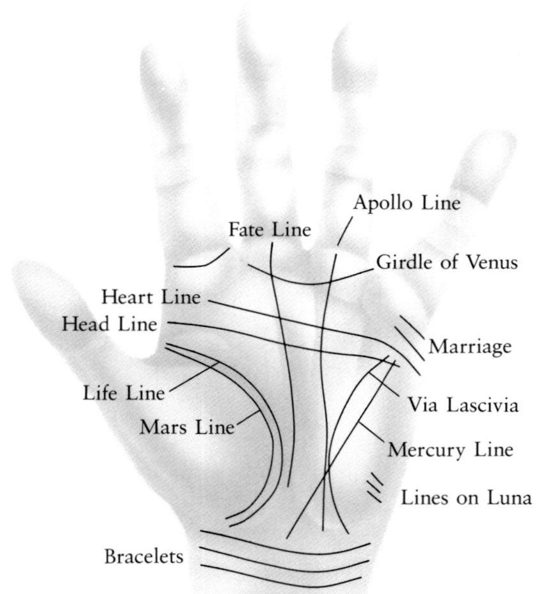

Lines of the Hand

The other lines of the hand are termed "secondary" or "subsidiary." These include the Girdle of Venus, Ring of Solomon, Mercury line, Via Lascivia, lines of Affection, Influence lines, and bracelets. All the lines have to be taken into account in a reading of the palm.

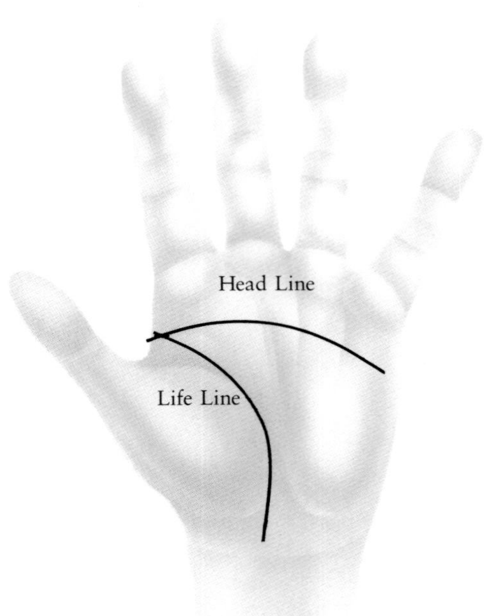

Life line in relation to the Head line

Life Line (vitality)

Course: Lower Mars to Venus and wrist
Signifies vitality, energy, drive

Appearance
Deep: energetic
Shallow: limited energy
Gaps: lapses of energy
Chains and islands: problems affecting vitality
Waviness: ebb and flow in energy
Duplication: accentuates energy and drive (this is called "Line of Mars")
Parallel lines: need for people and affection
Long: prolonged vitality
Short: easily fatigued
Starting close to head line: caution, timidity
Starting separately from head line: independence, rashness
Curves far out: penchant for activity
Curves close to thumb: intellectually active

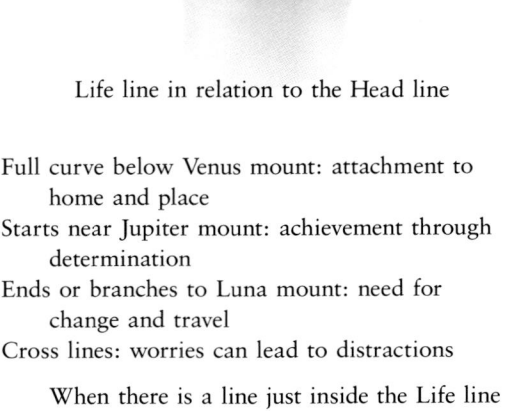

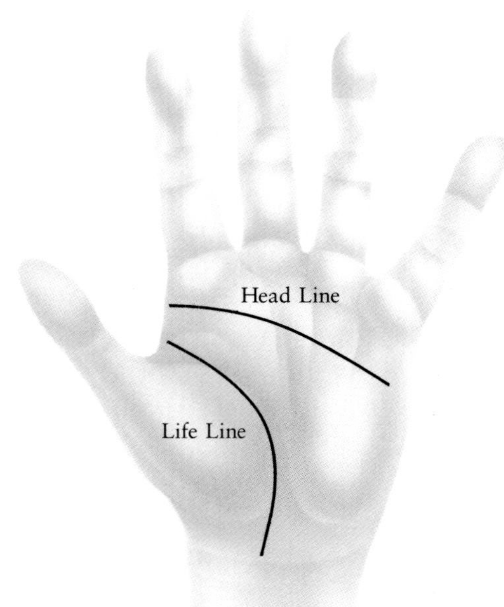

Life line in relation to the Head line

Full curve below Venus mount: attachment to home and place
Starts near Jupiter mount: achievement through determination
Ends or branches to Luna mount: need for change and travel
Cross lines: worries can lead to distractions

When there is a line just inside the Life line and paralleling it, this is called the Mars line and signifies strong drive.

The Life line has sometimes been used to indicate the course of the vital energies. This is done by dividing it into approximately eight- or ten-year periods, beginning with its origin at Lower Mars, swinging around the Venus mount, and ending at the edge of the wrist. The end of the line marks the age of death. One may also find the age at which events shown on the other lines will occur by noting the level of the particular marking with respect to the age point on the Life line. In general, modern palmists employ this age determination sparingly or not at all.

Head Line (*mind*)

Course: Lower Mars toward outer edge of palm (percussion edge)
Signifies attitudes

Appearance
Deep: thinking person
Shallow: practicality rather than brilliance

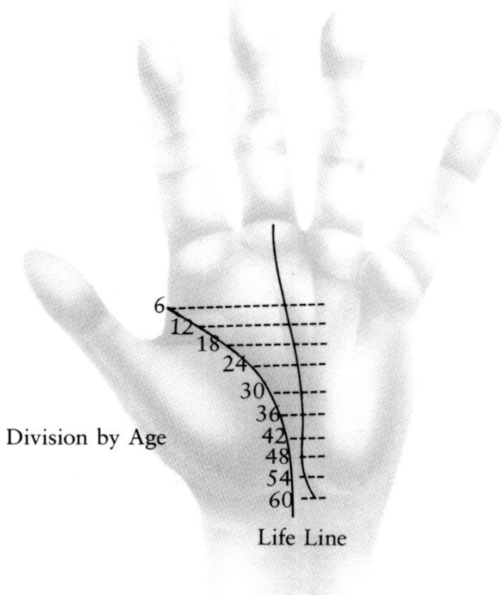

Line of Life

Gaps: lapses in thinking
Chains and islands: uncertainty
Waviness: varying directions of thought
Duplication: accentuation of mental abilities
Forked: broad perceptions
Parallel lines: accentuation of mental ability
Line associations: broad interests
Close to Life line: caution
Separate from Life line: independence
Joined to Heart line: unique personality
Branch to Heart line: logic, coldness
Straight: practicality
Slightly curved: flexibility
Sloping down: sensitivity, imagination
Starts at Lower Mars: tendency to irritability
With raised Lower Mars: drive to put across ideas
With flat Lower Mars: difficulty in using ideas
Branch to Luna: sensitivity of mind and imagination
Branch to Apollo: understanding of aesthetics
Branch to Mercury: scientific talents
Cross lines: challenges to decisions

Heart Line (*feeling*)

Course: outer edge of palm (percussion) toward inner edge
Signifies feeling, sympathy, emotion

Appearance
Deep: strong feelings

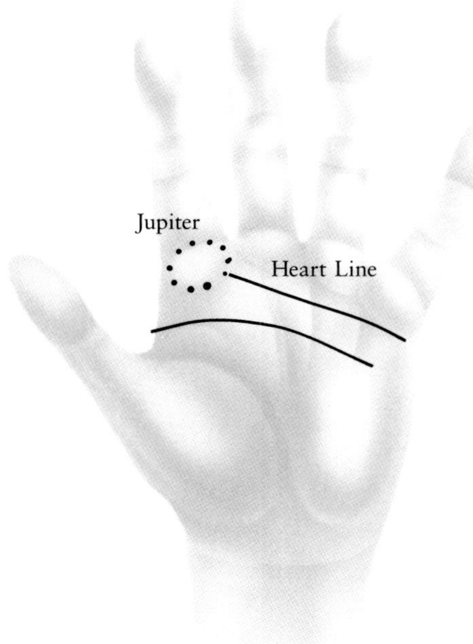

Heart Line

Shallow: lesser role given to feelings
Gaps: interruptions or loss in affection
Chains and islands: points of less interest in emotional activities
Waviness: uneven feelings
Duplication: accentuated feelings
Forked: warm-hearted emotions
Parallel lines: accentuation of feelings, danger of fickleness
Joined to Head line: unique personality
Branch to Head line: logical, cold
Branch to Life line: unafraid
Straight: idealistic affections
Curved: concrete attachments
Course high near fingers: superficial emotions
Course low near Head line: too much emotion
Branch toward Jupiter: idealism in love
Branch toward Saturn: realism in love

Fate Line (*destiny*)

Course: roughly vertical course from wrist to Saturn mount
Signifies destiny, purpose, productivity, sense of direction

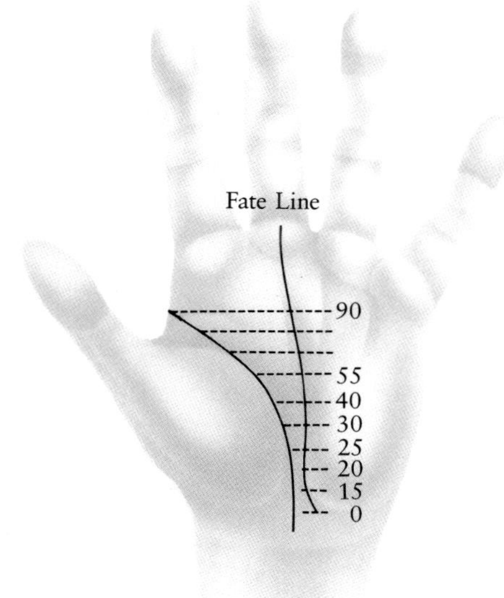

Line of Fate

Appearance
Deep: clear sense of direction
Shallow: uphill battle to success
Gaps: changes in course
Chains and islands: episodes of difficulty
Waviness: uncertainties in purpose

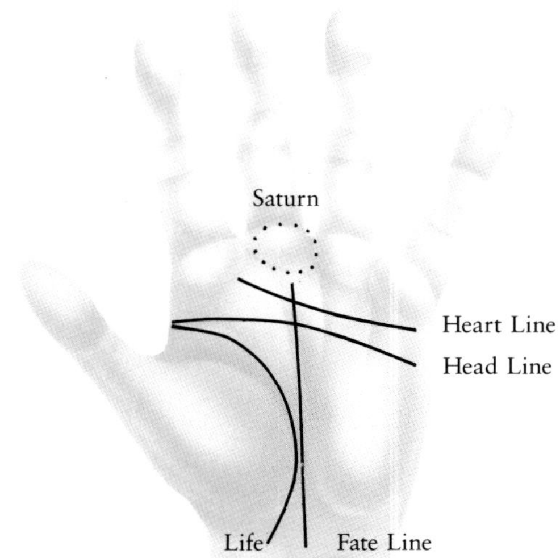

Fate Line to Saturn Mount

Duplication: can use other courses of action to substitute for a deficiency
Forked lines: various involvements
Parallel lines: sees opportunities
Starts near wrist: achievement through effort
Starts inside life line: constricted at beginning of life; apt to achieve with help of family or inheritance

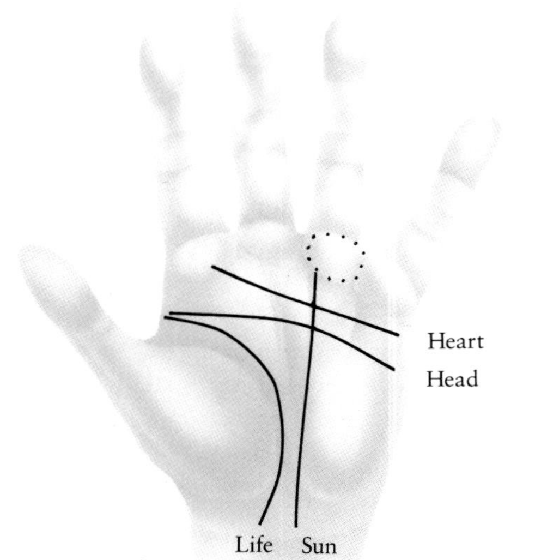

Fate Line to Apollo Mount

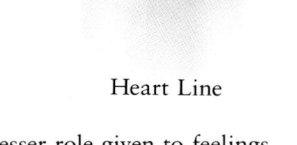

Branch to Head line: judgment plays role in course
Branch to Heart line: emotion can affect achievements
Straight: purposeful
Crooked or curved: can swing wide of mark on the way; the mount indicates area of activity
Curve toward Luna: career can be altered by emotion
Curve toward Venus: career can be altered by a love attachment
Curve toward Apollo: focus on arts and creativity

Curve toward Saturn: studiousness
Curve toward Jupiter: ambition may succeed, power apt to be gained
Curve toward Mercury: success through business
Long: steady march to achievement
Short: interruptions to achievement can be significant
Cross lines: interference on the way

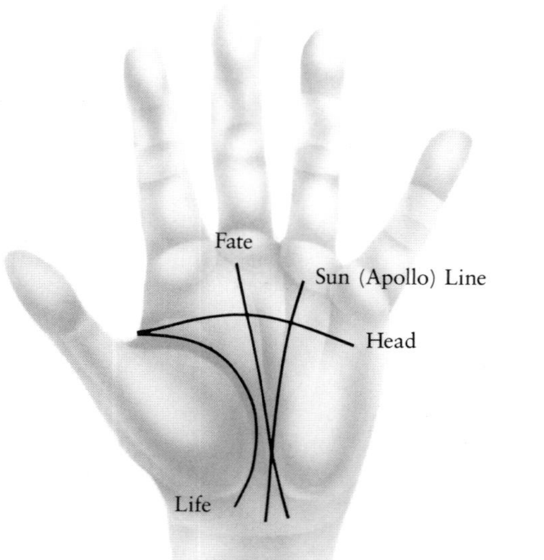

Apollo Line

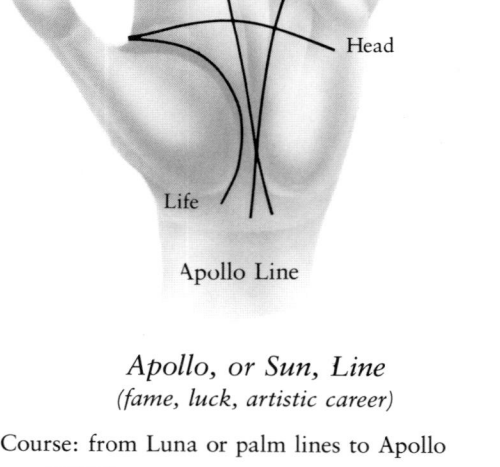

Apollo, or Sun, Line
(fame, luck, artistic career)

Course: from Luna or palm lines to Apollo mount
Signifies style, creativity, recognition

Appearance
Deep: perceptiveness
Shallow: perseverance rather than inspiration leads to creativity
Line absent: insecurity
Gaps: lapses in creativity
Chains and islands: problems in creativity
Waviness: unevenness in creativity
Duplication: different areas of creativity
Forked: recognition in more than one field
Parallel lines: accentuation of talent
Starts near wrist (between Venus and Luna): artistic enthusiasm and brilliance
Starts from Vitality line: dependence on family and friends in developing talents
Starts from Head line: intellectualization of talent
Starts from Heart line: artistry
Starts from Mercury line: business acumen in the arts
Starts from Fate line: artistic success
Straight: unimpeded achievement in the arts
Crooked: varying course on the way to artistic achievement
Near Luna: imaginative talent in the arts
Near Saturn: fame and fortune are desired
Near Mercury: material gain a prominent interest
Near Upper Mars: fame through individual's efforts
Near Venus: personal warmth plays a role in artistic success

Secondary Lines

These are lines that palmists use but consider of lesser significance.

Girdle of Venus
Beneath the long and ring fingers, usually below the mounts, there is sometimes seen a line of varying length and depth curving from the web between the ring and little fingers to the web between the long and index fingers. It is not seen often and is usually incomplete. It signifies emotionality and sensitivity, even a tendency to hysteria if strongly marked. Older books assign uncontrolled self-gratification to this feature.

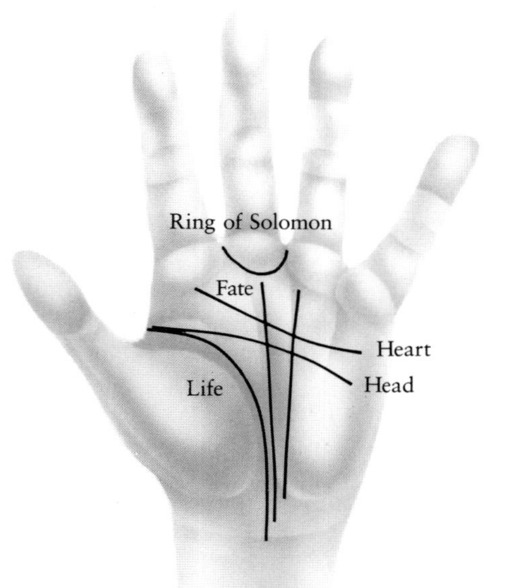

Ring of Solomon

Ring of Solomon
This curving line beneath the index finger running part or all of the way around the base of the finger on the Jupiter mount is supposed to indicate an understanding of and power to influence people. The line further announces skill in occult practices. It was named after the Hebrew king who is associated with wisdom and the subsequent Solomons who practiced magic. Sometimes palm readers designate as the Ring of Solomon a curving line between the index and long fingers that runs toward Lower Mars in the long web between the index finger and thumb.

Line of Mercury (Hepatica; Intuition)
This is a slanting, relatively straight line running outside the Apollo line, starting on Luna, or between Luna and Venus, or from the Saturn (fate) or Apollo (fame) lines. It may extend all the way to the Mercury mount or may stop before reaching it. When either deep and long or absent entirely, this line signifies good health. Broken features and other unfavorable markings are sometimes interpreted as incidents of poor health. The term *Hepatica* (liver) was assigned in the past centuries when the liver and its "humors" were a prominent part of medical thinking. Its present name refers to its proximity to the Mercury mount and finger. Some palmists consider this line an indicator of intuitive abilities.

Via Lascivia
This line lies beside the Mercury line. Older interpretations give this line a derogatory significance—such as unpalatable eroticism and dissipation. Modern palmists associate its presence with excitability. However, whether the Via Lascivia is a distinct, separate line with different meanings is in dispute.

Lines of Affection (Marriage)
On the percussion side of the hand, on the extreme outside at the level of the Mercury mount (seen when a fist is made), several short horizontal lines are usually associated with marriage or with bonds of affection. Few modern palmists assign consistent meanings to these.

Lines of Influence
On the Venus mount, the lines that run approximately parallel to the Life line are called lines of Influence, indicating the influence of other people on the life of the person. The nearer to the thumb side of the mount, the earlier in life the influences were exerted. A particularly clear line parallel and close to the Life line is termed the line of Mars (it accentuates energy), as already mentioned in the table summary of the Life line.

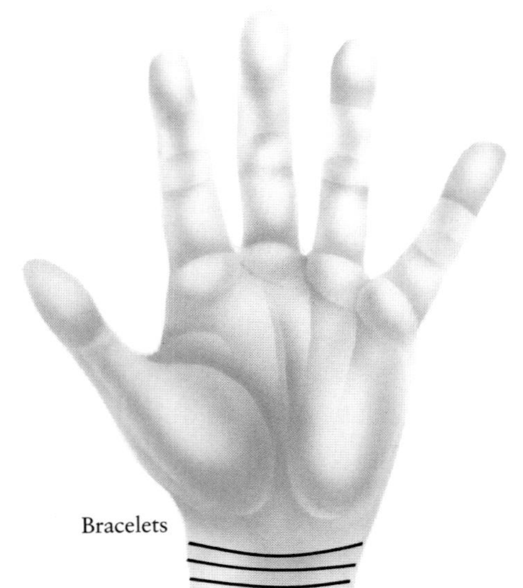

Bracelet Lines on the Wrist

Bracelets
A varying number of lines run across the wrist beyond the hand proper. Very little is written on their significance. Generally three are recognized, and the line directly at the base of the hand receives the principal focus. When particularly deep, clean, and noticeably curved in its center toward the interval between the Venus and Luna mounts, a potentially vigorous life marked by good fortune is announced. When chained, the line is associated with the need for perseverance. The more numerous the lines themselves, the more likely are vitality and healthy makeup. All three lines when well formed, clear, and unmarked are called the "Royal Bracelet" and signal a good chance for health and wealth.

Markings on the Hand

Various small, circumscribed markings may also be present on the palm. They may resemble a star, cross, square, circle, triangle, arrow, dot, or grille. Each of these shapes has a special significance by itself and according to where it occurs on the hand.

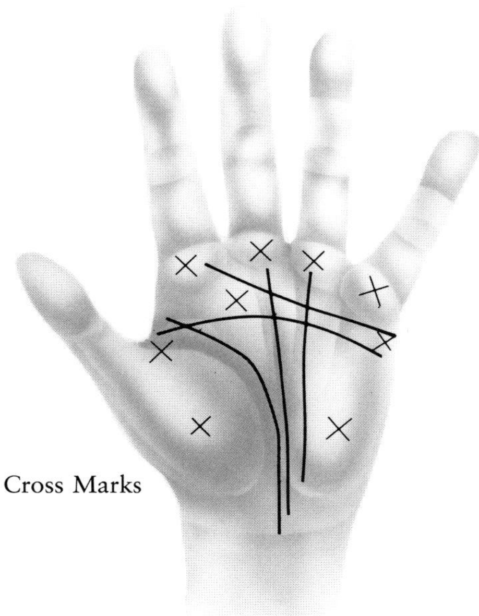

Cross Marks

Cross

The Mystic Cross, appearing between Head and Heart lines on palm middle signifies mysticism, metaphysics, danger of superstitiousness

On Jupiter mount: happy romantic relationship
On Saturn mount: gloominess
On Apollo mount: obstacles on way to achievement, disappointments
On Mercury mount: slyness
On Luna mount: danger of self-delusion
On Venus mount: intense love affair
On Plain of Mars: can generate enemies
On Life line: happiness at the indicated age period
On base phalanx of index finger: tendency to continence

Star

Signifies good fortune

On Jupiter: increased ambition, high likelihood of achievement
On Saturn: adaptability to obstacles, steadfast in danger, scholarship heightened
On Apollo: exceptional taste and style with probability of fame
On Mercury: especially articulate, perceptive in business and science

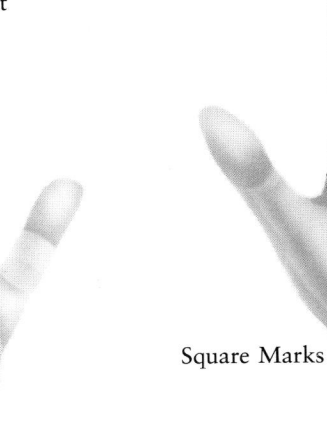

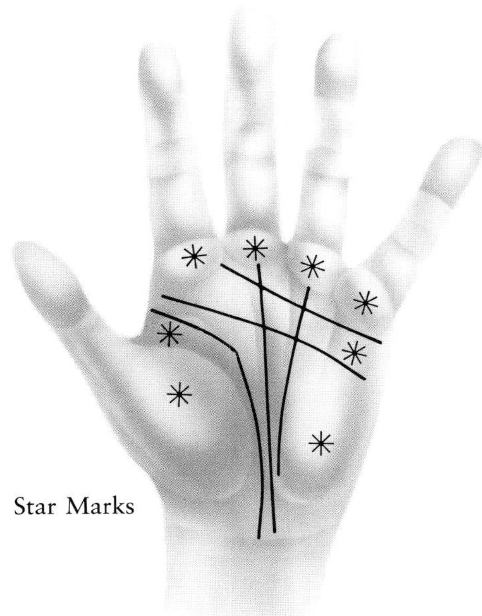

Star Marks

On Luna: exceptional imaginative powers
On Venus: happy outcome to love affairs
On Plain of Mars mount: good chance of honors through persistence
On end of Life line: material gain at the indicated age period
On palm middle: danger of an accident

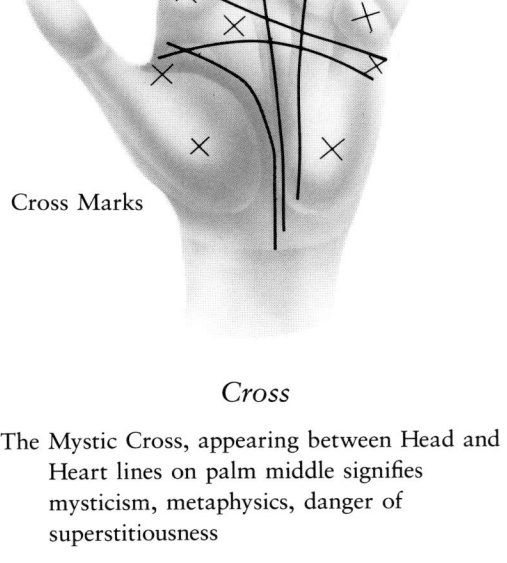

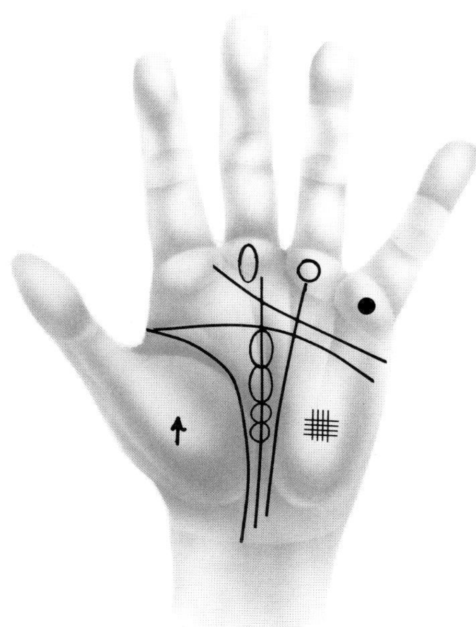

Chain, Circle, Grille, Arrow, and Dot Marks

Grille

Signifies nervous energy

On Jupiter: danger of self-defeating pride
On Saturn: depression or successful overcompensation for depression
On Apollo: tendency to self-display
On Mercury: deviousness
On Luna: hypersensitivity
On Venus: need for affection
On Mars: alertness to possible dangers
On palm middle: concentration on difficulties

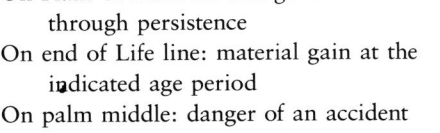

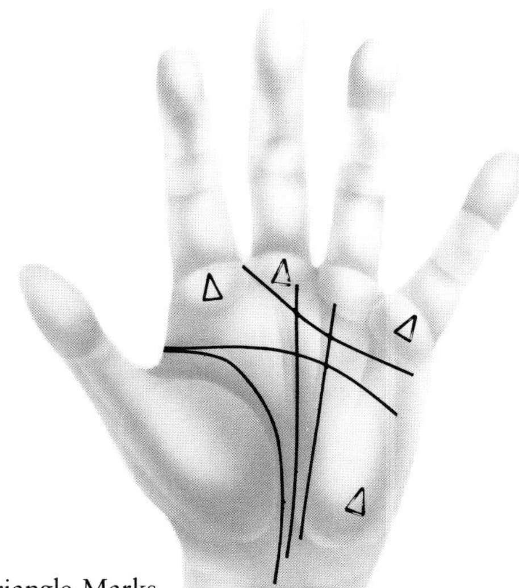

Triangle Marks

Triangle

Signifies skill

On Jupiter: leadership
On Saturn: scholarly capabilities
On Apollo: craftsmanship
On Mercury: verbal wit
On Luna: imagination used productively
On Venus: skill in romantic relationships
On Mars: self-control in meeting difficulties

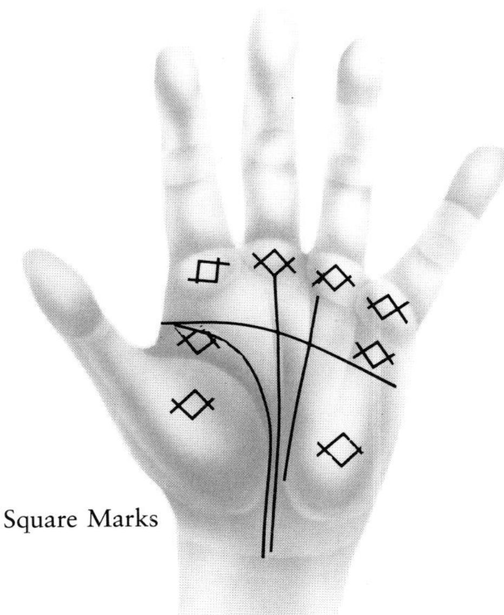

Square Marks

Square

Signifies protectiveness, moderation

On Jupiter: success easily acquired
On Saturn: less chance for gloom; occult abilities
On Apollo: emotional security
On Mercury: less tendency to unscrupulousness
On Luna: imagination kept in bounds
On Venus: balanced in love affairs
On Mars: adaptable

The significance of several other markings is more general:
Circle: heightens positive aspects of mount or line.
Chain: lessens strength of the line's meanings.
Island: divided energy.
Dot: a disorder in the significance of the line.
Arrow: achievement in the area governed by the mount or line.

Fingerprints

Palmists include fingerprints as a factor in their readings, and at least one chiromancer makes a full divination based solely on the prints. There are so many subdivisions and variations of each type of fingerprint that they have become the unique characteristic that identifies each person. However, for our purposes we will use only the three principal, basic arrangements: the arch, whorl, and loop.

Arch *(simplest configuration)*

Signifies rigidity, roughness, need for strong stimulus, materiality, danger of oppressiveness, violence

Whorl *(or circle; most complex configuration)*

Signifies domination, individualism, activism, danger of impetuosity, insensitivity, self-focus

Loop *(commonest configuration)*

Signifies control, reflection, adaptability, danger of unreliability

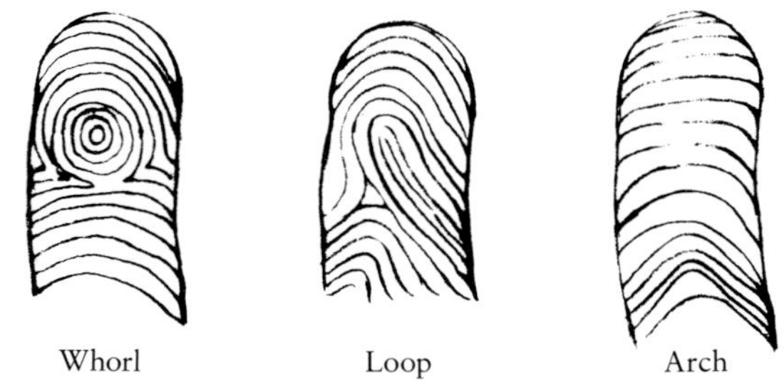

Types of Fingerprints

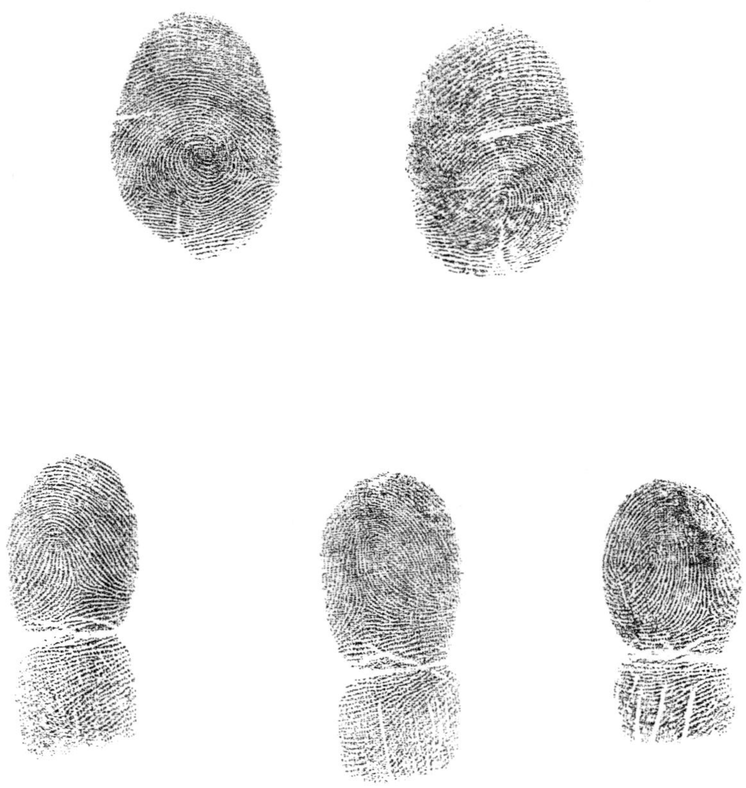

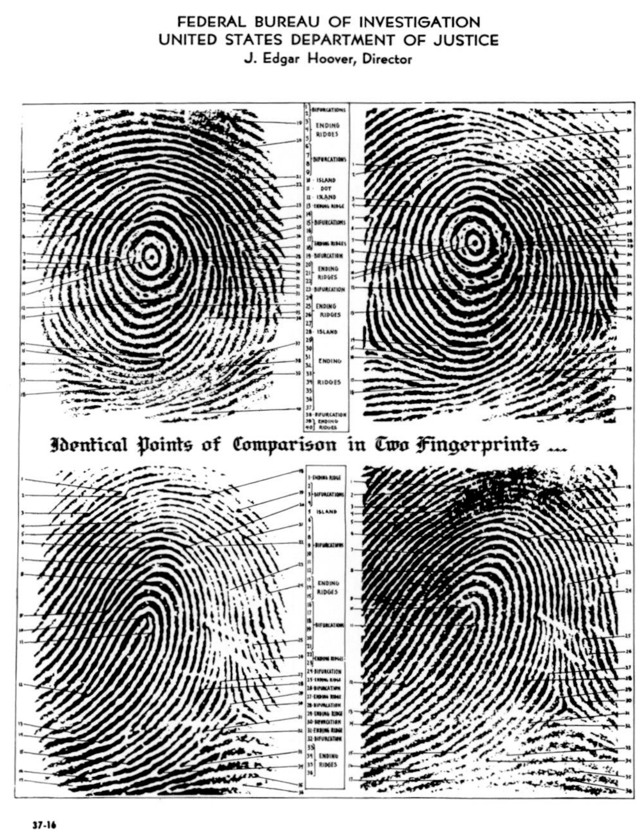

TOP: Examples of basic fingerprint types used in handreading. Left to right: whorl, loop, and arch.

ABOVE LEFT: Actual inked fingerprints. Top row: whorl and loop. Bottom row: arch, loop to right, loop to left.

ABOVE RIGHT: The uniqueness of fingerprints as identifying marks is widely accepted in the modern world and evidently was also recognized in prehistoric and ancient times. These prints from the FBI's files show the detailed classifications selected for identification—an art quite different from studying hands for what they reveal about character.

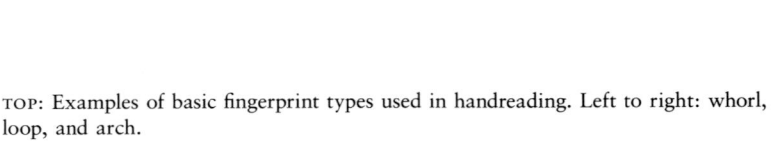

Postures

In addition to the shapes, configurations, irregularities, and furrows of hands that chiromancers use as indicators of personality, the postures in which the hands are held are also taken into consideration.

Postures of the Hands

Closed palm (half-clenched or kept in pockets): secretiveness

Hands held firmly at sides (palms in but not closed): self-containment, trustworthiness, carefulness, prudence

Hands hanging limply: malleable character

Hands hanging at side away from body but not limply: materialism

Fists held at sides: under pressure, determination

Fists held pugnaciously away from sides or across front: aggression, "chip-on-shoulder" attitude

Posture of display (one arm at chest or neck or behind head: the other on hip or waist): self-displaying, self-conscious appearance and manners

Postures of "stuffiness" (palm facing up, held stiffly across front): self-importance, lack of humor

Limp-wrist postures: hypersensitivity

Fidgety (continual movements, handling articles or clothing): uncertainty, anxiety

Avoidance movements (pulling away from contact): alertness, suspiciousness

Hands clasped quietly in front: temperance, poise

Hands clasped firmly or rubbed together: adroitness, evasiveness, deviousness, or merely tenseness

Hands clasped behind back: carefulness, timidity

Hand gestures (*mudras*) are an important part of the theology and life history of the Buddha, showing his works and services.

Reassuring Buddha. Nepalese, thirteenth century. Gilt copper. Height 18¾″. The Asia Society, New York City. Mr. and Mrs. John D. Rockefeller Collection.

LEFT: *Teaching Buddha.* North Indian, first half of the sixth century. Bronze. Height 27″. The Asia Society, New York City.

RIGHT: *Preaching Buddha.* Japanese, Kamakura period, c. thirteenth century. Wood. Height 47″. The Asia Society, New York City.

Meditating Buddha (*Great Amida Buddha*). Japanese, Kamakura period, 1253. Kamakura, Japan.

OPPOSITE LEFT: Back of the left hand used in the sample reading. Here it is clear that the measurement from the tip of the long finger to the large knuckle is equal to the length from the large knuckle to the level of the prominent wrist bone, indicating that the fingers are not shorter than the body of the hand. This view also shows the conical shape of the hand with fingers together.

OPPOSITE RIGHT: Left hand used in the sample reading, with the principal lines of the palm highlighted. The fingers appear to be shorter than the palm from this view.

1 = Fate line; 2 = Life line; 3 = branch from Life line to Lunar mount; 4 = Influence lines; 5 = line of Mars; 6 = Head line; 7 = fork of Head line; 8 = three short lines on Mercury mount; 9 = Upper Mars mount; 10 = Lower Mars mount; 11 = Heart line; 12 = Apollo line; 13 = branch from Apollo line to Heart line; 14 = Mercury line; 15 = branch from Mercury line to Fate line; 16 = Lunar lines; 17 = Marriage lines; 18 = Bracelets; 19 = Jupiter mount; 20 = Saturn mount; 21 = Apollo mount; 22 = Mercury mount; 23 = Venus mount; 24 = Lunar mount; 25 = Lascivia line.

Handreading Example

Now that we have defined each of the features of the hands, we shall try to interpret an example on the basis of this handreading system, bearing in mind that ours is only one of the techniques and that palmists are often in disagreement. The example shown here is a man's hand, chosen arbitrarily. We begin with observations on the general features. Since he is right-handed, we will read his left hand, the side that is supposed to show the inherited, basic nature of the person and the tendencies in his character. The predictive aspect of handreading consists of reporting on the likely directions in life as shown by the person's character (revealed through the lines, mounts, postures, and shape of the hand) and the dangers in his makeup that should be guarded against.

How shall we classify his hand type? The length of the back of the long finger appears to be equal to the length of the back of the hand, neither longer nor shorter, as befits a balanced personality. At first one may judge that the palm is wide and the fingers short, but measuring the back of the hand yields values that confirm the equal relationships between the middle finger and hand. The palm itself may be slightly long as compared with its width, thus offering us a mixed type of hand, difficult to classify and having both broad and long physical features. Versatility is the hallmark of this type.

The shape of the palm is conic, bulging at the percussion side; the composite fingers held together show a slight tapering from palm to tips. Extrapolating from these conic indications, our subject is apt to be skillful, original, and generous, suited to a creative or performing occupation. The negatives to be guarded against are impatience and superficiality. Since the hand is of mixed type, virtually any field is fair game to him. When relaxed, the hand is held with fingers held slightly apart, not too wide or too close, suggesting that he can reasonably hold on to possessions (they don't "slip through his fingers"), and yet he is not

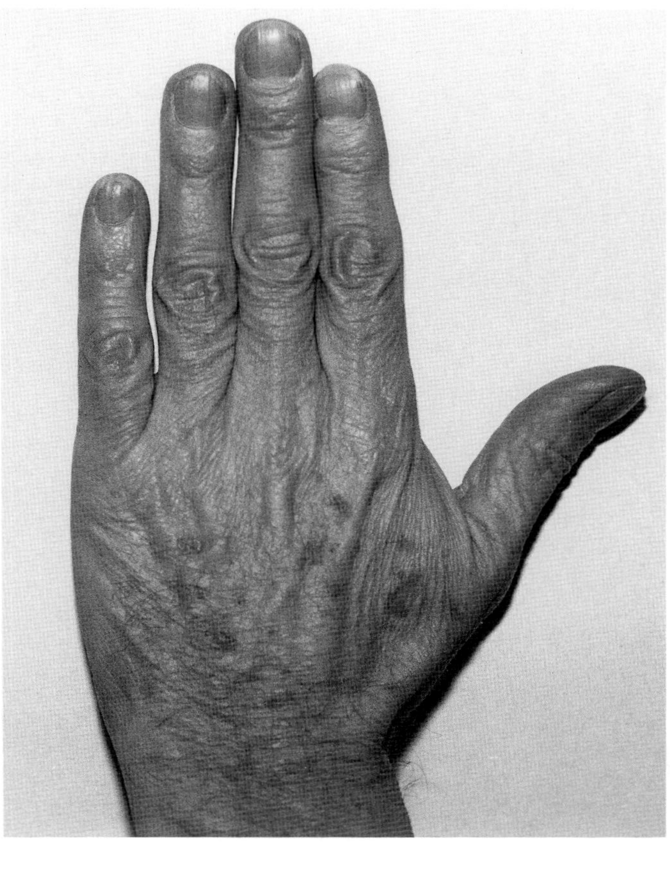

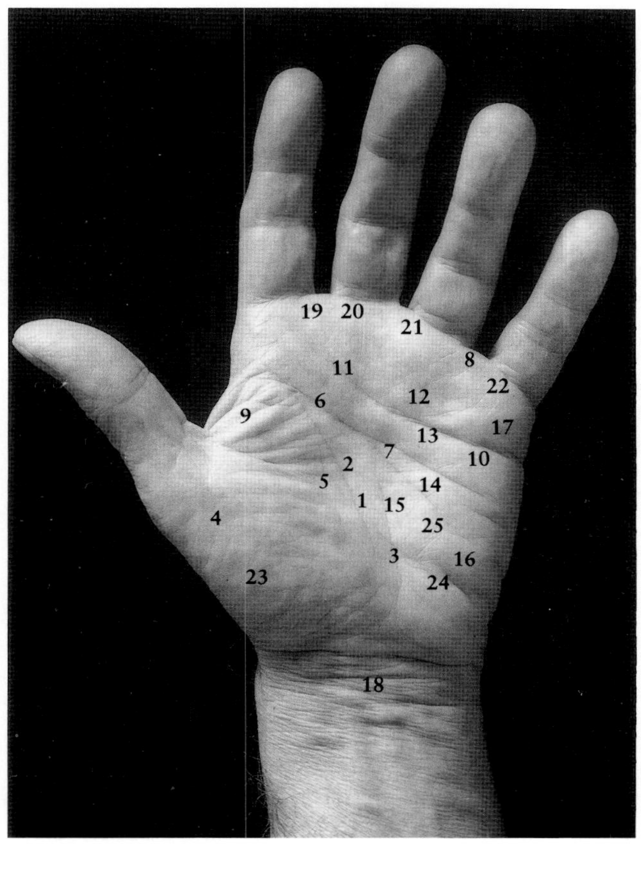

Jean-Baptiste Leprince. *A Necromancer.* 1770s. Oil on canvas, 31 × 25½". Stair Sainty Fine Art, Inc.

penurious, as would be shown if the fingers were held closely together.

The fingers are average, neither thick nor thin, so that this person probably does not swing to the extremes of either coolness or sensuality. The relative shortness of the fingers on the palm view would suggest that the person easily perceives the broad, essential core of projects. However, because the actual length of the fingers measured on the back of the hand does seem to be slightly more than is noted on the palm-side view, the hand conveys the person's ability also to retain some focus on details. The tendency to knobbiness of some of the fingers suggests good powers of concentration. The hazard here is that the person's broad perception may compete for attention with details, leading to incomplete performance.

Let us now examine the fingertips to assay the emotional patterns associated with each finger. Of the four types of configurations into which the fingertips of all persons can be classified, the conic (rounded) shape is here seen to be present on every finger. Thus a certain amount of consistency is apt to be part of the versatility, which might otherwise be in greater danger of dissipating energies.

In addition, the relatively average finger lengths also indicate that none of the extremes of traits governed by each digit will be found in this person. For instance, although the index (Jupiter) finger stands for ambition, pride, and assertiveness, this man is likely to possess these characteristics in only moderate degree. He is not apt to be swept away by anything.

The thumb, too, reveals a balance between the length of its base phalanx (reason) and the tip phalanx (will, action). In terms of the thumb's flexibility, there appears to be some resistance though not stiffness. Therefore, self-control and a degree of reserve are present; stubbornness must be guarded against.

However, the tip phalanx of the thumb when viewed from the side shows some flattening, even thinness, in its distal half, suggesting that the man's will is in danger of diffuseness. This again bears out our previous impressions. The waisted shape of the base phalanx connotes the ability to decide quickly and yet tactfully, but there can be a tendency to deviousness lingering in the wings.

The other fingers also presage a position between the extremes of the personality traits that they control. One or two of the features may be singled out in illustration. The approximately equal lengths of the index (Jupiter) and the ring (Apollo) fingers affirm our previous overall conclusions of balanced attitudes, drives, and performance, but the relatively longer tip phalanx on the Apollo finger reminds us that there may be more devotion to aesthetic theories than to their fulfillment. Principles may exceed performance.

On the little (Mercury) finger, the long tip signifies capabilities in medicine, law, or communications. The relatively short middle phalanx lets us know that business concerns in these fields are apt to be secondary or ineffective.

The nail shapes approach the tapered or "filbert" type. This indicates candor. Yet, we have just remarked that the waist-shaped base phalanx of the thumb suggests tact. How does one explain these potentially opposite traits? One possibility is that this person is inconsistent in his expressions to everyone, or else that he shows his different sides to different people, or that he may surround his candor with such tactful phraseology that he succeeds in achieving both. Indeed, he may actually have to take care lest he become insincere, manipulative, and devious.

The "moons" on the nails (which signify the person's degree of activism) are in conformity with the other mixed features of this hand. The thumb has a prominent moon. The index finger's moon is less noticeable; the long finger's moon is hardly visible. On the ring and little fingers, moons are absent entirely. It is worth noting that the larger moons are on the nails of the active side of the hand, reinforcing this trait; passivity is emphasized by absent moons on the fingers of the passive side of the hand. Thus, this person's will, a feature of the thumb, is enhanced by the thumbnail moon. The ambition shown in the index finger (Jupiter) is tempered by its smaller moon. The sobriety of Saturn (middle finger), still showing in the slightly visible but small moon, makes extreme seriousness or gloominess unlikely. The artistry and need for recognition indicated by the Apollo (ring) finger is either hidden or not pursued unless brought forth by others. The absence of any moon on the Mercury (little) finger implies a basic passivity in verbal expression, despite other aspects of this hand that point to talents in communication. Is he therefore essentially shy, modest, and reticent but with a strong drive to express himself?

A striking feature of this hand is the relatively prominent Venus mount. The fleshy Venus indicates a warm personality with feelings giving significant energy to his life's activities. This can lead to decisions based primarily on emotional attachments to people.

The Jupiter mount is relatively flat at the base of the index finger, suggesting that pride and ambition may be low in priority, but closer observation tells us that the Jupiter mount is actually present but displaced toward the middle finger. Of course, one can as well say that the Saturn mount is displaced towards Jupiter, and looking further onward one can see that a mount seemingly associated with the ring finger, Apollo, is also moved toward the middle finger. A controlling feature therefore is the shift of Jupiter and Apollo mounts toward Saturn. Therefore this person is most unlikely to throw off the shackles of duty, probity, and conscientiousness, for the convergence of the other mounts toward conforming Saturn would signal that this man is firm and responsible to family, friends, and work. Alternatively, the measure of ambition and leadership signified by Jupiter is not a consuming passion but rather a part of what is expected of him (Saturn). His work and studies (Saturn) will tend to have an artistry, as the shift of Apollo toward the middle finger suggests; but if the arts are pursued they are likely to be pursued with discipline and knowledge (due to the effects of Saturn).

The Mercury mount, which is shifted toward Apollo, suggests a preoccupation with aesthetics in speech and craft. The money-making propensities of Mercury can be capitalized on by using business principles in an artistic occupation—visual, musical, or literary. However, particularly striking are the three short vertical lines immediately at the base of the little finger, considered by many palmists to be associated with a strong talent for medicine. Involvement in any medical endeavors can have the undertones of philosophy (Saturn) or illustration (Apollo). But too much seriousness signaled by Saturn in everything has to be overcome.

Luna is well developed. Introspection and imagination therefore figure strongly in the person's thoughts and desires. Moreover, the several deep oblique lines on Luna may be indicative of a desire for participation in changes or in many travels. Indeed, the more this hand is examined, the more a reader would point to the strong influences of this mount. The Head line sends one of its forkings there; the Fate line too starts near Luna; even the Life line (Vitality) has a branch descending across the Fate line into Luna. Thoughts (Head), energies (Life), and purpose (Fate) all have the fantasy and imagination of Luna linked to them. The danger here lies in impracticality and dreaminess.

Upper Mars on the little finger's side of the hand is firm and clear. In spite of the versatility and ability to see both sides of an issue (shown in the large, forked Head line), others' attempts to control will meet passive but firm, even rigid resistance.

Lower Mars (thumb side) is so flat that the overlying skin is loose and lies in ridges. This person is not aggressive according to palmistry principles. He may stand firm but does not attack. There is danger, therefore, that he will not achieve, which fits with the Jupiter mount being displaced from the base of the index finger. He tends to rely on stubbornness once his decisions or principles are set, though only after carefully weighing the options (as seen in the forked Head line and the shift of mounts toward Saturn).

The fingerprints on the tips of Mercury (little), Apollo (ring), Saturn (middle), and thumb are of the loop type, signifying reflection and adaptability. Alternatively, the Jupiter (index) fingerprint is of the arch variety, which accents rigidity—rather than adjustment—materialism, slow arousal, and roughness. We saw previously that a low priority in pride and ambition accompanied the relative flatness of his Jupiter mount and the sense of duty and probity was announced by the displacement of the Jupiter mount toward Saturn. The presence of an arch fingerprint on this Jupiter finger, however, warns that a slow-to-arouse but stubborn roughness may lurk underneath and can be called forth if this man feels that his honesty or sense of duty is challenged. Beware of the hidden dragon.

Lines

The Life line is clearly marked, swinging wide of the thumb, showing enthusiasm for activity. About halfway around the hand the line fades out but is seen again at the base of the Venus mount as it trails out to the farthest edge of the wrist.

This interruption is considered a suggestion that a lessening of vigor or drive has occurred in the course of early middle age due to illness or psychological assault, followed by renewed vigor in later years. The Life line begins close to the Head line, signifying closeness to the family or perhaps shyness or timidity in early years. Indeed, the beginning of the line is actually even beyond the Head line, near the Jupiter mount, signaling outstanding achievement in childhood or early youth.

There is a branch from the Life line, just before it fades out, going across the Fate line into the mount of Luna. Thus, desire for travel, or else restlessness, occupies some of the energy of this person. Some palmists read this connecting line as a special Via Lascivia (indicating sensuality) rather than as a branch from the Life line, but since it stops and does not come from the Venus mount, most would assign this as a branch from vitality and not an intermount connection. What about the lines on the Venus mount, running vertically from the Life line toward the wrist? These are usually read as influence lines associated with the effects of persons on the directions and purposes of activity. One of these lines arising from, but not quite parallel to, the Life line could be interpreted as a line of Mars, which speaks of heightened energy and drive.

The numerous finer lines running toward the thumb on the Venus mount are supposed to be worry lines, indicating a worrisome nature or else worrisome events interfering with the unimpeded, purposeful drives.

The Head line is deep and forks in its outer trail. Its depth is in keeping with the other features in this hand, which announce the importance of mental activity. The Head line's separateness from the Heart line designates independence. The relative straightness emphasizes logical thinking. The forking corresponds with an ability to appreciate both sides of an argument, but the person must be on guard against indecision. However, the Head line is so well marked that the likely significance of the fork suggests an even approach to problems, with logic (straightness of the line) determining practical resolutions. The forking also gives further accent to the general versatility of this person—as previously noted.

Another characteristic that was noticed at the beginning

of the reading was the prominence of Luna. The sloping of the forks toward Luna emphasizes the part played by sensitivity and imagination. Creativity and interest in the arcane (or occult) would be considered probable interests of this person's mind. The relatively long Head line, with both forks reaching out toward the outer border of the hand, is again a restatement of mental versatility. However, this long line could also signal mere dilettantism.

The Heart line is as deep and clear as the Head line, except that there are some chains or islands in the outer segment, beneath the Mercury and Apollo mounts, indicating difficulties in love affairs. However, just above the Heart line at the outer border of the hand (seen only from the side) are two horizontal, clearly marked lines of affection, suggesting involvement in two or more such circumstances, according to some handreading principles. Since the Heart line has no waviness, feelings are steady. Attachments are apt to be based on a mixture of pragmatism and idealism, for the direction is straight from the outer hand border to its midpoint, where it curves gradually up toward Jupiter, announcing that the person has high expectations of others. Loyalty is also confirmed in this path to the Jupiter mount.

Heart and Head lines are separated, never touching each other. Thus intellectual activities can be carried on without being too influenced by emotions, and conversely, strong emotional attachments can be made without regard to reasoning. Thus, although this man can be objective when called upon for decisions, he can be irrational in the throes of passion. Because scientists, physicians, lawyers, and judges are most effective when they can keep these areas separated, the possessor of this hand would fit well into these professions, especially since an upward glance to the Mercury mount discovers three short vertical lines that have been read in many systems to be associated with medicine.

The Fate line (also called the Saturn line) is clearly seen starting near the wrist, curving from below the Life line toward the midpoint between Venus and Luna and then slanting straight upward across the head line and the heart line, where it becomes flanked by two other small lines, of which one (and maybe both) reaches the base of Saturn. Its origin close to Venus is considered to be a mark of strong early influences on the man's life and future direction. For instance, a parent or relative might have had an effect on how he was educated or on which career he chose. The pronounced Fate line means to some readers that the person is purposeful. Midway up the palm, where the Head line begins to fork, the Fate line becomes fainter, which means that there have been battles and obstacles to overcome. The two accompanying lines from there on suggest relative resourcefulness through bypassing or using obstacles in a positive way—a further confirmation of versatility in this hand's characteristics.

The Apollo line is clear, thin, but not deep. Talent is present but recognition and achievement are apt to result from perseverance rather than inspiration (the person is more influenced by Saturn than by Apollo). The Apollo line starts just below a fork of the Head line. This strong line announces a rich creative imagination. A career as a writer or an artist might be predicted, but the Fate line's course to a flat area beneath the Saturn mount might instead suggest to a handreader that artistry rather than art itself would be likely. The Apollo line deepens as it passes beyond the Heart line, forking into three distinct lines at the base of the ring (Apollo) finger. Recognition, therefore, is anticipated in several fields, especially in the later years of life. A small, oblique branch from Apollo to the Heart line in the interval on the palm between Head and Heart lines again accents dedication and feelings rather than talents as a means to achieving success, which further matches the fine, rather than deep, Apollo line.

The Mercury line is shallow and relatively faint but it starts at the lower fork of the Head line and either receives or sends down a thin but clear branch to the Fate line, just where the branch from the Life line crosses the Fate line and enters Luna (as described under the Life line). This branching to the Fate line is interpreted by some writers on palmistry as indicating that health problems have had or will have an influence on career or destiny.

Mention should be made of the lines on Luna. Clearly, in this hand Luna is an important symbol both in its prominence and in its association with lines. Interest in travel and in change are common readings of these markings. Imagination is also felt to be significant in this man's thinking. Other fine lines on Luna can have various interpretations on which palmists might differ widely. Are they part of the lines of Intuition (Lascivia)? Evidence of nervous concerns? A sense of unreality?

We end our reading by looking at the bracelets, the lines that cross the wrist. Here there are three. But while they are clear and well formed, they do not qualify as a Royal Bracelet because they are not altogether parallel and the bracelet line nearest to the palm manifests a number of chain markings. Perseverance is therefore needed by this man in order for him to achieve recognition and effectiveness.

A handreader could say that the principal characteristic of this man as seen in his left hand can be summarized accordingly—General attributes: versatile, expressive, original, imaginative, fair. Personality and attitudes: inner-directed, persevering, controlled, persuasive. Emotional features: steadfastness in attachments. Money and business: conflict between theory and pragmatism. Occupational suitability: medicine, science, teaching, communication, diplomacy. Hobbies and interests: travel, art, study. Negatives: diffuseness, dilettantism, pedantry, stubbornness, deviousness, verbosity.

Evaluation of Handreading

Direct forecasting now has few adherents among bona fide chiromancers. Questions about the validity of palmistry thus refer at the present time to correlations between the shape, size, lines, and surface of the hand and the mental and emotional makeup of a person.

Those who support handreading argue that the neural system and the skin are derived embryologically from the same tissue system ("primary germ layer") and therefore that it is scientifically comprehensible that the palm and the personality (which is a function of the central nervous system) would be connected.

Detractors point out that such reasoning would also make it proper to judge mental and emotional makeup on the arrangement of other skin appendages, such as hair, eyelashes, tooth enamel, ears, lips, etc. Indeed, there is an occult system that delineates character and the future according to the distribution of moles on the body. Most palmists would hardly want to place chiromancy in the same category.

Yet, say the apologists, hands are so much a part of daily activities, social intercourse, and general appearance—whether inherited or acquired—that the total makeup of each person is clearly bound to this exquisitely human anatomical feature. Body shapes as indicators of personality types have been classified by scientists, even to the extent of becoming psychological terms; for example, the short, thickset person (pyknic) is associated with extroverted swings in mood (cyclothymic); the tall, slender (asthenic) with introspective flattened emotions.

Detractors reply that even if they were to be accepted as statistically significant (and many investigators strongly reject such a conclusion), they would have no application to any particular individual human as an indication of his or her personality. All of us have seen pyknics who were even-tempered introverts and also physical asthenics who were dynamos of outgoing energy with swings of mood.

But there are medically accepted correlations between the appearance of the hand and internal conditions: clubbed fingers indicate lung disease and chronic ailments; a very red Luna mount suggests liver disease. No explanations have been found for these relatively simple connections. Thus the validity of the assignment of talents and deficiencies to hand configurations may have to wait much longer for scientific proof.

However, the antagonists point out that it is the biologists and physicians, not the palmists, who have described the correlation between certain features of the hand and pathological conditions. The fact that there are hundreds of proven observations whose precise mechanisms have not yet been explained is hardly an argument for the association of lines and shapes of the hands with mental traits. People have always been able to see the blush on the cheek of someone who was embarrassed, obviously indicating the connection between the blood vessels under the skin and the brain, while the minute network of pathways was only shown in recent centuries. Nevertheless, the observed association of thoughts and physical response was obvious, consistent, and clear. Only the precise mechanism remained to be established.

Still a number of medical studies have reported a high incidence of various patterns of the palmar lines and fingerprints in people with certain congenital defects and deficiencies. For instance, a simian line (one line across the palm instead of the usual two) is seen in those with particular congenital abnormalities far more often than in the normal population. Also, an excessive number of fingerprint ridges has been found in many people who have aberrations in their chromosomes. Therefore, the proponents of handreading assert, the assignment of particular traits and tendencies to the configuration of lines in the palm fits accepted biologic tenets.

However, the clues to chromosomal abnormalities that are found in various unusual configurations in the hand (whether inherited or acquired *in utero*) merely confirm the knowledge that some chemical and nervous-system properties are often genetically linked. Medical investigators may even look for these stigmas as leads to unrecognized conditions. But this has nothing to do with considering the appearance of the Heart line as a signal of the person's emotional makeup; the direction of the Head line as an indicator of mental processes; the length of the Life line as a sign of energy; the prominence of the Mercury mount as an announcement of communicative talents.

Finally, chiromancers claim that interpretations based on the hands do "work," whatever the eventual explanations may be; that the delineations seem to fit the actual personality and type of behavior; that whatever happens to the person later turns out to be what the palmist predicted according to the tendencies seen in the hand. The trouble with this argument, say the objectors, is that no controlled or even uncontrolled studies have been done to test these conclusions.

Of course, an objective evaluation would be difficult to accomplish under most conditions. As the anthropologist M. A. Park has observed, one problem is the self-fulfilling prophecy: the subject may try to become what the

Ben Shahn. *"I Never Dared to Dream."* The hands convey contemplation or cogitation in supporting the person's head. Norton Gallery of Art, West Palm Beach.

handreader says he or she is, or the person can act on the palmist's forecast and either cause the predicted happening to occur or behave in a way that allows the prophecy to be fulfilled. Indeed, opponents of palmistry often describe this mechanism to explain correct predictions.

The scientific community sees no factual basis for the methods of handreading that judge character or future behavior through the systems of palmistry as constituted in the past or present. The chiromancers consider the scientists prejudiced and actually unscientific in their conclusions, unwilling even to acknowledge their own findings of the biologic connections between personality and configurations on the hands.

I Ching

伏羲氏教民始分陰陽

I Ching

I may have naught
Though I have all;
The path is smooth,
Why do I fall?
The future lies
Not in what's read,
But how I tread
The road ahead.

The legendary Chinese Emperor Fu Hsi (c.2900 B.C.) holding the *pa kua* (yang-yin) symbol. Fu Hsi is presumed to have created the eight basic trigrams from which the sixty-four hexagrams of the *I Ching* were derived. Nineteenth century. Watercolor, 14 × 10″. Wellcome Institute Library, London.

The *I Ching,* or *Book of Changes,* is a collection of diagrams with accompanying interpretive texts. It serves a variety of functions. To some, it is a system of prediction, one of the oldest still in existence. Others view the book as a repository of universal wisdom, teaching correct conduct and giving guidance in all situations. Still others see it simply as a profound reflection of the mythology and philosophy of the ancient Chinese people.

The basic *I Ching* consists of sixty-four diagrams, each composed of six unbroken and broken lines (hexagrams) and accompanied by a title and a few Chinese characters, which are translated into coherent, though sometimes ambiguous, statements (the judgments). An interpretive comment accompanies each of the lines. To this fundamental pattern, myriad commentaries and explanations have been added over thousands of years as afterwords to the text. These appendages form a collection known as the "Ten Wings."

From the meanings of the Chinese characters a reader fathoms the answers to questions he or she poses. The interpretation gleaned from a hexagram, chosen by chance, is supposed to instruct the questioner on the proper course to be taken. The ritual of choosing one of the hexagrams (casting yarrow stalks in older times or coins in recent centuries) is performed by the questioner. Some commentators, notably Carl Jung, characterized this process itself as a means of clearing the questioner's mind of outside influences, allowing him to be receptive to repressed inner strivings.

The "answers" the *I Ching* offers are presumed to have predictive value because personal destiny, to the Chinese, is determined by the individual. If people can understand their own natures, needs, capabilities, and value systems, they can envision the correct path ahead. In response to the right question asked of the *I Ching,* the answer is open to each person's interpretation. The appropriate analysis will indicate the proper action. Thus, the future is dictated by choice—not by inevitability.

History of the I Ching

The origins of the hexagrams are not known. Perhaps they are derived from the line fissures in rocks where the ancient Chinese looked for patterns that might give clues to the future; or perhaps they come from the cracks in animal bones used in bone casting, another method of divination. One of the most ancient of divinatory practices involved observing the mosaic of lines on tortoises' shells. Did this ritual lead to the use of line symbols in forecasting? Or do the *I Ching* symbols merely represent the logical

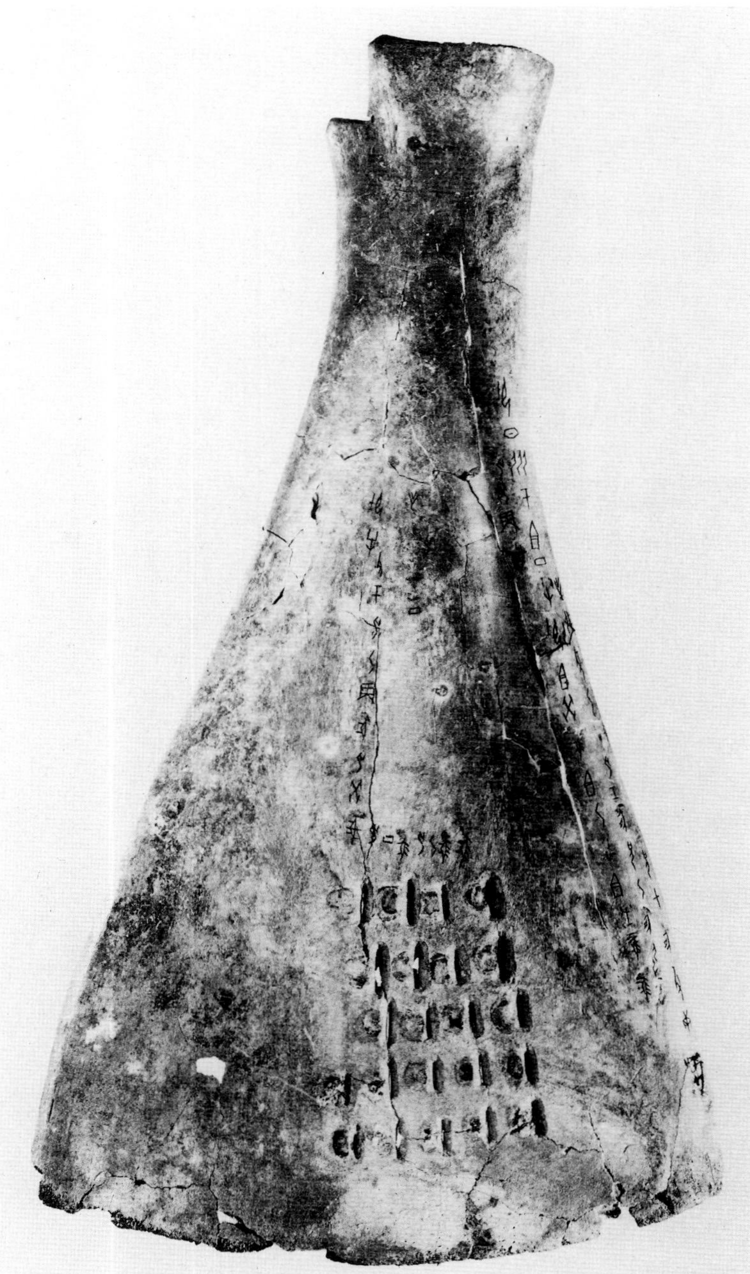

The ancient Chinese carved symbols on bones, known as "oracle bones," which may have been among the earliest forms of Chinese writing and divination. Shang dynasty (c.1500 B.C.).

employment of the simplest geometric form, the straight line, with its two properties, continuity and intermittence?

The Chinese have always seen a duality in the universe: the yang is the male principle—light, active, warm, dry, hard, positive; the yin is the female—dark, passive, cold, moist, soft, negative. These two forces are present in virtually everything. The legendary emperor Fu Hsi, who presumably lived in the third millennium B.C., is credited with having categorized these contending principles into a diagram of lines, the *Pa Kua* ("Eight Diagrams"): the unbroken line became synonymous with yang, the male force that initiates; the broken with yin, the female force that completes.

The way in which the single line became formed into the trigrams of the *I Ching* is also not known. One possibility is that each of the two lines was paired to make the four possible combinations (⚌ ⚍ ⚎ ⚏) and then increased by one line to yield eight trigrams (☰ ☱ ☲ ☳ ☴ ☵ ☶ ☷). Each of these trigrams became associated with a feature of nature (sky, earth, mountain, wind, lake, thunder, cloud, fire).

The development of the trigrams into six-line hexagrams has been attributed to a series of political events. In the generally accepted story, King Wên, the leader of the Chou people in the twelfth century B.C., was imprisoned by the infamous Emperor Chou Hsin of the Shang dynasty out of jealousy and fear of Wên's mounting influence. Wên is supposed to have been given his name (meaning "literary") because he was eager to learn. While incarcerated for about a year, Wên is presumed to have formed the sixty-four six-line hexagrams out of the trigrams. Although some scholars view the hexagrams as having existed before that time, virtually all agree that it was Wên himself who codified them, placed them in a structured order, named each, and added a very brief statement (later called the judgments) to each.

Wên never attained the throne. His son, the duke of Chou, after overcoming the Shang emperor, elevated his dead father to the rank of emperor and took for himself the title of Emperor Wû, thus founding the Chou dynasty. He also wrote explanations for each line of each of the sixty-four hexagrams. These comments consist of relatively few Chinese characters, which scholars and commentators have variously translated and interpreted.

The period from the fourth millennium B.C. to the mid-twelfth century B.C. was the period of ancient China's "high antiquity." It was early in this era that two of the very oldest Chinese classics were written, the *Shih Ching*, or *Book of Poetry*, and the even older *Shu Ching*, or *Book of*

History, both of which antedate the *I Ching.* The period starting in 1111 B.C., when the son of King Wên ousted the Shang ruler, and lasting into the sixth century B.C. is referred to as "middle antiquity," or the pre-Confucian era. The time of Confucius (551–479 B.C.) marks the start of "low antiquity" and the classical period of Chinese philosophy, when commentaries on the *I Ching* were considerably expanded.

The Chou dynasty (1111 B.C.–221 B.C.) lasted for almost nine centuries, but there were many upheavals, internecine wars, and relocations of political power, all of which affected the composition and transmission of the *I Ching.* The Chou era also witnessed the life and teachings of Lao-tse (c.604–531 B.C.), the seminal philosopher who preached the "natural way" (*Tao*), the doctrine of the natural, immutable laws of the universe, a philosophy that has correlations with the teachings in the *I Ching.*

Confucius further enlarged the *I Ching* with oral commentaries that were written down and collected by his pupils and disciples after his death. These comprise the greater part of the extensive Ten Wings. Scholars differ on precisely how much is attributable to Confucius, but certainly much of the text is considered to be the contribution of Confucius and his followers. Indeed, even the term "Image," the heading given to short verses accompanying the hexagrams in many versions, may have come from a misreading—according to some—of Confucius's name.

There are varied uses to which the *I Ching* has been put: a divinatory oracle, a standard of proper conduct, or a combination of predictive judgments and moral precepts. It has usually reflected the philosophical and ethical attitudes of the period. For instance, after Confucius, between the fifth and fourth centuries B.C., at the time of the philosopher Mo Ti, its nonmystical values were emphasized. In the fourth century B.C., Tsou Yen focused particularly on the moral principles. On the other hand, during the Ch'in and Han dynasties (221–206 B.C. and 206 B.C.–A.D. 221, respectively), its divination and mystical projections predominated.

The fluctuation in function between the instructive and the predictive has continued throughout history. Wang Pi and others in post-Han times (A.D. 226–249) returned the *I Ching* to a moral code that gradually became a standard for governing officials, even including the king. During the Sung dynasty, Shao Yung emphasized philosophical aspects. Still later, the *I Ching*'s predictive values were more prominent, as in the middle Sung years in the twelfth century A.D. when its oracular function was revived by the philosopher and philologist Chu Hsi. By the seventeenth century, a kind of synthesis had occurred (especially exemplified by the work of Wan I) between the mantic, mystic elements that had developed in the Han and Sung periods and Buddhist philosophy.

The commentaries by Confucius (551–479 B.C.), as reported by his disciples, were significant additions to the collected writings on the *I Ching.*

Throughout this long history, interpretations, commentaries, and appendices were added and collected in various ways. The *I Ching* was extensively codified in the Han period, and a particularly influential commentary by Chêng Hao was added during the Sung dynasty. Historical changes, cultural developments, and modifications in the systems of writing have altered the original text enough so that the *I Ching* as presently constituted and translated is not precisely the same as it was when Emperor Wên and the duke of Chou or other scholars in antique periods composed it. The earliest extant text, discovered in tomb excavations in the 1970s, dates to about 168 B.C. Today's version may represent the *I Ching* as it was compiled in about the seventh century A.D. and has been used ever since.

Until the late seventeenth and eighteenth centuries the Ten Wings had been kept together with the judgments and the lines. During the K'ang Hsi period (1662–1722) of the Ch'ing dynasty, the Ten Wings were placed in a separate section together with the commentaries of over two hundred contributors from the second century B.C. to the seventeenth century A.D. Both parts—the Ten Wings and Judgments and Lines—were then collated by a royal edict into a unified collection. This entire version was translated into German in the early twentieth century by Richard Wilhelm. In 1949 Cary Baynes translated Wilhelm's work into English. Before Baynes's rendition, there had been other English translations, of which the most noteworthy was by James Legge, who in 1882 completed an intensive study of the entire body of the *I Ching*. Also worth mentioning is the work of Regis and McClatchie in the nineteenth century. There have been thousands of studies, interpretations, and translations of the *I Ching*, but in the Western world the versions of Legge and Wilhelm are the best known.

At the present time it is difficult to assess the place of the *I Ching* in Western society. Little known to many people, it is nevertheless embraced by some as a means of arriving at helpful conclusions concerning a contemplated course of action. In Chinese culture it continues to be held in great reverence—as an oracle, a guide to ethical behavior, and a scholarly resource of Chinese thought, history, and philology.

ABOVE: Mi Yu-jen. *Cloudy Mountains* (detail). Sung dynasty (A.D. 1130). Painting on silk, 17³⁄₃₂ × 75¹⁵⁄₁₆″. During this time, the *I Ching* was valued as an oracle. The Cleveland Museum of Art. J. H. Wade Collection.

OPPOSITE: Tu Chin (active 1465–1487). *The Poet Lin P'u Walking in the Moonlight*. Ink and color on paper, 100″. The Cleveland Museum of Art. During the long history of the *I Ching* scholars added various interpretations and commentaries.

BELOW: A *pa kua* ("eight diagrams") tile piece showing the eight trigrams and the Chinese yang-yin symbol of duality of the universe. Musée de l'Homme, Paris.

The Trigrams

The eight three-line diagrams that are the basis of the *I Ching's* sixty-four hexagrams are listed in various orders depending upon the commentator. For instance, Legge has *Li* as the third trigram and *Tui* as the second, whereas Wilhelm places *Li* seventh and *Tui* eighth. The trigrams are also sometimes put into various arrangements according to their yang or yin spirit, the points on the compass, their opposite forces on a circle, and other symbolisms. Our listing is only one of the many standard sequences. However, in all of the arrangements, the actual line symbols, the names, and the meanings of each trigram are the same, no matter what their place is in the listing. The bottom line of the trigram represents the forces of earth; the middle line, the human influence; the top line, the power of heaven. Images from nature have also been assigned to each of the trigrams. In addition, other associations—such as familial positions and number symbols—have been made. Commentators have commonly seen the essential meaning of each hexagram in the interaction between the images of the upper and lower trigrams comprising the hexagram. For instance, in hexagram 3, *Chun* (interpreted as "difficulty in the beginning"; ䷂), *K'an* (☵) is the upper trigram, standing for the abyss, clouds, or danger. The lower trigram is *Chên* (☳), for thunder or arousing. *Chên* (thunder), as the bottom trigram, meets the downward movement of the upper trigram, *K'an* (clouds, danger). These two colliding symbolize confusion, until the rain falls, when the danger and the turbulence end.

Similarly, in hexagram 11, *T'ai* (peace; ䷊), the trigram *Ch'ien* (sky, strength) lies below *K'un* (earth, receptive) and tells the interpreter that heaven fills the earth's position and earth is up in the heavens, thus harmony is the status quo. But in hexagram 12, *P'i* (disharmony; ䷋), the opposite condition is present, for now *K'un* (mother, receptive) is supporting *Ch'ien* (father, strength). Disharmony and standstill are the result.

One may well wonder why the diagrammatic meanings of these hexagrams are not reversed, for in hexagram 12, with both heaven and earth in their natural positions (sky above and earth below), peace—not disharmony—might be expected. However, this is the way the sages constructed the hexagrams and named them.

Choosing and Reading the Hexagrams

In recent centuries, the hexagram for answering the question in mind is chosen by casting three coins, rather than by the more complex and ancient system of using yarrow sticks from the milfoil plant. Some say that the simplicity of the coin casting loses some of the mind-freeing benefits attained in the more lengthy, complicated yarrow ritual. Nevertheless, three coins are thrown. The head side is counted as 3, the tail side as 2. (A coin with a square hole in the center is preferred by the Chinese, with the smooth side designated as 3; the inscribed side as 2.) The

TRIGRAM	NAME	IMAGE	CHARACTERISTIC	FAMILY	NUMBER-SYMBOL
☰	*Ch'ien*	Heaven, Sky	Creative, Strong	Father	1
☳	*Chên*	Thunder, Spring	Moving, Arousing	Eldest son	4
☵	*K'an*	Water, Cloud, Abyss, Winter, Moon	Dangerous, Abysmal	Second son	6
☶	*Kên*	Mountain, Hill	Still, Resting	Youngest son	7
☷	*K'un*	Earth	Receptive, Yielding	Mother	8
☴	*Sun*	Wind, Wood	Gentle, Penetrating	Eldest daughter	5
☲	*Li*	Fire, Lightning, Summer, Sun	Clinging, Lighting up	Second daughter	3
☱	*Tui*	Lake, Marsh, River, Autumn	Joyful	Youngest daughter	2

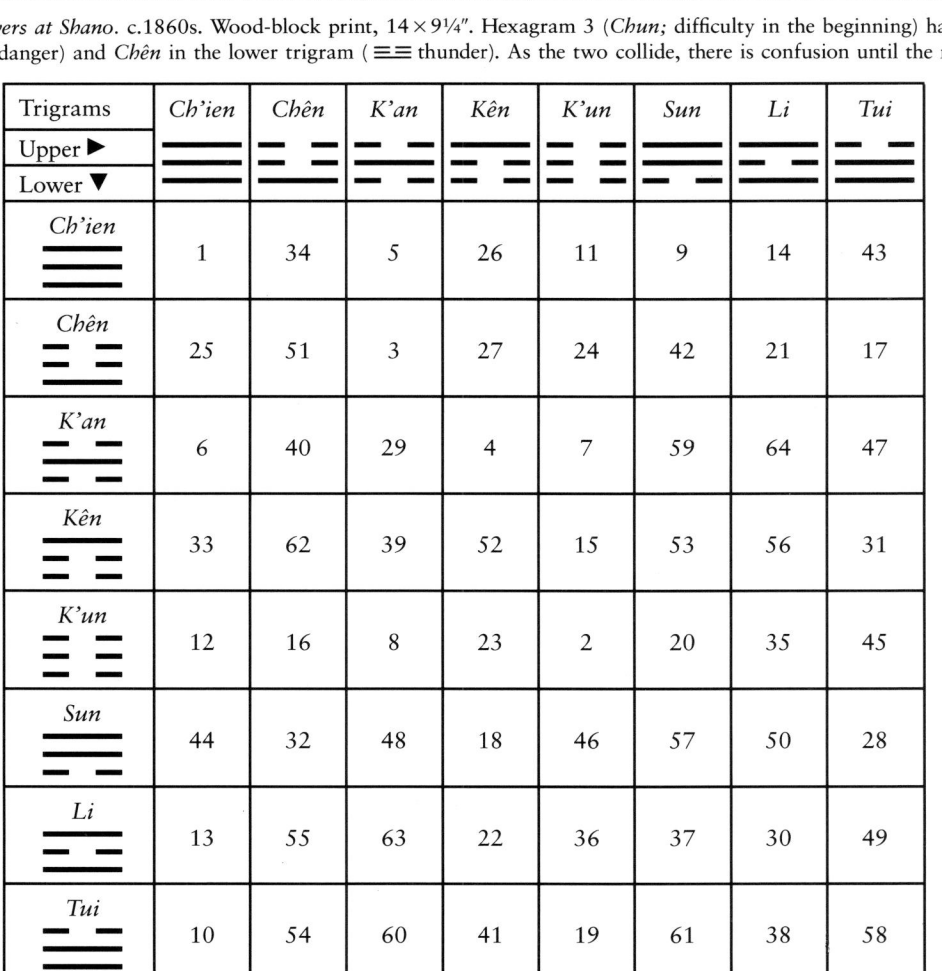

Hiroshige. *Light Showers at Shano.* c.1860s. Wood-block print, 14 × 9¼″. Hexagram 3 (*Chun;* difficulty in the beginning) has *K'an* in the upper trigram (☵ clouds, danger) and *Chên* in the lower trigram (☳ thunder). As the two collide, there is confusion until the rain falls.

Trigrams Upper ▶ Lower ▼	*Ch'ien* ☰	*Chên* ☳	*K'an* ☵	*Kên* ☶	*K'un* ☷	*Sun* ☴	*Li* ☲	*Tui* ☱
Ch'ien ☰	1	34	5	26	11	9	14	43
Chên ☳	25	51	3	27	24	42	21	17
K'an ☵	6	40	29	4	7	59	64	47
Kên ☶	33	62	39	52	15	53	56	31
K'un ☷	12	16	8	23	2	20	35	45
Sun ☴	44	32	48	18	46	57	50	28
Li ☲	13	55	63	22	36	37	30	49
Tui ☱	10	54	60	41	19	61	38	58

sum of the values of the three coins thrown is either an odd number (9 or 7) or an even one (8 or 6). These are the only results obtainable. An odd number is represented by a straight, unbroken line, which the questioner then draws as the first (bottom) line of the hexagram (—). An even number corresponds to a broken line (- -). A continuous line is called yang; a broken line is yin. If the odd number is 9, the straight line is designated "old yang"; if a 7, it is "young yang." The even number 6 is old yin; 8 is young yin. In keeping with much of the Chinese respectful attitude toward the old, old yang and old yin (9 and 6) have special significance, and it is only with these lines, also called "moving lines," that the hexagram can later be transformed.

After the first line is drawn, it is marked (usually with a small circle if it is an old yang; by a cross if an old yin: -o- and -x-). The coins are cast again to derive the next five lines. The first line is the bottom line (called also the "beginning") and the sixth line is the top. Thus, if a 6, a 7, and an 8 are thrown, the trigram formed is *K'an* ☵, signifying water. If a 6, an 8, and a 9 are then cast, the second or top trigram is *Kên* ☶, for mountain. The two trigrams together form the hexagram ䷃, with two "moving" 6s (marked with a cross) and one "moving" 9 (with a circle). A chart, very old in lineage, has been devised for identifying the hexagrams by assigning numbers to each possible trigram combination. These numbers of the hexagrams are presumably assigned according to the listing that King Wên introduced in the twelfth century B.C.:

On the chart we see that the lower trigram *K'an* ☵ when combined with the upper trigram, *Kên* ☶ yields the hexagram 4. *Mêng* is the name for hexagram 4, variously meaning "underdeveloped" or "unknown."

Using the example of hexagram 4, *Mêng,* we note that the first (or bottom) line we have already designated by a cross as a 6. In the commentaries on the lines under "Six at the bottom," meaning the bottom line was the result of a 6 produced in the casting, are Chinese characters (and English translations that we have rendered) offering the following: "As the unknown (or child) begins to develop (uncover) it is good to use discipline. If one removes restraints, it is a mistake." (After this statement in our translation are comments either to explain further or to offer an example of commentaries others have added through the centuries. We have included varying translations in only some of the hexagrams to illustrate the many ways that other commentators and translators have viewed the sparse Chinese words.)

The unbroken line in the second position of hexagram 4 is a 7 and the broken line in the third position is an 8. No further line statements apply, since these are both young yang and young yin. A 9 or a 6 would have to have been thrown in order for comments to apply. But the fourth line is another 6. "Six in the fourth place" has the Chinese characters for "wrapped, folly, blame." We have strung them together as: "Unrecognized folly brings humiliation." Appended are other translations by Baynes (after Wilhelm) and Legge.

The fifth line also has no corresponding statement because it is an 8. However, the top line is a 9, old yang. The Chinese words in our translation mean "strike, folly, not, bandit, benefit, defend, bandit." We put these together as: "Attack the unknown (or folly). No benefit to be an aggressor (robber or bandit). Benefit to defend against aggression." Wilhelm/Baynes and Legge interpret the individual words differently. (Their translations are indicated.)

Each hexagram is supposed to symbolize a condition of life, with the sixty-four diagrams altogether covering every circumstance that might be faced. Each line of the hexagram is a stage in the situation as expressed through imagery, metaphor, or abstraction in the statements accompanying the lines:

The first line (bottom) indicates the beginning of the circumstance as it is emerging.

The second line stands for the full internal development.

The third line represents the state of crisis, with the internal about to be externalized.

The fourth indicates the beginning of the external manifestation.

The fifth position is the fully developed external aspect.

The sixth line (top) marks the end of the process. The condition is then one of harmony or overdevelopment, ready for change to another set of conditions, for life is ever changing.

If one examines the line statements in all of the hexagrams, the consistency of these principles is revealed. For instance, virtually all the lines in the third position from the bottom announce an uncertainty, a perilous possibility, or a conflict.

Another factor in reading the hexagrams is the transposing of the moving lines (those with a 6 or 9 value) into their opposites: a 6 (broken line) can be transformed into an unbroken line; the 9s (unbroken) changed to broken lines. By this means, the hexagram originally chosen and used to answer a question can become a totally different hexagram with different judgments. The new hexagram then suggests what the eventual outcome may be if the advice given in the first hexagram is actually perceived and acted on. Since all situations in life are in a state of flux, a new circumstance awaits and follows every act. The newly formed diagram and its judgment now allow a glimpse of the possibilities and thereby further enable the questioner to reinforce his strengths and guard against his weaknesses.

The diagrammatic lines also have special significance in relation to each other, according to some views. The most

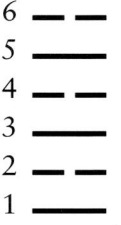

Hexagram 63 (*Chi Chi;* already completed) indicates that one should not go back over one's previous path. This is symbolized by a river already crossed. Dao Ji (A.D. 1641–1707). *Spring on Min River.* Hanging scroll, ink and color on paper. Height 15⅜″. The Cleveland Museum of Art.

"harmonious" arrangement has the undivided (yang) and divided (yin) lines alternating, so that the odd (yang) and the even (yin) correspond with the numbered positions, as for instance in a hexagram such as:

6 — —
5 ———
4 — —
3 ———
2 — —
1 ———

Moreover, the hexagram starts with a yang and alternates yang and yin from bottom to top. These relationships signify an especially favorable omen.

Within each hexagram's structure, lines 1 and 4 are considered to correlate with each other (they both make up the earth symbolization of the bottom line in the two trigrams composing a hexagram). Similarly, 2 is related to 5 (the central lines and therefore human metaphors in each trigram) and 3 and 6 correspond to each other (the tops or heaven images of the two trigrams).

The 2 and 5 correlation is of particular significance; if

the line 2 position is yin and the 5 is yang, this is considered a "complete" correlation, enhancing the power of the meaning of the entire hexagram. A hexagram's line 5 is the most important, often termed "the lord" of the diagram. Its correlative line 2 is also of special but lesser significance. Some interpretations focus entirely on these two central lines of the trigrams.

Commentators often consider one of the lines to be the hexagram's "ruler." Ruling lines have sometimes been further classified into "constituting" and "governing." The former indicates the essential meaning and may be in any of the six positions perceived as such by the interpreter. The governing line establishes the virtuous aspect of the hexagram. While it is almost always in the fifth position (thus being both lord and ruler), some have occasionally placed it in another position. Commentators pay special attention to these and many other properties and relationships of lines comprising each hexagram. When the unbroken and broken lines do not alternate or are not in the complete, harmonious arrangement, the influence may be inauspicious and the questioner is thereby warned to take steps to deal with the unfavorable conditions that are signaled.

Various strictures have become part of the customs of consulting the *I Ching*. The same specific questions asked of the chosen hexagram must not be repeated for an extended period of time—at least one to three months according to some. A particularly strong prohibition is also universally acknowledged against seeking counsel for a dishonest, harmful, or frivolous action. The *I Ching* is looked upon by its adepts as a sort of venerable benign sage of infinite wisdom. Thus the question should be formulated with care and sincerity. The answers require intense scrutiny and contemplation.

Iulian Shchutskii, who in the 1930s made an extensive translation of the *I Ching* into Russian (later translated into English by William MacDonald *et al.* in 1979), has summarized the philosophic basis of the code in seven fundamental teachings: the world is changeable and yet follows immutable laws; a polarity of opposites confronts and also synthesizes all things; the past, present, and future form one unitary system; understanding this unity of the cosmos leads to harmony; the internal and external contribute to each other; individual needs focus on both the self and the environment, and therefore the aim must be toward good for all parts, the self and society; the theoretical and practical are both properties of life.

Explanation of the Translation

We hope that our endeavor may contribute to understanding the nature of the *I Ching,* but it is not meant to supersede other translations of the original text, nor does it attempt to probe the complex insights that scholars have detected in the deceptively simple words and poetic images. It is instead an attempt to highlight the relatively sparse basic textual words (in Chinese and in English) on which all the later commentaries are based and from which many thousands of scholarly works were developed. Our assignment of particular English words to the Chinese characters is in effect a new translation, but we recognize that both the ancient and more recent meanings of some of them are not universally agreed upon by scholars.

In this presentation, the judgment for the hexagrams is shown first as it was originally written in individual Chinese characters, with the literally translated English word beneath it. Sometimes several words are also indicated as possible alternatives. Following the group of individual words is a more free translation, as literal as possible and yet understandable in modern English syntax. Sometimes the hexagram's name is also put in as part of the judgment in order for the latter to be clearer. For instance, hexagram 14, *Ta Yu,* with the title "Great Holdings," contains only two Chinese characters in the judgment. Their English equivalents are "great" and "enjoyment" (or "no obstruction"), but the overall meaning of each hexagram is supposed to affect all that follows, including both the judgment and the lines' statements. Therefore, "Great Holdings," the title, has been added, a practice that has been customary in the translations and the commentaries of scholars through the centuries.

The lines here are also accompanied by individual Chinese characters with their English equivalents, followed by their rendering into relatively grammatical English.

In this work, we have included only the name, judgment, and lines of each hexagram, leaving out the Ten Wings and the Images, the added commentary by Confucius. We are therefore presenting the skeleton of what later became the enlarged *I Ching*. It allows the reader to see how it all began, to peruse the original text (or at least as close to the original as we can get), to compare our

OPPOSITE: Zhu Zuchang. *Children with Crickets.* Modern period. Carved boxwood, 5 × 6″. Shanghai Museum of Art. Hexagram 4 (*Mêng;* underdeveloped) implies lack of development—as in a child—requiring discipline and understanding, but also can result in maturity and good fortune.

OVERLEAF: In the sample reading, hexagram 33 (*Tun;* retreat) was drawn from the casting of the coins, indicating that sometimes it is more favorable to retreat than to advance. After Li Zhaodao (A.D. 670–730). *The Emperor Ming Huang's Journey to Shu.* Ink and color on silk. Height 31¾″. National Palace Museum, Taipei.

青綠關山迥
崎嶇道路長
客人各結束行
李自周詳認
為名和利耶
識勞與忙年
陳失姓氏北宋
近乎唐
甲午新秋
御題

renderings with those of others, and to interpret the spare answers to questions. Of course, to get the full flavor of the *I Ching,* the numerous rich commentaries making up the Ten Wings should also be read. They consist of seven separate, extensive essays, two of which are in two parts, thus making ten treatises in all.

The paucity of the characters in the judgments and lines does not mean that the sense is impoverished. Sometimes only a few pictographs can convey extensive meanings. For example, in one place in the commentaries by Confucius, four characters from the judgment were translated by James Legge as, "If a man withdraws his mind from the love of beauty and applies it as sincerely to the love of the virtuous." The same Confucian treatise contains another passage with thirty-three Chinese characters that have been transposed into an English statement requiring about thirty words. Nevertheless, the leeway given to students and translators by the relatively few Chinese characters in the *I Ching* has led to a variety of interpretations by scholars from East and West.

Some of the versions in scholarly and popular monographs are often poetic and rich in imagery. The commentaries can be profound and perceptive. Our intention is not to review them for style, accuracy, or meaning. Each writer necessarily offers his own meanings of the ambiguities expressed in the translation. James Legge wrote that "the written characters are not representations of words but symbols of ideas, and that the combination of them in composition is not a representation of what the writer would say but of what he thinks." In this view, the translation of the Chinese characters into other languages is not a significant departure. Only a perception of what the original writer was thinking is what counts. But who can discover that? Many scholars and thinkers, including Confucius, have given their own opinions of what was meant by the original sages. We have no basis for either doubting or accepting their conclusions, but by listing the characters and presenting our own relatively literal summaries—together with a few examples of how others have read these same Chinese word symbols—we hope to enable readers to form their own ideas about what they mean. Many implications and meanings can be inferred from each hexagram. Our rendering of each Chinese character into an English word or phrase may differ from the translations that others make. We have used the Wade-Giles system of spelling Chinese names and words.

We have placed the English equivalents beneath or adjacent to each Chinese pictograph character, usually either as a noun or verb, for in the Chinese language the syntax depends on how the word is used in a sentence and in association with other words. Similarly, a noun may be singular or plural as it fits the sense of the phrase and the other words in juxtaposition. Thus, *man* may be used as *men. Danger* may apply best as *dangerous; lose* may be chosen over *loss.* At least five different Chinese characters can be translated as "*no, not, nothing.*" Four of them are now represented by one in modern Chinese. Such characteristics may account for the variety of translations. Moreover, the meanings of some of the individual Chinese pictographs have themselves changed through the history of the Chinese language.

We have also used some words interchangeably, choosing those that seemed to fit best. We employ *blame, mistake, regret, remorse, humiliation,* and *repentance* for the same Chinese character. *Superior person* is *righteous person. No obstruction* or *no obstacle* can also mean *potency, open way,* or even *enjoyment. Great good fortune* is our phrase for *supreme good fortune* (as rendered by Wilhelm/Baynes). *Great water* and *great river* are interchangeable in our version. We indicate *use, act,* and *move* as they seem to apply.

The term *superior person* may also need explanation. Recurring often in the judgments and lines, the two characters can be conveyed literally into English as "you" and "sir" (as a type of honorific title). Most English translations, including ours, render this combination as "superior person" or "superior man."

The same Chinese character may represent several nondescript words, such as *on, in, at, and, to, with, or,* and sometimes *is.* We render these as prepositions, conjunctions, and even verbs conforming to what we perceive to be the sense of the statement.

A few accepted symbolisms should be noted. All parts of the compass outside the central kingdom of China were symbolic of inferior areas at the time the *I Ching* was created. The north contained wild creatures; south was undeveloped; west, uncultured; east, the ghosts. Yellow and purple were the emperor's colors. Yellow was also the central hue of the five primary colors. Deep red meant people in power. Golden red implied nobles.

It should also be emphasized that Chinese proverbs in general, as in the *I Ching,* are often expressed in elliptical ways and therefore can be misinterpreted. While the essential meaning may be clear to the initiated, translators can sometimes stray unwittingly from the original intention. Often the reader may have considerable difficulty in fathoming what is meant. Commentators through the centuries have used the clues of history and of the inner symbolic structure of the diagrams with their assigned names to discover the implications in some of the judgments and lines. Even scholars steeped in Chinese history and lore differ among themselves on the meanings. Our rendering therefore is merely one of many. Since the original intentions of King Wên and the duke of Chou can only be surmised, our juxtaposition of the Chinese characters in the extant basic text, together with their possible English equivalents, may permit the reader to draw his or her own inferences and thereby receive added enjoyment and profit.

Sample Reading

We will take as our questioner Professor X. He was trying to decide whether to accept an offer for a new position in his native country at a higher salary and an upgraded rank. Here in the United States, with his wife and two children for almost twenty years, he had had a respectable position and reasonable income, but there was virtually no prospect for further advancement. In favor of his accepting the new appointment were the higher title and salary, his wife's general preference to return to her former homeland, and the likelihood that in the United States he had reached his professional limits. Arguing for staying were his present contentment with work and remuneration, his children's general preference to remain, and his own desire to perform and bring up his children here rather than in the relatively restrictive environment of his homeland.

On casting the coins, he first threw two heads and a tail for a total of 8 (3 + 3 + 2) and therefore a broken line at the bottom of the hexagram. The second casting yielded a 6 from three tails (2 + 2 + 2). This broken line was therefore a "moving line." The third was an unbroken line from two tails and a head (2 + 2 + 3), a 7. The fourth, fifth, and sixth were 9s (3 + 3 + 3) and therefore "moving" and unbroken lines. The resulting hexagram was 33:

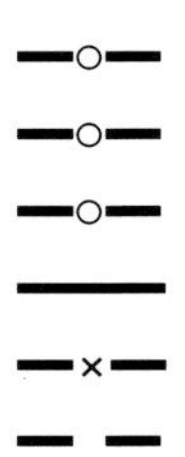

with its accompanying Chinese title meaning "retreat."

Professor X went about trying to apply the statements to his situation. The judgment in 33 is "No obstruction. In small things, benefit in perseverance." The "No obstruction" seemed to him to indicate that whatever his path might be he would meet no obstruction. But was his dilemma a small matter, as stated in the judgment? To him, it was a primary concern. Perhaps the "small" meant the lesser things in his activities. In those areas, it was important to persevere. Would the implication then be that the larger issues should not require persistence? Or did the phrase suggest that attention ought to be on lesser matters rather than on the consuming problem he had to resolve.

The title of the hexagram—always a significant part of the interpretation—is "Retreat." Thus support was given for turning away from further consideration of the proposal from abroad and toward a focus on the details of his present affairs, the small things. Perhaps he should "back off."

Examination of the lines helped to clarify the implied suggestions. The moving lines to be read were a 6 in the second place; 9s in the fourth, fifth, and sixth places. These are the only statements that are of significance under the rules.

A 6 in the second place says, "Holding firmly, you cannot be won over," an indication to him that the tempting offer should not draw him away. A 9 in the fourth place, in stating, "A favorable retreat brings good fortune to the superior man," suggested that refusing to advance was the proper decision for a superior person. The next sentence of the line reads, "It is unfortunate for the inferior person." The statement appeared to him to mean that a lesser man might be persuaded to take the new job by the lure of monetary gain and a higher position. A 9 in the fifth place emphasized the point further: "Perseverance brings good fortune," evidently counseling that steadfastness in resisting the blandishments offered was the proper course. Finally, the last line, a 9 in the sixth place, nailed it down for him with calming advice to pull back rather than to go forward—and without strain or stress: "Leisurely retreat. Some benefit (or nothing of no benefit)." The professor concluded that he was being cautioned to stay where he was, to keep to his mundane activities, to refrain from accepting the offer, and to do so without worry, in a "leisurely" manner.

How would things be likely to turn out if he followed the path as he saw it? The answer, according to the principles of the *I Ching,* was to be found by transposing each of the moving lines into their opposites and thereby forming a different hexagram. Therefore, the 6 in the second place (-x-) became an unbroken line (—); the 9s in the fourth, fifth, and sixth places became broken lines (≡≡). The new hexagram, consequently, was ䷭ (46; *Shêng*). Its title is "Elevation upward. Rising." Evidently in the end, no matter what he did, his outlook was favorable.

This reading is an instance of how the ambiguous wording of the *I Ching* can be used to confirm inner wishes. If otherwise inclined, Professor X could have interpreted the judgment and lines in the opposite way. "No obstruction" could have shown that the way ahead was open for him to go, rather than to stay. There was benefit only in adhering to the small items in his life, but the larger issues should not be approached with stubbornness. He could have seen "Holding firmly, you cannot be won over" as keeping to the correct line, which was to better his position, career, and remuneration. "Retreat" in the title and in the lines might have been viewed as a return to his place of origin. He could have concluded that the proper course would be to embrace his old society (to retreat) without haste. Furthermore, the promise offered by the new hexagram, after transforming the moving lines, of "elevation" and "rising" would seem to be more in keeping with the result of transferring to the more prestigious position abroad—where upward mobility was the hallmark of the proposed job. Yet, to the professor, hexagram 46 simply announced that all would go well and he might even achieve a higher position than he had anticipated by remaining where he was.

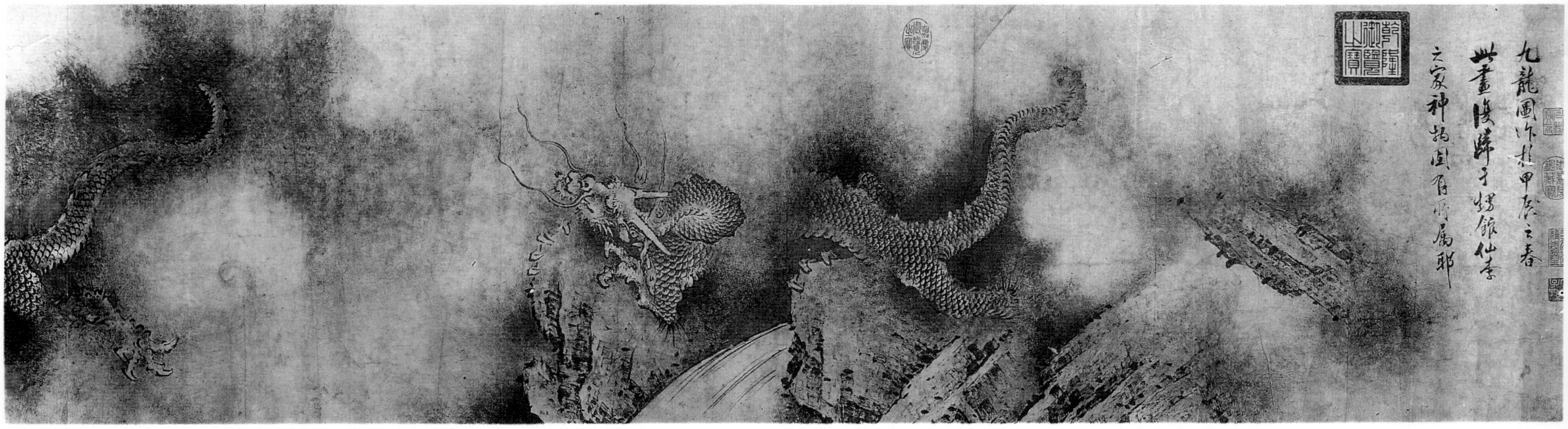

The Hexagrams

1 乾 Ch'ien ☰ (Strong. Creative. Yang principle)

The Judgment

元 亨 利
Greatness, Beginning No obstruction Benefit
貞
Perseverance, Justice
Greatness. No obstruction.
Benefit in perseverance

The Lines

Nine at the Bottom (Beginning)
潛 龍 勿用
Hidden Dragon Not Act
The dragon hides; do not act.

Nine in the Second Place
見 龍 在 田 利 見
See Dragon In, At Field Benefit, Auspicious See
大 人
Great Man, Person
See the dragon in the field.
It is auspicious to see the great man.

Nine in the Third Place
君 子 終日 乾
Superior Man or Person* All Day Consider, Ponder
乾 夕 惕 若
Consider, Ponder Night Self-examination As, Like
厲 无 咎
Danger, Seriousness No Blame, Mistake
The superior man keeps his mind attentive all day; considers the chances of danger.
Even at night he seriously examines himself.

Wilhelm/Baynes's translation speaks of being "creatively active" and at night "still beset with cares."

*Earliest translations referred only to "Man," but this Chinese character has no gender. It is an honorific title.

Nine in the Fourth Place
或 躍 在 淵
May, Or (implies options) Leap up In, At Deep water
无 咎
No Blame, Mistake
One may leap up while in deep water.
No mistake.

Nine in the Fifth Place
飛 龍 在 天 利
Flying Dragon In, At Heaven Benefit, Auspicious
見 大 人
See Great Man, Person
The dragon is flying in the heavens.
It is auspicious to see the great man.

Nine in the Sixth Place (Top)
亢 龍 有
Over, Uppermost Dragon Have
悔
Regret, Remorse, Repentance
With the dragon at the uppermost place, one may have reason to regret.
(The implication is that pride may be followed by a fall. Therefore, take heed.)

2 坤 K'un ☷ (Receptive. Follower. Yin principle)

The Judgment

元 亨 利 牝
Greatness, Beginning No obstruction Benefit Female
馬 之 貞 君 子 有 攸 往
Horse Of Perseverance Superior Man Have Far Go
先 迷 後 得
In the beginning, At first Loss Later Gain
主 利 西 南 得 朋
Indicate, Suggest Benefit West South Gain Friend
東 北 喪 朋 安 貞
East North Loss Friend Safe, Steady Perseverance
吉
Good fortune
Greatness. No obstruction.
Beneficial for the mare to be persevering.
If the superior man chooses to go, he loses at first and later gains; he mostly benefits.
To the Southwest he gains a friend.
To the Northeast he loses a friend.
With steadfast perseverance, he will have good fortune.

Wilhelm/Baynes's translation suggests that the mare symbolizes gentleness and devotion and is associated with the earth as distinguished from the dragon (mentioned in the first hexagram), which belongs to heaven.

The Lines

Six at the Bottom (Beginning)
履 霜 堅 冰 至
Step on Frost Hard, Firm Ice Arrive
If one steps onto frost, hard ice follows.

Six in the Second Place
直 方 大 不
Straight, Honest Square, Just Great, Big Not
習 无 不 利
Learn (Perform?) Nothing No Benefit
Honest ("straight"), just ("square"), righteous ("big"), even if one does not act, one will have much benefit ("nothing no benefit").

Six in the Third Place
含 章 可
Contain, Inside, Hidden Good quality Can, May
貞 或 從
Persistence, Perseverance Or, May Follow, Start
王 事 无 成 有 終
King Business No Success Have Result
Good qualities are inside.
One can be persevering.
If one starts on a large enterprise ("king's business"), one may have difficulty but will achieve a result.

Six in the Fourth Place
括 囊 无 咎 无 譽
Close, Tie Sack No Blame No Honor
Close the sack (implies "speak carefully").
No blame. No honor.

Six in the Fifth Place
黃 裳 元 吉
Yellow Cloth, Coat Great Good fortune
Yellow coat: great good fortune.
(The yellow coat was worn by royalty and therefore symbolized nobility.)

Six in the Sixth Place (Top)

龍 戰 于 野 其 血
Dragon Fight In, On Field The, Its Blood

玄 黃
Black Yellow

Dragons fighting in the field.
Blood over the universe.
("Black and yellow" symbolizes the universe.
An unfavorable omen is implied.)

3 屯 *Chun* ☳☵ (Difficulty in the beginning. Stay and prepare)

The Judgment

元 亨 利
Greatness No obstruction Benefit, Auspicious

貞 勿 用 有 攸 往
Perseverance Not Use, Act Have Far Go

利 建 侯
Benefit, Auspicious Establish Duke (the second of five ranks below the king)

Greatness. No obstruction. Benefit in perseverance.
Do not go too far.
Benefit to prepare and wait.
("Establish the Duke" implies reaching the second rank, high enough. It is not necessary to reach the top.)

Wilhelm/Baynes see this last phrase to mean "appointing helpers."

The Lines

Nine at the Bottom (Beginning)

磐 桓 利 居
Difficulty, Hesitant Advance Benefit Stay, Remain

貞 利 建 侯
Perseverance Benefit Establish Duke

Benefit to remain and persevere.
Benefit to go reasonably far.

Six in the Second Place

屯 如 邅 如 乘
Stay around As, Like Circle around As, Like Ride

馬 班 如 匪 寇 婚 媾 女
Horse Remain As, Like No Force Marriage Lady

貞 不 字 十 年
Perseverance No Marry (marriage) Ten Years

乃 字
Then Marry

Remain but be ready to go ("ride the horse around").
One cannot force the lady to marry (the implication is that she has lost either a husband or a betrothed) but maybe she will ten years later.

Six in the Third Place

即 鹿 无 虞
Follow (Hunt) Deer No Concern, Worry (or title of a

惟 入 于 林
hunting official) Only, In case In At Forest

ABOVE: The trigram *K'un* ☷ earth) is doubled to form hexagram 2 (*K'un*) to signify the yin principle of gentleness and receptivity. Chao Meng-fu. *Autumn Colors on the Chi'ao and Hua Mountains.* 1296. Ink and color on paper, 11¼ × 36¾″. National Palace Museum, Taipei.

OPPOSITE: The positions of the dragon described in the lines of hexagram 1 are metaphors for the auspiciousness of the circumstances. Chen Jung. *Nine Dragon Scroll.* Sung dynasty (mid-thirteenth century). Ink on paper. Height 18″. Courtesy Museum of Fine Arts, Boston.

中 君 子
Middle, Deep Superior Man
幾 不 如
Chance, Option, Risk Rather Than
舍 往 吝
Renounce, Leave, Yield Go Blame, Mistake

Hunt the deer without worry.
When in the deep forest, the superior man assesses the options rather than just goes away.
If one does go on (heedlessly is implied) then it is a mistake.

Six in the Fourth Place

乘 馬 班 如 求 婚 媾 往
Ride Horse Remain Like Ask Marriage Go
吉 无 不 利
Good fortune Nothing Not Benefit, Auspicious

Ride the horse. Remain (caution is implied).
If one asks her to marry, one can proceed with good fortune.
All is auspicious.

Legge's translation is: "the fourth line, divided, shows (its subject as a lady), the horses of whose chariot appear in retreat. She seeks, however (the help of) him who seeks her to be his wife. Advance will be fortunate; all will turn out advantageously."

Nine in the Fifth Place

屯 其 膏
Prepare, Store (sky?) His, The Treasure, Richness
小 貞 吉 大
Small, Lesser Perseverance Good fortune Large,
貞 凶
Major Perseverance, Persistence Misfortune, Disaster

Conserve energy ("store treasure").
Less persistence brings good fortune.
Great persistence brings misfortune.

Six in the Sixth Place (Top)

乘 馬 班 如 泣 血 漣 如
Ride Horse Stay Like Weep Blood Tears Like

Ride the horse. Remain in the same place.
Weep bloody tears (equivalent to "extreme sadness").

4 蒙 *Mêng*

(Undeveloped. Unknown. Uneducated. Unformed and Uninformed—like a child—Foolish)

The Judgment

亨 匪我 求 童 蒙
No obstruction Not I Ask, Request Child Unknown,
童 蒙
Undeveloped Child Unknown, Undeveloped Ask,
求 我 初 筮
Request I At first, Beginning Divination, Oracle
告 再 三 瀆
Answer, Tell Again Three Disrespect, Violate,
瀆 則
Profane Disrespect, Violate, Profane Then
不 告 利 貞
No Answer, Tell Benefit Persistence, Perseverance

No obstruction.
I do not seek the unknown ("I do not ask the child").
The unknown comes to me ("the child asks me").
At first a teacher may give an answer ("an oracle may answer").
If a pupil asks again and again and again, it is highly disrespectful and no answer need be given.
But there is benefit in persistence.

Legge's translation is: "Mang (indicates that in the case which it presupposes) there will be success. I do not (go and) seek the youthful and inexperienced, but he comes and seeks me. When he shows (the sincerity that marks the first recourse to divination), I instruct him. If he apply a second and third time, that is troublesome; and I do not instruct the troublesome. There will be advantage in being firm and correct."

The Lines

Six at the Bottom (Beginning)

發 蒙 利
Uncovered, Developed Unknown, Undeveloped Good
用 刑 人 用
Use, Act Punish, Discipline People Use, Act
説 桎 梏 以 往
Relieve, Remove Punishment Instrument With Go
吝
Blame, Mistake

As the unknown (or child) begins to develop ("uncover"), it is good to use discipline.
If one removes restraints, it will be a mistake.
("Punishment instrument" indicates fetters.)

Nine in the Second Place

包 蒙
Covered, Wrapped Unknown, Undeveloped
吉 納 婦 吉
Good fortune Receive, Marry Woman Good fortune
子 克 家
Son Take care Home (Family)

The unknown is enclosed (as in a container).
Good fortune.
Marry a woman. Good fortune.
The son can take care of the family.

Six in the Third Place

勿 用 取 女 見 金 夫
Not Use, Act Take Girl, Woman See Gold Husband,
不 有 躬 无 攸 利
Man Not Have Self No Further, Future Benefit

Do not marry a woman for her gold.
The husband will bow ("not have self"). No future benefits.
(The warning is that a rich wife will dominate.)

An alternative interpretation is: Do not marry a woman who, when she sees riches in a man, will not contain herself. No future benefit.

Six in the Fourth Place

困
Wrapped, Surrounded, Unknown
蒙 吝
Folly, Unknown Blame, Humiliation

Unrecognized folly brings humiliation.

Six in the Fifth Place

童 蒙 吉
Unknown, Child Folly, Unknown Good fortune

Although the child is foolish, he will have good fortune.

Another possibility is: The unrecognized folly will bring good fortune.

Nine in the Sixth Place (Top)

擊 蒙 不 利 爲 寇
Strike, Hit Folly No Benefit Far Robber, Bandit
利 禦 寇
Benefit Defend Robber, Bandit

Attack the unknown (or folly).
No benefit to be an aggressor ("bandit").
Benefit to defend against aggression.

5 需 *Hsü*

(Waiting. Patience. Need)

The Judgment

有 孚 光 亨 貞
Have Trust Brilliance No obstruction Perseverance
吉 利 涉 大
Good fortune Benefit Walk, Cross Big River, Water

Have trust. Brightness ahead.
No obstacle.
Perseverance brings good fortune.
Benefit to cross the great water.

The Lines

Nine at the Bottom (Beginning)

需 于 郊 利 用
Waiting At, In Suburbs, Outskirts Benefit Use, Act
恒 无 咎
Patience, Constancy No Blame, Mistake

Wait in the outskirts (in the wings).
Benefit to have patience.
No mistake.

Nine in the Second Place

需 于 沙 小 有
Waiting At, In Sand, Beach Small Have
有 終 吉
Criticism, Word Final Good fortune

Waiting in the sand (near the water, the place of danger), there is little criticism.
Finally, good fortune.

Nine in the Third Place

需 于 泥 致 寇 至
Waiting At, In Mud Bring Robber, Bandit Come

Waiting in the mud (implies "stuck in the mud") induces the enemy ("bandit") to come.

Six in the Fourth Place

需 于 血 出 自 穴
Waiting At, In Blood Out From Cave, Pit, Cavern

Waiting in blood (defeat is implied), one will finally escape from the pit.

Nine in the Fifth Place

需 于 酒 食 貞
Waiting At, In Wine Food Perseverance
吉
Good fortune

Waiting at the feast ("in wine and food") brings good fortune.

In hexagram 6 the trigram *Ch'ien* (☰ heaven) lies over *K'an* (☵ water, abysmal), a trigram of difficulty, to form the hexagram *Sung,* symbolizing disagreement—over which heaven rises. Kano Moranobu (1434–1530). *Shumoshiku Loving Lotus.* Muromachi period. Wash and ink on paper, 36 × 13″. Ogula Collection, Tokyo.

Six in the Sixth Place (Top)

入于 穴 有 不 速 之 客
In To Cave, Pit, Cavern Have Not Invited Of Guest

三 人 來 敬 之 終
Three People Come Respect, Honor It Final

吉
Good fortune

One gets into a pit (implies a limited or difficult position).
Three uninvited guests will arrive.
Respect them. Finally, good fortune.

6 訟 *Sung*

(Argument, Conflict—"conflict before authority," or "in litigation" is also implied)

The Judgment

有 孚 窒 惕
Have Trust Suffocation, Difficulty Warning, Wary

中 吉 終 凶 利 見
Middle Good fortune Final Misfortune Benefit See

大 人 不 利 涉 大
Big, Great Man Not Benefit Cross, Walk Big, Great

川
River, Water

Have trust but be wary of difficulty (or opposition).
Good fortune for part of the way ("middle").
Misfortune may be ahead ("finally").
Benefit to see the great man.
No benefit to cross the great water.

The Lines

Six at the Bottom (Beginning)

不 永 所 事 小 有
No Long Own Affair, Enterprise, Thing Small Have

言 終 吉
Criticism, Word Final Good fortune

If one does not continue the enterprise, one may receive criticism.
Finally good fortune.

Nine in the Second Place

不 克 訟
No Overcome, Win Save, Controversy, Sue

歸 而 逋 其
Back, Return Then Flee, Escape, Owe His, Its

邑 人 三 百 戶 无 眚
County People Three Hundred Family No Misfortune

One cannot win the argument ("do not enter the controversy or litigation").
Withdraw and flee the situation.
One's three hundred countrymen (implying that only a few) will have no misfortune.

Six in the Third Place

食 舊 德
Eat, Enjoy Old Morality, Virtues

貞 厲 終 吉
Perseverance, Persistence Danger Final Good fortune

或 從 王 事 无 成
If, Or, Perhaps Go King Business No Success

Depend on previous principles ("eat old virtues").

Persistence is dangerous but finally good fortune will come.
If one embarks upon a great enterprise ("king's business"), no success will come.

Nine in the Fourth Place

不 克 訟 復
No Overcome, Win Sue, Controversy Return
卽 命 渝 安
Far, Toward Fate, Destiny Change Equanimity, Quiet
貞 吉
Perseverance Good fortune

You cannot win the argument ("do not enter the controversy").
Turn away to follow fate.
Change to equanimity.
Perseverance will bring good fortune.

Nine in the Fifth Place

訟 元 吉
Sue, Controversy Great Good fortune

Entering the conflict will bring great good fortune.

Nine in the Sixth Place (Top)

或 錫 之 鞶 帶
If, Or, Perhaps Bestow It, Of Reward Belt (implies
終 朝 三 褫 之
high rank) End Day Three Remove It, Of

If one receives high rank (a "belt" from the king), it will finally be withdrawn again and again ("end of day three times").

Chu Hsi's version is: "Even if one receives reward from the king, if one spends one's time in controversy (or litigation) it will be taken away again and again."

7 師 *Shih*

(Army. Teacher. Leader)

The Judgment

貞 丈 人
Perseverance Father-in-law (older respected man)
吉 无 咎
Good fortune No Blame

Perseverance of the older, experienced man brings good fortune.
No blame.

The Lines

Six at the Bottom (Beginning)

師 出 以 律 否 藏
Army Out With Discipline No Good, Order
凶
Misfortune

An army moves with discipline. Without order there is misfortune.

Nine in the Second Place

在 師 中 吉 无
At, In Army Amidst, Middle Good fortune No
咎 王 三 錫 命
Blame King Three Bestow, Give Fate, Order

Being in the middle of the army is good fortune.
No blame.
The king awards honors ("orders") again and again ("three times").

Six in the Third Place

師 或 輿 尸 凶
Army If, Or, Perhaps Cart Corpses Misfortune

If the army (goes out to fight), (it will return) with corpses in the cart.

Shchutskii's version (as translated by MacDonald, Hasegawa, and Wilhelm): "A cart of corpses may be in the army. Misfortune."

Six in the Fourth Place

師 左 次 无 咎
Army Left Second choice No Blame, Harm

If the army retreats (as indicated by "left second choice," which implies going in the wrong direction), no blame will come.
(The implication is that a strategic retreat is wise.)

Six in the Fifth Place

田 有 禽 利
Field, Country Have Wild flying birds Benefit
執 言 无 咎 長 子 帥
Hold Say, Speech No Blame Elder Son Command
師 弟 子 輿 尸
Army Brother (Younger) Son Cart Corpses
貞 凶
Persistence Misfortune

The country is invaded ("has flying birds in the field").
Benefit to insist on speaking out. No blame.
The eldest son commanded the army.
The younger son will bring back corpses in the cart.
Persistence brings misfortune.
(The implication is that the older one should do the leading. The younger will lead to disaster.)

Six in the Sixth Place (Top)

大 君 有 命 開 國
Great King Have Order, Destiny Open Country
承 家 小 人 勿 用
Build Family Small Man No Use, Act

A great king gives orders, establishes ("opens") the country, and builds the families.
For these actions, do not use a lesser man.

8 比 *Pi*

(Selection. Mutual Support. Union—modern meanings include: Evaluate, Compare)

The Judgment

吉 原
Good fortune Beginning, Originally Oracle (originally
筮 元
meant "pray," or "tossing"—as of a coin) Greatness
永 貞 无 咎 不
Always Perseverance No Blame, Mistake No
寧 方 來 後
Equanimity, Quietude Nearly, About to Come Later
夫
Maybe (original meaning was "Male Adult")
凶
Misfortune

Good fortune.
At the beginning, the oracle forecasts greatness.
Continual perseverance is no mistake.
Instability ("no quietude") nearly arrives.
Later maybe misfortune.

The Lines

Six at the Bottom (Beginning)

有 孚 比 之 无 咎
Have Trust Follow, Support Of, It No Blame
有 孚 盈 缶 終 來 有
Have Trust Overflow Container Final Come Have
他 吉
Other Good fortune

Having trust brings support. No mistake.
Having much trust ("overflowing") in the end brings additional good fortune.

Six in the Second Place

比 之 自 內 貞
Follow, Support Of, It From Inside Perseverance
吉
Good fortune

Support from inside.
Perseverance. Good fortune.

Six in the Third Place

比 之 匪 人
Follow, Support Of, It No Man

One receives support from undesirable people ("no man" implies an undesirable person).

Six in the Fourth Place

外 比 之 貞
Outside Follow, Support Of, It Perseverance
吉
Good fortune

Support from outside. Perseverance. Good fortune.

Nine in the Fifth Place

顯 比 王 用
Open, Obvious Follow, Support King Use, Act
三 驅 失 前 禽 邑
Three Drive Loss Front Flying birds Country
人 不 誡 吉
Man No Alert, Warning Good fortune

Give open support.
The king drives the game from three sides, leaving one side open (to allow a chance for escape).
The country people need no warning.
Good fortune.
(This implies that the king, in kindness, leaves room for someone to avoid seizure. Therefore the subjects have no cause for concern).

Six in the Sixth Place (Top)

比 之 无 首 凶
Follow, Support Of, Or No Leader Misfortune

If there is no leader to support, it is unfortunate.

9 小畜 *Hsiao Ch'u*

(Stay awhile. Cultivate. Restraining Power)

The Judgment

亨 密 雲
No Obstruction Thick, Heavy Cloud

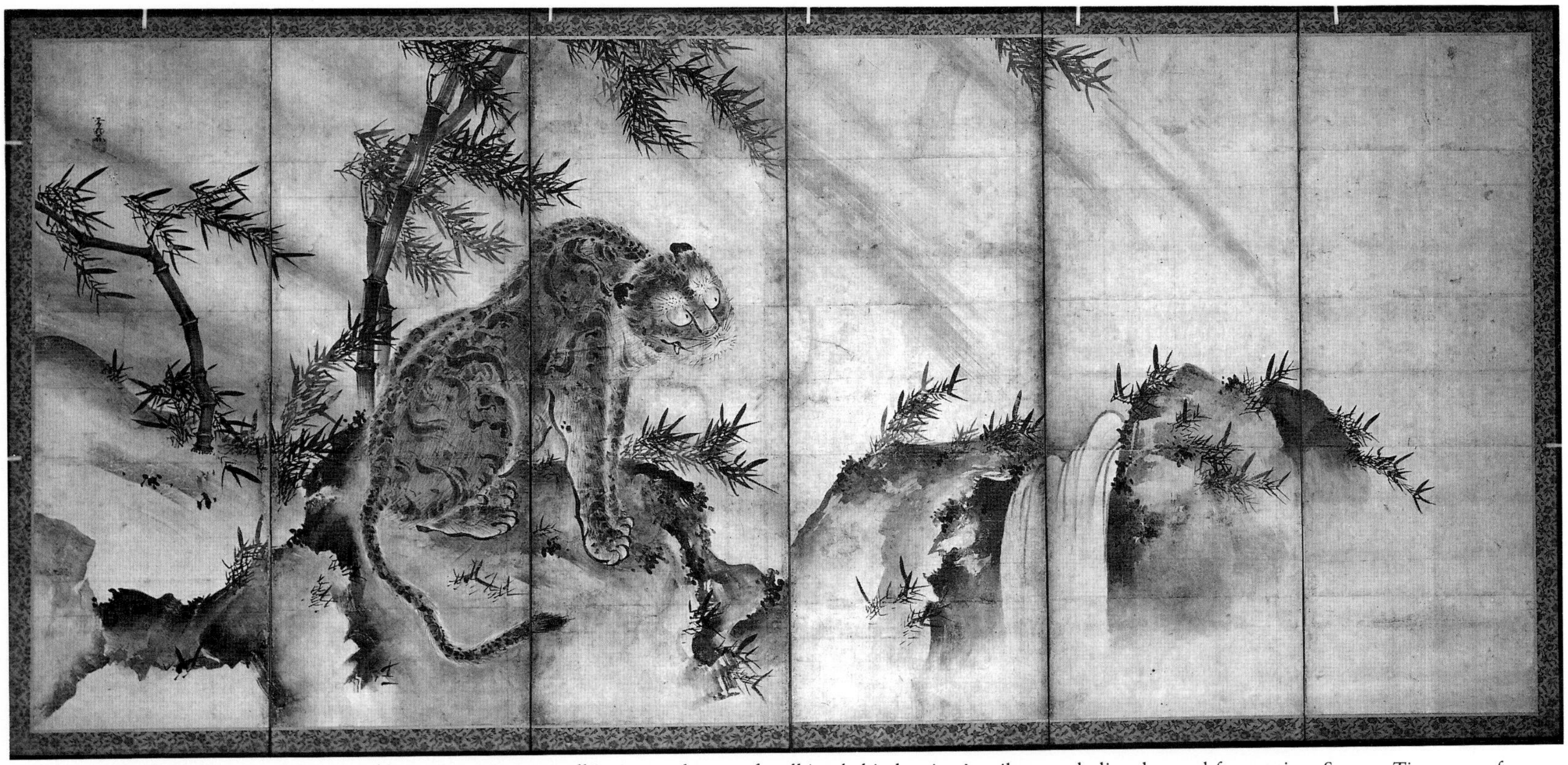

ABOVE: The Judgment and Lines of hexagram 10 (*Lu;* walking) uses the act of walking behind a tiger's tail to symbolize the need for caution. Sesson. *Tiger,* one of a pair of six-fold screens. Ashikaga period. Ink on paper. Length 133½″. The Cleveland Museum of Art.

OVERLEAF: The lines of hexagram 11 (*T'ai;* harmony) indicate that one should ford the river with prudence and with concern for others as an example of moderate behavior. Wu Bin (1591–1626). *The Five Hundred Arhats.* Ming dynasty. Section of handscroll, ink and light color on paper. Height 13¼″. The Cleveland Museum of Art.

不 雨 自 我 西 郊
No Rain From My West Outskirts, Suburbs

No obstruction.
Dense clouds but no rain from my Western outskirts.
(King Wên's origins were the suburbs not the capital city, where the tyrannical Emperor Chou Hsin had his court and where he held Wên a prisoner.)

The Lines

Nine at the Bottom (Beginning)

復 自 道 何 其
Return From Tao, Right way Why The, His
咎 吉
Blame, Mistake Good fortune

Returning to the right way, how can one be blamed!
Good fortune.

Nine in the Second Place

牽 復 吉
Pull Return Good fortune

Pull back and start again ("return")
Good fortune.

Nine in the Third Place

輿 說 輻 夫 妻
Cart Loss, Detach Wheel Husband Wife
反 目
Turn, Roll Eye

The wheels are detached from the wagon.
Husband and wife quarrel ("roll their eyes").

Six in the Fourth Place

有 孚 血 去 惕 出 无
Have Trust Blood Go Worry Out No
咎
Blame, Mistake

Go with trust into blood (implies danger) without worry.
No mistake.

Nine in the Fifth Place

有 孚 攣 如 富 以 其 鄰
Have Trust Hold As, Like Riches To His Neighbor

Have trust.
Offer to share one's riches with one's neighbor.

Nine in the Sixth Place (Top)

既 雨 既 處 尚
Already Rain Already Stopped Follow, Obey
德 載 婦 貞
Morality Caring Woman Persistence, Perseverance
厲 月 幾 望 君 子 征
Danger Moon Almost Full Superior Man Attack
凶
Misfortune

Rain may fall or stop (the implication is that the rain falls or stops as needed).
Follow moral principles in caring for a woman.
Persistence is dangerous.
The moon is nearly full.
If the superior man acts vigorously, misfortune comes.
(One implication is that the moon is ready to wane. Therefore, be cautious.)

10 履 *Lu*

(Walking. Treading—sometimes used as a noun, "shoe")

The Judgment

虎 尾 不 咥 人 亨
Tiger Tail No Bite Man, Person No obstruction

Walking behind the tiger's tail, one will not be bitten.
No obstruction (that is, the path is open).

The Lines

Nine at the Bottom (Beginning)

素 履 往 无 咎
Simple, Pure Walk Go No Blame

Walk sincerely. Go without blame.

Nine in the Second Place

履 道 坦 坦
Walk Road Flat, Smooth Flat, Smooth
幽 人 貞 吉
Quiet, Modest, Dark Man Perseverance Good fortune

The road is smooth and straight ("flat, flat").
The modest person ("dark man") should persevere.
Good fortune.

Six in the Third Place

眇 能 視 跛 能 履
Eye (One) Can See Limp, Lame Can Walk, Step
履 虎 尾 咥 人 凶 武
Walk, Step Tiger Tail Bite Man Misfortune Warlike,
人 爲 于 大 君
Fighting Man Becomes, For, As Your Great King

The halfblind can see ("one eye can see").
The lame can walk.
Walking behind the tiger's tail, one will be bitten.
Misfortune if a warlike man becomes your powerful king.
(The Chinese did not like to see a warrior become king. "Warlike" or "fighting" meant physically strong and brave but not necessarily wise.)

Shchutskii's translation is: "Even the blind can see! Even the lame can walk! But if you step on the tail of a tiger so that it bites you, there will be misfortune. The soldier nevertheless acts for the sake of a great sovereign."

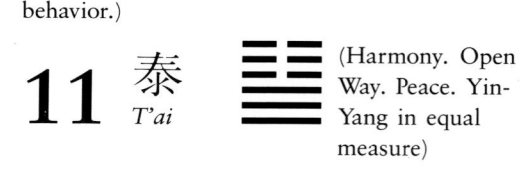

Nine in the Fourth Place

履 虎 尾 愬 愬 終
Walk, Step Tiger Tail Fearful Fearful Final
吉
Good fortune

Walking behind the tiger's tail is a fearful experience.
Finally good fortune.

Nine in the Fifth Place

夬 履 貞
Decisive Walk, Step Persistence, Perseverance
厲
Dangerous

Walk decisively, but persistence is dangerous.

Nine in the Sixth Place (Top)

視 履 考 祥
Observe, Look Walk, Step Become, Ahead Happiness
其 旋 元 吉
The Return Great Good fortune

Be observant of what lies ahead. Good fortune.
Be observant of what lies behind you. Great good fortune.

Another possible rendering is: Look ahead.
Good fortune.
Look behind (at the past). Great good fortune.
(The implication is to look back on one's own behavior.)

11 泰 *T'ai* ☷☰ (Harmony. Open Way. Peace. Yin-Yang in equal measure)

The Judgment

小 往 大 來 吉 亨
Small Go Big Come Good fortune No Obstruction

The small goes; the large comes.
Good fortune. No obstruction.

The Lines

Nine at the Bottom (Beginning)

拔 茅 茹 以 其
Lift, Pull up Ribbon grass Root With Its, His
彙 征 吉
Companion, Same kind Attack Good fortune

Pull up the entangled grass ("ribbon grass") by the roots, together with the same kind.
Advance. Good fortune.
(The implication is that interconnecting roots will be pulled up together.)

Nine in the Second Place

包 荒 用 馮
Contain, Bear with Dirty, Wild Use, Act Cross
河 不 遐 遺 朋
River, Water Not Remote, Distant Loss, Leave Friend
亡 得 尚 于 中 行
Disappear, Die Get Go At, To Middle Way

Bear the wilderness (or the unpleasant).
Ford the river ("cross").
Do not remain distant and leave your companions.
Benefit if one takes the middle way.

Wilhelm/Baynes's translation is: "Bearing with the uncultured in gentleness,
Fording the river with resolution,
Not neglecting what is distant,
Not regarding one's companion:
Thus one may manage to walk in the middle."

Nine in the Third Place

无 平 不 陂 无 往 不 復
No Plain Not Uneven terrain No Go Not Return
艱 貞 无 咎 勿 恤
Firm Perseverance No Blame Not Concern for
其 孚 于 食 有
Its, His Trust, Reputation At Eat, Have job Have
福
Good fortune

No flat plain without an uneven surface.
No going without a returning.
Firm perseverance is no mistake.
Do not have concern for your reputation.
Keep to your job.
Good fortune.

Six in the Fourth Place

翩 翩 不 富 以 其 鄰 不
Fly Fly Not Rich To Its, The Neighbor Not
戒 以 孚
Warning, Prohibition With Trust, Sincerity

Flitting to and fro, don't flaunt one's riches to neighbors.
Don't hold back ("prohibit") with sincerity.

Six in the Fifth Place

帝 乙 歸 妹
King I (apparently refers to "King I") Marry Sister
以 祉 元 吉
With Fortune, Happiness Great Good fortune

The king returns to the capital ("sister" here

may mean capital city).
Great good fortune.

There are many different interpretations. The capital of the Shang dynasty was called "Mei," a word that also means "sister." Some scholars identify the letter "I" with the first Shang monarch, Ch'êng T'ang of 1766 B.C., whereas others consider "sister" to mean a daughter married to either King Wên, originator of the hexagrams, or to King Wên's father.

Another interpretation is: "The king marries the sister (or daughter) of some other person."

Blofield's interpretation is: "By giving his daughter in marriage, the emperor attained felicity and extreme good fortune. . . . This was because of his impartiality in carrying out what he felt to be desirable. This suggests the need for impartiality in conducting our affairs."

Six in the Sixth Place (Top)

城 復 于 隍 勿 用 師
Wall Return, Back To Ditch, Moat Not Use Army
自 邑 告 命
Self, From Country Issue, Proclaim Command, Order
貞 吝
Perseverance Blame
The walls fall back into the moat.
Do not use the army.
Issue orders in your own country.
One may persevere and still be blamed.
(Implication is that one should keep to one's own boundaries.)

12 否 *P'i*

☷☰ (Unrest. Disharmony. Closed up. Standstill)

The Judgment

否 之 匪 人 不 利
Disharmony, Closed up Of No Man No Benefit
君 子 貞 大 往
Superior Man Perseverance Big, Great Go
小 來
Small Come
Disharmony occurs with an inferior man ("no man"). No benefit.
The superior man perseveres.
When the great goes, the small comes.

The Lines

Six at the Bottom (Beginning)

拔 茅 茹 以 其 彙
Pull up Ribbon grass Roots With Its Same kind,
貞 吉 亨
Group Perseverance Good fortune No obstruction
Pull up the ribbon grass by the roots.
All comes out together.
Perseverance. Good fortune. No obstruction.

Six in the Second Place

包 承 小 人 吉
Contained, Bear with Hold Small Man Good fortune
大 人 否 亨
Great Man Unrest, Upset, Closed up Enjoy
Be patient. Good fortune for the small man.
The great man may be upset but he will manage.

Six in the Third Place

包 羞
Contained, Bear with Shame
Tolerate shame.

Nine in the Fourth Place

有 命 无 咎 疇
Have Order, Fate No Blame Group, Companions
離 祉
Separate, Isolate Happiness, Blessings
Follow your destiny. No blame.
Be separate from the crowd ("group").
Blessings.

Legge's translation gives the opposite view that "companions will come and share."

Nine in the Fifth Place

休 否 大 人
At Rest, Standstill Closed up, Disharmony Great Man
吉 其 亡 其
Good fortune Its, The Die, Disappear, Loss Its, The
亡 繫 于 苞
Die, Disappear, Loss Tied At, To Deeply rooted
桑
Tree (Mulberry)
Unrest is at a standstill.
The great man will have good fortune.
Severe danger ("die its die").
Hold on to the mulberry tree (that is, something secure—a warning is implied here).

Nine in the Sixth Place (Top)

傾 否
Falling, Tilting Closed up, Disharmony, Unrest

The trigram *Li* (☲ fire) over the trigram *Ch'ien* (☰ heaven) yields hexagram 14 (*Ta Yu*; abundant possessions) of great power. Artist unknown. *Jigoku Soshi (Hell Scroll)*. Early Kamakura period, A.D. 1200. Color on paper. Height 10″. Tokyo National Museum.

先 否
Beginning Closed up, Disharmony, Unrest
後 喜
Later Happiness
Unrest is ending.
At the beginning, unrest.
Later, happiness.

13 同人 ䷌ *T'ung Jan*

(Same kind of people. Fellowship. Equality. Accommodation.)

The Judgment

同 人 于 野
Same Man, People At, In Field
亨 利 涉 大 川
No obstruction, Enjoyment Benefit Cross Great Water
利 君 子 貞
Benefit Superior Man Perseverance
Fellowship in the field brings enjoyment.
Benefit to cross the great water.
Benefit for the superior man to have perseverance.

The Lines

Nine at the Bottom (Beginning)
同 人 于 門 无 咎
Same Man, People At, In Door, Gate No Blame
Fellowship at the gate. No mistake.

Six in the Second Place
同 人 于 宗 吝
Same Man, People At, In Clan Regret
Fellowship within the clan. Regret.

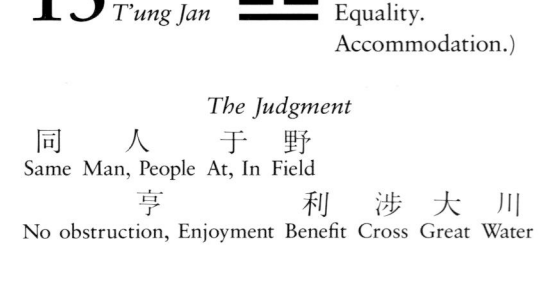

Nine in the Third Place
伏 戎 于 莽 升 其
Hide Soldier, Forces At, In Bushes Rise Its, The
高 陵 三 歲 不 興
High Hill Three Years No Prosperity, Rise up
Hiding forces are in the bushes.
Rise up to the high hill.
For three years, no prosperity.

Wilhelm/Baynes's translation is: "He hides weapons in the thicket.
He climbs the high hill in front of it.
For three years he does not rise up."

Nine in the Fourth Place
乘 其 墉 弗
Ride over, Clin Scale Its, The Wall Not
克 攻 吉
Overcome, Win Attack Good fortune
Climb over the wall but do not complete the attack.
Good fortune.

Nine in the Fifth Place
同 人 先 號 咷
Same Man, People Beginning Loudly Weep
而 後 笑 大 師 克
Then Later Laugh Great Army Overcome, Win
相 遇
Toward Meet
Men in fellowship weep loudly at the beginning and then laugh later as the great army wins and they meet each other again.

Nine in the Sixth Place (Top)
同 人 于 郊
Same Man, People At, In Outskirts, Countryside
无 悔
No Regret
Fellowship in the outskirts (or "countryside").
No regrets.

14 大有 ䷍ *Ta Yu*

(Abundant possessions. Great holdings)

The Judgment

大 有 元 亨
Great, Large Holdings Great Enjoyment
Abundant possessions. Great happiness.

The Lines

Nine at the Bottom (Beginning)
无 交 害 匪 咎
No Crossing, Near Harm No Blame, Regret
艱 則 无 咎
Difficulty Then No Blame, Regret
Stay away from ("don't cross") the harmful.
No blame.
Persist ("difficulty" implies need for much effort).
Then there will be no regret.

Nine in the Second Place
大 車 以 載 有 攸 往 无
Big Cart, Wagon With Load Have Far Go No
咎
Blame
The big cart is loaded.

One has far to go.
No blame.

Nine in the Third Place

公 用 亨
Duke, Noble, Prince Use, Act, Offer No obstruction,
于 天 子 小 人 弗
Enjoyment At, To Heaven Son Small, Petty Man Not
克
Overcome, Reach

A noble person offers without restraint to the king ("Heaven Son").
A lesser ("petty") man cannot go that far.
(The king was nominally the owner of everyone's possessions. The implication is that a truly noble person recognizes this principle. A less high-minded person holds back.)

Another interpretation is: A noble person can act with enjoyment with the king.
A lesser person cannot.

Nine in the Fourth Place

匪 其 彭 无 咎
Not Its, The Prosperous appearance No Blame

Do not show too much prosperity. No blame.

Wilhelm/Baynes's translation is: "He makes a difference
Between himself and his neighbor.
No blame."

Legge's is: "The fourth line, undivided, shows its subject keeping his great resources under restraint. There will be no error."

Six in the Fifth Place

厥 孚 交 如 威 如
Honesty Trust Crossing As, With Dignity As
吉
Good fortune

Honesty and trust crossing each other (or coming together) with dignity bring good fortune.

Nine in the Sixth Place (Top)

自 天 祐 之 吉
From Heaven Protection, Help Its, The Good fortune
无 不 利
No, Not, Nothing No, Not, Nothing Benefit

Help comes from heaven. Good fortune.
There will be benefit ("not no benefit" or "nothing of no benefit").

The trigrams *Kên* (☶ mountain) and *K'un* (☷ earth) combine two compatible aspects of nature to form hexagram 15 (*Ch'ien*; moderation). Chao Po-Chu (1120–1182). *River and Mountains in Autumn.* Section of the handscroll, ink and color on silk. Height 22½". Palace Museum, Beijing.

15 謙 *Ch'ien* ䷎ (Modesty, Humility)

The Judgment

謙 亨 君
Modesty, Humility No obstruction Superior
子 有 終
Man Have End

Modesty, no obstruction.
The superior man will have a good end.

The Lines

Six at the Bottom (Beginning)

謙 謙 君
Modesty, Humility Modesty, Humility Superior
子 用 涉 大 川 吉
Man Use, Act Cross Great Water Good fortune

The very modest superior man can cross the great water ("modesty" used twice indicates *very* modest).
Good fortune.

Six in the Second Place

鳴
Known, Recognized, Singing (as of a bird)
謙 貞 吉
Modesty, Humility Perseverance Good fortune

Modesty becomes recognized (like a bird's singing).
Perseverance brings good fortune.

Nine in the Third Place

勞 謙 君
Diligence, Hard work Modesty Superior
子 有 終 吉
Man Have Final Good fortune

Diligence. Modesty.
The superior man finally will have good fortune.

Six in the Fourth Place

无 不 利 撝 謙
No No Benefit Spread, Disperse Modesty

It is not without benefit to be modest in action ("spread modesty").

Six in the Fifth Place

不 富 以 其 鄰
Not Rich To, With, Toward Its, The Neighbor

利 用 侵 伐 无
Benefit Use, Act Invasion Attack No, Nothing
不 利
No, Nothing Benefit
Do not use wealth to show off to one's neighbors.
Benefit to invade and attack.
Some benefit in everything ("nothing no benefit").

Six in the Sixth Place (Top)
鳴
Known, Recognized, Singing (as of a bird)
謙 利 用 行
Modesty Benefit Use, Act Walking, Activity
師 征 邑
Army, Forces Attack, Act against Own
國
Colony, Country
Modesty becomes recognized.
Use one's forces to attack one's own colony (implication is not to go too far).

16 豫 *Yu* (Happiness. Harmony. Enthusiasm)

The Judgment
豫 利
Harmony, Happiness, Enthusiasm Benefit, Good
建 侯 行
Set up, Build up, Establish Duke, Noble, Vassal Move
師
Army, Forces
Harmony.
Benefit to set up vassals (or helpers) to move one's forces.

The Lines

Six at the Bottom (Beginning)
鳴
Singing, Expressing, Proclaiming
豫 凶
Happiness, Harmony, Enthusiasm Misfortune
Proclaiming happiness brings misfortune.
(Chinese consider restraint a virtue.)

Six in the Second Place
介 于 石 不 終 日
Character At, To Stone, Rock Not End Day
貞 吉
Perseverance Good fortune
Character like a rock, but not all the time ("not end day").
Perseverance brings good fortune.

Six in the Third Place
盱 豫
Look upward (Haughty) Happiness, Harmony,
悔 遲 有 悔
Enthusiasm Regret Delay, Lateness Have Regret
Looking with disdain at happiness brings regret.
Hesitation brings remorse.

Entirely different renderings are offered by others. For example, Wilhelm/Baynes:

"Enthusiasm that looks upward creates remorse. Hesitation brings remorse."

Legge: "The third line, divided, shows one looking up (for favors), while he indulges the feeling of pleasure and satisfaction. If he would understand!—If he be late in doing so, there will indeed be occasion for repentance."

Blofield: "To gaze reposefully brings regret; tardy action brings regret."

Nine in the Fourth Place
由 豫
Follow, From Happiness, Harmony, Enthusiasm
大 有 得 勿 疑 朋
Big, Great Have Gain Not Suspicion, Doubt Friend
盍 簪
Same kind Together
From enthusiasm comes great gain.
Do not be suspicious.
Friends of the same feather will come together.

Six in the Fifth Place
貞 疾 恒 不 死
Persistence Illness Always, Forever Not Dying
Continually ill, never dying.

Six in the Sixth Place (Top)
冥
Dark, Invisible, Unseen
豫
Happiness, Harmony, Enthusiasm
成 有 渝 无 咎
Success Have Change No Blame
Unseen happiness (or "hidden happiness").
Success brings change.
No blame.

Wilhelm/Baynes's translation is: "Deluded enthusiasm. But if after completion one changes, there is no blame."

Legge's is: "The topmost line, divided, shows its subject with darkened mind devoted to the pleasure and satisfaction (of the time); but if he changes his course even when it may be (considered as) completed, there will be no error."

Blofield's is: "Madcap repose. Fortunately a change takes place, so no blame is involved."

17 隨 *Sui* (Following)

The Judgment
元 亨 利 貞
Great No obstruction Benefit Perseverance
无 咎
No Blame, Mistake
Greatness. No obstruction.
Benefit in perseverance. No mistake.

The Lines

Nine at the Bottom (Beginning)
官 有 渝 貞
Officer, Authority Have Change Perseverance
吉 出 門 交 有 功
Good fortune Out Door Crossing Have Reward
Authority changes. (Implication is that all laws and power change.)
Perseverance brings good fortune.
Go out the door. Making friends brings rewards ("crossing" implies making contact).

Six in the Second Place
係 小 子 失
Tie up with, Connect with Small Son Loss
丈 夫
Great Man
If you connect with a lesser man ("small son") you lose the greater.

Six in the Third Place
係 丈 夫 失 小
Tie up with, Connect with Great Man Loss Small
子 隨 有 求 得 利
Son Follow Have Request Gain Benefit
居 貞
Reside, Possess Perseverance
If you connect with the greater man, you lose the lesser.
Follow to gain what one seeks ("request gain").
Benefit to maintain perseverance.

Nine in the Fourth Place
隨 有 獲
Follow Have Reward, Achievement
貞 凶 有 孚 在
Persistence, Perseverance Misfortune Have Trust At, To
道 以 明
Tao (Right path) With Brightness, Clarity, Sincerity
何 咎
How Blame
Following brings reward.
Persistence brings misfortune.
Have trust in the right path ("Tao").
With sincerity, how can one be blamed!

Nine in the Fifth Place
孚 于 嘉
Trust, Sincerity At, In Excellence, Goodness
吉
Good fortune
Trust in excellence.
Good fortune.

Six in the Sixth Place (Top)
拘 係 之 乃
Caught, Forced Tie up with, Bound Of, It Then
從 維 之 王 用
Follow, Obey Connection Of, It King Use, Act
亨 于 西 山
Worship At, In West Mountain
If firmly bound, then follow orders ("obey connection").
The king worships at the western mountain (signifies the central city or capital). This also implies that the king worships with sincerity. Some see in this line an allegory of the Chou dynasty, when loyal followers of the emperor were rewarded by being represented in the royal temple of ancestors on the "western mountain."

18 蠱 Ku

(Extreme corruption. Venom. When there are many poisonous creatures in a container, the one that is the most poisonous survives. This survivor is referred to as "*Ku*")

The Judgment

元 亨 利 涉 大
Greatness No obstruction Benefit Cross Big
川 先 甲
River, Water Before Beginning of a series (The first of
三 日 後
10 celestial items) Three Day After, Later
甲 三 日
Beginning of a series Three Day

Greatness. No obstruction.
Benefit to cross the great water.
Before starting, three days.
After starting, three days.

Six at the Bottom (Beginning)
幹 父 之 蠱
Tree trunk, Strength Father Of Venom (implies severe
有 子 考 无 咎 厲
mistake) Have Son Dead father No Blame Danger
終 吉
Final Good fortune
A strong father can make severe mistakes.
If he has a son, the dead father may not receive blame.
Danger but finally good fortune.

Nine in the Second Place
幹 母 之 蠱
Tree trunk, Strength Mother Of Venom (severe
不 可 貞
mistake) Not May, Can Perseverance, Persistence
A strong mother can make severe mistakes.
She must not persist.

Nine in the Third Place
幹 父 之 蠱
Tree trunk, Strength Father Of Venom (severe
小 有 悔 无 大 咎
mistake) Small Have Regret No Big, Great Blame
A strong father can make severe mistakes.
But have little regret. No major blame.

Six in the Fourth Place
裕 父 之 蠱
Loose, Leisure, Easy Father Of Venom (severe
往 吝
mistake) Go ahead See, Look Blame
A permissive father can make severe mistakes.
If he continues, he will see blame.

Six in the Fifth Place
幹 父 之 蠱
Tree trunk, Strength Father Of Venom (severe
用 譽
mistake) Use, Act Recognition, Honor
A strong father can make mistakes.
Nevertheless, act with honor.

Nine in the Sixth Place (Top)
不 事 王 侯 高
Not Work, Service, Thing King Duke High
尚 其 事
Character Its, The Work, Service, Thing
Do not be servile to the king and the nobles.
Keep high principles in one's work.

19 臨 Lin

(Coming. Approach)

The Judgment

元 亨 利 貞
Greatness No obstruction Benefit Perseverance
至 于 八 月 有
Toward, Arrival At, In Eight Month Have
凶
Misfortune

Greatness. No obstruction.
Benefit in perseverance.
As August arrives, there will be misfortune.

The Lines

Nine at the Bottom (Beginning)
咸 臨 貞 吉
All Coming, Approach Perseverance Good fortune
All approach together.
Perseverance brings good fortune.

Nine in the Second Place
咸 臨 吉 无 不 利
All Coming, Approach Good fortune No No Benefit
All approach together. Good fortune.
Everything will be favorable ("nothing no benefit").

Six in the Third Place
甘 臨 无 攸
Sweet, Tasteful, Easy Coming, Approach No Long
利 既 憂 之 无 咎
Benefit Then, Already Worry, Concern Of No Blame
Easy approach. No long term benefit.
If one is already concerned, no blame.

Six in the Fourth Place
至 臨 无
At the top, Arrival Coming, Approach No
咎
Blame, Error
Approach the top.
No blame (or error).

Six in the Fifth Place
臨 大 君 之
Wisdom Coming, Approach Great King Of
宜 吉
Harmonious, Comfortable Good fortune
A wise approach, as is due to a great king, brings good fortune (implies that people in high places should be approached with wisdom).

Six in the Sixth Place (Top)
敦 臨 吉
Honesty, Generosity Coming, Approach Good fortune
无 咎
No Blame, Mistake
An honest and generous approach brings good fortune.
No mistake.

20 觀 Kuan

(Observation. Look. View)

The Judgment

觀 盥 而
Observe, Look Hand washing, Preparation But, And
不 薦 有 孚 顒
Not Offer Have Trust, Sincerity Dignity, Respect
若
As, Like

Prepare but do not yet make the offering.
Be sincere and respectful (one washes one's hands before offering in worship).

The Lines

Six at the Bottom (Beginning)
童 觀 小 人 无 咎
Child Observation, View Small Man No Blame,
君 子 吝
Mistake Superior Man Blame, Mistake
A child's view, for the lesser man, brings no blame.
For the superior man, it is a mistake.

Six in the Second Place
闚 觀 利 女 貞
Peep Observation, Look Benefit Woman Perseverance
Peeping out to observe can be beneficial if a woman perseveres.

Six in the Third Place
觀 我 生 進 退
Observation, Look My Life Advance Retreat
Looking over my own life, I can choose to advance or retreat.

Six in the Fourth Place
觀 國 之 光
Observation Country Of Brightness, Light
利 用 賓 于 王
Benefit Use, Act Guest At, To King
Observing that the country is bright, one will benefit by going to the king (becoming a "guest of the king").

Nine in the Fifth Place
觀 我 生 君 子 无 咎
Observation, Look My Life Superior Man No Blame
In looking over his own life, the superior man is without blame.

Nine in the Sixth Place (Top)
觀 其 生 君
Observation, Look Its, His Life Superior
子 无 咎
Man No Blame
Looking over the life of another, the superior man is without blame. (The implication, in lines five and six together, is that one should look at both one's own behavior and that of others.)

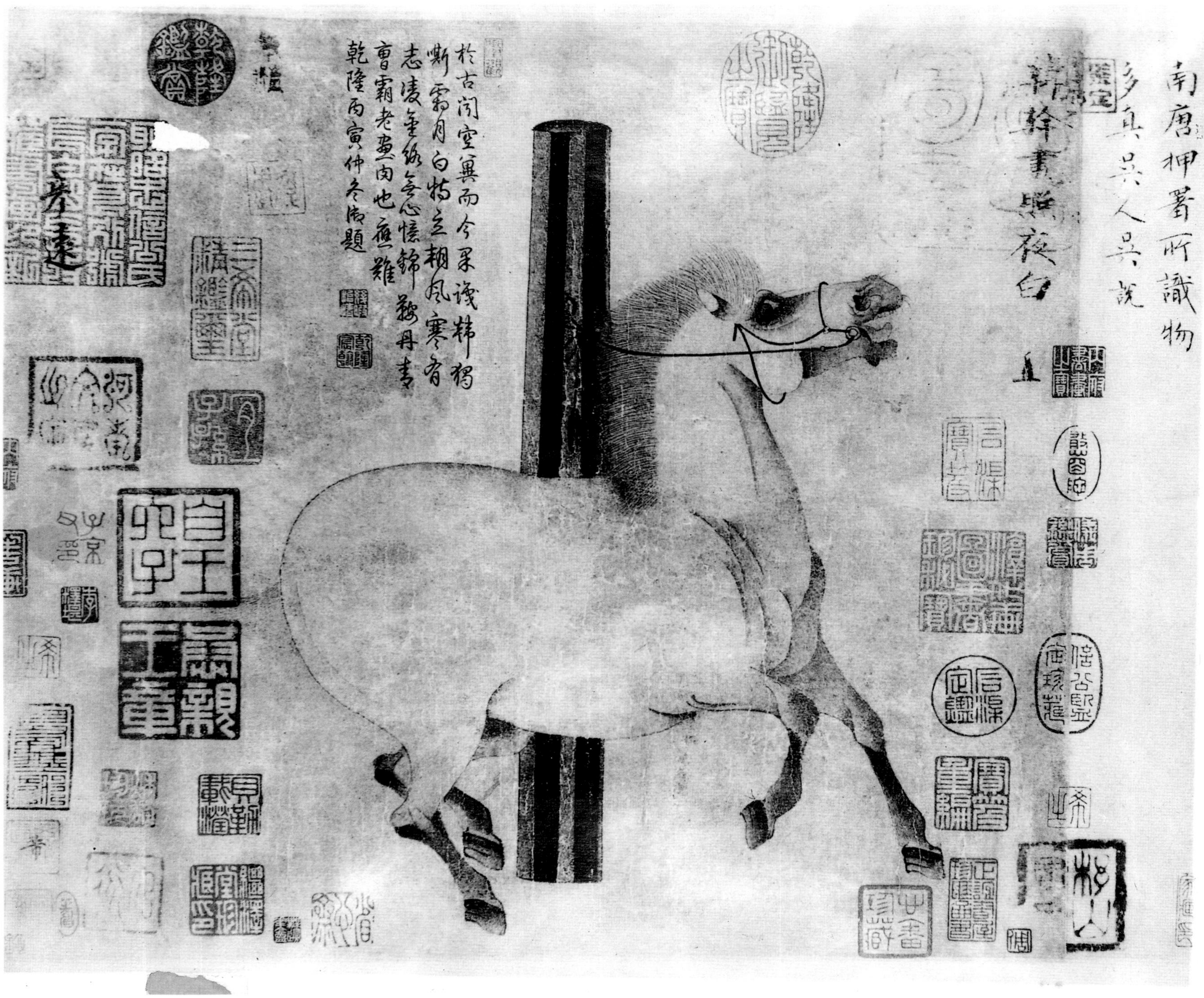

21 噬嗑 ䷔ *Shih Ho* (Biting. Chewing)

The Judgment

噬 嗑 亨
Biting, Chewing, Biting through No obstruction
利 用 獄
Benefit Use, Act Prison, Restraint

Carrying through ("biting through") clears the way ("no obstruction").
Benefit to use legal restraints ("prison").

The Lines

Nine at the Bottom (Beginning)

屨 校 滅 趾 无 咎
Walk, Step Shackle Covered Toe No Blame

Walking in shackles with toes covered (and therefore walking with difficulty), one will not be blamed.
(Shackling the feet was considered a punishment less severe than shackling the neck and therefore this line implies that the punishment ahead will not be severe.)

Six in the Second Place

噬 膚 滅 鼻 无
Biting Skin Covered, Not seen Nose No
咎
Blame, Mistake

Carrying through vigorously ("biting into the skin" so deeply that "the nose" of the biter is hidden) is not a mistake.

Six in the Third Place

噬 腊 肉 遇 毒
Biting Dried, Hard Meat Meet, Encounter Poison
小 吝 无 咎
Small Blame, Humiliation No Mistake, Blame

Carrying through a difficult enterprise, one may encounter hurt ("biting hard meat encounters poison").
Small humiliation. No mistake.

Nine in the Fourth Place

噬 乾 胏 得
Biting Dried, Hard Meat with bone Get, Gain
金 矢 利 艱
Golden Arrow Benefit Hard, Firm
貞 吉
Persistence, Perseverance Good fortune

OPPOSITE: The sixth line of hexagram 22 compares a person who is simple in manner and benevolent in aim with a white speeding horse. Hankan (A.D. 75). *The Night-Shining White Steed.* Album leaf, ink on paper. Height 11¾". Tang dynasty. The Metropolitan Museum of Art, New York City.

In hexagram 21, the sixth line refers to the extreme restrictions that occur when one's extremities or neck are shackled. Japanese. *Military Officer in Shackle.* Fifteenth century. Collection Marquis de Ganay, Paris.

Carrying through a very difficult enterprise ("biting into hard, bony meat") gains much reward ("golden arrow").
Benefit in firm persistence. Good fortune.

A different interpretation is given by Chu Hsi: "In the Chou dynasty, to reach a person in high position, one had to give a rich gift, symbolized by 'golden arrow.'"

Six in the Fifth Place

噬 乾 肉 得 黃
Biting Dried, Hard Meat Gain, Need Yellow
金 貞 厲 无 咎
Gold Persistence Danger No Blame, Mistake

Carrying through an enterprise ("biting hard meat") gains a reward ("yellow gold").
Persistence is dangerous but not a mistake.

Legge's translation is: "The fifth line, divided, shows one gnawing at dried flesh, and finding yellow gold. Let him be firm and correct, realising the peril (of his position). There will be no error."

Nine in the Sixth Place (Top)

何 校 滅 耳 凶
Hold Shackle Hidden, Covered Ear Misfortune

Being held in a neck shackle (in a "shackle" deeply enough to cover the ears) brings misfortune. (Shackling the neck was equivalent to capital punishment. It was much more severe than shackling the feet. The implication here is that the severest form of misfortune is ahead.)

22 賁 *Pi* ䷕ (Adornment. Shining)

The Judgment

亨 小 利 有 攸往
No obstruction Small Benefit Have Far Go

No obstruction.
Small benefit if one goes far.

Wilhelm/Baynes interprets this differently, suggesting the meaning that in small matters it is beneficial to proceed.

The Lines

Nine at the Bottom (Beginning)

賁 其 趾 舍 車 而
Adornment The Toe Leave Carriage, Cart But, And
徒
Walk
Adorn the toes. Leave the carriage and walk. (Implication may be to aim at humility, taking the more humble method of walking rather than riding.)

Six in the Second Place
賁 其 須
Adornment Its, The Face, Hair, Beard
Adorn the beard. (Implication is that one should pay attention to the way one appears.)

Nine in the Third Place
賁 如 濡 如
Adornment, Shining As Wetness, Waiting long As
永 貞 吉
Forever, Always Perseverance Good fortune
Bright and patient, always persevering, one will have good fortune.

Chu Hsi's interpretation is: "One cannot always remain safe. Be always persevering."

Six in the Fourth Place
賁 如 皤 如 白 馬
Adornment As Very white As, Like White Horse
翰 如 匪 寇
Speeding (as in flying) As, Like Not Robber, Bandit
婚 媾
Marriage
Adorned in white on a white, speeding horse, he comes to ask for marriage, not to force it. (Implication may be that the person of simplicity—"white"—in manner and action aims at fellowship, not hostility. "White" also signifies purity.)

Wilhelm/Baynes's translation is: "Grace or simplicity?
A white horse comes as if on wings.
He is not a robber.
He will woo at the right time."

Six in the Fifth Place
賁 于 丘 園 束 帛 戔
Adornment On, At Hill Garden Roll Silk Small
戔 吝 終 吉
Small Blame, Humiliation Final Good fortune
Adorn the gardens on the hill.
Although the roll of silk is meager ("small small") and humiliating, finally there will be good fortune. (Implication is that one should do one's best with what one has. Then even if one has very little, good fortune will come.)

Nine in the Sixth Place (Top)
白 賁 无 咎
White Adornment No Blame
Simplicity in style ("white adornment") merits no blame.

23 剝 *Po* ䷖ (Peeling off. Splitting)

The Judgment
不 利 有 攸 往
No Benefit Have Far Go
No benefit to go far.

The Lines

Six at the Bottom (Beginning)
剝 牀 以 足 蔑
Splitting Bed With Foot Destroy
貞 凶
Perseverance, Persistence Misfortune
Splitting the feet from the bed will destroy it.
Persistence in this brings misfortune.

Six in the Second Place
剝 牀 以 辨 蔑 貞
Splitting Bed With Leg, Trunk Destroy Perseverance,
凶
Persistence Misfortune
Splitting the legs from the bed will destroy it.
Persistence in this brings misfortune.

Six in the Third Place
剝 之 无 咎
Splitting Of, It No Blame
Splitting it apart brings no blame.

Six in the Fourth Place
剝 牀 以 膚 凶
Splitting Bed With Skin, Close Misfortune
Splitting the bed to the skin brings misfortune.

Six in the Fifth Place
貫 魚 以 宮 人 寵
Connect Fish With Palace People (female) Beloved
无 不 利
No, Nothing No Benefit
Many of the palace ladies are beloved (connected "like a line of fish").
Extreme benefit ("nothing no benefit").

Other interpretations include Wilhelm/Baynes's: "A shoal of fishes. Favor comes through the court ladies. Everything acts to further."

Legge's is: "Shows (its subject leading on the others like) a string of fishes, and (obtaining for them) the favor that lights on the inmates of the palace. There will be advantage every way."

Blofield's is: "A string of fishes symbolizing high favor enjoyed by maids in the palace—everything is favorable. (This implies that ultimately we shall be entirely free from blame.)"

Nine in the Sixth Place (Top)
碩 果 不 食 君 子 得
Big Fruit Not Eat Superior Man Get, Receive
輿 小 人 剝 廬
Carriage Small, Lesser Man Splitting House
The large fruit is not eaten (implication is to look but not to eat).
The superior man receives a carriage (he receives a reward because he does not take).
The lesser man's house splits apart. (Implication is that the omens are favorable to a superior man but unfavorable to an inferior person.)

24 復 *Fu* ䷗ (Return. Recovery)

The Judgment
亨 出 入 无 疾 朋
No obstruction Out Into No Sickness Friend
來 无 咎 反 復
Come No Blame Turn over Return, Recovery
其 道 七 日 來
Its, The Tao, Natural way Seven Day Come
復 利 有 攸 往
Return, Recovery Benefit Have Far Go
No obstruction.
In and out without harm ("sickness").
Friends come without criticism ("blame").
Go back and forth in the proper way (according to the Tao).
In seven days, recovery will come.
Benefit in going further.

The Lines

Nine at the Bottom (Beginning)
不 遠 復 无 祇 悔 元 吉
Not Far Return No Big Regret Great Good fortune
Return from nearby ("not far").
No great regret.
Great good fortune.

Six in the Second Place
休 復 吉
Good Return, Recovery Good fortune
Good recovery. Good fortune.

Six in the Third Place
頻 復 厲 无 咎
Frequent Return, Recovery Danger No Blame
Repeated recoveries (or returns).
Danger but no blame.

Six in the Fourth Place
中 行 獨 復
Middle, Amidst Walking Single Return
One walks in a crowd; one returns alone.

Six in the Fifth Place
敦 復 无 悔
Honesty Return, Recovery No Regret
A forthright return brings no regret.

Six in the Sixth Place (Top)
迷 復 凶 有 災
Loss Return, Recovery Misfortune Have Calamity
眚 用 行 師 終 有 大
Sickness Use, Act Movement Army Final Have Big
敗 以 其 國 君 凶
Defeat As, With Its, The Country King Misfortune
至 于 十 年 不 克 征
Arrive To Ten Year Not Overcome Attack
Losing the chance to return brings misfortune.
One will have a disaster ("calamity and disease").
If one moves the army ahead, there will finally be a major defeat.
The king of the country will have misfortune.
For up to ten years, attack will not be possible.

25 无妄 *Wu Wang* (Unanticipated. Innocence. Not Wished)

The Judgment

元 亨 利 貞
Greatness No obstruction Benefit Perseverance
其 匪 正 有 眚
Its, The Not Righteousness Have Harm, Eye-sickness
不 利 有 攸 往
Not Benefit Have Far Go

Greatness. No obstruction.
Benefit in perseverance.
If not righteous, harm will follow.
No benefit to go further.

Nine at the Bottom (Beginning)

无 妄 往 吉
Not Anticipated, Wished Go Good fortune

Not anticipated.
Go ahead. Good fortune.

Six in the Second Place

穫 不 菑 畬
No Plough Harvest No Weeding Ground,
則 利 有 攸 往
Soil Then Benefit Have Far, Long Go

Do not plough, anticipating the harvest; nor weed the soil.
There is benefit to having far to go.
(Implication is not to expect too much from the land. Have a long-range view.)

Six in the Third Place

无 妄 之 災 或
Not Anticipated, Wished Of, As Disaster Of, As
繫 之 牛 行 人 之
Tether Of, As Cow Walking Man, People Of, As
得 邑 人 之 災
Gain Country Man, People Of, As Disaster

Unanticipated disaster.
As with a tethered cow, the passerby ("walking man") takes it, and the farmer ("country man") has a disaster.

Nine in the Fourth Place

可 貞 无 咎
May, Can Perseverance No Blame

If one can persevere, there is no blame.

Nine in the Fifth Place

无 妄 之
Not Anticipated, Wished Of, As
疾
Generalized sickness
勿 藥 有 喜
Not Medication Have Happiness, Well-being

Unanticipated sickness.
Do not take the medication (or treatment).
You will get well.

Nine in the Sixth Place (Top)

无 妄 行 有
Not Anticipated, Wished Walking Have
眚 无 攸 利
Harm, Eye-sickness No Far, Long Benefit

Unanticipated.
Action ("walking") will cause severe trouble ("eye-sickness").
No long-term benefit.

26 大畜 *Ta Ch'u* (Cultivation of the large. Restraint of the large)

Ta means large. *Ch'u* means cow, horse, sheep, chicken, pig (as a noun); or follow, feed, cultivate (as a verb).

The Judgment

利 貞 不 家 食 吉
Benefit Perseverance Not Home Eat Good fortune
利 涉 大 川
Benefit Cross Great River, Water

Benefit in persevering.
Not eating at home brings good fortune. (This may be advising generosity, since eating at home means not sharing with others.)
Benefit to cross the great water.

A different interpretation is given by Chu Hsi: "Do not depend on your family" ("not eat at home"). Go outside ("cross the great water").

The Lines

Nine at the Bottom (Beginning)

有 厲 利 巳
Have Danger Benefit Stop

There is danger.
Benefit to halt.

Nine in the Second Place

輿 說 輹
Wagon Loss Central beam, Axletree

The wagon loses its central support.

Nine in the Third Place

良 馬 逐 利
Good Horse Chase, Run ahead Benefit
艱 貞
Firm, Persistent Perseverance Day, Say, Sun (The
日
characters for these three words are almost alike)
閑 輿 衛
At rest, Practice Wagon Protect, Guard
利 有
Benefit Have
攸 往
Far Go

A good horse tries to run ahead.
Benefit in firm, continued perseverance.
Protect the wagon by daily practice.
Benefit to go ahead.
(One implication may be that learning and performance are best preserved by continual use.)

Six in the Fourth Place

童 牛 之 牿 元 吉
Child Bull, Cow Of Band, Bar Great Good fortune

A horn-protector ("band") on the young bull brings great good fortune. (Implication is to keep potential force under restraint.)

Six in the Fifth Place

豶 豕 之 牙 吉
Castrated boar Boar Of Teeth, Tusks Good fortune

The tusks of a castrated boar.
Good fortune. (The implication may be that by castrating the boar, his potentially harmful tusks are made harmless; that prevention of danger keeps menace in check.)

Nine in the Sixth Place (Top)

何 天 之 衢 亨
How, What Heaven Of Wide road No obstruction

How broad is the way to heaven!
The path is open ("no obstruction").

27 頤 *I* (Corners of the Mouth. Nourishment. Feeding)

The Judgment

貞 吉 觀
Perseverance Good fortune Look
頤
Corners of the mouth, Feeding
自 求 口 實
Self Gain Mouth Full

Perseverance brings good fortune.
Look to one's own feeding and one will gain nourishment ("mouth full"; the implication is to look to one's own way of living for improvement in oneself).

The Lines

Nine at the Bottom (Beginning)

舍 爾 靈 龜 觀
Give away Your Magic Tortoise, Fortune Look
我 朵 頤 凶
My Drooping Corners of the mouth Misfortune

If you squander ("give away") your own substance ("magic tortoise" signifies fortune and independence), and then stare at what someone else has ("drooping mouth," meaning ready to begin to eat), you will have misfortune.

Six in the Second Place

顛 頤
Tilted, Tipsy Corners of the mouth, Nourishment
拂 經 于 丘
Against, Disregard Doctrine, Principles At, On Hill
頤 征
Corners of the mouth, Nourishment Attack
凶
Misfortune

Insecure ("tipsy") in nourishment.
Disregarding correct principles.
Nourishment is in higher places ("on the hill").
Try to conquer misfortune.
(Some translators see the meaning as being advice against seeking nourishment from either below or above one's station.)

Six in the Third Place

拂 頤
Against, Disregard Corners of the mouth,
貞 凶 十 年
Nourishment Perseverance Misfortune Ten Years
勿 用 无 攸 利
Not Use, Act No Far, Long Benefit

Persistence in disregarding nourishment brings misfortune.
Do not act for ten years.
No long-term benefit.

Six in the Fourth Place

顛 頤
Tilted, Tipsy Corners of the mouth, Nourishment
吉 虎 視 眈眈 其
Good fortune Tiger Look Fierce looking The, Its
欲 逐 逐 无 咎
Desire Chase Chase No Blame
Insecure nourishment. Good fortune.
Like a fierce-looking tiger, if one desires to jump ahead, one has no blame. (The implication is that if circumstances are uncertain, one has no blame in trying to further oneself.)

Six in the Fifth Place

拂 經 居
Against, Disregard Doctrine, Principles Remain
貞 吉 不 可 涉 大
Perseverance Good Fortune Not Can Cross Great
川
River, Water
Disregarding the correct principles, but• nevertheless remaining persevering, one will have good fortune.
You should not cross the great water.

Nine in the Sixth Place (Top)

由 頤
From, Depend Corners of the mouth, Feeding
厲 吉 利 涉 大
Danger Good fortune Benefit Cross Great
川
River, Water
Dependent feeding (depending on others) is dangerous.
But there is good fortune.
Benefit to cross the great water.

28 大過 *Ta Kuo*

(Excess. Too Much)

The Judgment

棟 橈 利 有
Ridgepole, Central beam Bend Benefit Have
攸 往 亨
Far Go No obstruction
The supporting beam bends.
Benefit to go far.
The way is open ("no obstruction").

The Lines

Six at the Bottom (Beginning)

藉 用 白 茅 无 咎
Rely on Use, Act White Rushes No Mistake, Blame
Rely on acting cleanly ("use white rushes").
No blame.

Nine in the Second Place

枯 楊 生 梯
Withered Poplar Grow Sprout, Root
老 夫
Old husband, Man
得 其 女 妻
Gain Its, His Girl, Young woman Wife No,
无 不 利
Nothing No Benefit
The withered poplar grows a sprout.
The old man gains a young girl as wife.
All is beneficial ("nothing no benefit").

Nine in the Third Place

棟 橈 凶
Ridgepole, Central beam Bend, Sag Misfortune
The supporting beam sags.
Misfortune.

Nine in the Fourth Place

棟 隆 吉
Ridgepole, Central beam Upward Good fortune
有 它 吝
Have Other Mistake, Blame
The supporting beam curves upward (implies that it is braced).
Good fortune.
But there may be other errors.

Nine in the Fifth Place

枯 楊 生 華 老 婦 得
Withered Poplar Grow Flower Old Woman Gain
其 士 夫 无 咎 无
Its, The Intellectual Husband No Blame No
譽
Honor, Praise
The withered poplar grows flowers.
The old woman gets a high-class husband ("intellectual").
No blame. No praise. (The implication may be that the situation is temporary.)

Six in the Sixth Place (Top)

過 涉
Excess, Too much Cross (Walking *in* the water is
滅
implied by this character) Disappear
頂 凶 无 咎
Top of the head Misfortune No blame
One walks into the water over one's head ("disappear top of the head").
Unfortunate but no blame.
(Implication is that if one does too much beyond one's capability, it is unfortunate, but one cannot be blamed for trying.)

29 坎 *K'an*

(Trap. Abyss. Depth)

The Judgment

習 坎 有 孚
Repeat, Redouble Trap, Abyss, Danger Have Sincere
維 心 亨
Only, Nothing but Heart, Inside No obstruction
行 有 尚
Walk, Move Have Honor, Fulfillment of a wish
The danger recurs ("trap repeated").
If you are nothing but sincere and honest in your heart, there is no obstruction.
Go ahead and get your wish fulfilled.

The Lines

Six at the Bottom (Beginning)

習 坎 入 于
Repeat, Redouble Trap, Abyss, Danger Into At
坎 窞 凶
Trap, Abyss, Danger Deep trap Misfortune
The danger recurs ("trap repeated").
Into a very deep trap.
Misfortune.

Nine in the Second Place

坎 有 險 求 小 得
Trap, Abyss, Danger Have Danger Seek Small Gain
The trap is dangerous.
Seek small gain.

Six in the Third Place

來 之 坎
Come, Approach Of Trap, Abyss, Depth
坎 險 且 枕 入 于
Trap, Abyss, Depth Danger And Obstacle Into At
坎 窞 勿 用
Trap, Abyss, Depth Deep trap Not Use, Act
Approach the deep abyss ("abyss, abyss").
Danger and obstacle are there.
Enter the very deep abyss ("abyss, deep abyss") but do not act.

Six in the Fourth Place

樽 酒 簋
Jug, Jar Wine Container of wood or bamboo for food
貳 用
Second in position, Better, Doubt Use, Act
缶 納 約 自
Earthen jar Accept, Receive Gift, Offering From
牖 終 无 咎
Window Finally No Blame
A jug of wine. A basket of food.
Or even an earthen jar. (These indicate simple objects.)
Receive offerings through the window (implies without the need for ceremony).
In the end, no blame. (Implication is that simple offerings without ceremony are not humiliating.)

Nine in the Fifth Place

坎 不 盈 祗
Trap, Abyss, Danger Not Full Respect, Pray, Only
既 平 无 咎
Then, And Level, Smooth No Blame
The trap is not full.
Pray for calm ("smooth").
No blame.

Wilhelm/Baynes's translation is: "The abyss is not filled to overflowing, it is filled only to the rim. No blame."

Six in the Sixth Place (Top)

係 用 徽 纆 寘 于
Bound, Tied up Use, Act Big Rope Put, Place In, At
叢 棘 三 歲 不 得 凶
Group Thorns Three Years No Gain Misfortune
Bound with large ropes.
Placed in a thorny bush ("group thorns").
For three years, no gain.
Misfortune.

30 離 *Li*

(Fire. Clinging. Brightness)

(The character for *Li* has several meanings, depending on how it is used and pronounced. Originally it may have meant "beauty." Now it is also used to mean "separate." *Li* also implies "adhering to" and therefore "clinging" as does a fire, according to the Chinese.)

Hexagram 30 (*Li*; fire), is formed by the trigram Li (☲ fire) doubled, emphasizing the brightness and clinging property of fire. *Hell Scene* from the handscroll *Jigoku Soshi*. Kamakura period (c. A.D.1200). Ink and color on paper. Height 10¾″. Seattle Art Museum.

The Judgment

利 貞 亨 畜
Benefit Perseverance No obstruction Feed
牝 牛 吉
Male Cattle Good fortune

Benefit in perseverance. No obstruction. Feed the bull. Good fortune.

The Lines

Nine at the Bottom (Beginning)

履 錯 然 敬 之
Walk, Step Wrong, Away As Respect It, The
无 咎
No Blame

Avoid it ("walk away"). Respect it. No blame.

Six in the Second Place

黃 離 元 吉
Yellow Fire, Brightness, Light Great Good fortune

Yellow brightness. Great good fortune. ("Yellow" implies correctness.)

Nine in the Third Place

日 昃 之 離 不 鼓
Sun Afternoon Of Fire, Brightness, Light Not Beat
缶 而 歌 則 大 耋 之
Pot And Sing Then, And Big Aged, Old age Of
嗟 凶
Bewail, Bemoan Misfortune

In the light of the afternoon sun, do not beat the pot and sing loudly, bewailing old age.
Misfortune. (Implication is to avoid loud complaints of growing old.)

Nine in the Fourth Place

突 如其 來 如 焚 如 死 如
Sudden As It Come As Burn As Die As
棄 如
Give up, Yield As

Suddenly it comes, burns, dies, and disappears. (Just like fire.)

Six in the Fifth Place

出 涕 沱 若 戚
Out Tears Draining from nose Like, Appears Sadness
嗟 若 吉
Bewail, Lament Like, Appears Good fortune

The appearance of crying ("out tears draining from the nose like"). Appearance of sadness and lamentation.
Good fortune. (Implication is that although the appearance of things is bad, good fortune is ahead.)

Nine in the Sixth Place (Top)

王 用 出 征 有 嘉
King Use, Act Out Attack Have Praise, Reward
折 首 獲 匪 其 醜
Broken Head Capture Bandit The Ugly, Nasty
无 咎
No Blame

If the king acts by attacking, there will be rewards and punishments ("broken heads").
He will capture the nasty bandit.
No blame.

Wilhelm/Baynes translates this line to mean that the king uses someone to march out and chastise; that the best course is to destroy the leaders and take prisoners.

31 咸 Hsien (Influence)

The Judgment

亨 利 貞 取
No obstruction Benefit Perseverance Marry, Take
女 吉
Woman Good fortune

No obstruction.
Benefit in perseverance.
If one marries a woman, there will be good fortune.

The Lines

Six at the Bottom (Beginning)

咸 其 拇
Influence The, Its Big toe

Influence is in the big toe (implication is that the influence is just beginning or is superficial).

Six in the Second Place

咸 其 腓 凶 居
Influence The, Its Leg (lower) Misfortune Stay
吉
Good fortune

Influence is in the lower leg (influence is increasing, up from the toe).
Misfortune.
Staying brings good fortune.

Nine in the Third Place

咸 其 股 執 其
Influence The, Its Thigh Hold, Keep The, Its
隨 往 吝
Follow Go Blame, Mistake

Influence is in the thigh (it advances further: from toe to leg to thigh).
Continue in the same way ("follow").
If you act differently ("go" away), it is a mistake.

Nine in the Fourth Place

貞 吉 悔
Perseverance Good fortune Persevere, Regret
亡 憧 憧 往 來
Die, Disappear Wavering, Irresolute Go Come
朋 從 爾 思
Friend, Same kind of person Follow Your Thought

Perseverance brings good fortune.
Regret disappears.
If indecisive ("wavering") and purposeless ("go come"), only your friends will follow your thoughts.

Nine in the Fifth Place

咸 其 脢 无 悔
Influence The, Its Back No Blame

Influence is in the back (suggesting that it has risen higher, reaching the upper back but not yet to the vital parts).

Another translator's version is that the back implies firmness and resistance to influence.

Six in the Sixth Place (Top)

咸 其 輔 頰 舌
Influence The, Its Bone Cheek Tongue

Influence is in the jaws ("cheekbones") and the tongue. (Speech is implied; in ancient China thinking and talking are inferior to doing.)

32 恒 Hêng (Endurance. Continuation. Maintenance)

The Judgment

亨 无 咎 利 貞
No obstruction No Blame Benefit Perseverance
利 有 攸 往
Benefit Have Far Go

No obstruction. No blame.
Benefit in perseverance.
Benefit to go far.

The Lines

Six at the Bottom (Beginning)

浚 恒
Deep, Digging Endurance, Continuation
貞 凶 无 攸 利
Perseverance, Persistence Misfortune No Long Benefit

Digging deeply and persistently brings misfortune.
No long-term benefit. (The implication is that trying to penetrate too deeply is not wise.)

Nine in the Second Place

悔 亡
Remorse, Regret Dies, Disappears

Remorse disappears.

Nine in the Third Place

不 恒 其 德
Not Endurance, Continuation The, Its Morality
或 承 之 羞
Or Take, Hold Of Disgrace, Shame
貞 吝
Perseverance, Persistence Blame

Discontinuing ("not continuing") one's morality will bring disgrace.
Persisting in this way brings misfortune.

Nine in the Fourth Place

田 无 禽
Field No Game, Birds

No game in the field. (The implication is that there is nothing to gain.)

Six in the Fifth Place

恒 其
Continuation, Endurance The, Its Morality
德 貞 婦 人
(Traditional ruler) Perseverance Woman Person,
吉 夫
People Good fortune Husband (Intellectual)
子 凶
Son (Sir) Misfortune ("Intellectual sir" indicates a gentleman)

Following the traditional rules of perseverance by a woman brings good fortune.
For a gentleman, it is misfortune. (The implication is that a woman should be steadfast in following rules, but not a man.)

Confucius suggested that a woman should cleave to one husband to the end but that a man might marry more than one woman. Other broader interpretations state that a woman should uphold traditions steadfastly but that a man should adapt to circumstances.

Six in the Sixth Place (Top)

振
Frequent movement, Repetition, Vibration

恒 凶
Continuation Misfortune

Agitation ("frequent movement") continued brings misfortune.

33 遯 *Tun* (Retreat)

The Judgment

亨 小 利 貞
No obstruction Small Benefit Perseverance

No obstruction. In small things, benefit in perseverance.

The Lines

Six at the Bottom (Beginning)

遯 尾 厲 勿 用 有
Retreat Tail Danger Not Use, Act Have

攸 往
Long, Far Go

Retreat at the rear ("tail") is dangerous. Do not go far away (or too far).

Six in the Second Place

執 之 用 黃 牛 之 革
Hold, Keep Of Use, Act Yellow Cattle Of Skin

莫 之 勝 說
Not Of Convince, Win Word

Holding firmly ("cattle of skin" means an ox hide) you cannot be won over ("win words"). ("Yellow" may refer to the middle or prudent way. If one holds to the correct line, one cannot be swayed.)

Nine in the Third Place

係 遯 有 疾 厲 畜
Bound, Tied Retreat Have Severe Danger Feed

臣 妾
Officials, Officers Second Wife, Concubine

吉
Good fortune

Restraining retreat is markedly dangerous.
Taking care of those in secondary position ("officers," "second wife") brings good fortune.
Wilhelm/Baynes's translation is: "A halted retreat
Is nerve-wracking and dangerous.
To retain people as men and maidservants
brings good fortune."

Legge's is: "Shows one retiring but bound, to his distress and peril. (If he were to deal with his binders as in) nourishing a servant or concubine, it would be fortunate for him."

Shchutskii's is: "For him who is connected with runaways there will be sickness and danger. For him who has male and female servants, good fortune."

Nine in the Fourth Place

好 遯 君 子
Good, Favorable Retreat King, Respected Son, Sir

吉 小 人 否
Good fortune Small Person Unfortunate

A favorable retreat brings good fortune to the superior man ("respected sir").
It is unfortunate for the inferior person.
(The implication is that the superior person knows when to withdraw.)

Nine in the Fifth Place

嘉 遯 貞 吉
Praise Retreat Perseverance Good fortune

Praiseworthy retreat. Perseverance brings good fortune.

Nine in the Sixth Place (Top)

肥 遯 无 不 利
Fatty, Leisure Retreat Not No Benefit

Leisurely retreat. Some benefit ("not no benefit").

34 大壯 *Ta Chuana* (Great Strength)

The Judgment

大 壯 利 貞
Great Strength Benefit Perseverance

Great strength. Benefit in perseverance.

The Lines

Nine at the Bottom (Beginning)

壯 于 趾 征 凶
Strength At, In Toe Attack, Conquer Misfortune

有 孚
Have Trust

Strength in the toes. Attack brings misfortune.
Have trust.

(See hexagram 31's bottom line, which deals with "influence in the toes," referring to the start of something. "Toes" may also indicate the lowest part of the body and symbolically the lowest class, which is here advised not to use force.)

Nine in the Second Place

貞 吉
Perseverance Good fortune

Perseverance brings good fortune.

Nine in the Third Place

小 人 用 壯 君 子
Small Person Use, Act Strength Superior Man, Person

用 罔 貞 厲
Use, Act Nothing Perseverance, Persistence Danger

羝 羊 觸 藩 羸
Male Goat Butt Hedge Wrapped, Constrained

其 角
The, Its Horn

The inferior person uses strength.
The superior person does not.
Persistence is dangerous.
The ram butts the hedge which entangles his horns. (Implication is that the use of force can be self-defeating.)

Nine in the Fourth Place

貞 吉 悔
Perseverance Good fortune Regret, Remorse

亡 藩 決 不
Die, Disappear Hedge Open Not

羸 壯 于 大 輿 之
Wrapped, Constrained Strength At, In Big Cart Of

輹
Axle

Perseverance brings good fortune.
Regret disappears. The hedge opens without entanglement.
Strength is in the axle (and therefore the hidden underpart) of the large cart.

Six in the Fifth Place

喪 羊 于 易
Lost Goat At, In Change (variously translated)

无 悔
No Regret

The goat is unexpectedly lost. No regret.

Legge's translation is: "Shows one who loses his ram (-like strength) in the ease of his position. (But) there will be occasion for repentance."

Six in the Sixth Place (Top)

羝 羊 觸 藩 不 能 退 不
Male Goat Butt Hedge Not Can Background Not

能 遂 无 攸 利 艱
Can Forward No Long Benefit Hard work

則 吉
Then, After Good fortune

The ram butts the hedge; cannot go backward or forward.
No long-term benefit by persisting.
Afterward, good fortune.

35 晉 *Chin* (Progress. Advance)

The Judgment

康 侯 用 錫 馬
Healthy, Rich Duke Use, Act Give Horse

蕃 庶 晝 日 三 接
Foreign Many, Common Daytime Day Three Receive

The honored noble ("rich duke") is given many exotic ("foreign") horses three times in a day (implication is "frequently"; a highly favorable meaning).

The Lines

Six at the Bottom (Beginning)

晉 如 摧
Progress, Advance As, Like Destroy, Check

如 貞 吉 罔 孚
As, Like Perseverance Good fortune No Trust

裕 无 咎
Wide open No Blame

One may advance but be checked.
Persevere. Good fortune.
If not trusted, remain open-minded.
No blame.

Six in the Second Place

晉 如 愁
Progress, Advance As, Like Sorrow, Sadness

如 貞 吉 受 茲
As, Like Perseverance Good fortune Receive This

介 福 于 其 王 母
Induce Happiness At The, Its King Mother

One may advance but there may be sadness.
Perseverance brings good fortune.

The line statement for six in the second place of hexagram 36 (*Ming I;* brightness diminishing) suggests that when in trouble, one should seek powerful and steadfast help, symbolized by a strong horse. *Horse.* Tang dynasty (A.D. 618–906). Glazed terra cotta. Height 30¼″. The Cleveland Museum of Art.

Receive that happiness that comes from one's ancestress ("king mother").

Six in the Third Place

衆 允 悔 亡
All Approve, Agree Remorse Die, Disappear
All approve. Remorse disappears.

Nine in the Fourth Place

晉 如 鼫 鼠
Progress, Advance As, Like Bad, Naughty Rodent
貞 厲
Perseverance, Persistence Danger
Advancing like a naughty rodent (sneakiness is implied), persistence is dangerous.

Wilhelm/Baynes translates the fourth Chinese character as "hamster." Legge calls it "marmot."

Six in the Fifth Place

悔 亡 失 得
Remorse, Regret Die, Disappear Loss Gain
勿 恤 往 吉
No Sympathy, Caring Go Good fortune
无 不 利
No, Not, Nothing No, Not, Nothing Benefit
Remorse disappears.
Lose or win, do not care.
Go forward. Good fortune.
Much benefit ("nothing no benefit").

Nine in the Sixth Place (Top)

晉 其 角 維 用
Progress, Advance The, Its Horn Only Use, Act
伐 邑 厲 吉 无 咎
Punish County Danger Good fortune No Blame,
貞 吝
Mistake Perseverance, Persistence Blame, Mistake
Attack ("advance the horns") only to punish the local region ("county").
There is danger but also good fortune.
No blame.
Persisting is a mistake (going too far is implied).

36 明夷 *Ming I* (Brightness diminishing. Obvious wound. Understanding lessened)

The Judgment

利 艱 貞
Benefit Firmness Perseverance
Benefit in firm perseverance.

The Lines

Nine at the Bottom (Beginning)

明 夷 于 飛
Brightness, Light Diminishing, Wounded In, At Fly
垂 其 翼 君 子 于
Drop, Lower Its, His Wing Superior Man In, At
行 三 日 不 食 有 攸 往
Walk, Action Three Day Not Eat Have Far Go
主 人 有 言
Master, Host Man Have Words
Brightness diminishes during flight.
Lower your wings.
The superior man continues on ("walks"), but does not eat for three days.
If you go far, the host may criticize ("have words"). (The implication is that if the conditions are not auspicious, one should adjust to them, "lower his wings." The superior man continues on his course and would rather starve than do the wrong thing.)

Six in the Second Place

明 夷
Brightness, Light Diminishing, Wounded
夷 于 左 股
Diminishing, Wounded At, In Left Thigh
用 拯 馬 壯 吉
Use, Act Save, Help Horse Strong Good fortune
Brightness diminishes.
Wounded in the left thigh (implies not a severe injury).
Give (or get) help with a strong horse.
Good fortune.
(Other implications could be that one should ride on a strong horse. The Chinese characters of this line may have been substituted for others, for there are similarities between riding a horse and a strong horse.)

Nine in the Third Place

明 夷
Brightness, Understanding Diminishing, Wounded
于 南 狩 得 其 大
At, In South Hunt Get, Gain The, Its Big, Great
首 不 可 疾 貞
Head No Can Extreme Perseverance, Persistence
Brightness diminishes.
Hunting in the wild ("south") gains a great prize ("big head").
One cannot go to the extremes of persistence.
(Originally the central kingdom was in the north. The south, therefore, was considered wild or crude.)

Six in the Fourth Place

入 于 左 腹 獲
Into At, In Left Belly, Side Gain, Get
明 夷 之
Brightness, Understanding Diminishing, Darkening Of
心 于 出 門 庭
Heart, Mind At, In Out Door, Gate Yard
One gets into the guts of the darkness ("into left side or belly of the darkness," in its very "heart"), by going outside the gate of the yard.
(One penetrates the meaning of darkness by moving outside one's own boundaries.)

Six in the Fifth Place

箕 子 之 明
Chi Sir, Prince Of, As Brightness, Understanding
夷 利 貞
Diminishing, Wrong Benefit Perseverance
As with Prince Chi, the understanding may be wrong.
But there is benefit in persisting in one's principles.
(Prince Chi, a storied sage in the tyrannical Chou Hsin dynasty, pretended he was insane in order to maintain his critical views of the ruling regime.)

Six in the Sixth Place (Top)

不 明 晦 初
Not Brightness, Light Darkness Beginning
登 于 天 後 入 于 地
Step up At, In Heaven Later Into At, In Earth
Not light but darkness ahead.
One may climb toward heaven, but later one may fall back to earth.

37 家人 *Chia Jên* (Family Member)

The Judgment

利 女 貞
Benefit Woman Perseverance
Benefit for a woman to be persevering.

The Lines

Nine at the Bottom (Beginning)

閑 有 家 悔 亡
Defense Have Family Remorse, Regret Die, Disappear
Defense within the circle of the family.
Remorse disappears.

Six in the Second Place

无 攸 遂 在 中
No Further, Far Forward At, In Amidst, Middle
饋 貞 吉
Feed, Serve Perseverance Good fortune
Do not move forward if one is in the midst of serving.
Perseverance brings good fortune.
(This might imply that one should attend to one's duties to their completion before taking on something else.)

Nine in the Third Place

家 人 嗃 嗃 悔
Family Person Strictness Strictness Remorse, Regret
厲 吉
Seriousness Good fortune
婦
Woman, Wife, Mother
子 嘻 終
Son, Child Lightness, Play around Final
吝
Blame, Regret
If the family members are too strict, one may take the blame too much to heart ("seriously").
But there is good fortune.
If the mother and child are frivolous ("play around"), regret will come in the end. (Lines imply that discipline needs moderation. But too little control is unwise.)

Six in the Fourth Place

富 家 大 吉
Riches Family Great Good fortune
Enrich one's family.
Great good fortune.

Nine in the Fifth Place

王 假 有 家 勿 恤
King Toward Have Family Not Sympathy, Worry
吉
Good fortune
The king becomes close to his family.
Do not worry. Good fortune will come. (Implies

that a king should first care for his family in order to take care of the country well. So also should the head of a household act.)

Nine in the Sixth Place (Top)

有 孚 威 如 終 吉
Have Trust, Sincerity Dignity As Final Good fortune
Be sincere and have dignity.
Finally good fortune.

38 睽 *K'uei* ䷥ (Disunity. Opposition. Disagreement. Difference)

The Judgment

小 事 吉
Small Thing Good fortune
In small things, good fortune.

The Lines

Nine at the Bottom (Beginning)

悔 亡 喪 馬
Remorse, Regret Die, Disappear Loss Horse
勿 逐 自 復 見 惡
Not Look, Seek Self Back See, Look at Evil
人 无 咎
Man, Person No Blame, Harm
Remorse disappears.
Do not search for the lost horse.
It will return by itself.
One may look at evil people, but there is no blame.

Nine in the Second Place

遇 主 于 巷 无 咎
Meet Master In Lane, By-way No Blame
If one meets one's master by chance ("in a by-way") there is no blame. (The implication is that a lord or master is not expected to be in a lesser street, but it should not be considered embarrassing.)

Six in the Third Place

見 輿 曳 其 牛
See, Look at Cart Overturn The, Its Ox
掣 其 人 天 且
Stop, Not moving The, Its Person, Man Heaven And
劓 无 初 有 終
Cut nose No Beginning Have End
See the cart overturned.
The ox cannot go forward.
A man may be naked and receive punishment ("cut nose") but what has begun will finally end. ("Person heaven" can indicate "naked" in common parlance in Chinese.)

Nine in the Fourth Place

睽 孤 遇 元
Difference, Opposition Alone Meet Great, First Man,
夫 交 孚 厲 无 咎
Husband Contact Trust Danger No Blame, Mistake
Alone in opposition, if one meets a high-minded man, both should trust each other.
There is danger but it is not a mistake.

Six in the Fifth Place

悔 亡
Remorse, Regret Die, Disappear
厥
Defect, Deficiency (this character has many possible

宗 噬 膚 往 何 咎
meanings) Origin, Ancestor Bite Skin Go How Blame
Remorse disappears.
If one bites through the skin of one's original defects and goes on, how can one be blamed.

Nine in the Sixth Place (Top)

睽 孤 見 豕
Disagreement, Opposition Alone See Pig
負
Covered, Held
塗 載 鬼 一 車 先
Mud Load Ghost One Cart Early
張 之 弧 後 說 之 弧 匪 寇
Open Of Bow Later Loosen Of Bow Not Robber
婚 媾 往 遇 雨 則 吉
Marry Marry Go Meet Rain Then Good fortune
Alone in opposition, one sees a pig covered with mud.
An entire cart is loaded with ghosts (this may mean it is empty).
At first, he draws his bow.
Later he loosens his bow.
He is not a robber, but one who wishes to join ("marry, marry").
Go ahead, receive the rainfall and then good fortune. (The implication may be that appearances can be deceiving. What seems to be hostile may actually be friendly. Another possibility is that the person with an unpopular opinion may look at all others as unsavory creatures whom he is ready to attack, only to realize that what he fancied is not there, "empty." The rainfall is a symbol of relief and also of good luck.)

39 蹇 *Chien* ䷦ (Difficulty. Obstruction)

The Judgment

利 西 南 不 利 東 北 利
Benefit West South Not Benefit East North Benefit
見 大 人 貞 吉
See Great Man, Person Perseverance Good fortune
Benefit in the southwest.
No benefit in the northeast.
Benefit to see the great man.
Perseverance brings good fortune. (There are many views on the significance of the compass points in the *I Ching*. Generally, the northeast suggests difficulty, peril, or retreat.)

The Lines

Six at the Bottom (Beginning)

往 蹇 來 譽
Go Difficulty, Obstruction Come Praise, Honor

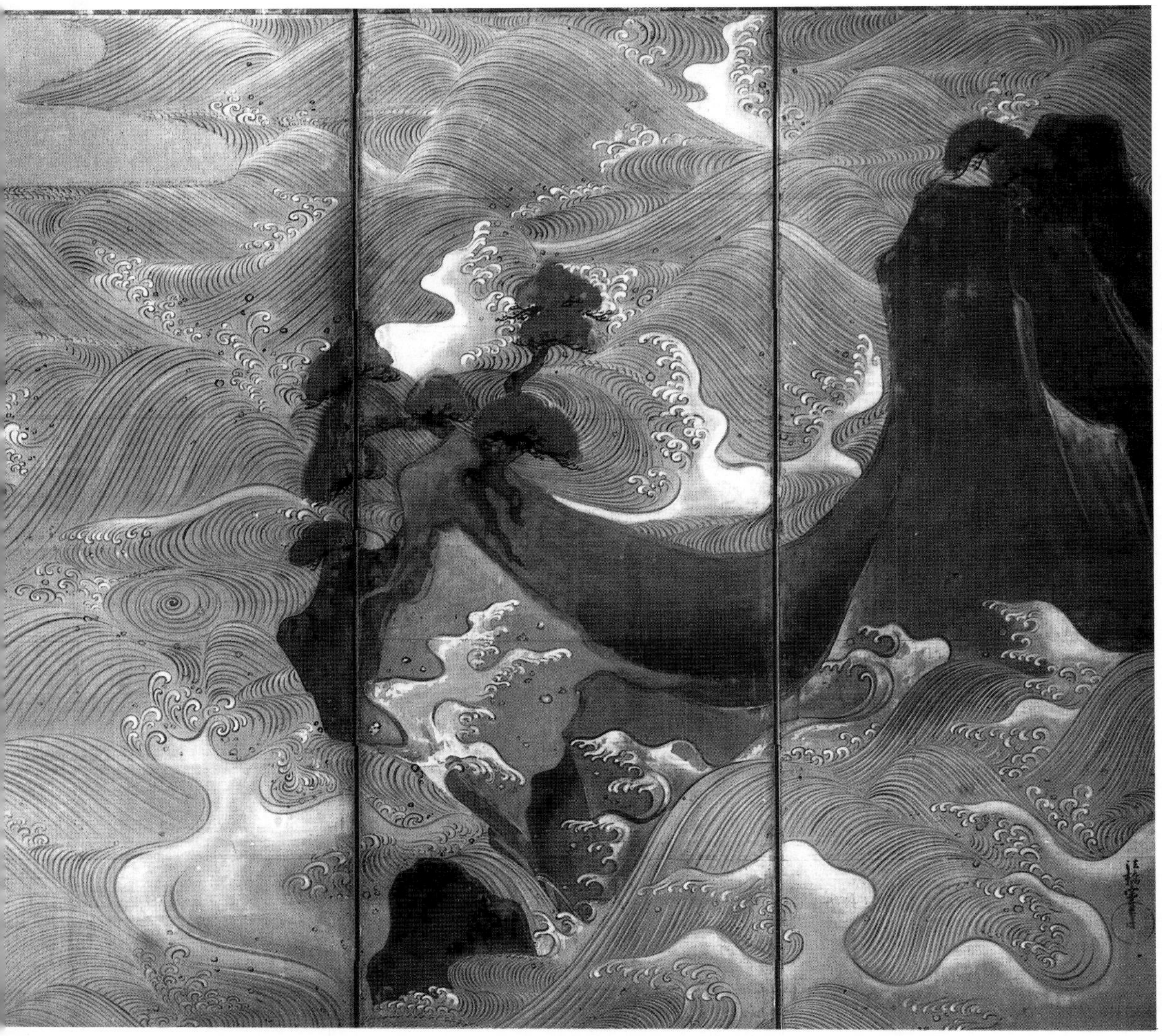

The trigram *K'an* (☵ abysmal) beneath and *Chên* (☳ thunder) above bring the rain, relief, and liberation of hexagram 40 (*Hsieh*). Nonomura Sōsatsu. *Waves at Matsushima* (painted screen). Early seventeenth century. Paper. Length 65½". Freer Gallery of Art, Washington, D.C.

Going ahead meets obstruction.
Honor will come.

Six in the Second Place

王 臣 蹇 蹇 匪 躬
King Officer Difficulty Difficulty Not Himself
之 故
The, Its Reason, Cause

The king's officer encounters difficulty upon difficulty.
He is not to blame ("not himself, the cause").

Nine in the Third Place

往 蹇 來 反
Go Difficulty Come Return

If going ahead meets difficulty, then turn back.

Six in the Fourth Place

往 蹇 來 連
Go Difficulty Come Union, Connection

If going ahead meets difficulty, come back to join with another.
(Implication is that together with an ally one can best meet difficulties.)

Nine in the Fifth Place

大 蹇 朋 來
Big Difficulty Friend Come

In the midst of great difficulty, friends will come.

Six in the Sixth Place (Top)

往 蹇 來 碩 吉
Go Difficulty Come Enormous Good fortune
利 見 大 人
Benefit See Great Man

Going ahead meets difficulty, but enormous good fortune will come.
Benefit to see the great man.

40 解 *Hsieh* ䷧ (Solution. Deliverance. Relief. Liberation)

The Judgment

利 西 南 无 所 往 其 來
Benefit West South No Place Go The, Its Come
復 吉 有 攸 往
Recover Good fortune Have Further, Far Go
夙 吉
Early morning Good fortune

Benefit in the southwest.
If there is no place to go, return ("come recover").
Good fortune.
If one goes far, go early in the day.
Good fortune.

The Lines

Six at the Bottom (Beginning)

无 咎
No Blame

No blame.

Nine in the Second Place

田 獲 三 狐 得 黃 矢
Field Catch Three Fox Gain Yellow Arrow
貞 吉
Perseverance Good fortune

If one catches many ("three") foxes in the field, one will gain a yellow arrow (implies reward).
Perseverance brings good fortune. ("Foxes" implies things crafty and undesirable.)

Six in the Third Place

負 且 乘 致 寇
Carry And, Also Ride Attract, Induce Robber, Bandit
至 貞 吝
Arrive Persistence, Perseverance Blame, Harm

If one carries something and also rides, this will induce a bandit to arrive.
Persistence will lead to harm.
(The implication is that one should not show off one's possessions.)

Nine in the Fourth Place

解 而
Relief, Deliverance And, But Great
拇 朋 至 斯 孚
toe, Thumb, Beginning Friend Arrive Then Trust

Relief at the beginning.
A friend will come.
Confidence follows.
(The character for "great toe" originally meant "beginning," according to some scholars. To others, the character means "thumb," suggesting massage and, therefore, smoothing over.)

Six in the Fifth Place

君 子 維 有 解
Superior Man, Person Only Have Relief, Deliverance
吉 有 孚 于 小 人
Good fortune Have Trust To, At Small Person

Only the superior person can deliver himself.
Good fortune.
Lowly people will then trust him.

Six in the Sixth Place (Top)

公 用 射 隼
Duke (Person in high position) Use, Act Shoot Hawk
于 高 墉 之 上 獲 之 无 不 利
At High Wall Of Top Catch Of Nothing No Benefit

The high official shoots at a hawk (implies a problem) at the top of a high wall, hits it, and receives much benefit ("nothing no benefit").
(The implication is that a person of high position must take aim even at a difficult problem to try to solve it. Much benefit will follow.)

41 損 *Sun* ䷨ (Decrease. Hurt. Harm. Injury)

The Judgment

有 孚 元 吉 无
Have Trust, Sincerity Great Good fortune No

咎 可 貞 利 有 攸 往
Blame May, Can Perseverance Benefit Have Far Go
Be sincere. Great good fortune. No blame.
One can persevere.
Benefit to go far.

The Lines

Nine at the Bottom (Beginning)
已 事 遄 往 无 咎
Past Thing, Thing done Quick Go No Blame, Regret
酌 損 之
Reflect, Consider Decrease, Harm It, Them
Past things have been hastily done.
Have no regrets. Reflect on whether one has harmed others. (Another interpretation might be: consider decreasing your goals.)

Nine in the Second Place
利 貞 征 凶
Benefit Perseverance Attack, Advance Misfortune
弗 損 益 之
Not Decrease Increase It
Benefit in perseverance.
Attack (or advance) brings misfortune.
Do not decrease or increase.

Six in the Third Place
三 人 行 則 損 一
Three Man, Person Walk Then Hurt, Decrease One
人 一 人 行 則 得
Man, Person One Man, Person Walk Then Gain
其 友
The, Its Friend
When three people walk together, one may drop out (or disagree).
When one person walks alone, he may gain a friend.

Six in the Fourth Place
損 其 疾 使
Decrease, Lessen The, Its Disease, Fault Make
遄 有 喜 无 咎
Quick Have Happiness No Blame, Mistake
If one lessens one's faults promptly, one will find happiness.
No blame.

Six in the Fifth Place
或 益 之 十 朋 之
May, Or Increase Of Ten Amount Of
龜 弗 克
Tortoise, Money, Luck Not Overcome
違 元 吉
Oppose, Against Great Good fortune
If someone gives you much ("ten amount") money, do not refuse it.
Great good fortune (which a tortoise symbolizes).

Another, similar interpretation is: if good luck comes your way, do not oppose it.
Wilhelm/Baynes's translation is: "Someone does indeed increase him.
Ten pairs of tortoises cannot oppose it. Supreme good fortune."

Nine in the Sixth Place (Top)
弗 損 益 之 无 咎 貞
Not Decrease Increase It No Blame Perseverance
吉 利 有 攸 往 得
Good fortune Benefit Have Far Go Get, Gain
臣 无 家
Official, Obedience No Home, Self, Family
Do not decrease or increase. No blame.
Perseverance brings good fortune.
Benefit to go further.
Get an assistant who is without selfishness ("no family"; the implication is that an assistant or official should take care of others before his own family).

Wilhelm/Baynes translates the last four characters as: "One obtains servants but no longer has a separate home."

Legge renders them as: "He will find ministers more than can be counted by their class."

42 益 *I* ䷩ (Increase)

The Judgment
利 有 攸 往 利 涉
Benefit Have Far Go Benefit Cross, Walk
大 川
Great Water
Benefit in going further.
Benefit in crossing the great water.

The Lines

Nine at the Bottom (Beginning)
利 用 爲 大 作 元
Benefit Use, Act For Big Action, Deed Great
吉 无 咎
Good fortune No Blame, Mistake
Benefit to aim at ("act for") great deeds.
Great good fortune.
No mistake.

Six in the Second Place
或 益 之 十 朋 之
Or, May Increase Of Ten Amount Of
龜 弗 克 違 永
Tortoise, Fortune Not Overcome Opposition Forever
貞 吉 王 用
Perseverance Good fortune King Use, Act
享 于 帝 吉
Worship At Emperor Good fortune
If much prosperity comes ("ten amount"), do not try to oppose it.
Perseverance always brings good fortune.
The king worships in the capital.
Good fortune. (The character meaning "king" or "emperor" may refer to a place, possibly the capital, according to some scholars. Others translate it as "God.")

Six in the Third Place
益 之 用 凶 事
Increase Of Use, Act Misfortune Thing, Business
无 咎 有 孚 中
No Blame Have Trust, Sincerity Middle
行 告 公 用
Way, Behavior Tell, Say Public Use, Act
圭
Jade insignia (implies sincerity)
Advantage can come from unfortunate things.
No blame.
Be sincere; follow the correct path ("middle way").
Speak out publicly with sincerity.

Six in the Fourth Place
中 行 告 公 從 利 用
Middle Way Tell Public Follow Benefit Use, Act
爲 依 遷 國
For, As Depend, Rely Move Country, Capital
Follow the right path ("middle way").
Tell the public to follow.
Benefit to move the capital; to undertake a major task. (The Chou court moved eastward. The line implies that this was the correct action).

Wilhelm/Baynes translates the first five characters: "If you walk in the middle and report to the prince, he will follow."

Legge renders them: "Its subject pursuing the due course. His advice to his prince is followed."

Nine in the Fifth Place
有 孚 惠 心 勿
Have Trust, Sincerity Give Heart Not
問 元 吉 有
Ask Great Good fortune Have
孚 惠 我 德
Trust, Sincerity Give My Virtue, Morality
Trust in a giving heart.
Do not ask. Great good fortune.
Being trustful enhances one's own virtue.

Nine in the Sixth Place (Top)
莫 益 之 或 擊 之 立
Not Increase It Or Strike, Hurt It Make, Build
心 勿 恆 凶
Mind, Heart Not Endure, Bear Misfortune
Neither increasing something nor diminishing it ("striking"), if one is continually changing one's mind, misfortune is the result.

Wilhelm/Baynes's translation is: "He brings increase to no one. Indeed, someone even strikes him. He does not keep his heart constantly steady. Misfortune."

Legge's is: "In the sixth line, undivided, we see one to whose increase none will contribute, while many will seek to assail him. He observes no regular rule in the ordering of his heart. There will be evil."

43 夬 *Kuai* ䷪ (Decisiveness. Determination. Resoluteness)

The Judgment
揚 于 王 庭 孚
Spread, Speak loudly At King Court Wide, Trust
號 有 厲 告 自
Cry out Have Serious, Weighty Plead Self, Own
邑 不 利 即
Country, City No Benefit Immediate
戎 利 有 攸 往
Army, Forces Benefit Have Far Go

Speak out loudly at the king's court.
Cry out strongly and plead for one's own region.
No benefit in arming immediately.
Benefit in pursuing the matter further.

The Lines

Nine at the Bottom (Beginning)

壯 于 前 趾 往 不 勝
Strength, Influence At Front Toe Go No Win

爲 咎
For, As Blame

There is some strength ("front toe" implies partial strength, not as much as the whole foot or the leg).
If you go ahead, you will not succeed ("win").
You will be blamed.

Nine in the Second Place

惕 號 莫
Alarm Cry, Sound No (This character can mean

夜 有 戎 勿 恤
"evening") Night Have Arms Not Worry, Concern

Alarms sound at evening and in the night.
Be ready ("have arms").
Do not be afraid.

Nine in the Third Place

壯 于 頑 有 凶
Strength At, In Cheekbone Have Misfortune

君 子 夬
Superior Man, Person Determination, Decisiveness

夬 獨
Determination, Decisiveness Single, Alone

行 遇 雨 若 濡 有 慍 无 咎
Walk Meet Rain If Wet Have Anger No Blame

Too powerful ("strength in the cheekbone," thus exposing one's strength), misfortune.
The superior man is decisive.
He walks alone, meets the rain, gets wet, may get angry.
No blame.

Wilhelm/Baynes translates the last four characters as: "And people murmur against him. No blame."

Nine in the Fourth Place

臀 无 膚 其 行
Thighs, Buttocks No Skin The Walk, Behavior

次 且 牽
Difficulty, Abnormality And Hold, Pull

羊 悔 亡
Goat, Sheep Remorse, Regret Die, Disappear

聞 言 不 信
Hear Word Not Belief

One is exposed ("no skin on the buttocks").
Moving ahead is difficult ("walking abnormal").
Be firm ("hold the goat").
Regret disappears.
Do not believe what you hear.

Both Wilhelm/Baynes and Legge consider characters eight and nine (which we translate as "hold" and "goat") to indicate being led like a sheep. They consider the last few characters to mean that if the words of this line are heard, they will not be believed.

Nine in the Fifth Place

莧 陸 夬 夬
Amaranth plant (Weeds) Decisive Decisive

中 行 无 咎
Middle Walk No Blame

Weeds ("amaranth plants") need much decisiveness.
Walk the middle way (that is, follow the golden mean).
No blame.
(The amaranth plants are oversupplied with the yin principle and therefore must be treated firmly.)

Six in the Sixth Place (Top)

无 號 終 有 凶
No Cry Final Have Misfortune

If one does not speak up ("cry out"), in the end misfortune will result.

Trigram *Sun* (☴ wind) blowing under trigram *Ch'ien* (☰ heaven) produces widespread effects, including gathering things together, as expressed in hexagram 44 (*Kou*). Hokusai. *A Gust of Wind at Ejiri.* Woodblock print from the *36 Views of Fuji.* Tokugawa Period, 1823–1839. The Metropolitan Museum of Art, New York City.

44 姤 *Kou* (Meeting)

The Judgment

女 壯 勿 用 取 女
Woman Strong Not Use, Act Marry Woman
The woman is too strong.
Do not marry her.

The Lines

Six at the Bottom (Beginning)

繫 于 金 柅 貞
Tether, Tied At Gold Brake Perseverance
吉 有 攸 往 見 凶
Good fortune Have Far Go See Misfortune
羸 豕 孚 蹢 躅
Weak, Thin Pig Behavior Hoof Hobbling
Held in check firmly ("tied up with a golden brake").
Perseverance brings good fortune.
If one tries to go far, one may meet misfortune.
Like a weak pig one will have difficulty in proceeding ("hoof hobbling").

Wilhelm/Baynes renders the last four characters as: "Even a lean pig has it in him to rage around."

Nine in the Second Place

包 有 魚 无 咎 不 利 賓
Container Have Fish No Blame No Benefit Guest
There are fish in the tank.
No blame but no benefit to others ("guests").
(Fish can have an undesirable connotation as a yin object; or it could refer to money.)

Nine in the Third Place

臀 无 膚 其 行
Thighs, Buttocks No Skin The Walk, Behavior
次 且 厲 无 大 咎
Second But, And Danger No Big Blame, Mistake
One is exposed ("no skin on the buttocks").
Proceeding ("walking") is difficult ("second but" means not right).
Danger but no great mistake.

Nine in the Fourth Place

包 无 魚 起 凶
Container, Tank No Fish Develop, Start Misfortune
No fish in the tank. Misfortune has begun.
(This can also imply that one has no money in his wallet.)

Nine in the Fifth Place

以 杞 包 瓜 含 章
With Willow Covered Melon Contain Principle,
有 隕 自 天
Rule Have Meteorite From Heaven
A well-covered melon ("with willows") retains its goodness ("principles").
It drops into one's possession like a meteorite from heaven.

Nine in the Sixth Place (Top)

姤 其 角 吝 无 咎
Meet The, Its Horn Blame No Blame, Mistake
He meets difficulties ("horns").
Some blame but no large error.

45 萃 *Ts'ui* (Gathering. Assembly. Union)

The Judgment

No obstruction King False, Borrow Have Temple
利 見 大 人 亨 利
Benefit See Great Man No obstruction Benefit
貞 用 大 牲
Perseverance Use, Act Big, Great Offering
吉 利 有 攸 往
Good fortune Benefit Have Far Go
No obstruction. The king manages to go to the temple.
Benefit to see the great man.
No obstruction. Benefit in perseverance.
Giving a large offering brings good fortune.
Benefit in going ahead.

The Lines

Six at the Bottom (Beginning)

有 孚 終 乃
Have Trust, Sincerity Not End Then
亂 乃 萃 若 號
Confusion, Chaos Then Gathering, Union If Cry out,
一 握 爲 笑 勿
Call out One Grasp (of the hand) As Laugh Not
恤 往 无 咎
Concern, Worry Go No Blame
Having sincerity, but not to the end, can lead to a mixture of chaos and order ("union").
If one calls out, one grasp of the hand can lead to laughter.
Do not worry. Go without blame.

Six in the Second Place

引 吉 无 咎
Draw, Induce Good fortune No Blame
孚 乃 利 用 禴
Sincerity, Trust Then Benefit Use, Act Worship
Cause ("induce") good fortune. No blame. If one is sincere, there is benefit in worship.

Six in the Third Place

萃 如 嗟 如 无 攸 利 往 无
Gathering, Union As Sigh As No Far Benefit Go No
咎 小 吝
Blame Small Mistake, Humiliation
Gathering together and sighing (implies sadness).
No long-term benefit.
Go without blame.
Minor humiliation.

Nine in the Fourth Place

大 吉 无 咎
Great Good fortune No Blame
Great good fortune.
No blame.

Nine in the Fifth Place

萃 有 位 无 咎
Gathering, Union Have Position, Status No Blame
匪 孚 元 永
Not Sincerity Beginning, Greatness Always, Forever
貞 悔 亡
Perseverance Remorse, Regret Die, Disappear

Gathering together while in a favorable position, brings no blame.
Even if not sincere, if one maintains perseverance always, remorse will disappear.

Legge sees the sixth, seventh, eighth, and ninth characters to mean, "If you do not have confidence in him, let him see to it that (his virtue) be great, long-continued and firmly correct."

Six in the Sixth Place

齎 咨 涕 洟 无 咎
Farewell, Separate Lamentation Cry Tears No Blame
Parting with lamentation and the shedding of tears brings no blame.

46 升 *Shêng* (Elevation. Pushing upward. Rising)

The Judgment

元 亨 用 見 大
Greatness No obstruction Use, Act See Great
人 勿 恤 南 征
Man, Person Not Worry, Concern South Attack,
吉
Advance Good fortune
Greatness. No obstruction.
You can see the great man.
Do not worry.
Advance toward the south (implies a less-developed area).
Good fortune.

The Lines

Six at the Bottom (Beginning)

允 升 大
Permission, Allow Upward, Rising Great
吉
Good fortune.
Allow upward movement.
Great good fortune.

Nine in the Second Place

孚 乃 利 用
Sincerity, Trust Then Benefit Use, Act
禴 无 咎
Enjoyment, No obstruction No Mistake, Blame
Sincerity is the best form of worship.
No mistake.
("Uses enjoyment" means worships.)

Nine in the Third Place

升 虛 邑
Pushing upward Empty Country, City
Pushing upward reaches an empty city.

Six in the Fourth Place

王 用 亨
King Use, Act Enjoyment, No obstruction
于 岐 山 吉 无 咎
At Ch'i Mountain Good fortune No Blame, Mistake
The king worships ("uses enjoyment") at Ch'i Mountain (implies that this is an appropriate action).
Good fortune.
No mistake.

(The implication in this historical allusion is that pushing upward achieves a reward.)

Six in the Fifth Place

貞 吉
Perseverance Good fortune
升 階
Pushing upward, Rising Rank
Perseverance brings good fortune and promotion up through the ranks (or up the ladder).

Six in the Sixth Place (Top)

冥 升 利
Blind, In darkness Pushing upward Benefit
于 不 息 之 貞
At, In No Rest Of Perseverance
Blindly pushing upward, one benefits from unremitting ("no rest") perseverance.

47 困 *K'un* (Oppression. Exhaustion. Surrounded)

The Judgment

亨 貞 大
No obstruction Perseverance Great
人 吉 无 咎 有
Man, Person Good fortune No Blame Have
言 不 信
Word No Belief
No obstruction. Perseverance.
The great man will have good fortune.
No blame.
Criticism ("have words") will not be believed.

Legge translates the last four characters: "If he make speeches, his words cannot be made good."

The Lines

Six at the Bottom (Beginning)

臀 困 于 株
Buttocks, Bottom Oppression At, In Root
木 入 于 幽 谷 三 歳 不 覿
Tree Enter At, In Deep Valley Three Year Not See
Sitting (on one's "buttocks") oppressed at the stump of a tree, one enters into a gloomy depression ("deep valley").
For three years one cannot see out.
(Implies deep involvement in one's own thoughts, unable to look beyond oneself.)

Nine in the Second Place

困 于 酒 食
Oppression, Surrounded At, In Wine Food
朱 紱 方 來 利 用
Golden red Silk rope or band Just Come Benefit Use,
亨 祀 征
Act Enjoyment, No obstruction Pray Attack
凶 无 咎
Misfortune No Blame
Surrounded by wine and food, the nobles (or political rewards) are about to come.
Benefit comes from worship ("use enjoyment").
Praying counters ("attacks") misfortune.
No blame.

Wilhelm/Baynes indicates that a prince wore scarlet knee bands. Their interpretation suggests that help will come from a noble.

Six in the Third Place

困 于
Oppression, Surrounded At, In Stone, Rock
據 于 蒺 蔾 入
Depend, Lean on At, In Thorn Plant Into At, In
其 宮 不 見 其 妻
The, Its Palace, Home Not See The, Its Wife
凶
Misfortune
Surrounded by rocks, he depends on thistles (implies hurtful things).
He enters the palace and does not see his wife (implies "not even" his wife is there, as all is empty).
Misfortune.

Wilhelm/Baynes uses "home" instead of "palace." Legge keeps the word "palace."

Nine in the Fourth Place

來 徐 徐 困
Come, Move Slow Slow Oppressed, Surrounded
于 金 車 吝 有 終
In, At Golden Cart Blame, Humiliation Have End
He moves along very slowly, oppressed, in a golden carriage (implies surrounded by riches or in a high court position but not progressing well).
Humiliation will finally end.

Nine in the Fifth Place

劓 刖 困 于 赤
Nose cut Feet cut Oppression In, At Deep red
紱 乃 徐 有 說 利
Silk band Then Slow Have Happiness Benefit
用 祭 祀
Use, Act Pray Offering
Nose cut off, feet cut off (that is, punished), oppressed by the authorities (those with "deep red silk bands"), one will obtain pleasure nevertheless.
Benefit to use prayer and offerings.

Six in the Sixth Place (Top)

困 于 葛 藟
Oppressed, Surrounded In, At Creeping Vines
于 臲 卼 曰
In, At Hazardous Look, Appearance Call, Say
動 悔 有 悔 征
Move Regret Have Regret Attack, Advance
吉
Good fortune
Entangled in creeping vines in a hazardous situation, one may say, "Moving ahead will bring regret."
If one feels repentance and goes ahead nevertheless, one will have good fortune.

48 井 *Ching* (The Well)

The Judgment

改 邑 不 改 井 无
Change Country, City Not Change Well No
喪 无 得 往 來 井 井 汔
Loss No Gain, Increase Go Come Well Well Draw
至 亦 未 繘 井
up Arrival, Come Also Not Rope Well
羸 其 瓶 凶
Hurt, Weaken The, Its Jug, Vessel Misfortune
The country may change but not the wells.
Whether there is loss or increase of water, people will go and come and draw up water from the wells.
If the rope does not reach or the jug breaks, misfortune results.

The Lines

Six at the Bottom (Beginning)

井 泥 不 食 舊 井 无 禽
Well Mud Not Feed Old Well No Bird
The well with muddy water cannot be drunk from.
Not even a bird can use an old well.

Nine in the Second Place

井 谷 射 鮒 甕 敝 漏
Well Valley, Inside Shoot Fish Jug Broken Leak
Fish can be shot inside a well, but a broken jug leaks.
(The implication is that it is easy to shoot fish inside a well, but if water is put into a broken jug, one cannot stop the water from leaking out.)

Nine in the Third Place

井 渫 不 食 爲 我 心 惻
Well Clean Not Feed Far My Heart Pity, Sorrow
可 用 汲 王 明
May Use Draw up King Understanding,
並 受
Enlightenment And, Both Receive, Enjoy
其 福
The, Its Fortune, Luck
The well is clean but not drunk from.
Sorrow is in my heart for the water could be used.
If the king is enlightened, both he and the people will enjoy the benefit ("fortune").

Six in the Fourth Place

井 甃 无 咎
Well Smooth, Lined No Blame, Mistake
The well is repaired ("smooth" or "lined").
No mistake.

Nine in the Fifth Place

井 洌 寒 泉 食
Well Clear Cold Spring Feed
The well is clear. Its spring is cold.
Drink.

Six in the Sixth Place (Top)

井 收 勿 幕 有
Well Receive Not Contained Have
孚 元 吉
Sincerity, Trust Great Good fortune
One can draw from a well that is not covered ("contained").
Be sincere.
Great good fortune.
(The implication is that if one does not hide one's ideas, they can be used.)

49 革 *Ko* (Change. Revolution. Renovate)

(Some scholars believe that the character for *Ko* originally meant an animal skin that could be "molted.")

The Judgment

巳 日 乃 孚 元
Later Day Then, After Trust, Sincerity Great No
亨 利 貞 悔
obstruction Benefit Perseverance Regret, Remorse Die,
亡
Disappear
In due time ("later days after"), trust will come.
There is a wide-open path ("great no obstruction").
Benefit in perseverance.
Regret will disappear.

The Lines

Nine at the Bottom (Beginning)
鞏 用 黃 牛 之
Firmness, Defense Use, Act Yellow Cattle Of
革
Renovate, Hide (of an animal)
Defend with ox hide (implies strength). (The implication is that one should hold firmly to one's course. "Yellow cattle" is a term distinguishing cows and oxen from the water buffalo type of cattle.)

Wilhelm/Baynes considers "yellow" to indicate moderation and "cattle" to refer to docility. Their commentary, as translated, implies that no action should be taken.

Six in the Second Place
巳 日 乃 革 之 征
Later Day Then, After Change Of, It Attack,
吉 无 咎
Advance Good fortune No Blame, Mistake
In due time ("later days after"), one can make changes.
Advancing brings good fortune.
No mistake.

Another interpretation could be: Wait until the proper time to advance changes. Good fortune. No mistake.

Nine in the Third Place
征 凶 貞
Attack, Advance Misfortune Perseverance
厲 革 言
Danger Change Word, Speak
三 就 有 孚
Three Times, Occasions Have Trust
Advance brings misfortune.
Persistence is dangerous.
Consider ("speak of") change again and again ("three times").
Then one will gain trust.

Wilhelm/Baynes and Legge both translate the last character to mean "belief," as in, "Men will believe him."

Nine in the Fourth Place
悔 亡 有
Remorse, Regret Die, Disappear Have Trust,
孚 改 命 吉
Sincerity Correct Order Good fortune
Regrets disappear.
Have belief ("trust") in correcting conditions ("order").
Good fortune.
(Some scholars translate the sixth character as "form of government"; others use "ordinances.")

Nine in the Fifth Place
大 人 虎 變 未
Great Man, Person Tiger Transformation Not
占 有 孚
Divination, Forecast Have, Gain Trust
The great person can make large transformations (that is, like a tiger who changes his stripes).
No divination is needed.
He will receive trust.

Six in the Sixth Place (Top)
君 子 豹 變
Superior Man, Person Panther Transformation
小 人 革 面 征
Small Man, Person Change Face Advance, Attack
凶 居 貞 吉
Misfortune Stay Perseverance Good fortune
The superior person makes attractive transformations (like a panther, which implies beauty).
The inferior person only gives the appearance of change ("changes face").
Advance brings misfortune.
Stay. Perseverance brings good fortune.

50 鼎 *Ting* (The Cauldron)

The Judgment

元 吉 亨
Greatness Good fortune No obstruction
Greatness. Good fortune. No obstruction.

The Lines

Six at the Bottom (Beginning)
鼎 顛 趾 利 出
Cauldron Tilted up Leg, Toe Benefit Out
否 得 妾 以 其
Difficult, Bad Gain, Take Concubine With The,
子 无 咎
His Son No Blame
The cauldron is tilted over ("legs tilted up." This was usually done to clean the utensil).
Benefit to remove the bad contents.
Take a concubine for the sake of begetting a son.
No blame.
(The implication is that benefits can be derived from lesser circumstances.)

Nine in the Second Place
鼎 有 實 我 仇 有
Cauldron Have Full My, Me Enemy, Partner Have
疾 不 我 能 卽
Sick Not My, Me Can Finish, Help, Solve
吉
Good fortune
The cauldron is full.
My enemies (or partners) are envious ("sick").
I cannot help that.
Good fortune.

Wilhelm/Baynes translates the fifth word as "comrades."

Nine in the Third Place
鼎 耳 革 其
Cauldron Ear, Handle Change, Remove The, Its
行 塞 雉 膏 不 食 方
Way, Walk Obstructed Pheasant Fat Not Eat Just
雨 虧 悔 終
Rain Defect, Lack Regret, Remorse Final
吉
Good fortune
The cauldron's handles are removed.
The way is obstructed (that is, one cannot lift the cauldron to deliver the food).
The food ("pheasant fat") is not eaten.
Rain is about to fall ("just rain").
Remorse is not complete ("lacking").
Finally good fortune.
(The fall of rain implies relief.)

Nine in the Fourth Place
鼎 折 足 覆 公 餗
Cauldron Loss, Broken Leg Overturn Official Food
其 形 渥 凶
The, Its Figure, Body Soiled Misfortune
The cauldron, with leg broken, overturns, spills the official's food, and soils his person.
Misfortune.
(Some scholars consider the characters for "food," "figure," and "soiled" together to mean heavy punishment.)

Six in the Fifth Place
鼎 黃 耳 金 鉉
Cauldron Yellow Ear, Handle Gold Rod (carrying
利 貞
rod) Benefit Perseverance
The cauldron has yellow handles and golden carrying rods.
Benefit in perseverance.
("Yellow" implies moderation and modesty. The golden carrying rod suggests that the action or conduct is praiseworthy.)

Nine in the Sixth Place (Top)
鼎 玉 鉉 大 吉 无
Cauldron Jade Rod Great Good fortune Nothing
不 利
No Benefit
The cauldron has jade carrying rods.

Ting ("the cauldron"), hexagram 50, is one of only two hexagrams to feature material objects, rather than abstractions or persons, in its title. Its position, contents, and appearance are used in the lines of the hexagram to forecast favorable or unfavorable conditions. *Ting*. Late Shang (thirteenth–eleventh century B.C.). Inscribed bronze. Height 14″. Asian Art Museum of San Francisco. Avery Brundage Collection.

Hexagram 51, formed by the trigram *Chên* (☳ ; thunder) doubled, symbolizes danger, which must not allow a superior man to be deterred from the right paths.
Tenjin Engi (detail). Kamakura period (thirteenth century). 28′3¾″ × 11¾″. The Metropolitan Museum of Art, New York City.

Good fortune. Everything benefits ("nothing no benefit"). (Jade is very hard, but soft in appearance. The implication is that if the strong person also shows gentleness, he will have good fortune, no matter what happens.)

51 震 *Chên* ䷲ (Tremors. Vibrations. Shaking—these words can imply a thunderclap.)

The Judgment

亨 震 來
No obstruction Shaking (as of thunder) Come
虩 虩 笑 言
"Foo" "Foo" Laughter, Cheer Talk, Words
啞 啞 震 驚 百
"Ha" "Ha" Shaking, Thunderclap Terror Hundred
里 不 喪 匕 鬯
Miles Not Harm Spoon, Ladle Sacrificial wine

No obstruction.
A thunderclap comes, causing words of fear ("foo foo").
Yet cheerful words can induce laughter ("ha ha").
Thunderclaps can terrify over a hundred miles, but they must not alter one's proper action ("spoon and sacrificial wine," signifying worship or libation).

The Lines

Nine at the Bottom (Beginning)

震 來 虩 虩 後
Shaking, Thunderclap Come "Foo" "Foo" Later
笑 言 啞 啞 吉
Laughter Words "Ha" "Ha" Good fortune

A thunderclap comes, causing words of fear ("foo foo").
After, words of laughter ("ha ha").
Good fortune.

Six in the Second Place

震 來 厲 億
Shaking, Thunderclap Come Danger Billions
喪 貝 躋 于
Loss Treasure Walk up, Climb up At
九 陵 勿 逐 七 日 得
Nine Hill Not Chase, Pursue Seven Day Gain

Thunderclaps come with danger.
Much ("billions") treasure is lost.
Climb to the highest hill ("ninth hill").
Do not pursue it.
Gain will come in seven days.

Six in the Third Place

震 蘇 蘇
Thunderclap Feeling of fear Feeling of fear
震 行 无
Thunderclap Go, Walk No
眚
Severe illness ("eye disease"), Trouble

Thunderclaps make one tremble ("feeling of fear" repeated).
If one proceeds carefully ("going in thunder"), no serious trouble will result.

Nine in the Fourth Place

震 遂 泥
Thunderclap Reach, Comply Mud

The shock of thunder is caught in the mud.

Six in the Fifth Place

震 往 來 厲 億
Shaking, Thunderclap Go Come Danger Billions
无 喪 有 事
No Harm Have, Keep Thing, Something

Thunder shocks go and come. Danger.
The many will receive no harm, only minor trouble ("have something").

Wilhelm/Baynes translates the last two characters to mean: "Yet there are things to be done."

Six in the Sixth Place (Top)

震 索 索 視
Shaking, Thunderclap Distraught, Fearful Look
矍 矍 征 凶
Anxiety Anxiety Attack Misfortune
震 不 于 其 躬 于 其
Shaking, Thunderclap Not At The Self At, In The
鄰 无 咎 婚 媾
Neighbor No Blame Marriage Combination
有 言
Have, Receive Word

The shock of thunder makes one distraught and look around with much anxiety ("anxiety anxiety").
Taking aggressive action brings misfortune.
If the thunderbolt does not fall on you but on your neighbor, there is no blame.
In close connections ("marriage combination"), there may be arguments ("have words").

52 艮 *Kên* ䷳ (Keeping Still. Mountains. Halted)

The Judgment

艮 其 背 不 獲
Keeping still, Halted The, Its, His Back Not Get to
其 身 行 其 庭
The, Its, His Body Walk The, Its, His Courtyard
不 見 其 人 无 咎
Not See The, Its, His Person No Blame

Keeping one's back still, not in touch with ("getting to") one's own body, one walks into the courtyard and sees no people there.
No blame. (The implication is that with total control of oneself—so that one doesn't even feel one's body—one is untouched by what goes on around.)

The Lines

Six at the Bottom (Beginning)

艮 其 趾 无
Keeping still, Halted The, Its, His Toe No
咎 利 永
Blame Benefit Forever, Always
貞
Perseverance, Persistence

Keeping still before one has even started ("keeping the toes still"), one has no blame.
Benefit in continuing always on this course ("always perseverance").

Six in the Second Place

艮 其 腓 不
Keeping still, Halted The, Its, His Leg Not
拯 其 隨 其
Save, Help The, Its, His Follow, Like The, Its, His
心 不 快
Heart Not Happy, Quick

Keeping one's legs still (or halted), one cannot help the one he follows.
He is unhappy in his heart.

Nine in the Third Place

艮 其 限 列
Keeping still The, Its, His Waist, Loins Hurt, Split
其 寅 厲
The, Its, His Hip, Lower back Danger
熏 心
Burned, Suffocated Heart

Keeping one's waist still can hurt the hip.
There is danger that the heart can be severely troubled.

Wilhelm/Baynes's translation is: "The heart suffocates."

Legge's is: "The heart glows with suppressed excitement."

Six in the Fourth Place

艮 其
Keeping still, Halted The, Its, His
身 无 咎
Body, Torso, Trunk No Blame

Keeping one's torso still, one has no blame.

Six in the Fifth Place

艮 其 輔 言
Keeping still, Halted The, Its, His Mouth, Jaw Word
有 序 悔 亡
Have Order Regret, Remove Die, Disappear

Keeping his mouth still, his words are orderly.
Regret disappears. (The implication is that by controlling or limiting one's speech—"mouth"—one's words will be orderly and one will not regret what one says.)

Nine in the Sixth Place (Top)

敦 艮 吉
Honesty Keeping still, Halted Good fortune

Keeping still (or quiet) with honesty brings good fortune.

53 漸 *Chien* ䷴ (Gradual Progress. Development)

The Judgment

女 歸
Woman Return (implies marriage)
吉 利 貞
Good fortune Benefit Perseverance

The girl marries. Good fortune.
Benefit in perseverance. (The basic meaning of the second character in the judgment is "return." It implies returning to one's residence, a place to belong to, and therefore marriage.)

Hexagram 52, formed by doubling the trigram for mountain, *Kên* (☶), repeatedly counsels that one should remain still and controlled. *Spring Landscape in Sunlight.* Ashikaga period. One of a pair of six-fold screens; ink, color, gold, silver, and gesso on paper. Length 124½″. Kongo-ji, Osaka.

The Lines

Six at the Bottom (Beginning)

鴻 漸 于
Wild goose, Water goose Gradual progress At, In
干 小 子 厲 有 言 无 咎
Shore Small Son Danger Have Word No Blame

The wild goose flies toward the shore ("gradually progresses").
The fellow ("small son") is in danger.
He may receive criticism but there is no blame.
("Small son" resembles the English slang for "guy" or "chap.")

Six in the Second Place

鴻 漸 于
Wild goose, Water goose Gradual progress At, In
磐 飲 食 衎 衎 吉
Stone, Rock Drink Eat Happy Happy Good fortune

The wild goose gradually flies over the rocks (or to the cliff—that is, further inland).
He may eat and drink very happily.
Good fortune.
(The wild or water goose may symbolize someone in a lower rather than a higher position. The rocks may indicate a distance from the usual abode at the water's edge, but still near home. Others view the wild goose as the emblem of faithfulness.)

Nine in the Third Place

鴻 漸 于
Wild goose, Water goose Gradual progress At, In
陸 夫 征 不
Inland Husband Attack (the army is implied) Not
復 婦 孕 不 育
Return Woman Pregnant Not Feed, Nurture
凶 利 禦 寇
Misfortune Benefit Defense Robber, Bandit

The wild goose gradually flies inland.
The husband is away in the army and does not return.
The wife is pregnant. The child does not survive ("not feed").
Misfortune.
Benefit to resist intruders ("robbers").

Wilhelm/Baynes translates the fourth character as "plateau."
Legge, as "dry plains."

Six in the Fourth Place

鴻 漸 于
Wild goose, Water goose Gradual progress At, In
木 或 得 其 桷
Tree Or, If Get The, Its, His Flat branch
无 咎
No Blame, Mistake

The wild goose gradually flies to the trees (or woods).
If it stays on a flat branch, it is no mistake.

Nine in the Fifth Place

鴻 漸 于
Wild goose, Water goose Gradual progression At, In
陵 婦 三 歲 不 孕 終
Hill Woman Three Year Not Pregnant Final
莫 之 勝 吉
Nothing, Not Of Win, Succeed Good fortune

The wild goose gradually flies to the hilltop.
The woman does not become pregnant for three years.
Finally nothing can stop her from succeeding.
Good fortune.

Nine in the Sixth Place (Top)

鴻 漸 于
Wild goose, Water goose Gradual progress At, In
陸 其 羽 可 用 爲
Inland The, Its Feather May Use, Act As, For
儀 吉
Formal ceremony Good fortune

The wild goose gradually flies further inland.
Its feathers can be used in a sacred ceremony (that is, at least its feathers can be used).

Legge states that the goose was part of ancient Chinese marriage ceremonies and also that it may symbolize gradual progression. He translates the fourth character as "large heights."

Wilhelm/Baynes suggests that the lines are metaphors for the gradual progression through life, which finally ends. If a man strives to improve himself, his life can benefit others. They translate the fourth character as "cloud heights."

Chu Hsi believes that the fourth character (which we translate literally as "inland") originally referred to clouds.

54 歸妹 *Kuei Mei* ䷵ (Marrying Maiden)

The Judgment

征 凶 无 攸 利
Attack, Advance Misfortune No Long Benefit
Going ahead brings misfortune.
No long-term benefit.

The Lines

Nine at the Bottom (Beginning)
歸 妹 以 娣
Marrying (Return) Maiden With Younger sister
跛 能 履 征 吉
Lame Can Walk Attack, Advance Good fortune
The marrying maiden is in a secondary position ("younger sister").
But a lame man can still walk.
Going ahead brings good fortune.
(The younger sister in ancient tradition often married the same man as her elder sister but was therefore a secondary spouse. Some commentators have inferred that here she is a concubine. The implication of the line, therefore, is that one does not have to reach the highest position to do well.)

Nine in the Second Place
眇 能 視 利 幽
Halfblind, One-eyed Can See Benefit Dark, Hidden
人 之 貞
Person Of Perseverance
The one-eyed can still see.
Benefit for the unrecognized ("dark" or "hidden") person to be persevering.

Wilhelm/Baynes calls the fifth and sixth characters "solitary man."

Legge calls them "solitary widow."

Six in the Third Place
歸 妹 以 須 反
Marrying Maiden With Mean star (*Hsu*) Reverse
歸 以 娣
Marrying With Younger sister
The marrying maiden is a naughty girl ("mean star").
She returns to her parents' home ("reverse return").

Wilhelm/Baynes's translation is: "The marrying maiden as a slave, she marries as a concubine."

Legge's is: "The third line, divided, shows the younger sister who was to be married off in a mean position. She returns and accepts an ancillary position."

Nine in the Fourth Place
歸 妹 愆 期 遲 歸
Marrying Maiden Delay Time Late Marrying
有 時
Have Time
The marrying maiden delays her marriage.
There is time for a later marriage.

Six in the Fifth Place
帝 乙 歸 妹 其
King Daughter Marrying Maiden The, Its, His
君 之 袂 不 如 其
King, You Of Cloth Not As The, Its, His
娣 之 袂 良 月 幾 望
Younger sister Of Cloth Goodness Moon Almost Full
吉
Good fortune
The king gives his daughter in marriage.
The king's clothing is not as gorgeous as the younger sister's.
The moon is almost full.
Good fortune.
(The implication may be that nobility is not shown by outward display.)

Chu Hsi interprets this line to mean that the king does not focus on his raiments but rather on his morality. "The moon is almost full" signifies high principle.

Legge explains: "The fifth line, divided, reminds us of the marrying of the younger sister of (King) Ti Yi, when the sleeves of the princess were not equal to those of the (still) younger sister who accompanied her in an inferior position."

Wilhelm/Baynes indicates: "The embroidered garments of the princess were not as gorgeous as those of the serving maid."

Six in the Sixth Place
女 承 筐 无 實 士 刲
Woman Hold Basket Not Full Soldier Cut, Kill
羊 无 血 无 攸 利
Sheep, Lamb, Goat No Blood No Long Benefit
The woman holds the basket, but there is nothing inside.
The soldier kills the lamb. No blood flows (indicating that the sheep is already dead and the killing unnecessary).
No long-term benefit.
(The implication is that a marriage between the parties is inauspicious. Keeping in mind the name of the hexagram, this sixth line suggests that the ritual offerings by both the man and the woman are not fulfilled. The basket is empty and the lamb already slaughtered before the ceremony.)

55 豐 *Fêng* ䷶ (Richness. Abundance. Fullness)

The Judgment

亨 王 假 之 勿
No obstruction King Get, Borrow It, Of Not
憂 宜 日 中
Worry Should Sun, Day Center, Middle
No obstruction.
The king achieves abundance ("gets it").
Have no worry.
One should eat at midday.

The Lines

Nine at the Bottom (Beginning)
遇 其 配 主 雖 旬
Meet The, Its Destiny Master Although Ten (days or
无 咎 往 有 尚
years) No Blame Go Have Expectation, Recognition
Meet the destined leader.
Although it may take a long time ("ten days or years"), it is not a mistake.
Go forward with good expectations.

Legge translates the last character as "approval."

Six in the Second Place
豐 其 蔀 日 中 見
Fullness The, Its Cover, Hide Sun Middle See
斗 往 得 疑 疾 有 孚
Pole star Go Get Odd Disease Have Honesty, Trust
發 若 吉
Happen, Start As, Like Good fortune
A thick ("full") cover hides the sun at midday (darkness is implied).
One can see the pole star (so dark is it that a bright star can be seen at midday).
If one goes ahead, one will receive mistrust ("get an odd disease").
But starting out with honesty brings good fortune.

Nine in the Third Place
豐 其 沛 日
Fullness The, Its Sufficiency, Banners Sun

中 見 沫 折 其 右
Middle See Small star Broken The, Its Right
肱 无 咎
Arm No Blame
Banners fully cover the sun at midday.
One can see a small star (so dark that even a small star can be seen).
One may have a disaster ("broken right arm") and yet no blame.

Nine in the Fourth Place
豐 其 蔀 日 中 見
Fullness The, Its Cover, Hide Sun Middle See
斗 遇 其 夷
Pole star Meet The, Its Hidden (varying translations)
主 吉
Master Good fortune
A thick cover hides the sun at midday,
One can see the pole star.
One meets the unrecognized leader.
Good fortune.

Six in the Fifth Place
來 章 有 慶 譽
Come Brightness Have Celebration Honor
吉
Good fortune
Brightness comes (that is, darkness lifts).
One will receive congratulations ("celebration") and honor.
Good fortune.

Six in the Sixth Place (Top)
豐 其 屋 蔀 其
Fullness, Abundance The, Its House Cover The, Its
家 闚 其 戶 闃 其
Home Peep, Look The, Its Gate, Door Quiet The, Its
无 人 三 歲 不 覿 凶
No Person Three Year Not See Misfortune
The house is opulent ("abundant, rich") but the home is screened off ("covered").
Peering through the gate, one finds it quiet with no one inside.
For three years, one will not see anyone.
Misfortune.
(The implication is that even in abundance, one needs family. Some commentaries suggest the meaning that in the midst of abundance one can alienate others and be isolated.)

56 旅 *Lü* (Traveler. Stranger. Wanderer)

The Judgment
小 亨 旅
Small No obstruction, Enjoyment Traveler
貞 吉
Perseverance Good fortune
Little enjoyment for the traveler.
Perseverance brings good fortune.

The Lines

Six at the Bottom (Beginning)
旅 瑣 瑣 斯 其
Traveler Small things Small things That, This The, Its
所 取 災
Place, Way Get Disaster
If the traveler gets involved in many trivial things, that may well lead to disaster.

Six in the Second Place
旅 卽 次 懷 其
Traveler Almost at Inn Hold, Keep The, Its
資 得 童 僕
Capital, Money Get Child, Youngster Servant
貞
Perseverance, Loyalty
The traveler reaching the inn should keep his money with him and get a loyal young servant.

Nine in the Third Place
旅 焚 其 次 喪 其 童
Traveler Burn The Inn Loss The Child, Youngster
僕 貞 厲
Servant Perseverance, Persistence Danger
The traveler finds the inn on fire.
He loses his young servant.
Persistence is dangerous.

Nine in the Fourth Place
旅 于 處 得 其 資
Traveler At Place, Spot Get The, Its Capital, Money
斧 我 心 不 快
Axe My Heart Not Happiness
The traveler reaches some place.
He may obtain his valuables ("money axe").
Yet his heart is not happy.
(The implication may be that he is still a stranger.)

Six in the Fifth Place
射 雉 一 矢 亡
Shoot Pheasant One Arrow Die, Disappear
終 以 譽 命
Final With Honor, Praise Life, Fame
He kills ("shoots die") the pheasant with one arrow.
In the end, praise and fame (or high position).

Legge considers the third, fourth, and fifth characters to mean, "He will lose his arrow."

Nine in the Sixth Place (Top)
鳥 焚 其 巢 旅 人 先
Bird Burn The, Its Nest Traveler Person Beginning
笑 後 號 咷 喪 牛
Laughter Later Loud shout Cry Loss Cattle
于 易 凶
At, In Carelessness, Ease, Change Misfortune
The bird's nest burns.
The traveler laughs at the beginning but later cries out loudly.
Through carelessness he loses his belongings ("cattle").
Misfortune.

Another possible interpretation is: He loses his belongings as things change.

Wilhelm/Baynes suggests that "cattle" or "cow" signifies modesty and adaptability.

Legge renders "cattle" as "oxlike docility."

57 巽 *Sun* (Obedience. Yielding)

(Some have named this hexagram "Gentle, Penetrating Wind," the title of the trigram *Sun*, which when doubled forms this 57th hexagram).

The Judgment
小 亨 利 有
Small No obstruction, Enjoyment Benefit Have
攸 往 利 見 大 人
Far Go Benefit See Great Man
Little enjoyment. (Another translation may be: success in small things.)
Benefit to go further.
Benefit to see the great man.

The Lines

Six at the Bottom (Beginning)
進 退 利 武
Forward Backward Benefit Warrior, Fighting man
人 之 貞
Person, Man Of Perseverance
Going to and fro (implies indecisiveness).
Benefit in acting like a warrior, showing perseverance.

Nine in the Second Place
巽 在 牀 下 用
Obedience, Yielding At Bed Beneath, Lower Use,
史 巫 紛
Act Official Witch, Shaman Numerous, Profuse
若 吉 无 咎
Like, As Good fortune No Blame
Yield from a lower position ("at bed beneath").
Use numerous official magicians.
Good fortune. No blame.

Wilhelm/Baynes calls the sixth and seventh characters "priests and magicians."

Legge renders them "diviners and exorcists."

Nine in the Third Place
頻
Pained expression (also can mean frequent)
巽 吝
Obedience, Yielding Blame
Yielding but with complaint warrants blame.
(Some have translated the first two characters to mean repeated penetration.)

Six in the Fourth Place
悔 亡 田
Remorse, Regret Die, Disappear Land, Field
獲 三 品
Gain Three, Third Rank, Class
Remorse disappears.
Hunting (implied in the term "field") will gain a middle result (the "third of five ranks").

A different translation offers: "The hunt is successful because three kinds of game are caught."

Nine in the Fifth Place
貞 吉 悔
Perseverance Good fortune Remorse, Regret
亡 无 不 利 无 初
Die, Disappear Nothing No Benefit No Beginning
有 終 先 庚
Have End Before Change (also has other meanings)
三 日 後 庚 三 日 吉
Three Day After Change Three Day Good fortune
Perseverance brings good fortune.
Remorse disappears.
Everything benefits ("nothing no benefit").
There is no beginning but there is an end.
Before making a change, three days.
After the change, three days.
Good fortune. (The implication is that we should ponder long enough—"three days"—before and after making a change. This may refer to an admired practice of waiting three days before announcing a regulation, in order to explain its meaning; then waiting three days after the announcement before enforcement to allow the public to get accustomed to the idea.)

Nine in the Sixth Place (Top)
巽 在 牀
Obedience, Yielding At, In Bed, Couch
下 喪 其 資
Beneath, Lower Loss The, Its, His Capital, Money
斧 貞 凶
Axe Perseverance, Persistence Misfortune
Yield from a lower position (that is, act in a low key).
One's possessions ("money axe") are lost.
Persistence brings misfortune.

Legge's translation indicates "penetration beneath a couch and having lost the axe with which he executed his decisions."

58 兌 *Tui*

(Happiness. Joyfulness)

The Judgment

亨 利 貞
No obstruction Benefit Perseverance
No obstruction.
Benefit in perseverance.

The Lines

Nine at the Bottom (Beginning)
和 兌
Harmony, Contentment Happiness, Joyfulness
吉
Good fortune
Harmonious joy.
Good fortune.

Nine in the Second Place
孚 兌
Sincerity, Trust Happiness, Joyfulness
吉 悔 亡
Good fortune Remorse Die, Disappear
Sincere joy.
Good fortune.
Remorse disappears.

Six in the Third Place
來 兌 凶
Come Happiness Misfortune
Anticipating joy (that is, expecting joy or offering joy with an ulterior motive) brings misfortune.

Nine in the Fourth Place
商 兌 未
Discuss, Evaluate, Weigh Happiness Not
寧 介 疾
Peaceful, Quiet, Stable Between, Separate Disease, Bad
有 喜
Have Joy
Weighing (evaluating) happiness is not a peaceful pursuit.
Separate out the bad and you will have joy.

Nine in the Fifth Place
孚 于 剝
Trust, Sincerity At, In Decay, Peeling, Disintegration
有 厲
Have Danger
Trusting in decay is dangerous.
(Implies to be wary of what can injure.)

Six in the Sixth Place (Top)
引 兌
Pull, Induce, Draw Happiness
Produce happiness (either in others or draw it to you).

59 渙 *Huan*

(Diffusion. Dissolution. Dispersion. Scattering)

The Judgment

亨 王 假 有 廟
No obstruction King Come Have Temple
利 涉 大 川 利 貞
Benefit Cross Great Water Benefit Perseverance
No obstruction.
The king comes to the temple (implies praying).
Benefit to cross the great water.
Benefit in perseverance.
(The third character can also mean "borrow" or "false." The old meaning, however, was "come.")

The Lines

Six at the Bottom (Beginning)
用 拯 馬 壯 吉
Use, Act Save, Help Horse Strong Good fortune
Using a strong horse to help brings good fortune.

Nine in the Second Place
渙 奔 其
Dissolution, Dispersion Run The, Its, His
机 悔 亡
Support, Chance Remorse, Regret Die, Disappear
When dissolution occurs, run to a support.
Regret disappears.

Another interpretation can be that dissolution depends on chance.

Six in the Third Place
渙 其 躬 无
Dissolution, Dispersion The, Its, His Self No
悔
Regret, Remorse
Spread yourself ("disperse its self").
No regret.
(This can also be referring to self-renunciation.)

Six in the Fourth Place
渙 其
Dissolution, Dispersion The, Its, His
羣 元 吉
Group, Organization Great Good fortune
渙 有 丘 匪
Dissolution, Dispersion Have Hill, Mound Not
夷 所 思
Others, Foreign For Think
Disperse the group. Great good fortune.
Dispersion leads to another grouping ("have hill").
Others cannot think of this (that is, ordinary minds may not realize this).
One implication is that dispersal or scattering of a group can lead to their reforming again.
Another view sees the dispersal as a dissolution of a hill of problems.

Nine in the Fifth Place
渙 汗 其 大
Dispersion, Scattering Sweat The, Its, His Big
號 渙 王 居
Shout, Order Dissolution, Dispersion King Residence
无 咎
No Blame
Disperse with vigor ("sweat") the loud shout from the king's palace.
No blame.

Another interpretation has been that once an order goes out, like sweat, it cannot go back.

A different implication has been that a great edict marks a recovery in the same way that sweating signifies a favorable crisis in an illness.
Sweat can also imply the reaction of fear.

Another translation suggests a meaning related to scattering of the contents of the royal granary.

Nine in the Sixth Place (Top)
渙 其 血
Dissolution, Dispersion The, Its, His Blood
去 逖 出 无 咎
Go Far Out No Blame
Disperse harmful things ("blood" implies trauma).
Go far away. No blame.

Another possibility is: If you enter with trauma, go out with care.

One commentary considers "blood" to refer to the wounds of fear from which one should separate oneself.

Still another explanation implies that "blood" symbolizes danger, which one should avoid.

Hexagram 56 (*Lü;* the traveler) forecasts good and bad fortune according to the attitudes described: overemphasis on trivialities, care of possessions, reaction to unexpected catastrophe, precision in aims. Fukae Roshu (A.D. 1699–1757). *The Pass Through the Mountains.* Tokugawa period. Height 53⅜″. The Cleveland Museum of Art.

OVERLEAF: The trigram *Tui* (☱ river, lake) lies under the trigram *Sun* (☴ wood, wind) to form hexagram 61, (*Shung Fu*; sincerity, understanding).

60 節 *Chieh* ䷻ (Control. Self-Limitation. Self-Restraint)

The Judgment

亨 苦
No obstruction Extreme, Bitter, Severe

節
Control, Limitation, Restraint

不 可 貞
Not Can Perseverance, Persistence

No obstruction (that is, the path is open). Excessive self-control ("bitter limitation") cannot last ("persist").

The Lines

Nine at the Bottom (Beginning)

不 出 戶 庭 无 咎
Not Out Door, Gate Courtyard No Blame

Not going outside of the house ("door courtyard") is without blame.

Nine in the Second Place

不 出 門 庭 凶
Not Out Door Courtyard Misfortune

Not going outside beyond the door and the courtyard brings misfortune.

Six in the Third Place

不 節 若
Not Limitation, Control, Restraint Like, As

則 嗟 若 无 咎
Then Limitation Like, As No Blame

If one does not exert self-control, then one will have reason to lament.
But there is no blame.

Six in the Fourth Place

安 節
Peace, Contentment Control, Limitation, Restraint
亨
No obstruction

Peaceful self-control leads to enjoyment (or an open path).

Nine in the Fifth Place

甘 節
Sweetness Control, Limitation, Restraint
吉 往 有 尚
Good fortune Go Have Respect, Admiration, Follow

Pleasant ("sweet") self-control brings good fortune.
Going ahead brings admiration.

Six in the Sixth Place (Top)

苦 節
Extreme, Bitter, Severe Control, Limitation
貞 凶
Perseverance, Persistence Misfortune
悔 亡
Regret, Remorse Die, Disappear

Persisting in extreme self-restraint brings misfortune.
Regret will disappear.

61 中孚 *Chung Fu* ䷼ (True Sincerity. Understanding. Inner Sincerity)

The Judgment

豚 魚 吉 利 涉 大
Pig Fish, Dolphin Good fortune Benefit Cross Great
川 利 貞
Water Benefit Perseverance

True sincerity influences even the least intelligent. Good fortune.
Benefit to embark on great enterprises ("cross the great water").
Benefit in perseverance.

An alternate view: Understanding ("pig fish") brings good fortune.
Still another possibility: True sincerity affects all of low or high intelligence.
(There are many different meanings attached to the first two characters and the implication of the entire judgment.
The "pig fish" is poisonous, and understanding is needed to remove its poison in order to eat it.
Others classify "pigs" and "fishes" as the least intelligent of animals. On the other hand, some see in "pigs" low intelligence and in "dolphins" high intelligence.
Therefore, the translation depends on how one assigns the meanings to the two characters.)

The Lines

Nine at the Bottom (Beginning)

虞 吉 有
Evaluate, Consider Good fortune Have
他 不 燕
Other, Outside Not Place

Consider (that is, before acting). Good fortune.
Having something else ("outside") is disquieting.
(The implication is that having one's mind on something besides the project at hand is disturbing.)

Legge translates the first character to indicate resting within oneself.

Wilhelm/Baynes sees the meaning as referring to a prepared state of mind.

Nine in the Second Place

鳴 鶴 在 陰 其 子
Sing, Call Crane At, In Shade The, Its Son
和 之 我 有 好
With, Together Of I, My Have Good Duke, High
爵 吾 與 爾 靡 之
position, Cup I, My With, And Thee Divide, Share Of

A crane is singing in the shade.
Her offspring ("son") sings with her.
I have a good position ("duke") and will share it with you.
(Others have translated the twelfth character as "cup" or "goblet" instead of "position.")

Six in the Third Place

得 敵 或 鼓
Get, Find Enemy, Antagonist Or, If To drum (for an
或 罷 或 泣
attack) Or, If Stop, Retreat Or, If Cry, Weep
或 歌
Or, If Sing

Face your enemy.
Advance or retreat; weep or sing.
(The implication is that if you face things squarely, you can do as you wish.
Some have translated the second character as "friend" instead of "enemy.")

Six in the Fourth Place

月 幾 望 馬 匹 亡
Moon Almost Full Horse Pair, Both Loss, Disappear
无 咎
No Blame

The moon is almost full (that is, almost perfect).
Losses can occur (the "pair" or "team of horses" runs away).
No blame.
(The implication is that if things are too perfect, expect something to happen, but it won't be very bad.)

Nine in the Fifth Place

有 孚 攣 如无 咎
Have Trust, Sincerity Hold, Link As No Blame

Have trust. Hold together. No blame.

Nine in the Sixth Place (Top)

翰 音 登 于
Flat Sound, Song, Shout Step, Reach, Upward At, In
天 貞 凶
Heaven Perseverance, Persistence Misfortune

The sound of song (or shouting) flies up to heaven.
But persisting brings misfortune.

Here again many different translations and interpretations have been offered by scholars. For instance:
Sound alone does not achieve results.

The first two characters signify a cock's crowing, which may reach heaven, but not necessarily the cock itself.

"Heaven" often implies the king. Therefore misfortune will be the lot of nobles or officials who seek to rival the king's fame.

Even a good sound can be bad if it is too much.

62 小過 *Hsiao Kuo* ䷽ (Excess of the Small. Minor Excess)

The Judgment

亨 利 貞 可 小
No obstruction Benefit Perseverance Can Small
事 不 可 大 事 飛 鳥 遺 之
Thing Not Can Big Thing Fly Bird Remain Of
音 不 宜 上 宜
Sound Not Proper, Fitting Up Proper,
下 大 吉
Fitting Down Great Good fortune

No obstruction.
Profit in perseverance.
One can do small things.
One cannot do large things.
A bird may fly away; the sound remains (that is, its influence).
It is not proper to strive upward.
It is proper to stay down.
Great good fortune.

The Lines

Six at the Bottom (Beginning)

飛 鳥 以 凶
Fly Bird With Misfortune

The flying bird meets with misfortune.

Six in the Second Place

過 貞
Overmuch, Pass over The, Its, His
祖 遇 其
Ancestor, Grandfather Meet, Come The, Its,
妣 不 及 其 君
His Ancestress, Grandmother Not Reach The King
遇 其 臣 无 咎
Meet The Official, Minister No Blame, Mistake

If one passes by the grandfather, then meet the grandmother.
If one does not reach the king, then meet the minister.
No mistake.
(The implication is that if one cannot reach the topmost position, one should be content with the lesser.)

Nine in the Third Place

弗 過 防
Not Overmuch, Pass over Prevention, Precaution
之 從 或 戕 之 凶
Of, It Follow, Obey Or Kill Of, It Misfortune

Do not neglect precautions.
Someone may follow and harm you.
Misfortune.

Nine in the Fourth Place

无 咎 弗 過 遇 之
No Blame Not Overmuch, Pass over Meet Of, It
往 厲 必 戒 勿 用
Go Danger Must Restrain No Use, Act
永 貞
Always, Forever Persistence, Perseverance

No blame.
Do not do too much.
Dangerous to go ahead.
One must restrain oneself.
Do not continue to persist.

Wilhelm/Baynes groups the words to give a slightly different meaning: "one must be on guard, not act, and be constantly persevering."

Six in the Fifth Place

密 雲 不 雨 自 我 西
Thick, Dense Cloud Not Rain From My West
郊 公 弋
Border, Outskirts Duke, Prince Army or Ship in
取 彼 在 穴
Motion Get, Gain His At, In Cave

Dense clouds but no rain.
From his western borders, the prince's army gets to them in their hidden spot ("cave"; the west was where the enemy resided).

Wilhelm/Baynes suggests that the prince shoots and hits the person in the cave.

Legge indicates the shooting of an arrow at a bird in a cave.

Six in the Sixth Place (Top)

弗 遇 過 之 飛
Not Meet Overmuch, Pass over Of, It Fly
鳥 離 之 凶
Bird Separate, Leave Of, It Misfortune
是 謂 災 眚
Is Name, Call Disaster Sick

Do not do too much.
The flying bird leaves.
Misfortune.
One can call this situation "injury and disaster."

63 既濟 ䷾ (Already Completed. After Completion)

Chi Chi

The Judgment

亨 小 利
No obstruction, Enjoyment Small Benefit
貞 初 吉
Perseverance Beginning Good fortune
終 亂
End, Final Disaster, Chaos

Enjoy the small (or small successes: "no obstruction in the small").
Benefit in perseverance.
At the beginning, good fortune.
At the end, disaster.

The Lines

Nine at the Bottom (Beginning)

曳 其 輪 濡 其
Pull, Brake The, Its, His Wheel Wet The, Its, His
尾 无 咎
Tail No Blame

Pull back on your wheels (that is, slow down) or you will wet your tail (that is, you will be retarded).
No blame.
(The implication is that going too rapidly can meet resistance just as a wet tail slows one's forward movement.)

Six in the Second Place

婦 喪 其 茀 勿
Woman Loss The, Its Jewelry, Curtain Not
逐 七 日 得
Chase, Pursue Seven Day Gain, Get

A woman loses her jewelry.
Do not pursue it.
In seven days she will get it back.
(Several interpretors have translated the fourth character as "curtain" or "carriage screen" instead of "jewelry.")

Nine in the Third Place

高 宗 伐
High, Illustrious Family heritage, Ancestor Attack
鬼 方 三 年 克
Devil, Ghost Area Three Year Conquer
之 小 人 勿 用
Of, It Small Man, Person Not Use, Act

The king attacks the enemy area ("devils").
In three years, he conquers it.
Small (or inferior) men should not be used for this.
(*Gao-Chung*, "Illustrious Ancestor," was a dynastic title and therefore referred to the king.)

Six in the Fourth Place

繻 有 衣 袽 終
Leak, Silken, Wetness Have Cloth Rag All
日 戒
Day Warning, Alert

When there is wetness, have a cloth rag ready.
Be alert all day. (The first character has had widely divergent translations.)

Wilhelm/Baynes's translation is: "The finest clothes turn to rags."

Nine in the Fifth Place

東 鄰 殺 牛 不 如
East Neighbor Slaughter Cattle, Ox, Cow Not Like,
西 鄰 之 禴 祭
As West Neighbor Of, It Lesser Offering, Worship
實 受 其
True, Substantial Receive The, Its, His
福
Fortune, Reward

The eastern neighbor can make a large offering ("slaughter an ox").
It is not better than the western neighbor's lesser offering which receives true reward.
(The implication is that what is given in sincerity is more praiseworthy than its size.)

Six in the Sixth Place (Top)

濡 其 首 厲
Wet The, Its, His Head Danger

If one wets one's head, there is danger.
(The implication is that submersion in water over one's head is dangerous. This in turn suggests that excess in anything is perilous. One commentary interprets the line as a caution against turning back once a stream is crossed lest one get into the water again.)

64 未濟 ䷿ (Before Completion. Not Yet Finished)

Wei Chi

The Judgment

亨 小 狐 汔
No obstruction Small Fox Almost
濟 濡 其
Completed, Finished Wet The, Its,
尾 无 攸 利
His Tail No Long Benefit

Smooth pathway ("no obstruction").
The cunning person ("little fox") has almost reached his goal ("almost completed").
He meets resistance ("wets his tail").
No long-term benefit.

The Lines

Six at the Bottom (Beginning)

濡 其 尾 吝
Wet The, Its, His Tail Blame, Humiliation

He wets his tail. Humiliation.
(Explanations of this line vary. To some it suggests that one cannot go too fast. Others see the meaning as cautioning those with a lack of experience. Still another views the line as a warning that the times are unsettled.)

Nine in the Second Place

曳 其 輪 貞
Pull, Brake The, Its, His Wheel Perseverance
吉
Good fortune

Slow down ("brake the wheels").
Perseverance brings good fortune.

Six in the Third Place

未 濟 征 凶
Not yet Completed, Finished Attack Misfortune
利 涉 大 川
Benefit Cross Great Water

If one is not yet prepared ("finished"), attack brings misfortune.
Benefit to cross the great water (that is, to embark on a large enterprise).
(Some have interpreted the line to mean that when the chance arises, go forward. Others refer to the necessity of acting within one's own borders.)

Nine in the Fourth Place

貞 吉 悔 亡
Perseverance Good fortune Remorse Disappear
震 用 伐 鬼
Shock, Large force Use, Act Attack Devil
方 三 年 有 賞 于
Area Three Year Have Gift, Tribute At, In
大 國
Big Country

Perseverance brings good fortune.
Remorse disappears.
Use a large force in attacking enemies ("devil area").
In three years, the larger country will receive tribute.
(Historically, China was the larger country in its wars with enemy lands. Tribute was given to the conqueror. Therefore, the line predicts that the larger country will have conquered the smaller in three years, as implied by its receiving tribute.)

Six in the Fifth Place

貞 吉 无 悔 君
Perseverance Good fortune No Regret Superior
子 之 光 有 孚
Man, Person Of Glory, Light Have Sincerity, Trust
吉
Good fortune

Perseverance brings good fortune.
No regrets.
It is the glory of the superior man that he is sincere.
Good fortune.

Nine in the Sixth Place (Top)

有 孚 于 飲 酒 无
Have Trust, Sincerity At, In Drink Wine No
咎 濡 其 首 有
Blame Wet The, Its, His Head Have
孚 失 是
Trust, Sincerity Loss Correctness, Righteousness

If one celebrates ("trust in drinking wine"), no blame.
If this is excessive ("wets the head"), one loses the trust of others and one's own rectitude.
(Commentators have pointed to the "already completed" attitude in the previous hexagram as contrasted with the "not yet completed" meaning in this, the last of the hexagrams. Thus, nothing ends. Change continues.)

Tea-Lea

Reading

ABOVE: William Sydney Mount. *Dregs in the Cup*. 1838. Oil on canvas, 42 × 52″. New-York Historical Society. Evidently, the diviner's reading of the tea leaves has hit home, causing the fashionable client mild embarrassment.

OPPOSITE: Ink-blot number three of the ten standardized Rorschach images employed in psychological testing. Color print by Hans Huber. Courtesy Rorschach Institute.

Tea-Leaf Reading

Those shapes I see
In clouds on high,
All come from *me,*
Not to *my eye.*

Tasseography, or reading derived from cup dregs, resembles divination by observing movements, ripples, and colors of water in pools, streams, and containers (hydromancy) or by examining the dregs in a wine glass (olimancy). When tea-leaf reading began is not known, though in the West tea was not imported until the 1600s. Tea-leaf forecasting has long been associated with gypsies, although there are almost no references or documentation available on its history.

Watching clouds is a well-known pastime. For centuries, it was also a method of forecasting. What one person sees as a chariot another might picture as a mountain, another as a bear, still another as a band of angels. The visualizations thus come from within the observer. In the early twentieth century, a collection of irregular ink-blots was organized into a special test whereby a person would report what he or she saw in these otherwise meaningless configurations. The responses were tabulated, systematized, and correlated with the known psychological makeup of the viewer and the results of a clinical course. This procedure was eventually refined into a formal mechanism for helping psychiatrists and psychologists to discover the emotions and thought patterns of patients. It is known as the Rorschach Test, after the name of its originator, the Swiss Hermann Rorschach. Indeed, the activity of perceiving visual symbols in otherwise formless patterns, whether in clouds, vegetation, pebbles, sand, or other materials, is itself a sort of Rorschach test.

So it is with looking at patterns of tea-leaf bits or coffee grounds in a cup. What we see there—or rather what we choose to visualize—is a reflection of our state of mind at that time. We often differ markedly from others in the figures we discover in the same pattern of dregs as each of us puts together from the chance arrangements whatever suits the moment, although we may be totally unaware of the significance of the choices we have made. Wishes, fears, anticipation, frustration, past experience, present emotional state—all may play a role. The images that emerge we call forth ourselves. Of course, it may require a psychiatrist or psychologist to seek dispassionately the significance of our visualizations.

Teacup forecasters believe that they can connect the symbols that a person sees with his or her problems and subsequent experiences. In these general goals tea-leaf readers superficially resemble the Rorschach investigators but they differ markedly in that they do not make systematic studies of the associations or test the accuracy of the correlations. Furthermore, if the tea-leaf reader performs the readings rather than the client, the analogy is not really applicable.

However, when the requesting person actually does the imagining, clues can sometimes be discovered that reveal the psychic and emotional condition of that person. This in turn may explain the direction in which the person wishes or fears to go, the events which he or she suspects will occur in the future, the acts which he or she feels obligated to perform. In these respects, the subject may be prognosticating either knowingly or unknowingly. (One way of combining the methods of self-examination with divination by a tea-leaf reader would be to have the client report the images he or she sees in the cup and then to have the reader evaluate their significance.)

An entire lexicon of symbols has been passed on by tea-leaf and coffee readers and other occultists. The innumerable dictionaries of patterns in the residues are similar to dream books (glossaries of dream imagery and its meanings). However, although many of the meanings attributed to the dreamed images are the same as the associations assigned to the tea and coffee dregs, a fair proportion have quite different implications. For example, dogs visualized in a cup of tea leaves are equated with reliable friends and rewards, but they forecast treachery in some dream books. The image of a dragon in a teacup warns of terror ahead but with an eventual good result. In dream books, it often signals wealth and advancement. A horse ridden or running prognosticates good news to the tea-reader. The same figure in a dream is seen by some as a risk in business; to Freudians, it is a symbol of sexual intercourse or of sex itself. The rabbit in tasseography merely displays its well-known trait of timidity. Dream books consider the animal's appearance to predict favorable ventures and victory over enemies. The tortoise means false flattery when in the cup; a long life and good fortune in the dream lexicon. The form of a lion in the teacup residues tells of help by powerful friends and favorable contacts with people in high places. The same animal is seen as a father or other authoritative figure in psychiatric analyses of dreams.

In this candid nineteenth-century documentary photograph, an older woman is sharing the wisdom of the tea leaves.

OPPOSITE: Arthur I. Keller. *Women at Tea.* c.1890. Watercolor on paper, 17½ × 12″. Private collection.

BELOW: Henri Matisse. *Tea.* 1919. Oil on canvas, 55 × 83″. Collection Mr. and Mrs. David Loew, Beverly Hills, California. The institution of afternoon tea has often been a time for personal revelations.

Formal tea-leaf reading is surrounded by rituals that require the participants to brew and drink the contents before looking at the remnants in the cup. Readers place emphasis on the treasured utensils used in this process. Chinese porcelain teapot, from a service sent to Mount Vernon in 1757 and used by George Washington. Height 6½″. The Mount Vernon Ladies Association Collection.

Technique of Tea-Leaf Reading

To get the most meaningful information about the future, the petitioner is asked by the tea-leaf reader to have a particular purpose for consulting the teacup. Career? Romance? Contemplated venture? Journey? Illness?

Preferably, one particular cup should be reserved for divination. Tea leaves that are too fine may not make recognizable patterns. Arranging coffee grounds also often requires several attempts in order to obtain pronounced images. Coffee readings therefore sometimes result in more abstract pronouncements because the objects may not show up as vividly.

The petitioner is supposed to clear his or her mind of extraneous thoughts at the outset. The contents of the cup are to be drunk as the session starts, allowing a little fluid to remain in order to distribute the dregs. The cup is held in the left hand, twirled around three times, inverted to empty the remaining liquid, and then placed upright again. If the leaves or grounds are too thick to show any patterns at all, the process is repeated with fresh contents. If three such attempts are unsuccessful the reading is abandoned. The future is not meant to be revealed at that time.

"The tea leaves say you should go into insurance, but I say forget the tea leaves and go into whatever makes you happy."

The reading is begun immediately after the cup has been drained. The meanings of each of the objects perceived are obtained from a dictionary of established symbols and also by intuition. All over the world, gypsies are believed to possess this intuition to a high degree and therefore to be especially talented readers. Capitalizing on this reputation, tea and coffee restaurants have sometimes given themselves appropriate names, such as Gypsy Tea Room, Genuine Gypsy Tea Reading, Original Gypsy Tea Room, First Gypsy Tea Place, Authentic Gypsy Tea Tavern, and similar labels. Of course, the reader hired by the establishment may turn out to be anything but a gypsy.

The assigned meaning of each symbol has to be modified according to its position in the cup, its clarity, and its contiguity to adjacent shapes. For instance, an object lying in isolation signals its full basic meaning; obscured by grounds it assumes negative values; surrounded by dots, it takes on monetary overtones. Figures at the top of the cup near the rim have more positive and agreeable connotations than the same patterns on the bottom. Also, the significance of a particular image depends on the person's cultural background, occupation, and personal experiences. To an observing Christian, the cross inspires associations that a Muslim or Jew would probably not see. Someone who has been in an accident at sea may look upon the image of a ship or an anchor as representing tragedy and danger rather than good tidings and luck.

A few observers who are familiar with the uses of the Rorschach Test have taken up some of its general implications in evaluating the psychological makeup of the person doing the tea-leaf reading. Concentration mainly on the overall shape of only the largest masses in the dregs is said to reflect a practical but pedestrian personality. Attention to varieties of images throughout the cup and within individual "blobs" signals an active, curious mind. Attention to both the whole and the parts goes with a well-balanced nature.

The following list is a composite drawn selectively from treatises on tasseography, gypsy tea-leaf readings, and manuals of fortune-telling. The divinatory significance of any particular symbol imagined by the reader or client can vary with the lexicon and the interpreter. One is also free to assign one's own special meaning to an image.

Animals and Creatures

Alligator: danger of deceit.
Ball: uncertainty; good or bad fortune will follow.
Bat: deceit by friends.
Bee: success, loyalty, gathering of friends if there are several images, influencing an audience.
Bird: fortunate outcome. (A flying bird means good tidings. A bird at rest or standing means a happy landing. The owl, however, connotes the presence of failure.)
Bull: aggression and insensitivity.
Butterfly: enjoyment; the dissipation of money, when surrounded with dots.
Cat: hostile friend about to strike.
Chicken or Rooster: chattering is senseless; pomposity is noisy.
Cow: comfort and nurture.
Crab: watery associations; beware of the shy person with sharp claws.
Deer: treachery.
Dog: reliable friends. (A running dog means a rewarding meeting lies ahead. A dog lying down means be careful not to speak ill of a friend. A dog at the bottom of the cup means a friend is in need of help.)
Donkey: faithfulness, patience.
Dragon: terror ahead, but with a good outcome.
Elephant: achievement by perseverance; wisdom.
Fish: supreme good fortune; travel over water.
Fox: cleverness in others is not always well-intentioned.
Frog or Toad: avoid pomposity.
Goat: hidden enemies.
Horse: news. (A walking horse means news arrives slowly; a running horse or horse being ridden means good news will arrive soon.)
Lion: extreme good luck; help from powerful friends; good relationships with people in high position; favorable ventures ahead.
Mouse or Rat: robbery; loss; untrustworthy friends.
Parrot: gossip.
Peacock: increase in material possessions. (When the peacock's tail is open it signifies land or real estate. A peacock surrounded by dots means money.)
Pig: uncertain success; good and bad aspects to the events ahead.
Rabbit: timidity.
Snake: hostility; danger; falseness. (When near the top of the cup the snake means overcoming deceit. At the bottom of the cup it means losing to deceit. The snake is differentiated from a road or a curved line by the presence of the snake's head.)
Spider: cleverness and persistence.
Swan: quiet contentment.
Tortoise or Turtle: danger of being fooled by flattery.

Geometric Shapes

Circle or Ring: success and good fortune; marriage.
Cross: unsuccessful outcome; someone hostile; chance of illness.
Dot: money; usually a good omen; adds financial involvement to its contiguous symbols.
Line or Road: Seen merely as a line, it means advancement but with some interruptions if the line is broken. (If seen as a road, it is a path to the future, winding or straight. The associated meanings depend on which symbol crosses it or is present at the end. For instance, surrounded by dots, the line or road means monetary progress. A cross at one end indicates an upset of expectations.)
Polygon: even-handedness; balance.
Rectangle or Square: confinement or restriction; if seen as a coffin, means a death among associates or family.
Triangle: meanings depend upon the position of the apex; if pointing toward the rim, it suggests successful plans; if toward the bottom, it means failure of plans.

Letters of the Alphabet

Any letter that is seen is the first letter of the name of someone who is or will be influential.

Numbers

1: ambition; enthusiasm; leadership.
2: friendship; favorable partnership.
3: involvement in writing, music, or public relations.
4: hard work; research project; settlement of dispute.
5: significant changes; speaking or entertainment event.
6: harmony; good domestic relations.
7: a spiritual experience; an intuitive decision.
8: executive endeavor; prudent business plans.
9: insightful forecast; an altruistic enterprise.

Objects

Acorn: good luck and good health.
Airplane: unplanned trip; high achievement.
Anchor: success in business, social affairs, and travel.
Arrow: highly significant event, with potential danger.
Axe: problems that must be handled.
Bed: mental preoccupation. (If the image is clear and tidy, it means logical solution; if irregular or obscure, it means sloppy reasoning.)
Bell: news and significant information to arrive.
Boat or Ship: resolution of difficulty; chance to avoid trouble.
Book: controversy when the book is open; information sought but not obtained, when closed.
Boot or Shoe: shielded from unwelcome events.
Bottle: health concerns; the outlook depends upon adjacent symbols.
Bread or Breadloaf: accent on material things.
Bridge: grand opportunity ahead.
Bush: friends.
Cabbage: jealousy.
Cage: desire to escape convention.
Car: travel; interest in possessions.
Castle: attainment of authority or relationship with authoritative figure.
Cat: danger of unsuspected treachery.
Chain: law or authority will assert itself.
Chair: surcease; improvement in position.
Church: morality needs reinforcement; code of ethics must be followed.
Clock: unnecessary delay; final resolution ahead.
Clown: entertainment with serious purpose.
Crown: supreme success; valuable gift.
Cup: introspection; contentment; quiet ease.
Cymbal: good news to be announced.
Dagger, Knife, or Sword: danger (when pointed up to the rim, it means hazard to oneself; pointing down, it means danger to others); need for control of rashness.
Door: obstacle ahead that needs knowledge to be overcome.
Drum: dissension; slander; gossip.
Egg: supreme good fortune.
Engine or locomotive: pent-up energy needs expression.
Fairy or Angel: desire to do good; unrealistic expectations but eventual satisfaction.
Fan: inexplicable event will bring reward.
Feather: uncertainty; lack of focus.
Fly: worry; disturbance.
Flag: warning of danger ahead.
Flower: success.
Fountain: good omen; devotion; abundance.
Fruits: good fortune.
Garden: gathering of people with pleasurable intentions.
Garland: honor.
Gate: possibilities ahead will depend on how one uses them; the gate is both an entrance and an exit.
Glass: honesty and incorruptibility.
Grass: joy, ease, idleness.
Gun: danger of hostility by oneself or from others.
Hammer: fortitude in the face of attack; perseverance in overcoming difficulty; danger of insensitivity.
Harp: peace; affection.
Hat: new opportunities.
Heart shape: love and money. (The associations depend on adjacent symbols.)
Horn (musical instrument): communication, either for good or ill.
Horn (of an animal): domination or subjugation.
Horseshoe: a legacy.
Hourglass: urgency; use the present advantageously.
House or Building: security—domestic and commercial.
Jewel: attention. (A bracelet means a liaison lies ahead; an earring means a need for attention; a necklace means reception of admiration.)
Jug, Vase, Pail, or Pot: influence; service; generosity.
Kettle, Teapot, or Coffee Pot: domestic serenity.
Key: insight; perception of meanings and opportunities.
Kite: speculation.
Ladder: advancement step by step.
Lamp or Candle: desire to be enlightened; perseverance will bring understanding.
Leaves: mixed significance. (Falling leaves means danger of illness; a fern leaf means disloyalty in self or others; a fig leaf means slander; a garland of leaves means honor; a grape leaf means anger; several leaves means favorable events; a thistle means beware of hidden hostility.)
Letter or Envelope: news and information ahead.
Lock: obstruction.
Mask: danger of deception.
Mountain: high goal.
Mushroom: expansion; advancement.
Nail: danger of injustice.
Needle: love affairs.
Nurse: chance of illness in those who surround one.
Oyster: prosperity and joy.
Package: unexpected happening.
Pen or Inkwell: disturbing news.
Pencil: business affairs; temporary arrangements.
Pipe: satisfaction; minor but pleasant events.
Purse: material gain.
Racket (for tennis): good fortune for a friend; winning a dispute.

Samples of tea were first brought from the Far East to Europe in the seventeenth century. The date of the first tea-leaf reading is not known. Chien Hsuano (1235–1300). *Tea Connoisseurs.* Painting on silk. Osaka Municipal Museum.

Rake: personal affairs need organization.
Saucer: debts.
Saw: danger of dissension caused by outside factors.
Scales: litigation; a fair decision is needed.
Scepter: financial strain.
Scissors: dissension.
Scythe: faithfulness. (When partly covered, it means danger to relationships.)
Spade or shovel: achievement only after diligence.
Spoon: in need of money or personal satisfactions.
Table: a gathering of people, social or business, depending upon adjacent symbols.
Tent: love affairs, with stormy periods.
Telescope: concern with the future; perceptive forecasting.
Trident: good outcome in business and travel.
Tree: favorable state of health; fruition of plans. (Two trees close together means a close attachment; separate trees means a separation will occur; many trees means excellent health ahead.)
Trunk: necessity to prepare for travel.
Umbrella: in need of aid and security. (When open, it means security will be achieved; when closed, it means security delayed.)
Violin: self-sufficiency; danger of self-centeredness.
Volcano: strong emotions with potential for harm.
Wall: obstruction to be overcome; favorable outcome.
Watch: proposals—commercial or personal.
Wheel: recovery after trials, hard work, or illness.
Windmill: achievement by adaptability and steadfastness.
Wings: important news coming.
Yoke: danger of being entrapped or enslaved.

Body Parts

Ear: secrets.
Eye: caution is needed.
Face: good luck, if of a stranger; uncertainty in outcome of plans if face is familiar or one's own.
Foot: danger; pain; disappointment.
Hand: caution in love and business.
Mustache: suspicion and intrigue.
Nose: beware of deceit, gossip, and failure in investment.

People

Baby, Child, or Cradle: minor concerns; someone entering the family; love affair.
Man: visitor; someone bringing gifts.
Mermaid: immorality beckons.
Rider or Jockey on a Horse or Vehicle: good news ahead; an event related to foreign travel.
Walking person: good business; new friendships; new ventures.
Woman: courtship; happiness.

The Sky

Cloud: obstacles, doubts, problems unresolved.
Comet: new and unexpected relationship.
Moon: love, when full; change, when half or crescent; obstacles to love and fortune, when covered.
Star: variable fortune. (When six-pointed, it means highly favorable fortune; five-pointed means favorable but with unexpected features; many-pointed means chance for success but with undesirable accompaniment.)
Sun: full success and power.

Sample Reading

The question posed by the petitioner in a sample tea-leaf reading was, "Is my love quest going to be fulfilled?" The images seen in the tea-leaf bits in the cup were reported by the questioner to be: the letter L, a road, an eagle, a snake, a swan, a horseshoe, a duck on water, a tree, a man with a shield and a sword, and birds in flight.

The diviner could then construct a reply. If the person is pursuing a particular courtship or contemplating one, it may be that someone whose name begins with L will be influential in its outcome, or the letter may represent the cherished person's initial. Chances of wishes being fulfilled are very good (road, eagle), with minor diversions from the goal (waviness of the road). Quiet contentment (swan) is more apt to be the reward than is passionate fire. The general good fortune (duck on the water) may not be perceived at first (horseshoe). A healthy relationship (tree) is highly likely. Two possible dangers are present. Deceit (snake) by the object of affection can be imminent. A second hazard is that someone will come upon the scene (man with a shield and sword) who will jeopardize the quest by distracting or harming the loved one—but not the petitioner. Yet, good news should be on the way (birds in flight) and it will be soon (if they are nearer the top of the cup than the bottom).

The tasseologist might offer an additional general evaluation. Since the petitioner had described only discrete individual images and saw no overall shape, object, or figure in the total collection of dregs (for instance, a face formed by the total outline was described by another observer present at the reading), the analyst might suggest that the questioner is concentrating more on parts of the situation than on the whole. Is it possible, asks the diviner, that you are placing too much emphasis on the projected romance itself? What about the actual person to whom you are directing your thoughts? Are you clear on what you really want? Are you seeking immediate satisfaction? Someone to fill a present void? Or is this the person with whom you would wish to spend a month, years, a lifetime? What is your real objective? The big picture?

Different images may be seen in this same arrangement by different people. Furthermore, using the same shapes and even the same lexicon of meanings for the figures, another interpreter might develop an entirely different scenario. The possibilities are endless.

The cup with the actual dregs used in the sample tea-leaf reading.

Dreams

Dreams

I myself am everyone,
Yet no one else am I;
The dreams I see
Are tales of me
My truth, my need, my lie.

OPPOSITE: Hyman Bloom. *Apparition of a Danger.* 1951. Oil on canvas, 54¼ × 43¼″. The Hirshhorn Museum and Sculpture Garden, Washington, D.C. An apparition is an exceptional appearance seen while awake; a dream is a series of images seen while asleep. Both are visions created by the mind.

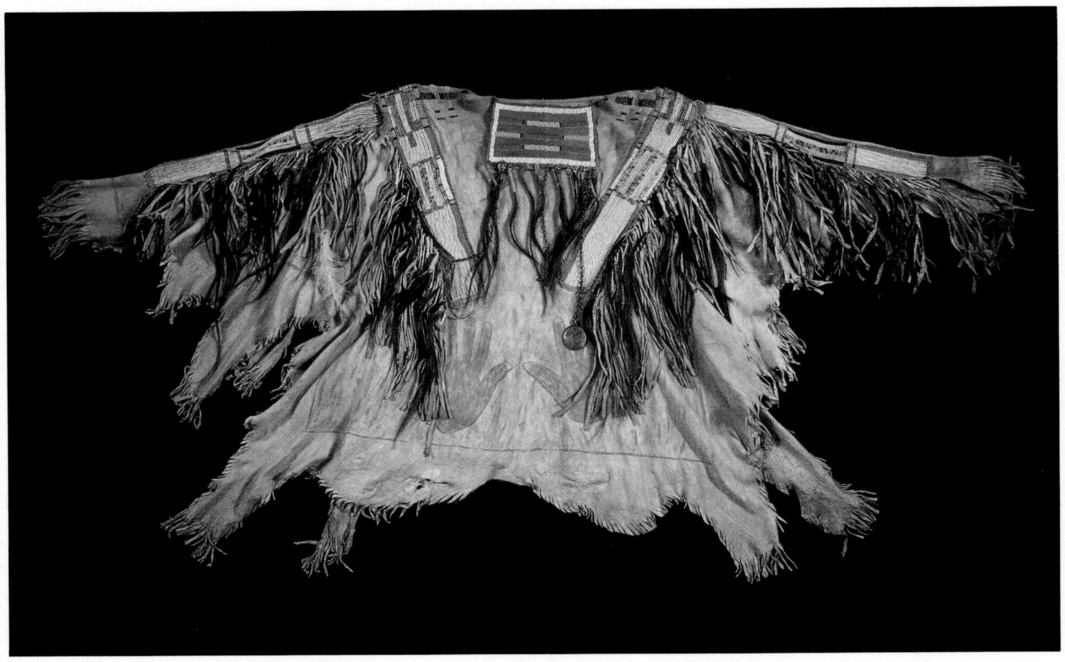

A "dream vision" shirt worn by a member of the Crow tribe to induce dreams (or visions), which are remembered as important messages and symbols. Acquired by the Smithsonian Institution in 1899 from Crow Indians in Montana. 70″ width (at shoulders). Smithsonian Institution, Washington, D.C.

All creatures sleep or else exhibit temporary cessations of awareness and of motion that resemble what we call sleep. Mammals, particularly the family of which humans are classified as members, apparently have to sleep at some time for short or long intervals (each species has its own special pattern). Why must creatures sleep? Many explanations have been offered by investigators, but no universally accepted theory is at hand, except that some kind of recharging of energies or perhaps resorting of received images is required through the suspension of physical activity and consciousness.

Is dreaming a necessary part of sleep? Most of us certainly have observed motions and sounds in our pets that suggest that the animals are under the spell of a dream. Studies of human sleep have correlated some dreaming with rapid eye movements (REM) and similar phenomena have been observed in sleeping animals. Moreover, people who claim that they never dream also have been shown to have the same types of REM as those who do. People may forget dreams or prefer to forget them—as we all often do—but apparently dreaming is an integral part of the sleep process in everybody.

As to why we dream and what dreams tell us, myriad explanations have been

ABOVE: Frederick Leighton. *Flaming June*. 1895. Oil on canvas, 47½ × 47½″. Museo de Arte de Ponce, Puerto Rico.

OVERLEAF: Illustration from *Le Nimi—Jataka*. Burmese. Nineteenth century. Gouache on paper. Musée Guimet, Paris. This tale of Buddha depicts an elaborate dream sequence.

offered from the earliest times to the present day. In this chapter we will review the history of dream interpretation to help explain how methods of dream prognostication developed. Since many of the systems that we use now are in principle the same as those that were followed far back in time, our historical survey is in itself a presentation of the modern techniques of interpreting dreams.

History

Prehistoric and Preliterate Cultures

Although we may believe that prehistoric people had dreams, we do not know what they dreamed or what they thought about the images. However, the customs of certain societies existing today might offer clues to the attitudes of early humans. Of course, the beliefs and practices of some of the present-day indigenous cultures in the Americas, Africa, Asia, Australia, and the Pacific islands may merely represent evolution and modifications in each society over thousands of years.

Two general types of dreams in these cultures are those that are important to the society and those of personal significance to the dreamer. In both groups, the dreams may be spontaneous or induced, but those considered of general import are usually brought on by special rites—involving fasting, meditation, regimens, and even the intake of drugs. Both adults and children try to produce these dreams, which can elevate their status. A shaman or witch doctor, for instance, is often self-chosen by a divine decision revealed in dreams.

Among some cultures the mundane replaying of daily activities predominates in dreams. In others, dreams are mystical and complex. Dream life and the real world are usually recognized to be different, but some peoples evaluate both to be equally important. A dream of adultery is a punishable offense in some societies, perhaps even requiring restitution to the offended husband. If the sleeper sees an act of sorcery against someone else, he or she is duty-bound to inform the intended target, who can then take steps to nullify the bewitchment. On the other hand, some groups feel no shame for dreaming about violations of ethical codes. Indeed, they enjoy these experiences and try to carry them to full satisfaction.

Although the spirit may leave the body during slumber it must return before awakening. The journey is often to the world of dead ancestors, where the dreamer may receive instruction. Moreover, if someone dreams of having suffered a disaster or death, the person's spirit is considered to have had the experience and has therefore been lost. A shaman is needed to rescue the spirit and set things right. Sometimes, however, as with the North American Iroquois, dream scenarios may have opposite meanings: joyful dreams may indicate sadness ahead; misfortune in a dream may be announcing good tidings. This same reversal of significance was also a common characteristic of dream interpretation in many ancient civilizations—notably Mesopotamia, Greece, and Rome.

Alternatively, instead of the dreamer's own spirit leaving, outside spirits may enter the body during sleep. An animal or object can appear so vividly and so prove its worth in a dream that forever afterward it becomes the totem, talisman, or amulet of the dreamer. The Sioux Native Americans place the blame for asocial behavior on evil spirits that entered the offending person's dreams and stimulated unacceptable actions. Usually, however, it is the dreamer's guardian spirit—often a dead ancestor—who is responsible for directing the dreams and for advising, warning, and healing.

Some of the attitudes among these cultures resemble the theories of contemporary psychotherapists. The Huron peoples of North America consider dreams to show the wishes of the soul and to give satisfaction in the revelations. Freudians might look upon this belief as implying that opposition to the soul's needs can cause sickness. The Kurds in Asia find that a person of good conscience will be rewarded by having pleasing images during sleep. In one African tribe, the dream of an elephant being killed is held to be a prediction that a chief, who is equivalent to a great animal, will die. One might characterize such a dream as a hostile wish.

The Iroquois and others try to get rid of distressing images by acting out what was dreamed, often in elaborate rites. The mere recital of disturbing experiences (often overtly sexual) is supposed to give relief. The practices of shamans and witch doctors encourage such unburdening. The value of "confession" is evidently well understood. However, other groups, such as the Maricopa of the American West, are cautioned not to reveal what they have learned in a dream, lest the guardian spirit be offended by the disclosure and withhold further information.

In most traditional cultures of the world, the dream itself is held to be of prime importance. Sleeping life coexists with waking life and plays a highly influential role in the ideology and the activities of the tribe and the person.

The Far East

Both in the traditions and in the ancient writings of Indian culture, dreams were considered to be an integral part of the personality. The reality of this world, which was the waking state, was matched by the simultaneous reality of another spiritual world, and between the two was sleep, in a middle world, which could look both ways and yet was of neither.

The levels of consciousness were classified variously

depending upon the society and its adherence to Hindu, Tibetan, Buddhist, or other religious doctrines. For instance, in the Upanishads, the ancient Hindu religious commentaries, four separate states were recognized. The awake condition contained cognition of outward surroundings. Dreaming represented the personal spiritual life of inward cognition. Deep sleep, void of dreams, was an integration of the other two cognitions. In this stage a person might also be able to achieve the fourth and highest state, beyond all cognition, a merging with the universal mind.

In the ancient Hindu yoga tradition human experience was composed of seven entities—each of which had its own category of dreams—that had to be passed through in order to achieve the highest level of spirituality. In the first three divisions, the dreams responded to physical needs and desires and reenacted daily activities, pictured the astral travel of the soul to familiar or strange places, and overcame fear of death through knowledge and understanding. The fourth entity contained perceptions connected with artistic creation. However, the potential to concentrate on superior works was to be resisted lest the mind be tempted to remain there and thus interrupt the spiritual journey. The fifth body was the storehouse of dreams into which the person entered for the first time the area of universality, where the great myths had been fashioned and experienced. The dreams in the next highest level, the sixth, were the place where the religions and broad philosophies originated. Finally, when the spirit reached the seventh state, nirvana, there was no longer thought or feeling or affirmation or denial. The dream was of nonexistence. It was purely spiritual and everlasting.

All the types of dreams in Indian and related cultures were considered to be part of consciousness and therefore awareness was considered to be maintained while the dreaming was going on. Also, the soul in its voyage through the levels of consciousness and beyond the physical body was able to perceive the future. Communication from the mystical world of the spirit brought forth the content of dreams, but the actual images could be derived from either mundane daily experiences or from universal spiritual interconnections. Telepathic influences from one person to another and travel by the soul during sleep were accepted.

Thus, dreams revealed the past and the future, illuminated the dreamer's character traits, and presented the demands of conscience. The individual was expected to aim at finding the meaning of the dreamed images. Yet, professional dream readers were always plentiful. Over the centuries many reported symbols were sometimes collected into "dream books." The Hindu *Brahmavaivarta Purana,* for example, paid much attention to the images and scenarios in dreams. Elaborate lexicons were built up through both oral tradition and written works.

Among the Chinese, dreamed images were examined in order to determine what the dreamer was thinking and how he or she should proceed in life. Thus a type of "unconscious mind" was apparently recognized. The tendency to categorize all things in nature and all human activities included putting the images of dreams into categories. Just as the number 5 continually recurred in Chinese systems as the basis for most classifications, dreams also were divided into five types: ordinary, contemplative, waking, joyous, and fearful. In Buddhism, which began in India and flourished in China, five dreams announced to the Buddha his eventual mission to spread enlightenment.

Yet, the problem of what a dream really is occupied the philosophers. Chuang-tzu of the fourth century B.C., a disciple of Lao-tse, the founder of Taoism, voiced the dilemma: are we in our supposed real life merely in fact dreaming, to be awakened into a new life? When dreaming that he was a butterfly, Chuang-tzu had no thought of being anything else, but when he awakened he wondered whether he was a man who had dreamed of being a butterfly or whether he was actually a butterfly who was now dreaming that he was a man.

The ancient Egyptians postulated that there are two divisions of a person's soul. The vital spark that energizes the live body leaves after death to become a ghost, whereas the eternal spirit present in life continues to hover over the body when it dies and accompanies the person into the afterlife. The ancient Chinese also believed that a material soul is attached to the body, controlling its functions, but that it dies with the body. A spiritual soul (*hun*), however, could leave during sleep and continue to exist after death.

To the Chinese, dream interpretation could also be influenced by the astrological configurations at the time of dreaming, by the bodily and mental state, the time of day, the season, and the geographic location of both the sleeper and the dream's reader. Incubation—sleeping in a holy place after rites of preparation—was a practice followed by the Chinese. Evidently by the late Middle Ages (Ming dynasty) it was common for officials to rely on dreams induced while sleeping in a sanctuary for advice on how to act in circumstances that they were about to encounter. It is likely that the populace also engaged in seeking similar guidance.

Mesopotamia

In ancient Mesopotamia (Babylon, Assyria, and other kingdoms) dream lore was considered to be highly important, and the skill of dream interpreters evidently gained wide renown.

It was believed that the profusion of surrounding invisible spirits became visible in dreams and thereby was helpful in understanding otherwise inexplicable happenings. Dreaming provided the means of finding a place in the overall cosmic scheme. Astrological omens applied almost exclusively to the royal dynasty, important personages, and large-scale events. On the other hand, dreams were experienced by everyone and had meaning for each person. The images seen by someone in a dream were assumed to be causally linked to the future as messages from the surrounding spirits and deities. Indeed, all dreams were believed to be what we would call supernatural.

One category of dreams reported by Mesopotamian commentators comprised religious communications from the gods, who thereby expressed their wishes or gave orders on matters of high importance, such as restoring a temple or participating in a special ceremony honoring the god. Portentious messages during sleep were usually sent by the gods to announce happy circumstances or to warn against improper behavior by the sleeper. This advice might be couched in symbolism that required interpretation. Unfavorable visions were believed to be inspired by demons, but sometimes were accompanied by indications or even direct depictions of how an undesirable event could be prevented or how evil spirits could be exorcised. Such beliefs were similar to those of early Christian writers, who thought that evil dreams were sent by the Devil. A second type of dreams had more mundane connotations, but these were also held to come through outside spiritual agencies.

Several factors, it was believed, produced dreaming. Dreams could be sought actively, ordered directly, or received spontaneously. For example, one might sleep in a temple dedicated to the dream deity after praying for a good dream. Makhir, the god of dreams, could be importuned for a vision during sleep. In at least one instance a ruler ordered a priest himself to dream about the future of the dynasty. Most often, dreams came spontaneously, sometimes in forthright terms, more often in devious guises needing interpretation by experts, of whom the priests were the most reliable.

Of the three types of priests, the *baru,* the seer-prognosticators, were most important. Indeed, Shamash, the sun-god, was referred to as *baru terêti,* seer of the transmitted lore. Various self-styled magicians (the *ensi* in Sumerian times) and soothsayers—many of whom were women—also plied a trade in translating the symbols, images, and actions portrayed in dreams. Explanations given to the dreamer by a priest or secular interpreter were sometimes enough to alleviate anxiety and to enable the client to extricate himself or herself from the difficulty that had been exposed in the vision—a process that calls to mind dream interpretation by modern Freudian psychiatrists.

Much of what we now know of ancient Babylon and Assyria comes from the twentieth-century discovery of clay tablets from the library of Ashurbanipal, king of Assyria in the seventh century B.C. The summaries of dreams and meanings that appear in some of the tablets refer to much earlier lore, possibly dating as far back as 5000 B.C. Individual symbols were linked to future events. The numerous and detailed items were evidently scrutinized carefully for their significance. A dream of visiting the dead meant that one's own life would be shortened, but restoring a god's statue foretold aging—perhaps indicating that the dreamer would have a long life. Teeth falling out or being pulled presaged illness; a dog urinating was unfavorable; fire announced trouble. However, a vision of eating excrement was favorable; a dream about fish indicated strength. Of course, the significance of subject matter in dreams probably depends in large measure on the cultural symbols of the society. For example the association of the dead with a short life in the Babylonian texts had a different meaning in the civilization of ancient Elam, where images of the dead in a dream signified good luck.

The legends and myths of ancient Mesopotamia were replete with the significance of dreams. Gilgamesh, Sumerian hero of the archetypal epic, was assured of success in three dreams, as interpreted by his mother, a priestess of the sun-god. The great deluge (predating the flood of Noah's time) was predicted in a dream by Utu-napishtim, the wise old man. The Sumerian King Gudea of 2500 B.C. erected a grand temple in Ur in response to heaven's wish expressed in a dream. In the seventh century B.C., Ashurbanipal pressed on in battle at the urgings of the goddess Ishtar, who appeared in a dream. The goddess assured the king that he would not lose his determination nor fail in strength. The contents of the dream were communicated to the troops to cheer them on to victory.

Egypt

Dream lore in ancient Egypt was similar in some respects to that of Mesopotamia. Some have inferred from the biblical story of Joseph, who was descended from Mesopotamian Hebrew forebears, that Mesopotamian dream interpreters were thought to be superior. That the pharaoh earnestly sought an explanation for his dreams, however, indicates that in Egypt dreams were also held in high repute.

As in Babylon, many dreams were brought on through rituals and incantations. Alongside daily existence there was thought to be a world of gods and demons not perceivable except in sleep, when a heightened sensitivity enabled the dreamer to see and receive messages from the deities. To keep away unpleasant images and to produce favorable ones, elaborate magical methods were used, such as placing written words and sayings in a dead animal or under a particular spot on the ground. The focus of dream interpretation was principally on future happenings, advice, and warnings—as in Babylon and Assyria—rather than on the character of the sleeping person. Of course, when the dreamer petitioned the gods to foretell how to overcome a deficiency or fulfill a desire, he or she was in a sense revealing psychological conflicts.

There are a number of examples of messages from the gods. Plutarch reported the story that the gods directed the

"Jacob's Dream" from the *Saint Louis Psalter.* 1256. Illumination on vellum. Bibliothèque Nationale, Paris. Jacob dreamed of a ladder to heaven on which angels traveled—an indication to him that although he would have "ups and downs," God had forgiven him for his deception of his brother Esau.

pharaoh Ptolemy Soter to return a colossus statue to its rightful place in Alexandria. Thutmose IV was promised kingship if he cleared away sand covering the sphinx. Dreams could also be metaphorical. The seers interpreted the appearance of two serpents in a dream by Tonutamen as a prediction that he would one day become the ruler of upper and lower Egypt.

Healing dreams (dreams that effected healing processes) were forerunners of the Greek incubation treatment in Asclepian temples. Imhotep, the presumed architect of the pyramids of Saqqara, was deified (and later replaced by the Greek Asclepius) as a god who appeared in dreams to cure illnesses. Dream healing also occurred in temples to Isis at Philae, the oracles at Thebes, and other shrines.

Virtually all the gods played a role in dreams. However, just as Babylon had its Makhir, the special god of dreams, Egypt had Bes, a household deity effective in domestic affairs, in childbirth, and also in dreaming. He could hold off the demons of the night who caused bad visions and also bring satisfying dreams associated with joy.

Hundreds of dreams are mentioned in surviving Egyptian writings, especially in the Chester Beatty Papyrus in the British Museum, but there do not seem to have been the systematic compilations that were made in Mesopotamia and later in Greece. Most of the recorded dream interpretations appear to have been directed to royalty, but everyone was acknowledged as being capable of dreaming, so that although dream encyclopedias may not have existed, as far as we know, standard associations developed between images and their significance. For instance, a dream about sawing wood meant the death of one's enemies; about falling teeth presaged a death in the family; about buttocks announced the imminent death of a parent.

Although there were similarities between Mesopotamian and Egyptian dream lore, some distinct differences in the meanings of the symbols did exist. For instance, in one Egyptian burial ceremony the priest "opened the mouth" of the deceased to let the vital spirit in or out, as if it were a step in awakening to a new life after death. Thus, images of the dead in a dream had a favorable significance, even forecasting happiness and longevity. Sexual intercourse with one's mother was a sort of reenactment of the activities of the gods and of the mandatory incestuous marriages of the pharaohs. It was therefore a favorable indication of the loyalty of one's relatives in contradistinction to its unfavorable implications in Mesopotamian society.

Some generally accepted images and voiced instructions in a dream were unambiguous enough to permit the dreamer to recognize the message, but the visions were often confusing and, as in many other cultures, special dream interpreters were needed.

Ancient Hebrews

The Hebrews, whose history is intertwined with that of Mesopotamia and Egypt, had similar attitudes toward dreams to those held by their rulers. Some dreams were God-sent and good. Others were caused by evil spirits and bad. In dreams God gave orders through angels or voices, offered warnings, and healed the sick and troubled. Just as in Mesopotamian and Egyptian lore, Talmudic commentators also differentiated between visions from the deity (the meaningful dreams of truth) and from those called evil (of no significance and false).

However, some characteristics were peculiar to the monotheistic Hebrews. As people who considered themselves chosen to spread God's word, they felt that Jehovah spoke more clearly to them. Evidently others also shared that view, for biblical accounts suggest that they were regarded as superior dream interpreters. Some historians note that the dreams reported by the Hebrews were relatively direct messages from the deity, whereas the preponderance of enigmatic dreams in the Old Testament were experienced by non-Jews, who therefore were in need of explanation by the prophets or other prominent biblical figures.

Nevertheless, evidently not all the dreams of the Jews were clearly understood, for there were many soothsayers in Jerusalem and other parts of Palestine. One Talmudist of the late Hellenistic period even wrote of the interpretations of his own dream by twenty-four different dream readers. To counterbalance those who invoked gods other than the one and only Jehovah, there were the pious and true prophets. Jeremiah inveighed against the false interpreters of dreams that were not God-sent. The Bible contains passages that condemn dream readers who misinterpret or recite false dreams and pretend to prophesy in order to lead the children of Israel to worship idols and other gods besides Jehovah.

Most of the dreams reported in the Bible represent advice, promises, and warnings from God or his angel messengers. If there is a prophet among you, Jehovah proclaimed, I will appear and speak to him in a dream. Indeed, God did make himself known to Solomon while he slept. When Solomon thanked the Lord for his past favors to him and to the Jews, he asked for understanding and judgment in order to lead well. For this worthy intention, Jehovah granted his wish—and therefore in a sense showed the prospective future course.

Two dreams were particularly significant in the life of Jacob. In his flight from Canaan, where he had deceitfully pretended to be his brother Esau in order to receive Isaac's inheritance, he dreamed of a ladder leading from heaven to earth with angels ascending and descending. Jacob felt that the very appearance of God was a sign of absolution from his sin. In the second dream, disturbed by guilt, he wrestled with an angel in a man's form, finally gaining supremacy.

Jehovah then informed him that he was henceforth to call himself "Israel"—he who has prevailed. Some analyses of this vision portray the contest as a struggle of Jacob with himself—between his good and bad natures—a "coming to grips" with his past transgressions. Because of this dream, Jacob was later able to approach Esau, now without fear but instead with repentance.

Perhaps the best-known dreams of the Old Testament concern Joseph, Jacob's youngest son. As a youngster, he had a dream that the sheaves of wheat of his brothers bent before his own, and that the sun, moon, and stars also bowed to him. Apparently he did not perceive the meaning until Jacob, with a rebuke, explained that the boy had dreamed himself into a position above his father, mother, and brothers. Some say that this scenario was a description of Joseph's own view of himself, unconscious or conscious, as someone whom God had chosen for supremacy. The various well-known dreams in the story of Joseph were dreamed by others—the baker, wine steward, and the pharaoh—and seen as prophecies by Joseph. In particular, the repeated visions of seven lean cattle devouring the fat ones and similar situations were interpreted as presentiments of seven years of plenty followed by seven of famine. Some scholars have wondered whether the pharaoh himself held the same worrisome view of probable future events but could not perceive their explanation until it was analyzed by Joseph. This inability of a dreamer to perceive the meaning of the symbols in a dream is a common characteristic, according to modern psychoanalytic teachings.

Dreams from Jehovah did not come to everyone. Even as powerful a personage as King Saul was unable to pray himself into a prophetic and counseling dream from God.

OPPOSITE: Egyptian stela. Third century B.C. Ny Carlsberg Glyptothek, Copenhagen. On the stone a jabiru bird symbolizes the spiritual part of a person, which remains during dreams and after death (here being embalmed with the corpse).

"The Sacrifice of Isaac" from the *Manuscript of Saint Gregory of Nazianzus.* The Courtauld Institute, London. The middle panel depicts the dream of Jacob, in which Jacob struggled with the angel. The top panel shows the Sacrifice of Isaac. The bottom panel depicts the Anointing of David.

Job, on the other hand, had so many fearful and disturbing nightmares that he implored the Lord to spare him those images. Many of the visions of the prophets were forecasts of doom but some were glowing promises of the future.

The most active forecaster and dream interpreter mentioned in the Bible seems to have been Daniel. The details in the stories of his analysis of Nebuchadnezzar's nightmares, his explanations of the handwriting on the wall to Belshazzar, and his survival in the den of lions testify to the high position and respect he gained in the courts of his Babylonian and Persian captors. Especially striking was his ability to prompt Nebuchadnezzar to recall a dream of the destruction of a huge idol that disturbed the king considerably but which he had mostly forgotten. Daniel explained that the dream announced the conquest and dismemberment of the Babylonian empire into four separate kingdoms. Some equate the rock that destroyed the statue with the later Christian Church or with the power of God. Of considerable importance to Nebuchadnezzar's spiritual life was a dream of the scattering of leaves and fruit from a great tree, whose trunk was chopped across leaving only a stump. Daniel's prediction came true that the king would go mad and recover only when he acknowledged the one God.

Daniel himself also had dreams that have been variously interpreted. His dreams of a ram and a goat are said to have foretold the later conquests by Alexander the Great (symbolized by the ram's larger horns) and of Antiochus IV (by the goat's smaller horns). His dream of four beasts being overcome by a man is believed to have announced the future Messiah. Gabriel appeared to Daniel in another dream to forecast a time when a Messiah would

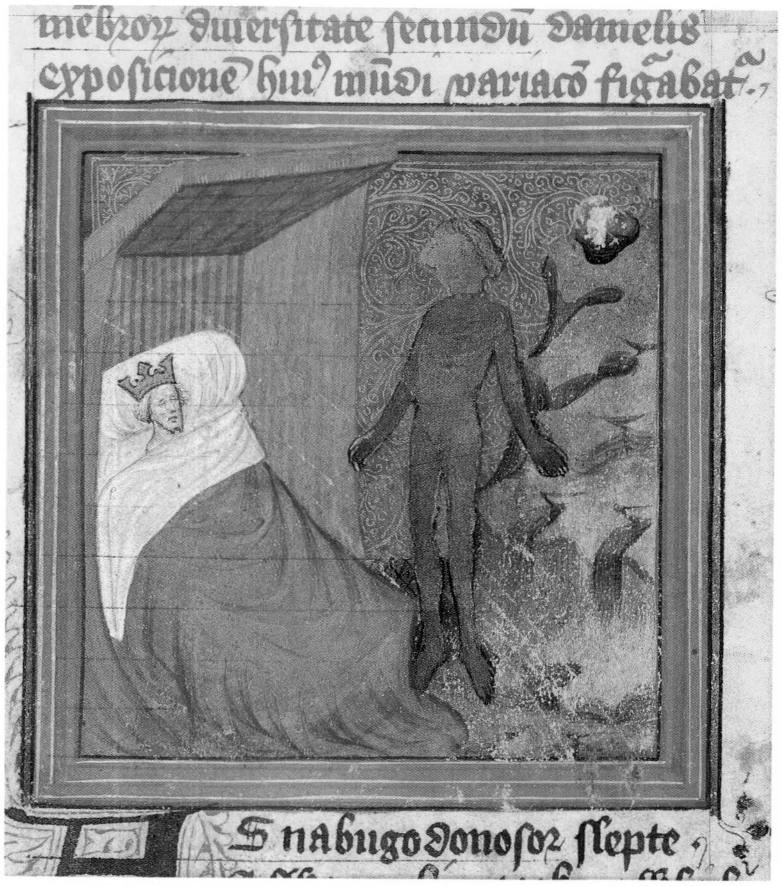

ABOVE: *Nebuchadnezzar's Dream*. The Bodleian Library, Oxford. Nebuchadnezzar's dream of a huge idol about to be destroyed was interpreted by Daniel as a sign that the Babylonian empire would soon be dismembered.

OPPOSITE: John Martin. *The Feast of Belshazzar*. 1820. Oil on canvas, 31½×47¼". Yale Center for British Art, New Haven. It was at Belshazzar's feast that Daniel foretold the imminent destruction of the King that the handwriting on the wall prognosticated.

BELOW: *Vision of Charlemagne*. Charlemagne (742–814), whose domain became the foundation of the Holy Roman Empire, had regular dream interpreters as part of his retinue. Bibliothèque Nationale, Paris.

come to redeem the Jewish people and resurrect Jerusalem. The angel also warned of an eventual Day of Judgment. All of Daniel's prophecies rested on his belief in the supremacy of Jehovah, who could cause even the most powerful to fall, elevate the lowliest, and protect the pious from harm.

Although most visions in sleep were thought by the

peoples of Mesopotamia, Egypt, and Palestine to be supernaturally inspired, some "natural" or ordinary dreams were also recorded. Isaiah, for example, spoke of the fulfillment of desires, as when a hungry man envisions during sleep that he is eating or satisfying the thirst that he had before he slept. In Ecclesiastes it is recognized that dreams could arise out of the day's mundane activities. Sexual encounters during dreams, including the erotic visions of Incubus and Succubus demons, do not seem to have been considered sinful by the Hebrews—an attitude that certainly seems to presage Freudian concepts of unconscious sexual drives.

Head of Hypnos. Egyptian. Third–first century B.C. The British Museum, London. Hypnos was the Greek god of sleep and the twin brother of death.

Greece and Rome

Both supernatural and natural dreams were acknowledged by the ancient Greeks and Romans, but secular interpretations were given greater prominence. For probably the first time, philosopher-scientists attempted systematically to understand the mechanisms of dreaming without resorting to purely religious explanations. Yet, although their analyses were in accordance with the science of the period, they were in some respects still related to what we would call the supernatural. The existence of a person's soul was considered a fact and the presence of a universal soul of the cosmos was accepted dogma. They accepted, too, that the soul was under the body's control except during sleep, when the soul was unrestricted and could express itself.

Dreams were thought to be communications from the gods, messages from the soul, or disorders inside the body. Reports of dreams and their predictions were put into collections, which were often consulted to help understand the meanings of the images. Their prophetic value was generally accepted, with a few notable exceptions. The Epicureans, for instance, attached only corporeal significance to dreaming.

Homer's definition, in the eighth century B.C., of dreams as messengers from the gods was acceptable ideology virtually through all of later Greco-Roman history. The Orphic concept that visualized each person's soul as free during sleep to communicate with the deities was maintained in one way or another in the philosophies of the Pythagoreans and Plato and also in plays and poetry.

Homer's recitals and the poetry of Hesiod reveal the Greek view that dream images were derived in a genealogical line from Hypnos (sleep), Thanatos (death), Ker (doom), Moros (ill fortune), and originally Chaos (disorder), mythological figures who antedated the time of the gods of Olympus. The dramatist Euripides, using a different lineage, connected dreams to the underworld as "black-winged" children of Chthon, goddess of the underparts of the earth. The playwright Aeschylus credited the mythological god Prometheus, who brought humans fire and was punished by the other gods for that generosity, with the invention and interpretation of dreams. In the

F. Sim. *Prometheus.* Nineteenth century. Wood engraving. Best known for the punishment inflicted on him for bringing fire to mankind, the Greek god Prometheus also imparted to humans the skill of interpreting dreams.

Odyssey, dreams were placed in a village just adjacent to the abode of the souls of the dead—therefore not quite among the living and yet not of the dead, as a sort of bridge between life and death. Homer assigned two gates through which the dreams left the underworld to enter into humans. True images came by way of the Gate of Horn; the false passed through the Gate of Ivory.

Later Roman writers perpetuated the tradition of regarding dreams as having supernatural origins. Virgil depicted a tree of dreams growing among visions that haunt people in sleep. To Ovid, sleep was a god, Somnus, in a house surrounded by mythical demons, in an area of mists and silence. To Lucian, dreams were located on an island where they were indistinct and outside the real world.

Thus there tended to be a linkage between dreams and darkness—it was thought dreams could be dissipated by light and the sun (Helios). Some have inferred a corresponding implication that the images in dreams could be better handled when they were brought out into daylight, but that view may merely be grafting modern beliefs onto ancient theory.

The Philosopher-Scientists

Pythagoras (580–500 B.C.), whose teachings are known through the works of his pupils and followers, attributed meaningful dreams to demons and meaningless images to disorders of the functions of the body. It was commonly believed in his time that the soul was active during sleep. Even the poet Pindar, who considered dreams to be of little significance, averred that the soul could judge things correctly while a person was asleep. Indeed, he guessed that human lives themselves might merely be dreams. Heraclitus of the late sixth century B.C. taught that the suspension of senses in sleep gave the soul free rein, but that the soul performs according to its own rules in dreams, which are not necessarily rational and therefore not part of reality. Yet, since each soul is part of the soul of the universe, dreams can predict what lies ahead. His belief was deterministic in that he envisaged there was an overall plan for everything in the cosmos. Democritus in the fifth century B.C., in keeping with his concept that invisible atoms exist throughout the universe and constitute all its objects, including humans, postulated that images too were ever-present and penetrated into each person's body wherein they appeared as dreams.

Plato, in the fourth century B.C., accepted the notion that demons brought dreams but ascribed the character of a dream to the particular part of the soul of the sleeping person that was in ascendancy. He classified the soul into three divisions—reason, passion (or anger), and desire (or wish). If reason was in control, the dream was truthful but might be obscure and therefore require skill to be

OPPOSITE LEFT: *Plato.* Vatican Museum, Rome. Plato accepted supernatural causes for dreams but attributed the origin of the images seen to the soul of the sleeping person.

OPPOSITE RIGHT: *Aristotle.* Aristotle believed that dreams were caused by disorders of the heart, but also that they could reveal the previously unnoticed.

LEFT: *Cicero.* Museo Capitolino, Rome. Cicero mocked those who interpreted dreams as reliable forms of prognostication.

understood. When either passion or desire was predominant, a dream became confusing, sometimes producing monstrous behavior that would not have been countenanced during the waking state. This reasoning suggests to some that Plato may have recognized that dream images can represent a person's repressed desires and drives. But he also attributed some of the events in dreams to the residual movements carried over from the waking state.

Of the Greek philosophers, Aristotle (384–322 B.C.) offered the most extensive explanations of the process of dreaming. He believed that dreams were an affliction of the heart, for in his physiology the heart, not the brain, was the source of sensation and emotions. Our languages still connect "heart" with feeling. We say, "I know in my heart"; "have a heart"; "my heart's desire." Aristotle had a physiological explanation for the bodily mechanics of dreaming: what a person sees while awake remains in the body during sleep as an image, which is carried through the bloodstream. Dream images are seen as if they are unclear reflections in a stream whose waters are in motion. If the blood flow is turbulent, the scenes appear more confused. Stimuli from the outside are multiplied in intensity. For instance, a slight sound in the vicinity of a sleeper might become a loud thunderclap in a dream. Stimuli from inside the body are also heightened and can show up as conflicts, such as dreams of fire, flood, and war, indicating changes that may be announcing the presence of physical disorders that are undetected in the waking state. Dreams therefore can be useful to the physician as clues to undetected abnormalities and to prognosis. They could also have general predictive value by revealing the hitherto unknown probabilities in people, activities, and surroundings that escape perception during consciousness. Despite these mainly secular associations, Aristotle's system contained some religious explanations as well. For example, he reasoned that since everyone dreams, demons probably initiate the process, for gods would not be likely to visit unworthy persons.

The Stoic philosophers, followers of Zeno of Citium who lived in the fourth century B.C., saw dreams as being spiritual in origin. Some were divine and others the result of emanations from objects and creatures that were transmitted to the sleeper. These philosophers (named Stoics after the columns, the *stoa,* around which the group usually gathered) subscribed to a predetermined universal plan connecting all things, and therefore they subscribed to divination practices, including interpreting portents in the sky or dreams.

Many Roman rulers were either staunch Stoics or shared their beliefs. According to Plutarch, Julius Caesar's wife, Calpurnia, received warning in a dream that her husband would be killed if he went to the Senate. Augustus clearly believed in the power of dreams and had a law passed requiring public disclosure of any dream that pertained to the state. Other emperors, as for instance Tiberius, Caligula, and Domitian, ostensibly saw in dreams the circumstances of their own deaths. Nero's night visions, reported by his court soothsayer, Artemon, were persistent horrors: seeing ants crawl over his body, being dragged by his wife into a hidden place, standing locked inside the statues of gods. Modern psycho-historians have analyzed his dreams as being unconscious self-punishment for the well-known sadistic acts he committed. Others think that the dreams reported by the emperors were often merely part of devious political maneuvers.

Yet, there were also those who dissented from dream divination. Epicurean philosophers, who followed the principles of Epicurus (whose writings we know about mainly from the works of Lucretius in the first century B.C.), taught that truth could best be found through observation and perception; that the gods exist because people believe in them but they have no inherent power; that the universe is made up of atoms. According to the Epicureans, dreams had no predictive powers, rather they represented physical forces in the body. In the first century A.D., Petronius, the trusted advisor of Nero, considered dreams to be fabrications of each person's mind—an astonishing precursor of today's attitudes. He wrote in his *Somnia*: "Dreams, dreams that deride us with their fleeting shadows. They do not come from the temples of the gods. Each man creates his own dreams."

Cicero (106–43 B.C.) was one of the most outspoken critics of divination by dreams. If gods wished to communicate with humans, he reasoned, they would do so during the day as well as at night. They would seek to appeal to the intellect not to confuse through obscure symbols. The mere fact that dream images have myriad meanings, depending on the dreamer and the interpreter, shows their lack of value. Dreams are not sent by the gods but instead arise from the thoughts and happenings of the day. Yet, even though Cicero was not convinced that dreams had any value, he seemed to take into consideration a particular dream he had that Octavius would attain power.

One of the noteworthy commentaries about dreams after the time of Cicero was by Macrobius, in the fourth century A.D. He used the "Dream of Scipio," an essay about Roman morality attributed to Cicero, as a foil for his opinions. In the course of his commentary, he classified dreams into five types: the predictive allegory (the Greek *oneiros* or Latin *somnium*); the clear prediction (*horama* or *visio*); the dream oracle from the gods (*chrematiomos* or *oraculum*); the nonpredictive allegory or straightforward scenario (*enhypnion* or *insomnium*); the nonpredictive nightmare (*fantasma* or *visium*). Macrobius believed that bodily states were one cause or influence over dream content, but he also believed in the spiritual origin of dreams.

Dreams in Medicine

The idea that dreams are connected to health and illness was evidently widely accepted in Greece and Rome. For instance, the Hippocratic writings include a full treatise on dreams, although it may have actually been composed a century after Hippocrates. In addition to the separate segment on dreams, interspersed among other parts of the collection are recommendations to physicians to elicit from their patients the subject matter of visions during sleep, together with associated emotional reactions. From these bits of information, it is suggested, one may prognosticate and prescribe treatment.

The nature and time of the dream was believed to affect its meaning. At the height of an illness during a crisis, images of coldness merely showed that a chill was occurring. The same image during recovery might signify that a chill and relapse were in the offing. Some Hippocratic accounts warned that a dream could be prodromic, the first indication that disease was present before the symptoms. When an athlete, for example, reported that he dreamed of standing in a marsh, his trainer needed to recognize that he had an excess of fluid in his body and that he should be bled.

The ideas in the Hippocratic writings collected in Alexandria were continued in later centuries. The anatomist and teacher Herophilus of the fourth century B.C., who considered himself a disciple of Hippocratic doctrines, classified dreams into the god-sent (*theopemptoi*), prophecies from the soul (*physikoi*), and representations of bodily conditions of the humors (*synkrimatikoi*). Rufus of Ephesus of the second century A.D. was another noteworthy disciple of the tradition. He emphasized the need for every physician to take into consideration the nature of his patient's dreams.

Perhaps the most influential medical authority of the Roman era was Galen. He endorsed Hippocratic teachings for virtually all aspects of medicine, including the emphasis on the therapeutic powers of dreams.

Galen (no one knows what his first name actually was, although some historians later inserted the prename of Claudius, but without verifiable correctness) was personally affected by the power of his own dreams and those of others. He was started on his career in medicine by his father, Nikon, who had a dream about Asclepius, the god of medicine, and sent his son to be taught by Satyrus, a respected physician in their home city of Pergamum. A few years later, Asclepius appeared again in a dream, this time to Galen, and instructed him to cut open a blood vessel in his hand to relieve a severe internal infection. Galen reported that after that maneuver he recovered. On at least two other occasions, divine visions during sleep influenced his life: he heeded a warning to remain at home in Rome rather than to accompany his patron the Emperor Marcus Aurelius on a military campaign, and he was stimulated to complete a medical treatise that he had started after being scolded in a dream into finishing it. Galen also paid attention to those dreams by his patients that advised them to drink particular concoctions or to apply special ointments.

Galen placed much store in the mundane scenarios and symbols that came to a sleeper, which he attributed to derangements of the body. When properly interpreted, he believed, dreams announced a preponderance of one or more humors, whose proportions determined health or illness. Although Galen by no means originated the humoral concepts of physiology (they were almost a thousand years old by his time), he did emphasize and expand the theories. His unrivaled influence during the subsequent fifteen hundred years or so helped to maintain the standard basis

RIGHT: *Hippocrates.* 1825. Line engraving. (Imagined depiction.) Among the writings attributed to Hippocrates was advice to the physician to find out the subject matter of the dreams of patients as a help in diagnosis and treatment.

BELOW: A miniature of Galen teaching from the *Therapeutica.* Venetian. 1500. Wellcome Institute Library, London. Galen, in the second century A.D., affirmed the teachings of Hippocrates of the third century B.C., emphasizing the importance of dreams in medicine.

of diagnosis and treatment according to the presumed imbalance of the four humors: yellow bile from the liver; black bile from the spleen; phlegm from the brain; blood in the heart and vessels.

However, Galen was essentially a pragmatist. Within the competing philosophies of medicine—Methodism, Dogmatism, Pneumatism, Empiricism, and others—he counted himself an eclectic, choosing from each what he saw to be the effective practices. To Galen therefore dreams were one useful tool for discovering the nature of a person's disease and the proper direction for treatment.

The preponderance of dreams analyzed by Galen were

secular in content. He perceived the mechanism of dreaming to be a movement by the person's soul into the interior of the body and mind, where it observed the body's physiological state and formed correlating imagery that the sleeper saw as dreams. Since these visions were manifestations of what was needed to resolve any unhealthy conditions, they were often looked upon by Galen as expressions of wishes by the soul. Some moderns have evaluated this theory as a recognition by the ancients that dreams could be depictions of "wish fulfillment"—a tenet of Freudian and other present-day systems of psychology.

The Healing Shrines

Physicians and patients alike attached special importance to the visions seen during sleep in the Asclepieions, the temples where the god Asclepius visited his petitioners.

This phenomenon was a striking example of the mingling of religiosity with rationality in dreams. Dream therapies had been practiced in Mesopotamia and Egypt and were even mentioned in the Bible. In the Greek world, healing shrines of Amphiaraus at Oropus and of Trophonius in Lebadia were also famous, but the widely distributed Asclepieion temples eventually became the prevailing sanctuaries to which rich and poor could go when medicine's capabilities were insufficient. Not only was there no rivalry between doctors and Asclepian priests, but the physicians frequently set up their offices (*iatreia*) near the precincts of the temples. Asclepius, who evidently began as a human warrior-leader in the Trojan War, receiving mention in Homer's *Iliad,* was later raised to the status of a demigod and eventually a god. Myths abounded concerning Asclepius but all in some way connected him with healing. He was considered to be a son of Apollo, the sun-god, who was himself a patron of health, disease, and healing. Asclepius was later merged with deities of other cultures, as for example with the Egyptian Imhotep, becoming Asclepius-Imouthes.

Adjacent to some of the temple compounds, there were elaborate buildings and arrangements for relaxation and entertainment, of which the famous amphitheater of

The Greek amphitheater near the Asclepian temple at Epidaurus (built 380 B.C.). Supplicants visited the theater for entertainment before sleeping in the temple.

An imagined reconstruction of the Asclepian temple at Epidaurus in Greece. Sick people went to the temple to dream of the healing god Asclepius, who would cure them during sleep. The rotonda (left) was the area for purification; the abaton (center), for dreaming; the temple (right), for worship.

Epidaurus is an outstanding example. However, the central focus was the *abaton,* where the primary function of incubation was acted out. Here, after preparation that included bathing in the *tholos,* the suppliant went to sleep for the purpose of dreaming of Asclepius, who would treat, advise, or prognosticate. No clear evidence is found that the petitioner took any preliminary drugs or underwent hypnosis, but the patient must have already been impressed by the ritual, imposing architecture, and religious mystical atmosphere in the semidarkness, together with the widespread reputation such a shrine had of accomplishing cures, all reinforced by the visible votive offerings and lists of previous successes. By the time the god ministered to the patient, he or she may have well been in a mood to believe in the hoped-for alleviation of symptoms.

There is some question of whether the god always appeared in a dream or whether the priest in the garb of Asclepius, sometimes attended by a retinue standing in for his daughter, Hygeia, and other members of the god's family, visited the dozing or half-awake suppliant. A variety of treatments might be administered or prescribed: a particular regimen of activity; a plant or animal remedy; an actual or symbolic action, such as the opening of an abscess, applying an ointment, or laying on of hands. Sometimes the accompanying snake, the standard representation of Asclepius himself, might lick the affected part. Fanciful manipulations also could occur during the dream states, as for instance a decapitation of the person's head and then its replacement with the symptoms gone.

On awakening in the morning, the patient expected to be free of the medical problem. Reports by commentators of failures are few but they do exist, and some people had to return many times before being healed. Models of parts of the body that had been successfully treated—for instance, statuettes of legs, hands, breasts, intestines, and a variety of other areas—were on display in Asclepieions, thereby acting as further reassurance to others who came to be treated.

Much of what we know of the Asclepian temples comes from the diaries of Aelius Aristides, a contemporary of Galen's and a highly regarded orator whose principal focus in life seems to have been his illnesses. Virtually every system in Aristides's body exhibited a derangement at one time or another, varying from vomiting and diarrhea to cough and constipation; chills and sweating to debility and dryness; growths and eruptions on the skin to headaches and mouth pains; clear attacks of anxiety but also major illnesses, such as smallpox. The descriptions of his symptoms and their subsequent course suggest that although at least some of his sicknesses were indeed organic abnormalities, many more were probably of psychological origin (psychosomatic in today's terminology), and even the physically pathological states were often associated with emotional reactions that Aristides did not differentiate from disease itself.

Aristides described in detail in his *Sacred Tales* about 130 of his dreams, most of which either were actually experienced within Asclepian temples or were about Asclepius the god. Although Asclepius, whom Aristides often referred to as his savior, was his special deity, he also obtained healing benefits from other gods, among them Zeus, the highest god in the pantheon; Apollo, father of Asclepius; Athena, patron goddess of some diseases; and even the Egyptian gods Serapis and Isis. He looked upon all his dreams as divine messages, some of which were forthright advice to consume or apply particular substances or to act in a variety of ways—perhaps to exercise or to rest. Often the images, words, and scenarios were more subtle and were interpreted by Aristides to signify how he was to proceed in treatment as a divine prescription.

Asclepius, for instance, indicated in a dream that a particular drug containing salt should be applied to a tumor of the thigh, which led to its disappearance. At another time, despite the expressed misgivings of his doctor, Aristides prevailed upon him to administer an enema, as suggested by a dream, which was followed by immediate recovery. In response to entreaties from Aristides to save his declining father, Asclepius advised him to speak some particular phrases. After they were recited, the man's health was restored. On the other hand, Aristides interpreted a dream he had of having a bone stuck in his throat to mean that blood should be drawn from the ankle, a rather elliptical conclusion.

A contemporary of Galen's, Aristides probably never met him, although he subscribed to the Galenic opinion that dreams could forewarn of impending illness. Aristides was contemptuous of physicians, ridiculing their ineffectiveness. Yet, many of the remedies he employed at the direction of the gods in fact corresponded to the medical practices of his time.

Aristides looked upon most popular dream interpreters as charlatans or ignoramuses. His own interpretations of dreams, however, were mostly in accordance with accepted traditional meanings. A dream of being restrained or obstructed meant prolonged illness; a rising sun was beneficial to the hopeless; the image of a monument would lead to recovery. Like Jacob's dream in the Old Testament, moving up a ladder presaged advancement but with risk; descending the steps announced fault or failure.

Artemidorus

Artemidorus Daldianus, a professional soothsayer in the second century A.D., became the most influential dream interpreter of all time. Even in the twentieth century Sigmund Freud paid attention to the *Oneirocritica,* a series of five books in which Artemidorus collected all the reports of dreams that he could find and in which he summarized the theories and practical methods of explaining the meanings of dreams. In the collection, Artemidorus wrote: "I have not only made special efforts to obtain every book on the interpretation of dreams but also have kept company for many years with the much-disdained soothsayers of the marketplace." His purpose was "to fight against those who wish to abolish divination." By studying every work on dreams that he could discover during his many travels, he aimed to prove the validity of dreams as a method of prediction by describing their actual fulfillment in historical reports and by his own observations. Another goal of his was to help those who needed advice but were unable to obtain reliable interpretations of their dreams. In his writings, he also referred to other kinds of visions, oracles, fantasies, and apparitions, and there is some evidence that he was the author of works on palmistry and augury, but dreams were his principal concern.

Thus, three of the outstanding writers on dreams lived in the same century in the Greco-Roman world, and yet in all likelihood they never met each other. Aristides was an illustrious orator of the upper class, and Galen was perhaps the star physician of his generation, eventually becoming the personal doctor to two emperors. On the other hand, Artemidorus, a professional soothsayer, was educated and knowledgeable but clearly of lower rank. His class position was so far below that of the other two, and his occupation so denigrated by them, that there was little chance for intercommunication. Galen's commentaries, however, referred to Aristides's health history and to the dream books of Artemidorus.

Especially because Artemidorus codified and systemized virtually all the ideas and methods of past dream interpreters, his treatise was useful to subsequent students of dreams. Indeed, in the sixteenth century, not long after the invention of printing from movable type, the *Oneirocritica* was published in Venice (in Greek), Basel (in Latin), and Lyons (in French). Later English editions were reprinted repeatedly, and translations into many languages continued through the centuries.

In keeping with long-standing custom, Artemidorus classified dreams into the predictive and the nonpredictive. His main focus was the predictive group. One significant difference, however, from previous writings was Artemidorus's effort to match dream symbols with what actually happened to the dreamer afterward. He tried to verify personally the presumed meanings of the objects, people, and scenes seen in the dreams with later events and was candid in recounting errors in his own and others' prognoses.

The obvious forthright experiences during sleep wherein a future happening was clearly enacted or forecasted he called "theorematical." Here no soothsayer was needed. But the "allegories"—the objects and scenes that were indirect, subtle, and symbolic—required interpretation. Each of these headings was further divided and subdivided according to the subject matter. For example, allegories could be about oneself only or about others as well as oneself; about public places and structures; even about the cosmic actions of sea, earth, and sky. The attribution of prophetic meaning to dream symbols formed the bulk of his five books.

For proper interpretation, several prerequisites were essential. In the first place, a report of the entire dream was needed. The first four of the five books in the *Oneirocritica* contained mainly individual symbols and their significance. Only the last book gave full dream descriptions (in the form of instructions to his son on the methodology). A second necessity for correct interpretation was information on all the specifics surrounding the dream and the dreamer, for the same image might have a different or even opposite meaning, depending upon its conformity to the makeup of the person and of the society.

Artemidorus categorized the factors into six groups: nature, laws, custom, time, occupation, and name. If the activities occurring in a dream conformed to the usual behavior of the dreamer or were in accordance with the laws of nature and humans, the omen was auspicious; the contrary if not. The common customs appearing in dreams were favorable portents: honoring the gods, caring for children, sexual congress, being awake by day and asleep at night. A person's name might affect the dream's meaning. Acrostics and numerological associations of a name in the dream could reveal the underlying sense that might not at first be apparent. The time of occurrence also influenced the significance. For instance, the dreams at the end of sleep were likely to be important. This emphasis on the hypnagogic state just before awakening or at dawn was a legacy from the Homeric myth of the Gates of Horn and Ivory through which dream images passed from the underworld into the sleeper. Only after midnight was the Horn passage open to the path of truth.

The same dream could mean or predict different things, depending upon the dreamer's finances, health, age, and status. For instance, highly placed and "moral" people were more apt to have dreams of importance; government officials to dream of the state and country. Let us take the example of a dream that is about the dreamer's birth. To the poorer person, the omen is good, for like an infant he will have someone to look after him. For a rich man, the outlook is bad. He will be dominated by others, as a baby is under someone else's control. The working person will become unemployed, just as infants do not work. The slave will be treated kindly and his misdeeds overlooked, as is the attitude toward infants. But he will not become a free man, because a baby is ruled by others. Since newborns do not walk, run, or physically overcome others, an athlete who has such a dream will lose out. The traveler will return home to his own land, the place where a baby is born. The sick will die, for like infants the dead are wrapped and laid on the ground and life ends as it began. The fugitive cannot flee successfully; he is a counterpart of infants, who cannot overcome obstructions or stand steadily. The plaintiff in a suit cannot win his argument as newborns cannot speak. But the defendant will win or receive a light sentence even if convicted, just as children are forgiven.

Artemidorus's methods of interpretation applied a number of mechanisms—all of which were virtually standard practices—including wordplay and puns, symbols, and analogies. The image of a camel was equated with the thigh because the derivation of the Greek word for that animal is "bent thigh." Artemidorus repeated the report that Aristander, Alexander the Great's soothsayer, had interpreted his master's dream of a satyr (*satyros*) as a prophecy that Alexander would conquer the city of Tyre. By putting together the two as parts of the Greek word, *sa* (your) and *Tyros* (Tyre) the forecaster announced that Tyre would be Alexander's. We now use in everyday language many of the traditional dream metaphors that Artemidorus inherited and maintained, as for example, the "ship of state" and "smooth sailing" for its course.

The symbols and analogies Artemidorus codified were almost endless. For instance, rivers and streams represented blood flow; polluted places, the bowels. The body parts symbolized objects and activities: the mouth meant a house; teeth, the inhabitants and also possessions. Loss of teeth by a debtor indicated the paying off of his debts; if without pain it signaled payment through conscientiousness and current earnings. When pain was the accompaniment, the payment could be made only by selling possessions. Springs were analogous to urine. If a spring seemed to be held up, urinary difficulty was predicted. Earth was equivalent to flesh, so that scorched land meant abnormal dryness.

Dreams involving the beard were highly significant. While beards were common among the ancient Greeks, during early Roman times clean-shaven visages became fashionable, until in the second century A.D. Emperor Hadrian, a noted Grecophile, restored the style of sporting facial hair. A thick beard was a good portent for a philosopher or an orator or a merchant (as a symbol of dignity and forcefulness). However, the act of having the beard shaved off or pulled was unfavorable, signifying shame. A woman who dreamed of having a beard could have a variety of expectations: if married, she would be separated, for she would be then acting as both husband and wife; if a widow, she would marry again (merging with a husband); if pregnant, she would bear a male child, identifying with him when he was grown up and wearing a beard; if involved in litigation, she would prevail, for she would be highly respected by the court.

There certainly had been compilations of dream symbolism before—such as the ancient Mesopotamian tablets; certain presumed Egyptian papyri; very early Greek handbooks; the work of Aristander, Alexander the Great's diviner, referred to by Pliny, Plutarch, and Artemidorus; the reported writings of Artemon, Nero's soothsayer. However, the encyclopedic accomplishment of Artemidorus remained the standard source in the many subsequent centuries. Just as Artemidorus had studied many writings on dreams, from

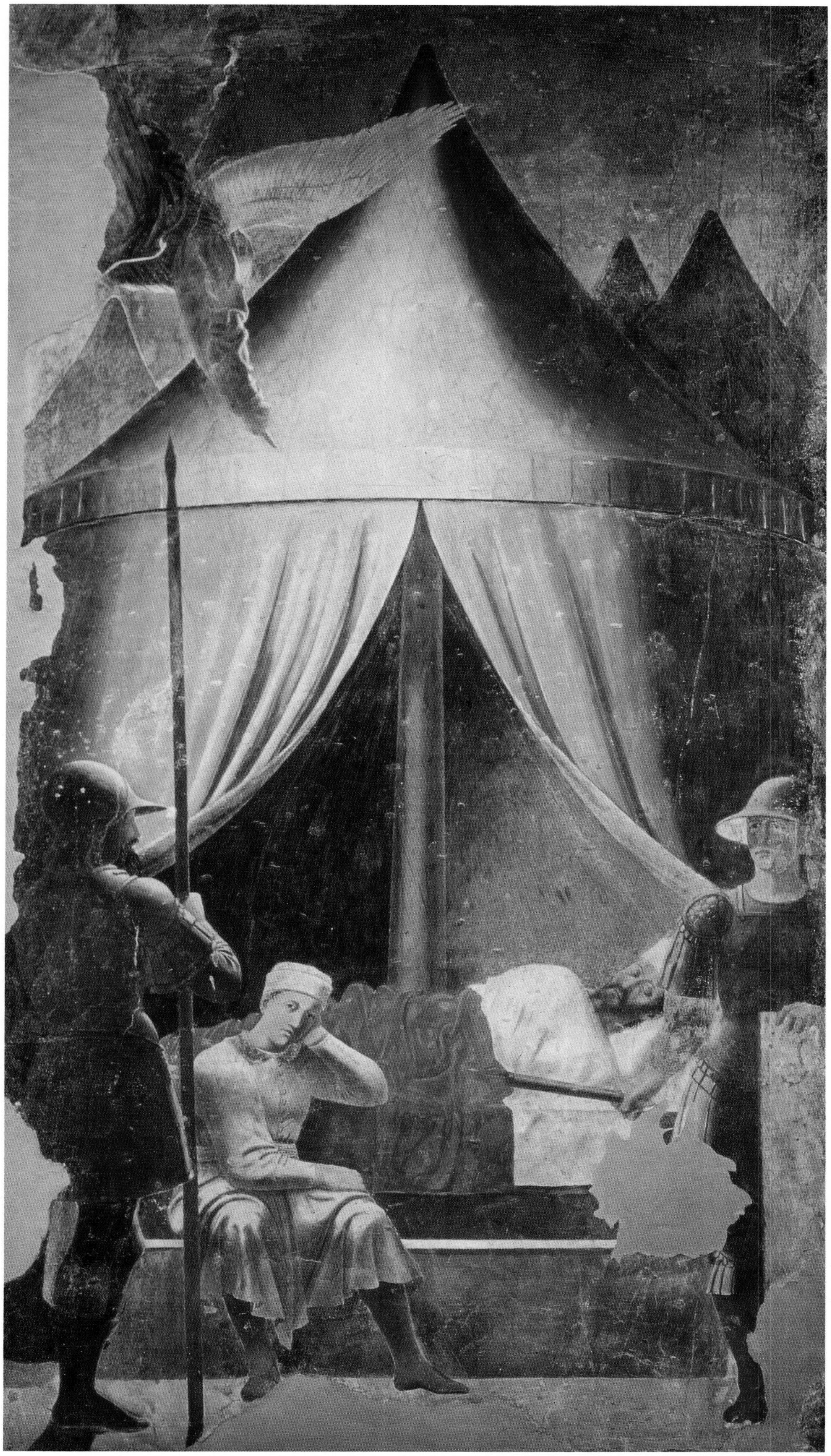

Piero della Francesca. *Dream of Constantine.* 1453–1454. Fresco. San Francesco, Arezzo. It is said that the Emperor Constantine was converted to Christianity from paganism after dreaming of a flaming crucifix promising him victory over his rivals.

OPPOSITE: Alexander the Great at Tyre, 332 B.C. The conquest of Tyre had been foreseen in a dream interpreted by Alexander's soothsayer.

the ancient Assyro-Babylonian and Egyptian periods to the contemporary texts of his time, so also did students and practitioners of dream lore after him develop their own dream books. Investigators have found compilations throughout the Byzantine era, and of course also long afterward, composed in either verse or prose, in Greek, Latin, and Arabic. There was much mutual borrowing and duplication of textual material. Scholars differ widely on the datings, sources, and authorships. For example, one of the earliest dream books to appear after Artemidorus has had its date of origin variously assigned from the second century to the seventh century A.D. Some dream books were later translated into many languages—among them French, Italian, German, and even Welsh. It is not known how much influence each of them had but even as the numbers increased into recent centuries, most still harked back to the organization and content of the books by Artemidorus.

The principle Artemidorus based his conclusions on, the association of images and their outcomes, is in accordance with present scientific methods, but various essential ingredients were missing. For example, he took at face value all the reports, from the past and from his clients, of the correctness of the predictions. There was no evaluation of the frequency of the confirmations of the prophecies as compared with the number of failures. The collection of observations rested on untested a priori assumptions that the visions reported and subsequent happenings had to be related. Skepticism and challenge, which are necessary to arrive scientifically at a perception of factual associations, were absent. Nevertheless, in terms of his times, his pursuit of correlations between symbols and future events was a unique, honest attempt. Even in his cynical advice to his son to convince clients and to respond to their needs he was forthright: Artemidorus emphasized that no matter how he impressed the customer, he was never to delude himself.

Early Christianity

Dreams continued to play an important role in Christian thinking, but the early Church, as it battled against the influence of pagan magic, had difficulty in deciding whether to accept predictive suggestions in dreams. Which were divine and true, rather than impious and false? Part of the dilemma lay in the prominent mention of dream interpretation in both the Old and the New Testament. The Gospel of Saint Matthew indicated that an angel from God informed Joseph in a dream that Mary would conceive a special son through the agency of the Holy Spirit. Appearing in dreams, an angel of the Lord warned the three wise men not to return to Herod to report the birth of Jesus, cautioned the Holy Family to flee from Herod, and eventually advised Joseph while he was in Egypt that he could return to Israel. Moreover, at the beginning of the Passion, some commentators reported that the wife of Pontius Pilate had importuned her husband in vain to spare Jesus rather than Barabbas because of the dreams she was experiencing.

Tertullian (c. A.D. 155–222), an early North African convert to Christianity, tried to reconcile pagan philosophy with the ideas of the Church. He postulated that dreams came from God, nature, and demons. In sleep, the soul, having left the body in a condition resembling death, remained active and in a state of "ecstasy" (a word meaning "to step out"), perceiving but not causing all the images and emotions experienced in dreams, whether divine or mundane. Origen, a Christian bishop of the second century and a staunch intellectual defender of the faith, allowed that some but not all dreams came from God. He wrestled with the problems presented by dreams: to differentiate among the divine, the earthly but predictive, the foolish, and the evil.

The significance of dreams received challenges from both anti-Christians and the devout. Celsus, a second-century Roman Platonist philosopher (not to be confused with the Roman encyclopedist of the first century), opposed Christianity itself and asserted that the idea that dreams come from a Christian God was a delusion carried over from the Old Testament, in which the Jews had shown themselves to be mere charlatans. He called Jesus a despicable sorcerer.

A noteworthy Church father, Gregory of Nyssa of the fourth century, sought to counter pagan objections to Christianity and aimed at rational explanations of dreams. Yet, he concluded that his analyses owed much to Platonic and Aristotelian views. While acknowledging that some dreams were inspired by God, most were caused by the experiences, thoughts, and food consumed during the waking hours. In keeping with early Greek theories, he described the mechanism of sleep as a suspension of the mind and feelings during sleep, which allowed the soul to be in control. Because the senses and intelligence were inoperative, one might see absurdities as well as scenes from the memory of images perceived when awake. Moreover, stimuli from within the body could uncover unrecognized disorders and predict the course of a person's health, as Hippocrates and Galen had theorized. Even more significant were Gregory's beliefs that dreams could reveal a person's character, expressing the anger and lust within. The drives for self-preservation that impelled animals were paralleled by sexual and other sinful wishes of people resulting from modifications during sleep of virtuous human impulses. Gregory's explanations thus can be seen to affirm the "wild beast" that Plato had postulated as one of the parts of the soul.

Theories of dreaming by other Church fathers in these early Christian centuries also seemed to have had resemblances to Platonist ideas. Synesius of Cyrene, for example, wrote a book in the late fourth century on

Saint Augustine of Hippo (North Africa). The prominent church philosopher (A.D. 354–430) is shown teaching from one of his writings in this illumination from a twelfth-century manuscript. Augustine's conversion to Christianity was predicted in one of his dreams.

dreams, in which he concluded that during sleep the soul obtained from God a view of the future. The mind received and stored information from the waking state, but the soul, freed in sleep, could see things to come. This faculty was possible because each person's soul was part of the universal soul of the cosmos, under God, a prevalent attitude among the thinkers, philosophers, and scientists of medieval times. Indeed, the word *universe* in several languages literally means "turned into one."

A noteworthy instance of the important role played by a dream in the history of the Church was the conversion of Constantine in the fourth century, an event that had a profound effect on the dissemination of Christianity in Europe. Before a crucial battle, Constantine is reported to have dreamed of a flaming cross accompanied by the phrase "*in hoc signo vinces*" ("under this sign, you will conquer").

Perhaps the most influential of early Church leaders was Augustine of Hippo (A.D. 354–430), whose *Confessions* had lasting impact on Christian philosophy. He contended intensively with the purposes and meanings of dreams. In his own life, a dream had predicted his conversion to Christianity. Yet, in keeping with his honesty and sincere pursuit of truth, he acknowledged that he was unable to resolve the dilemmas in a way that was satisfactory either to himself or to others: "I have not solved but complicated the question," he wrote. This very recognition of his difficulty has served as an admonition to thinkers ever since. In Augustine's view, if one could not explain with reasonable certainty even the common daily occurrence of dreaming, one should not rush to offer opinions on larger questions beyond one's own range of experience—an activity that both ancients and moderns have often engaged in. The chief problems for Augustine were how to differentiate between divine and mundane dreams; the God-inspired and demon-caused; the predictive and ordinary.

Medieval Europe

Ambivalent attitudes toward dreams were displayed by the medieval Church. For example, Pope Gregory II of the eighth century castigated the practice of dream interpretation, threatening the death penalty for those who disobeyed his mandate. Nevertheless, Church officials sometimes used the content of dreams by those accused of heresy as evidence of having consorted with the Devil. Pope Leo IX in the eleventh century was plagued by visions during sleep, which he assumed were Devil-sent.

Many writings and historical records indicate that both the general populace and the noble class believed in the prophetic value of dreams. Charlemagne even had an official dream interpreter. The practices of incubation in healing shrines of pagan times continued to be observed at caves, churches, and holy places during the Christian Era, although the Virgin Mary and various saints now replaced the god Asclepius. Medieval and Renaissance literature was filled with allusions to valid predictions that came to sleepers. *The Song of Roland, The Romance of the Rose,* the tales of King Arthur and the Round Table, Chaucer's *Canterbury Tales, Decameron* by Boccaccio, Dante's *Divine Comedy,* miracle plays, and many other prose and poetic works are merely a few of the many examples. Indeed, Rabelais in his *Gargantua* and *Pantagruel* recited, with irony, the history of dream interpretation.

Those who wrote about the causes, mechanisms, and meanings of dreams continued to follow generally the ancient theories of Aristotle and Plato and other Greek philosophers. The explanations of a few of the contributors may serve as examples.

Hildegard of Bingen, a thoughtful, poetic abbess of the twelfth century, made an analogy between the moon and the soul of a person. Just as the moon gives brightness to the night, the soul enlightens the sleeping person, often showing the way ahead through its ability to see the truth. In the same manner as clouds and storms can darken the moonlight, the Devil can obscure the dream through indecent images.

To Thomas Aquinas in the thirteenth century dreams could be both prophetic and causes of the future. Aristotle had also suggested that dreams could influence a person to act in particular ways and therefore in a measure produce future happenings. Aquinas believed that a dream and a future event might both arise from the same antecedent cause, in keeping with the kinship between the universe and each human. He saw nothing immoral in dream interpretation, for since God teaches through dreams, one could learn by trying to understand the images.

Anatomic and physiologic explanations for dreams were offered by the Christian philosopher and teacher Albertus Magnus (1200–1280). He believed that a special sense-perception connecting each person with the universe and

ABOVE: An illumination from the French fifteenth-century *Romance of the Rose* by Guillaume Lorris and Jean de Meun, a tale of thirteenth-century Europe in which a dream anticipated future events. The British Museum, London.

OPPOSITE ABOVE: The dreams of Childeric, the fifth-century Merovingian ruler, about specific animals were interpreted by his wife to mean that his offspring would be noble (unicorns, leopards, lions); his grandchildren would be ferocious (bears); the last of his line (dogs) would be lecherous, unvirtuous, and in conflict with each other until they were overthrown. Bibliothèque Nationale, Paris.

OPPOSITE BELOW: *Saint Hildegard, Abbess of Bingen.* A twelfth-century abbess, Hildegard was a scholar and theologian who had many visions of the cosmos, one of which was recorded in her treatise *Scivias,* probably illustrated under her supervision, showing the universe as oval, with the earth at the center surrounded by clouds. The sun is a large bright star surmounted by a row of starry planets. Courtesy Abtei St. Hildegard, Rüdesheim—Ebingen, Germany.

Saint Thomas Aquinas, philosopher and theologian of the thirteenth century, believed dreams had predictive and instructive values. 1438–1445. Lunette fresco, San Marco Museum, Florence.

OPPOSITE: *Youth Sleeping Under a Willow Tree.* Persian. Late sixteenth century. $8^{3}/_{16} \times 4^{7}/_{8}''$. The Cleveland Museum of Art. J. H. Wade Collection.

possessed by all was located in a center of the forebrain. There stimuli transmitted by the five senses were carried by the bloodstream, the same mechanism for transmitting "sense impressions" that Aristotle had described. Albertus called the terminus the *cellula phantastica* (also *imaginatio*), which had the function of constructing dreams.

A disciple of Albertus's, Arnald of Villanova (1235–1312), subscribed to his mentor's views, classifying the causes of night visions into those of external, divine origin and those whose source was the body. As a physician, he was much concerned with the medical significance of dreams, ascribing the nature of the images to the mix of the four humors, as Hippocrates and Galen had done. The dreams of rain and wetness signified a preponderance of phlegm; thunder and shooting stars, yellow bile; doom and terrors, black bile; red-colored objects, blood.

Islam

The ambivalent attitudes of the Christian Church toward dreams were not mirrored by the clergy of Islam, who looked upon them as highly important, privileged interchanges between Allah and humans, for divine revelations had been recorded in the Koran and in the later commentaries. The Arabic and Persian words for dreaming meant "to see in sleep." Dream interpretation (*tâbir*) was a science integrated into medical practice.

The Prophet himself repeatedly interpreted the night visions of his followers and recited his own dreams. Of highest significance was the dream of the announcement by the archangel Gabriel that Muhammad had been designated as the messenger of Allah. In the same dream Muhammad was shown the Koran, which would be transmitted to him. A dream also foretold that Mecca would become the holy city of Islam. Differing interpretations of Muhammad's dreams became one basis for a major split of Muslims into the Sunni and Shiite sects.

There was a problem in discriminating between the true and the false, but certainly false images were dreamed by those of immoral and hostile attitudes, drunkards, consumers of particular foods (among them, lentils and salted meats), and children, whose visions in the main were held to be meaningless or trivial—except very small children whose descriptions were still untainted by worldliness.

To obtain valid and favorable dreams, special rules were sometimes followed. Sleeping on the right side was most apt to prompt good dreams; lying on the left less useful (whereas Pythagoras had advised the left side for receiving satisfying images in sleep). Reclining on the back or the stomach were least favored in Muslim dream theory. Before retiring at night, one was well advised to pray to Allah for protection against evil dreams fomented by wily

Satan and to solicit the fortunate, true images from the deity. Other favored rituals included washing, eating moderately—neither too much nor starving—and reciting passages from the Koran, especially those that spoke of the sun, the night, the fig, and the olive.

Both the dreamer and the dream reader had duties when it came to exploring the meaning of a dream. The petitioner was expected to report accurately, truthfully, clearly, and completely. Dissimulation was sinful. The interpreter, as the inheritor of a sacred tradition, had to be upright, devout, and humbly aware of his position as an agent of Allah, just as Joseph in Egypt and Daniel in Babylon had been. The only motive permissible was a search for the true meaning that the deity intended to impart. Skillful dream reading was a calling bestowed on only a few. The *moabbir* (the analyst) was expected to recite prescribed prayers before each session.

Evaluation was known to depend upon considerable insight. The primary requirements were judgment and tact, not merely an acquaintanceship with symbols and their traditional associations. Moreover, the practitioner of this noble science was enjoined to possess much knowledge of people and things. An understanding of the sacred and profane worlds, methods of augury in many lands, language, customs, laws, religion, and even the etymology of words were necessary in order to unravel dreams and to apply their meanings appropriately in each instance. Most important was information concerning the petitioner, virtually the same characteristics as had been emphasized by Artemidorus in Greco-Roman times: name, birth place, age, position, religion, surrounding circumstances, domicile, habits, and also the person's reliability as a reporter.

The surroundings during the actual reading of the dream were also significant. A consultation in a public place was to be avoided if possible. Both the recounting of the visions and their elucidation needed to be out of the earshot of women, children, enemies, and the potentially jealous. The presence of some creatures during the interview was a good omen, because the Koran stated that Allah had created animals. Indeed, passages in the Koran were referred to very frequently in order to find out whether a dream was favorable or not. Explanations of a dream of the Koran itself depended upon which chapters (*suras*) were involved. Generally, such a dream presaged truthfulness, safety, and success. The value of a dream also varied according to the gender, marital state, and financial status of the person: more good dreams came to males than females; to chaste married women over unchaste single females; to rich men rather than to the poor—possibly because the more wealthy would be in a better position to distribute alms, a required action under Islam.

Dreams came from Allah, Satan, or stimuli from inside and outside the body. A vision was highly likely to be true and therefore divinely sent if an angel brought the message, for Satan and his minions were powerless to insinuate themselves in place of heavenly figures. These dreams, the *ahkám*—corresponding to the *oneiros* or *somnium* of Greco-Roman times—could be an illumination of present happenings, revelations of the future, warnings of danger, or inspiration that spurred an action by the sleeper. The false, unsound dreams, the *ahlám* or *azghás*—matching the *enhypnion* or *insomnium*—were either transmitted by Satan's evil spirits who falsely simulated a prophecy or else were caused by physical derangements inside the body and in the environment, such as extreme heat or cold, loud sounds, or objects touching, striking, or piercing the skin.

In contrast to the reliance that the Greek physicians had placed on the prodromic and diagnostic significance of images seen in sleep, such imagery was not held to be

Satan and to solicit the fortunate, true images from the deity. Other favored rituals included washing, eating moderately—neither too much nor starving—and reciting passages from the Koran, especially those that spoke of the sun, the night, the fig, and the olive.

Both the dreamer and the dream reader had duties when it came to exploring the meaning of a dream. The petitioner was expected to report accurately, truthfully, clearly, and completely. Dissimulation was sinful. The interpreter, as the inheritor of a sacred tradition, had to be upright, devout, and humbly aware of his position as an agent of Allah, just as Joseph in Egypt and Daniel in Babylon had been. The only motive permissible was a search for the true meaning that the deity intended to impart. Skillful dream reading was a calling bestowed on only a few. The *moabbir* (the analyst) was expected to recite prescribed prayers before each session.

Evaluation was known to depend upon considerable insight. The primary requirements were judgment and tact, not merely an acquaintanceship with symbols and their traditional associations. Moreover, the practitioner of this noble science was enjoined to possess much knowledge of people and things. An understanding of the sacred and profane worlds, methods of augury in many lands, language, customs, laws, religion, and even the etymology of words were necessary in order to unravel dreams and to apply their meanings appropriately in each instance. Most important was information concerning the petitioner, virtually the same characteristics as had been emphasized by Artemidorus in Greco-Roman times: name, birth place, age, position, religion, surrounding circumstances, domicile, habits, and also the person's reliability as a reporter.

The surroundings during the actual reading of the dream were also significant. A consultation in a public place was to be avoided if possible. Both the recounting of the visions and their elucidation needed to be out of the earshot of women, children, enemies, and the potentially jealous. The presence of some creatures during the interview was a good omen, because the Koran stated that Allah had created animals. Indeed, passages in the Koran were referred to very frequently in order to find out whether a dream was favorable or not. Explanations of a dream of the Koran itself depended upon which chapters (*suras*) were involved. Generally, such a dream presaged truthfulness, safety, and success. The value of a dream also varied according to the gender, marital state, and financial status of the person: more good dreams came to males than females; to chaste married women over unchaste single females; to rich men rather than to the poor—possibly because the more wealthy would be in a better position to distribute alms, a required action under Islam.

Dreams came from Allah, Satan, or stimuli from inside and outside the body. A vision was highly likely to be true and therefore divinely sent if an angel brought the message, for Satan and his minions were powerless to insinuate themselves in place of heavenly figures. These dreams, the *ahkám*—corresponding to the *oneiros* or *somnium* of Greco-Roman times—could be an illumination of present happenings, revelations of the future, warnings of danger, or inspiration that spurred an action by the sleeper. The false, unsound dreams, the *ahlám* or *azghás*—matching the *enhypnion* or *insomnium*—were either transmitted by Satan's evil spirits who falsely simulated a prophecy or else were caused by physical derangements inside the body and in the environment, such as extreme heat or cold, loud sounds, or objects touching, striking, or piercing the skin.

In contrast to the reliance that the Greek physicians had placed on the prodromic and diagnostic significance of images seen in sleep, such imagery was not held to be

زان سخن هوش را تمامی داد
گوش را حلقهٔ غلامی داد
آن امین خدای در تنزیل
وین امین خرد بعقل دلیل
دو امین بر امانتی گنجور
در شب تیره آن سراج منیر
برق کردار بر براق نشست
گردن از طوق آن کمند نتافت

ABOVE: A Persian thirteenth-century kashan dish showing a sleeper awakening and in the hypnagogic state, surrounded by five princes, who symbolize the five organs of spiritual perception, signed by Sayyid Shans-al-din al-Hasani. Iranian. Diameter 12⅞″. Freer Gallery, Washington, D.C.

OPPOSITE: "The Ascension of Mohammed" (also referred to as "The Night Journey"). Miniature from the *Khamsa* by Nizami. 1539–43. The British Library, London. Dreams played a significant role in the development of Mohammed's theology.

significant in Muslim medicine. Muslim physicians expected that a person's special interests, occupation, and intense emotional concerns would cause related images to appear in dreams: battle and armaments to a soldier, merchandise to a merchant, the beloved to the lovesick, food to the hungry, drink to the thirsty, erotic activities to the sexually frustrated.

Interpreters employed analogies and wordplay and made cultural associations. Some images in dreams were observed more closely by Muslims than by others before them. For instance, the species of animals and plants and the types of inanimate objects that appeared in dreams were examined minutely for their biological and technical classifications, each property of which had bearing on the dream's significance. Numbers also played a role. A bird crying out three times might be a good sign, but not if the calls were fewer or more frequent. Sometimes complex numerological associations yielded underlying meanings. The number 3 could indicate a secret revealed; 4, the sky and stars; 6, the angels and the sacred; 7, the harvest (perhaps harkening back to the pharaoh's dream in the Old Testament as intepreted by Joseph).

Just as the prophet Daniel had enabled Nebuchadnezzar to recall the dream he had forgotten, the Muslim *moabbirs* often had their own ways of reawakening the memory of a lost dream, in a sort of free association that Freud was later to develop and elaborate. For example, the petitioner might be instructed to touch any part of his body of his own choosing. From these gestures, a list of corresponding subjects was compiled to serve as a guide to discover what the dream probably consisted of. These seem to have been based on the similarities in shape between body parts and objects. The head meant mountains; hair, grass; ears, caves; arms, trees. Forgetting a dream was due to sinfulness, stubbornness, or purposelessness.

Although some of the associations were the same or similar to the lexicon developed by Artemidorus (for example, a book was equated with wisdom), others were unique to Muslim culture, such as a tiger corresponding to illness. The principle of contraries was also observed: sadness could mean joy; fear, freedom, a prevalent method of other ancient systems.

Dream books, filled with symbols and interpretations, were abundant. In one work (*Tâbir ul Caderi*), fully 600 interpretations were collected from over 7,000 other writings. The oldest may have been by Ibn Sirin, considered one of the most reliable and perceptive authorities, in the latter part of the seventh century. Another very popular treatise was the "Complete Dream Book" (*Kámil ul Tâbir*) put together for a ruler. One of the much-used sources, originally completed some time between the ninth and eleventh centuries, was a Byzantine collection of interpretations attributed to Achmet, whose precise identity has not been clearly established. He was a Christian or a Muslim who wrote in Arabic, probably at the behest of Caliph al-Mamuṅ, and may have been his official dream interpreter.

Although Christian Europe also produced many widely used dream books containing lists of associations between symbols and future happenings, they were sometimes considered part of the folklore of the lower classes or were condemned as impious and superstitious. On the other hand, in Muslim society, since dream interpretation was a much-admired and sanctioned endeavor, compendiums of symbols and treatises on dream reading were held in high repute by commoners, governmental officials, religious leaders, and scholars.

The Reformation and the Renaissance

Although there was an increasing intellectual conflict between the scientific and the mystical as the fifteenth and sixteenth centuries developed, dreams in a sense occupied a special position, encompassing both the secular and the spiritual. For instance, opposition to occultism was not synonymous with rejecting the significance of dreams, and a favorable attitude toward astrology did not need to be mirrored by a spiritual view of the meaning of dreams. The

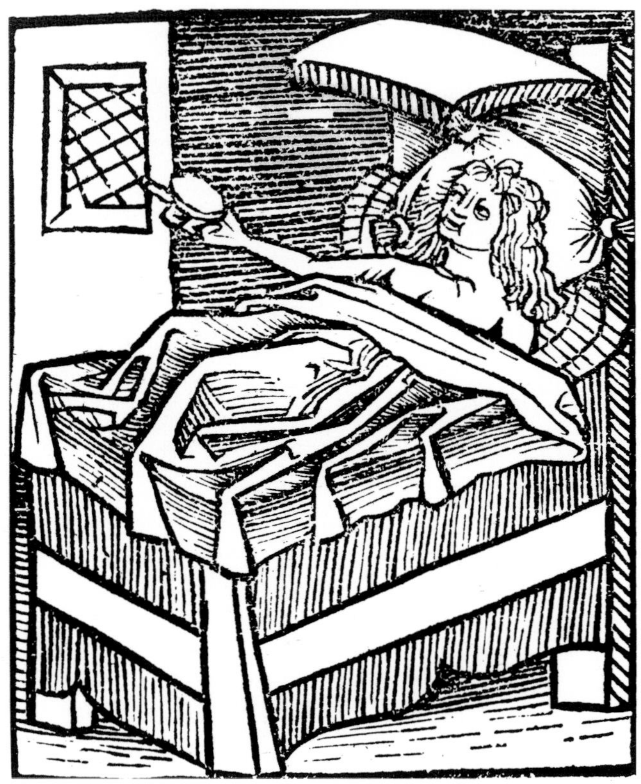

ABOVE: An illustration from the *Ortus Sanitatis*. 1491. National Library of Medicine. In order to have pleasant dreams, a sleeper might hold and gaze on particular stones or gems that were supposed to possess magical properties.

OPPOSITE: Sir Joseph Paton. *Luther at Erfurt*. 1861. Martin Luther found that differentiating between the divine and satanic nature of dreams was so difficult that he prayed to have no dreams.

ABOVE: Albrecht Dürer's *Das Traumgesicht* ("Dream Vision") depicts great dark clouds of water striking the earth—a vision he saw in a dream that shocked him, possibly signaling a depressed mood. c.1525. Watercolor on paper, 30 × 42″. Kunsthistorisches Museum, Vienna.

OPPOSITE: The delights and terrors, rewards and punishments, real and fanciful images—virtually all the types of scenes seen in dreams appear in the Hieronymus Bosch painting *The Garden of Delights* (detail). c.1503–1504. 86⅝ × 38⅛″. The Prado, Madrid.

Catholic Church's ambivalence was also matched by the attempts of Martin Luther to evaluate dreaming. He believed that the Devil could be responsible for sinful images in dreams but he encountered difficulty in trying to separate the Satanic from the divine. Like Job in the Old Testament, who importuned Jehovah to spare him disturbing images at night, Luther begged God to send him no dreams at all. The Protestant leader John Calvin acknowledged that divine messages came during sleep, but his opinion was that they were usually in the form of symbols rather than direct communications.

As the Renaissance brought a revival of interest in the ancient Greco-Roman writers, the explanations of dreaming offered by Plato, Aristotle, and others also became better known. The principles and practices of Artemidorus were widely used by virtually all interpreters of dreams. The occult historian and practitioner Henry Cornelius Agrippa von Nettesheim engaged in dream reading along with his many other pursuits in astrology, magic, medicine, law, and diplomacy. His interpretations referred to the macrocosmic-microcosmic relationship between the soul and the universe that had been part of Greco-Roman scientific and occultist thinking.

The same universal interconnections were also emphasized by Jerome Cardan, the mathematician, writer, and mystic, but he stressed the tenet that dreams originate in the sleeping person himself or herself. He even devised methods, including the application of particular medications, to induce various kinds of dreams. Although for the most part he employed the system summarized by Artemidorus and Macrobius, he underlined the part played by emotions—especially fear, passion, love, and delight—in determining the nature of the images. However, he was also convinced of the predictive value of those dreams that were caused by a combination of astrological influences and the sleeper's state of mind. His *Somniorum Libri III* contained a detailed presentation of his theories and practices, including a description of some of his own experiences. In one passage he claimed that a disturbing dream persisted night after night, spurring him to finish his book and even revealing to him the plan and organization of the treatise. When the work was completed, the dreams ended.

Paracelsus, one of the most influential thinkers and practitioners of medicine in the Renaissance, applied his unique mixture of the mystical and the rational to his highly significant medical theory and practice. Some of his contributions altered the concepts and methods of medicine and chemistry for centuries. On the subject of dreams, he followed many of the explanations offered by Plato and Aristotle. The spirit, liberated during sleep, could perceive the past and future, for it was part of the universal soul of the cosmos—the microcosm in contact with the macrocosm. By this means, a person could give and receive messages from the spirits of the dead and also of the living. In addition, Paracelsus subscribed to the beliefs seen in primitive cultures that the soul could wander but must return before the sleeper awakened lest the person die, deprived of the vital force. However, in at least one observation he seems to have been among the first to use the word *unconscious* (*unbewusst*) to mean the part of a person's mind that lies hidden but active in his psychological makeup—the *subconscious* in Freudian terms.

By the time of the Renaissance, society in general, not just theologians and philosophers, displayed a panoply of attitudes toward the implications of dreaming. There were those who believed implicitly in their prophetic use; others were uncertain and fearful; some were impressed but wary; some condemned them as impious, favoring incarceration and even death for interpreters. However, many were not dissuaded from dealing in dreams. Elaborate rites were developed in order to bring on evil night images. The blood of bats, fish bones, shells, animal fat, special plants—some of which we now know were probably narcotic or hallucinogenic—were applied externally or consumed to elicit the sinful scenarios. Modern psychologists might view these aims as expressions of desires, the search for satisfactions otherwise unobtainable.

Literary works were filled with examples of the significance of dreams. Even Montaigne, who was skeptical of their importance, did not reject their significance altogether. Dante, Boccaccio, Chaucer, and many others had used dreams in both form and substance to present ideas and plot. The same tradition continued throughout the Renaissance and afterward. Dreams played an essential role in several of Shakespeare's plays, especially *Hamlet, Julius Caesar, Macbeth,* and *Richard III.* Artists portrayed dreams and dreamers. No matter how scientists, theologians, and leaders viewed the process of dreaming, writers and painters revealed the deep concerns, which virtually all people had, with the reasons for dreaming and what the scenes meant.

In keeping with this interest, books and pamphlets multiplied, summarizing the purported predictive meanings of dreamed symbols. Specific nights were held to be the best times for dreaming of the future—notably Halloween, the night of All Saints' Day, and Midsummer Eve. The Eve of Saint Agnes (on the cusp between the zodiac signs of Capricorn and Aquarius) gave girls a chance to see their future husbands during sleep. Particular activities at bedtime heightened the likelihood of receiving omens, such as eating herring or cakes baked according to prescribed formulas; placing under the pillow a sprig of mistletoe or handwritten love poems. Some brochures claimed to be based on mythical writings of biblical prophets, ancient Egyptian papyri, famous magicians of the past, and oriental mystics, but most of the associations and rituals were clearly inherited from the five books of Artemidorus of the second century and their summary two hundred years later by Macrobius.

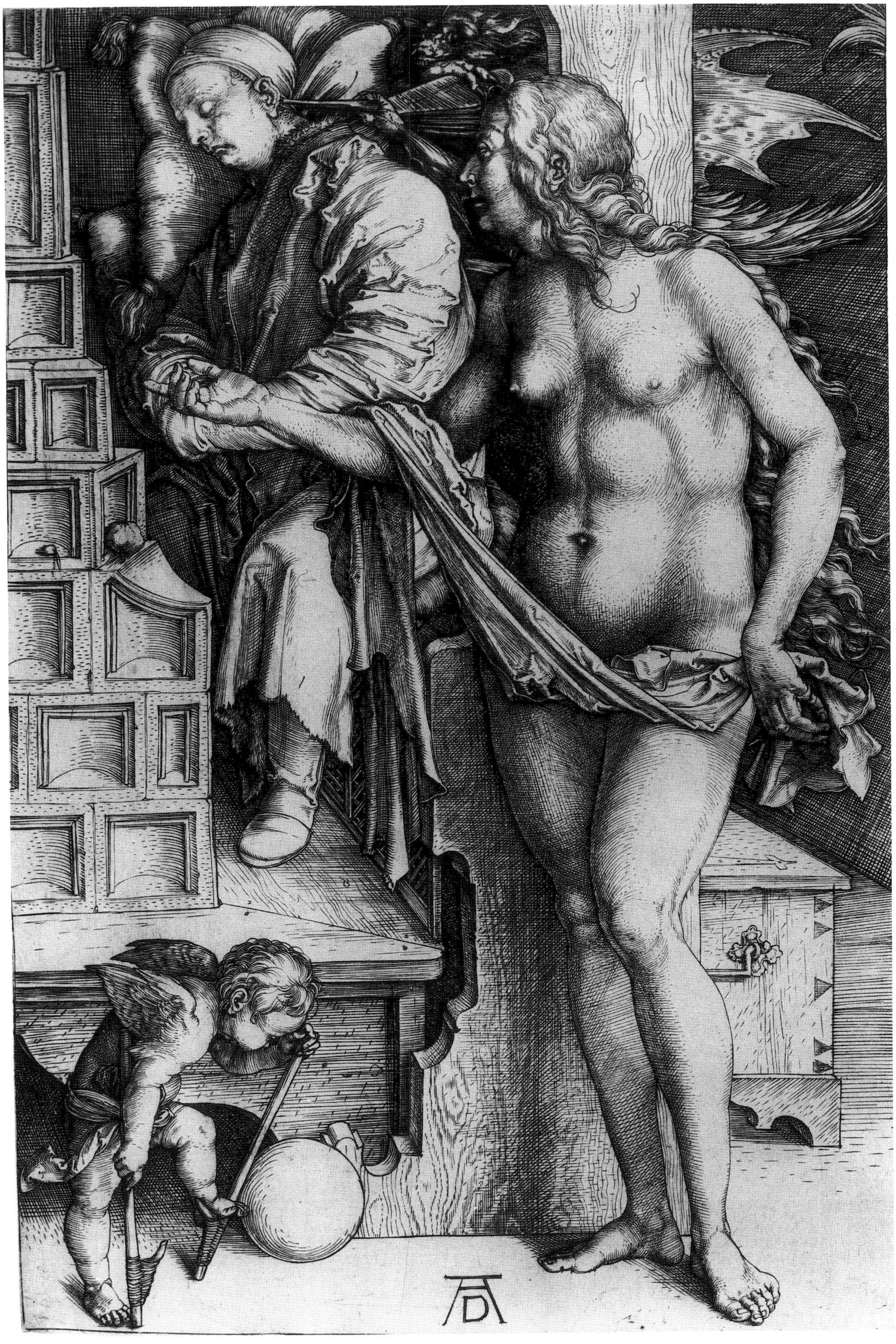

Albrecht Dürer.
The Dream of the Doctor. 1497.
Engraving,
7½ × 3¾". The doctor in this scene is being both tempted and instructed during his dream.

The Seventeenth and Eighteenth Centuries

In the centuries of "Science" and "Enlightenment" there was an increasing tendency to give mechanistic explanations for dreams. The Copernican theory had removed the earth and its creatures from the center of the universe and correspondingly diminished their position in the cosmos. Yet, at the same time, the Renaissance had renewed interest in the human being, including the structure and function of the body. Dreaming was among the activities that were examined for secular and rational causes by writers and philosophers, not only by scientists. For instance, Robert Burton, whose life spanned the last decades of the sixteenth century and the first half of the seventeenth century, declared in his *Anatomy of Melancholy* that dreams are fashioned by the dreamer not by gods or spirits. The English philosopher Thomas Hobbes (1588–1679) looked at dreams in a matter-of-fact way, explaining that the images resulted from outside stimuli—as Aristotle and others had also in part concluded. Heat on a person's body was reflected in the fiery events experienced in sleep; a cold draft might call up scenarios of a storm.

These centuries saw outstanding advances in knowledge of the human body—among them, the physics and chemistry of respiration, digestion, circulation, and metabolism, and the structure of lymphatic and other systems. Nevertheless, the heritage of speculative theories remained. William Harvey (1578–1657), whose elegant experiments proved that the blood circulates continuously through the arteries and veins and thereby demolished the long-held concept described in the second century A.D. by Galen, was himself a follower of most of Galen's doctrines, believing, for example, that a "vital spirit" was concocted in the heart. Indeed, while the investigators increasingly revealed the inner workings of living organisms, public reliance on ancient mysticism was widespread. John Wesley (1703–1791), the founder of Methodism, in conformity with the new scientific spirit of the age, subscribed to somatic and psychological causes for dreams, but he also acknowledged the influence of angels and demons in fashioning the imagery.

Although experiments and studies on many bodily functions were pursued, dreaming appears to have been approached by reasoning and conjecture rather than by investigation. The secular rationalists themselves evidently were unable to define to their own satisfaction the differences between the waking state and dream imaging.

René Descartes (1596–1650), a professed mechanist, stated the now famous declaration "*je pense donc je suis,*" (I think, therefore I am). But to him the question still remained, am I a dream or a reality? He might have lengthened his celebrated sentence, to "*mais qu'est-ce que je suis?*" ("but *what* am I?"). And as the medieval philosopher and churchman Saint Augustine had given prime significance to a dream for his conversion, as Galen's entrance into a career of medicine had depended upon his father's dream, so did Descartes credit his dreams for his philosophical development.

Frans Hals. *Descartes.* 1649. Oil on canvas, 29⅞ × 26¾". Musée du Louvre, Paris. René Descartes claimed that three particular dreams suggested to him the proper path that he should follow in his intellectual endeavors.

Descartes reached the conclusion that his dreams together suggested his path ahead: to combine faith in his own individuality with intellectual reality, to merge the separate drives of emotion and reason, to accommodate all the dualities of life, internal and external, through the capability that human beings possess of integrating divergent forces. In his efforts to find an anatomical region responsible for each physiological activity, he placed the soul in the pineal gland located at the base of the brain.

The French mathematical genius Blaise Pascal (1623–1664) separated dreaming from being awake only on the basis of the duration of the images seen: evanescent in the dream, constant in the awake state. Like the Chinese philosopher Chuang-tzu in the fourth century B.C., Pascal wondered whether life itself was a dream that ended with the awakening at death. Another mathematical scientist, the German Gottfried Leibniz (1646–1716), who invented calculus at virtually the same time as Isaac Newton, saw

Title page, *Anatomy of Melancholy* by Robert Burton (1577–1640), English clergyman and writer. This treatise deals with the causes and treatment of melancholy. The author perceptively states that dreams come from within the mind of a person, not from outside spirits or gods.

Francisco Goya. *The Sleep of Reason Produces Monsters.* No. 43 from *Los Caprichos.* 1799. Etching. During sleep and dreaming the imagination is unrestricted by the reason that is in control during waking. Horrors and monstrosities have full sway. Goya's image has become an iconic metaphor for the suspension of reason.

dreams as merely recollections of past experiences and thoughts, forgotten but always present in the psyche. The English philosopher and physician David Hartley (1705–1757) subscribed to the same ideas but gave particular importance to the condition of the gastrointestinal tract as a determining factor in producing dream images. He further emphasized the inconstancy and inconsistency of dreams, as did Pascal, as one of the reasons that dreams were forgotten during the waking state. Significantly, however, he also attributed a useful purpose to dreaming—the unscrambling of images and associations in order to protect against mental illness. Johann von Goethe (1749–1832), the German literary leader, also ascribed a healing power to dreaming, averring that sometimes dreams elevated his spirits and relieved him of depression.

Such scientific approaches to dreams were continued by philosophers before and after the French Revolution. Voltaire (1694–1778) considered dreams an expression of human desires and terrors, a characteristic of all peoples, both primitive and sophisticated. Projected meanings and prophecies were superstitious beliefs added in hindsight. He is said to have composed part of a poem during a dream but this endeavor he attributed to his own mental processes, not to supernatural causes. In his evaluation, if an event was foretold correctly it was remembered. When a dream prediction wasn't fulfilled, it was simply forgotten. The essayist Jean-Jacques Rousseau (1712–1778) was more interested in daydreams than the dreams of sleep, but he did credit psychological impulses for the content of his reveries. Thomas Paine (1737–1809), the American political philosopher, in keeping with his secular, rationalist principles, suggested that common-sense reasons could account for premonitions and prophetic dreams.

Nevertheless, dreams loomed large in literature, both as literary metaphors (as in John Bunyan's *Pilgrim's Progress* in 1678) and elements of plot (as in Shakespeare's plays), and their occult significance was often emphasized by writers and the readers. The experience of the writer Jacques Cazotte was often cited as an example of dream prognostication. He had dreamed of his own execution well before he was arrested and guillotined in 1792 during the French Revolution. Of course, there are those who evaluate this case history as an instance of premonition arising from real perceptions of the circumstances of the time and a reasonable concomitant fear.

More dream books than ever were published in Europe and America, for the most part echoing the lexicon that had been developed by Artemidorus in the Greco-Roman period. A few publications acknowledged that every dream could have diverse interpretations and was therefore open to self-delusion by the dreamer and deceit by the soothsayer. However, most were offered as authentic methods of predicting the future, based on presumed ancient truths, and sometimes were accompanied by explanations of other systems, such as palmistry, numerology, astrology, and a variety of mystical practices.

The English physician Thomas Browne (1605–1682) pointed out in his *Religio Medici* that science responds only to what can be observed and rationally explained. Belief in what the senses contradict is in the realm of religion. The two types of thinking are separate, coexisting, and incapable of being applied to each other. But to him, belief in the significance of the images seen during sleep represented an illusion, not faith.

The Nineteenth Century

In the nineteenth century, the separation between faith and science became more and more noticeable and the attribution of dreams to divine or supernatural causes steadily diminished—with the notable exception of the ever-continuing popular belief in prophecy through mystical agencies and dream books. Studies on dreaming also began to be more systematic, although speculation and reasoning rather than organized observation and evaluation were still a prominent part of the investigations.

Dreams contain both wish fulfillment and images called forth by guilt, as shown in these visions of a sleeper at Christmastime. Phiz. *Our Christmas Dream* from the *Illustrated London News*. January 4, 1845.

Henri Fuseli. *Nightmare.* 1781. Oil on canvas, 40 × 50″. Detroit Institute of the Arts. Gift of Mr. and Mrs. Bert L. Smokler and Mr. and Mrs. Lawrence A. Fleischman.

Scientific studies on sleep itself were focused principally on sleep talking, sleepwalking, and similar activity. Observers noted relationships among dreams, the unconscious, sleep, and hypnosis, but they were not clear about the connections. Anton Mesmer (1734–1815) thought that an "animal magnetism" present in all humans could be harnessed, through proper methods, to alter the state of consciousness and produce healing. His techniques ("mesmerism"), involving transferences of magnetism by the laying on of hands and creating of a suitable ambience for expectations of healing, evolved into the rituals that we now call hypnotism. Physicians such as the Scottish surgeon James Braid (?1795–1860) used hypnotism—a term he introduced—to produce insensitivity to pain. Others, such as the English doctor John Elliotson (1791–1868) and the French Jean-Martin Charcot (1825–1893), treated physical

Illustration from Anton Mesmer's *L'Antimagnetisme.* 1784. A scene depicting a group session in which Anton Mesmer used his concept of "animal magnetism" to benefit his patients. His methods (later called hypnotism) were evaluated by students of dreams as being akin to dreaming in recalling past experiences.

symptoms and mental aberrations by the same system. Mesmer and his followers poorly understood what they were doing and were ridiculed. They often indulged in excesses that bordered on charlatanism. However, hypnotism became a well-respected psychological method in medicine and was later employed by Freud and others. It was the recollection of forgotten past feelings and experiences under hypnosis that particularly interested the students of dreams.

The German physiologist Wilhelm Wundt (1832–1920), one of the earliest experimental psychologists, explained dreams—along with sleep and hypnosis—on psychological grounds and embraced the theory taught by Aristotle and those before him that external stimuli, internal emotional conditions, and the memory of previous events formed the images during sleep. Others, such as James Sully (1842–1923) and Henri Bergson (1859–1941), essentially belonged to the same school of thought. Hippolyte Bernheim and Auguste Forel (1848–1931) defined sleep, hypnosis, and dreaming as states in which two forms of consciousness operated simultaneously. A sleeper or a hypnotized subject each had an awareness that was separate from, but just as real as, the waking consciousness. To these physiological investigators somnambulism was a form of behavior akin to hallucinations engendered by drugs. However, Emil Gutheil and Pierre Janet, among others, offered the view in 1889 that unacceptable drives in the person were responsible for impelling the sleeper to talk, walk, and dream. These concepts were similar to the later teachings of Freud.

The unconscious as a separate inner world within each person, operating according to its own rules and purposes,

Sean Grandville (Jean-Ignace-Isidore Gérard; 1803–1847). *First Dream. Crime and Expiation.* Lithograph. The Metropolitan Museum of Art, New York City. Philip Hofer Collection.

gained ground as an explanation for the content of dreams. The word "unconscious" to refer to the deeper makeup of the human psyche began to appear in the late eighteenth century, especially in German and English writings, but Paracelsus during the early sixteenth century may have actually been the first to use it. Romantic writers, such as J. P. F. Richter (1763–1825), explained this hidden mental world as a type of memory in which impressions and ideas were present but not always, or even never, perceived by the conscious mind.

Sean Grandville. *Second Dream. A Promenade in the Sky.* Lithograph. The Metropolitan Museum of Art, New York City. Philip Hofer Collection.

Many understood, as did the ancients, that ordinarily unacceptable scenes readily appeared during sleep, when the censorship of the awake mind was absent. Some asserted that these behaviors were apparent to the dreamer as violations of decency, but most writers, such as the pioneering sex psychologist Havelock Ellis (1859–1939) and the essayist William Hazlitt, noted the suspension of conscience. William Dean Howells (1837–1920), the American novelist and critic, pointed out that *un*morality, not *im*morality, was the characteristic of the attitudes of

ABOVE LEFT: George Caleb Bingham. *Dull Story*. 1853. Oil on canvas. 50½ × 39⅛". Saint Louis Art Museum. Eliza McMillan Fund.

ABOVE RIGHT: Thomas Couture. *Day Dreams*. Oil on canvas, 47⁷⁄₁₆ × 35½". The Walters Art Gallery, Baltimore.

OPPOSITE: J. Perry after William Blake. *O How I Dreamt of Things Impossible*. Etching. The British Museum, London.

sleepers in their dreams, a conception that prefigured a tenet of Freud's. Indeed, because dreams were unfettered, Howells found that they could have oracular powers by virtue of their perceptive revelations.

On the other hand, there were the extreme mechanists, who gave exclusively physiological explanations for dreams and characterized them as irrational and meaningless. Francis Crick, the corecipient in 1962 of the Nobel Prize for developing the structure of DNA, the genetic code in the living cell, has subscribed to the view that dreams are merely parades of images that serve to unscramble during sleep the highly organized computerlike processes performed by the brain's nerve connections. The philosopher and poet George Santayana (1863–1952) observed, "Nothing could be madder, more irresponsible, more dangerous than this guidance of men by dreams." Contrarily, a pioneering German scientist, F. A. Kekulé (1829–1896), advised his colleagues, "Let us learn to dream," as a method of seeing the truth. He claimed that the circular structure of the benzene ring, a fundamental basis for organic chemistry, came to him in a dream. However, according to at least one historian, he seems to

Ralph Waldo Emerson. The famed American essayist and philosopher, suggested that dreams could reveal to the person the strengths and weaknesses of character. c.1888.

have previously had visualizations of this image. It is not certain whether this far-reaching conception was the result of a dream vision, a flash of waking insight, or a gradual development.

Francois Magendie (1783–1855) was an experimental physiologist who denigrated the psychological importance of dreaming. His research led to many significant advances, such as the differentiation between the sensory and motor nerves of the spinal cord. In keeping with his strict principles of scientific procedure, in which he avoided speculation and based conclusions only on verifiable observations, he decried the extravagant claims for meanings in dreams. Others too sought somatic reasons for dreams. American psychologist G. T. Ladd (1842–1921) studied the way sights that are seen before sleep might be impressed on the retina and remain there to appear in a dream. An extreme form of an interconnection between the body and dream images was proposed in 1886 by Philippe Tissié. To Tissié, each group of organs led to specific types of dreams. Dysfunctions of the heart produced visions of anxiety; poor lungs led to scenes of suffocation, confinement, or the impulse to flee; intestinal trouble brought on revulsion; sexual organs originated eroticism. Robert Grey, Robert MacNish, and other physiologists expressed similar views on the stimulation by bodily states and external factors of images in dreams, which were themselves the recollection of past events and feelings.

In the last decade of the century, Mary Calkins, after reviewing in detail the 375 dreams of two people over a six-week period, reported that the contents were derived from the experiences and thoughts of waking hours. The events and people had all been known to the dreamers. Dilemmas in the mind were infrequently shown directly, and she did not find evidence of disguised representations of psychological conflicts. Her conclusion was that dreams were not useful as clues to the psychological makeup of the dreamers.

The French scholar and archaeologist Alfred Maury (1817–1892) studied his own dreams to examine the effects of arbitrary stimuli on causing particular visions. For instance, when he deliberately burned a match close to his face before going to sleep, he found that he dreamed of an explosion. The draft from a window while he was asleep called forth scenes of sailing at sea. The accidental pressure of a bed rail on his neck during the night brought a dream of being guillotined. The Marquis Hervey de St. Denys (1823–1892), a student of Chinese culture, similarly experimented with consciously inducing dreams by dwelling on particular thoughts before the onset of sleep. He stated that the process of dreaming often connected disparate memories in random fashion. Visiting a painter at home and then, at another time, at his studio where he was painting an undraped model provoked a dream of the sudden and inappropriate appearance of a nude woman among a group of friends at a social gathering.

At the other extreme of exploring the causes and mechanics of dreaming were the Romanticists. They held to the ancient idea of an attunement between each individual person's soul and the soul of the cosmos. Some, such as Carl Gustav Carus (1789–1869), a Swedish physician and philosopher, were at the forefront. Many scientists, philosophers, and writers maintained the concept of a macrocosm-microcosm relationship in their approach to dreams as the means by which the unconscious was in touch with the universal mind and soul. Of course, a mystic such as William Blake, many of whose pictures echoed dreamlike images, would be expected to receive inspiration from dreams. In fact, he introduced in 1789 a significant advance in the technique of engraving, which he claimed his dead brother had explained to him in a dream.

Others who were not romanticists also valued the usefulness of dreams. The mathematical scientist the Marquis de Condorcet (1743–1794), in a vision while sleeping, found the solution to an equation that theretofore had eluded him. Johannes Purkinje (1789–1869), the innovative Czech microscopist and physiologist, spoke of the release afforded by dreams to the soul, enabling it to create not just new ideas but also situations that calmed and enlivened the agitated and depressed mind. Friedrich Nietzsche also saw dreams as rewards not receivable in real life.

Poets, novelists, painters, and others found inspiration and instruction in their own visions in sleep and gave dreams prominent roles in their works. Victor Hugo wrote about dream symbols in one of his poems, and Edgar Allan Poe often used dreams for his subject matter. The musician Giuseppe Tartini had even dreamed that the Devil played for him on a violin the theme of a piece that he later composed. To Maurice Maeterlinck (winner of the Nobel Prize for literature in 1911) all time—past, present, and future—meet during sleep, enabling us to be in touch with the continuum of existence. The transcendental philosophy of Ralph Waldo Emerson taught that one should seek within oneself the weaknesses and also the "spark of divinity" present in all humans. He maintained that dreams contain these truths if read skillfully.

Robert Louis Stevenson went so far as to induce himself, through concentration on specific thoughts and images before going to sleep, into having complicated dream scenarios, which became the plots of his short stories and novels. Some have claimed that these visions were actually deliriums brought on by fever or chronic illness, but his descriptions of how he planned the mingling of daytime fantasies, nighttime dreams, and the creative process indicate that they were the result of conscious efforts. Evidently the artist Piranesi did receive the inspiration for his pictures in a bout of delirium during an illness.

Drugs played a part in the creative efforts of some writers. Thomas De Quincey, for example, is known to have taken opium from which he acknowledged he derived special dreams later used in his literary works. In his *Confessions of an English Opium-Eater* of 1821 he detailed these experiences. Samuel Taylor Coleridge claimed that his entire *Kubla Khan* was composed in 1813 during sleep produced by opium, of which he could recall part but not all, because he had not written it down immediately. Of course, the effects of drugs on the images in sleep have been well known from the times of antiquity. When anesthesia was developed in the nineteenth century, the dreams of the anesthetized person were not considered unusual. The discoverer of nitrous oxide ("laughing gas") as an anesthetic agent, the chemist Humphry Davy, reported in 1799 that it induced an impression in the subject of possessing new and unique insight. The hallucinatory visions that many different chemicals impart were often construed to be a pathway to universal wisdom that was not transmissible during the drug-free state. Widespread utilization of drugs to produce sights and feelings reached its peak in the twentieth century.

The prevalent medical and rationalist opinions toward dreams were summarized by the Scottish physician John Abercrombie (1780–1844). The fact that dreams are beyond alteration while they are occurring, in contrast to the activities of a person awake who can choose to modify his or her own behavior, puts the two types of experiences into separate worlds. During sleep, when the distracting stimuli of reality are suspended, the mind is sometimes able to perceive the traits of others and the connections between events not otherwise noticed—a type of forecasting not unlike the conclusions that Aristotle reached. Some recognized that hidden desires could appear in the dream world. One may add that in popular sentiment and among artistic creators there was also an inchoate belief that dreams represented a communion with the natural forces of the world.

Robert Louis Stevenson. The famed English writer tried to induce in himself dreams that he could use as stories for his novels. c.1888.

Sigmund Freud.

The Twentieth Century

Freud

The publication of an extraordinary work in 1900 at the very start of the twentieth century, *The Interpretation of Dreams* by Sigmund Freud (1856–1939), for generations after changed much of the thinking about dreams—and, indeed, almost every facet of intellectual inquiry. As revolutionary as that seminal book was, the way had been prepared for thousands of years. Freud himself surveyed the past contributions in a chapter of the book.

By the end of the nineteenth century, along with various developments in philosophy, medicine, and science, a number of traditional attitudes about dreaming were still adhered to: namely, endorsement of the prognostic uses of dreams in medicine, as presented by the Hippocratics, Galen, and others, and faith in the healing power of dreams, as exhibited by the Asclepian and other dream-incubation systems. Freud also paid considerable attention to the compilation and explanations of dreams given by Artemidorus of the second century A.D.

By the twentieth century, the mechanism of sleep—its causes, purposes, and visions—was beginning to be studied. Most important, writers and scholars had accepted the existence in each person of an unconscious life, in which desires are manifested in dreams.

Yet, many occultists continued the long-standing tradition of seeing in dreams a path of communication between God and humans, a representation of the spiritual force in the cosmos, to which all living things belong. The prophetic value of dreams continued to be stressed by the mystics. Even some mechanists also subscribed to the validity of prediction because they observed that when the sleeping mind was let loose from the distractions and restrictions of reality, it could detect otherwise unnoticed patterns of events. This view in essence was similar to the theories advanced by Aristotle in the fourth century B.C.

Freud integrated traditional explanations into his own unique way of looking at dreaming and constructed a systematized conceptual framework for understanding the mental processes of humans and for relieving their distressing mental and emotional symptoms. According to Freud, the mind functions on three levels: the unconscious or subconscious, the conscience or censor, and the conscious. The unconscious, inhabited by past repressions of drives and fears, is always operating—awake or asleep—fueling our daily thoughts and behavior. The censor contains our principles of social, intellectual, and emotional morality, which are formed, beginning very early in life, by the approbation and disapproval of parents, family, friends, and teachers. Conflict between these two divisions of the mind affects and steers the development and functioning of the ego. Later Freud organized the mind structurally, into the id (subconscious), superego (censor), and ego.

The sick and the well mind use the same mechanisms. The psychotic person fails to distinguish between the real and the imaginary worlds, or is so affected by the struggle between the conscience and inner strivings that anxiety becomes insupportable to the person. Sometimes the person possesses so weak a conscience and such strong unconscious drives that the ego performs as the unconscious dictates, without the restraints of conscience and societal norms. All three functional divisions of the mind contribute to the formation of dreams. The unconscious makes itself felt through imagery, the superego modifies and disguises the images coming from the unconscious to make them acceptable to the ego, sleeping or awake. In the scenarios of our dreams, each of us is not the passive observer that we seem to be but rather the deus ex machina who actually forms and manipulates the symbols.

Dreams mirror repressed desires that are unfulfilled. "To their deaf pillows infected minds will discharge their secrets," said Shakespeare in *Macbeth*. The visions arise from both childhood and recent experiences. The dream's main function therefore is to satisfy strivings or mollify fears. According to Freud, almost all these urgings are sexual or aggressive. (This emphasis on sex produced considerable opposition to Freud's ideas and provoked

Giorgio de Chirico. *Gare Montparnasse.* 1914. Oil on canvas, $55\frac{1}{8} \times 72\frac{5}{8}$". Collection, The Museum of Modern Art, New York City. J. T. Soby Bequest. Surrealism ("beyond realism") and dreams have similarities in their incongruous images and links to the subconscious, but paintings are created by the mind awake, dreams by the mind during sleep.

resistance, condemnation, and mockery.) Freud taught that the basic drives of humans, perhaps of all living creatures, aim at survival: of the individual's life through nourishment; of the individual's acceptance by society through sanctioned behavior; of the species through sexual procreation. The child focuses progressively and sequentially on the parts of the body that are associated with each of the impulses to survive. The mouth receives sustenance through the suckling of the infant. Next, defecatory control, and therefore the anus, become a major concern to the child, in order to receive approbation from the parent. Then, sexual stirrings and the genitals draw attention. These urges and their organs enter the content of dreams.

"Average" dreams—often referred to as "ordinary" or "mundane" in ancient writings—also are fulfillments in Freudian psychology, but they are usually about more immediate necessities and of less fundamental significance. For example, thirst may call forth images of drinking; the requirement to keep an urgent appointment may be satisfied by a scene in which the dreamer is already there. Indeed, many stimuli, inside and outside the sleeper, can set off dreaming, but in Freud's theory these are merely triggers, incorporated sometimes into the dream scenario, but the actual message of the dream is prompted by the unconscious.

To Freud, dream imagery represented a compromise between what the repressed hidden strivings demand and what the conscience allows to form. If the unconscious

Carl Gustav Jung. Jung emphasized the similarities in the dreams of varied cultures, suggesting that dream images are biologically inherited.

energy (the libido) is able to prevail over the censorship so that the unacceptable thought images are about to break through, then the anxiety engendered awakens the dreamer. Since sleep is physiologically essential to the health of mind and body, dreams in Freud's system are the "guardians of sleep," affording satisfactions to desires that are unrealized or unacknowledged during the conscious, awake state. Dreams protect the sleeper from having to confront forbidden drives, which otherwise would cause the person to awaken. Sometimes the secret wishes come out far enough to be the horrifying scenes of nightmares. The closer our dreams are to the actual unacceptable urgings, the more likely we are to forget them—that is, to repress them.

The unconscious drives, if allowed to show themselves (the "latent dream"), would disturb the sleeper and therefore are altered, producing the manifest dream scenario. The process by which the mind reconciles the latent dream (the representation of unconscious demands) with the manifest dream (the actual visions seen) is called "dream-work." Essentially there is a concretization of thoughts into images so that they can be modified into less threatening thoughts. For instance, instead of the murder of one's father or mother (arising from a deep-seated hostility and destructive wish), one may dream of observing the death of that person or else the killing of a dragon (symbolizing the father) or of a cow (the mother). Of course, much more subtle and complex substitutions also occupy dream scenarios.

The sleeper's mind, Freud suggested, frequently brings together several disparate images—for example, the head of one person on the body of another—and merges several events into a single plot. This action of superimposition and combination is called "condensation." Another kind of work that is characteristic of dreams is "displacement." Here the forbidden elements are deemphasized while less significant and neutral details are elevated into prominent positions, so that morally unacceptable thoughts can be either skimmed over or made to seem unimportant. The analyst therefore has to be alert to these displacements and to offer questions concerning what may seem at first to be minor points in the dream. Another process, which Freud called "secondary elaboration," involves filling in gaps while a dream is going on or is recalled later and recited. Elaboration may also complicate a scenario, so that its basic content is further disguised. For instance, while asleep, we may think that we are awake and that what we have just witnessed was itself a dream, although we are still sleeping and dreaming (a dream within a dream). These types of modifications all aim at distorting and veiling the undesirable wishes from the unconscious.

Dream images have their own grammar. For instance, time is often shown through space relationships. A person or an action may be seen spatially occurring in front of or behind another, rather than chronologically before or after. Walking through rooms can symbolize going back into past events. One person or object may be used to stand for a totally different person or thing because of similarities in a particular characteristic. Similarly, morality may be signified by a church; passion by fire; shame by nakedness. An accident or an obstruction may be meant to show anticipated difficulties. Symbols are also at times the opposite of what is to be conveyed. The vision of a wish fulfilled may merely be covering up a self-doubt. Riches may suggest a feeling of poverty; strength a fear of weakness. Freud also found that puns, slang, and common expressions could be associated with concepts, as did the ancients. The image of a lamp may express the idea of joy, as in the saying "light of my life."

Freud's interest in so-called primitive cultures and their myths and artifacts paralleled his recognition that the objects of mythology and folklore were also often represented in dreams. He believed that human instincts were universal but, in contradistinction to Carl Jung, one of his early disciples, he did not subscribe to notions of mystical inherited origins or a collective unconscious. To Freud, the feelings, thoughts, and events experienced in childhood, not biologically transmitted symbols, were the inhabitants of the unconscious. Culture not evolution determined the nature of dream images.

Norbert Lyons, a journalist who wrote a history of the invention of the agricultural reaper, called Freudianism, "Neo-Calvinism," because it characterized the basic nature of humans, the id, as amoral and antisocial, just as Calvin had categorized all humans as "sinners" from birth. Whereas Rousseau had considered the natural state to be "good," Freud and Calvin considered it "bad."

The principal aim of dream interpretation for Freud was to discover what a patient was suppressing, in order to alleviate the distress occupying the person. Freud's main goal was to heal. A related benefit was advancing the understanding of mental mechanisms of all humans and their societies. Scientific validation of the association between the symbols in manifest dreams and their hidden latent content was not his main concern. He was convinced and took for granted, on the basis of his own observations and the reports of others through the centuries, that uncovering specific underlying unconscious wishes was necessary to achieving a therapeutic result. Dreams were an important clue. Through the technique of free association and skillful questioning in order to discover meanings in the dreams reported, the therapist was to open up to the patient a path of thought that could lead to recollections and perceptions of what was repressed, unrecognized, and producing the disturbed feelings and actions—that is, the neurotic symptoms.

At first, Freud also tried hypnosis as a means of reaching the buried material, the drives that he called inhibited in their aims. Later he found the method insufficiently rewarding. Pursuing the content of dreams, however, through "free association" was more useful to him. He asked the patient to let the mind wander and to follow each thought with another, seemingly at random. But Freud considered these unrestricted musings to be anything but "free," for it was the person's own thinking that made the connections. Sooner or later, he believed that the process would bring to the fore recollections that had been forgotten—"suppressed" in Freud's terms. If the patient felt a strong emotion or a sudden insight as he or she voiced a name, object, or activity, then both the person and the analyst had a chance to follow through to the forces that had created the dream, the hidden drives and conflicts, and perhaps even to reconstruct the past events.

Freud was an organicist in that he looked upon thinking as a physiochemical reaction, including neurotic imagings. However, he considered the state of the current biological knowledge to be so far from being capable of physiologically treating the causes of the mental troubles that it behooved physicians to study the manifestations of these physiological processes in order to help the suffering patients.

Alfred Adler. Adler was the founder of the School of Individual Psychology in 1913.

Freud used his own dreams and symptoms as examples of mechanisms, just as Montaigne, the sixteenth-century essayist, had probed himself to understand mankind. The problem for Freud, as Erich Fromm (b. 1900) later pointed out, was that each of us, and Freud was no exception, often unwittingly prevents the shattering revelations in the unconscious from reaching our consciousness. Some of Freud's analysis of himself therefore was apt to be a rationalization too, a misinterpretation of significant parts. However, that very deficiency of his was itself a confirmation of Freud's teachings.

Dissenters and Legatees of Freudianism

A number of disciples and followers of Freud disagreed with some of his theories and practices. Their chief objections were that Freud arbitrarily used dreams to support his theories rather than to examine their validity; that his conclusions were derived from neurotic rather than healthy processes; that he assigned only sexual meanings to the symbols, since very little else was given an important role or any part at all in his philosophy.

Alfred Adler (1870–1937), a leading figure in the

coterie that gathered around Freud, substituted ambition for sexual drive as the prime motivator and "self-assertion" rather than unfulfilled wishes as the energizer prompting the content of dreams. The universal motive was the quest for power. This might take the form of a "superiority complex," acting in a domineering manner, or striving at all costs to win.

To Adler, dreaming has the purpose of allowing people to feel powerful. The symbols are meant to be vivid and exaggerated expressions rather than disguises. By means of such created scenes, people learn and plan to overcome perceived difficulties. The unconscious urges are merely echoes of conscious compulsions, basic in all humans. Adler argued that dreams anticipate what the person is likely to do and therefore have predictive value. The images and scenarios affect bodily functions—particularly the adrenals and other glands of internal secretion—which in turn engender moods. These psychological feelings prompt us to act out unconscious impulses. This concept of the interaction between organs and thoughts recalls the theories of Tissié in the nineteenth century, who postulated mechanistic connections between dreams and specific organs. The images come from the unconscious part of the mind, which prepares for future behavior and instructs us on the way problems can be met. Dreams reveal one's "lifeline," thereby mirroring the compensatory actions that a person is likely to perform.

Carl Gustav Jung (1875–1961) became one of the sharpest dissenters of Freudian dream interpretation. Originally chosen by Freud to disseminate the doctrines of psychoanalysis widely beyond the boundaries of Austria and Freud's inner circle, Jung moved resolutely to a different intellectual position. He challenged Freud's theory of the psychosexual development of the child and deemed the unconscious a repository of attitudes and images inherited from early prehistoric humans. Both Freud and Jung accepted the biological origin of fundamental human psychological requirements. Indeed, Freud summarized these impulses as the need to survive and to procreate, inherent in all the infantile wishes. Jung, however, saw these feelings as originating in the cultural history of the race, inhabiting the psychological makeup of each person. Images from the unconscious that appeared in dreams did not represent the fulfillment of wishes. Instead, they were a collection of religious, spiritual, and societal associations from the earliest experiences of humankind.

Jung also categorized dream images. The "archetypical" symbols, the most important, appear in all cultures and have similar significance everywhere. For example, Jung emphasized the male and female components in all things, which he termed "the animus" (the male figures of wisdom and strength) and "the anima" (the woman in various guises as creator, nurturer, and destroyer). Other examples of universal symbols are versions of

Salvador Dali. *Apparition of Face and Fruit Dish on a Beach*. 1938. Oil on canvas, 43½ × 57″. Wadsworth Atheneum, Hartford, Conn. Ella Gallup Sumner and Mary Catkin Sumner Collection.

René Magritte. *Time Transfixed.* Oil on canvas, 57½ × 38½″. The Art Institute of Chicago. Winterbotham Collection.

devilish, dark, and hidden things. Some symbols, however, are peculiar to the individual person, varying according to the dreamer's personal constellation of people, past events, immediate societal environment, and internal bodily functions. Since the unconscious was usually superior to the conscious, it could also be prescient, predicting what was ahead.

A mystical aura overlay Jung's concept of the collective unconscious. Wisdom came from revelation, seldom from thinking out something for oneself. A voice beyond the capacity of the human organism came from the world soul, the common possession of the mind as handed down through evolution. The unconscious, as revealed in dreams, contained the essential truth of the macrocosm and microcosm.

Jung considered the conscious and unconscious minds to be separate. Together they added up to the whole. The psychic properties of feeling, thinking, receiving sensation, and intuition followed the principles of the conservation of energy, the first law of thermodynamics. If there was a smaller proportion of one of the four in one sector of the mind, more would be found in the other. Dreams especially supplied the missing property and thereby helped achieve harmony.

Below we briefly compare Freud, Adler, and Jung's attitudes toward dreams:
The dream's focus:

Freud: Repressed past frustrations of wish fulfillment.
Adler: Overcoming future obstacles to active self-assertion.
Jung: Present psychological concerns, inherited in our biological makeup and forming the collective unconscious.

The purpose of dreams:
Freud: To express the conflict between unconscious drives and the conscious imperatives of reality.
Adler: To examine problems ahead and rehearse their solution.
Jung: To attune us to our psychic inheritance.

The cause of dreams:
Freud: Repressions of infantile strivings from the past.
Adler: Anticipation of problems ahead.
Jung: Promptings of our biological inheritance.

The function of dreams:
Freud: Guardians of sleep, affording satisfactions and allowing us to continue sleeping.
Adler: Instructors in effective attitudes.
Jung: Guides to our human makeup.

Activities of the mind during sleep:
Freud: Modify images to make them palatable and satisfying.
Adler: Allow the person to see difficulties more clearly.
Jung: Reveal the human connections to the universe.

Wilhelm Stekel (1868–1940), a disciple of Freud's, integrated into his system the principles of both Freud and Jung. He postulated that dreams contain religious and mystical morality (as advanced by Jung) that aim to better us. At the same time, the instinct-directed sexual drives in dreams (as promulgated by Freud) look into the past's asocial, infantile impulses. Stekel found confrontation in human nature (as Pythagoras and Plato also had concluded) that dreams attempt to harmonize: good and evil, maleness and femaleness, strength and weakness, advance and retreat, love and hate.

Many staunch followers of Freudian psychology developed their own evaluations of dreams. For example, Otto Rank (1884–1937) considered sleep to resemble the beginnings of life, when the sleeper, like the unborn infant, has suspended physical and mental activity. Rank suggested that images of water in a dream signify birth, since humans are descended from water creatures and the newborn emerge from the liquid environment of the amniotic fluid. Other followers and dissenters—Jung among them—similarly linked birth, death, and resurrection. Fantasies in dreams, like beliefs in an afterlife, were considered to be a longing for the prebirth existence in the future. To the psychiatrist Nandor Fodor, birth and death were always active in the unconscious. Humans continually were visualizing the death of one type of life for another. Erich Fromm called sleep the "brother of death" and concluded that the insights of the dreamer's mind predict the future—a quality that Plato and Aristotle had bestowed on the sleeper's "soul."

The psychobiological school of Adolph Meyer (1866–1950) attributed human personality to a combination of biological, psychological, and social factors, and the experiences throughout a person's lifetime. The Freudian reliance on infantile psychosexual development was one but not the only fundamental principle. Dreams therefore would be expected to contain pluralistic meanings. In the "interpersonal psychology" of Harry Stack Sullivan (1892–1949), the interactions between the child and parents and the interrelationships with other people during adulthood were more influential determinants of behavior than infantile strivings. The contemporary psychiatrist Karen Horney emphasizes the social and cultural origins of attitudes and actions and correspondingly therefore the individualistic dream content of each person.

Another supporter of Freudian contributions who took issue with some of the basic tenets of dream interpretation was Calvin Hall, a proponent of "cognitive psychology." He concluded that the images in dreams were meant to clarify rather than hide from the sleeper the presence of inner drives—a position diametrically opposed to Freud's. The purpose of dream images was not to deceive but instead to reveal to the person in pungent, forceful, and recognizable symbols the source of conflict. He subscribed to the lessons

Henri Rousseau. *The Dream*. 1910. Oil on canvas, $80\frac{1}{2} \times 117\frac{1}{2}''$. Collection, The Museum of Modern Art, New York City. Gift of Nelson A. Rockefeller.

taught by Freud that symbols were concretizations of abstract ideas, that dreaming represents regressions to childhood experiences and strivings, that free association was often useful in discovering the origin of disturbing feelings, and that the meanings of dreams often lay in wordplay and the recall of myths of the culture. However, he maintained that since both symbolic and explicit representations of distasteful thoughts and acts appear in dreams and that since the numerous puns, slang words, and figures of speech in dreams are well known to the dreamer and are used every day (for example, "tool" for the phallus; "box" for the vagina), the person's mind selects images to suit his or her own information and biases.

Several followers of general psychoanalytic theory offered various methods of establishing consistent implications in the symbols and scenes of dreams. David Foulkes presented the elements of a dream as if they were the grammatical parts of a sentence. The whole dream scenario was analogous to a complete sentence. He offered this grammar of dream language as a means of systematizing the contents and applying rules of interpretation that would permit a consistent understanding of every dream. His approach supported Freudian principles by extending the basic tenets into more quantitative terms. The resulting scoring became quite intricate. Although his fundamental principles were straightforward, the eventual structure resulted in complicated diagrams and a network of mathematical symbols. Without challenging its validity, many investigators and clinicians found the system too complex.

Others also formed scoring methods, expressing the content of dreams by letters of the alphabet and mathematical symbols and sometimes assigning numerical values to particular types of images. Calvin Hall and Robert Van de Castle summarized many of the scales that were devised and presented their own scoring of actions, emotions, scenes, people, and objects that comprised dreams. These classifications had the purpose of systematizing the contents of dreams so that their psychological import could be assessed and compared. For the most part, the analyses adhered to the fundamental attitudes of Freud toward dreams: their origin in the unconscious; the presence of conflict between reality and strivings; the satisfaction of desires.

Stephen LaBerge has argued that we can learn to engage in "lucid dreaming," thereby maintaining awareness that the images are merely dreams and therefore able to be directed or altered to suit our wishes. According to this conception, dreams are just as expressive of our desires as they are in Freudian teachings, but they also allow the conscious and unconscious states to meet. They therefore give us a better indication of how to deal with our problems. In that sense, they may be predictive of our future actions.

The Physiologists

Physiological psychologists principally attend to the mechanism rather than to the substantive content of dreams. "Behaviorist psychology," originated by Thomas B. Watson (1856–1922), derived its concepts largely from the conditioned reflex experiments of Ivan Pavlov in the late nineteenth and early twentieth centuries. Our attitudes, feelings, and actions could all be explained on the basis of their continual association with repeated stimuli from the outside. Like Pavlov's dogs, humans are conditioned to think and respond through a habit pattern. The content of dreams, however, did not figure in Pavlovian studies.

A highly important advance in understanding the process of dreaming came from the chance discovery by Eugene Aserinsky in the 1950s that sudden peaks of electrical activity appeared in the tracings of the electroencephalographs (tracings of electrical patterns in the brain) of sleeping persons at the same time that rapid eye movements (REM) were occurring behind the closed eyelids. Aserinsky, Nathaniel Kleitman, and William Dement reported that these jerky motions of the eyes coincide with dreaming and last from ten to forty minutes at a time. However, they recur at intervals of about one hour or more throughout the night. During longer periods of slumber, the eye motions are slow or absent and are accompanied only uncommonly by dream images. REM occupy about 20 percent of the total sleeping time.

The people being studied were awakened and asked to describe immediately any dreams they were having. The dreaming during REM activity was remembered best—often vividly. The dreams in the quiescent periods, when they did occur, were recalled uncertainly. Of course, the investigators did not know whether there had actually been thoughts or images at those deep levels of sleep or whether they were simply too deep to be available to the conscious recollection of the awakened sleeper. Yet, the implication was strong that dream-free states existed and were marked by slow electrical impulses, just as active dreaming matched the vigorous tracings. Also, it could not be known for certain whether the rapid eye movements were responses to the images seen by the "mind's eye" or merely represented bursts of mental activity causing both the eye movements and the dreams.

Experimental interruptions of the REM cycles often were reported to be followed on subsequent nights by more frequent and longer stretches of REM tracings, as if the organism had to make up for the previous deprivation of dreaming. The same total number of interruptions of the slow tracing sleep apparently did not necessitate more time spent in nonactive slumber. The investigators concluded that disruptions of dreaming could lead to psychological disorders. Other workers challenged this conclusion and

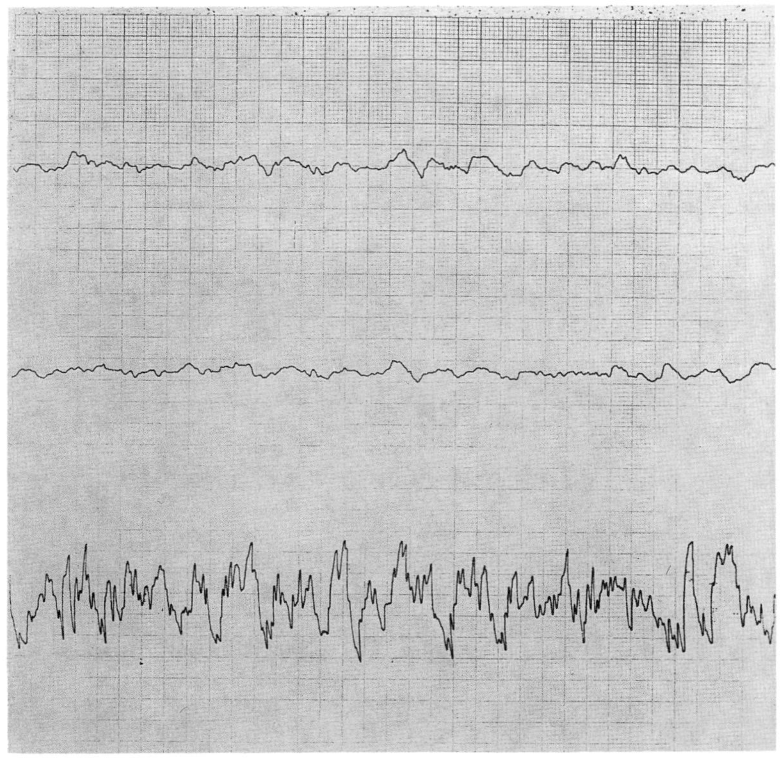

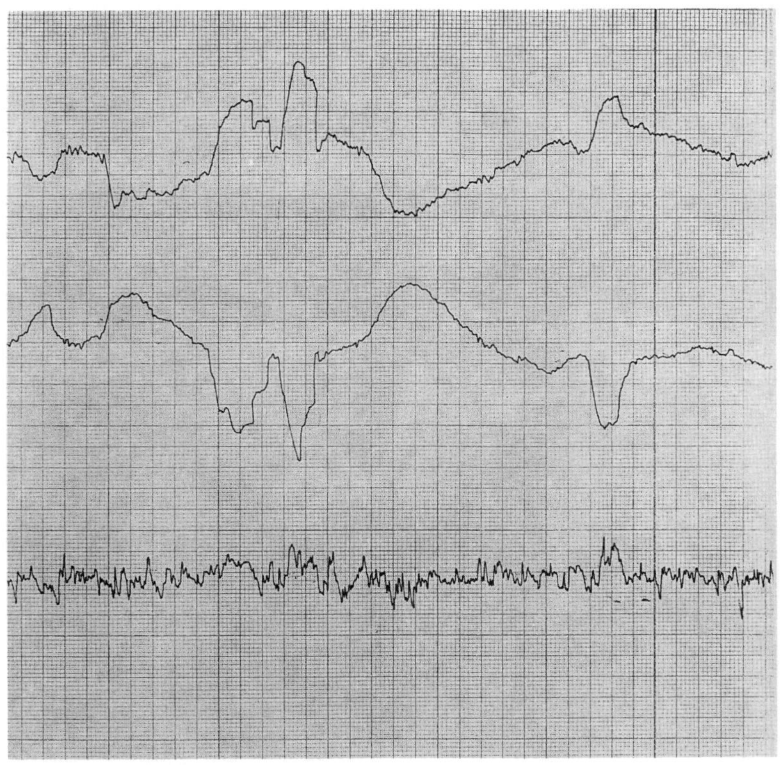

Two graphs recording the electricity of left- and right-eye movements during sleep (REM). The lower graph shows REM activity during sleep, when dreaming occurs. The upper graph shows almost no eye movement during sleep without dreams. The bottom tracing on each graph represents the electroencephalogram, which records brainwave activity (rapid frequency during dreams; slower frequency—longer peaks and valleys—during sleep without dreams). Courtesy Mount Sinai Medical Center Sleep Lab, Department of Psychiatry, New York City.

even implied that depressions were actually improved when the dream process was curtailed.

The journalist Douglas Hand reported on Ernest Hartmann's investigations, which showed that nightmares occurred principally during REM sleep and awakened the sleeper in vivid recall of the dream. On the other hand, although frightening dreams could also happen during the period of the slow eye movements, the person awakened with only the feeling of terror but without a trace of the images. After comparing the psychological makeup, as determined by a battery of tests, of those who had many nightmares with those who experienced them rarely or not at all, Hartmann concluded that terrifying dreams are an indication of creativity in the personality. These persons have in common with schizophrenic patients a tendency to merge fantasy and reality.

One group of investigators equated the activities of the brain with the functioning of a computer. As a gigantically complex instrument of neural mechanisms, according to this concept, the brain requires periods of sleep for sorting out its overburdened interconnections, just as computers have to be reprogrammed at intervals in order to maintain them in efficient working order. These readjustments of a computer have to be done while the machine is still attached to its electrical power source but in an "off-line" status, so that it cannot receive or deliver information while the erasures are being performed. During slumber, the human computer brain also is "off-line," protected from both incoming stimuli and outgoing communications. Similarly, the dreaming marked by REM recordings represents the shedding of excessive and inappropriate images from the memory. The mind is thus cleared of useless material and prepared for the next day's reception of sensory stimuli, just as the machines have to receive new or modified instructions.

The subscribers to this highly mechanical view emphasized that the computer model of complex interconnected programs was merely analogous to the mind and by no means identical. It was a means of understanding the probable significance of dreams not a blueprint of mental functions. For instance, the transmission of nerve impulses and the process of thinking are chemical reactions, not in the same category as the passage of electricity through wires, chips, and mechanical devices. Actually, the burgeoning information on the workings of the brain, including dreams, memory, and REM, has begun to instruct designers of computers on possible ways to develop ever more innovative, complex, and efficient machines.

That hallucinations could be produced by drugs was well known for many centuries. Thus some attributed the occurrence of visions during the normal sleeping state to the effects of hormones and other physiochemical phenomena in the body. The numerous chemical processes associated with the flow of neural impulses along the nerve cells in the brain would therefore be responsible for the snatches of scenes and objects that the sleeper would see as dreams—particularly during the REM period. It was noted that there are striking similarities between the timeless, bizarre, and incongruous experiences under drugs—LSD, mescaline, and others—and the images produced in dreaming. Drugs therefore would merely represent additions, stimulators, and modifiers of the normal continual chemical transactions that produce dreams.

Mystics

Many of the same attitudes prominent in ancient times toward dreams continue. Those who are convinced of the validity of preconception, precognition, ESP, and telepathy subscribe to the importance of dreams as a spiritual dimension of the human psyche. Instead of a belief in the actual entrance of demons and deities into the sleeper's mind, as had been accepted among earlier cultures, there is an assumption that each person has the capability of communicating with the world soul. The great religious mystics might be unique in receiving divine revelations but every human, through dreams, can understand basic truths of humankind and see ahead, under the proper conditions and frame of mind. Indeed, dream thoughts can also be transmitted from person to person in a telepathic communication—as in the legends of ancient India. Also, some mystics continue to subscribe to the belief held by some of the earliest cultures that the spiritual part of a person's physical structure—the "astral body"—can leave to wander during sleep.

Mystical approaches to dreams are typified by the doctrines of Edgar Cayce, the influential occultist whose main writings were published in the first few decades of the twentieth century. Cayce argued that there is a universal life force in the cosmos. Each person's mind is an expression of that energy. Our minds create our physical reality. The conscious mind is our mentality. The unconscious is ever present and hidden within us on two levels. The subconscious part contains the forgotten and repressed past, including former lives that each of us has lived, for our present existence is only the most recent of our previous existences. The superconscious level of the unconscious mind overlies all as a universal soul, of which each human forms a part. It is visualized in dreams as advice and warnings. Although Cayce's structure showed resemblances to the three-dimensional psyche promulgated by Freud, Adler, and Jung, it also had its own unique characteristics. Thus, to Cayce the subconscious division of the unconscious also has three levels: the personal, previously lived experiences; the collective unconscious of the race, as presented by Jung; the telepathic contributions from all other minds presently existing.

According to Cayce, dreams occur through several

Henry Fuseli. *Titania and Bottom*. c.1790. Oil on canvas, 85½ × 108½″. The Tate Gallery, London.

mechanisms. The intuitive reasoning by the unconscious mind attempts to extract a unifying principle out of the seemingly disjointed scenes and objects that float before us during sleep. The spiritual (superconscious) and subconscious parts, together with the conscious thinking, interact in the search for meaningful relationships and correlations among the images stimulated by physical factors in our bodies, externally induced sensory impressions, mental processes remaining in our consciousness, and emotional difficulties from our childhood. Our thoughts, arising from all these sources, are projected into dreams, which therefore reveal the state of the body, mind, and soul.

In the tenets of Cayce and his followers, among them Mark Thurston, the dream fulfills a number of purposes. Most importantly, it shows the dreamer his or her true self: the unvarnished motivations, rather than the rationalizations of wishes and behavior. In one of the dreams interpreted by Cayce, for instance, the dreamer's actual carnal designs on a woman appeared frankly, thereby forcing the person to see through his own self-delusion that he was acting impersonally during the conscious, awake state. A dream offers each of us the chance to choose among several possible pathways—all of which can show up in the scenarios. The dreamer also may be shown the solution to a problem, personal or occupational. The oft-cited experiences (referred to earlier in this chapter) of Kekulé the scientist, Robert Louis Stevenson the novelist, and Coleridge the poet are examples of the way difficulties can be resolved and works created during sleep. One legend about Cayce was circulated—that he was able to learn the complicated contents of books that he placed under his pillow before going to sleep.

A highly significant function of dreaming, in the teachings of Cayce, is insight into God's law. The dream instructs in moral thought and action. This powerful attunement to the deity was called by Cayce "natural," not "supernatural," for his philosophy considered this capability of being in touch with God and the universe a biological property possessed by all human beings.

Here are a few examples of interpretations by Cayce. A woman dreamed that she drove a car over a cliff—wanting to put on the emergency brake but failing to do so. The meaning: she was being told that if one knows what is the right action and does not do it, one will be punished. A man who dreamed he undressed while in church, for which he was mocked by the parishioners, was thereby warned that changes in his theological thinking would call forth ridicule. Dreaming a boy was run over by a car was a way for a dreamer to see himself in danger of running over himself. In another dream scenario, a person dove into the surf but found he had gotten caught headfirst in the sand: here the ocean represented physical life; diving precipitously into life's experiences could entrap one. Wade in, do not dive, was Cayce's advice.

Thus in twentieth-century dream interpretation, rational analysis (the natural) has traveled side by side with mysticism (the supernatural).

Evaluation

From the very beginning of human history until the last decade of the twentieth century, dreaming has been given supernatural, psychological, and physiological explanations—often all at the same time. The mystics for the most part have viewed dreams as communications from deities, the world soul of the cosmos, or the inner spiritual soul of the sleeper. All three types of messages show the dreamer what lies ahead. Psychological theorists also have subscribed to forecasting through dreams but mostly as the actions that the person would be likely to take when awake, under the emotional proddings produced by the scenarios he or she saw while asleep. The physiologists have evaluated dreams as manifestations of biochemical processes in the brain, which serve up images to the sleeping person's "inner eye" and are accompanied by rapid eye movements (REM). Some investigators have even designated one specific area of the midbrain, the pons, as the initiator of the scenes seen in sleep. The stimulant is supposed to be a chemical, acetylcholine, one of the normal substances of the body. In these mechanical conceptions, dreaming is a clearing activity. The images merely represent the discharge of neural impulses in the course of shedding overburdensome impressions and preparing for the reception of the new stimuli of the next day.

But no observers have been able to explain why we sleep, except to express the general opinion that slumbering is necessary in order to recharge our mental energies. We also know little of the mechanism and physiological changes specific to sleep. Moreover, it is not even clear whether the dreamed images come first and then the rapid movement of the eyes looking at the visions, or whether the REM are merely part of the same physiological process, with the eye movements and the dream scenes both produced by the same rush of impulses through the nervous tissue of the brain.

Whatever the origin of dreaming may be, dream interpreters believe that it is the person's own mind that strings the images together. Gods or spirits or chemicals or conscience may impel the flow, but each of us makes the connections. Even if the objects and events are chance appearances and therefore meaningless, as claimed by Crick and others, the dreamer's mind fashions the connections among them to form the dream scenario. The mystics give the directorial role to the deities or to the immaterial spirit of the person, but the sleeper is the playwright. To the psychologists, the director, writer, actors, and audience are one. Some cultures even allow for the souls of outside persons to enter and become the actors. The play is the adjustment or resolution of conflicting forces within each of us.

The reading of dreams therefore depends on the preconceived principles of the interpreter. The occultist, psychologist, physiologist, or the dreamer who interprets his own dream perceives particular signals. Thus, the dream is meaningless or instructive or therapeutic; a reenactment of the past, a depiction of the present, or a forecast of the future—or all together.

Selected Bibliography

Adler, Alfred. *The Practice and Theory of Individual Psychology* (transl. P. Radin). London: Littlefield, 1973.

Agrippa, Henry Cornelius. *The Philosophy of Natural Magic.* Secaucus, N.J.: University Books, 1974.

Allen, Richard Hinckley. *Star Names, Their Lore and Meaning.* New York: Dover Publications, 1963.

Appleby, Derek. *Horary Astrology.* Wellingborough, England: The Aquarian Press, 1985.

Artemidorus. *The Key to Dreams in the Five Books of the Interpretation of Dreams and Visions* (transl. and comm. H. Vidal). Paris: Editions de la Sirene, 1921.

Aserinsky, E., and Kleitman, N. "Regularly Occurring Periods of Eye Motility, and Concomitant Phenomena During Sleep." *Science* 118 (1953), pp. 273.

Baker, Robert H. *Introducing the Constellations.* New York: Viking Press, 1961.

Baynes, Cary F. (transl. from the German of Richard Wilhelm). *The I Ching or Book of Changes.* New York and London: Bollingen Press, 1950 and 1951.

Béguin, A. *L'Âme Romantique et le Rêve.* Paris: Conti, 1939.

Behr, Carl. *Aelius Aristides and the Sacred Tales.* Amsterdam: Hakkert, 1968.

Bischoff, Erich. *Babylonisch-Astrales im Weltbilde des Thalmud und Midrasch.* Leipzig: J. C. Hinrichs, 1907.

Bloch, Raymond. *La Divination dans l'Antiquité.* Paris: Presses Universitaires de France, 1984.

Blofeld, J. (transl.). *The Book of Changes.* London and New York: Arco Publishing, 1965.

Bouché-Leclercq, A. *L'Astrologie Grecque.* Paris, 1899.

———. *The Interpretation of Dreams (Oneirocritica).* Paris: Ernest Ledoux, 1899.

Brainerd, Charles J. *Origins of the Number Concept.* New York and London: Holt, Rinehart, and Winston, 1979.

Bram, Jean Rhys (transl.). *Ancient Astrology. Theory and Practice. The Mathesis of Firmicus Maternus.* Park Ridge, N.J.: Noyes Press, 1975.

Brinton, Daniel Garrison. "The Origin of Sacred Numbers." *American Anthropologist* 7 (1894), pp. 168.

Brook, Stephen. *Oxford Book of Dreams.* New York: Oxford University Press, 1983.

Browne, Alice. "Descartes's Dreams." *Journal of the Warburg and Courtauld Institutes* 40 (1977), pp. 256–273.

Budge, E. A. Wallis. *Egyptian Magic.* New York: Dover Publications, 1971.

Bunker, Dusty. *Dream Cycles.* Rockport, Mass.: Para Research, 1981.

Burke, James T. *Ancient Hindu Astrology for the Modern Western Astrologer.* Miami, Fla.: Hermetician Press, 1986.

Campbell, Joseph. *The Mythic Image.* Princeton, N.J.: Princeton University Press, 1974.

Capp, Bernard. *Astrology and the Popular Press, 1500–1800.* Ithaca, N.Y.: Cornell University Press, 1979.

Cartwright, Rosalind. *Night Life, Explorations in Dreaming.* Englewood Cliffs, N.J.: Prentice-Hall, 1977.

Case, Paul Foster. *The Tarot.* Richmond, Va.: Macy Publishing Co., 1947.

Cavendish, Richard. *A History of Magic.* New York: Taplinger, 1977.

———. *The Tarot.* New York: Harper and Row, 1975.

Chou, Hung-hsiang. "Chinese Oracle Bones." *Scientific American* 204 (April 1979), pp. 134–147.

Christian, Paul. *The History and Practice of Magic.* New York: Citadel Press, 1969.

Cicero, Marcus Tullius. "The Dream of Scipio," in *On the Good Life* (transl. M. Grant). New York: Penguin Books, 1971.

Cohen, D. *Sleep and Dreaming: Origins, Nature and Functions.* Elmsford, N.Y.: Pergamon Press, 1981.

Constant, Alphonse Louis (Eliphas Lèvi). *The Great Secret: or, Occultism Unveiled.* New York: Samuel Weiser, 1969.

———. *The Mysteries of the Qabalah or Occult Agreement of the Two Testaments: As Contained in the Prophecy of Ezekiel and St. John.* New York: Samuel Weiser, 1974.

Copernicus, N. *On the Revolutions of the Heavenly Spheres* (transl. A. M. Duncan). New York: Barnes and Noble, 1976.

Cornell, Howard Leslie. *Encyclopedia of Medical Astrology.* New York: Samuel Weiser, 1972.

Craig, Katherine. *The Fabric of Dreams, Dream Lore, and Dream Interpretation, Ancient and Modern.* London: Darby Books, Reprint of 1918 edition.

Crowley, Aleister. "A Description of the Cards of the Tarot, with Their Attributions; Including a Method of Divination by Their Use." *The Equinox,* vol. 1, no. 8 (September 1912), pp. 143–210.

Culver, Roger B., and Ianna, Philip A. *The Gemini Syndrome: Star Wars of the Oldest Kind.* Tucson, Ariz.: Pachart Publishing House, 1980.

Cumont, Franz. *Astrology and Religion Among the Greeks and Romans* (transl. J. B. Baker). New York: Dover Books, 1960.

Curry, Patrick (ed.). *Astrology, Science and Society.* New Hampshire: Boydell Press, 1987.

D'Allemagne, Henry René. *Les Cartes à Jouer du Quatorzième au Vingtième Siècle.* Paris, 1906.

Davison, R. C. *The Technique of Prediction.* Essex, England: L. N. Fowler and Co., 1979.

Davison, Ronald C. *Astrology: The Classic Guide to Understanding Your Horoscope.* California: CRCS Publications, 1988.

De Givry, Emile Grillot. *Witchcraft, Magic, and Alchemy.* New York: Dover Publications, 1971.

DeLuce, Robert. *Complete Method of Prediction.* New York: ASI Publishers, 1978.

Dement, W. C. "A Life in Sleep Research," in *New Perspectives in Sleep Research, Intra-Science Symposium* 3 (February 1981).

DeVore, Nicholas. *Encyclopedia of Astrology.* New Jersey: Littlefield, Adams, and Co., 1976.

Dick, Hugh G. "Students of Physic and Astrology. A Survey of Astrological Medicine in the Age of Science." *Journal of the History of Medicine and Allied Sciences* (July 1946), pp. 419–433.

Diskin, Clay. "An Epicurean Interpretation of Dreams." *American Journal of Philosophy* 101 (1980), pp. 342–365.

Doane, Doris Chase, and Keyes, King. *How to Read Tarot Cards.* New York: Funk and Wagnalls, 1968.

Dorlon, Pierre. *Secrets of the Gypsies.* New York: Ballantine Books, 1977.

Douglas, Alfred. *The Tarot.* New York: Taplinger Publishing Co., 1972.

Dracon, Richard. *Napoleon's Book of Fate.* Secaucus, N.J.: Citadel Press, 1977.

Dreyer, J. L. E. *A History of Astronomy from Thales to Kepler.* New York: Dover Publications, 1953.

Dubs, Homer. "The Beginnings of Chinese Astronomy." *Journal of the American Oriental Society* 57 (1958), pp. 295–300.

Dummett, Michael. *The Visconti-Sforza Tarot Cards.* New York: George Braziller, Inc., 1986.

Eliade, Mircea. *Cosmos and History.* New York: Harper and Row, 1959.

Forster, E. S. (transl.), and Ross, W. D. (ed.). *The Works of Aristotle Translated into English.* Oxford, England: Oxford University Press, 1931.

Foulkes, David. *A Grammar of Dreams.* New York: Basic Books, The Harvester Press, 1978.

Frazer, James. *The Golden Bough.* New York: Macmillan, 1922.

French, Peter J. *John Dee: The World of An Elizabethan Magus.* London: Routledge and Kegan Paul, 1972.

Freud, Sigmund. *Interpretation of Dreams* (transl. James Strachey). New York: Avon Books, 1983.

Gauquelin, Michel. *The Scientific Basis of Astrology* (transl. James Hughes). New York: Stein and Day, 1969.

Gérardin, Lucien. *Le Mystère des Nombres.* St. Jean-De-Braye, France:

Editions Dangler, 1985.

Gettings, Fred. *The Book of Tarot.* London: Triune Books, 1973.

Gibson, Walter Brown, and Gibson, Litzka R. *The Complete Illustrated Book of the Psychic Sciences.* Garden City, N.Y.: Doubleday, 1966.

Goldstein, Bernard R. *The Arabic Version of Ptolemy's Planetary Hypothesis.* Philadelphia: American Philosophical Society, 1967.

Goold, G. P. (ed.). *Manilius: Astronomica.* Cambridge, Mass.: Harvard University Press (Loeb Classical Library), 1977.

Graves, F. D. *The Windows of Tarot.* Dobbs Ferry, N.Y.: Morgan and Morgan, 1973.

Graves, Robert. *The Greek Myths.* New York: Penguin Books, 1955.

Grinstein, Alexander. *Sigmund Freud's Dreams.* New York: International University Press, 1980.

Gulevich, G., Dement, W. C., and Johnson, I. "Psychiatric and EEG Observation on a Case of Prolonged (264 Hours) Wakefulness." *Archives of General Psychiatry* 15 (1966), pp. 29–35.

Haining, Peter (ed.). *The Magicians: The Occult in Fact and Fiction.* New York: Taplinger, 1972.

Hall, Calvin, and Van De Castle, R. L. *The Content Analysis of Dreams*, New York: Appleton-Century-Crofts, 1966.

Hamon, Count Louis (Cheiro). *Mysteries and Romances of the World's Greatest Occultists.* London: Herbert Jenkins, 1935.

Hand, Robert. *Horoscope Symbols.* Rockport, Mass.: Para Research, 1981.

———. *Planets in Transit.* Gloucester, Mass.: Para Research, 1976.

Hannah, Robert. "Manilius, the Mother of the Gods, and the *Megalensiu.*" *Labomus* 45 (1986), pp. 864–872.

Heath, Thomas. *Aristarchus of Samos.* Oxford, England: Oxford University Press, 1913.

Highbarger, E. L. *The Gates of Dreams: An Archaeological Examination of the Aeneid.* Baltimore: Johns Hopkins University Press, 1940.

Hofstätter, Hans H. *Symbolismus und die Kunst der Jahrhundertwende.* Köln: Dumont Buchverlag, 1978.

Holden, Ralph William. *The Elements of House Division.* Essex, England: L. N. Fowler and Co., 1977.

Holroyd, Stuart. *Magic, Words, and Numbers.* Garden City, N.Y.: Doubleday, 1975.

Hopper, Grace Murray. "The Ungenerated 7 as an Index to Pythagorean Number Theory." *American Mathematical Monthly* 43 (August–September 1936), pp. 409–413.

Hopper, Vincent Foster. *Medieval Number Symbolism: Its Sources, Meaning, and Influence on Thought and Expression.* New York: Cooper Square, 1969.

Howe, Ellic. *Urania's Children. The Strange World of the Astrologers.* London: William Kimber, 1967.

Hoyle, Fred. *On Stonehenge.* San Francisco, Cal.: W. H. Freeman, 1977.

Innes, Brian. *The Tarot.* London: Orbis Publishing, 1977.

John of Salisbury. *The Statesman's Book of John of Salisbury* (transl. J. Dickinson). New York: Russell and Russell, 1963.

Jones, Marc Edmund. *How to Learn Astrology.* Boulder, Col.: Shambhala Publications, 1977.

Jung, C. G. *Dream Analysis* (ed. W. McGuire). London: Routledge and Kegan Paul, 1984.

———. *Man and His Symbols.* New York: Doubleday, 1964.

———. *Psychology and the Occult.* Princeton, N.J.: Princeton University Press, 1978.

Kaplan, Stuart R. *Encyclopedia of Tarot.* New York: U.S. Games Systems, 1985.

———. *Tarot Classic.* London: Robert Hale, 1972.

Kennedy, E. S., and Pingree, David. *The Astrological History of Māshā' Allāh.* Cambridge, Mass.: Harvard University Press, 1971.

Kepler, Johannes. *The Harmonies of the World,* in *Great Books of the Western World,* vol. 16. Chicago, Ill.: Encyclopaedia Britannica, 1952.

Kies, Cosette N. *The Occult in the Western World: An Annotated Bibliography.* Library Professional Publications, 1986.

King, Francis. *Palmistry.* New York: Crescent Books, Crown Publishers, 1987.

Kleitman, N. *Sleep and Wakefulness.* Chicago, Ill.: Chicago University Press, 1963.

Knapp, Bettina. *Dream and Image.* Troy, N.Y.: Whitston Publishing Co., 1979.

Koestler, Arthur. *The Sleepwalkers.* Harmondsworth, England: Penguin Books, 1964.

Kuper, Adam. "A Structural Approach to Dreams." *Man* 14 (1979), pp. 645–662.

LaBerge, Stephen. *Lucid Dreaming.* Los Angeles, Cal.: Jeremy Tarcher, 1985.

Lama Anagarika Govinda. *The Inner Structure of the I Ching.* New York and Tokyo: Wheelwright Press and John Weatherhill, 1981.

Larousse Encyclopedia of Astrology. London: Hamlyn Publishing Group, 1968.

Lau, Theodora. *The Handbook of Chinese Horoscopes.* New York: Harper and Row, 1979.

Lease, Emory B. "The Number 3: Mysterious, Mystic, Magic." *Classical Philology* 14 (1919), pp. 56–73.

Leek, Sybil. *Numerology.* New York: Collier, 1969.

Legge, James (transl.). *I Ching: Book of Change.* New York: Bantam Books, 1983.

Lemay, R. "The Teaching of Astronomy in Medieval Universities, Principally at Paris in the 14th Century." *Manuscripta* 20 (1976), pp. 197–217.

———. "Astrology, a Formal Course in European Universities." *Clio* 13 (1978), pp. 1–13.

Leo, Alan. *Esoteric Astrology.* Albuquerque, N.M.: Sun Publications, 1981.

Leo, Alan, and Robson, Vivian E. *Alan Leo's Dictionary of Astrology.* Albuquerque, N.M.: Sun Publications, 1981.

Lèvi, Eliphas. *The Book of Splendors.* New York: Aquarian Press, Samuel Weiser, 1973.

Lindsay, Jack. *The Origins of Astrology.* New York: Barnes and Noble, 1971.

Loewe, Michael, and Blacker, Carmen (eds.). *Oracles and Divination.* Boulder, Col.: Shambhala Publications, 1981.

Loomis, A. L., Harvey, E. N., and Hobart, G. "Potential Rhythms of the Cerebral Cortex During Sleep." *Science* 71 (1935), pp. 597–598.

Lorenze, Dora Masie. *Tools of Astrology: Houses.* Topanga, Cal.: Eomega Press, 1973.

Luck, Georg (ed.). *Arcana Mundi: Magic and the Occult in the Greek and Roman Worlds.* Baltimore, Md.: Johns Hopkins University Press, 1985.

Mackenzie, Norman, *Dreams and Dreaming.* New York: Vanguard Press, 1965.

MacNeice, Louis. *Astrology.* New York: Doubleday, 1964.

Macrobius. *Commentary on the Dream of Scipio* (transl. and intro. W. A. Stahl). New York: Columbia University Press, 1952.

Mair, G. R. (transl.). *Phenomena of Aratus.* Cambridge, Mass.: Loeb Classical Library, 1921.

Mathers, MacGregor S. L. *The Kabbalah Unveiled.* London: Routledge and Kegan Paul, 1951.

McIntosh, Christopher. *Astrologers and Their Creed: An Historical Outline.* London: Hutchinson and Co., 1969.

———. *Eliphas Lèvi and the French Occult Revival.* London: Rider, 1975.

Megary, A. L. *An Investigation into the Mystery and the History of Dreams.* Albuquerque, N.M.: American Institute for Psychological Research, 1985.

Merkel, Ingrid, and Debus, Allen G. (eds.). *Hermeticism and the Renaissance.* London and Toronto: Associated University Presses, 1988.

Morinus, J. B. *Morinus System of Interpretation.* New York: American Federation of Astrologers, 1974–1975.

Needham, Joseph, and Ling, Wang. *Science and Civilization in China.* Vol. 3: "Mathematics in the Sciences of the Heavens and Earth." Cambridge, England: Cambridge University Press, 1959.

Neugebauer, Otto. *The Exact Sciences in Antiquity.* Providence, R.I.: Brown University Press, 1957.

Neugebauer, Otto, and Van Hoesen, H. B. *Greek Horoscopes.* Philadelphia, Pa.: American Philosophical Society, 1959.

North, J. D. *Horoscopes and History.* London: The Warburg Institute, 1986.

Oberhelman, Steven M. "The Diagnostic Dream in Ancient Medical Theory and Practice." *Bulletin of the History of Medicine* 61 (1987), pp. 47–60.

———. "Galen, On Diagnosis From Dreams." *Journal of History of Medicine and Allied Sciences* 38 (1983), pp. 36.

———. "The Interpretation of Prescriptive Dreams in Ancient Greek Medicine." *Journal of History of Medicine and Allied Sciences* 36 (1981), pp. 416–424.

———. *The Oneirocriticon of Achmet.* Binghamton, N.Y.: State University of New York, 1989.

Onians, Richard Broxton. *The Origins of European Thought About the Body, the Mind, the Soul, the World, Time, and Fate.* New York: Cambridge University Press, 1988.

Pack, Robert (ed.) *Artemidorus of Daldis. Oneirocriticon Libri V.* Leipzig: Taubner, 1963.

Panekoek, A. *A History of Astronomy.* London: Allen and Unwin, 1961.

Papus (Gerard Encausse). *The Qabalah: Secret Tradition of the West.* Wellingborough, England: Thorsons, 1977.

———. *The Tarot of the Bohemians* (transl. A. P. Morton). New York: Arcanum Books, 1958. North Hollywood, Cal.: Wilshire Book Co., 1970.

Paracelsus. *The Hermetic and Alchemical Writings of Aureolus Phillippus Theophrastus Bombastus of Hohenheim.* New Hyde Park, N.Y.: University Books, 1967.

Parker, Derek. *Familiar to All: William Lilly and Astrology in the Seventeenth Century.* London: Jonathan Cape, 1975.

Parker, Derek, and Parker, Julia. *A History of Astrology.* London: André Deutsch Ltd and Oregon Press Ltd, 1983.

Poulle, E. "Horoscopes Princiers des 14me et 15me Siècles." *Bulletin de la société nationale des antiquaires de France* (séance de 12 février 1969), pp. 63–77.

Préaud, Maxime. *Les Astrologues à la Fin du Moyen Age.* France: J. C. Lattès, 1984.

Pruckner, H. *Studien zu den Astrologischen Schriften des Heinrich von Langenstein.* Leipzig and Berlin, 1933.

Putscher, Marielene. "Die Himmelsleiter Verwandlung eines Traums in der Geschichte." *Clio* 13 (1978), pp. 13–39.

Rachleff, Owen. *Exploring the Bible.* New York: Abbeville, 1981.

———. *Sky Diamonds.* New York: Popular Library and Hawthorne Books, 1976.

Ratcliff, A. J. *A History of Dreams: A Brief Account of Dream Theories with a Chapter on the Dream in Literature.* Darby, Pa.: Arden Library, 1979.

Regardie, Israel. *The Golden Dawn: An Account of the Teachings, Rites, and Ceremonies of the Order of the Golden Dawn.* St. Paul: Lewellyn, 1971.

———. *The Tree of Life: A Study in Magic.* New York: Samuel Weiser, 1971.

Reiner, E., and Pingree, D. *Enuma Anu Enlil Tablet 63, The Venus Tablet of Ammisaduqa.* Malibu, Cal.: Udena Publishers, 1975.

Reynolds, Roger E. "At Sixes and Sevens, and Eights and Nines." *Speculum* 54 (1974), pp. 669–684.

Rignac, Jean. *Les Lignes de la Main.* France: Librairie Générale Francaise, 1973.

Robbins, F. E. (ed. and transl.). *Ptolemy: Tetrabiblos.* London: Heinemann (Loeb Classical Library), 1940.

Rudhyar, Dane. *The Practice of Astrology.* Boulder, Col.: Shambhala Publications, 1978.

Rycroft, Charles. *The Innocence of Dreams.* New York: Pantheon Books, 1979.

Saint Germain, Comte C. de. *Practical Astrology. The Language of the Stars.* Hollywood, Cal.: Newcastle Publishing Co., 1973.

Samuelson, Harding V. *Numerology for the Millions.* Los Angeles, Cal.: Sherborne Press, 1970.

Sandbach, John. *Astrology, Alchemy, and the Tarot.* Birmingham, Mi.: Seek-It Publications, 1982.

Sarton, George. *A History of Science.* Cambridge, Mass.: Harvard University Press, 1952.

Sayce, A. H. "Astronomy and Astrology of the Babylonians with Translations of the Tablets." *Transactions of the Society of Biblical Archeology* 3 (1874), pp. 145–339.

Scarborough, John. "Hermetic and Related Texts in Antiquity," in *Hermeticism and the Renaissance,* (ed. Ingrid Merkel and Allen G. Debus). New Jersey: Associated University Press, 1988.

Schiller, Francis. "Semantics of Sleep." *Bulletin of the History of Medicine* 56 (Fall 1982), pp. 377–391.

Scholem, Gershon. *On the Kabbalah and Its Symbolism.* New York: Schocken Books, 1965.

Schott, Heinz. "Traum und Geschichte zur Freudschen Geschichte auffassung im Kontext der Traumdeutung." *Sudhoffs Archiv* 64 (1980), pp. 298–312.

Seligmann, Kurt. *The History of Magic.* New York: Pantheon Books, 1948.

———. *Magic, Supernaturalism, and Religion.* New York: Pantheon Books, 1973.

Shchutzkii, Iulien K. *Researches on the I Ching* (transl. W. MacDonald and Tsuyoshi Hasegawa). Princeton, N.J.: Princeton University Press, 1979.

Sherrill, W. A., and Chu, W. K. *An Anthology of I Ching.* London: Routledge and Kegan Paul, 1978.

Shulman, Sandra. *Encyclopedie Illustrée de l'Astrologie.* Pully, Switzerland: Jean F. Gonthier, 1977.

Shumaker, Wayne. *The Occult Sciences in the Renaissance.* Berkeley, Cal.: University of California Press, 1972.

Smith, Richard Furnald. *Prelude to Science: An Exploration of Magic and Divination.* New York: Scribner's, 1975.

Spence, Lewis. *Encyclopedia of Occultism.* New York: University Books, 1956.

Stekel, Wilhelm. *The Interpretation of Dreams* (transl. E. and C. Paul). New York: Washington Square Press, 1967.

Stern, Jesse. *Edgar Cayce—The Sleeping Prophet.* New York: Doubleday, 1967.

Tester, Jim. *A History of Western Astrology.* Rochester, N.Y.: Boydell and Brewer, 1989.

Thom, A. "Stonehenge." *Journal for the History of Astronomy* (1974), pp. 71–98.

Thompson, C. J. S. *The Mystery and Romance of Astrology.* London: Brentano's Ltd., 1929.

Thorndike, Lynn. *A History of Magic and Experimental Sciences.* New York: Columbia University Press, 1923–1958.

Thurston, Mark A. *How to Interpret Your Dreams.* Virginia Beach: A.R.E. Press, 1978.

Toomer, G. J. (ed. and comm.). *Ptolemy's Almagest.* London: Duckworth, 1984.

Toulmin, Stephen, and Goodfield, June. *The Fabric of the Heavens: The Development of Astronomy and Dynamics.* New York: Harper and Brothers, 1961.

Van de Kemp, Hendrika. "The Dream in Periodical Literature, 1860–1910." *Journal of the History of Behavioral Science* 17 (1981), pp. 88–113.

Vickers, Brian. *Occult and Scientific Mentalities in the Renaissance.* Cambridge, Mass.: Harvard University Press, 1984.

Waite, Arthur Edward. "The Great Symbols of the Tarot." *The Occult Review,* Vol. 43, No. 2 (Feb. 1926), pp. 83–91.

———. *The Pictorial Key to the Tarot.* New York: University Books, 1961.

Walker, Barbara G. *The Secrets of the Tarot: Origins, History, and Symbolism.* New York: Harper and Row, 1984.

Waltham, Clae. *I Ching, Arranged from the Work of James Legge.* New York: Ace Books, 1960.

Wang, Robert. *The Qabalistic Tarot.* York Beach, Me.: Samuel Weiser, 1983.

Westcott, William Wynn. *Numbers: Their Occult Power and Mystic Virtues.* London, 1890.

White, Robert. *The Interpretation of Dreams: The Oneirocritica by Artemidorus.* Park Ridge, N.J.: Noyes Press, 1975.

Wilhelm, Hellmut. *Heaven, Earth, and Man in the Book of Changes.* Seattle: University of Washington Press, 1977.

Wilson, Colin. *The Occult.* New York: Vantage Books, 1973.

Wing, R. L. *The I Ching Workbook.* New York: Doubleday, 1979.

Wisdom, J. O. "Three Dreams of Descartes." *International Journal of Psychoanalysis* 28 (1947), pp. 11–18.

Wolff, Werner. *The Dream, Mirror of Conscience. A History of Dream Interpretation from 2000 B.C. and a New Theory of Dream Synthesis.* New York: Grune and Stratton, 1952.

Yates, Frances Amelia. *The Occult Philosophy in the Elizabethan Age.* London: Routledge and Kegan Paul, 1979.

Zain, C. C. (Elbert Benjamine). *Mundane Astrology.* Los Angeles, Cal.: The Church of Light, 1962.

———. *Sacred Tarot.* Los Angeles, Cal.: Church of Light, 1969.

Index

Numbers in italics denote illustrations.

A

Abercrombie, John, 405
Abu-Ma'shar, *see* Albumasar
Achillinus, Alexander, 252, *252*
Achs, Ruth, 256
Acusmatici, 163
Adams, Evangeline, 89, 93
Adams, John J., 88
Adler, Alfred, *409,* 409–10, 417
Aeschylus, 368
Affection, lines of, palm, 266, 268
Agrippa von Nettesheim, Henry Cornelius, 60–61, 69, 174, 392
ahkām (*hukm*): dream type, 385; judgment, 52
ahlám, dream type, 385
air (Greek element), 34, 36, 162; zodiac signs associated with, *96,* 108, 136
Albertus Magnus, 56, 382–84
Albumasar, 48, *52;* manuscript illustrations, *48, 112, 124*
alchemy, 48, 56, 61, 88, 167, *172,* 206, 210
Alcott, Henry Steel, 89
Alexander VI, Pope, 61
Alexander the Great, 28, 29, 32, 33, *35,* 248, 365, 377; at Tyre, *379*
Alexandria, 33, 35, 36–37, 48, 60, 164, 372
algebra, 160, 164, 167
Alice in Wonderland (Carroll), 180
Alliette, *see* Etteilla
Allen, G., 118
Allen, William Frederick ("Alan Leo"), 92, 93
All's Well That Ends Well (Shakespeare), 69
Almagest (Ptolemy), 44, 48; *Epitome of, 61*
Alphonsine Tables, 52, 60
Alphonso XI of Castile, King, 201
Al-Kwarizmi, 48
American Indians: dream mythology, 357; dream shirt, Crow, *355; see also* Pre-Columbians
Amman, Jost, woodcut by, *73*
Anatomy of Melancholy (Burton), 394, *395*
Anderson, Carl, 89
Anga Vidya, 247
Anglicus, Bartholomeus, *Liber de Proprietatibus, 155*
angular distance measurement, *60*
angular houses, horoscope, 118, 120–21, 133
animal entrails, reading of, 9, *38,* 247
animal magnetism, of Mesmer, 398, *399*
Antares (star), 113
anthroposophy, 92
L'Antimagnetisme (Mesmer), *399*
Antiochus IV, King of Syria, 365
antiscion aspects, 127
Apian, Peter, *Cosmographia, 35*
Apollo, rule over ring finger, 248, 253, 256, 263
Apollo (Sun) line, palm, 268, 277
Apollo mount, palm, *253, 254,* 263, 264, 266, 275–76
Apollonius of Perga, 36, 52
Apparition of a Danger (Bloom), *354*
Apparition of Face and Fruit Dish on a Beach (Dali), *410–11*
Aquarian tarot deck, court cards, *218*
Aquarius, *58,* 107, 108, 115–16, *116;* Age of, 37, *37,* 107; Persian depiction, *51;* primary in House XI, 121; Saturn as ruler of, *103,* 104, 116; Uranus as ruler of, 105, 116
Aquinas, Thomas, *see* Saint Thomas Aquinas
Arabian Nights, The, 48
Arabic numerals, 164; manuscript, *165*
"Arabic parts" of the horoscope, 48, 128
Arabic writings and translations, 48, *48, 52, 59, 124, 131,* 164, 250, 252, 389
archaeoastronomers, 21
Archimedes, 36, 37
Areas of Life spread, tarot, 229
Aries, *106,* 107, 108, 109; Age of, 37, *37,* 107, 109; compared to Leo, 111, 114; compared to Sagittarius, 114; Mars as ruler of, 97, *97,* 100, 109; Pluto as ruler of, 105, 109; primary in House I, 120; sun in, *108,* 108
Aristander, 377
Aristarchus, 36–37, 44, 76
Aristides, 375–76
Aristotle, 33, *35,* 36, 56, 57, 73, 160, 164, 167, 247–48, 250, *370,* 394; cosmological system of, 33–34, *35,* 80; his cosmology accepted by Church, 34, 52; pseudo-works, 53; view of dreams, 371, 382–84, 392, 399, 405–6, 413
arithmetic, 160, 167
Armenian manuscript, mathematical table, *166*
armillary sphere, *45*
Arnald of Villanova, 56, 384
Arnason Republican Automatons (Grosz), *190*
Artemidorus, 376–80, 385, 389, 392, 397, 406
Artemon, 371, 377
Arthur, King, and Round Table, legend of, 382
Art of Divining (Rothman), *253*
ascendant point, horoscope diagram, 108, 127
ascendant sign, 108, 132, 146, 148, 154; defined, 17, 95; importance of, 127, 136; ruling planet, 132, 136; in synastry, 130–31
"The Ascension of Mohammed" (from *Khamsa*), *386*
Ascension of Propitious Stars and Sources of Sovereignity, The (Matali), *113, 131*
Asclepius, 247, 363, 372, 374–75, 382, 406; healing shrines of, 363, 374–76, *374–75*
Aserinsky, Eugene, 416
Ashmole, Elias, 72
Ashurbanipal, King of Assyria, 24, 29, 361
aspects, astrological, 17, 77, 96, 97, 122–27, *123;* antiscia, 127; in Chinese astrology, 143; contraparallel, 126; and delineation of chart, 132, 133, 148–50; effects of, 122; in Mesopotamian astrology, 28; midpoint, 127, *127;* minor, 122, 123–26; parallel, 126; Ptolemaic system of, *41–43,* 44; quincunx, 122, 123, *126;* semisextile, 122, *123,* 126; semisquare, 122, *123,* 126; sextile, 96, 122–23, *123;* square, 96, 122, 123, *123;* of three or four planets (grand trine, T-cross, grand cross, yod), 126, *126;* trine, 96, 122, 123, *123;* validity questioned, 154; *see also* conjunction; opposition
Association for Research and Cosmecology, 93
Assyrians, 24, 29, 360, 361; astrolabe, *24*
asthenics, 278
"astral body," 417
astrobiology, 92
astrolabes, *24, 54, 59, 94*
Astrologer of the Nineteenth Century, The, 90
astrologi, 45
Astrologia Gallica, Louis XIV horoscope from, *71*
astrological prediction, 53, 128–31; Chinese reading, 145; Indian (Hindu), 138–39; sample reading (Colette), 146, 150–51
—**methods of,** 128–29, 131; progressions, 128–29, 131, 150–51; solar arc, solar return, 131; transits, 129, 151; Uranian system, 131
—**purposes of,** 129–31; electional (favorable timing of action), 129; horary (advisability of action), 129–30; synastry (relationships), 130–31
astrology, 9–10, 13–155, 174, 235; arguments for and against, 152–55; vs. astronomy, 21, 44, 71, 80, 88, 154; basis of, 17; and cabala, 61, 89, *168, 172;* Chinese, 29, 33, 93, *140–42,* 143; and chiromancy, 252–53, 256; defined, 21; and dreams, 360, 392, 397; Indian, 29–30, 33, 107, 138–39, *138–39;* interrogatory, 48; in medieval university curricula, 56; methodology of, 41, 44, 95–128; roots of, 21; terminology of, 17, 21; Uranian system of, 93, 105, 127
—**divisions of,** 17–19; electional, 19, 48, 129; genethliacal (natal), 19, 28, 48; horary, 19, 48, 129–30; judicial, 17–19, 52; medical, 19, 48, *53–55,* 65, 71, 72, 137, 252
—**history of,** 21–93; early Christian era, 44–45, 250; Egypt, 30–32; Greek and Hellenistic period, 32–37, 38, 248; Islam, 45–52; Mesopotamia, 24–30, 360; Middle Ages, 52–57; 19th and 20th centuries, 88–93; post-Renaissance rationalism, 73–88; Pre-Columbians, 23–24; prehistoric peoples, 21–23; Ptolemy, 41–44; Renaissance, 57–72; Rome, 38–41; West-East/East-West transmissions, 33, 48, 52
—**modern branches of,** 88–93; mystical, 88, 89–92; psychological, 88, 92–93; statistical, 88, 92; symbolist, 88, 89; traditional, 88–89, 93, 96
Astro-Meteorological Society, 89
Astronomer, The (Vermeer), *95*
Astronomiae, Wandsbek, illustration from, *73*
Astronomica (Manilius), 41
astronomical clocks, 16th century, *66, 70*
astronomy, 9–10, 17, 76; Arabic/Islamic, 48; vs. astrology, 21, 44, 71, 80, 88, 154; Copernican, 76–80; 18th century instruments, *16;* emergence of modern, 80–82, 85–86, 88; Greek, 36–37; Ptolemaic, 41–44; Renaissance, 60, 65, 71
Astro-Theology (Denham), 87
Aszalay, Joseph, 255
Atlas Coelestis, 74–75
atmospheric refraction, 80
augury, 9, 38, *40,* 248; from liver, *38,* 247
Augustine of Hippo, *see* Saint Augustine
Augustus, Emperor, 38, 115, 371; coin, *38*
Autumn Colors on the Chi'ao and Hua Mountains (Chao Meng-fu), *301*
Avenzoar, 48
Averroes, 48, 56, *162*
Avicenna, 52, 56, 57, 250
azghás (dream type), 385
Aztec concept of Zodiac Man, *23*

B

Babylonia(ns), 9, 19, 24–30, 32, 33, 360, 361, 365; calendar, 29; cuneiform tablets, *25,* 29; sexigesimal system, 160
"Babylonian numbers," in horoscopes, 29
Bacon, Sir Francis, 69
Bacon, Roger, 56
Baghdad, 48
Balzac, Honoré de, 256
Barbault, André, 92
Barrett, Francis, 89
baru, of Babylonia, 9, 24, 361
Baughan, Rosa, 89
Bayeux tapestry, detail showing comet, *84*
Baynes, Cary, 286, 290, 296
Beamish, Richard, *Psychology of the Hand, 256*
Beatty (Chester) Papyrus, 363
Becket, Thomas, 250
Behair, Caspar, astronomical clock of, *70*
Bell, Charles, *255*
Belot, Jean-Baptiste, 255
Belshazzar, Daniel's prognostication, *365, 366*
Bembo, Bonifacio, *205*
Benjamine, Elbert (Zain), 210
Bergson, Henri, 209, 399
Bernheim, Hippolyte, 399
Berossus, 29
Berry, Duke of, *Très Riches Heures, 55*
Besant, Annie, 89
Beware-Danger American Dream #4, The (Indiana), *192*
Bezold, Carl von, 93
Bible, 27, 44, 164, 168, 174, 206, 243–45, 255, 363, 374, 380; of Luther, woodcut from, *65;* Vivian, dedication page of, *251; see also* New Testament; Old Testament
Biblical prophets, 9, 168, *243,* 365
Bingham, George Caleb, *Dull Story, 403*
biochemical processes, and dreams, 417, 419
biquintile aspect, 122
birth (in horoscope): vs. conception, and ascendant sign, 127; place and time of, 118
birth horoscope, *see* natal horoscope
Birth Name (numerology), 178, 188
Birth Number, 178, 188, 191, 193
Blake, William, 89, 404; etching after, *402*
Blavatsky, Helena, 89
Bloom, Hyman, *Apparition of a Danger, 354*
Boccaccio, 382, 392
body parts: chiromancy and, 253; dream interconnections with, 404, 410; in dream symbolism, 363, 377, 384, 389; planetary associations with, 100, 104, 105, *137;* zodiacal associations with, 41, *55, 55,* 61, 97, 137, *137*
body shape, and personality, 278
Boethius, *De Arithmetica Musica, 160*
Bogomil tomb sculpture, ink rubbing from, *250*
Bok, Bart, 93
Boke of Astronomy, miniature from, *102*
Boll, Franz, 93
Bologna, University of, 56
Bonatti, Guido, *Liber Astronomicus, 18*
Book of Fate, The (author uncertain), 88
Book of History (*Shu Ching*), 284
Book of Poetry (*Shih Ching*), 284
Book of Revelation, 167, 181–87, 206, 210
Book of Stars and Constellations (al-Sufi), *114*
Book of Thoth, 201; tarot decks, 206, 210, *220*
books of hours, astrological illuminations in, *55, 110, 113, 116*
Bosch, Hieronymus, *The Garden of Delights, 391*

Botticelli, Sandro, *The Rite of Spring, 179; Saint Augustine, 45*
Bouché-LeClerq, Auguste, 93
Brahe, Tycho, 77, *77, 78,* 80; drawing by, *77;* observatory of, *77, 79*
Brahmavaivarta Purana, 360
Braid, James, 398
Brhatsāmudrikāsastra, diagram of palm, *246*
Browne, Sir Thomas, 72, 397
Bruno, Giordano, *65,* 167
Buch von der Haand (Hartlieb), 250
Buddha: diagram of hand of, *246;* hand gestures and their meaning, *271–72; Le Nimi-Jataka* dream sequence, *358–59*
Buddhism, 285, 357, 360
bull (constellation), 31; *see also* Taurus
Bunyan, John, 397
Burdell, Claude, 205
Burton, Robert, 69, 394, 395
Butler, Samuel, *Hudibras,* 72; W. F. Douglas illustration for, *71*

C

cabala, cabalism, 29, 61, 160, 168–74; and astrology, 61, 89, 168, *172;* Sephiroth Tree, *169,* 170–71, 209; and tarot, 206, 208–9, 210, 225; terminology, 168, 174; texts, *167–68, 172–73*
Cabala, Speculum Artis (Michelspacher), *172*
cadent houses, in horoscope, 118, 120–21, 133
Caesar, Julius, 113, 371
Cagliostro, Count Alessandro di (Giuseppe Balsamo), *87,* 87–88; tarot deck of, *222*
Cairo, Egypt, 48, 52
calendars, 29, 31, 37, 60, 64; perpetual, *67*
calendrical knowledge: Babylonian, 29; Egyptian, 31; Greek, 29, 37; prehistoric peoples, 21, *22*
Caligula, Emperor, 371
Calkins, Mary, 404
Callippus, 33
Calpurnia, 371
Calvin, John, 64, 392, 409
Campagnola, Giulio, engraving by, *97*
Campin, Robert, *Saint Barbara, 186*
Cancer, *58,* 108, 109, *110,* 111; Moon as ruler of, 99, 111; primary in House IV, 120
Canon (Avicenna), 250
Canterbury Tales, The (Chaucer), *54, 55–56,* 382
Capricorn, *58,* 107, 108, 115, *115,* 116; on Augustan coin, 38, *38;* Persian depiction, *51;* primary in House X, 121; Saturn as ruler of, *103,* 104, 115; Uranus as ruler of, *105,* 115
Caravaggio, *The Fortune Teller, 238*
Cardan, Jerome, 253, 392
cards: origins of, 200–1; uses of, 201; *see also* tarot
career choices, 92, *102,* 127, 152, 154
Carti di Baldini, 205
Carus, Carl Gustav, *255, 255,* 404
Case, Paul Foster, 174, 209, 210
Cassiopeia (constellation), 29
Castor (star), 109
Catholic Church, 88; and astrology, 45, 48, 56, 61, 64, 73, 250; and Copernican system, 76–77, 82; and dreams, 380–81, 382, 384, 389; and numerology, 164, 167; and tarot, 205
Cavendish, Richard, 174
Cayce, Edgar, 417–19
Cazotte, Jacques, 397
Cecco d'Ascoli, 56
Celestial Map: Northern Hemisphere (Dürer), *65*
Celestial Science of Astrology (Sibly), *87*
Cellarius, Andrew, *78;* engravings by, *42–43, 74–75, 78*
Celsus (Roman encyclopedist), 61, 380
Celsus (Roman Platonist philosopher), 380
Celtic associations with tarot cards, 201, 210
Celtic cross spread, tarot, 224, 226–27; sample reading, 230, *231,* 232
Chaldean priest-astrologers, 24
Chao Meng-fu, *Autumn Colors on the Chi'ao and Hua Mountains, 301*
Chao Po-Chu, *River and Mountains in Autumn, 307*
character traits, *see* personality
Charcot, Jean-Martin, 398
Chariot (tarot card), 200, 212, *214*
Charlemagne, Emperor, 382; vision of, *366*
Charles II, King of England, 72
Charles VI, King of France, 205
Chartres Cathedral, stained glass window, *117*
Chaucer, Geoffrey, *The Canterbury Tales, 54, 55–56,* 382
Cheiro (*pseudonym* of Count Louis Hamon), 256
Chên (*I Ching* hexagram), *328,* 329
Chên (*I Ching* trigram), 266, 288–89, 320–21
Chêng Hao, 285
Chen Jung, *Nine Dragon Scroll, 298*
Chia Jên (*I Ching* hexagram), 319–20
Chichén-Itzá, 23–24
Chi Chi (*I Ching* hexagram), *291,* 339
Chieh (*I Ching* hexagram), 333–37
Ch'ien (*I Ching* hexagram 1, Greatness, Beginning, Benefit), 298, *298*
Ch'ien (*I Ching* hexagram 15, Modesty, Humility), *307,* 307–8
Ch'ien (*I Ching* trigram), 266, 288–89, 301, 306, 321
Chien (*I Ching* hexagram 39, Difficulty, Obstruction), 320–21
Chien (*I Ching* hexagram 53, Gradual Progress, Development), 329–30
Chien Hsuano, *Tea Connoisseurs, 350*
Ch'ien-lung, Emperor, zodiac jade plate, *143*
Childeric, Merovingian king, dreams of, *382*
Children with Crickets (Zhu Zuchang), *292*
Childrey, Joshua, 73
Chin (*I Ching* hexagram), 317–19
China, 201; astrology, 29, 33, 93, *140–42,* 143, *145;* color symbolism, 296; Communist, 29, 93; dream interpretation, 360; eras of antiquity, 284–85; oracle bones, *284;* palmistry, 266; thumb print clay seal, *241;* writings and philosophy, 29, 162, 284–86; *see also I Ching;* yang and yin
Ch'in dynasty, 285
Chinese Year, 143, 144; animal figures, *140–42,* 143
Ching (*I Ching* hexagram), 325
Ch'ing dynasty, 286
chirology, 239
chiromancy, 247–57; astrology and, 252–53, 256; medical, 252–53, 256; origin of term, 247; *see also* handreading; palm
Choisnard, Paul, 89, 92
Chou dynasty, 284, 285
Chou Hsin, Emperor, 284
Christian, Paul (Jean-Baptiste Pitois), 89, 208
Christianity, 29, 33, 48; Aristotelian philosophy accepted by, 34, 52, 382; and astrology, 44–45, 48, *52–53,* 56, 61, 64, 73, 250; and cabala, 168, 171–74; and chiromancy, 250; and Copernican system, 76–77, 82; Crusades, 48, 52, 201; and dream interpretation, 361, 380–81, 382–84; early, 44–45, 164, 250, 361, 380–81; and Islam, 48; medieval, 52, 56, 160, 164, 382; mysticism, 44, 160, 164, 167, 171–74; and numerology, 164, 167; Renaissance, 61, 64, 65; and tarot, 201, 205, 206
chromosomal abnormalities, and hand, 278
Chuang-tzu, 360, 394
Chu Hsi, 285
Chun (*I Ching* hexagram), 288, *289,* 299–300
Chung Fu (*I Ching* hexagram), *336–37,* 337–38
Cicero, 38, 41, 248, *371,* 372
Circular spread, tarot, 228
clairvoyance, 9, 10
Classic tarot (deck), 205
Clement (Alexandrian writer), 44
Clement VII, Pope, 64
Cloudy Mountains (Mi Yu-jen), *286–87*
Codex Vaticanus, illustration from, *23*
coffee readings, 344, 348
Coleridge, Samuel Taylor, 405, 418
Colette, Sidonie-Gabrielle, *146, 193;* horoscope, 146–51; numerological reading, 191–92
collective unconscious, 408, 413, 417
comets, 44, 60, 85, 93; Bayeux tapestry, *84*
Committee for the Scientific Investigation of Claims of the Paranormal, 93
compatibilities, assessment of: in astrology, 130–31; in numerology, 189
concentric spheres, *see* spheres
Condorcet, Marquis Antoine Nicholas de, 405
Confessions (Saint Augustine), 381
Confessions of an English Opium-Eater (De Quincey), 405
Confucius, *285;* commentaries, 285, 293, 296, *299*
conjunction (aspect), 96, 97, 122, *123,* 154; defined, 28; in Indian astrology, 139; in Mesopotamian astrology, 28
conscience (censor), 360, 401, 406, 407–8
conscious mind, 406–10, 415, 417–18; Adlerian, 410; Freudian, 406–9, 413, 415; Jungian, 410–13
consciousness, states of, 398–400, 409; Freudian teaching, 406–9; Hindu, 357–60
Constant, Alphonse Louis, *see* Lèvi, Eliphas
Constantine, Emperor, dream of, *378,* 381
constellations, 15–17, 95, 153; ancient knowledge of, 21, 24, 28, 31; in Greek cosmology, 33; naming of, 31; *see also* zodiac signs
contraparallel, planets in, 126
converse progression, 131
Cooke, Christopher, 89
Copernican system, 65, 73, *74–76,* 76–77, 80, 82, 394
Copernicus, Nicolaus, 44, 76, *78,* 80
Cordova, Spain, 48, 52
Cornell, Joseph, *Sun Box, 98*
Corvus, Andreas (Barthelemy Cocles), 252
cosmic rays, 152, 153
Cosmobiological Society, 93
cosmogeny, 21
Cosmographia (Apian), *35*
cosmology: Aristotelian, 33–34, 36, 52, 80; of Dante, *57;* Platonic, 33, 36; Pythagorean, 32–33, *33*
Cossa, Francesco del, Zodiac frescoes, *107, 110*
"counter earth," postulated by Pythagoras, 33, 185
court cards, tarot, 200, *207, 218, 220–21;* as significators, 225; *see also* king; knight; page; queen
Couture, Thomas, *Day Dreams, 403*
Creation of Adam (Michelangelo), *244–45*
Crick, Francis, 304, 419
crocodile, Egyptian constellation, 31
Crowley, Aleister, 89, 174, 209, 210; Thoth tarot deck, 210, *220*
Crow tribal "dream vision" shirt, *355*
Culpeper, Nicholas, 72
Culver, Roger, 93
Cummins, Harold, 257
Cumont, Franz, 93
cuneiform texts, *25,* 29, *158,* 361
cups, Lesser Arcana suit, 200, 210, 217, *218,* 219, *222–23;* reading, 226
cusp, (horoscope) defined, 96; planets near, 96, 132, 136
cyclothymics, 278
Cyromancia Aristotelis, 247, 250

D

Dali, Salvadore, *Apparition of Face and Fruit Dish on a Beach, 410–11*
Daniel (prophet), 29, 365–66, 385, 389
Dante Alighieri, *56,* 164, 184, 382, 392; cosmic concept of, 57, *57*
Dao Ji, *Spring on Min River, 291*
D'Arpentigny, Stanislas, 256, 260
Davy, Humphrey, 405
Day Dreams (Couture), *403*
day-for-year progressed chart, 128, 131
days: Egyptian division into 24 segments, 31; of the week, naming of, 29, 32
De Arithmetica Musica (Boethius), *160*
Death (tarot card), 200, 213, *215*
Decameron (Boccaccio), 382
decan system, 31–32, 164
de Chirico, Giorgio, *Gare Montparnasse, 407*
decimal system, 167
De Divinatione (Cicero), 41
Dee, John, 69, 174; *General and Rare Memorials, 68*
de Gébelin, Antoine Court, 200, 201, 205, 206, 208, 213
De Harmonia Mundi (Giorgi), *167*
delineation, of horoscopes, 97, 118, 132–36, 152; Chinese, 145; sample (Colette), 145–51
Dement, William, 416
Democritus, 370
Demuth, Charles, *"I Saw the Figure 5 in Gold," 195*
Denham, William, 87
De Nova Logica (Lull), *173*
De Quincey, Thomas, 405
De Revolutionibus Orbium Coelestium (Copernicus), 76, *76*
dermatoglyphics, 257
Desbarrolles, Adolphe, 256; *Mystères de la Main, 254,* 256
Descartes, René, 84, 394; Hals portrait, *394*
descendant point, in horoscope diagram, 108
descendant sign, 132, 136, 147; defined, 17
De Sphaera, manuscript miniatures, *99, 103*
determinism, 370, 371; *see also* predestination
"detriment," planets in, 97, 108, *131*
Devil (tarot card), 200, 213, *215*
diseases: chiromancy and, 256–57; classification in astrological medicine, 55, 72, 137; hand and finger correlations, 278
Divine Comedy (Dante), *57,* 164, 382
Dobyns, Zipporah, 128
Doctor Faustus (Marlowe), 69; title page, *168*
Dominoes (Lawrence), *192*
Domitian, Emperor, 371
Douglas, Sir William Fetter, *Hudibras and Ralph visiting the Astrologer, 71*
Dream, The (Rousseau), *414–15*
dream books, 344, 360, 376–80, 389, 392, 397
Dream of Constantine (Francesca), *378*
Dream of the Doctor, The (Dürer), *393*
dreams, 206, 235, 353–419; Adler's

views on, 410, 413; Cayce's views on, 417–19; "condemnation" in, 408; creative inspiration obtained from, 392, 397, 404, 405, 418; "displacements" in, 408; Freud's views on, 374, 399, 403, 406–9, 413–15; fueled by repressed hidden desires for wish fulfillment, 371, 374, 399, 401–3, 405, 406–8, 409, 413; healing, 363, 374–76, 382, 385, 387, 406; Jung's views on, 410–13; literary allusions, 382, 392, 397, 405; and Moon's position in Zodiac, 99; physiological studies of, 416–17; "secondary elaboration" in, 408; symbols, 376–77
—**causation of**: deity/God-sent, 361, 363, 368, 371, 372, 380, 381, 382, 385, 392, 419; demon/devil-caused, 361, 363, 370, 371, 381, 385, 392; drug-induced, 357, 392, 405; induced, 357, 374–75, 392, 404; invoked, 361; physiological/somatic origins, 371, 372–73, 382–84, 397, 403, 404, 417, 419; psychological origins, 371, 374, 389, 392, 397, 399, 404, 406–10, 419; spontaneous, 357, 361; supernatural, 361, 367, 368, 370, 372, 397
—**classification of**: five Chinese types, 360; by Macrobius, 372; predictive vs. nonpredictive, 372, 376, 381; theorematical vs. allegorical, 376
—**imagery,** 344, 377, 389; body parts, 363, 377, 384, 389; Freudian, 407–9, 413–15; Jungian, 410
—**interpretation of,** 356, 357–419; Adlerian, 409–10; American Indian mythology, 357; ancient China, 360; ancient Egypt, 360, 361–63, 367, 374; ancient Greece and Rome, 368–74; ancient Hebrews, 363–67; ancient India, 360; Aristides, 375–76; Aristotle and, 371, 382–84, 392, 399, 405, 406, 413; Artemidorus, 376–80, 389, 392; Cayce, 418, 419; in early Christianity, 361, 380–81; evaluation of, 419; free association, 389, 409, 415; Freudian, 406–9; Galen, 372–74, 376; in Islam, 384–89; Jungian, 410–13; medieval views, 382–84; Mesopotamian lore, 360–61, 363, 367, 374; Plato, 370–71, 392, 413; Renaissance and Reformation, 382, 389–92; 17th and 18th centuries, 394–97; 19th century, 397–405; 20th century, 406–19
—**prognostication from,** 356, 361, 368, 371–72, 380–81, 384–85, 389, 392, 397, 405, 406, 413; Adlerian, 410; Jungian, 413; medical uses of, 371, 372, 373, 376, 380, 385, 406; Egypt, 363, 374; Greece, 363, 374–76, 385
"dream vision" shirt, Crow, *355*
Dregs in the Cup (Mount), *342*
Dresden Codex, *159*
drugs, 417; and dreams, 357, 392, 405, 417
Dryden, John, 69
Dulazzi, Aldo, *Pope Gregory XIII's Meeting to Reform the Calendar, 64*
Dull Story (Bingham), *403*
Dumas, Alexandre, 256
Dummet, Michael, 201
Dura Europas Synagogue, painted tile from, *115*
Dürer, Albrecht: *Celestial Map, Northern Hemisphere, 65; The Dream of the Doctor, 393;* Knight and Page *tarocchi* card, *204; Das Traumgesicht* ("Dream Vision"), *390*

E

earth (Greek element), 34, 36; zodiac signs associated with, *96,* 108, 136
earth (planet): circumference measured, 37; concept of as flat, 32; Greek spherical view of, 32, *36,* 37; medieval Church view of, 52; revolution around sun, 76, *96, 108;* rotation of, 76; rotational "wobble" of, 37, *37,* 154; seasons, *96; see also* geocentric systems
Ebertin, Reinhold, 93
"eccentrics," 28, 95; *see also* planets
eclipses, 29, 60; lunar, 28, 128; Ptolemaic view of, 44; solar, 128
ecliptic, solar, 28, *96;* defined, 15, 95; house divisions of, 44, 118; north (ascending) and south (descending) nodes on, 128
Egypt, ancient, 24, 160, 247; astronomy, *30–31,* 30–32; *decan* system, 31–32; dream interpretation, 360, 361–63, 367; dream therapy, 363, 374; *jabiru* bird stela, *364;* tarot card origin attributed to, 200–1, 206, 208, 210; tarot cards, *223;* two-finger amulet, *247;* view of cosmos, *32*
eight, in numerology, 183, 185
Eight Bells Folly: Memorial for Hart Crane (Hartley), *183*
Einstein, Albert, 178
Eisler, Richard, 93
Elam, dream interpretation in, 361
electional astrology, 19, 48, 129
electromagnetic waves, 152, 153
elements, five Chinese, 143, 144, 181
elements, four Greek, 33, 34, 36, 137, 162, *172,* 180, 256; Arabic reemphasis on, 48; house associations, *96,* 118, 120–21; zodiac sign associations (triplicity), *96,* 108, 109–16, 147
eleven, number, 186
Eliot, T. S., 210
Elizabeth I, Queen of England, 69, 174
Elliotson, John, 398
Ellis, Havelock, 401
Emerson, Ralph Waldo, *404,* 405
Empedocles, 36
Emperor (King) (tarot card), *199,* 200, *202,* 211–12, *214*
Emperor Ming Husang's Journey to Shu (Li Zhaodao), *294–95*
Empress (Queen) (tarot card), *199,* 200, *203,* 211, *214*
Encausse, Gerard, *see* Papus
Encyclopedia Londinensis, Milky Way diagram, *85*
Encyclopedia of Tarot (Kaplan), 210
enhypnion (nonpredictive dream), 376, 385
Enlightenment, Age of, 84, 255, 394
ephemerides (astronomical tables), 17, 60, 96
Epicureans, 41, 368, 371–72
Epicurus, *34,* 41, 371–72
epicycles, planetary, 36, 77
Epidaurus, amphitheater at, *374*
Epitome of Ptolemy's Almagest (Müller), *61*
Equal House system, horoscopic, 118
equinoxes, 37; precession of, 37, *37,* 107, 154
Erasmus of Rotterdam, 60
Eratosthenes, 36, 116, 180, 327
Escher, Maurits Cornelis, *Hand with Reflecting Globe, 257*
ESP (extrasensory perception), 417
"ether" ("fifth essence"), 34
Etruscans: augury, 38, *38,* bronze mirror, *161*
Etteilla (Alliette), 206; tarot deck, 206, 208, *222*
Euclid, 36, 52, 163
Eudoxus, 33, 34, 88
Eugénie, Empress, 256
Euripides, 368
"exaltation," planets in, 97, 108
Ezekiel (Michelangelo), *243*

F

Fagan, Cyrus, 118
"fall," planets in, 97, 108
Fate line, palm, *253,* 266, 267–68, 277
Faucheux (French astrologer), 89
Faulds, Henry, 257
Faust in His Study (Rembrandt), *170*
Feast of Belshazzar, The (Martin), *366–67*
Female Pope (tarot card) *see* High Priestess
Fêng (*I Ching* hexagram), 331–32
Ficino, Marsilio, 61, 171
Fibbia, Prince François, 205
fiery trygon, 108
Figulus, Publius Nigidus, 38, 164
fingernails, 260, 263, 275; moons, 263, 275
fingerprints, 257, 270, 276, 278; basic types of, 270, *270*
fingers, 239, 256; association of Greco-Roman gods and planets with, 248, 252, 253; classification of types, 262–63; features considered in palmistry, 260; in handreading example, *273,* 275; mounts at base of, 264–65; zodiacal associations with, 252, 255
fingertips, 260, 275
fire (Greek element), 34, 36, 162; Pythagorean central, 33, *33;* Stoics' view of, 41; zodiac signs associated with, 96, 108, 136
First Dream. Crime and Expiation (Grandville), *400*
five, as mystical number, 164, 181; in Chinese culture, 143, 181, 360
Five Hundred Arhats, The (Wu Bin), *304–5*
Flaming June (Leighton), *356*
Flemish zodiac sign tapestry, *125*
Fleury, Robert, *Galileo Before the Holy Office, 82*
Flinck, G., *The Legacy of Isaac, 245*
Fludd, Robert, 174, *174,* 255; *Utriusque Cosmi Minoris et Majores Technica Historia, 69, 175–77*
Fodor, Nandor, 413
Fool (Madman) (tarot card), *199,* 200, *203, 207, 209,* 211, *214, 220, 221*
Forel, Auguste, 399
Formalhaut, 89
Fortune, Dion, 174
Fortune Teller, The (Caravaggio), *238*
Fortune-Teller and the Soldier, The (Vecchia), *259*
Foulkes, David, 415
four, as mystical number, 180–81, 183; *see also* elements, four; humors; qualities, four
Francesca, Piero della, *Dream of Constantine, 378*
Francis I, King of France, 65
Frederick II of Sicily, Emperor, 57, 250
free-association technique, 389, 409, 415
free will and choice, issue of, 17, 41, 44–45, 56, 73, 80, 153
Freud, Sigmund, 92, 200, 376, 389, 392, 399, 403, *406,* 406–9, 410, 413–15, 417
Freudians, 344, 357, 361, 367, 374, 409–10, 413
Friday, origin of word, 29
Fromm, Erich, 409, 413
From Ritual to Romance (Weston), 210
Fu (*I Ching* hexagram), 312
Fu Hsi, Emperor, *282,* 284
Fukae Roshu, *The Pass Through the Mountains, 334–35*
Fuseli, Henry: *Nightmare, 398; Titania and Bottom, 418*

G

Gadbury, John, 13
galaxy, spiral, 17
Galen, 48, 61, 248, 372–74, *373,* 375, 376, 380, 384, 394, 406
Galileo Before the Holy Office (Fleury), *82*
Galileo Galilei, 76, *78,* 82, 167, 183
Galle, Johann, 88
Gallego, Fernando, Salamanca fresco, *99*
Galton, Francis, *255,* 257
Gandāvyūha, illustration from, *246*
Gardener, Martin, 93
Gare Montparnasse (de Chirico), *407*
Gargantua and Pantagruel (Rabelais), 65, 382
Garnett, Richard (A. G. Trent), 92
Gauquelin, Michel and Françoise, 92, 118, 152, 154–55
Gaurico, Luca, 61
Gauthier de Metz, *Image of the World, 54*
Gauthier-Villar, Henri, 191, 193
Geber, al- (Jabir ibn-Hayyan), 167
gematria, 164, 167, 171, 174
Gemini, *55, 58,* 92, 108, 109, *110;* Mercury as ruler of, *18, 99,* 100, 109; primary in House III, 120
General and Rare Memorials (Dee), *68*
genethliacal (natal) astrology, 19, 28, 48; *see also* natal horoscopes
geocentric systems, *57, 66,* 76, *77;* Greek, 33, 36, *36;* of Ptolemy, *42–43,* 44, *61, 65*
geometry, 164, 167; Pythagorean, 162–63, 185
George III, King of England, 85
Gerard of Cremona, 52
Gérôme, Jean-Léon, paintings by, *40, 248–49*
Gettings, Fred, 256
Gilgamesh, Epic of, 109, 361
Giorgi, Francesco, *De Harmonia Mundi,* 167
girdle of Venus, palm, *253,* 266, 268
Gleadow, Rupert, 93
Gnosticism, 44, 160, 164, 168, 206
Goad, Joshua, 73
Goethe, Johann Wolfgang von, 87, 397
Golden Dawn, Hermetic Order of the, 89, 174, 206, 209–10; tarot cards, 209–10, *210*
Goldschmidt tarot cards, *199, 202–3*
Golem, tale of, 168
Goudeket, Maurice, 191, 193
Goya, Francisco, *The Sleep of Reason Produces Monsters, 396*
grand cross (aspect), 126, *126*
Grandes Heures of the Duke of Rohan, *113*
grand quintile (aspect), 126
grand trine (aspect), 126, *126*
Grandville, Sean (Jean-Ignace-Isidore Gerard), dream lithographs of, *400–1*
gravity, 152, 153; Newton's law of, 84
Greater Arcana, tarot deck, 171, 200, 201, 209, *214–15;* attitude of churches toward, 205; Book of Thoth deck, 206, 210, *220;* cards listed, 200; famous decks, 205–6; Golden Dawn cards, 209–10, *210;* Goldschmidt cards, *199, 202–3;* Gringonneur cards, 205, *207;* images, meanings of specific cards, 211–16; Marseilles deck, 205, *214–15;* Napoleon deck cards, *221;* preparation of cards, 225; reading, 225–29; Visconti-Sforza cards, *198,* 205, *235*
Great Pyramid, 31
Greece, ancient, 9, 24, 28, 29, 38; calendar, 29, 37; cosmology, 32–37, *33, 35, 36; decan* system, 31–32; dream interpretation in, 368–71, 372; dream therapy, 363, 374–76, 385; manuscript translation and transmittal via East, 33, 48, 52; naming of zodiac constellations, *30,* 31; numerology, 32, 33, 160–63; palmistry, 247–48
Gregorian calendar, 29, 64
Gregory II, Pope, 382
Gregory of Nyssa, 380
Grey, Robert, 404
Gringonneur, Jacquemin, 205; tarot card deck, *207*

Grosseteste, Robert, 56
Grosz, George, *Republican Automatons, 190*
Guaita, Marquis Stanislas de, 208
Gudea, King of Sumerians, 361
Guide to the Perplexed, A (Maimonides), *59*
Gust of Wind at Ejiri, A (Hokusai), *323*
Gutheil, Emil, 399
gypsies, 201, 248, 252; tea-leaf reading, 343, 348
Gypsy spread, tarot, 228

H

Hadrian, Emperor, 377
Hail Caesar: We Who Are about to Die, Salute You (Gérôme), *248–49*
Hall, Calvin, 413, 415
Halley, Edmund, *84,* 85; Comet of, 85
Hals, Frans, *Descartes, 394*
Hamon, Count Louis (Cheiro), 256
Hand, Douglas, 417
Hand, Robert, 93
handreading, 10, 206, 235, 237–79; and astrology, 252–53, *256;* Chinese, 266; evaluation of, 278–79; example, 273–77; of past vs. present, 253; predictive, rejections of, 255–56, 257, 278; *see also* chiromancy
—**features used in:** fingerprint as modifier, 257, 270; finger types and classification, 260, 262–63; German 15th-century illustrations, *250, 252;* hand types and classifications, 260, 261; mounts, *253, 254,* 264–65; palm lines, 248, *253, 254,* 266–68; palm markings, 269; plains, 265
—**history of,** 241–57; ancient Greece and Rome, 247–48; Bible, 243–45; earliest reference in Indian writings, 247; early Christian era, 250; Middle Ages, 250–52; 19th and 20th centuries, 255–57; post-Renaissance, 255; Renaissance, 252–53
Hands of Children, The (Spier), 257
hand types, 255–56, 260; classifications, 261
Hand with Reflecting Globe (Escher), *257*
Han dynasty, 285
Hanged Man (tarot card), 200, 206, 213, *215*
Hankan, *The Night-Shining White Steed, 310*
Hansen, Heinrich, *Tycho Brahe's Observatory at Night, 79*
Harmonia Macrocosmica, frontispiece of, *78*
Harold, King of England, *84,* 85
Harper, Rita, 256
Harris, Lady Frieda, 210
Hartley, David, 397
Hartley, Marsden, *Eight Bells Folly: Memorial for Hart Crane, 183*
Hartlieb, Johannes, 250
Hartmann, Ernest, 417
Hartmann, William, 92
Harun al-Rashid, caliph of Baghdad, 48
Harvey, William, 65, 253, 394
Hasani, Sayyid Shans-al-din al-, dish of, *387*
Hasidic Judaism, 171, 194
Hastings, Battle of, 85
Hathor, temple of, at Dendera, *30*
Hazlitt, William, 401
Head line, palm, 248, *253, 254,* 266, 267, 276–77, 278
healing shrines and dreams, 363, 374–76, 382, 406
Heart line, palm, 248, *254,* 266, 267, 277, 278
Hebrew alphabet: and numerals, 168, 170; and tarot cards, 174, 206, 209
Hebrews, ancient, 29, 170; astrology, *26,* 29; cabala, 29, *168,* 168–71; calendar, 29; dream interpretation, 363–67
Hebrew tetragrammaton, 171–74, 206, 208–9
Heindel, Max, 92
heliocentric systems, 76, 77; of Aristarchus, 36, 44, 76; of Copernicus, 65, 73, *74–76,* 76–77, 80, 82; of Pythagoras, 33, 76
Hellenistic period, 21, 28, 29, 30, 31, 32, 33, 36–37, 38
Hell Scroll (Jigoku Soshi), 306, 315
Hêng (*I Ching* hexagram), 316–17
Henry II, King of England, 250
Henry VIII, King of England, 69; clock of, *66*
Henry, Duke of Saxony and Bavaria, star mantle of, *53*
hepatoscopy, *see* liver, reading of
Heraclitus, 36, 370
herbals, in astrological medicine, 72, 137
Hermes Trismegistus, 168, 171, 206
Hermetica, 171
Hermeticism, 168, 174; *see also* Golden Dawn
Hermit (tarot card), 200, 212, *214, 220, 235*
Herophilus, 372
Herschel, William, 85, 88, 105, *105,* 153, 257; Milky Way diagram of, *85;* telescope of, *85*
Hesiod, 32, 368
hexagrams of *I Ching,* 283, 298–339; basis of, 284, 288; choosing for reading, 283, 288–90; history of, 284, 285; meanings of, 288, 296; reading, 290–93, 296; reading example, 297; ruling (constituting and governing) lines, 293; *see also specific hexagrams*
Hicks, Edward, *Noah's Ark, 179*
Hierophant (tarot card), 200, 212; *see also* Pope
High Priestess (Female Pope) (tarot card), 200, 211, *214, 235*
Hildegard of Bingen, Abbess, 382; *Scivias, 382*
Hinduism, 357; astrology, *see* India, astrology
Hindu playing cards, 201, 206
Hipparchus, 36, 37, 154
Hippocrates, 372, *373,* 380, 384, 406
Hiroshige, *Light Showers at Shano, 289*
Historia Animalium (Aristotle), 248
History of Magic (Constant), 89
Hobbes, Thomas, 394
Hokusai, *A Gust of Wind at Ejiri, 323*
Holden, R. W., 118
Homé, Diegus, perpetual calendar of, *67*
Homer, 32, 368, 370, 374, 377
homocentric sphere models of cosmos, 33; *see also* geocentric systems; spheres, concentric
Hone, Margaret, 92
Honnecourt, Villard de, *Lion and Porcupine, 111*
horary astrology, 19, 48, 129–30, *130*
Horney, Karen, 413
Horoscope of Napoleon III, The (Vogt), *88*
horoscopes, 17–19, 206; "Arabic parts" of, 48, 128; ascendant sign in, 17, 95, 108, 127, 132, 136, 146, 148, 154; before and after discovery of Uranus, Neptune, Pluto, 85–87, 105, 153; beginnings of, 21, 28, 29, 33, 38; birth (natal, genethliacal), *see* natal horoscopes; descendant sign in, 108, 132, 136, 147; history of, 29, 41, 48, 53–56, 61, *69,* 80; horary, 129, *130;* Moon's significance in, 129–30, 136; plotting of, 96, 97, 108, 118; prime mover, 132, 136, 148; progressed, 128–29, 131, 150–51; reading of, *see* delineation; ruling planet of, 132, 136; significance of precession of the equinoxes for, 37, 154; Sun-sign in, 37, 93, 95, 99, 108, 127, 136, 154; two or more persons' comparison (synastry), 130–31; uses of, 48, 53, 129–31
—**diagrammatic wheel of,** 17, 96, *96,* 108, 118, 132; angles, 132, 136, 146, 154; axes of (horizontal and vertical), 108, 118; houses of, *see* houses; points on, 108, 127–28, 132, 136
—**examples of specific persons:** Colette, *147,* 146–51; Iskandar, *46–47;* Kepler's for Wallenstein, *80;* Louis XIV, *71;* Louis XVI and Marie Antoinette, *86*
—**parts of,** 48, 96, 132, 136; "Arabian," 48, 128; planets, 95–96, 97–105, 108, 118, 132, 136; zodiac signs, 95–96, 97, 107–16, 118; *see also* aspects, astrological; houses; planets; zodiac signs
Horse (Tang dynasty terra cotta), *318*
Horseshoe spread, tarot, 227; sample reading, 233, *234*
Hortus Deliciarum (Herrade de Landsberg), *182*
Hours of the Duchess of Burgundy, 110
House of Wisdom (Baghdad), 48
houses (astrological divisions of the sky), 17, 44, 77, 93, 96, 118–21, *121;* angular, 118, 120–21, 133; cadent, 118, 120–21, 133; in Chinese astrology, 143; criticism of, 153–54; elements and qualities held by, *96,* 118, 120–21; fixed location of, 118; Greek origin of, 33; in Indian astrology, 138; numbering in horoscope wheel, 118, *121;* primary zodiac signs for, *96,* 118, 120–21; role in horoscope, 96, 118; succedent, 118, 120–21, 133
—**planets and, in horoscope,** *96,* 97, 118, 132, 136; absence of planets from, 132, 133, *133,* 136; distribution of planets in, 132–33, *133,* 146; effects listed, 120–21; effects, sample reading (Colette), 147–50
—**systems of,** 96, 118; Equal House, 118; Koch, 93, *119;* Placidian, 61, 93; Regiomontanus, 60, 93
House I, 111, 120, *121;* angular, 118, 120, 133; in horary horoscope, 130; ruled by Mars, 100, 120; ruled by Pluto, 105
House II, 120, *121;* in horary horoscope, 130; ruled by Venus, 100, 120; succedent, 118, 120, 133
House III, 120, *121;* cadent, 118, 120, 133; ruled by Mercury, 100, 120
House IV, 120, *121;* angular, 118, 120, 133; ruled by Moon, 99, 120
House V, 120, *121;* ruled by Sun, 99, 120; Saturn in, 72; succedent, 118, 120, 133
House VI, 120, *121;* cadent, 118, 120, 133; ruled by Mercury, 100, 120
House VII, 120, *121;* angular, 118, 120, 133; in horary horoscope, 130; ruled by Venus, 100, 120; in synastry, 130
House VIII, 120, *121;* ruled by Mars, 100, 120; ruled by Pluto, 105, 120; succedent, 118, 120, 133
House IX, 120–21, *121;* cadent, 118, 120, 133; ruled by Jupiter, 100, 121
House X, 121, *121;* angular, 118, 121, 133; ruled by Saturn, 104, 121
House XI, 121, *121;* ruled by Saturn, 104, 121; ruled by Uranus, 105, 121; succedent, 118, 121, 133
House XII, 121, *121;* cadent, 118, 121, 133; ruled by Jupiter, 100, 121; ruled by Neptune, 105, 121
Howells, William Dean, 401–3
Hsiao Ch'u (*I Ching* hexagram), 302–3
Hsiao Kuo (*I Ching* hexagram), 338–39
Hsieh (*I Ching* hexagram), *320–21,* 321
Hsien (*I Ching* hexagram), 316
Hsü (*I Ching* hexagram), 300–1
Huan (*I Ching* hexagram), 333
Hudibras (Butler), 72; W. F. Douglas illustration for, *71*
Hugo, Victor, 405
hukm (*ahkām*), 52
Humanist Journal, The, 93
Hume, David, 84
humors, four, 137, 180, *180,* 372, 384
Hunting Cards of Ambras, queen of falcons, *206*
Huron Indians, 357
hydromancy, 343
hyleg (Part of Fortune), 48, 128
Hypnos, Head of (Egyptian sculpture), *368*
hypnosis, hypnotism, 398–99, 409

I

I (*I Ching* hexagram 27, Corners of the Mouth, Nourishment, Feeding), 313–14
I (*I Ching* hexagram 42, Increase), 322
Iamblichus, 164, 208
Ianna, Philip, 93
Ibn Sina, 250; *see also* Avicenna
Ibn Sirin, 389
I Ching, 224, 235, 281–339; basis of, 283; commentaries, 285–86, 288, 293, 296, *299;* correspondence of Chinese palmistry to, 266; as divinatory oracle, 283, 285; functions of, 283, 285; fundamental teachings of, 293; history of, 284–86; image, 285, 293; judgments, 283, 284, 286, 293, 296; lines of, broken vs. single, 283, 284, 286, 288, 290–91, 293, 296; as moral code for correct conduct, 283, 285; reading, 290–93, 296; reading example, 297; ruling (constituting and governing) lines of, 293; symbolisms (color, compass), 296; Ten Wings of, 283, 285, 286, 296, *299;* translations of, 286, 293, 296; *see also* hexagrams; trigrams; *and see specific hexagrams and trigrams*
identical twins, 118
Iliad (Homer), 374
Image of the World (Gauthier de Metz), *54*
Imhotep, 363, 374
Imum Coeli (IC; nadir of celestial sphere), 17, 108, 118, *119,* 127, 132, 136, 147
incubation: Asclepian treatment, 363, 374–76, 382, 406; Chinese custom of, 360
Indagine, John, 253
India, 417; astrology, 29–30, 33, 107, *135,* 138–39, *138–39,* 247; cards and card games, 201; dreams, and levels of consciousness, 357–60; laws of Manu, 247; palmistry, 247
Indiana, Robert, *The Beware-Danger American Dream #4, 192*
"I never dared to dream" (Shahn), *297*
Influence, lines of, palm, 266, 268
ink-blot test, 343–44; Rorschach, *343,* 344, 348
Inner Drive (in numerology), 188
insomnium (nonpredictive dream), 376, 385
intercepted zodiac signs, 132, 133
Interpretation of Dreams, The (Freud), 406
interrogatory astrology, 48
In the House of a Diviner (Longhi), *240*
Introduction to Arithmetic (treatise), 164
Introduction to Dermatoglyphics, An (Cummins and Midlov), 257
Iroquois Indians, 357
Isadore of Seville, Saint, 164
Isaiah (prophet), 29, 367
"I Saw the Figure 5 in Gold" (Demuth), *195*
Ishtar (Mesopotamian goddess), *23,* 24, 100, 109, 111, 361
Iskandar of Shiraz, horoscope of, *46–47*
Islam: astrology and sciences, 45–52, *46–51,* 53, *112–14, 124, 131;* dream

interpretation, 384–89; Greco-Roman writings translated and transmitted by, 48, 52; *"naib"* card game, 201; numerology, 164–67; Sabians, 93; Sunni vs. Shiite split, 384

J

Jacob (biblical character): deceiving Isaac, 245, *245*, 363; the wrestler, dreams of, *362*, 363–64, *365*, 376
Jacob ben Tarik, 48
"Jacob's Dream," from *Saint Louis Psalter, 362*
Jacob's staff, *60*
Jain cosmological chart, *134*
Jamnapattra of Prince Navanibal Singh, illustration from, *106*
Janet, Pierre, 93
Jayne, Charles, Jr., 93
Jerome, Lawrence, 93
Jewish culture and tradition, 29; astronomer-astrologers in Baghdad, 48; attitudes toward astrology, 29; mysticism and cabala, 168–71; in Spain (Cordova), 48; tarot origins speculated on, 201, 206; *see also* Hebrews, ancient
Jigoku Soshi (*Hell Scroll*), *306; Hell scene, 315*
Johannes Trimethius, Abbot, 174, 205
John of Salisbury, 56, 250
John of Seville, 52
Jones, Marc Edmund, 93, 133
Joseph (biblical character), dream interpretation by, 364, 380, 385, 389
Josephine, Empress, 256
Joseph of Ulm, drawing by, *98*
Journey of the Magi (Sassetta), *27*
Judgment (tarot card), *198*, 200, *210, 215*, 216
judicial astrology, 17–19, 52
Juggler (tarot card), *see* Magician
Julian calendar, 29
Julius Caesar (Shakespeare), 69
Julius II, Pope, 64, *64*
Jung, Carl Gustav, 92–93, 152, 154, 235, 257, 283, 408, *408*, 410–13, 417; and *I Ching,* 283
Jupiter, 29, 100, *102;* astrological symbol, 100; beneficent, 97, 138; body parts assigned to, 100; in Capricorn, 115; and choice of career, 92, *102*, 152, 154; in conjunction with Saturn in Pisces (in A.D. 747), 116; conjunctions of, 122; discovery of moons of, 183; domiciled in Houses IX and XII, 100, 121; in Gemini, 109; in Leo, 111; in Libra, 113; in opposition to Moon, 123; rule over index finger, in chiromancy, 248, 253, 256, 262; ruling Pisces, 100, 116; ruling Sagittarius, 100, 114, *124;* in Scorpio, 114, *125;* slow-moving, 97, 100, 108, 129; in square with Mars, 123; in trine with Venus, 123; in Virgo, 113
Jupiter mount, palm, *253, 254*, 260, 262, 264, 266, 275–76
Jupiterian personality, 97, 100
Justice (tarot card), 200, 212, *214*
Juvenal, 41, 248

K

Kalender and Compost of Shepherds, 64–65
Kámil ul Tābir (dream book), 389
K'an (*I Ching* hexagram), 314
K'an (*I Ching* trigram), 266, 288–89, 290, 320–21
K'ang Hsi period, 286, 299
Kano Moranobu, *Shumoshiku Loving Lotus, 301*
Kaplan, Stuart R., 210
Kāsīnātha, *Lagnacandrika, 138–39*
Kekulé, F. A., 403–4, 418
Keller, Arthur I., *Women at Tea, 346*
Kên (*I Ching* hexagram), 329, *330–31*
Kên (*I Ching* trigram), 266, 288–89, 290, 307, 330–31
Kepler, Johannes, 44, 76, 77, 116, 118, 174; laws of planetary motion, 80; *Mysterium Cosmographicum, 81;* Wallenstein horoscope of, *80*
Khamsa (Nizami), *386*
Kidinnu, 29
Kindi, al- (abu-Yūsuf Ya'qūb ibn-Ishāq), 252
king (court card, Lesser Arcana), 200, *200*, 216, 217, *218*, 219, *221*
kite (aspect), 126
Klee, Paul, *182*
Kleitman, Nathaniel, 416
knight (court card, Lesser Arcana), 200, *204, 207*, 216, 217, *218*, 219, *220*
Knight Templars, 206
Ko (*I Ching* hexagram), 326
Koch, Walter, 93
Koran, 384–85
Korean divination, ancient, 201
Kou (*I Ching* hexagram), *321*, 324
Krafft, K. E., 92
Kratzer, Nicholas, astronomical clock of, *66*
Ku (*I Ching* hexagram), 309
Kuai (*I Ching* hexagram), 322–23
Kuan (*I Ching* hexagram), 309
Kubla Khan (Coleridge), 405
K'uei (*I Ching* hexagram), 320
Kuei Mei (*I Ching* hexagram), 331
K'un (*I Ching* hexagram 2, Receptive, Follower, Yin Principle), 298–99, *301*
K'un (*I Ching* hexagram 47, Oppression, Exhaustion, Surrounded), 325
K'un (*I Ching* trigram), 266, 288–89, 301, 307
Kunst Chiromantia des Hartlieb, Die, 250
Kurds, 357

L

Laberge, Stephen, 415
Ladd, G. T., 404
Lagnacandrika (Kāsīnātha), *138–39*
Lakhovsky, G., 92
Landsberg, Herrade de, *Hortus Deliciarum, 182*
Laodicaea, Council of, 45
Lao-tse, 285, 360
Laplace, Pierre de, 88
LaRousse's encyclopedia, 118
Last Supper, 187
Last Supper (Leonardo da Vinci), *187*
Laussel, Venus of, *20*, 30
Lavater, Johann, 255
Lawrence, Jacob, *Dominoes, 192*
leap years, Western vs. Chinese, 143
Legacy of Isaac, The (Flinck), *245*
Legge, James, 286, 288, 290, 296
Leibniz, Gottfried, 394–95
Leighton, Frederick, *Flaming June, 356*
Lemay, Richard, 52
Le Nimi—Jataka, illustration from, *358–59*
Leo, *55, 58*, 108, 111, *111;* compared to Aquarius, 116; compared to Aries, 111, 114; compared to Sagittarius, 114; primary in House V, 120; Sun as ruler of, 99, 111, *135*
Leo IX, Pope, 382
Leo X, Pope, 182
Leo, Alan (William Frederick Allen), 92, 93
Leonardo da Vinci, *Last Supper, 187*
Leprince, Jean-Baptiste, *A Necromancer, 274*
Lesser Arcana, tarot deck, 200, 201, 209–10; attitude of churches toward, 205; Book of Thoth deck, 206, 210, *220;* court cards, 200, *207, 218, 220–21* (*see also* king; knight; page; queen); famous decks, 205–6; Golden Dawn cards, *210;* Goldschmidt cards, *199, 202–3;* images and meanings of cards, 216–21; Marseilles deck, *222–23;* Napoleon deck, *221;* numbered cards, 200, 208–9, 217, 219–21, *222–23;* preparation of cards, 225; reading, 225–29; suits of, 200, 210, *218, 222–23;* Visconti-Sforza cards, *235*
Lesson Year (in numerology), 188–89
Leverrier, U. J., 88
Lèvi, Eliphas (Alphonse Louis Constant), 89, 174, 201, 206, 208–9, 210
Levi, Herta, 257
Li (*I Ching* hexagram), 314–16, *315*
Li (*I Ching* trigram), 266, 288–89, 306, 315
Liber Astronomicus (Bonatti), *18*
Liber de Gentili et tribus sapientibus (Lull), *173*
Liber de Proprieratibus (Anglicus), *155*
Libra, 55, *58*, 108, 113, *113;* Mars in, 97, 113; primary in House VII, 120; Venus as ruler of, 100, *101*, 113
Life and Opinions of Tristram Shandy (Sterne), 87
Life line (Vitality line), palm, 248, *253, 254*, 266–67, 276, 278
Life Path, 178, 188, 189, 193
lightning, Ptolemaic view of, 44
Light Showers at Shano (Hiroshige), *289*
Lilly, William, 71–72, *72*
Lin (*I Ching* hexagram), 309
lion (constellation), 31; *see also* Leo
Lion and Porcupine (Honnecourt), *111*
liver, reading of, *38*, 247
Li Zhaodao, *The Emperor Ming Husang's Journey to Shu, 294–95*
Locke, John, 84
Lokman *Sahinsahname, 50*
London, great fire of 1666, *73;* prediction of, 72
Longhi, Pietro, *In the House of a Diviner, 240*
Lorris, Guillaume, 383
Louis XIV, King of France, 71, 201; horoscope of, *71*
Louis XVI, King of France, 87; horoscope of, *86*
Lover(s) (tarot card), 200, 212, *214*
Lowell, Sir Percival, 88, 105, *105*
Lü (*I Ching* hexagram 10, Walking, Treading), *303*, 303–4
Lü (*I Ching* hexagram 56, Traveler, Stranger, Wanderer), 332, *334–35*
Lucian, 370
Lucretius, 372
Lull, Ramon, cabala text illustrations, *173*
"luminaries," 95
Luna mount, palm, 253, *254*, 264, 265, 266, 276–77
lunar calendars, 29, 31, 143
Lunar Mansions (Indian astrology), 30
Luther, Martin, 64, 182, 392; Bible of, *65*
Luther at Erfurt (Paton), *388*
Lyons, Norbert, 409

M

Macbeth (Shakespeare), 406
McClatchie, Regis, and Canon, 285
MacNish, Robert, 404
Macrobius, 372, 392
Madman (tarot card), *see* Fool
Maeterlinck, Maurice, 405
Magendie, François, 404
Magi (three Wise Men), *27*, 29, 44, 116, 380
magic, 52, 60–61, 88, 206; and dreams, 361; Faust as symbol of, *168, 170;* numerical, 160; *see also* cabala
Magician (Juggler) (tarot card), 200, 211, *214*
Magritte, René, *Time Transfixed, 412*
Maimonides, 48; *A Guide to the Perplexed, 59*
Mamun, al- (Abbas Abdullah al-Mamun), 48, 389
Manetho, 32
Manichaeans, 164
Manilius, Marcus, 41, 44
Mansūr, caliph of Baghdad, 48
Mantegna *tarocchi* cards, 205, *208, 209*
Manuscript of Saint Gregory of Nazianzus, 365
Marc Antony, 38
Marco Polo, 29
Maricopa Indians, 357
Marie Antoinette, Queen, horoscope of, *86*
Marlowe, Christopher, 69; *Doctor Faustus,* 69, *168*
marriage: five as number of, 180, 181; palm lines of, *250;* six as number of, 181; Sun-Moon aspect in, 93; use of synastry to assess compatibility, 130–31
Mars, 29, *99*, 100; in Aquarius, 116; astrological symbol, 100; body parts assigned to, 100; in Cancer, 111; in Capricorn, 115; and choice of career, 92, 152, 154; domiciled in Houses I and VIII, 100, 120; fast-moving, 97, 100, 108, 129; in Libra, 97, 113; malefic, 97, 138; near Moon, at eclipse, 29; in opposition to Moon, 122–23; in Pisces, 116; ruling Aries, 97, *99*, 100, 109; ruling Scorpio, *99*, 100, 114; in Sagittarius, 114; in sextile with Saturn, 123; in square with Jupiter, 123; in square with Uranus, 123; Venus in conjunction with, 29; in Virgo, 113
Mars, Plain of, palm, *254*, 265
Marseilles tarot deck, 205, *214–15, 223, 231*
Mars mounts, palm, 264, 265, 266, 276
Martian personality traits, 100
Martin, John, *The Feast of Belshazzar, 366–67*
Masha'allah, 48, 52
masons, masonics, 206, 210
Masque of the Red Death (Poe), 199
Mass of Bolsena (Raphael), *64*
master number (numerology), 178
Matali al-sa'ada wa-manabi 'al-Siyada, 113, 131
materialistic (secular) approach to prediction, 9–10
Maternus, Julius Firmicus, 44
Mathematical Syntaxis (Ptolemy), 32, 44
mathematici, 45, 163
mathematics, 160, 164, 167; Armenian manuscript, *166;* in astrology, 28, 33, 92, 93; Pre-Columbian notations, *159;* sexigesimal (Babylonia), 160; Pythagorean, 33, 162–63
Mathers, Samuel Liddell (MacGregor), 174, 209, 210
Matisse, Henri, *Tea, 347*
Maury, Alfred, 404
Maya, 23–24, 159
Mazarin, Cardinal Jules, 205
medical astrology, 19, 48, 53–55, 65, 71, 72, 137, 252
medical chiromancy, 252–53, 256
Medici, Cosimo de', 61, 171, 174
Medici family, 61, 64
medicine, 9, 32, 48, 61, 137, 153, 163, 252, 253, 389, 394, 398–99; four competing philosophies of, 372–73; numerology and, 162
—**dreams and,** 371, 372–76, 385, 392, 397, 405, 409; diagnostic theories and uses, 371, 372–73, 384, 385; prognostic uses, 371, 372, 373, 376, 380, 406; therapeutic uses (healing dreams), 363, 374–76, 382, 385, 406
Medium Coeli (MC; midheaven, zenith of celestial sphere), 17, 97, 108, 118, *119*, 127, 132, 136; in synastry, 130–31

megaliths, 21, *22*
Melampus, 248
Mêng (*I Ching* hexagram), 290, *292,* 300
mental illness, chiromancy and, *256–57*
Mercurial personality traits, 100
Mercury, 17, 29, 36, *56, 99,* 99–100; in Aquarius, 116; aspect to Sun, 97; astrological symbol, 99; beneficent or malefic potential, 97, 138; body parts assigned to, 100; in Cancer, 111; in Capricorn, 115; conjunctions of, 122; domiciled in Houses III and VI, 100, 120; fast-moving, 97, 99, 108, 129; in Leo, 111; in Libra, 113; as moderator of Saturn, 61; in opposition to Moon, 123; in Pisces, 116; rule over little finger, in chiromancy, 248, 253, 263; ruling Gemini, *18, 99,* 100, 109; ruling Virgo, *18, 99,* 100, 111; in Sagittarius, 114; Salamanca fresco by Gallego, *99;* Venus in conjunction with, 29
Mercury line, palm, 266, 268, 277
Mercury mount, palm, *253, 254,* 263, 264, 266, 276
Mesmer, Anton, 398–99; *L'Antimagnetisme, 399*
Mesopotamia, 9, 24–30, 32, 33, 160, 247, 360–61, 363, 367, 374; cuneiform tablets, *25,* 29, *158,* 361, 377; *see also* Assyria; Babylonia; Sumeria
Messahala, *see* Masha'allah
metempsychosis, 163
Meteorologist and Medical Botany or Herbal Guide to Health (Simmonite), 88
Methan, John, 250
"method of the Arabs," 52
Meton's calendar, 29
Meun, Jean de, 383
Meyer, Adolph, 413
Michelangelo, 64; *Creation of Adam, 244–45; Ezekiel, 243*
Michele, Parrasio, 205
Michelspacher, M., *Cabala Speculum Artis, 172*
Middle Ages, 9, 52–57, 76, 160, 164; astrological depictions, *52–55, 117;* cabala mysticism, 29, 160; dream interpretation, 382–84; Islam, 48; *see also* Islam
midheaven, on horoscope wheel, 127, 130–31, 132, 136, 147; *see also Medium Coeli*
Midloo, Charles, 257
midpoint aspect, 127, *127*
Milky Way, diagram by Herschel, *85*
Military Officer in Shackle, 311
Minchiate-Florentine Tarot, 206
mind, 392; in astrological theory, 56 (*see also* free will); Cayce's structure, 417; Freudian parts of, 406; in Freudian theory, 406–8, 417; line of, in palmistry, *253* (*see also* Head line); vs. soul, in sleep, 380–81; *see also* conscious mind; unconscious mind
Ming dynasty, 360; scroll, *304–5*
Ming I (*I Ching* hexagram), 319; horse as symbol of, *318*
Mitelli, Giuseppe Maria, 205
Mi Yu-jen, *Cloudy Mountains, 286–87*
moabbirs (dream analysts), 385, 389
Monday, origin of word, 29
Monde Primitif, Le (de Gébelin), 206
Montaigne, Michel Eyquem de, 392, 409
month-for-year progression, 128
months, Roman naming of, 181
Moon, 17, 71, 95–96, 99; in Aquarius, *51,* 116; in Aries, 109; astrological symbol, 99; beneficent, 97, 138; in Capricorn, *51,* 115, 116; classified as planet in astrology, 96, 97; in conjunction with Sun, 122; conjunctions of, 122; course of, 80; domiciled in House IV, 99, 120; eclipses of, 28; fast-moving, 97, 99, 108, 129; in Gemini, 109; goddess (medieval drawing), *98;* in Greek cosmology, 33, *35,* 37, 99; Indian symbolism, 30; in Leo, 111; in Libra, 113; masculine in Mesopotamian mythology, 99; nodes of, on ecliptic, 128, 132, 136, 139, 150; in numerology, 180; in opposition to Jupiter, 123; in opposition to Mars, 122–23; in opposition to Mercury, 123; in Pisces, 116; in Ptolemaic system, 44; ruling Cancer, 99, 111; in Sagittarius, *51,* 114, *124;* in Scorpio, 114; in sextile with Uranus, 123; significance in horoscope, 136; significance in horary horoscope, 129–30; soul analogy, 382; in Virgo, 111
Moon (tarot card), 200, *215,* 216
Morgan-Greer tarot deck, court cards, *218*
Morrison, Richard ("Zadkiel"), 88–89, 92
Moses de Leon, 170
Mo Ti (Chinese philosopher), 285
Mount, William Sidney, *Dregs in the Cup, 342*
mounts, palm, *see* palm
Muhammad, 384; "Night Journey" ("Ascension of Mohammed") from *Khamsa, 386*
Müller, Jan Harmensz, drawing by, *104*
Müller, Johann, *see* Regiomontanus
mundane astrology, 19, 28
Munis al-Ahrar (Persian poetry anthology), leaf from, *51*
"music of the spheres," 80, 162
Mylius, Johann, *Opus Medico, 171*
Mystères de la main, Les (Desbarolles), *254,* 256
Mysterium Cosmographicum (Kepler), *81*
mysticism, 9–10, 29, 32, 60–61, 88, 89–92, 93, 154, 167–68, 253, 389, 394, 406, 417–19; Christian, 44, 160, 164, 167, 171–74; Jewish, 168–71; Jungian, 92, 413; in numbers, 33, 160, 164–68, 174; Pythagorean, 32–33, 162–63, 167, 174; *see also* cabala, cabalism

nadir, *see Imum Coeli*
nakshatras, 30
names, in numerology, 178, 188, 191
Napir, John, 167
Napoleon I Bonaparte, Emperor, 256
Napoleon III, Emperor, 256
Napoleon tarot deck, *221*
natal (genethliacal) astrology, 19, 28, 48
natal horoscope, 17, 71, 87, 89, 92, 96, 128; beginnings of, 28, 29, 33, 38; history of, 38, 48, 61; sample (Colette), 146–50; time and place of birth in, 118, 127
Nataraja, statue of, *246*
Nativities (Placidus), *41*
natural astrology, 17; *see also* astronomy
Nebuchadnezzar, dream of, 365, 389
Nebuchadnezzar's Dream 365, 366
Nechepso, King of Egypt, 31
Necromancer, A (Leprince), *274*
Neolithic cultures, 21
Neoplatonism, 44, 61, 84, 164, 168, 185
Neopythagoreans, 164, 168
Neptune, 97, *104,* 105; astrological symbol, 105; in Cancer, 111; discovery of, 86, 88; domiciled in House XII, 105, 121; in Gemini, 109; in Leo, 111; in Libra, 113; ruling Pisces, 105, 116; in Sagittarius, 114; in Scorpio, 114; slow-moving, 105, 108, 129; still distant from Capricorn and Aquarius, 115, 116; in Virgo, 113
Neptunian personality traits, 105
Nero, Emperor, 38, 371, 372, 377
Neugebauer, Otto, 44, 93
Newgrange, prehistoric site, Ireland, *242*
newspaper horoscopes, 152
New Testament, 29, 44, 164, 167, 380
Newton, Sir Isaac, 77, 82–85, 153, 394; laws of motion, inertia, gravity, 82–84; *Principia Mathematica, 82, 82;* telescope of, *83*
Newton, Robert, 44
Nicea, Council of, 45
Nichomachus, *160,* 164
Nicoullaud, Charles, 89
Nietzsche, Friedrich, 405
Nightmare (Fuseli), *398*
Night-Shining White Steed, The (Hankan), *310*
nine, in numerology, 184, 185
Nine Dragon Scroll (Chen Jung), *298*
nirvana, 360
Nizami, *Khamsa,* miniature from, *386*
Noah's Ark (Hicks), *179*
nodes, Moon's, on ecliptic, 127–28, 132, 136, 139, 150
Nonmura Sōsatsu, *Waves at Matsushima, 320–21*
Normand, Mlle, 256
North Star (pole star), 31; measuring the angle of, *31*
Nostradamus (Michel de Nostredame), *63*
nova, 80
numerals: Arabic, 164, *165;* Roman, *163*
numerology, 10, 157–95, 208, 235, 397; basis of, 159; evaluation of, 194; meanings and associations, 180–87; mechanics of, 178; modern practice of, 174; principles of interpretation, 188–89; sample reading (Colette), 191–93
—**history of,** 160–74; ancient Greece and Rome, 32, 33, 160–64; the cabala, 29, 168–74; early Christian era, 164; Islam, 164–67; Middle Ages, 29, 160, 164; modern era, 174; Renaissance, 167–68, 171

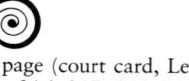

occultism, 29, 45, 52, 56, 60, 65, 84, 87–88, 89, 92, 93, 154, 160, 167–68, 174, 206, 344, 389, 406, 417, 419; groups, 206; *see also* cabala, cabalism
Octavian, 38, 372; *see also* Augustus, Emperor
octile aspect, 122
Odyssey (Homer), 370
O How I Dreamt of Things Impossible (Perry, after Blake), *402*
Old, Walter Gorn ("Sepharial"), 92
Old Testament, 29, 168, 243; dreams described in, 363–67, 376, 380, 385, 389
olimancy, 343
one, as mystical number, 178, 179
Oneirocritica (Artemidorus), 376–77
Oneiros (predictive dream), 376, 385
opposition (aspect), 96, 122–23, *123*
Opus Mathematicum (Taisnier), 253
Opus Medico (Mylius), *171*
oracle bones, *284*
orbits, planetary, *see* planets, orbits of
Order of Saint Francis, 56
Origen, Bishop, 380
Orpheus (Etruscan bronze mirror), *161*
Ortus Sanitatis, illustration from, *389*
Our Christmas Dream (*Illustrated London News*), *397*
out-of-the-body experience, 417, 419; *see also* soul, travel during sleep
Ovid, 370
Oxford University, 56, 72

page (court card, Lesser Arcana), 200, 216, 217, *218,* 219, 220, *235*
Paine, Thomas, 397
pa kua ("Eight Diagrams"), *282,* 284, *287*
Palazzo Schifanoia (Ferrara) frescoes of Costa, *107, 110*
palm, *264–69, 273;* in handreading example, *273, 275–76;* lines, 248, *253, 254,* 266–68; markings (cross, star, grille, triangle, square), 269; mounts and plains, *253, 254,* 264–65, 266; planetary rulerships, 252, 253, *254,* 256, 264–65; zodiacal associations, 252, 255
palmistry, 10, 206, 397; *see also* chiromancy; handreading
Panaetius, 41
Papus (Gerard Encausse), 89, 208, 209, 210, 392; tarot deck court cards, *218*
Paracelsus (Philippus Bombastus von Hohenheim), 61, *62,* 253, 400
parallel, planets in, 126
Park, M. A., 278
Part of Fortune (*hyleg*), 48, 128, 132, 136, 150
Partridge, John (John Hewson), 73, 87
Pascal, Blaise, 394, 397
Pass Through the Mountains, The (Fukae Roshu), *334–35*
Path of Destiny (numerology), 178, 188
Paton, Sir Joseph, *Luther at Erfurt, 388*
Paul II, Pope, 61
Paul III, Pope, 64, 76
Pavlov, Ivan, 416
Pearce, Alfred, 89
pentacles, Lesser Arcana suit, 200, 210, *218,* 219–21, *222–23;* reading, 226
peregrine planet, 97
Perry, J., *O How I Dreamt of Things Impossible, 402*
Persia, 164, 247; ancient, 24, 32; dream depictions, *385, 387;* zodiac sign depictions, *49, 51*
personality traits: body shapes and, 278; chiromantic associations, 253, 255–57, 260–70, 278–79; governed by planets, 96, 97, 138; hand posture and, 271; manifestations governed by zodiac signs, 96, 108, 138; numerological associations, 178–86; tarot associations, 211–21
Personal Month (numerology), 189
Personal Number, 178, 188, 189
Personal Year (numerology), 188–89, 191, 193
Petosiris, 31
Petronius, 372
Pfaff, Julius, 88
Phaedrus (Plato), 33
Philo Judaeus, 164
Philolaus, 33
photoperiodism, 152
physical traits, 97, 108; association with Sun sign and ascending zodiac sign, 65; *see also* body parts; body shape
Physiognomische Fragmente (Lavater), 255
physiognomy, 247, 250
physiology, study of dreams, 416–17, 419
Pi (*I Ching* hexagram 8, Selection, Mutual Support, Union), 302
P'i (*I Ching* hexagram 12, Disharmony, Unrest, Closed up, Standstill), 288, 305–6
Pi (*I Ching* hexagram 22, Adornment, Shining), *310,* 311–12
Pico della Mirandola, Giovanni, 61, 171
Pictorial Key to the Tarot, The (Waite), 209
Pierre de Lorrain, 61
Pilgrim's Progress, The (Bunyan), 397
Pillars of Judgment (*or* Force), Mercy (*or* Form), and Mildness, in Sephiroth, 171
Pindar, 370
Piranesi, Giambattista, 405
Pisces, *55, 58,* 107, 108, 116, *117;* Age of, 37, *37,* 107, 116; conjunction of Jupiter and Saturn in (A.D. 747), 116; Jupiter as ruler of, 100, 116; Neptune as ruler of, 105, 116; Pluto as ruler of, 105; primary in House XII, 121

Pitois, Jean-Baptiste (Paul Christian), 89, 208
Placidian house system, 61, 93
Placidus de Titis, 61; *Nativities, 41*
planets, 15, 17, 85–86, 95–96, 97–105; beneficent vs. malefic, 97, 138; body parts assigned to, 100, 104, 105, *137;* in Chinese astrology, 29, 143; and disease, 137; epicycles of, 36, 77; 15th-century European depictions of, *99, 101–4, 155;* five outer, and historical events, 93; in Indian astrology, 138–39, *138–39;* peregrine, 97; personality traits governed by, 96, 97, 138; "rule" over ancient herbals, 137; rulerships in palmistry, 252, 253, *254,* 256, 264–65; slow vs. fast-moving, and relative influence, 97, 105, 129; *see also specific planets*
—**history of concepts and knowledge of:** ancient Egypt, 31; ancient Greek cosmology, 33, 34, *35–36,* 36–37; ancient Mesopotamia, *24, 25,* 28, 29; Christian dogma, 56; Copernicus, *74–76,* 76; discovery of Uranus, Neptune, Pluto, 85–86, 88, 93, 105; Kepler's laws, 80, *81;* Ptolemaic system, *42–43,* 44
—**in horoscope,** *96,* 97, 97–105, 108, 118, 132, 136; absence from houses and zodiac signs, 132, 133, *133,* 136; in angular vs. cadent vs. succedent houses, 118; in antiscion, 127; aspects of, 17, 28, 77, 96, 97, 122–27, 154 (*see also* aspects, astrological); clustering of, 132–33, *133,* 146; clustering effects listed, 120–21; in conjunction, 28, 29, 97, 122, *123,* 139, 154; in detriment, 97, 108, *131;* domiciles in houses, 97, 120–21; in exaltation, 97, 108; in fall, 97, 108; hemispheric distribution, 132, 146; in mutual reception, 132, 136, 148; near the cusp, 96, 132, 136; in opposition, 96, 122–23, *123;* overall distribution patterns, *133;* in parallel and contraparallel, 126; plotting, 96, 97, 108, 118; prime movers ("in oriental appearance"), 132, 136, 148; retrograde motion, 97, 132, 136, 146; rulerships over zodiac signs, *96,* 97, *108, 131,* 132, 136, *155;* sample reading (Colette), 147–50; stellium of, 132, 133
—**movement of,** 97, 108; apparent, 15, 97; in geocentric system, 33, 34, 36, 77; in heliocentric (solar) system, 17, 36–37, 76, 80; retrograde, 28, 36, 97
—**orbits of,** 76, 97; Brahe's drawing, *77;* concentric spheres concept, 33–34, *35,* 57, *57;* Kepler's law, 80
Planet Venus, The (Hausbuch Master), *101*
Plato, 32, 33, *34, 35, 160,* 163, *370;* concept of soul and universal soul, 33, 368, 370, 380; view of cosmos, 33, 36; view of dreams, 370–71, 392, 413
Platonism, 44, 163, 164, 167, 380
Pliny, 377
Plotinus, 44
Plutarch, 363, 371, 377
Pluto, 17, 97, 105; assigned to Houses I and VIII, 105, 120; astrological symbol, 105; in Cancer, 111; discovery of, 86, 88; in Libra, 113; ruling Aries, 105, 109; ruling Pisces, 105; ruling Scorpio, 105, 114; in Sagittarius, 114; slow-moving, 105, 108, 129; still distant from Capricorn, Aquarius, and Pisces, 115, 116; in Virgo, 113
Plutonian personality traits, 105
Po (I Ching hexagram), 312
Poe, Edgar Allan, 199, 405
Poet Lin P'u Walking in the Moonlight (Tu Chin), *286*
polarities of zodiac signs, *96,* 108, 109–16, 136, 147; Chinese, 143, 144
pole star, *see* North Star
Pollux (star), 109
Pompeii: mosaic, *34;* wall painting, *39*
Pontius Pilate, 380
Pope (tarot card), *199,* 200, *202,* 212, *214*
Pope Gregory XIII's Meeting to Reform the Calendar (Dulazzi), *64*
Porphyry, 44
Porta, Giovanni della, 252
Posidonius, 41
Praetorius, Johannes, 255
Prayer (Shahn), *184*
precession of the equinoxes, 37, *37,* 107, 154
precognition, 10, 417
Pre-Columbians: astronomy of, *23,* 23–24; mathematics, *159*
predestination, vs. free will, 17, 41, 44–45, 56, 73, 80, 370, 371; and grace of God, 205
prehistoric peoples, 21–23, 241–43
primary direction technique of astrological prediction, 128
prime mover, horoscope, 132, 136, 148
primitive cultures of present, 21–23; dreams in, 357
"Primum Mobile" cosmic sphere, in system of concentric spheres, *35, 57*
Princely Hunting Cards of Ambras, queen of falcons, *206*
Principia Mathematica (Newton), 82, *82*
Problemata (Aristotle), 248
progressions, in astrological prediction, 128–29, 131; sample reading (Colette), 150–51
Prometheus (Sim), *369*
Prophetic Messenger, The (almanac), *90–91*
Protestantism, 64, 167, 205
Psalter of Blanche of Castille, 54
psychiatry, 344; Freudian dream interpretation, 361, 374, 406–9
psychoanalysis, 92, 224, 410, 415; and dreams, 364, 408–9
psychohistory, 371
psychological astrology, 88, 92–93
psychology, 344, 374, 392, 399, 419; Adlerian, 410; behaviorist, 416; cognitive, 413; Freudian, 406–9, 410, 413; Jungian, 410; physiological, 416
Psychonomy of the Hand (Beamish), *256*
Ptolemaic system, *42–43,* 44; Bible woodcut, *65;* extension by Regiomontanus, 60, *61*
Ptolemy, Claudius, 32, *41,* 41–44, 52, 73, *78,* 88, 154; Arabic transmittal of his writings, 48
Ptolemy Soter, pharaoh, 363
Purbach, George, 60
Purkinjê, Johannes L., 257, 405
Pythagoras, 32–33, *34, 160,* 160–63, *162,* 174, 370, 384, 413; cosmic system of, 33, *33;* moving earth of, 33, 76; "music of the spheres," 80, 162
Pythagoreanism, 160, 162–64, 167, 174, 178, 180–83, 185, 194, 368, 370
Pythagorean theorem, 163

Q

quadriplicity, of zodiac signs, 108, 136
qualities: four (hot, cold, dry, moist), 48, 137, *172,* 180; three astrological (cardinal, fixed, mutable), 33, 108, 118, 136, 147, 256; four astrological, zodiac sign associations, 108, 109–16; house associations, 118, 120–21
queen (court card, Lesser Arcana), 200, 216, 217, *218,* 219, *220, 221*
quincunx (aspect), 122, 123, *123*
quintile (aspect), 122

R

Rabelais, François, 65, 382
Rank, Otto, 431
Raphael: *Mass of Bolsena* (detail), *64; School of Athens* (details), *35, 162*
Raphael's Almanac, Prophetic Messenger, and Weather Guide (Smith), 88–89
rapid eye movements (REM), 355, 416–17, 419; graphs, *416*
rationalism, 60, 73, 84, 87, 394, 397, 405
Reading the Palm (ceramic, after Beyer), *258*
Reformation, Protestant, 64, 167, 392
refraction, atmospheric, 80
Regardie, Israel, 210
Regiomontanus (Johann Müller), 60, *61,* 64, 93
reincarnation, 139, 163, 417; and north mode of Moon orbit, 128
Religio Medici (Browne), 397
Rembrandt van Rijn, *Faust in His Study, 170*
Renaissance, 48, 76, 167–68, 252–53, 394; astrology and astronomy, *57–72;* cabala mysticism, 29, 61, 168, 171; dream interpretation, 382, 392
retrograde motion, of planets, 28, 36, 97, 132, 136, 146
Revelation of St. John, 167, 181–87, 206, 210
Rheticus, George Joachim, 76
Richter, J. P. F., 400
ring of Solomon, palm, 266, 268
rising sign, *see* ascendant sign
Rite of Spring, The (Botticelli), *179*
River and Mountains in Autumn (Chao Po-Chu), *307*
Roemer, Olaus, *16*
Rohan, Cardinal Louis René Édouard de, 88
Rohan Master, *Les Grandes Heures* of the Duke of Rohan, *113*
Rolleston, Frances, 89
Roman calendar, 29
Romance of the Rose, The, 382, *383*
Rome, ancient, 9; astrology, *38,* 38–41, 248; augury, 9, *40;* counters, *163; decan* system, 32; dream interpretation, 368, 370, 371–74, 376; manuscript translation and transmittal via East, 33, 48, 52; numerology, 163–64; palmistry, 248; Pompeii mosaics, *34, 39*
Rorschach, Hermann, 344
Rorschach test, 344, 348; ink blot, *343*
Rosicrucians, 206, 208, 210
Rothman, John, 253; *Art of Divining, 253*
Rousseau, Henri, *The Dream, 414–15*
Rousseau, Jean-Jacques, 397, 409
Royal Society of London, 72, 87
Royal spread, tarot, 227
Rubens, Peter Paul, *The Three Graces, 179*
Rudhyar, Dane, 92
Rufus of Ephesus, 372

S

Sabian Assembly, 93
Sacred Tales (Aristides), 375
"Sacrifice of Isaac" from *Manuscript of Saint Gregory of Nazianzus, 365*
Sadhu, Monni, 174
Sagittarius, *55, 58,* 108, 114; compared to Aries and Leo, 114; Islamic depictions of, *51, 114, 124;* Jupiter as ruler of, 100, 114; primary in House IX, 121
Sahinsahname (Lokman), illustration from, *50*
Saint Augustine, 45, *45, 78,* 164, 167, 381, *381,* 394
Saint Barbara (Campin), *186*
St. Denis, Marquis Hervey de, 404
Saint Germain, Count de, 87, 88
Saint Louis Psalter, "Jacob's Dream," *362*
Saint Paul, 245
Saint Thomas Aquinas, 56, *56,* 164, 167, 182, 250, 382, *384*
Saladin, sultan of Egypt, 48, 52
Sardulakarnavadana (Buddhist tale), 247
Sassetta, *Journey of the Magi, 27*
Satanic Beast, the, 167, 181–82, 210
Saturday, origin of word, 29
Saturn, 29, 88, 100, *103,* 104; in Aries, 109; astrological symbol, 100; body parts assigned to, 104; in Cancer, 111; in conjunction with Jupiter in Pisces (in A.D. 747), 116; in conjunction with Sun, 122; domiciled in Houses X and XI, 104, 121; in House V, 72; in Leo, 111; in Libra, 113; malefic, 97, 138; Mercury as moderator of, 61; in Pisces, 116; rule over middle finger, in chiromancy, 248, 253, 262; ruling Aquarius, *103,* 104, 116; ruling Capricorn, *103,* 104, 115; in Sagittarius, 114; in Scorpio, 114; in sextile with Mars, 123; slow-moving, 97, 100, 108, 129; in trine with Venus, 123; in Virgo, 111–13
Saturnian personality traits, 104
Saturn mount, palm, *254,* 262, 264, 266, 275–76
Saul, King, 363
Saunders, Richard, *72,* 255
Savoy, Bona of, 205
Saxl, Fritz, 93
School of Athens (Raphael), *35, 162*
Scivias (Hildegard of Bingen), *382*
Scorel, Jan van, portrait of Paracelsus by, *62*
Scorpio, *58,* 108, *113,* 113–14; Aquarius compared to, 116; Jupiter in, 114, *124;* Mars as ruler of, *99,* 100, 114; Pluto as ruler of, 105, 114; primary in House VII, 120
Scot, Michael, *56–57,* 250
Scott, Sir Walter, 89
secondary progression (*or* direction), 128; sample reading (Colette), 150–51
Second Dream. A Promenade in the Sky (Grandville), *401*
Secret of Secrets (pseudo-Aristotelian work), 53
secular (materialistic) approach, 9–10
Selva, Henry, 89
semisextile (aspect), 122, *123,* 126
semisquare (aspect), 122, *123,* 126
"Sepharial" (Walter Gorn Old), 92
Sepher Bahri (Book of Clarity), 168, 170
Sepher Yetzirah (Book of Creation *or* Formation), 168, 170
Sephiroth Tree, *169,* 170–71, 209
septile (aspect), 122
Septimus Severus, Emperor, 38–39
Servetus, Michael, 65
sesquiquadrate (aspect), 122, 126
Sesson, *Tiger, 303*
S'Eun-Ho, Chinese Emperor, 201
seven, as mystical number, 164, 167, 182–85; in astrology, 85, 183; relationship with number four, 180, 183
Seven-card spread, tarot, 228
Seven Liberal Arts, The (Herrade de Landsberg), *182*
Seven-point spread, tarot, 229
seventeen, number, 167
Seventh-card spread, tarot, 228
Seville, Spain, 52
sextile (aspect), 96, 122, 123, *123*
Sforza, Duke Francesco, 205
shadow rod, ancient Egyptian, *31*
Shahn, Ben: *Prayer, 184; "I never dared to dream," 279*
Shakespeare, William, 69, 185, 392, 397, 406
shamanism, 357
Shang dynasty, 284, 285; bronze cauldron (*Ting*), *324;* oracle bone, *284*
Shao Yung, 285
Shchutskii, Iulien, 293

Shêng (*I Ching* hexagram), 324–25
Shih (*I Ching* hexagram), 302
Shih Ching (*Book of Poetry*), 284
ShihHo (*I Ching* hexagram), 310–11, *311*
Short Papus spread, tarot, 228
Shu ching (*Book of History*), 284
Shumoshiku Loving Lotus (Kano Moranobu), *301*
Sibly, Ebenezer, 87
sidereal year and zodiac, 37, 107, 138
Sieggrun, Fredrich, 93
significator, in tarot, 225
Silverstris, Bernard, 52
Sim, F., *Prometheus, 369*
simian line, palm, 241, 278
Simmonite, William, 88
Simon ben Jochai, 170
Simon Magnus, 164
Sioux Indians, 357
Sirius (star), 31, *115*
Sistine Chapel frescoes, Michelangelo, *243–45*
six, in numerology, 181–82
Sixtus IV, Pope, 60, 61
Sixtus V, Pope, 61
sleep, 355, 380–81, 408, 419; mind vs. soul in, 380–81; "off-line" state of brain in, 417; studies of, 355, 398, 406, 416–17
Sleep of Reason Produces Monsters, The (Goya), 396
Smith, Pamela Colman, 209
Smith, Robert Cross ("Raphael"), 88–89
Socrates, 33, *34*
solar arc method of prediction, 131
solar calendars, 29, 31
Solar personality, 97, 99
solar return method of prediction, 131
solar system, 17, 73, 76–77, 80–82
solar year, 15, 29, 31; sidereal vs. tropical, 37
Solomon, King, 363
solstice point, on horoscope wheel, 127
somnambulism, 398, 399
Somniorum Libri III (Cardan), 392
somnium (predictive dream), 376, 385
Song of Roland, The, 382
soothsayers, 9, 38–39, *39,* 361, 363, 376
Sothis (star), 31
soul, 163, 394, 404–5; ancient Chinese concept of, 360; ancient Egyptian concept of, 360; ancient Greek concepts, 33, 368, 370–71, 380; dreaming and, 360, 368, 370–71, 372, 373, 380–81, 382, 404–5, 417, 419; exempt from influence of stars, 56; travel during sleep, 357, 360, 380, 392, 417, 419; universal, 33, 360, 368, 370, 381, 392, 404, 417, 419; in yoga tradition, 360
Soul Urge (numerology), 188, 193
Spain, Islam in, 45, 48, 52, 201
Spenser, Edmund, 199
Sphaera Mundi manuscript illumination, *36*
spheres, concentric, cosmological systems of, 33–34, *35, 57, 57*
Spier, Julius, 256
spiral galaxy, 17
spiritual (mystical) approach, 9–10
Spring Landscape in Sunlight (Kongo-ji), *330–31*
Spring on Min River (Dao Ji), *291*
square (aspect), 96, 122, 123, *123*
Stanhope, Lady Hester Lucy, 88
Star(s) (tarot card), 200, 213, *215,* 216
Star of Bethlehem, 27, 29, 116
Star of Jacob, 29
stars, 15–17, 80, 95–96, 153; Arabic tables of, 48; distances of, 37; Egyptian knowledge of, 31; fixed, 17, 24, 31, 33, 36, *76,* 80; in Greek cosmology, 33, 34, 36–37; medieval Christian views of, 56; Mesopotamian lists, 28; new (nova, supernova), 80; in Ptolemaic system, 44; seen to "impel but not compel," 44, 73, 80, 153 (*see also* free will)
statistical astrology, 88, 92
Steiner, Rudolf, 92
Stekel, Wilhelm, 413
stellium, of planets, 132, 133
Sterne, Laurence, 87
Stevenson, Robert Louis, 405, *405,* 418
Stoicism, 34, 41, 371
Stonehenge, 21, *22*
Strength (tarot card), 200, 213, *215*
subconscious, 392, 406, 417–18
succedent houses, in horoscope, 118, 120–21, 133
Sufi, Abd al-Rahman al, 114
Sui (*I Ching* hexagram), 308
Suleiman the Magnificent, Ottoman Emperor, 167
Sullivan, Harry Stack, 413
Sully, James, 399
Sumeria(ns), 24, 28, 361; cuneiform tablet, *158*
Sun, 15–17, 95–96, 99; apparent movement of, 15, *96;* in Aquarius, 115, 116; in Aries, *108,* 109; astrological symbol, 99; beneficent, 97; classified as planet in astrology, 96, 97; conjunctions with Moon, Saturn, Venus, 122; in Copernican system, *74–76,* 76; domiciled in House V, 99, 120; earth revolution around, 76, *96, 108;* ecliptic of, 15, 28, 95, *96;* fast-moving, 97, 99, 108; in Greek cosmology, 33, *35–36,* 36–37; movement in galaxy, 17; in Ptolemaic system, 44; relationship to zodiac signs, 37, 95, 99, 108, *108,* 127, 154; rule over ring finger, in chiromancy, 253 (*see also* Apollo); ruling Leo, 99, 111, *135;* in Scorpio, 114; *see also* heliocentric systems
Sun (Apollo) line, in palmistry, 268
Sun (*I Ching* hexagram 41, Decrease, Hurt, Harm, Injury), *301,* 321–22
Sun (*I Ching* hexagram 57, Obedience), 332–33
Sun (*I Ching* trigram), 266, 288–89, 320, 336–37
Sun (tarot card), *198,* 200, *215,* 216
Sun Box (Cornell), *98*
Sunday, origin of word, 29
Sung (*I Ching* hexagram), *301,* 301–2
Sung dynasty, 285; paintings, *286–87, 298*
Sun-Moon aspect, in marriages, 93
Sun-sign, 37, 93, 99, 108, 132, 136, 154; vs. ascendant sign, relative importance, 127; defined, 95; in synastry, 130–31
superconscious level of unconscious mind, 417–18
supernova, 80
Surrealism, 407
Swift, Jonathan, 87
swords, Lesser Arcana suit, 200, 210, 216–17, *218, 222–23;* reading, 225–26
Sylvester II, Pope, 52
symbolism, astrological, 88, 89, 93
synastry, 130–31
synchronicity (of Jung), 92, 152
Synesius of Cyrene, 44, 380
Syntaxis (Ptolemy), 32, 44

T

Tābir (dream interpretation), 384
Tābir ul Caderi (dream book), 389
Ta Ch'u (*I Ching* hexagram), 313
Ta Chuana (*I Ching* hexagram), 317
T'ai (*I Ching* hexagram), 288, 304–5, *304–5*
Taisnier, Johannes, 253
Takiuddin in his Observatory at Galata, from Lokman, *Sahinsahname, 50*
Ta Kuo (*I Ching* hexagram), 314
Talmud, 363
Tang dynasty, terra cotta *Horse, 318*
Tao, Taoism, 285, 360
tarot, 10, 89, 174, 197–235, 252; basis of, 199, 210; and cabala, 206, 208–9, 210, 225; cards (*see* Greater Arcana; Lesser Arcana; tarot decks); evaluation of, 235; history of, 200–10; origin of word, 200–1; reading, 224, *225–29;* sample reading, 230–34; self-reading, 224, 235; significator card, 225; spreads, 224, 225, 226–29; upright vs. reversed image positions, 224
Tarot, Its Occult Signification, Use for Fortune-Telling, and Method of Play, The (Mathers), 209
tarot decks: famous, 205–6; meanings of cards, 216–21, 224; modern, 206–10; preparation, 224–25; shuffling and cutting methods, 225; storing, 224; *see also* Greater Arcana; Lesser Arcana
Tarot des Bohémiens, Le (Papus), 208
Tarot des Imagiers du Moyen Age, Le (Wirth), 208
Tarot Divinatoire, Le (Papus), 208
Tartini, Giuseppe, 405
tasseography, 252, 343–44; *see also* tea-leaf reading
Taurus, *55, 107,* 108, 109; Age of, 37, 109; Aquarius compared to, 116; primary in House II, 120; Venus as ruler of, 100, 109
Ta Yu (*I Ching* hexagram), *303,* 306–7
T-cross (aspect), 126, *126*
Tea (Matisse), *347*
Tea Connoisseurs (Chien Hsuano), *350*
tea-leaf reading, 10, 235, 252, 343–44, *345;* reading, 349–50; sample, 351; technique, 348
teapot, Chinese porcelain (Mount Vernon), *347*
telepathy, 417
telescopes: of Galileo, 82; of Newton, *83;* reflecting, of Herschel, *85,* 88
Temperance (tarot), 200, 213, *215*
ten, as mystical number, 33, 164, 167, 185–86; nodes of Tree of Life (cabala), 168, *169,* 170–71
Ten Wings of *I Ching,* 283, 285, 286, 296, *299*
tertiary progression, 128
Tertullian, 44–45, 380
Tetrabiblos (Ptolemy), 44, 48
tetragrammaton, 171–74, 206, 208–9, *225*
Thales of Miletus, 32, 162
Theagenes, 38
Theophrastus, *34*
Theosophical Society, 89, 92
theosophy movement, 89–92, 174, 206
Therapeutica, miniature from, *373*
thirteen, in numerology, 187
thirty-three, in numerology, 186–87
Thomism, 56
Thoth (Egyptian god), 53; *see also* Book of Thoth
Thrasyllus, 39
three, as mystical number, 164, 179, 180
Three Graces, The (Rubens), *179*
thumb, mount at base of, *see* Venus mount
thumb print, on Chinese clay seal, *241*
Thunderbolt (tarot card), *see* Tower
Thursday, origin of word, 29
Thurston, Mark, 418
Thutmose, pharaoh, 363
Tiberius, Emperor, 39, 371
Tiberto, Antioco, 253
Tibetan doctrine, 357
Tiger (Sesson), *303*
Timaeus (Plato), 33
Time Transfixed (Magritte), *412*
Ting (*I Ching* hexagram), 326; Shang bronze, *324*
Tissie, Philippe, 404, 410
Titania and Bottom (Fuseli), *414*
Tobey, Carl Payne, 92
Toledo, Spain, 52
Toledo Tables, 52
Tonutamen, 363
Torah, 168, *181*
Torella (astrologer), 61
Tower (Thunderbolt) (tarot card), 200, 213, *215*
traditional astrology, 88–89, 93, 96
transits, in astrological prediction, 129; sample reading, 151
Traumgesicht, Das ("Dream Vision," Dürer), *390*
Travels of Sir John Mandeville, The, illumination from, *94*
Tree of Life, 168, *169,* 170–71, 209
Tree of Life spread, tarot, 229
Trent, A. G. ("Richard Garnett"), 92
Très Riches Heures of the Duke of Berry, *55*
trigrams of *I Ching,* 266, 288–89; meanings of, 288; origin of, 284; tile, *287*
trine (aspect), 96, 122, 123, *123*
Trinity, 164, 180
triplicity, of zodiac signs, *96,* 108, 136
Trithemius, Abbot Johannes, 60
tropical year, 37, 107
Tsou Yen, 285
Ts'ui (*I Ching* hexagram), 324
Tu Chin, *The Poet Lin P'u Walking in the Moonlight, 286*
Tuesday, origin of word, 29
Tui (*I Ching* hexagram), 333
Tui (*I Ching* trigram), 266, 288–89, 336–37
Tun (*I Ching* hexagram), *294–95,* 317
T'ung (*I Ching* hexagram), 306
Twain, Mark, 259
twelve, as mystical number, 164, 167, 187
twenty-two, as mystical number, 170–71, 186, 206, 209
Twenty-two Paths, Tree of Life, 168, *169,* 170–71
twins, 118
two, as mystical number, 164, 178, *179,* 180

U

unconscious mind, 360, 392, 398, 399–400, 404, 406–10, 415, 417–18; Adlerian, 410; the collective unconscious, 408, 413, 417; Freudian, 406–9, 413, 415; Jungian, 410–13; superconscious level of Cayce, 417–18
unified systems of divination, 174; Etteilla, 206; Golden Dawn, 174, 209; Lèvi, 174, 206, 208–9
U.S. Games Systems, Inc., tarot cards, 210, *218, 231, 234*
Universe (tarot card), *see* World
university curricula of past: astrology in, 56; chiromancy in, *255*
Upanishads, 360
Ur, temple of (ziggurat), *28,* 361
Uranian mind and personality, 105
Uranian system of astrology, 93, 105, 127; prediction in, 131
Uranus, 88, 97, 104–5; in Aries, 109; astrological symbol, 104–5; body parts assigned to, 105; in Cancer, 111; discovery of, 85–86, 88, 93; domiciled in House XI, 105, 121; in Leo, 111; in Libra, 113; in Pisces, 116; ruling Aquarius, 105, 116; ruling Capricorn, 105, 115; in Scorpio, 114; in sextile with Moon, 123; slow-moving, 97, 105, 108, 129; in square with Mars, 123; in Virgo, 113
Urban VIII, Pope, 61
Utriusque Cosmi Minoris et Majores Technica Historia (Fludd), *69, 175–77*
Utu-napishtim, 361

V

Valens, Vettius, 41
Van de Castle, Robert, 415
Vaschide, N., 255
Vecchia, Piero Della, *The Fortune-Teller and the Soldier, 259*
Vedas, 30, 109, 247
Venetian-Lombardi tarot deck, 205
Venus, 29, 36, 97, 100, *101,* 138; in Aquarius, 116; in Aries, 109; astrological sign, 100; body parts assigned to, 100; in Cancer, 111; in Capricorn, 115; in conjunction with Sun, 122; conjunctions of, 122; domiciled in Houses II and VII, 100, 120; fast-moving, 97, 100, 108, 129; in Leo, 111; Mars in conjunction with, 29; Mercury in conjunction with, 29; Mesopotamian, *see* Ishtar; in Pisces, 116; rule over thumb, in chiromancy, 248, 253; ruling Libra, 100, *101,* 113; ruling Taurus, 100, 109; in Sagittarius, 114; in Scorpio, 114; in trine with Jupiter, 123; in trine with Saturn, 123
Venusian personality, 97, 100
Venus mount, palm, 253, *253, 254,* 260, 264, 265, 266, 275
Venus of Laussel, *20,* 30
Vercors (Jean Bruller), 9
Vermeer, Jan, *The Astronomer, 95*
vernal equinox, 37, 107
Vespasian, Emperor, 115
Via Lascivia, in palmistry, 266, 268, 276, 277
Villefranche, Jean-Baptiste Morin de, 71
Virgil, 370; medieval depictions, *51, 56*
Virgo, *55,* 108, 111, *112,* 113; Mercury as ruler of, *18, 99,* 100, 111; primary in House VI, 120
Visconti, Filippo Maria, 205
Visconti-Sforza tarot cards, *198,* 205, *235*
Vitality line, palm, *see* Life line
Vivian Bible, dedication page of, *251*
Vogt, Johannes Karl, 88
Volguine, Alexandre, 89
Vollrath, Hugo, 92
Voltaire, (Jean François Arouet), 397

W

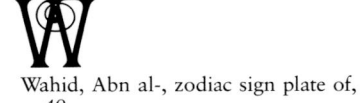

Wahid, Abn al-, zodiac sign plate of, *49*
Waite, Arthur E., 209–10
Waite-Rider tarot deck, 209–10; court cards, *218*
Waite-Smith tarot deck, 209–10
Wallenstein, Duke Albrecht von, Kepler's horoscope for, *80*
"wanderers," 17, 95; *see also* planets
wands (batons), Lesser Arcana suit, 200, 210, *218,* 219, *222–23;* reading, 226
Wang, Robert, 174, 210
Wang Pi, 285
Wan I, 285
Warburg, Aby, 93
"The Waste Land" (Eliot), 210
water (Greek element), 34, 36, 162; zodiac signs associated with, *96,* 108, 136
Watson, Thomas B., 416
Waves at Matsushima (Nonomura Sōsatsu), *320–21*
weather prediction, 92, 93
Wednesday, origin of word, 29
week, seven-day, origin of, 29
Wei Chi (*I Ching* hexagram), 339
Wên, King of Chou (posthumously Emperor of China), 284, 285, 296
Wesley, John, 394
Westcott, Wyn, 174
Weston, Jessie, 210
Wharton, George, 72
Wheel of Fortune (tarot card), 200, 212–13, *214, 221*
Wilhelm, Richard, 286, 288, 290, 296
William of Conches, 52
William the Conqueror, 85
Wilson, James, 88
Wirth, Oswald, 208, 209
Witte, Alfred, 93
"wobble" of earth's rotation, 37, *37,* 154
Wolff, Ruth, 256
Women at Tea (Keller), *346*
wood, as fifth Chinese element, 143, 144, 181
Woodman, William, 174
World (Universe) (tarot card), 200, *210, 215,* 216
Wû, Emperor of China (duke of Chou), 284–85, 296
Wu Bin, *The Five Hundred Arhats, 304–5*
Wundt, Wilhelm, 399
Wun Wang (*I Ching* hexagram), 313

Y

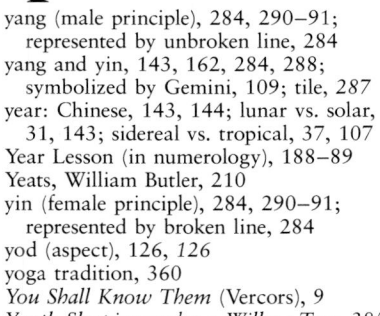

yang (male principle), 284, 290–91; represented by unbroken line, 284
yang and yin, 143, 162, 284, 288; symbolized by Gemini, 109; tile, *287*
year: Chinese, 143, 144; lunar vs. solar, 31, 143; sidereal vs. tropical, 37, 107
Year Lesson (in numerology), 188–89
Yeats, William Butler, 210
yin (female principle), 284, 290–91; represented by broken line, 284
yod (aspect), 126, *126*
yoga tradition, 360
You Shall Know Them (Vercors), 9
Youth Sleeping under a Willow Tree, 385
Yu (*I Ching* hexagram), 308

Z

Zadkiel (Richard Morrison), 88–89, 92
Zadkiel's Almanac (Morrison), 89
Zain, C. C. (Elbert Benjamine), 210
Zavattari, Francesco, 205
zenith, 127; *see also Medium Coeli*
Zeno of Citium, *34,* 371
zero, concept of, 159, 164
Zhu Zuchang, *Children with Crickets, 292*
ziggurats, 24, *28*
zodiac, 17, 77; sidereal, 138
"Zodiac Man," 41, *55,* 61, *137;* Aztec, *23*
zodiac signs (constellations), 15–17, *58,* 80, 95–96, *96,* 107–16, 153, 164, 225; animal designations for, 31, 143; ascendant, 17, 95, 108, 127, 132, 136, 143, 146, 148, 154; Chinese, *140–42,* 143, 144; chiromantic associations, 252, 255, 256; *decan* system, 31–32; descendant, 17, 132, 136, 147; elements of, 33, *96,* 108, 136, 147; 15th-century European depictions of, *99, 101, 103, 107, 110, 113, 116, 155;* Flemish tapestry, *125;* Greek/Hellenistic views of, *30,* 31, 33, *36;* Hebrew mosaic, *26;* in Indian astrology, *106,* 107, *135,* 138; influence on parts of the body, 41, 55, *55,* 61, 97, 137, *137;* "intercepted," 132, 133; in Islamic depictions, *46–49, 51, 112–14, 124, 131;* manifestation of personality traits governed by, 96, 108, 138; medieval depictions, *53, 55, 117;* plotting in horoscope wheel, 96, *96,* 108, 118; polarities of (positive/masculine vs. negative/feminine), *96,* 108, 136, 147; primary house associations for, 96, 118, 120–21; quadriplicity of, 108, 136; qualities of (cardinal/initiating; fixed/term; mutable/adaptable), 33, 108, 136, 147; and Sun-sign, correlation, 37, 95, 99, 108, *108,* 127, 154; Temple of Hathor ceiling, *30;* triplicity of (association with elements), *96,* 108, 136; tropical vs. sidereal systems, 37, 107; and "wobble" of earth and precession of the equinoxes, 37, *37,* 154; *see also specific signs of the zodiac*
—**and planets, in horoscope,** *96,* 97, 108, 132, 136; absence of planets from signs, 132, 136; planets' rulerships, *96,* 97, 108, *131, 155;* Ptolemaic system of aspects, *42–43,* 44; in sample reading (Colette), 148–50; *see also* aspects, astrological
Zohar (Book of Splendor *or* Brightness), 168, 170
Zoroastrians, 164

Credits

Text Credit

Quotations from *The I Ching or Book of Changes.* The Richard Wilhelm translation rendered into English by Cary F. Baynes, Bollingen Series XIX. Copyright © 1950, © 1967, © renewed 1977 by Princeton University Press. UK & Commonwealth rights Copyright by Arkana Books.

Photograph Credits

The Albertina, Vienna: 393, Asian Art Museum, San Francisco: 336–37. David Berman: 182 above left. The Bettmann Archive: 16, 105 left, 345. Cartamancie Grimaud: 222, 223, 231. Edizioni il Meneghello, Italy: 221. The Granger Collection: 35 above right, 45, 64 above, 65 above, 76, 81, 105 above, 146, 369–70, 373, 381, 384, 404, 405. Hirmer Fotoarchiv: 374. Kepler Kommission, Munich: 72 left. Mary Evans Picture Library: 35 above left, 56 above, 84 below, 86, 193, 255 below, 285, 379. The Metropolitan Museum of Art: 328. © Morgan Press, Inc. Illustrated by David Palladini: 218 below. © 1979 Morgan Press, Inc.: 218 above. Courtesy Philosophical Research Society, Los Angeles: 41. Photo MAS, Barcelona: 99. © *The New Yorker:* 348. Photos by Philip Pocock: 214–15, 222–23, 231, 234, 273, 351. Ann Ronan Picture Gallery: 35 below left, 69, 80, 85 above. The Smithsonian Institution, Washington, D.C.: 83. Courtesy of Time, Inc.: 32. Austin Underwood: 22. University Museum, University of Pennsylvania: 28. UPI/Bettmann Newsphotos: 408, 409. U.S. Games Systems, Inc. Illustrated by Robert Wang: 210. Copyright U.S. Games Systems, Inc.: 210, 214–15, 218 second row, 220, 234, 235. Copyright © 1971 U.S. Games Systems, Inc.: 218 third row. Courtesy of World Health Organization: 406. Zentralbibliothek, Zurich: 180.

Original Drawings by Martin Hardy: 33, 37, 96, 108, 127, 140–41, 169, 262, 263–69.

Species rise and species fall,
The way has just begun;
Mankind is learned by seeking all,
Or just by probing one.